Englishness

Englishness

Politics and Culture 1880–1920

Second Edition

EDITED BY ROBERT COLLS
AND PHILIP DODD

AFTERWORD BY WILL SELF

B L O O M S B U R Y
LONDON • NEW DELHI • NEW YORK • SYDNEY

Bloomsbury Academic

An imprint of Bloomsbury Publishing Plc

50 Bedford Square	1385 Broadway
London	New York
WC1B 3DP	NY 10018
UK	USA

www.bloomsbury.com

Bloomsbury is a registered trade mark of Bloomsbury Publishing Plc

First published by Croom Helm, 1986

Second edition published by Bloomsbury Academic, 2014

© Robert Colls, Philip Dodd, 1986, 2014

British Library Cataloguing-in-Publication Data
A catalogue record for this book is available from the British Library.

ISBN: HB: 978-1-4725-2753-0
PB: 978-1-4725-2267-2
ePDF: 978-1-4725-2569-7
ePub: 978-1-4725-2334-1

Library of Congress Cataloging-in-Publication Data
Englishness: politics and culture 1880–1920/edited by Robert Colls and Philip Dodd; afterword by Will Self. – [Second edition].
pages cm
Includes bibliographical references and index.
ISBN 978-1-4725-2753-0 (hardback) – ISBN 978-1-4725-2267-2 (pbk.) –
ISBN 978-1-4725-2569-7 (epdf) – ISBN 978-1-4725-2334-1 (epub)
1. England–Civilization–20th century. 2. England–Civilization–19th century.
3. National characteristics, English. I. Colls, Robert. II. Dodd, Philip, 1949-
DA566.4.E54 2014
941.08–dc 3
2014004144

Typeset by Deanta Global Publishing Services, Chennai, India

CONTENTS

LIST OF CONTRIBUTORS

D. George Boyce is emeritus professor in the University of Swansea, UK. He has published and edited books and articles on British, Irish and Imperial history, including *Nationalism in Ireland* (3rd. ed., 1995), *The Irish Question in British Politics, 1868–1996* (2nd. ed., 1996), *Decolonisation and the British Empire, 1775–1997* (London, 1999), *The Falklands War of 1982* (2005), *The Ulster Crisis* (co-edited with Alan O'Day, 2006), and *Gladstone and Ireland: politics, religion and nationality in the Victorian Age* (co-edited with Alan O'Day, 2010). He is working on the political ideas of the Victorian novelist Charles Lever (1806–1872) and read a paper on 'Lever, the Landlords and the Union' at the Lever Bicentenary Conference, University of Pisa, 2006, which was published in Anglistica Pisana, Vol. IV, 2007. He is also editing a collection of letters written by an Irish officer who served in the Crimean War of 1854–56.

Peter Brooker is emeritus professor in the Department of Culture, Film and Media, the University of Nottingham, UK. Between 2008 and 2010, he was professorial fellow at the Centre for Modernist Studies, University of Sussex, UK. He has written widely on modernism and contemporary writing and is the author of *Bertolt Brecht: Dialectics, Poetry, Politics* (1989), *New York Fictions* (1996), *Modernity and Metropolis* (2004), *Bohemia in London* (2004, 2007), and *A Glossary of Cultural Theory* (1999, 2002). He edited *Modernism/Postmodernism* (1992) and more recently co-edited *The Oxford Handbook of Modernisms* (2010). He was principal investigator on the AHRC Modernist Magazines Project (2005-2010) and lead editor of the three-volume *Oxford Critical and Cultural History of Modernist Magazines*. He served between 2005 and 2011 as chair of the Raymond Williams Society and is currently working on a biofiction of 3 years in the life of Ford Madox Ford.

Robert Colls is professor of Cultural History in the International Centre for Sports History and Culture at De Montfort University, Leicester, UK. Before that, he taught at Vaughan College in the University of Leicester's Department of Adult Education, and was professor of English History in the School of Historical Studies. He has held fellowships at Yale, Dortmund, and St John's College, Oxford. His most recent book is *George Orwell. English Rebel* (2013).

Jeremy Crump joined the Home Office in 1986, having completed a PhD in social history at Warwick University. After his career in the civil service which also included time in the Treasury, the Cabinet Office and the National Policing Improvement Agency, he worked for the IT company, Cisco Systems. He has been a visitor at Leeds University Business School, the Oxford Internet Institute and Nuffield College, Oxford. He is an associate of the Centre for the Analysis of Social Media at Demos and a fellow of the British Computer Society. In 2013, Jeremy resumed research on the social history of sport and popular culture at De Montfort University, Leicester, UK, where he is a visiting fellow.

Hugh Cunningham is emeritus professor of Social History at the University of Kent, UK. His work has covered the histories of leisure, patriotism, national identity, childhood and philanthropy. 'The language of patriotism, 1750–1914', *History Workshop Journal*, No. 12 (1981), explored the rise and decline of radical expressions of patriotism. His books include *The Children of the Poor: Representations of Childhood since the Seventeenth Century; Children and Childhood in Western Society since 1500; The Challenge of Democracy: Britain 1832-1918; The Invention of Childhood; Grace Darling: Victorian Heroine; and Time, Work and Leisure: Changing Lives in England since 1700.*

Philip Dodd is former director of the Institute of Contemporary Arts, former editor of the BFI's *Sight and Sound*, chairman of Made in China (UK) Ltd, and a regular BBC broadcaster. His work on national identity has taken many forms, including the Demos pamphlet *The Battle Over Britain*; the exhibition *Spellbound; Art and Film* at the Hayward Gallery, and his involvement as creative consultant in the UK Pavilion at the 2010 Shanghai Expo. He has been visiting professor at King's College, London, UK, and currently holds the same post at the University of the Arts, London, UK.

Brian Doyle (1943–1997). Brian's work on the historical and ideological formation of the discipline of English culminated in his influential book *English and Englishness* (1989). In later years, his interests had turned towards what he called 'changing the culture of Cultural Studies', mounting an explicitly humanistic critique of the professionalization of the discipline and its concern with high theory.

Alun Howkins is a professor emeritus of Social History, University of Sussex, UK, and a honorary professor in the School of History, University of East Anglia, UK. He was born in rural Oxfordshire and left school at the age of 15 to work on the land. After a variety of jobs he went to Ruskin College, Oxford, as a trade union student. From there he did a BA at Oxford and a PhD at the University of Essex. His doctorate was published as *Poor Labouring Men. Rural radicalism in Norfolk 1872–1924* in 1985.

This was followed by *Reshaping Rural England* (1991, 2003) and *The Death of Rural England* (2003). He was a founder editor of *History Workshop Journal* and has remained a member of the editorial board ever since. He is a past president of the British Agricultural History Society. He is currently a Trustee of Diss Corn Hall in Norfolk and is working on its history and the history of its associated townscape. He is also working on the early history of socialism in Kings Lynn.

Alice Jane Mackay is a freelance consultant and oral historian working with local groups and organisations to preserve and enhance community archive collections and make hidden historical sources more widely known. She is a member and director of Waltham Forest Oral History Workshop, London's longest-established oral history group, with an archive of more than 600 recordings. Previously a library manager, it was her work at Ruskin College, Oxford, and as librarian of the City Literary Institute and Bishopsgate Institute in London that led her to focus on encouraging wider public involvement with archives and local heritage. She is currently working on an oral history project exploring the influence of Kingsley Hall in Bromley-by-Bow and its founders, socialist feminists, pacifists and educationalists Muriel and Doris Lester, on the lives and families of the people who took part in its activities.

Dennis Smith is emeritus professor of Sociology of University of Loughborough, UK. He is currently investigating the different ways that avant-garde writers such as Oscar Wilde and Jean Améry, and radical politicians such as Nelson Mandela and Aung San Suu Kyi, have fed the experience of brutal incarceration into their lives and philosophies. This historical and comparative research into the phenomenology of humiliation traces the long struggle for political and artistic freedom from West to East and from North to South. This latest project builds upon decades of research on forced social and social-psychological displacement leading to books and articles on Zygmunt Bauman, historical sociology, Norbert Elias, modernity, Barrington Moore, how cities shape our politics and culture, the chronically bad fit between capitalism and democracy, the ways that globalization lays the seeds of humiliation, and the interplay between fear and anger in recession-ridden Europe.

Pat Thane is research professor of Contemporary History, Kings College, London, UK. Her publications include *The Foundations of the Welfare State* (2nd ed. 1996); *Old Age in England: Past Experiences, Present Issues* (2000); *Women and Ageing in British Society since 1500* (co-edited with Lynn Coelho, 2001); *The Long History of Old Age* (editor, 2005); *Britain's Pensions Crisis: History and Policy* (co-edited with Hugh Pemberton and Noel Whiteside, 2006); *Unequal Britain: Equalities in*

Britain since 1945 (editor, 2010); *Women and Citizenship in Britain and Ireland in the Twentieth Century: What Difference did the Vote Make?* (co-edited with Esther Breitenbach, 2010); *Happy Families? History and Family Policy* (2010). She is a convenor of History and Policy (www.historyandpolicy.org).

Peter Widdowson (1942–2009). Peter was at the forefront of theoretical debates about literature in English universities and polytechnics and an internationally renowned scholar on Thomas Hardy. He was a co-founder of *Literature and History* (1975), later editor of 'Reading English' and author of books on Thomas Hardy and Graham Swift, among many others.

Stephen Yeo taught at Sussex University between 1966 and 1989, before becoming principal of Ruskin College in Oxford from 1989 to 1997. Since then, he has worked closely with the Co-operative College in Manchester, chairing its Board and now chairing the Co-operative Heritage Trust which looks after the National Co-operative Archive and the Pioneers Museum in Rochdale. His interests are in the social history and current practice of labour, co-operative, adult education, community-publishing, worker-writing, transition towns and other social movements.

LIST OF CONTRIBUTORS
IN 1986

D. G. Boyce, Department of Political Theory and Government, University College, Swansea

Peter Brooker, School of Humanities, Thames Polytechnic

Robert Colls, Department of Adult Education, University of Leicester

Jeremy Crump, Lutterworth Community College, Leicestershire

Hugh Cunningham, Faculty of Humanities, University of Kent

Philip Dodd, Department of English, University of Leicester

Brian Doyle, Department of Behavioural and Communication Studies, Polytechnic of Wales

Alun Howkins, School of Cultural and Community Studies, University of Sussex

Alice Jane Mackay, Social Science and Administration Department, Goldsmiths' College, London

Dennis Smith, Department of Sociology and Social History, Aston University

Pat Thane, Social Science and Administration Department, Goldsmiths' College, London

Peter Widdowson, Faculty of Humanities, Middlesex Polytechnic

Stephen Yeo, School of Social Sciences, University of Sussex

PREFACE

We should say at the outset that we do not see 'Englishness' as an obvious or in any way, natural propensity of the people who now live, or have lived in the territory that has come to be England. The English are an old nation and that there were (and are) critical phases in the long history of national consciousness is clear, but that these phases flowed simply one into another, or that the Englishness they produced stood for the same things, or that the English were (and are) a people with a resolved identity, is not. Englishness has had to be made and re-made in and through history, within available practices and relationships, and existing symbols and ideas. That symbols and ideas recur does not ensure that their meaning is the same. Meaning is not solely a property of genealogy, but a matter of present context and practical life.

Apart from the problem of mistaking a repetition of ideas and symbols for resolution or continuity of meaning, there is an additional problem: a reticence to discuss the English as a nationalistic people at all. The received wisdom is that the English are patriotic rather than nationalistic. Popular nationalism is the vulgar face of other peoples, some because they are oppressed and need it, and some because they just like that sort of thing. The English do not need nationalism and do not like it; they are so sure of themselves that they need hardly discuss the matter. As one historian recently remarked, 'English identity was not in doubt,' and, with such strength, 'there was no need to show excessive devotion to St. George.' (Keith Robbins, *The Eclipse of a Great Power. Modern Britain 1870–1975*, 1983, pp. 8–9). This volume of chapters is, in part, an attempt to make it clear that such innocence is culpable.

We chose to focus on 1880–1920 because we, as well as others (e.g., Stuart Hall and Enoch Powell) believe that it is within the shadow of that period, and its meanings, that we still live. Of course, there were dominant voices in the making of this Englishness. It is to these voices that this volume pays its major attention. 'Some Examples of Englishness 1880–1920' might have been a more modest title than the present one. There are omissions. Because we could not find a suitable and willing contributor, there is no account of what 'the Empire', or a part of it, thought of the English. And we decided to exclude the monarchy and sport, two subjects which have been given attention in the recent volume edited by Eric Hobsbawm and Terence

Ranger, *The Invention of Tradition*. After the two chapters by the editors which map the two areas of the volume, the cultural politics of England and its political culture, the succeeding chapters address particular aspects of those areas in some detail. The decision to organize the volume in its present form is due to our belief that it is impossible and wrong to see culture and politics as autonomous domains. Indeed a number of chapters in this volume suggest that our definitions of politics and of culture were forged during the years 1880–1920.

One last note. While our conviction is that a volume such as this one will make appeals to an unexamined English national identity (which can include 'British' identity too) more difficult, we are also aware that this volume may appear to be a negative act – an act of dispossession. To such an accusation, which we have often levelled at ourselves, our response is three-fold. First, it is important to write the history of a national identity which has remained unexamined – some would say wilfully so. Second, without such a history the diverse identities available within these islands are doomed to starvation and malformation. Third, this volume is a necessary prelude to another one which might help to make an adequate identity for us all. Until that further work can be done, this volume will address the England we know.

We wish to gratefully acknowledge The Twenty-Seven Foundation for their financial assistance in the publication of this book. We should like to thank for their invaluable assistance in the making of this volume, Kate Green and Nicola Kirby.

Robert Colls and Philip Dodd

Introduction to the second edition

Philip Dodd: It is 1982. I am baffled, like others, by the Falklands War – or rather by the speed with which the Conservative government and Labour opposition have come together in a time of war. Although the war against the Argentine junta is declared in the name of the United Kingdom, the appeal seems to be to a sense of England and Englishness, to Sir Francis Drake and the naval battles against the Armada. I keep asking myself: how can it be that such an appeal to this 'ancestral memory' of England and Englishness is so quickly understood and answered, bulldozing aside the authority of dissenting voices.

Around the same time, I am reading Alasdair's Macintyre's magisterial *After Virtue (1981)* where he argues that, in terms of our moral life and language, we are living as if after an earthquake. We have simply fragments of moral languages – often contradictory and sometimes incommensurable – with which to order our lives. I feel something similar about the matter of England and Englishness. We have fragments left from earlier stories. And not merely on the political terrain. At the time I am teaching twentieth-century literature in a provincial university. Even among liberals, England and Englishness often seemed to be the horizon beyond which it was difficult to see. Contemporary playwrights such as Howard Brenton and David Hare were haunted by World War II and by the popular Englishness they found in Angus Calder's *The People's War*; the celebrated novelists of that time, Martin Amis, Julian Barnes and Ian McEwan, were marinaded in an unexamined Englishness, filtered by Philip Larkin (McEwan would go on in *On Chesil Beach* to write a novel in homage to Larkin's poem 'Church Going').

If the unexamined life is not a life worth living, I just felt somewhat similar about Englishness. It had to be examined; a whiff of history needed to be let in.

Robert Colls: It was at this time that you stopped me in Leicester University library and asked if I knew of a book on the making of the English nation that was similar to E. P. Thompson's *The Making of the English Working Class*. I didn't. I wasn't interested in nationalism and of course on the face of it that book was about class consciousness not Englishness. The idea that old established nation-states like this one might still be in the making was new – to me at least. I understood that new nations had to be made, and were being made as part of the process of de-colonization, but it seemed 'England' had been there for so long and was so well established that although one might question what went on there, questioning the very idea of the country itself did seem, and continues to seem, very odd. My first degree at Sussex was based on modular choice and I never elected to do the long run history of any country, let alone England or Great Britain. For my PhD at York, which was on eighteenth and nineteenth century coalminers, it never occurred to me to think about their regional or national identity – even though, looking back, blending 'true-bred pitmen' with Thompson's idea of the 'freeborn Englishman' would have made a good chapter. Later, though more by luck than by design (there was precious little design in doing PhDs in those days), my supervisor showed me, indirectly, the 'cultural turn' in the study of nations.

PD: Part of the problem was that – is that – most of the disciplines were ill-equipped to interrogate Englishness. England and Englishness were the paradigm within which some of them breathed. Even for the more 'promiscuous' disciplines, the kinds and range of knowledge necessary to try to grasp the construction of Englishness and the institutions that incarnated it was huge, as we found out.

RC: Yes. At Leicester there was actually a department founded on an idea of Englishness as formulated by the local historian W. G. Hoskins but which, up to the 1980s at least, remained entirely unexamined. In 1982, many young historians looked to 'social history' for a radical lead and Thompson was seen as the model even though he was not someone who was easy to learn from. Still, there were straws in the wind. Establishment historians continued to write elegantly if unthinkingly about the national character – Robert Blake's *The English World* comes to mind – but others were finding new ways of thinking about it. I suppose George Orwell was a key figure here with his war-time patriotism and his taste for what he called 'semi-sociological' cultural criticism. I try to explain this in my *George Orwell English Rebel* (2013). And Philip Bounds' *Orwell and Marxism* (2009) and Alexandra Harris' *Romantic Moderns* (2010) both showed us how there were significant levels of interest in Englishness in 1930s England – especially on the Popular Front-left – which carried over into the 1940s. But after the war there was a generation of writers who stopped thinking about it – at least historically. Our book was published one generation on from them, in 1986, and led a revival of interest, but our first impulse came from the outside. Tom Nairn's *The Break Up of Britain* (1977) for example was important in making me think about British identity as an outside force willed on the constituent nations of these islands, as was Tony Curtis' *Wales: the imagined nation* (1986), and G. A. Williams' *When Was Wales?* (1985). Williams was my PhD supervisor at York. In 1974, under his influence, I abandoned work on my doctorate in order to write what eventually became *The Collier's Rant: Song and Culture in the Industrial Village* (1977). This was a cultural history of North East England written (one might say) in the Welsh national way – or at any rate in the Gwyn Williams Welsh National Way (sounds like a path in the Brecon Beacons). Gwyn was not trying to present Welsh national identity as something odd, or alien, or outside the historical experience of being Welsh. On the contrary; he was trying to present it as something that belonged to that experience.

Like the Irish and the Scots, the Welsh were much more comfortable than the English in writing unselfconsciously about 'The People', but looking back, I think Thompson had influenced Gwyn to see class at the heart of what Antonio Gramsci had called the 'national question'. It is worth a footnote that Gwyn had been one of the first British Marxists to recognize Gramsci's importance.

Nairn's essays on Enoch Powell, and on the Foreign Office's country house at Weston Park, were very different in that by looking at England from the outside – as a Scots nationalist and a Marxist – he presented Englishness as something contrived, a deception if you like, practiced on the English by a neo-colonial elite. *New Left Review's* interviews with Raymond Williams in *Politics and Letters* (1981), Martin Wiener's *English Culture and the Decline of the Industrial Spirit* (1981), and Benedict Anderson's *Imagined Communities* (1983), also broke the Anglo-British circle by stepping outside it. J. H. Grainger's *Patriotisms* (1986) also stepped out; only in his case the vantage point was not the break-up of Britain but its holding-together. Grainger called the holding force 'patriotism' but accepted that it included much else besides, including 'national self-reproach, self approbation and identification'.

All these historians were deconstructing the cultural history of nations, albeit with different levels of personal identification and commitment.

The political scientists on the other hand had been deconstructing the nation-state for years. E. P. Thompson's 'The Peculiarities of the English' (1965) was, I think, the first sweeping, long range account of English history I'd read where what England was, and what England could be, seemed up for discussion. His antagonists at *New Left Review*, Nairn and Perry Anderson, were more political scientists than historians and they injected Gramsci into those mid 1960s debates through the idea of a 'hegemonic' national culture: 'The hegemonic class is the primary determinant of consciousness, character, and customs throughout a society' (Perry Anderson, 'Origins of the Present

Crisis', *New Left Review*, 1964, 39). Hans Kohn's *Nationalism* (1971) and Ernest Gellner's *Nations and Nationalism* (1983) also concentrated on what was later termed the 'cultural turn'. Kohn saw in nationalism 'a state of mind' – lots of room for cultural criticism there – while Gellner saw the nation as a powerful 'system of ideas and signs'. Edward Said's *Orientalism* (1985) followed Benedict Anderson's astonishingly fertile concept of nations as imagined communities, while Corrigan and Sayer's *The Great Arch* (1985) identified the state itself as the most potent and sustained source of that imagining. Historians still fought shy of 'deconstruction' as a word, but from their number the most powerful example of it was Terence Ranger and Eric Hobsbawm's *The Invention of Tradition* (1983) – an edited work that unpicked the origins and meanings of nineteenth-century national traditions from Scottish tartans and Welsh *eisteddfodau* to British coronations and Indian *durbars*.

All these writers were making new waves, but Thompson's *The Making* was the one you asked about. How did you come to want a history like that?

PD: You are right to say that E. P. Thompson threw a shadow over us – protective and looming. But I had my doubts that he could be helpful, for three reasons. At the opening of *The Making of the English Working Class*, he had written that out of respect he would not deal with the Scottish working class. This had always struck me as odd – as if there was not serious interpenetration between the English and the Scots, not least in the working class movements. I had always been fond of the comment of Daniel Defoe, someone often called 'the father of the English novel', that the English were a 'mongrel' bunch. We are that, and I certainly wanted our Englishness volume to register that at as many points as possible.

Second, Edward Thompson's English were largely indifferent to vulgar pleasure – yet *The Making of the English Working Class* was published in 1963, around the same time that mass package holidays began to become affordable and desirable to the English and that English pop exploded into the air. It's also worth reminding ourselves that we may have been working on *Englishness: Politics and Culture* at a time which had more than its fair share of political conflict – from Ireland to the miners' strikes – but it was also the era of the pleasure-seeking *Sun*, of *Dynasty* and *Dallas* on prime-time television. I felt and feel that any account of the English and Englishness that does not register the attraction to the English of common pleasures is only telling a part of the story. It was in the 1980s that Tony Benn sneered at the working-class English who bought their own homes and fitted Georgian door knockers. How vulgar!

Third, there is something primordial about the English experience of industrialisation in Thompson's book – so goes the implicit argument, it was the first development and it is the model for all other developments. I remember bumping into one of the best writers on Englishness in the street 2 or 3 years ago. She knew I spent part of my time in China and told me that she had been reading Thompson's book and that she felt that it also helped to make sense of the contemporary Chinese experience – the move from country to city, of industrialisation. To put it mildly I disagree, but her judgement reminded me that there is a view that English history provides the paradigm for all other historical experiences. I wanted our book to have a sense of the complexity of the history of England and of Englishness without the error of thinking that it could provide *the* model for the experiences of other cultures and nations. One way of ensuring English megalomania did not creep in was to have a variety of voices. What was it Wallace Stevens called one of his poems? 'Thirteen Ways of Looking at a Blackbird'. That is what I at least was aiming for.

RC: Did you want a book on Englishness for teaching purposes?

PD: No; very rarely for teaching. But I think the other thing was that we were both teaching in an English provincial city which by 1982 was absorbing a large Asian population, displaced from East Africa.

RC: Sure.

PD: And of course both of us came from working class families – I came from a mining family, you from a shipyard family – and because of that I'd never really felt wholly English. In fact in cultural terms I'd been brought up as an American. My father adored everything American. I remember that the late Stuart Hall said to me after our book came out that it was written from 'a class position' and, for good or bad, there is truth in that.

RC: My father loved American music too, and with my mother his Ginger to her Fred, they never stopped ballroom dancing right to the end. America always seemed a natural part of me.

And then there was Leicester. Talk about the English constitution! It stands now to be the first city with an Asian majority. At first, Leicester Asians had been told by the town council not to bother coming (from Kenya and Uganda) but come they did and by the early 1980s they were growing as a visible presence.

And yes, the 1980s were very divided years, filled with appeals for national unity in the face of so much division – over Scottish and Welsh devolution (referendum March 1979); over The Falklands War (April to June 1982); over the installation of American Cruise missiles (1981–84); over the first privatizations of resources that had once been seen as national assets (1982–86); over the miners' strike, which was connected to those privatizations as well as to some older class and regional struggles (March 1984 to March

1985); over Northern Ireland (the Anglo-Irish Accord failed in 1985); and over rising immigration and Britain's continuing membership of the European Union. All these highly divisive issues rumbled on through the decade.

The missiles were particularly worrying. I had heard from people in the Workers' Educational Association that there had been a meeting of all voluntary services at County Hall where a junior government minister had told them that a nuclear war could be fought and won if only the nation was sufficiently prepared. In the event of a nuclear strike, the government booklet *Protect and Survive* told us how long we had to whitewash the windows and scuttle under the kitchen table. Like you, we had very young children at the time and I for one took that sort of state madness personally. At one point my wife and I talked about emigrating for the sake of the children.

The dominant histories of England and Englishness had been written with such a powerful sense of unity and continuity that they left almost nothing open for discussion. In them, history more or less began with William the Conqueror in 1066 and reached its peak with David Niven in 1945. What could be fairer than that? I exaggerate, but only slightly. And in the face of a lifetime's iteration, so the story went, once our island history was learned there was nothing more to think about. The glorious revolution of 1689, for instance, was a revolution alright but once it was resolved, as the constitutional historian George Burton Adams put it in 1920: 'the foundation[s] upon which the constitution rests, the supremacy of the law, the sovereignty of the nation, are never again called in question. All the later progress consists in more and more complete application of these principles' (*Constitutional History of England*). When talking about that shadowy thing they called the constitution, constitutional lawyers were in fact talking about national identity. In other words, in the Anglo-British tradition, your identity was recognized for you, before you, in a functioning constitution. Dicey in 1885, and Wade in 1964, both recognized that in order to function, the constitution had to be recognized, and in order to be recognized, it had to function (*Introduction to the Study of the Law of the Constitution*, 1885, 1964 edition).

According to the lawyers and historians therefore, constitutional history *was us*. England was our fate and although our generation of historians and others reacted against that sort of writing with niche works of deconstruction, the constitutional model still dominated the long run view of who we are and who we were. In a sense I think it still does.

PD: It is important to remember too that other kinds of writing and what we then called cultural practice were also addressing Englishness and being saturated by it. It was one of those moments when Englishness was the field on which battle was joined. Just remember the cinema with Hugh Hudson's

Chariots of Fire set against Hanif Kureishi/Stephen Frears' Channel 4 funded *My Beautiful Launderette*, even if on reflection they both shared an interest in looking at national identity from the perspective of an 'outsider' (the Jewish athlete in Hudson's film; the gay Pakistani-English young man in *Launderette*, a modern version of the English dandy – see also *The Buddha of Suburbia*).

Or in the art world, there was Peter Fuller's use of John Ruskin (Fuller founded the influential magazine, *Modern Painters*) to mount a defence of English art against a globalised art market. In the theatre was Caryl Churchill's *Light Shining in Buckinghamshire*, with its shades of Christopher Hill on the English revolution, and even Howard Brenton's *The Romans in Britain*, the 'infamous' play taken to court for indecency, had shades of Matthew Arnold in its understanding of the Celts and an English protagonist, Chichester, whose Englishness the war in Ireland dismantles.

And there was of course for those who liked it, Cultural Studies, which enjoyed an extraordinary authority inside the academy in the 1980s. One way of reading it was to say that in its absorption in popular culture, it insulated all forms of Englishness from interrogation – rather it celebrated them, all the way from Dick Hebdige's *Subcultures: The Meaning of Style* (1979) to much of the work coming out of the Centre for Contemporary Cultural Studies at Birmingham. One of the key volumes published by CCCS was *Working Class Culture* edited by Chas Critcher *et al* but on the cover it used a photograph by Ian Berry from a project called The English! To use a cliché, Englishness was almost always the elephant in the room at that time. The most important volume to be precipitated by CCCS was Paul Gilroy's *There Aint No Black in the Union Jack* but that was more concerned with Britain than England and Englishness. Only Patrick Wright's *On Living in an Old Country* talked of Englishness, but seemed sublimely unaware of the globalising tendencies of the Thatcher regime. The 'old country' was melting into thin air.

RC: Mrs Thatcher portrayed herself as a Little Englander but as the miners found out, markets were global or they were nothing.

The times demanded a different kind of history but nobody seemed to be writing it. Then you pop up and suggest we write something for ourselves. But where to start? We certainly didn't have the time or resources to re-write the whole history of Englishness, though there was one other group at that time which was trying to do just that. Raphael Samuel's History Workshop movement was talking about long run English history as part of a frankly socialist project and making the case – through the very practice of writing history – that English history no less than Welsh history or Scottish history belonged to the people. It was at about this time that we went to the Oxford History Workshop on Patriotism. Do you remember?

PD: Yes. March 1984; lots of radically inflected 'workshops' on this and that, but nothing joined up, least of all in the long run sense you mention . . .

RC: . . . like a great harvest-home of peasant-writers in chunky sweaters. But there was much for us to learn. Rodney Hilton told us that medieval peasants had no sense of national identity, and Christopher Hill told us how the 'Norman Yoke' idea of English resistance to the Conqueror reached down into popular consciousness during the Civil War. From my notes, we went to papers by Peter Furtado on the 'Language of Patriotism', Simon Binney on 'Shakespeare's England', Peter Bailey on 'Music Hall', Stephen Yeo on 'Socialism', and Richard Gott on 'A J P Taylor's Little Englandism' – all great stuff but it occurred to me that only Gott and Yeo seemed to believe in the country they were talking about.

We enjoyed the call for history-from-below but drove home none the wiser; we still didn't know what to do with long run history.

PD: No, hold on . . . there was something else. I think the problem with the history from below narrative – which to some extent we shared and which found its political manifestation at that time in Tony Benn – lies in its opposition to the elite Englishness of Matthew Arnold and Oxbridge and the Anglican Church and all that, and in its replacement by a people's kind of Englishness which seemed to inhabit a parallel universe. In this narrative, the ruling class had their history while the working class had their *oppositional* history running underneath, from the Civil War through to the Tolpuddle Martyrs through to the Suffragettes and so on. What we were trying to do, in our ham-fisted way I admit, was to see what wove them together. And we came to the conclusion that the force which held them together was an account of what it was to be English. How the people (rather than 'The English People') actually related to the histories was a moot point but our wager was to argue that a new Englishness had been invented in the late-nineteenth century. I remember we started the volume with a quotation from Richard Shannon:

> The characteristic 'Englishness' of English culture was made then very much what it is now. The quip that all the oldest English traditions were invented in the last quarter of the 19th century has great point. (*The Crisis of Imperialism 1865–1915*, 1976)

RC: We had to take on the fact that parallel histories are not necessarily in opposition to each other. Liberalism as a history of liberty drove *both* popular and elite versions of the Anglo-British narrative – and could run either or both ways. John Burrow's *A Liberal Descent: Victorian Historians and the English Past* (1981) was very helpful in this. The History Workshop movement on the other hand had declared for the popular narrative at the outset and therefore was less flexible, tending to think that if you just dug down into the people's experiences you would find the answer in ten thousand local studies.

Then there was the question of what went into our volume. Where, for instance, was Empire?

PD: The comforting part of this conversation is saying where other people were wrong, or their judgement awry; the more discomforting part is to say what's wrong with what we did. In any queue of people critical of our book, I'd be near the head of the queue. I want to talk about a couple of absences, because I think they are revealing of the framework within which we worked in the 1980s and how what has changed subsequently forces us to re-examine the paradigm which was then ours. Jorge Luis Borges puts it rather more eloquently when he says that the present changes everything in the past.

You are right to suggest that we should have given a separate chapter to the British Empire, which would have allowed us to think how Englishness in particular was partly shaped by its interaction with the Empire. One reason was that we simply couldn't find a contributor who felt capable of doing this. But also I think we felt, or at least I ought to talk of myself, that class was being undervalued as a variable at that time – race and gender seemed more fruitful forms of interrogation – and we wanted to reinstate the power of class. The project paid a cost for our determination.

RC: In a private communication very early on, Neal Ascherson said the cutting edge of English national identity was race and pointed out that we didn't have a chapter on it

PD: We didn't want a separate chapter on race because that felt to ghettoize. So we tried to integrate it. I still think that was the better strategy, for all its faults.

But what is truly missing from the book – and a chapter on the Empire might have at least highlighted this – is any serious engagement with religion, particularly the cultural and political resonances of religion. *Englishness* came out in 1986 and three years later 'the Rushdie Affair' erupted. That made it impossible not to notice the importance of Islam to English history. What flabbergasts me, looking back, is how we could have ignored the extent to which England's engagement with Islam was so important during the period 1880 to 1920.

From my teaching I knew very well the story of Sir Richard Burton who in 1856 disguised himself and went on a pilgrimage to Mecca. Why didn't either of us, or all of us, remember that Britain occupied Egypt in 1882? From then on Britain's and England's sense of themselves were shaped partly by their engagement with Egypt and that part of the world. It was Lord Cromer who claimed the title of 'the greatest Mohammedan ruler in the world' for King George V. A recent book, Diane Robinson-Dunn's *The Harem, Slavery and*

British Imperial Culture: Anglo-Muslim Relations in the Late Nineteenth Century has persuaded me how important Islam was to the remaking of English national identity in the late-nineteenth century.

We can feel the reverberation of Islam in that period in our present lives. After the 7/7 bombing some Muslims set up a not-for-profit foundation to combat what they saw as Islamic extremism and they called it the Quilliam Foundation. This was in honour of the memory of a Manx solicitor Muslim-convert who was active in the late-nineteenth century and who argued for 'the reasonableness of Islam'. Now I don't think we should reduce history to a matter of finding the pre-conditions of the present. But, good as we are at finding the mote in other people's eyes, the absence of religion from the book is, to put it mildly, surprising. In retrospect, the early 1980s feels like a very secular moment. Recently that splendid radical Mike Davis has said that Pentecostalism is the greatest social movement of the poor in the world. I just don't think many on the left – and that's how we saw ourselves – were alert in the 1980s to the central role that religion played and still plays in global life and even in the ways that England and Englishness were defined.

The other, equally important, blank in the book is the relationship between Englishness and China and I am surprised that I didn't acknowledge this because I was a student of Thomas de Quincey's *Confessions of an English Opium Eater* which was part of a larger narrative in which Englishness defined itself 'against the Orient'. On the other hand, the early 1980s were not a time when China featured much in the intellectual imagination of Britain. Mao Ze Dong had died in 1976 and, to be frank, the economic and cultural opening up that took place after 1979 (during the 1980s there were ten times more book translated into Chinese than in the previous 30 years) had not made its way into the wider world, at least not into my imagination.

Yet that's not an excuse. The period 1880–1920 and the discourse about Englishness were steeped in things Chinese. The Second Opium War was as recent as 1860 and Hong Kong was leased to Britain for 99 years in 1899.

China was also ripening once again in our imagination during this time. Fu Manchu, the Chinese 'devil' with the brow like Shakespeare and brain of Satan, an invention in 1911 of the Birmingham working-class novelist Sax Rohmer, was in his way as important a figure of the 'other' as was Bram Stoker's Dracula, another invention the period. Fu Manchu was fixed on global domination often by way of London. It was in Limehouse, London's old Chinatown by the East End docks, that Manchu had his subterraneous layer and extended his financial tendrils. Fu Manchu was just part of the Yellow Peril moral panic that overtook England during the period that our book was centred on; and against which Englishness defined itself. It's worth saying that Fu Manchu metamorphosed into a Maoist-dressed *Dr No* in the 1960s film of the Ian Fleming novel.

But the most resonant element of China and Englishness during the late-nineteenth century can be seen in that strange book – M. P. Shiel's 1898 *The Yellow Danger*. I have just been re-reading it for something I have done for the BBC. Here is the way it imagines the Chinese invasion over the white cliffs of Dover.

> The Chinese host was to resemble a flight of locusts, covering the entire sky from horizon to horizon, each member of which was armed with some implement, not so much for the purpose of killing, as for the purpose of protracting his own death, while the rest of the host pressed forward, blighting as they went.

Here the Chinese are imagined as a blind collective, unlike the English in their staunch individuality. Jump to the present and we still have an obsession with Chinese numbers, a fear that they will overwhelm us – and a sense of their otherness. There are 642 recent books with 'China' and 'power' in the title and 444 with the words 'China' and 'rise'. If in the period of the first Yellow Peril the fear was that Chinese men from Limehouse were going to corrupt English women (the Chinese were also blamed for the Spanish flu epidemic after the World War I, just after around 100,000 had been conscripted as non combatants in Britain's WW1 army), now our fear is that China's invisible financial power will overwhelm us. *Plus ça change* as the French say.

RC: One part of my chapter deals with Empire, but not on its own terms. As for Islam, it's true it was a big presence in the British Empire – in India and Africa especially – but I don't think it's quite as true that Islam or even the Empire was a major influence on most British people. Compared to many other European countries, the British enjoyed a historically positive relationship with Islam. China was different, though the Yellow Peril scare was carefully orchestrated by the press and not long-lived. But yes; we should have included more of these subjects. The *Raj*, after all, to some extent modelled itself on the old Mughal Empire.

What about our methods? We kept saying we wanted to 'deconstruct' but failed to acknowledge that compared to now, the study of Englishness in 1880–1920 was very different. Then, it was the authenticity of sources and the sincerity of advocacy that seemed to matter most. In university teaching now, 'deconstruction', usually with and against a ubiquitous 'Other', is the new sincerity. And because everything has been, or will be, 'constructed', identifying constructions and their 'contradictions' seems to be about as far as academics are prepared to go. Statements of value or preference are few and far between, while theories of 'otherness', it seems to me, are totally devoid of practical political use.

PD: *Englishness: Politics and Culture* seems so marked by the moment in which it was written. I am used to saying this about important works on

Englishness: I have just re-read George Dangerfield's *The Strange Death of Liberal England*, a study of pre-World War I England published in 1935. It is so clearly a product of the 1930s which wanted to cleanse Englishness of that taint of Imperialism that so marked the pre-war years. But even our modest book is marked by the moment in which it was written. It is so monitored by race, class, gender, those three omnipresent variables in the cultural arguments of the 1980s, and whose paces we put Englishness through.

I have been wondering how I would do the book now. I know it would be profoundly different – not least because I have spent the last 25 years in London and not a little of that time on an airplane to Asia. It is a commonplace to say that England and Englishness look different from, say, China, but commonplaces can be true. But the serious reason I would re-imagine the book top to toe is because my intellectual judgement has changed so considerably. I wish now I had taken more heed of an aside in Alun Howkins' splendid essay in our book – when he mentions the movement of Englishness from north to south in the late-nineteenth century, and the fact that London became a financial centre. I think Howkins' aside opens up vast vistas given what has happened in the subsequent one hundred years. England may have had to relinquish its physical hold over the Empire but it has become the heart of a global financial empire. Last year I read Nicolas Shaxson's *Treasure Islands: Tax Havens and the Men who stole the World*. It is a simply brilliant account of how most tax havens in the world are former British colonies and how London is the heart of a global financial network. I think there is an umbilical cord connecting Howkins' aside and Shaxson's thesis.

What was born in the late-nineteenth century and continues to grow (and choke us) is a global Englishness centred on financial institutions. I think people educated in the humanities like us are not well-prepared to think how Lloyds is a bearer of Englishness, globally. Humanities-trained people are much more comfortable analysing cricket and Englishness (although sport is also absent from our book).

Anyway, what this leaves me to say is that if I was re-imagining the book now, I would conjugate it less in terms of class, race and gender and more in terms of England and Englishness' relationship with the globe. I still think that the English too often think that we are the centre of the world. *Our indebtedness* to that world is still less interrogated – what we made out of resources we begged, borrowed or stole, from here, there and everywhere.

Let's just take, as we might have done, Englishness and the United States, just in the field of literature. Oscar Wilde or Bernard Shaw, there is dispute who is the author, said we were separated by common language. The volume has an essay on the invention of English literature but I think we did not see how central to the invention of modern English literature were the Americans T. S. Eliot and Henry James. Also we might have considered how technology and its industrialisation (think early cinema) were helping to construct Englishness, at home and abroad (think Charlie Chaplin and, slightly later, Alfred Hitchcock, both of whom went to the US).

Another chapter might have centred on Englishness and Europe. Just take the subject of English art. There was Roger Fry's seminal 1910 exhibition of European post-impressionism which helped to re-route the Englishness of modern English art or the fact that Walter Sickert – the bearer of so much talk of Englishness and English art, from his Camden Town murder paintings to his music hall paintings – was born in Munich and had European painterly affiliations.

A third chapter might have centred on Englishness and Asia. I have already mentioned China and Englishness but just think of the way Joseph Conrad defines Englishness against Malaysia (foreshadowing Somerset Maugham and Anthony Burgess). Or look at Bernard Leach, the great bearer of Englishness and the English handmade crafts, in the wake of George Sturt's *The Wheelwright's Shop* – a writer who would be so important to F. R. Leavis. Scratch the surface and you'll see that Leach was born in Hong Kong and spent some of his early years in Japan. When he returned there he took with him the lessons of William Morris and a certain account of Englishness. But there was also the influence of Japan on Leach. Just read Tanya Harrod's brilliant *British Crafts in the Twentieth Century* to see how the Englishness of English crafts during our period was invested with an Asian aesthetic.

RC: What a great work our last book will be. Yes, the world is one place – never more so than in 1880–1920 – and it is always fascinating to pull the global threads and see where they originate. But it's more interesting to see where they go than where they came from. After all, as Ian Buruma shows (*Voltaire's Coconuts*, 1999) there was a time when men in different parts of the world were devoted to the English blazer, or sports jacket – but quite rightly it's the adaptations not the origins that capture his attention. Same for cricket, or ballroom dancing: once indisputably 'English', apparently, and forever locked in meaning against the 'Other' of course, but now indisputably Indian or Australian or Japanese or Russian as well. There are no autochthonous cultures.

If we were doing the volume again I'd certainly want to include a chapter on the many-coloured coat of Englishness, but in the end I'd want to come back to these islands and the political settlement which we used to call *the* constitution but which was far more complicated and interesting than what the definite article might suggest – and which, in fact, had change written into its very definition. Looking back, we could have done with the riches of the *Oxford History of the British Empire* when we started out, especially Andrew Porter's

Nineteenth Century and Judith Brown's *Twentieth Century* volumes. Peter Cain and A. G. Hopkins' gentlemanly capitalism theory of British imperialism (1993) would have been indispensable too – as would Bernard Porter's notion of the British as *Absent-Minded Imperialists* (2006). At the other end of the scale, Elizabeth Edwards' (2012) micro study of 55,000 English amateur photographs taken between 1885 and 1918 would have told us much – while for me Peter Mandler's forays into 'Olden Time' and at least two *Past and Present* pieces, Hopkins' 'Back to the Future. From National to Imperial History' (1997), and Paul Readman's 'The Place of the Past in English Culture' (2005), would have steadied my historical sense of the project as a whole. Michael Billig's *Banal Nationalism* (1995) is an innovative work which would have addressed the idea of the 'unexamined life'. So, along with Empire, and the photographs, and the long run considerations, I'd want to include Nairn on the Scots, Williams on the Welsh, Patrick Joyce on the role of the industrial regions in balancing the cultural deficit of London (*Visions of the People,* 1991), Jon Lawrence on party discourse (*Speaking for the People,* 1998), and, connected with all these matters, a chapter on the English folk revival by Georgina Boyes (*The Imagined Village* 1993), and a chapter from Richard Holt on modern sport – a peculiarity of the English if ever there was one. In many ways, Holt's *Sport and the British* (1989) was a treatise on national and regional identities without saying so.

PD: But at the time, it wasn't easy to find contributors for the book was it? As well as Empire I recall it was especially difficult to find people prepared to write on women. Only Pat Thane and Alice Jane Mackay took up the challenge. Like a lot of people who took up this book, including us, they were doing something well outside their comfort zone.

RC: It proved just as hard to find a publisher. They just didn't get it. I can remember you sitting in my office taking to a publisher on the telephone. After you had carefully explained what you meant by 'Englishness'; and after you had carefully explained what you meant by 'deconstruction'; I remember him saying '*Deconstruct England? Well what do you want to go and do that for?*'

You were holding the phone to me and we were holding our sides laughing, but it wasn't funny. Books were being published on everything except a subject whose time had come. We lacked contacts, I guess. I knew David Croom because Croom Helm had published me in 1977. But the terms were harsh. We had to seek a subsidy – which we gladly received from the Twenty Seven Foundation, a charity for needy books. And I must say the finished product looked terrible. The book was produced by camera copying of word processed pages. It was so hard to read I don't know how we got reviewed. Although they didn't all think alike or write alike, the contributors wrote brilliantly – way beyond their titles and with bibliographies that almost founded Englishness as a new subject: Howkins on 'The Discovery of Rural England', Brian Doyle on 'The Invention of English', Peter Brooker and

Peter Widdowson on 'A Literature for England', Jeremy Crump on 'The Reception of Elgar 1898–1935', Thane and Mackay on 'The Englishwoman', David George Boyce on 'Marginal Britons: the Irish', Dennis Smith on 'The Liberal Inheritance', Hugh Cunningham on 'The Conservative Party and Patriotism', and Stephen Yeo on 'Socialism, the State and some Oppositional Englishness'. Our own chapters swept through institutional and ideological features – far too fast in my case. Looking at the list now there was so much we left out, but at least what we left in addressed some of the carriers of modern cultural authority in these islands.

After that – and I'm not claiming causal connection here – there was a trickle of fine but disconnected work on English national identity, including Gerald Newman's outstanding *The Rise of English Nationalism* (1987), Raphael Samuel's various essays and workshop gleanings starting with *Patriotisms* (1989), and Alison Light's wonderful *Forever England: Femininity, Literature and Conservatism between the Wars* (1991). But the big splash came in 1992 with Linda Colley's *Britons: Forging the Nation 1707–1837*. This hit the spot. Colley wasn't trying to write about Englishness. Nor was she too bothered about current dilemmas (she stops in 1837). And she wasn't fussed about 'hegemony' and all that either, though she describes it well enough. She may have taken the concept of the reactive 'other' too far, but she knew what she wanted to say about the making of the eighteenth century British nation-state and said it best. If we were doing the book now I'd invite Linda Colley to write a chapter called *Britons*. Ah Dr Hindsight! You always write the best histories.

Then the avalanche began. Best sellers included Jeremy Paxman's skimming work, *The English. A Portrait of a People* (1998) and Norman Davies' general round-up, *The Isles* (1999). Davies ends with five great remonstrances, or propositions, on a state which in his opinion was never a nation-state like other nation-states. Particularly noteworthy, albeit with much smaller readerships, were David Gervais' *Versions of Englishness in Modern Writing* (1993), David Matless' *Landscape and Englishness* (1998), Stefan Collini's *English Pasts* (1999), Paul Langford's *Englishness Identified* (2000), and Peter Mandler's *The English National Character* (2006). Englishness went mediaeval in 1996 with Thorlac Turville-Petre's *England the Nation* followed by Adrian Hastings' *The Construction of Nationhood* (1997), Patrick Wormald's *The Making of English Law* (1999), and Andrea Ruddick's *English Identity and Political Culture in the Fourteenth Century* (2013). Twenty years on, Mandler (2006) reviewed the field to find Colls and Dodd ('preceding even Colley') 'frankly Gramscian' – which was fair.

Political scientists continued to make outstanding contributions. David Miller's *On Nationality* (1995) and Anthony Smith's *The Ethnic Origins of Nations* (1988) would have helped us enormously if they had been available in 1982 – with Miller's searching re-statement of national identity as the key to the nation-state, and Smith's study of national 'myth symbol complexes' almost before nation-states began. He quotes Emile Durkheim: 'There can be no society which does not feel the need of upholding and reaffirming at regular intervals the collective sentiments and the collective ideas which make its unity and personality'. Bhabha's *Nation and Narration* (1990) invoked another great Frenchman of the period by republishing Ernest Renan's Sorbonne lecture of 1882 'What Is A Nation?' Arthur Aughey's *The Politics of Englishness* (2007) reminded us of the importance of iteration in all these matters, while Krishan Kumar's *The Making of National Identity* (2003) acknowledged our work by making 1880–1920 the crux of his argument. Shlomo Sand stretched 'invention' to its farthest limits with his *The Invention of the Jewish People* in 2009 and *The Invention of the Land of Israel* in 2013. Roger Scruton's *England. An Elegy* (2002) showed a rare touch of love in these matters. I took it as a sure sign that our book had been either remembered or forgotten when Simon Featherstone called his book *Englishness* in 2009.

PD: So, we're writing a book about national identity at a moment when world markets begin to open up. Everything that is solid melts into air said Marx about an earlier phase of globalization, and it's as if Hegel, too, may have been right in his comment about the Owl of Minerva – that history, like the owl, flies only at dusk. In other words, in the 1980s we were coming to the end of an epoch in English history. Unlike Roger Scruton, what we were writing was not an elegy because I don't think either of us felt elegiac, but something was passing and we were marking it

RC: We were marking something, and it wasn't just Mrs Thatcher. The General Agreements on Tariffs and Trade (GATT) had been laying the global economic groundwork for over a generation and, once they went on stream and we were living in a free trade world, much else followed. But equally we were young enough, and foolish enough, maybe, to think the changes were temporary or could be reversed. As a result our book looked both ways: to an Englishness that had been 'invented' between 1880 and 1920, and to a new transnational market liberalism that was undermining that settlement far more effectively, and far more ruthlessly, than anything left-wing academics could dream up. What's happened since is the opening up of a country which at the time we were writing still had borders.

PD: That is why I'd want a volume about England, Englishness and the globe. England and Englishness were forged and marinaded in their engagement with the rest of the world. The English had never respected borders – culturally, politically or economically – for good and bad. The 1980s were the last gasp of the postwar settlement, and that settlement allowed too many of us to forget, or underestimate, that global England. It is important to say that the book nudged me into thinking about it

RC: In those days we had to explain our terms; now you can read about the deconstructed Englishness of everything including dancing, brewing, gardening, painting, fashion, dress, design, pop music, ethnicity, the Sea, the Cinema, citizenship, schooling, Auden, Betjeman, Anglo Saxons, Philip Larkin, George Orwell and Mother Goose. David Edgar might feel 'queasy' attending a festival of Englishness (*The Guardian*, 21 October 2013) but there's no shortage of people who want to know about it and of course we can be sure that of those 85,186 football fans who felt queasy watching a different festival of Englishness at Wembley the week before, very few would be feeling sick for cultural reasons.

You name it and it's the Englishness of something or its other. I even had another go in 2002 with my *Identity of England*. Mandler's 2006 review article described national identity as 'a subject of rapt fascination' among academics. In June 2012, Ed Miliband gave a keynote speech on Englishness. All prime ministers in recent years have returned to national identity again and again – although without profit.

PD: Do you think that one of the ways you and I have developed differently, given your loyalties in terms of your teaching and writing, and my loyalties in terms of my writing, cultural work with China, and broadcasting, is that I'm much more focused on England in the world, and you're much more focused on England in England. Is that fair?

RC: Seems so.

PD: It's not meant to be one better than the other, but I think that since 1986 you and I are good examples of how England has been pulled both ways – globally and locally.

There is probably another book to be written about why there has been a flood of books about Englishness over the last 30 years – from the academic through to the political to the popular. Let me just suggest one reason. I think that those who used to feel they had the right 'to speak for England' have become anxious over the last 30 years that they have lost authority – and this especially applies to the political class. I see the noise around Englishness as partly an attempt by the political elite to regain the power to speak for England. This is perfectly clear if you look at speeches and strategies by the last three Labour leaders Tony Blair, Gordon Brown and, as you mention, Ed Miliband. I remember well during the Labour government being sent a speech on national identity by a very senior minister. I lost count of the number of times we were 'a beacon to the world'. I crossed each and every one of them out. They referred back to the Armada and reinforced the sense that we were an example to the world. I think this is a very hard habit to kick. It was very noticeable in Ed Miliband's recent speech on Englishness that he made the habitual reference to an outward looking England and Englishness. But at no point did he put flesh on that particular bone. Inevitably, given the dimunition in authority of the political class, he did not try to root Englishness in metropolitan political institutions. He rooted Englishness in 'the people' and the Blitz spirit. For me, the problem with this is two-fold. The English cannot be simply summoned up or called into action by UKIP or by another political movement. The 'English' are not there, already formed.

Also, no longer do I think that Blitz spirit references are helpful. In the Blitz, the English (not to mention the rest of the UK) was under attack by an external enemy. I am not sure how this is to be reconciled with an outward looking Englishness.

I was born in a small mining village in Yorkshire, Grimethorpe, whose industry was taken away by Thatcher's government and by globalization. I was there recently and the first person I met was Polish. This is now the world of England.

I am always haunted by Bertolt Brecht's dictum 'Start from the bad new things, not the good old things'. I am not sure that the new things are always bad but for me a sense of Englishness has to start from here.

Englishness: Culture and Politics tells us where we came from. We need more than a new book to chart the future.

RC: It's an interesting proposition, but historians don't do futures. To put another point of view, it seems to me that social democracies can't survive the permanent instability that stems from the free flow of labour and capital in a European supra-state of 28 countries and 500 million people. I believe in intelligent interventions of the nation-state in order to make civil society stronger and private lives more agreeable for the many and, in order to be able to do that you need proper borders, citizens' rights, national insurance, and a social democratic movement that keeps as close as it can to the majority sensibility. I used to believe that this is what socialists believed too. In that sense my politics haven't changed much since when we first met. I don't see 'little England' as a term of abuse.

PD: But you know the response to that; let me give you a Chinese story.

I asked a Chinese friend of mine who owns an animation company in Beijing 'what do you do in your spare time?' because he seems to me to work 23 hours a day. He said, 'Oh it's fine Philip, I am doing a digital reconstruction of the Imperial Gardens in Beijing as they were before you burnt them down in the late nineteenth century'. So the truth is, in that sense, England has been 'out there' in the world for a long time. We may have forgotten it but others have not.

Also, both of us know that at its best English socialism has understood its connections with – and indebtedness to – the rest of the world. You just need to read Sara Bonjioni's *A Year Without 'Made in China': One Family's True Life Adventure in the Global Economy'* (2008) to see how much of our daily lives are dependent on Chinese workers. Borders are complex things in the economic sphere – not to mention the cultural one.

RC: Oh dear this is going to sound terribly boring but I think that social democracy's stability depends on its propensity to make sustainable political settlements that are fair and trusted, and it seems to me that the more you move away from the nation-state model, with borders, and mutuality, the more difficult such settlements become.

PD: Obviously, bearing down on Englishness now is a matter closer to home than China: the prospect of Scottish independence. It's true as you say that Tom Nairn's book was an early influence on us, but the problem with Tom's argument, as I see it, was that he saw England only as a diseased elite society. He wanted the break-up of Britain and if that happens won't the whole question of what England is come to the fore yet again?

RC: If Scotland votes for independence England will be thrown back on its own imagining. At first I think that might bring us and the Welsh closer together but over time I think the problem of a gargantuan London/South-East region will move centre stage. The other English and Welsh regions might come to see that a good part of Scotland's problem is their problem too – though how far this goes also depends on whether the Scots take their independence and how they manage it. The English political elite (it's different in Scotland) have no idea how to respond to what most people think. Their key political relationship, as you know only too well, is with the London political-media-intelligentsia.

It is important to democracies that states and nations stay in touch. Looking back, I suppose our book tried to examine one moment in that relationship – a moment of renewal, if you like. I can't really remember now what I thought I was doing with the book at the time other than stumbling forward. I don't think talk of 'deconstruction' or 'invention' makes what people did in the past any less interesting, or any less authentic, nor do I think I was trying to reveal a political deception or anything like that. But I *was* aware how cramped and pinched this particular vision of Englishness looked, and how many English people were actually excluded from it. Paradoxically, I learned from doing the book just how important liberalism was to the new Englishness and, out of that, what came later, the social democratic sense of self.

PD: I'm in part embarrassed by the book now because I think we shared some of the elite assumption – that we had the answers. The volume is so sublimely confident of its strategy: that if only we show the people that Englishness is 'invented', then, like that moment in the *Wizard of Oz* when Dorothy sees that the wizard is only a small man behind a curtain, all illusions would fall way. This was too often the problem of the left, and it is the problem I suppose of rationality too, really, that identity is lived in your body, in your demeanor, in your expressions, in your language. It is lived everywhere as well as your head and I think at least for me now, whatever its many virtues, from all the contributors, the book's weakness is that it suffered from the kind of smugness that thought it could simply undermine settled identities without offering an alternative of how to live.

RC: Is that an invitation to try again?

Select bibliography

Adams, George Burton, *Constitutional History of England* (London: Cape, 1920).

Alexander, Claire E., *The Art of Being Black: The Creation of Black British Youth Identities* (Oxford: Clarendon Press, 1996).

Anderson, Benedict, *Imagined Communities: Reflections on the Origin and Spread of Nationalism* (London: Verso, 1983).

Anderson, Perry, 'Origins of the Present Crisis', *New Left Review*, 23 (1964).

Aughey, Arthur, *The Politics of Englishness* (Manchester: Manchester University Press, 2007).

Augusteijn, Joost and Storm, Eric (eds), *Region and State in Nineteenth-Century Europe: Nation-Building, Regional Identities and Separatism* (Basingstoke: Palgrave Macmillan, 2012).

Baxendale, John, *Priestley's England. J. B. Priestley and English Culture* (Manchester: Manchester University Press, 2007).

Baycroft, Timothy and Hewitson, Mark (eds), *What Is A Nation? Europe 1789–1914* (Oxford: Oxford University Press, 2006).

Bhabha, Homi K., *Nation and Narration* (London: Routledge, 1990).

Billig, Michael, *Banal Nationalism* (London: Sage, 1995).

Blake, Robert (ed.), *The English World: History, Character, and People* (London: Thames & Hudson, 1982).

Bonjioni, Sara, *A Year Without 'Made in China': One Family's True Life Adventure in the Global Economy* (London: John Wiley, 2008).

Bounds, Philip, *Orwell and Marxism* (London: I. B. Tauris, 2009).

Boyes, Georgina, *The Imagined Village: Culture, Ideology and the English Folk Revival* (Manchester: Manchester University Press, 1993).

Brenton, Howard, *The Romans in Britain* (National Theatre, 1980).

Brockliss, Lawrence and Eastwood, David (eds), *A Union of Multiple Identities: The British Isles, c.1750–1850* (Manchester: Manchester University Press, 1997).

Brown, Judith (ed.), *Oxford History of the British Empire, vol. iii, The Twentieth Century* (Oxford: Oxford University Press, 2001).

Burrow, J. W., *A Liberal Descent. Victorian Historians and the English Past* (Cambridge: Cambridge University Press, 1981).

Buruma, Ian, *Voltaire's Coconuts: Anglomania in Europe* (London: Weidenfeld and Nicolson, 2001).

Butterfield, Herbert, *The Englishman and his History* (Cambridge: Cambridge University Press, 1944).

Cain, Peter and Hopkins, A. G., *British Imperialism: Innovation and Expansion 1688–1914* (London: Longman, 1993).

Calder, Angus, *The People's War* (London: Pantheon Books, 1969).

Cannadine, David, *Ornamentalism: How the British Saw their Empire* (Oxford: Oxford University Press, 2001).

Carey, John, *The Intellectuals and the Masses: Pride and Prejudice among the Literary Intelligentsia 1880–1939* (London: Faber & Faber, 1992).

Churchill, Caryl, *Light Shining in Buckinghamshire* (Royal Court Theatre, 1976).

Clarke, John, Critcher, Charles and Johnson, Richard (eds), *Working Class Culture: Studies in History and Theory* (London: Hutchinson, 1979).

Colley, Linda, *Britons: Forging the Nation 1707–1837* (London: Pimlico, 1992).

Collini, Stefan, *English Pasts* (Oxford: Oxford University Press, 1999).

Colls, Robert, *The Collier's Rant*: *Song and Culture in the Industrial Village* (London: Croom Helm, 1977).

—*Identity of England* (Oxford: Oxford University Press, 2002).

—'Gael and Northumbrian: Separatism and Regionalism in the UK 1890–1920', in Augusteijn and Storm, *Region and State* (Basingstoke: Palgrave Macmillan, 2012).

—*George Orwell English Rebel* (Oxford: Oxford University Press, 2013).

Corrigan, Philip and Sayer, Derek, *The Great Arch: English State Formation as Cultural Revolution* (Oxford: Basil Blackwell, 1985).

Curtis, Tony (ed.), *Wales: The Imagined Nation. Essays in Cultural and National Identity* (Bridgend: Poetry Wales Press, 1986).

Dangerfield, George, *The Strange Death of Liberal England* (London: Constable, 1935).

Davies, Norman, *The Isles*: *A History* (Oxford: Oxford University Press, 1999).

Davis, Mike, *Planet of the Slums* (London: Verso, 2007).

Dicey, A. V., *Introduction to the Study of the Law of the Constitution* (1885), with a *Commentary* by E. C. S. Wade (London: Macmillan, 1964).

Dodd, Philip, 'Art, History and Englishness: An Open Letter', *Modern Painters*, 1iv (1988/89): 40–1.

—*The Battle Over Britain* (London: Demos, 1995).

—'Modern Stories', in Ian Christie and Philip Dodd (eds), *Spellbound: Art and Film* (London: BFI, 1996).

Edwards, Elizabeth, *The Camera as Historian: Amateur Photographs and the Historical Imagination 1885–1918* (Durham: Duke University Press, 2012).

Featherstone, Simon, *Englishness: Twentieth-Century Popular Culture and the Forming of English Identity* (Edinburgh: Edinburgh University Press, 2009).

Fuller, Peter, *Beyond the Crisis in Art* (London: Writers and Readers, 1981).

Gellner, Ernest, *Nations and Nationalism* (Oxford: Basil Blackwell, 1983).

Gervais, David, *Literary Englands: Versions of 'Englishness' in Modern Writing* (Cambridge: Cambridge University Press, 1993).

Gilroy, Paul, '*There Ain't No Black in the Union Jack*': *The Cultural Politics of Race and Nation* (London: Hutchinson, 1987).

Grainger, J. H., *Patriotisms. Britain 1900–1939* (London: Routledge & Kegan Paul, 1986).

Gramsci, Antonio, Hoare, Quintin and Nowell-Smith, Geoffrey, *Selections from the Prison Notebooks* (London: Lawrence & Wishart, 1971).

Hall, Catherine, *Civilizing Subjects: Metropole and Colony in the English Imagination 1830–1867* (Cambridge: Polity Press, 2002).

Harris, Alexandra, *Romantic Moderns: English Writers, Artists and the Imagination from Virginia Woolf to John Piper* (London: Thames & Hudson, 2010).

Harrod, Tanya, *The Crafts in Britain in the Twentieth Century* (New Haven: Yale University Press, 1999).

Hastings, Adrian, *The Construction of Nationhood: Ethnicity, Religion and Nationalism* (Cambridge: Cambridge University Press, 1997).

Hebdige, Dick, *Subcultures: The Meaning of Style* (London: Routledge, 1979).

Holt, Richard, *Sport and the British* (Oxford: Oxford University Press, 1989).

Hopkins, A. G., 'Back to the Future. From National to Imperial History', *Past and Present*, 164 (1999).

Hudson, Hugh, director, *Chariots of Fire* (film 1981).

Joyce, Patrick, *Visions of the People: Industrial England and the Question of Class* (Cambridge: Cambridge University Press, 1991).

Kidd, Colin, 'North Britishness and the Nature of 18c British Patriotisms', *The Historical Journal*, 39, 2 (1996).

—*British Identities before Nationalism: Ethnicity and Nationhood in the Atlantic World 1600–1800* (Cambridge: Cambridge University Press, 1999).

Kohn, Hans, *Nationalism: Its Meaning and History* (New York: Van Nostrand Reinhold, 1971).

Krishna, Sanjav, *Reading the Global: Perspectives on Britain's Empire in Asia* (New York: Columbia University Press, 2007).

Kumar, Krishan, *The Making of English National Identity* (Cambridge: Cambridge University Press, 2003).

Kureishi, Hanif, *The Buddha of Suburbia* (London: Faber & Faber, 1990).

Kureishi, Hanif and Frears, Stephen, director, *My Beautiful Launderette* (film 1985).

Langford, Paul, *Englishness Identified: Manners and Character 1650–1850* (Oxford: Oxford University Press, 2000).

Lawrence, Jon, *Speaking for the People: Party, Language and Popular Politics in England 1867–1914* (Cambridge: Cambridge University Press, 1998).

Light, Alison, *Forever England: Femininity, Literature and Conservatism between the Wars* (London: Routledge, 1991).

Macintyre, Alasdair, *After Virtue: A Study in Moral Theology* (Notre Dame: University of Notre Dame Press, 1981).

Mandler, Peter, *The English National Character: The History of an Idea from Edmund Burke to Tony Blair* (New Haven: Yale University Press, 2006).

—'What is "National Identity"? Definitions and Applications in Modern British Historiography', *Modern Intellectual History*, 3, 2 (2006).

—'Revisiting Olden Time', in T. String and M. Bull (eds), *Tudorism* (Oxford: Oxford University Press, 2011).

Matless, David, *Landscape and Englishness* (London: Reaktion, 1998).

McEwan, Ian, *On Chesil Beach* (London: Cape, 2007).

Miller, David, *On Nationality* (Oxford: Clarendon Press, 1995).

Nairn, Tom, *The Break Up of Britain: Crisis and Neo-Nationalism* (London: New Left Books, 1977).

Newman, Gerald, *The Rise of English Nationalism: A Cultural History 1740–1830* (London: Weidenfeld & Nicolson, 1987).

Paxman, Jeremy, *The English: A Portrait of a People* (London: Michael Joseph, 1998).

Pevsner, Nikolaus, *The Englishness of English Art* (London: Architectural Press, 1956).

Pond, Allan, 'Beyond Memory's Reach: The Peculiarities of English Radicalism', *The Quarterly Review*, 2, 4 (Winter 2008).

Porter, Andrew (ed.), *Oxford History of the British Empire, vol. iii, Nineteenth Century* (Oxford: Oxford University Press, 2001).

Porter, Bernard, *The Absent-Minded Imperialists: Empire, Society and Culture in Britain* (Oxford: Oxford University Press, 2006).

Porter, Roy (ed.), *Myths of the English* (Cambridge: Polity Press, 1992).

Quincey, Thomas De, 'Confessions of an English Opium-Eater: Being An Extract from the Life of a Scholar', *London Magzine* (September/October 1821).

Ranger, T. O. and Hobsbawm, E. J. (eds), *The Invention of Tradition* (Cambridge: Cambridge University Press, 1983).

Readman, Paul, 'The Place of the Past in English Culture', *Past and Present*, 186 (2005).

Renan, Ernest, 'What Is A Nation?' (1882), in Bhabha, *Nation and Narration* (London: Methuen, 1990).

Richards, Jeffrey, *Films and British National Identity* (Manchester: Manchester University Press, 1997).

Robinson-Dunn, Diane, *The Harem, Slavery and British Imperial Culture: Anglo-Muslim Relations in the Late Nineteenth Century* (Manchester: Manchester University Press, 2006).

Rohmer, Sax (A. H. S. Ward), *The Mystery of Dr Fu-Manchu* (1913).

Ruddick, Andrea, *English Identity and Political Culture in the Fourteenth Century* (Cambridge: Cambridge University Press, 2013).

Rushdie, Salman, *The Satanic Verses* (Harmondsworth: Penguin, 1988).

Said, Edward, *Orientalism* (London: Peregrine, 1985).

Samuel, Raphael (ed.), *Patriotisms: The Making and Unmaking of British National Identity, vol. ii, Minorities and Outsiders* (London: Routledge, 1989).

Samuel, Raphael, *Theatres of Memory, vol. i, Past and Present in Contemporary Culture* (London: Verso, 1994).

—*Theatres of Memory, vol. ii, Island Stories: Unravelling Britain* (London: Verso, 1998).

Sand, Shlomo, *The Invention of the Jewish People* (London: Verso, 2010).

—*The Invention of the Land of Israel* (London: Verso, 2013).

Schwarz, Bill (ed.), *The Expansion of England: Race, Ethnicity, and Cultural History* (London: Routledge, 1996).

Scruton, Roger, *England: An Elegy* (London: Pimlico, 2001).

Shannon, Richard, *The Crisis of Imperialism 1865–1915* (London: Hart-Davis, MacGibbon, 1976).

Shaxson, Nicolas, *Treasure Islands: Tax Havens and the Men who Stole the World* (London: Vintage, 2012).

Shiel, M. P., *The Yellow Danger* (1898).
Smith, Anthony, *The Ethnic Origins of Nations* (Oxford: Basil Blackwell, 1988).
Snell, K. D. M., *Parish and Belonging: Community, Identity and Welfare in England and Wales 1700–1950* (Cambridge: Cambridge University Press, 2006).
Stoker, Bram, *Dracula* (1897).
Sturt, George, *The Wheelwright's Shop* (Cambridge: Cambridge University Press, 1923).
Thompson, E. P., *The Making of the English Working Class* (London: Gollancz, 1963).
—'The Peculiarities of the English', *Socialist Register*, 2 (1965).
—*Customs in Common* (London: Penguin, 1993).
Turville-Petre, Thorlac, *England the Nation. Language, Literature and National Identity 1290–1340* (Oxford: Clarendon Press, 1996).
Weight, Richard, *Patriots. National Identity in Britain 1940–2000* (London: Macmillan, 2002).
Wiener, Martin J., *English Culture and the Decline of the Industrial Spirit 1850–1980* (Cambridge: Cambridge University Press, 1981).
Williams, G. A., 'The Concept of "Egemonia" in the thought of Antonio Gramsci'. Some notes on interpretation', *Journal of the History of Ideas*, 21 (1960).
—*When Was Wales?* (Harmondsworth: Penguin, 1985).
Williams, Raymond, *Politics and Letters: Interviews with New Left Review* (London: Verso, 1981).
Wormald, Patrick, *The Making of English Law: King Alfred to the Twelfth Century, vol. i, Legislation and it Limits* (Oxford: Blackwell 1999).
Wright, Patrick, *On Living in an Old Country* (London: Verso, 1985).

Apart from a very few minor revisions, the text is unchanged from the 1987 edition.

CHAPTER ONE

Englishness and the national culture

Philip Dodd

The characteristic "Englishness" of English culture was made then very much what it is now. The quip that all the oldest English traditions were invented in the last quarter of the nineteenth century has great point.[1]

RICHARD SHANNON, *The Crisis of Imperialism*

Richard Shannon's judgement is central to the argument of this chapter, even if 'invented' does not adequately register the complex and overlapping processes of invention, transformation and recovery which characterized the remaking of English identity and the national culture in the later years of the nineteenth century. Complementing Robert Colls' argument which follows, this chapter argues that Englishness and the 'English spirit' were the preoccupation not only of the political culture, but also of what we might now call the institutions and practices of a cultural politics. Indeed an Englishness sited exclusively – or even primarily – in political institutions would hardly have established itself as the centre and circumference of our thinking about ourselves and our history. Certainly one does not have to think for long to acknowledge that many of our educational and, more generally, cultural traditions and institutions were forged in the later part of the nineteenth century. For instance, the tools without which this study is unimaginable – *The New English Dictionary* (1884–1928) and the *Dictionary of National Biography* (1885–1900) – are also among its objects of study; and the academic disciplines out of which the two editors write, English Literature and History, were fashioned in their present forms during this period.

I

To understand *whose* account of Englishness and the national culture was authorized during this period, and *how* it was authorized, some words from Edward Said's impressive study of the colonization and representation by Europe of the Orient are helpful. Said's argument is that,

> without examining Orientalism as a discourse one cannot possibly understand the enormously systematic discipline by which European culture was able to manage – and even produce – the Orient politically, sociologically, militarily, ideologically, scientifically and imaginatively during the post-Enlightenment period.[2]

To translate Said's argument for our purposes: a great deal of the power of the dominant version of Englishness during the last years of the nineteenth century and the early years of the twentieth century lay in its ability to represent both itself to others and those others to themselves. Such representation worked by a process of inclusion, exclusion and transformation of elements of the cultural life of these islands. What constituted knowledge, the control and dissemination of that knowledge to different groups, the legitimate spheres and identity of those groups, their repertoire of appropriate actions, idioms and convictions – all were the subject, *within the framework of the national culture and its needs,* of scrutiny, license and control.

But before we embark on a mapping of this English national culture and its constituent parts, one thing needs to be said. Although there is certainly evidence to support the thesis that Englishness and the national culture were reconstituted in order to incorporate and neuter various social groups – for example, the working class, women, the Irish – who threatened the dominant social order, it is unhelpful for two reasons to see the reconstitution as a simple matter of the imposition of an identity by the dominant on the subordinate. First, the remaking of class, gender and national identity was undertaken at such a variety of social locations and by such various groups that it is difficult to talk of a common intention. It was, for instance, undertaken not only within the new state schools and within the new public schools and ancient (and new) universities, but also by quite a remarkable number of groups, professional and otherwise, who took it upon themselves for various reasons to explore and 'colonise' others. What these groups shared was not necessarily a common intention, but (often) an interlocking membership and an overlapping vocabulary of evaluation. The other reason why 'imposition' is too simple is that the establishment of hegemony involves negotiation and 'active consent' on the part of the subordinated.[3] Take, for instance, the case of women who, as Virginia Woolf said, 'are, perhaps, the most discussed animal in the universe'.[4] It is undoubtedly true that a separate spheres ideology was elaborated by professional males during the last quarter of the nineteenth century; but it is also true that at least some of the groups of women most opposed to male domination often proclaimed women's moral superiority: 'while they challenged women's traditional roles, they adopted much of the traditional conception of womanhood, which they, like the anti-feminists, saw as rooted in women's domestic situation and above all in her potential if not her actual maternity'.[5] Not any identity can be imposed, then; it must at least be consented to. And even to acknowledge this is still to ignore completely oppositional identities and practices forged by the subordinated groups – or at least, and this is what my argument does, to note such identities and practices only when they were forged within and against those offered to them from above.

What I propose to do is to build a general argument about the national culture and the English around particular instances. The chapter is in two parts. First, I examine the identity and 'place' within the national culture of a number of social groups, during a period when 'class loyalties and conflicts [were] set in a genuinely national framework for the first time'.[6] The groups chosen for scrutiny are the working class and the Celts. (Needless to say, other groups have powerful claims for attention.)[7] Second, I trace, through the examples of the English language and the National Theatre (with sideway glances at the *Dictionary of National Biography* and the National Portrait Gallery), how the cultural history and contemporary life of the English were stabilized and articulated anew.

II

First, a brief sketch of the dominant English. The centrality of educational institutions for the control and dissemination of a national identity hardly needs stressing, and was especially clear during the later years of the nineteenth century with the dramatic reorganization and extension of state education. But what is interesting is that, as the new 'national system of education' began to be held responsible for the (ill-) health of the national culture,[8] the 'English spirit' was seen *not* to reside in such institutions – as one might expect – but to be incarnate elsewhere. Compare two comments, one from the end, one from the beginning, of the period. In 1929, Bernard Darwin, in one of a large number of books around that time about the public school system, said that, whatever one's views of it, 'it is really to a great extent the English character that we are criticising'.[9] And in 1869,

Matthew Arnold argued in *Culture and Anarchy* that to belong to the national life one had to belong or to affiliate to certain English institutions: the Anglican Church and Oxford or Cambridge University. Arnold's definition was sufficiently flexible to accommodate John Milton, sufficiently definite to exclude the culture of the nonconformists.[10] The argument that the history of the working class, and of women, as well as certain bourgeois data have often been buried out of sight of the 'national mind' may seem to attest to the power of Arnold's and his successors' equation of Englishness with certain institutions.[11]

The establishment of those educational institutions identified by Matthew Arnold and Bernard Darwin as custodians and transmitters of English culture entailed substantial change on the part of each of the institutions. First, the ancient universities. During the late-nineteenth century, their constituency changed from landed and clerical families to professional and rich business ones, and their graduates increasingly selected careers in the secular professions – including the academic one.[12] Certainly the responsibility of the ancient universities to the nation was an important matter for debate. When criticisms were made of their curriculum by scientists, the frame of reference was not those institutions' inadequate sense of what constituted knowledge, but the nation: 'That the ancient universities are keeping the nation back there cannot be a doubt.' Or when their serviceableness was called into question it was, according to James Bryce, who was later to be a Liberal minister, a matter of 'how to make the universities serviceable to the whole nation, instead of only to the upper classes'.[13] Needless to say, such service did not mean they had to acknowledge responsibility for the educational needs of *all* men and women; although one ought to add that the rhetoric of national service was, to a degree, coercive and successful (for instance, in the University Extension Movement). It could also lead Mark Pattison, Rector of Lincoln College, Oxford, to say that a National University should be 'co-extensive with the nation; it should be the common source of the whole of the higher (or secondary) education for the country'.[14] The price exacted by Pattison for Oxford's acknowledgement of its national responsibilities was high: the agreement that it was *the* source of all higher instruction, a centre of, and authority on, the national culture. In *Oxford and Working-Class Education* (1908), it was stated that 'The Trade Union Secretary and the 'Labour Member' need an Oxford education as much . . . as the Civil Servant or the barrister'.[15]

The shift of national authority to the (ancient) universities – their establishment as custodians of the national culture – may be encapsulated in the example of the school subject History which was made compulsory in 1900 in secondary schools. What is interesting in this context is that the authorship of History textbooks moved from upper middle-class amateurs to school-teachers and finally to academics. Almost all the texts written to respond to the education codes at the end of the century were produced by academics. Not only is what counts as History important, but also who controls what, who is representing whom and in what circumstances.[16] In short what was authorized as History for the new national education constituency was under the control of a particular specialized group. As we shall see, all geographical locations in England are equal but some are more equal than others. For instance, the 'essential' England may have been represented as 'rural', but it is noteworthy how many of the figures who represented it as such derived their authority from metropolitan centres such as Oxford.[17]

In order to join Oxford and Cambridge as the guardians of English cultural life, the public schools also had to undergo change. For instance, the 'old boy' consciousness was inculcated in the later-nineteenth century – fewer than five per cent of Thomas Arnold's 'old boys' sent their sons to Rugby[18] – and the relationship of the schools to Oxford and Cambridge was intensified: between 1855 and 1899 four fifths of Oxford and Cambridge students were public schoolboys, a greater percentage than ever before. Perhaps the most important change was the one that prised the schools from their local attachments. As Brian Simon has shown, the most significant condition for the 'transformation of an endowed grammar school into a public school was the exclusion of local foundationers – the sons of tradesmen, farmers or workers'. Alienated from their locality, and 'transformed into residential schools, servicing a single class', the schools were fit to play their role as the guardians of English cultural life.[19]

But these schools did not, of course, select only in terms of class but also – like Oxford and Cambridge – in terms of gender. (The cornerstone of the curriculum, classics, was seen as unsuitable for women.) A great deal has usefully been written about the public school system, but what is important to this argument is its construction of masculinity, and its exclusion of women – within the terms of the argument, the exclusion of certain qualities which had been ceded to the female. Indeed one might go so far to argue that the core of the curriculum *was* masculinity:

> "Manliness", a substantive widely favoured by prelates on speechdays and headmasters on Sundays, embraced antithetical values – success, aggression, and ruthlessness, yet victory within the rules, courtesy in triumph, compassion for the defeated. The concept contained the substance not only of Spencerian functionalism but also the chivalric romanticism of an English Bayard: egotism coexisted uneasily with altruism.[20]

But before discussing masculinity it is worth noting that the absence of women – of 'female' qualities – was remedied by reconstituting male relationships within the institution. Fagging, which acted in this way, involved 'wholly domestic chores, considered totally "feminine", in a period when no male would ever in other circumstances make toast and tea or lay and light a fire'.[21] Such reconstituted male relationships were also at the core of what has been called the homoerotic writing of World War I, which was organized around the simultaneous exclusion of women and inclusion of those qualities which were seen as female: 'the other ranks [during the war] were equivalent to the younger boys, and as at school, one generally admired them from a distance'; 'What inspired such passion was . . . good looks, innocence, vulnerability, protection and admiration. The object was mutual affection, protection and admiration.'[22]

Masculinity itself, which was best articulated in the public schools in the recently institutionalized games (which had themselves by 1929 become part of the 'English [educational] tradition'), is as interesting for what it excludes as what it includes. In 1872, W. Turley in the journal *The Dark Blue* urged support for masculinity, relating nationhood, gender and appropriate activity in his argument that 'a nation of effeminate enfeebled bookworms scarcely forms the most effective bulwark of a nation's liberties'.[23] 'Vigorous, manly and English' was the popular collocation. The identification of the English with the masculine could even determine matters of literary style. Given that males had at least to read and write (but not too much), they must cultivate a 'masculine' style, as many of the books on style made clear. For instance, Arthur Quiller-Couch could say in one of a series of lectures at the University of Cambridge: 'Generally use transitive verbs, that strike their objects and use them in the active voice. . . . For as a rough law, by his use of the straight verb and by economy of adjectives, you can tell a man's style, if it be masculine or neuter, writing or composition'.[24] In the arguments of the Oxford historian, E. A. Freeman – with his love of pre-Conquest England – the distinguishing characteristic of the English and of his [sic] language was, according to J. A. Burrow, 'its honest . . . manliness and simplicity'. Freeman wished to purge the language of 'effeminate Latin or French words'. Alfred Austin, the poet, was a good example of a 'concrete individual Englishman', according to the *Quarterly Review,* for he wrote a 'poetry of commonsense and healthy directness'. Such a climate may help to clarify the significance of the condemnations which, say, Lawrence's *The Rainbow* (1915) suffered when attention was given to its 'morbidly perverted ingenuity of style'.[25] What such a judgement did was to link the (un-English) 'ingenious' style of *The Rainbow* with the conviction that Lawrence was 'unmanly' (the *OED* notes that the first occurrence of 'perverted' in a sexual sense is 1906; Partridge's *Slang Dictionary* gives 1918 as the date at which perverted began to be used in certain social circles to mean 'buggered'). The dominant English licensed to other groups and to other nationalities those 'female' qualities which it did not acknowledge itself to possess. As recently as 1973, Professor William Walsh could write in his book *Commonwealth Literature* that Indians do not write in a 'direct, masculine way', but with 'Indian tenderness'.[26]

It is not surprising that one response of female writers during 1880–1920 to the masculine norm was to recognize it and to devalue it, and to go on to identify a superior *female* form of writing. Summarizing such a view, Elaine Showalter argues that its proponents saw women as disadvantaged – 'not as a deprived sub-culture forced to use the dominant tongue, but as a superior race, forced to operate on a lower level'.[27] As we shall see elsewhere, a subordinated group often gained a degree of autonomy at the cost of accepting the terms of the argument set by the dominant group.

Men, then, that is, gentlemen, recognized each other through a shared repertoire of activity, gesture and idiom, including pronunciation, 'for whose standardisation in the late nineteenth century (at the expense of regional accents) the public school system was largely responsible'.[28] Mark Girouard's *The Return of Camelot: Chivalry and the English Gentleman* has traced the establishment of a code for gentlemen, one which structured their interpretation of their behaviour if not the behaviour itself. For instance, Captain Scott in his expedition – which had been named the National Antarctic Expedition – was described by *The Times* as 'chivalrous in his conduct'; and Roland Huntford's *Scott and Amundsen* has argued persuasively that Scott's representation of his group's behaviour was organized in terms of the chivalric code.[29] Certainly its reach was extensive; it could, for example, license imperial endeavour (*Heart of Darkness* [1902]: 'from Sir Francis Drake to Sir John Franklin, knights all, titled and untitled . . . they had all gone out on that stream, bearing the sword, and often the torch'); it could authorize the male's adoption of an attitude of responsibility towards the female – and appropriate female behaviour; and it could also articulate for various reform movements an appropriate stance towards those whom they wished to colonize. The success of the Primrose League, founded in 1883 as an auxiliary social and educational organization to support Conservatism, was due, according to Brian Simon, to the fact that its 'techniques, ritual and feudal overtones chimed in with traditional practices and attitudes among sectors of the rural population'. The power of the code might be judged by noting how even its opponents paid it the compliment of using its vocabulary to influence their audience. For instance, Edward Carpenter argued that the habits of the gentleman and lady must be left behind if there was any desire to 'win the honorable title of man or woman in the world's Modern Chivalry'.[30]

The dominant English cultural ideal of the late-nineteenth century was then sited in certain institutions which underwent transformation, served 'national' not local needs, gained authority to define themselves and others, and inculcated appropriate (male) behaviour defining its function in and to the national culture: 'Yet some who tried/In vain to earn a colour while at Eton,/Have found a place upon an English side/That can't be beaten'.[31]

III

But, of course, an Englishness centred exclusively on such institutions could hardly hope to mobilize the people in its defence. What about the others? The quotation from J. A. Mangan above on masculinity, which refers to Herbert Spencer and functionalism gives us a clue. Certainly there was little dispute about the adequacy of society-as-organism analogies during the period[32]:

> From each member in a biological organism are demanded certain functional activities for the support of the life of the organism. . . . In a body which is in health and functions economically, every one contributes to the life of the organism according to its powers. . . . Each limb, each cell has a "right" to its due supply of blood. (1909)

> to consider that phenomenon in the life of the national organism which in Nature is known as disease . . . the second step in the establishment of scientific politics is the application of society as an organism. (1904)

The provenance of the analogy is not of primary concern here. What is important is that the analogy offered to resolve the tension between a hierarchical educational and social order and the concept of a horizontal community (Benedict Anderson's recent description of the self-perception of a national community),[33] by positing that social groups had different *not* unequal responsibilities and functions: 'Each limb, each cell has a "right" to its *due supply* of blood' (my emphasis). I want to trace the identity and place offered to two groups within the national culture: the working class and the 'Celts.'

First, the working class, its identity, its educational needs and its appropriate sphere of action. Study of that class took on epidemic proportions during this period, drawing on old representations for new purposes. Indeed, concern with that class often translated itself into observation and study. One of the major forms of that study was the 'Into Unknown England' writing of the late-nineteenth century and early-twentieth century, in which the older traditions of personal exploration blended 'into the newer techniques of sociological analysis,'[34] and which included works such as Charles Booth's *Life and Labour of the People in London* (1889–1903), Rider Haggard's *Rural England* (1902) and Robert Sherard's *The White Slaves of England* (1897). Central to such works and others was the construction of class as a *cultural* formation. As Gareth Stedman Jones has said, 'it was only at the beginning of the twentieth century – in London at least – that middle-class observers began to realize that the working class was not simply without culture or morality, but in fact possessed a "culture" of its own.'[35] Even the East End – that den of 'mystery' – *began* to be seen in new terms: 'Its real people labour, they do not loaf; they toil, they do not thieve. Labour here is very laborious.'[36]

The people who were seen and studied were, as the quotation suggests, construed predominantly in terms of their (manual) labour. And, with women increasingly consigned to the home, the working class as a class was identified as male. When female labour was glimpsed, the maleness of the observer was put into question: 'Indeed no part of this work is work for women, and his manhood is ashamed who sees these poor females swinging their heavy hammers.'[37] The illegitimate deduction that what was the essential characteristic of the (male) working class was its *physicality* – articulated in its work and pleasures – was drawn from the fact that the majority of the class worked as manual labourers. Working-mens' bodies – the suffering inscribed upon them by their work or their wonderful vigour and strength – carried positive meaning, and continued to do so in that extension of the 'Unknown England' tradition, the British documentary film movement of the 1920s and 1930s, which celebrated the worker as 'a heroic figure' and 'the ardour and bravery of common labour.'[38] The noun Labour, in the sense of 'the general body of labourers and operatives . . . with regard to its political interests and claims,' made its first appearance in 1880, according to the *OED*.

For the travellers into unknown England, the working class led lives which were congruent with their physical nature. This is Charles Booth, drawing on a vocabulary whose oppositions (natural/artificial) were traditional by the late-nineteenth century: 'I see nothing improbable in the general view that the simple natural lives of working-class people tend to their own and their children's happiness more than the artificial complicated existence of the rich.'[39] But the meaning of such a vocabulary is not exhausted by identifying its etymology. Consider the translation of Booth's vocabulary by his co-worker, Beatrice Webb. Writing about Bacup, which she visited in disguise in 1883, Beatrice Webb shared Booth's vocabulary: Bacup 'knows nothing of the complexities of modern life'; it has no place for 'complicated motives.' She went on to elaborate the implications for its inhabitants: they lack 'the far-stretching imagination of cosmopolitanism, don't realise the existence of a larger world.'[40] And in such a judgement the working class were fixed; their strengths were inseparable from what they were constitutionally unsuited for. Their way of life was simple (not complex), their mode of address direct (not sophisticated), their skills practical (not theoretical), their appropriate sphere of activity local (not national). What, in short, such a vocabulary as Booth's and Webb's did was to fix working-class concerns and competence and ratify the mental/manual distinction. Compare Sylvia Pankhurst on Annie Kenney, a cotton operative, and a recruit to the Women's Social and Political Union: 'Her lack of perspective, her very intellectual limitations, lent her a certain directness of purpose – when she became an instrument of a more powerful mind.'[41] It comes as no surprise to find that the *OED* lists as one of the emergent late-nineteenth century meanings of *manual*: 'Now esp of physical labour, an occupation etc., as opposed to *mental, theoretical.*' It is, of course, important to acknowledge, if only in parenthesis, that the emphasis on the 'localism' of the working class did answer to one of its strengths: the extraordinary development through the nineteenth century of 'Co-operative Centres and halls, Working Mens' Clubs and a plethora of small *often highly local initiatives* organized by women and men for their own cultural and political purposes.'[42]

The contours of the identity of the (male) working class sketched above, and the vocabulary which articulated it, can be seen in other accounts of that class during the period. I want to look briefly at two of them. First, the University Extension Movement. Although, as Brian Doyle says in his chapter in this volume, the University Extension Movement failed to penetrate seriously the working-class, what it did do was to confirm a particular account of what constituted working-class identity. If the social explorers and 'settlers' used the language of *terra incognita* to describe their journeys into working-class lives, so too did working-class people, when they wished to describe the education they were offered by the Extension Movement: 'I have lived in Cleveland about eighteen years of my life, but find it true that I am now in a strange country. I mean however to know it'; or, 'I was always buying books, picking them up here and there and everywhere . . . but of course I couldn't have found my way alone. I should have got lost in the wilderness or stuck in a bog.' What these metaphors suggest is that the cost exacted of the working class for the granting to them their own culture was the ceding of knowledge and learning to their masters. Such a surrender must have been particularly easy, given the interpenetration of knowledge and certain class habits – for instance, of demeanour and pronunciation. (This is not to deny that matters of skill and practice – which the best will in the world will not wish away – were involved.) The consequence was that teachers and students granted to each other and claimed for themselves a particular terrain of experience and knowledge. What is striking is the overlap of vocabulary with that sketched above. Students would sometimes oppose book knowledge to their own 'ingenuity with practical work'; and teachers and observers would oppose the 'dumb insight and sensibility' of the working-class male and his ability 'to think in the concrete' to the academic's ability to 'think in abstract and general terms of culture.'[43]

Such vocabulary extended to formal educational institutions. A practising schools inspector as well as one of those lobbying on behalf of State intervention in education, Matthew Arnold articulated clearly his conviction that educational needs had to be weighed in relation to the 'evident proximate destination' of a particular social group: 'To the middle class the grand aim of education should be to give largeness of soul and personal dignity; to the lower class, feeling, gentleness, humanity.' Arnold's assignment of certain needs to the working class led him to propose a curriculum which stressed *affective* material: 'Good poetry . . . implies the evolution so helpful in making principles operative. Hence its extreme importance to all of us; but in our elementary schools its importance seems to me at present extraordinary.'[44] As if she set out to see how the position with which we associate Arnold operated in practice, Jacqueline Rose in *The Case of Peter Pan: or the Impossibility of Children's Fiction* examines the transformation and transmission of Barrie's *Peter and Wendy,* accepted in 1915 as a reader for use in schools. She shows how the rewriting excised not only its pseudo-classicism but its associated forms of linguistic style. Jacqueline Rose goes on to show how appropriate styles of writing and reading were outlined for different groups: for elementary schoolchildren, 'a direct, simple, unaffected style,' a vocabulary based on 'concrete objects,' a literature centred on 'physical actions.'[45] Of course, the meaning of 'appropriate education' could always be inflected differently, as it was during and after the 1909 strike at Ruskin College, Oxford, by working-class students who also wanted an education for their class: 'the establishment of a network of labour colleges through the country . . . a huge educational structure entirely devoted to the interests of the working class.'[46]

But the interest of this argument is in the nature of the invitation to the working class to take its place in the national culture. Across the practices surveyed, the continuity of vocabulary and thinking is impressive; the working class was acknowledged and its essential identity and nature fixed. Slowly such a way of thinking would become simple common sense. To attest to this, here are two quotations, one about William (Lord) Beveridge in 1940, whose career encompasses membership of the Liberal government in the early 1900s; the other is from David Storey, who was marketed as a working-class novelist in the 1960s[47]:

> But as of old, Beveridge is obstinately convinced that he and his class have to do the job [of planning production], and the Trade Unionists have to be ignored and the wage earner ordered to work . . . he agrees that there must be a revolution in the economic structure of society; but it must be guided by persons with training and knowledge.

> I was brought up in a mining village where everyone worked with their hands and the few who didn't were looked on rather as poor, weedy inferior beings, and all the pleasures, desires and ambitions which were socially acceptable were purely physical. Everything was exterior and immediate.

IV

But it was one thing to invite into the national culture an *English* working class, it was quite another to invite the marginalized peoples – the Irish, Scots and Welsh – to rejoice in such a national culture. Unambiguous solutions were, of course, on offer. Here is a judgement about the language and culture of Wales, simply a 'geographical expression,' according to one bishop:

> the Welsh language is the curse of Wales. Its prevalence and the ignorance of English have excluded and even now exclude the Welsh people from the civilization, the improvement, and the material prosperity of their English neighbours . . . we can only observe as a matter of fact that Welsh music and poetry have not had the slightest effect in civilizing the Welsh people.[48]

That is a third leader in *The Times* in response to correspondence on Matthew Arnold's rejection of an invitation to address the Eisteddfod, and, more generally, on Arnold's Oxford lectures published in *The Cornhill Magazine* (1866) and collected as *On the Study of Celtic Literature* (1867). These lectures were delivered and published at around the same time as *Culture and Anarchy*, which centred on Englishness. Arnold's complementary series of lectures of the 1860s is a reminder that the definition of the English is inseparable from that of the non-English; Englishness is not so much a category as a relationship. Delivered at Oxford, the home in the 1860s of the Saxonism of Freeman, Arnold's lectures aimed to establish the contribution of the Celt to English culture. Why these lectures are useful is that they contain the substance of the Celticism argument of the following years, and were seen as seminal contributions to the debate. In reference to *The Times's* damnation of the Welsh quoted above, Alfred Nutt, who edited Arnold's essays in 1910, said: 'If it is impossible [now] for such stuff as this to appear in any self-respecting newspaper, it is chiefly thanks to the spirit induced by Arnold's work.'[49]

Arnold fixed the essential character of a people in its literature, and 'read off' the national character of the Welsh and Irish from Celtic literature, his designation for the writing of the Welsh and Irish. After the initial opposition which seemed to favour the Celts – the 'impassive dullness' of the English, the 'lively Celtic nature' – Arnold described the cost of such a nature, the absence of 'steadiness, patience, sanity.' The shift to the political followed immediately: 'The skilful and resolute appliance of means to ends which is needed both to make progress in material civilisation, and also to *form powerful States*, is just what the Celt has least turn for' (my emphasis).

Given that the Celts were not capable of governing themselves what was their place within the national life? Arnold's answer was to claim that the matter of the minority nation's cultural identity was separable from the matter of the minority nation's political control of its cultural institutions. He proposed that the 'provincial nationalisms' had to be swallowed up at the level of the political and licensed as cultural contributions to English culture.[50] And with such an argument Arnold laid, at the very least, the groundwork for the assimilation of Irish, Scots and Welsh writers into the emergent discipline of English literature.

What Arnold did was to offer the core/periphery relationship as the appropriate one between the 'metropolitan' English culture and the 'provincial' cultures of the other nations.[51] Citing Arnold, the *OED* offers as one of the meanings of 'provincial', 'wanting the culture and polish of the capital.' (One might suggest that Joyce's refusal to exile himself in England was a rejection of his fate as a 'provincial' writer, to play jester at the court of the English, his description of Wilde's fate.) The cultural life of Scotland or Wales or Ireland could have no meaning other than in its satellite relationship with the cultural life of England. Developing this position, T. S. Eliot in 1919 – he would later use the phrase 'satellite cultures' – asked

'Was there a Scottish literature?' and answered in the negative: 'When we assume that a literature exists we assume a great deal: we suppose that there is one of the five or six (at most) great organic formations of history. We do not suppose merely a "history", for there might be a history of Tamil literature.' England is, of course, one of the great organic formations.[52]

The autonomous contribution of the Celts to civilization was confined to the past. According to Arnold, 'Wales, where the past still lives, where every place has its tradition, every name its poetry and where the people, the genuine people, still knows this past, this tradition, this poetry, and lives with it, and clings to it.' The 'genuine' Celts 'cling' to the past. In short, they could not face the present.[53] Their contribution to the present fixed, and their identity secured in the past, the Celts were rewarded by Arnold with his recommendation that they deserved to become the object of study of the English, in the form of a Chair of Celtic languages at Oxford or Cambridge. And within 10 years of Arnold's lectures – and this is not to attribute to them simple causal significance – the first chair of Celtic literature *was* established at Oxford University, in 1877. Like other ways of life which were fixed as objects of study – the School for Modern Oriental Studies was established in London in 1916 – Welsh became a subject of and for the English (even in the Welsh colleges, Welsh was taught in *English* until after World War I).[54] Although such a bald judgement ignores the enterprises instituted by Welsh cultural nationalists during this period – for instance, the University Colleges of Bangor and Cardiff were established in the early 1880s, and in 1907 a National Library and a National Museum were opened – what is important to stress is that at least a number of the premises of the cultural nationalists ratified rather than challenged Arnold's terms of reference. For example, if Arnold stressed the Celts' embodiment of 'the spiritual quality implicit in the concept of the "noble savage",' so did some minority nationalists themselves who often contrasted 'English decrepitude and decadence' to 'native "nature and thought"'.[55] Most important, Arnold's culturalist argument, his conviction that each nation had certain essential characteristics, was often accepted by the nationalists – at a great cost. Gwyn Williams' *When Was Wales?* brilliantly shows how the Welsh Wales of the cultural nationalists neither could nor can accommodate or articulate the experiences of industrial (often South) Wales: 'the more arrogant, extreme or paranoid exponents of Welshness simply refuse to see any "culture" at all in English-speaking Wales, or else they dismiss it as "British" or even "English"'.[56]

Or take the example of Ireland. After the failure of 'politics' with Parnell – politics defined in exclusively parliamentary terms; the replacement in 1881 of the Land League by the Irish National League was the 'complete eclipse by a purely parliamentary substitute of what had been a semi-revolutionary organization'[57] – the search for an Irish cultural identity was pursued. Through such institutions as the Gaelic League (1893), the Gaelic Athletics Association (1884), and the National Literary Society (1892) what was sought was an Irish cultural identity unsullied by, and morally superior to, English culture: 'Let us put our shoulder to the wheel, one and all, to make the National Literary Society strong and useful. . . . We may not, so, bring Ireland freedom, but assuredly with God's help, *let politics sink or swim,* so we shall make ourselves worthy of it.'[58] The search for a 'pure' or essential Ireland – which legitimised and was in turn legitimised by an essential England – often led the nationalists away from weighing the complex relationship (subordination) of Ireland to England and towards a Gaelic Ireland. 'The Necessity of De-Anglicising Ireland' was the title of the Protestant Douglas Hyde's 1892 lecture to the National Literary Society.[59] The cultural nationalists' pursuit of an 'Irish' Ireland also meant that they were unable to recognize the actual diverse cultural identities within Ireland itself. In short, it is extraordinary how far some of the terms of Arnold's arguments about Celticism – language, the primacy of the cultural, the siting of value in the past – were replicated in the arguments of at least some of the cultural nationalists of Wales and of Ireland. Both sides sought an *essential* identity for the Celts.

The extensiveness of the colonization by the English of the Celts – of the bestowal of identity by the core on the periphery – can be measured by a very brief mention of what may seem far removed from Celticism, the artistic colonies which were established in the 1880s and 1890s, particularly the Newlyn School, and (later) the St Ives colony. (Given the argument of this chapter, the word 'colony' – their own description – is unsurprising.) The general orientation of these colonists might lead one to assume they are part of that penetration of working-class England, which has been described above. It is certainly true that they often celebrated the 'immemorial' customs of communities and the dignity of certain kinds of manual labour – for instance, of the fisherman, 'a heroic figure.'[60] But what was more determining was their construction of Cornwall as Celtic. Inspired by the example of those artistic colonies in Celtic Brittany, the colonists – 'we cannot claim to have been the discoverers of this artistic Klondyke' (Stanhope Forbes) – stabilized and fixed the identity of the Cornish as that of ancient communities, closer to nature than was metropolitan England.[61] Absent was the recent experience of the Cornish – of mass emigration, of a declining tin mining industry, of the decimation of the fishing industry by European competition.[62] Newlyn was a 'primitive' place; and Cornwall was full of a 'simple and harmless folk.' Like Arnold for whom the 'genuine' Celt 'clings' to the past, for the colonists the genuine Cornwall was to be found in the past. The writings of Stanhope Forbes – the founder of the Newlyn School – were full 'of fear that [the traditional attire of the fisherman] was passing away with other old-fashioned and paintable things,' and that 'quaint old houses' were to be replaced by cottages that 'ape the pretentiousness of modern villadom.'[63]

But what is crucial is that this desire to fix the life of the periphery, of those whom they painted, co-existed with – or was the necessary complement of – the artists' affiliation to metropolitan institutions, especially the Royal Academy, one of those 'national' centres of authority. (The National Trust for Places of Historic and Natural Beauty, founded in 1895, gained part of its authority from the fact that three out of four Vice-Presidents of the National Trust were members of the Royal Academy.) The Newlyn paintings 'were conceived in Royal Academy terms' – and were painted for exhibition there. As early as 1888, Forbes wrote that 'the RA this year may best be described as the "triumph of Newlyn"'.[64] The lasting power of this metropolitan representation is attested to in Dennis Farr's 1978 contribution to *The Oxford History of English Art, English Art 1870–1940*: 'Cornwall in the 1880s must have been still quite primitive, unspoilt, and akin to Brittany in both its terrain and peasant life.'[65] The fate of Cornwall at the hands of the colonists may be taken as a metaphor for the general relationship between the Celts and English. The Celts are licensed their unique contribution to, and place in the national culture: the cost is that they know their peripheral place as the subject of the metropolitan centre.

V

The colonization of 'others' – two instances of which have been mapped – was the necessary complement of the definition of the dominant English. What was common to both these colonizations was the recognition that identity must be secured at the cultural as well as – or indeed as an alternative to – the political level. But what was the national culture in which these groups found their present place? What was the cultural heritage to which the English were heirs? How was a single heritage to accommodate the experiences of the distinct groups? The pattern again was that of inclusion, simple exclusion, and transformation – of the stabilization of the present and past across a range of institutions and practices. As we suggested earlier, this section will focus on two matters: one taken from the field of scholarship, the other from the arts.

Consider the English language, spoken and written, and how its meanings, past and present, were made and remade. First, the present. The Society for Pure English (founded in 1913) was instituted with the conviction that the imperial duties of English taxed its strength:

> It would seem that no other language can ever have had its central force so dissipated – and even this does not exhaust the description of our special peril, because there is furthermore this most obnoxious condition, namely, that wherever our countrymen are settled abroad there are alongside of them communities of other-speaking races, who, maintaining amongst themselves their native speech, learn yet enough of ours to imitate it, and establishing among themselves all kinds of blundering corruptions, through habitual intercourse infect therewith the neighbouring English.[66]

(It is perhaps important to mention that American English was among the mongrel tongues.) The horror of contamination is clear. What is also evident is that such celebration of the English language – it was the touchstone of all other languages – co-existed with a sense of its vulnerability. If the language was threatened without, it was also threatened within. The Society was happy with compulsory state education since it 'provides a machinery which can be and is used to counteract the uncontrolable [sic] natural trend and growth of language.'[67] The title of the Society for Pure English encapsulates its limitations. Committed to pure English and simply refusing to acknowledge the varieties of English, the Society allowed the excluded elements to remain undefined and thus free to be made into centres of opposition and resistance. Dialect (as much a class as a regional matter) could and did act to emphasize the solidarity of subordinated groups, provided the idiom for cultural initiatives (e.g., Cockney in the music hall), and generated large bodies of writing.

The elements of language which were excluded by the Society were found some useful work by other strands of language scholarship which developed in the period immediately prior to 1880–1920, and in the period itself. The Philological Society founded in 1842, which originated the plan for the New English Dictionary (to which this argument will return), gave prominent attention to dialect. And in 1873 Walter Skeat – who 3 years later was to be given the Bosworth Chair of Anglo-Saxon at Oxford – undertook the secretaryship of the newly founded Dialect Society, which had the objective of collecting lists of dialect words from published books and from field work – material which was eventually used for the *English Dialect Dictionary* edited by Joseph Wright. Like many other projects initiated during this period, the *Dialect Dictionary's* importance was voiced in terms of service to the nation: 'a work of great national importance,' announced the advertisement appealing for material for the *EDD*.[68] It was organized by county, and the *Dictionary* and other publications stressed the rural character of 'pure' dialects. Dialect needed to be 'preserved'; that is, it was of the *past,* not an acceptable medium of present communication.[69] Certain urban dialects (such as Cockney which was at the centre of the London Music Hall – 'an indigenous entertainment by Cockneys largely for Cockneys') were not accorded the status of a dialect.[70] (Recent dialect words were excluded from the *New English Dictionary.*) The rich diversity of the English language was a matter of the past – but dialects did have their place. If the Society for Pure English's position on 'impure' English was not unlike that of *The Times* on the Welsh language, then the position of Henry Cecil Wyld on dialects was not unlike Matthew Arnold's on the Celts. Wyld, who was later to become Merton Professor of English Language at Oxford, was clear that the dominant English language was to be identified with certain English institutions – the Court, the Church, the Bar, the older universities and the great public schools – but, as with Arnold, Wyld was eager to offer a place to the subordinated:

> When one dialect obtains the dignity of becoming the channel of all
> that is worthiest in the national literature and the national civilisation,

the other less favoured dialects shrink into obscurity and insignificance. The latter preserve, however, this advantage, considered as types of linguistic development, that the primitive conditions under which language exists and changes are more faithfully represented in them than in the cultivated dialect.[71]

The analogy with the Celts is sustained. Dialect had the virtues of the 'primitive', and its contribution to the past which had made the present was acknowledged. But dialect had to recognize its subordinate position and give way to the standard. Indeed the one function of the 'pure' dialects of the past was the judging and disciplining of present mongrel dialects.

Interest in the history of English, as the quotation from Wyld suggests, is never far from concern with the present state of language. And nowhere is this more evident than in the debate around the *New English Dictionary*. General reading in nineteenth-century works on the language very quickly makes it clear that the renewed interest was in part the result of the recognition of the 'vastly increased distribution of English in the last hundred years. . . . English may become the most widely spoken language on earth.'[72] Richard Trench, author of two seminal books on language, claimed that language is a 'moral barometer, which indicates and permanently marks the rise and fall of a nation's life'; 'it is the collective work of the whole nation, the result of the united contribution of all.'[73] It was within such assumptions, and with the societies which helped to found those assumptions – such as the Early English Text Society (1864), and the Wyclif Society (1881) – that the debate around the *NED* was prosecuted.

When James Murray, the editor of the *NED*, entered into negotiations with Oxford University Press, he found himself under pressure from the Delegates, and especially Benjamin Jowett, Master of Balliol College, Oxford, to make the Dictionary a source of cultural authority. This could not have been welcome advice to a man who identified himself as a Whig, Dissenter and Scotsman and claimed that his own interest in language was initiated by his realization that 'the constructions he had been scolded for at school . . . as "bad grammar" by English standards were in fact "good grammar" in Scotch'.[74] From the Delegates Murray had to contend with the insistence that the function of the Dictionary was to establish a standard of right and wrong; that quotations should be as far as possible drawn from great writers; that slang terms and scientific words should be limited to such as were found in literature; and that its title should be 'A New Dictionary showing the history of the language from the earliest times,' with the stress on language and not on words.[75] One of the matters of interest which arise from these arguments is the tension between the historical scholarship upon which Englishness was in part reconstructed in the last quarter of the nineteenth century and the uses to which others wished to put it. As Murray said, the Delegates 'could not grasp that this [the setting of a standard of good literary usage] is not the province of an historical dictionary.'[76] The other

relevant matter to note from Murray's skirmishes with Oxford and the Press
is that what has come down to us as the *Oxford English Dictionary* met
initial indifference or downright hostility in Oxford. One might generalize
the case. So many of the scholarly initiatives of the late-nineteenth century –
the *NED,* the *DNB,* the discipline of English literature – which are now
seen as 'Oxford' or 'Cambridge' projects and which have helped to bestow
on those universities their reputation as centres of cultural authority – were
initiated and sustained elsewhere.

That the *New English Dictionary* was subject to the pressures outlined
above should not lead us to assume that the project itself – as conceived
and sustained – was ideologically neutral. Murray, as has been mentioned,
described himself as a Whig, and within limits wished to insist on English
liberty: 'we do not all think alike, walk alike, dress alike, write alike or
dine alike; why should we not use our liberty in speech also, so long as
the purpose of speech, to be intelligible, and its grace, are not interfered
with?'[77] But what the *NED* enshrined was not the vision of a number of
autonomous and equally valued histories but a national Whig history of the
language, whose starting point was '1150 and its early history.' For Murray,
the 'English Dictionary, like the English Constitution, was the creation of no
one man, and of no one age; it is a growth that has slowly developed down
the ages.'[78] The clearest statement of this conviction is to be found in Murray's
contribution to the eleventh edition of the *Encyclopaedia Britannica:*

> This evolution [of the language] appears so gradual in English that we
> can nowhere draw distinct lines separating its successive stages, we
> recognise these stages as merely temporary phases of an individual whole,
> and speak of the English language as used alike by Cynewolf, by Chaucer,
> by Shakespeare, and by Tennyson.[79]

What such a description did was naturalize the social transmission of the
language; what the *NED* did was to offer to establish its 'evolution' and
continuity, eliding the complex history of the language. It is at least arguable
that the establishment of a 'single' language was the necessary prerequisite for
the institution of a national literary tradition which in turn became the 'true'
bearer of the language. The study of literature was all the language study
that was necessary. As a recent commentator has said: the *NED* gives the
impression 'that it was the giants of literature who formed our language.'
Also its 'normal limitations of one or two quotations per sense per century
is inadequate to account for the regional and stylisic variety of usage at any
stage in the history of the language.'[80]

Before we turn away from language and briefly towards other institutions
which offered to hold the English to a single and continuous history, it is
worth noting that in *Imagined Communities,* Benedict Anderson argues that
'Language is not an instrument of exclusion: in principle, anyone can learn
a language.'[81] At one level this may be true (an English person can learn

French), but at another level the statement begs the question of what it is to learn a language. Not all ways of speaking and writing the language are equally acceptable or authorized. James Joyce's *Ulysses* was as much denigrated for its violation of the norms of the English language as for its obscenity: 'All the conventions of organized prose which have grown with our race and out of our racial consciousness which have been reverently handed on by the masters . . . have been cast aside as so much dross.'[82]

By the time he died, in 1941, Joyce had become an honorary Englishman. The English ambassador – not the Irish one – attended his funeral. One way such an outstanding representative from the 'periphery' as Joyce could gain English status was through his incorporation into English literature. For outstanding representatives in other spheres, there was always the *Dictionary of National Biography* or the National Portrait Gallery (which gained a permanent home in 1896). Although both enterprises declared that they wished to honour *British* subjects (the *DNB* added 'foreigners' eminent in British life and important figures from the colonies), both were in fact dominated by the English and simply recognized outstanding contributions from the 'peripheries.' It is, of course, important to add that neither enterprise, despite the explicit claim of the NPG 'to aid . . . the study of national history,'[83] actually registered the diverse contributions of the English to English life. As one recent commentator has noted, there was an over-attachment to politicians, civil servants and the military and a neglect of the business-world. A marginalization of a different order was that of women. Their presence was negligible and, according to Sidney Lee, the second editor of the DNB, was unlikely to increase: 'Women will not, I regret, have much claim on the attention of the national biographer for a very long time to come.'[84]

VI

The new initiatives in learning and scholarship without which the reconstruction of Englishness was inconceivable were complemented by new institutions and patterns of production and consumption in the field of the arts. Given the attention to the arts in other chapters in this volume, what I propose to do is to examine a single element of the arts, the theatre, in terms of the general argument of this chapter, and show how the various theatrical sectors were offered a place in the national culture and fixed in relationship to a metropolitan core – the projected national theatre.

Serious agitation for a National Theatre began again in the 1870s, at a time when new work was produced which could not be accommodated within the commercial theatre. Matthew Arnold, who, as we have seen, understood what would count as the national culture, wrote: 'the theatre is irresistible; organize the theatre.' Arnold went on to argue that the 'state, the nation in its collective and corporate character, does well to concern itself about an influence so important to national life and manners as the theatre.'[85] A historian of the National Theatre summarizes the general agitation thus:

> The claims were now seen to be threefold: firstly, for a working memorial to Shakespeare in the capital of the British Empire; secondly, as Irving had pleaded, for an "exemplary theatre" that would provide a permanent machine or factory for the production of plays on the highest artistic level; and thirdly, as in Matthew Arnold's vision, for a central organisation able to spread throughout the country an appreciation of great drama as a major factor in education.[86]

What is common to these claims is the conviction that a certain metropolitan institution should define and bear (the drama of) the national culture and be the core from which what is of value should be disseminated to the rest of the country.

The debates continued through the last decades of the nineteenth century, especially through the writings and agitation of William Archer, defender and translator of Ibsen. Archer's conviction that the general public could not be immediately converted to the 'new' drama led him to advocate, in the words of the critic John Stokes, 'the establishment of a cadre of little theatres which would cater for the discriminating minority alone.' Archer asked, have not playwrights 'again and again found themselves continuously sacrificing artistic considerations to the necessity of conciliating the masses'?[87] When he published in 1907 (in conjunction with Granville Barker, a Fabian and member of the executive committee between 1907 and 1912) *A National Theatre: Schemes and Estimates*, he was at pains to stress the character of the institution. While it would break 'completely and unequivocally, from the ideals and traditions of the profit-making stage,' the National Theatre 'IS NOT AN ADVANCED THEATRE . . . but forms part, and an indispensable part, of the main army of progress. It will neither compete with the outpost theatres nor relieve them of their function.'[88]

Two issues central to my general argument about the national culture arise out of the debate about the role of theatres. First, as has been mentioned, the stress on the establishment of a centre of authority which would license what constituted great drama; second, the renunciation by such an institution of engagement with new drama (G. B. Shaw declared that Archer and Granville Barker's selection of plays was obsolete)[89]; and third, implicit in the first two, the definition of the function of the National Theatre and that of others. The National Theatre would not deprive the 'advanced' theatre of its place; avant-gardism was licensed. The relative ease with which it was (sometimes) accommodated is evident in an anecdote about Shaw's play about the English/Irish relationship, *John Bull's Other Island*, produced at the centre of avant-gardism, the Royal Court Theatre:

> Beatrice Webb persuaded the Prime Minister, A. J. Balfour, to see it; in turn he invited the Opposition leaders, Sir Henry Campbell-Bannermann

and H. H. Asquith, and King Edward VII commanded an evening performance on 11 March 1905. For this occasion Verdenne hired special furniture from Maples for the Royal Box. . . . Max Beerbohm dated Shaw's popularity from that night, after which his plays became "a fashionable craze".[90]

Although certain works – literary as well as dramatic – did prove more resistant to incorporation than did Shaw's – the modernism of Joyce, for instance, was more difficult for the dominant culture to assimilate than Woolf's or Eliot's[91] – the force of the argument remains. The various sectors of the artistic life of the period – like education and scholarship, and the larger national culture of which they were all part – were stabilized and fixed (always precariously) in terms of their different functions and related audiences. Elite/mass and avant-garde/commercial were not pairs of oppositional terms but pairs of complementary ones. Each ratified the sphere and responsibilities of the other. Disengaged from the contemporary culture, the artistic institutions of the national culture simply gathered up and acted as custodians of the best of the national past.[92]

This argument has tried to do two things. First, it has traced how the cultural identities of the dominant English and of the subordinated groups were articulated during this period; and second, it has showed how the diverse cultural histories and contemporary cultural life of these islands were organized and stabilized as a national culture. Englishness was appropriated by and became the responsibility of certain narrowly defined groups and their institutions, and yet meaning and function were (con) ceded to subordinated groups and institutions. But the places offered to the subordinated groups were, it is clear, no simple gift. For instance, the acknowledgement that women had their own 'culture', their own sphere of activity became, as is clear in the history of the suffragette movement, a demand that they knew their place:

> Passion ran high on both sides: that was the meaning of the "Cat and Mouse" Act, above all of its retention of forcible feeding. The House of Commons was almost hysterical in its susceptibility to its prestige. . . . The long inequality of the sexes had bitten deeply into them, they had grown up with it in every relation of life. What from men might have been received as a commonplace of political controversy, from women was an intolerable impertinence, an unpardonable offence.[93]

One might say that the suffragette movement resisted, to use the vocabulary of my argument, the representations offered to them; they wished to represent themselves, *to make themselves present*.[94]

Inseparable from their power to represent themselves and others, the dominant English had the power, I have also argued, to say what the national culture had been and *was*. The past tense is important, for what is clear is that during 1880–1920 the conviction that English culture was to be found in the past was stabilized. The *past* cultural activities and attributes of the people were edited and then acknowledged, as contributions to the evolution of the English national culture which had produced the present. Nowhere was this more evident than through the establishment of a national literary tradition within the emergent discipline of English literature. Professor Sidney Lee, second editor of the *DNB* and Professor of English at London University, made the matter plain in his inaugural lecture.

> Current writing which awaits the final verdict does not claim the attention of the lecture room. The student may well be advised if in his leisure he attempts to appraise current writing by the standard of the old literature which has stood time's test.[95]

Everyone had a place in the national culture, and had contributed to the past which had become a settled present. The people of these islands with their diverse cultural identities were invited to take their place, and become spectators of a culture already complete and represented for them by its trustees. In the face of such an invitation it may well be appropriate to reply that 'only those directly concerned can speak in a practical way on their own behalf.'[96]

Notes

1 Richard Shannon, *The Crisis of Imperialism 1865–1915* (St Albans: Paladin, 1976), pp. 12–13.

2 Edward Said, *Orientalism* (London and Henley: Routledge & Kegan Paul, 1978), p. 3.

3 A. Gramsci, *Selections from the Prison Notebooks*, eds. Q. Hoare and Geoffrey Nowell Smith (London: Lawrence and Wishart, 1971), p. 244. The trajectory of my argument is generally indebted to Gramsci.

4 Virginia Woolf, *A Room of One's Own* (1929) in *'A Room of One's Own' and 'Three Guineas'*, intro. Hermione Lee (London: Hogarth P., 1984), p. 25.

5 Olive Banks, *Faces of Feminism: A Study of Feminism as a Social Movement* (Oxford: Martin Robertson, 1981), p. 96.

6 David Cannadine, 'The Context, Performance and Meaning of Ritual: The British Monarchy and the 'Invention of Tradition', c.1820–1977', in *The Invention of Tradition*, eds. Eric Hobsbawm and Terence Ranger (Cambridge: C.U.P., 1983), p. 122.

7 'Youth', which was seen during this period as a universal grouping which included everyone of a certain age-range, is the most important group not to be given a chapter in this volume.

8 'The economic, political, social and moral welfare of the community depend mainly on the development of a national system of education', *Report of the Committee . . . to inquire into the position of the Classics* (1921), quoted in

Richard Jenkyns, *The Victorians and Ancient Greece* (Oxford: Basil Blackwell, 1980), p. 345. It is important to acknowledge that there was fierce resistance, in some quarters, to national state educations, from, for example the National Education League.

9 Bernard Darwin, *The English School* (1929), quoted in Martin J. Wiener, *English Culture and the Decline of the Industrial Spirit* (Cambridge: C.U.P., 1981), p. 21.

10 Matthew Arnold, *Culture and Anarchy, The Complete Prose Works of Matthew Arnold*, ed. R. H. Super (Ann Arbor: U. of Michigan Press, 1965), V, Preface.

11 See Tom Nairn, *The Break-up of Britain: Crisis and Neo-Nationalism*, 2nd expanded edn (London: Verso, 1981), p. 46, on the bourgeois data.

12 T. W. Heyck, *The Transformation of Intellectual Life in Victorian England* (London and Canberra: Croom Helm, 1982), p. 183.

13 H. W. Armstrong, 'The Place that Chemistry must take in Public Esteem,' an address to Manchester University Chemical Society, 1906 quoted in Michael Sanderson, *The University and British Industry 1850–1970* (London: Routledge & Kegan Paul, 1972), p. 31; James Bryce, 'The Future of the English Universities,' quoted in Heyck, *The Transformation of Intellectual Life*, p. 185.

14 Quoted in Brian Simon, *Education and the Labour Movement 1870–1920* (London: Lawrence and Wishart, 1974), p. 187.

15 Quoted in Simon, *Education and the Labour Movement*, p. 314.

16 John M. Mackenzie, *Propaganda and Empire: The Manipulation of British Public Opinion, 1880–1960* (Manchester: Manchester U. P., 1984), pp. 175–6. Although not all of the books would have been produced by Oxford or Cambridge academics, one should not underestimate the power of these institutions to define for other universities what constituted knowledge. Jack Simmons records the incredulity of some people in Leicester that the city should consider a university: Oxford and Cambridge and London were the *real* universities: *Leicester Past and Present* (London: Methuen, 1974), II, 73. On the continuing power of Oxford after World War I, see Francis Mulhearn's introduction to Regis Debray, *Teachers, Writers, Celebrities: The Intellectuals of Modern France*, trans. David Macey (London: Verso, 1981), pp. xvii–xviii.

17 See the chapter by Brooker and Widdowson in this volume.

18 J. R. de S. Honey, 'Tom Brown's Universe: The Nature and Limits of the Victorian Public Schools Community', in *The Victorian Public School: Studies in the Development of an Education Institution*, eds. Brian Simon and Ian Bradley (Dublin: Gill and MacMillan, 1975), p. 20.

19 Simon, *Education and the Labour Movement*, pp. 101–2.

20 J. A. Mangan, *Athleticism in the Victorian and Edwardian Public School: The Emergence and Consolidation of an Educational Ideology* (Cambridge: C.U.P., 1981), p. 135.

21 Isabel Quigly, *The Heirs of Tom Brown* (London: Chatto and Windus, 1982), p. 7.

22 Paul Fussell, *The Great War and Modern Memory* (Oxford: O.U.P., 1975), pp. 272–3.

23 Cyril Norwood, quoted in Mangan, *Athleticism,* p. 7; W. Turley, quoted in Mangan, *Athleticism*, p. 189.

24 *On the Art of Writing* (1916), quoted in Ken Worpole, *Dockers and Detectives: Popular Reading: Popular Writing* (London: Verso, 1983), p. 40.

25 E. A. Freeman, in J. W. Burrow, *A Liberal Descent: Victorian Historians and the English Past* (Cambridge: C.U.P. 1981), pp. 209–12; *Quarterly Review* is quoted in C. K. Stead, *The New Poetic* (London: Penguin, 1967), p. 75; James Douglas, *The Star,* is quoted in *D.H. Lawrence: The Critical Heritage*, ed. R. P. Draper (London: Routledge & Kegan Paul, 1970), p. 93.

26 *William Walsh, Commonwealth Literature* (Oxford: O.U.P. 1973), pp. 1, 10. I am indebted to Aleid Fokkema for the reference.

27 Elaine Showalter, *A Literature of their Own: British Women Novelists from Brontë to Lessing*, rev. edn (London: Virago P., 1982), p. 259.

28 J. R. de S. Honey, 'Tom Brown's Universe,' *The Victorian Public School*, eds. Simon and Bradley, p. 21.

29 Mark Girouard, *The Return to Camelot: Chivalry and the English Gentleman* (New Haven and London: Yale U.P., 1981), p. 6; Roland Huntford, *Scott and Amundsen* (London: Hodder and Stoughton, 1979).

30 Edward Carpenter, *Woman and her Place in a Free Society* (Manchester: Labour Press Soc., 1894), p. 28.

31 E. W. Hornung, 'Lord's Leave 1915,' quoted in Mangan, *Athleticism,* p. 193.

32 J. A. Hobson, *The Crisis of Liberalism: New Issues of Democracy* (London: King & Son, 1909), pp. 80–1; Charles H. Harvey, *The Biology of British Politics* (London: Swan Sonnenschein, 1904), p. 95.

33 Benedict Anderson, *Imagined Communities: Reflections on the Origin and Spread of Nationalism* (London: Verso, 1983), p. 16.

34 *Into Unknown England: Selections from the Social Explorers*, ed. Peter Keating (London: Fontana, 1976), p. 10.

35 Gareth Stedman Jones (ed.), 'Working Class Culture and Working Class Politics in London, 1870–1900: Notes on the Remaking of a Working Class', in *Languages of Class: Studies in English Working Class History 1832–1982* (Cambridge: C.U.P. 1983), pp. 183, 219. Another 'residual' tradition – of seeing the working class as animals, as cultureless – was still active. For its roots, see F. S. Schwarzbach, 'Terra Incognita – An Image of the City in English Literature, 1820–55', in *The Art of Travel,* ed. Philip Dodd (London: Frank Cass, 1982).

36 George Haw, 'Weekly Sun Literary Supplement' (1896) quoted Peter Keating, 'Fact and Fiction in the East End', in *The Victorian City: Images and Realities*, eds. H. J. Dyos and Michael Wolff (London and Boston: Routledge & Kegan Paul, 1973), II, 600.

37 Sherard, 'The Chainmakers of Cradley Heath', Keating, *Into Unknown England*, p. 180.

38 See Robert Colls and Philip Dodd, 'Representing the Nation: Documentary Film, 1930–45', *Screen*, 26 (1985), 21–33.

39 Charles Booth, *Life and Labour of the People in London*, Keating, *Into Unknown England*, p. 127.

40 *Glitter Around and Darkness Within: The Diary of Beatrice Webb, vol.1, 1873–1892*, eds. Norman and Jeanne Mackenzie (London: Virago, 1982), pp. 183–4. The diary entry is for 31 October 1886.

41 E. Sylvia Pankhurst, *The Suffrage Movement: An Intimate Account of Persons and Ideals* (1931) (London: Virago, 1977), p. 186.

42 Worpole, *Dockers and Detectives*, p. 96. My emphasis.

43 'Travellers in a Strange Country: Responses of Working-Class Students to the University Extension Movement 1873–1910', *History Workshop Journal*, no.12 repr. Sheila Rowbotham, *Dreams and Dilemmas: Collected Writings* (London: Virago, 1983), pp. 267–305. All quotations in the paragraph are taken from this essay.

44 Matthew Arnold, *A French Eton* (1863–4) and *What Her Majesty's Inspectors Say 1880–81,* both quoted Brian Hollingsworth, 'The Mother Tongue and the Public Schools in the 1860s', *British Journal of Educational Studies*, 22 (1974), 319–20.

45 Jacqueline Rose, *The Case of Peter Pan: or the Impossibility of Children's Fiction* (London: Macmillan, 1984), pp. 117–20.

46 Simon, *Education and the Labour Movement,* p. 324.

47 Beatrice Webb writing of Beveridge, quoted 'Why is the Labour Party in a mess?' Jones, *Languages of Class: Studies in English Working Class History 1832–1982*, p. 245; David Storey, *The Times*, 28 November 1963, p. 15.

48 The Bishop is quoted in Gwyn A. Williams, *When Was Wales? A History of the Welsh* (Harmondsworth: Penguin, 1985), p. 229; Arnold quotes the leader in his 'Introduction,' *On the Study of Celtic Literature, Lectures and Essays in Criticism, The Complete Works of Matthew Arnold*, III, 391. The relative neglect of Scotland by Arnold and others may be due to the fact that nationalism in Scotland reappeared only later in this period. See Nairn, *The Break-Up of Britain*, p. 95.

49 Quoted Rachel Bromwich, *Matthew Arnold and Celtic Literature: A Retrospect 1865–1965* (Oxford: Clarendon P., 1965), p. 38.

50 Matthew Arnold, *Complete Prose Works*, III, 295, 296, 344, 345.

51 For this phrase I am indebted to Michael Hechter, *Internal Colonialism: The Celtic Fringe in British National Development 1536–1966* (London: Routledge & Kegan Paul, 1975).

52 Eliot's essay was published in the *Athenaeum* (1 August 1919). I take the reference from Cairns Craig, 'Peripheries', *Cencrastus*, 9 (1982), 3–9.

53 Matthew Arnold, *Complete Prose Works,* III, 291.

54 Ned Thomas, 'Renan, Arnold, Unamuno: philology and the minority languages', *Bradford Occasional Papers*, 4 (1984), 8.

55 John S. Kelly, 'The Fall of Parnell and the Rise of Irish Literature: An Investigation', *Anglo-Irish Studies*, 2 (1976), 14.

56 Williams, *When Was Wales?*, p. 236.

57 Michael Davitt, quoted Kelly, 'Fall of Parnell,' p. 6.

58 *United Ireland,* quoted Kelly, 'Fall of Parnell,' p. 17.

59 That the Irish Republican Brotherhood demanded political, as well as cultural freedom marked them out as different from some of the cultural nationalists – but the IRB did want, with other nationalists, an Ireland 'not merely free but Gaelic as well'. Tim Pat Coogan, *The IRA,* rev. edn (London: Fontana, 1980), p. 35.

60 Caroline Fox and Francis Greenacre, *Artists of the Newlyn School (1880–1900)* Exhibition Catalogue of Newlyn Orion Galleries, 1979. The description is Norman Garstin's, quoted p. 31.

61 Mrs Lionel Birch, *Stanhope Forbes ARA and Elizabeth Stanhope, ARWS* (London: Cassell, n. d.), p. 26.

62 See for example F. E. Halliday, *A History of Cornwall* (London: Duckworth, 1959).

63 Such sentiments are commonplace in the writings of the painters. See, for the quoted phrases, Birch, *Stanhope Forbes ARA,* p. 27 and *Artists of the Newlyn School,* p. 66.

64 *Artists of the Newlyn School,* pp. 28, 60–1.

65 Dennis Farr, *English Art 1870–1940* (Oxford: Clarendon P., 1978), p. 40.

66 Society for Pure English, *Tract XXI,* partly repr. in *The English Language Vol.2: Essays by Linguists and Men of Letters 1858–1964,* selected and edited W. F. Bolton and D. Crystal (Cambridge: C.U.P., 1969), pp. 88, 93.

67 Society for Pure English, repr. Bolton and Crystal, *The English Language Vol.2,* p. 93.

68 From Joseph Wright's letter to newspapers appealing for material for the *EDD,* quoted Elizabeth Mary Wright, *The Life of Joseph Wright* (London: O.U.P., 1932), II, 357.

69 The *preservation* of *pure* dialects is everywhere recommended. See, for example, Wright's piece in *Notes and Queries* (1870) and Elizabeth Mary Wright, *Rustic Speech and Folk-Lore* (London: O.U.P., 1913), p. 1.

70 William Matthews, *Cockney Past and Present: A Short History of the Dialect of London* (London and Boston: Routledge & Kegan Paul, 1938), p. 83.

71 Henry Cecil Wyld, *The Historical Study of the Mother Tongue: An Introduction to Philological Method* (London: John Murray, 1920), p. 358. First pub. 1906.

72 Thomas Watts, 'On the Probable Future Position of the English Language,' (1850), quoted Hans Aarsleff, *The Study of Language in England 1780–1860* (London: Athlone P., 1983), p. 222.

73 Trench, quoted Aarsleff, pp. 240–1.

74 K. M. Elisabeth Murray, *Caught in the Web of Words: James A. H. Murray and the Oxford English Dictionary* (Oxford: O.U.P., 1979), pp. 51, 181.

75 Murray, *Caught in the Web of Words,* chs 8–13.

76 Murray, *Caught in the Web of Words,* p. 223.

77 Ibid., p. 189.

78   Ibid., p. 187.

79   *Encylopaedia Britannica: A Dictionary of Arts, Sciences, Literature and General Information*, 11th edn (Cambridge: C. U. P., 1910), p. 587. James Murray is joint author with Hilda Murray.

80   *TLS*, 13 October 1972, pp. 1211–12.

81   Anderson, *Imagined Communities*, p. 122.

82   Harold Jackson in *Today*, quoted *James Joyce: Critical Heritage*, ed. Robert H. Denning (London: Routledge & Kegan Paul, 1970), I, 48.

83   *The National Portrait Gallery*, ed. Lionel Cast (London: Cassell, 1901); Philological Society is quoted in Murray, *Caught in the Web of Words*, p. 137.

84   Sidney Lee quoted 'George Smith and the *DNB*,' *TLS* 24 December 1971, 1593–95. The recent commentator is David Cannadine in a review of the *DNB 1961–1970, London Review of Books*, 3–16 December 1981, pp. 3–6. The *DNB* was bequeathed to Oxford University Press by Smith's family in 1917.

85   Matthew Arnold, 'The French Play in London,' quoted James Woodfield, *English Theatre in Transition 1889–1914* (London: Croom Helm, 1984), p. 96. This is not the place to outline the importance of the theatre during this period. For a sketch, see the introduction to *Theatres of the Left 1880–1935: Workers Theatre in Britain and America*, eds. Raphael Samuel, Ewan MacColl and Stuart Cosgrave (London: Routledge & Kegan Paul, 1985).

86   Geoffrey Whitworth, *The Making of a National Theatre* (London: Faber & Faber, 1951), p. 37.

87   John Stokes, *Resistible Theatres: Enterprise and Experiment in the Late Nineteenth Century* (London: Elek, 1972), p. 9.

88   Quoted Woodfield, *English Theatre in Transition*, p. 99. Only recently have historians begun to be interested in the popular and/or political theatre which Archer and Granville Barker would not acknowledge. See, *Theatres of the Left 1880–1935*, eds. Samuel, MacColl and Cosgrave.

89   Quoted Woodfield, *English Theatre in Transition*, p. 100.

90   Ibid., p. 77. It is interesting to note that the English Stage Society, the main support of theatrical avant-gardism before the advent of the Royal Court, was largely officered by Fabians. See *Theatres of the Left*, ed. Samuel et al., p. 9.

91   Patrick Parrinder, 'The Strange Necessity: James Joyce's Rejection in England 1914–30', in *James Joyce: New Perspectives*, ed. Colin McCabe (Sussex: Harvester P., 1982), pp. 151–67.

92   That the National Theatre was not established during the period of this volume does not materially affect the argument which is centred on the dominant ways of conceiving the national culture and its constituent parts. An account of a later institution such as the Arts Council would confirm my argument. Robert Hutchison has shown how the concern during World War II with taking the arts to the people and supporting arts produced by the people evaporates in the 1950s, and is replaced with a policy of supporting certain metropolitan centres of excellence: *The Politics of the Arts Council* (London: Sinclair Browne, 1982), p. 100.

93   E. Sylvia Pankhurst, *The Suffragette Movement*, p. 454.

94 Raymond Williams, *Towards 2000* (London: Chatto & Windus 1983), pp. 114–19 discusses the various meanings of 'representation'.

95 Sidney Lee, 'The Place of English Literature in the Modern University', in *Elizabethan and Other Essays by Sir Sidney Lee*, ed. Frederick Boas (Oxford: Clarendon P., 1929), p. 4.

96 Gilles Deleuze in conversation with Michel Foucault, *L'Arc* (1972) quoted Alan Sheridan *Michel Foucault: The Will to Truth* (London: Tavistock, 1980), p. 114.

CHAPTER TWO

Englishness and the political culture

Robert Colls

The first stirrings of a popular national consciousness occurred in the four-teenth century, in the writings and fighting experiences of the Hundred Years War.[1] The French were the enemies within and without the Realm, and their national myths grew with ours. In England, the writing and anecdote of the fourteenth and fifteenth centuries was reformulated in the sixteenth century on behalf of a swelling Tudor state. By then, a Catholic world-order was seen to surround a beleaguered Protestant nation-state: Catholics, and the Irish, were now the enemies within and without. The true English, and their Reformed Religion, stood alone. Later, in the next century some of these notions were mobilized by Parliament and Commonwealth.[2] The Civil War was fought as a patriotic war for 'traditional' English liberties. These liberties were by now seen as constitutional as well as religious, and passed way beyond Tudor state Protestantism back to Alfred, England's great king, whose democratic patrimony was broken by the Norman Yoke.[3] Norman lords, and other tyrants, Catholics and continentals and their sympathizers, were all now seen as the enemy within and without. The true English were not only free; they were also Protestant and free, and warred with the Irish to stay that way. The 'Settlement' of 1688 settled not the nation but the dominant modes of political Englishness – confident enough now to incorporate Scotland (1707) and Ireland (1801) in formal union. Reflections on the revolution in France in the 1790s challenged this confidence, but it remained intact. Early-nineteenth-century radicalism had many variants, the most interesting of which was Paineite and Chartist radicalism and its fusion with working-class consciousness; but to a greater or lesser degree the dominant modes of political Englishness – emerging as a cluster of ideas called Liberalism – worked within the settlement of 1688.

A capacious Liberalism remained the dominant force within the political culture between 1880 and 1920. Other views had to accommodate, or be accommodated by, this one. However, between 1880 and 1920, Liberalism represented the English to themselves and to others in ways which were increasingly regarded as inadequate for a nation facing serious social issues within, and carrying a large and growing Empire without. To many, the logic of domestic and Imperial responsibilities, and threats, demanded a more visceral idea of the central state. At first, the idea of such a state was difficult for Liberal ideology to accept, but later Liberalism embraced the idea with speed and invention. This chapter will examine these developments and the new political culture of state and nation which emerged. The following section maps the view of nineteenth-century Liberalism as the historical incarnation of an ideal English freedom from 1688. Section two shows how this notion of freedom was seen to lend the British state a peculiarly 'English' capacity for healing rifts and absorbing its constituents. Sections three and four centre on Ireland and Empire as constituencies difficult to absorb, and the ways in which national identity had to be reformulated to face them. Section five emphasizes the feelings of vulnerability which attended this reformulation, and section six ends the chapter with the entrenchment of the state as the proper expression of subjectivity, sociality and nationhood. After 1920 the resources of English polity are seen to reside less in a diverse civil freedom and more in a corporate national efficiency.

1688 and a Liberal freedom

In 1908 the Charity Organization Society interviewed Mr J. Fisher, a London building foreman. When asked how his casual labourers managed to live, he answered it was 'a thing which I never could understand'; when asked if they applied to the workhouse, he answered:

> No, they would lose their votes. They are English you see.[4]

How the Liberals of the C.O.S. must have enjoyed this answer. If England presented its labourers with a struggle to subsist, Englishness gave them the mettle to survive as a free people.

Nineteenth-century Liberalism represented English freedom as an ideal force, deep within the national character and capable of universal dissemination as England's special gift to the world. Some fifty years before Mr Fisher's splendid answer, the Liberal historian, Henry Buckle, whose *History of Civilization* was reprinted regularly throughout the period, had divided social determinants into two kinds: the 'material' and the 'ideological'. For Buckle, advanced countries defined themselves as societies which had reduced the importance of material determinants, and raised the importance of their 'mental and imaginative' resources. His view that only Liberalism, by freeing these resources, could offer advanced countries a true civilization was accompanied by complementary ideas about the benefits of a true, liberal, higher education for individuals.[5] London's building labourers, impoverished but independent, clearly showed that the Liberal idea of Englishness was, in Buckle's words, 'impossible to stifle':

> in England the course of affairs . . . since the sixteenth century, had diffused among the people a knowledge of their own resources, and a skill and independence in the use of them . . .
> . . . so early as the eleventh century . . . [circumstances] began to affect our national character, and had assisted in imparting to it that sturdy boldness . . . those habits of foresight, and of cautious reserve, to which the English mind owes its leading peculiarities.[6]

The peculiarities of this 'English mind', or this 'Anglo Saxon mind',[7] centred on the idea of the English as a free people. The Liberal ethos both made, and was made by, this mind. Liberalism matched Englishness, and they had demonstrated consanguinity in the expansion of freedom to an ideally free, but historically growing freer, people. Specific freedoms – free subjects, free speech, free ideas, free religion, free contracts, free enterprise, free markets, free trade – were the *historic* Liberal inducements of an *ideal* Englishness.

The major site of that freeing process was Parliament. Parliament's first moves against arbitrary royal decree had been coincident with the growth of English as the nation's official language.[8] Parliament was the English word made free and sovereign: in its discourse, stone, and ceremonial, the Palace of Westminster (rebuilt 1840–52) stood to specify the very meaning of the English as a nation. It stood for them, and above them.

> The power and jurisdiction of parliament are so transcendent and absolute, that it cannot be confined, either for causes or persons, within any bounds.[9]

The period from the 1620s to the 1680s has long been regarded as the Parliament's decisive years. From the revised histories of Sir Edward Coke's Society of Antiquaries (f. 1572) – which fed Charles I's Parliamentary opposition through the dangerous years with a confidence in themselves and their institution – to its later victories, Parliament encompassed the proper dimensions of English freedom.[10] The final settlement of a 'constitutional monarchy' in the Glorious Revolution of 1688–89 was seen as the climax of Parliamentary national duty. The idea of English freedom had been defined, the history of English continuity had been preserved, and the resolved nation could proceed once more. Macaulay's great *History of England* (1848–55),

which began *from the Accession of James II* and explained this story anew
to the Victorians, stood with Buckle's *History* in popularity and influence:

> Our liberty is neither Greek nor Roman; but essentially English. It has a
> character of its own . . .
>
> . . . [it was] indeed difficult to conceive the full amount of the impetus
> given to English civilization by the expulsion of the House of Stuart . . .
> . . . the reign of William III . . . [was] the most successful and the most
> splendid recorded in the history of any country.[11]

Liberal freedom was cast as the English, in history, clawing back margins
of freedom from an arbitrary state. Freedom in this sense could be weighed
in discrete units: as a *prima facie* case, the fewer units which went to the
state, and the more units which went to a freer people, the better it was.
It was this interpretation of historical basics which so well suited popular
political economy from Adam Smith onwards, where the freedom of
peoples was a precondition for the wealth of nations. Discrete political man
had paved the way for discrete economic man where independence, and
freedom from the state became recast as private (commercial) rather than
public (constitutional) virtues. Nevertheless, in spite of this shift of popular
meaning from the constitutional to the commercial, the settlement of
1688–89 was cast as the decisive event for both.

However, to highlight the decisive years at the point of settlement, as
Liberalism did, was less than candid. A political movement which cherished the
history of the seventeenth century but which had its prime ministers kneel before
the monarch, was facing some contradictions when stripped to its ideological
essentials. A Liberal political culture which celebrated the disarming of one
arbitrary power – the monarch – by the arming of another – Parliament – could
be seen not as a myth of freedom at all but the swapping of one arbitrary power
for another. Rebellion, regicide, the restoration of Charles II, the expulsion of
James II, the invitation of William and Mary – in other words, the arbitrary
handling of monarchs – constituted actions whose implications were avoided
but not resolved by concentration on the single happy-ending of 1688. The sins
of Oliver Cromwell as an arbitrary power comparable with the Stuarts could
be absolved by Restoration in 1660, or put to one side because Parliament
itself had suffered by him, but other aspects of the record were indisputable.
Because Liberalism saw English freedom not only as an ideal but also as an
ideal willed by the English in their history, a rebellious *pre*-1688 'Liberalism'
had to explain itself to a settled *post*-1688 'Liberalism'.

Of course, it could never explain itself in ways which equally satisfied
both 'Liberalisms'. Edmund Burke and Thomas Paine were the historical
poles of nineteenth-century debate on these matters. They and all their
successors had to begin by accepting the validity of 1688. To Burke, the
glory of 1688 lay in his representation of it as the end of a series of extreme
acts necessary to restabilize the constitution and, once carried through, not

to be repeated. To Paine, the glory of 1688 lay in the fact of precedent, that if it was willed to overthrow the State then, it could be willed again.[12] Paine in particular understood the contradiction between an ideal freedom and Parliament's own historical arbitrariness:

> In England, it is said that money cannot be taken out of the pockets of the people without their consent:
> But who authorized, or who could authorize the parliament of 1688 to control and take away the freedom of posterity?[13]

During the later-nineteenth century constitutional lawyers continued the argument, albeit in calmer tones than Burke and Paine. Maitland had no doubt that in the first instance Charles I had been acting unlawfully, but, given the drive for constitutional continuity demonstrated by lawyers since 1702, he was at pains to show that 1688–89 had been a proper *revolution*. Lawyers had always taken the view, and still took the view when Maitland delivered his lectures in 1888, that Charles II had immediately succeeded his father in 1649. All those Acts of the Long Parliament which had not received the king's assent were invalid. However, William III's first Assembly and the 'Convention Parliament' which it advised William to call were of the same status – they had not received royal assent. James II had burned the writs for a succeeding Parliament and took with him the Great Seal. Parliament could not invite itself; its acts of dissolution and reconstruction were 'irregular', or, as Paineites preferred to remember it, revolutionary. Maitland affirmed this:

> It seems to me that we must treat the Revolution as a revolution, a very necessary and wisely conducted revolution, but still a revolution. We cannot work it into our constitutional law.

This did not make Maitland a Paineite, although we can see some common points of departure. Rather he was merely insisting on some academic rigour across the bland surface of historical continuities. In matters political, Maitland took the long view of national, institutional essences, which put him with Burke:

> Constitutional history, should, to my mind, be a history not of parties, but of institutions, not of struggles, but of results; the struggles are evanescent, the results are permanent.

Following Burke and Maitland, George Burton Adams (Professor of History at Yale) declared that 1688–89 had been a revolution, but a once and for all revolution:

> The foundations upon which the constitution rests, the supremacy of the law, the sovereignty of the nation, are never again called in question.

... it was a revolution fully justified. ... Its purpose was only to remove obstacles from the way, that the political progress of the people might go on naturally in the same path which for centuries it had been following.[14]

This conservative reading of a royal revolution ('King in Parliament') could be challenged by degrees depending on how closely the challenger wished to scrutinize the subsequent relationship between Parliament and People. Staying close to Paine for Paine's own day, Buckle had reckoned that the achievements of 1688 had nearly been squandered by a repressive Parliament between the 1790s and 1820s. Later Liberals, the Hammonds among them, followed his lead.[15] But for the middle years of the nineteenth century, with Paine buried and the dark days gone, the People – if not all of their Parliamentary representatives – had held onto their Englishness to find the light with Liberalism (small 'l' and large 'L'). 1828, 1832, 1846, the reforming Gladstonian administrations, had marked huge blows for freedom. Even Chartism could die only to be absorbed in the commonplace remark that five of their six demands had been eventually granted by a Parliament and State which had cleansed itself and recovered its right relationship with the People.[16] The (male) People had been allowed entry into Parliament, largely in Liberal colours. But they entered a conservative place because Burke's reading and not Paine's dominated its understanding of English freedom, and the relationship of state and revolution upon which it was founded.

It was not that Burke's view of English freedom had privileged his 'history' of settlement over Paine's rebellious 'ideal', but more that Burke had enclosed the ideal within his history and refused to comprehend it in any other way. For the ideal had the unpleasant habit of spontaneity, and it was the spontaneous and combustible energies of revolution that were no longer to be countenanced – in this country at least.

The English state took the same view of revolution as the Roman Church took of miracles. It believed in them – indeed it was founded on one albeit one of a different order – but it did not welcome them, and was in no hurry to acknowledge them. What was heresy today might be truth tomorrow; it all depended on time and the long run. All political energies, after Burke, now had to go through the mill of 1688. And it was a rich and subtle mill to be ground in. The ideal was not denied, but when manifest it had to stand the test of continuity. In a state where the existing structures and conventions of power were themselves parts of the Constitution, the status quo interpreted the precedents, and tested the continuity, and by so doing presented 1688 as the *historically achieved ideal* of 'freedom'. The English may have had to snatch at freedom to save it, they may even have managed to make it grow, but in its essence their freedom had already been achieved. Their way of life, their national character, their liberties, existed primarily as *things* to be defended rather than as processes to be lived or to be realized.

Their present had to constantly measure itself against someone else's past. Mr Fisher's building labourers may have found it hard to live, their present relationships may have been exploitative, but they had the past thing of freedom. Slung between an historic Parliament and the English ideal, between those in power who preserved the history and interpreted the ideal and those in whose name it was done, lay the 'resolved' nation.

As a postscript to this section a word needs to be said about Samuel Smiles' brand of extreme Individualism which most threatened the 1688 paradigm from within its own Liberal framework. This Individualism nearly succeeded in splitting the ideal from the historic by pushing the units of (individual) freedom against the state as far as they could go, and by so doing appeared to give back to the people, as individuals, their spontaneity to make and remake the state:

> The Government of a nation is usually found to be but the reflex of individuals composing it . . .
> . . . the worth and strength of a State depend far less upon the form of its institutions than upon the character of its men. For the nation is only an aggregate of individual conditions, and civilization itself is but a question of the personal improvement of the men, women and children of whom society is composed.[17]

However, the cutting-edge of this theory and its capacity to break with ideals in history and rely instead upon individuals in the present, was blunted by the good fortune of the English to have the idealist-historicist mix deep within themselves. Self-help and the freedom it engendered might indeed be a universal quality, but it also had to be quintessentially English. Freedom '. . . has in all times been a marked feature in the English character, and furnishes the true measure of our power as a nation'.[18]

The absorbing qualities of the State

In fact, 'the true measure' of the power of the English state lay in its qualities of healing and absorption. The Liberal ethos saw the seventeenth-century Parliamentarians as having made no real break. Liberalism misconceived the Middle Ages in order to come to terms with feudalism, and it admitted the replacement of dynasties in order to come to terms with royalty: Simon de Montfort became an honorary Liberal, William III joined de Montfort, and Magna Carta touched tips with the Bill of Rights. Everything since then, and in a reformulated way everything before then, was cast in continuity. The Industrial Revolution and Democracy were not ruptures so much as the long run clearing up of anomalies (against patronage) and the expansion of potentials (through freedom). The constitutionalist Professor Adams thought that 'All the later progress consists in more and more complete application of these principles in actual government, the more complete carrying of them out in practice'; Gardiner's *Student's History* (1892) typically concentrated on the evolution of a constitution and gave scant attention to population, manufacturing and commerce.[19] If Edwardian society unsuccessfully divided wealth across classes, 5 per cent owned 87 per cent,[20] the Liberal ethos successfully dispersed power across time. There was a place for everyone in its history of the Settlement: the monarchy was restored; the gentry were secured; the middle classes rose; the working classes rose with them; emigrants flocked to England for its liberties, safety, and prosperity.[21] The new system carried all before it, and its absorbent state produced a nation without martyrs or shrines that had any popular meaning other than the Liberal one.[22] Even Cromwell's statue could be eventually raised in 1899 in the precinct of the Palace of Westminster, a gift of Lord Rosebery the former Liberal Prime Minister. Fabian and Marxist socialists, as opposed to each other as to the political order, were both hopeful of some blend of economics with that fact upon which they could all agree, the historic continuity of the English character:

> The Fabian Society accepts the conditions imposed on it by human nature and by the national character and political circumstances of the English people . . . gradual, peaceful changes, as against revolution, conflict with the army and police, and martyrdom. . . . The Fabian Society therefore begs those Socialists who are looking forward to a sensational historical crisis, to join some other Society.[23]

But what other society was there to join? H. M. Hyndman, leader of the Marxist S.D.F., thought that,

> Patriotism is part of our heritage; self restraint necessarily comes from the exercise of political power. . . . We are ready enough to talk about justice to others. . . . Let the people of these islands . . . now be just to themselves. . . . Thus only shall the England of whose past we are all proud, and of whose future all are confident, clear herself from that shortsighted system which now stunts the physical and intellectual growth of the great majority.[24]

It was in its capacity to heal and absorb, and in its resolving myths of continuity and longevity that Liberalism, and its Parliament, made claim for the idea of Englishness.

Of course this is a necessarily schematic account of the Liberal ethos. Looked at in detail there were gaps and anomalies and differences of emphasis, but the Liberal memory of the political nation predominated. Some would prefer to call it the 'Whig' memory.[25] This is not to say that Tories and High Churchmen could not subscribe. Tory-voting historians like Stubbs and Froude wrote within its widest margins. So did Liberal-voting republicans like Freeman. In the 1880–1920 period, as Dennis Smith's chapter in this volume indicates, this Liberal ethos was breaking up to take Conservative and Labour party formulations. At times the Liberal ethos appears to be such a capacious view that it is without margins at all. Perhaps its exponents were more united on what threatened it than what constituted it – corruption? industry and town? Ireland? From within Liberalism's libertarian centre, proper Liberals like Mill, Smiles, Cobden, Bright and Green all had their differences with it.[26] So did the working-class radicals, and socialists; and New Liberals. But their opposition and dissent more often stemmed from taking Liberal freedom at its face value rather than real value, and asking more of it than Capitalism could possibly give.

The most insistent petitioners upon liberal Capitalism were the working class. It has to be accepted that their petitions were mainly about the admission of working-class males into the political culture. Women had fitfully claimed their place – as with Chartism and Owenism[27] – but they had to make the Women's Social and Political Union in 1903 before a mass and explicitly female politics could begin, for Liberal freedom was a *manly* sentiment, permanently serving, but rarely admitting, a named femininity. The entry of working-class males into electoral politics was granted with some misgivings but no real rupture. After all, freedom was their birthright. Achieved before, outside their power, it had at first been entrusted to patricians. The extension of the franchise – 'Reform' – had at first been opposed as an illegitimate demand on the past, but it is easy to see how it could be cast in historical continuity. It was merely an extension of near-perfection. The problems came after the franchise. Although plural voting remained, in principle all males were now equally invested with a single vote, but not all men were equal. The simple level ground of electoral rights had to coexist with an uneven national culture which, as Philip Dodd made plain in the last chapter, began to operate by new methods of exclusion and the fixing of function. The political male nation was indivisible, but the national culture was based upon an unequal diversity of functions. By this system the physicality of male manual workers ('salt of the earth') could be respected, and their intellectual capacity for organization could be allowed, so long as both facets knew their place. If working-class males wished to go further and journey into the heartlands of the national culture where all the fixing and ordering happened, then the *right* to journey (if not the means) could only be by affiliation. The Liberal party was quick to seek the affiliation of independent working-class politics.[28] The Labour party convinced itself that it could only travel by full affiliation to a political culture where the omnicompetence of Parliament was the crucial passport. The same was true of journeys into other heartlands than the political one – the professions, finance, business, government service, the arts, education. When the class travelled as a class, they had to affiliate; when they travelled as individuals, even like enormously talented individuals like D. H. Lawrence, the road was impossibly rough or miserable. For example,

Ruskin College was founded in 1899 for working-class men; the College was built in Oxford, but

> the Ruskin Students come to Oxford, not as mendicant pilgrims go to Jerusalem, to worship at her ancient shrines and marvel at her sacred relics, but as Paul went to Rome, to conquer in a battle of ideals.[29]

However, it was only six years after its foundation that the University began to busy itself in trying to establish formal affiliations and change the College's rubric. University Chancellor Lord Curzon's overtures were rebuffed in 1907 by Principal and students alike, but the interference continued and in 1909 most of the students struck, and ten of them left to found their own 'unaffiliated' Central Labour College. They were in no doubt that their refusal to affiliate culturally was a political act. They were pleased to call themselves 'Plebs':

> Our answer to those who would swing the reactionary rod over the mental life of the working class, is only this: we neither want your crumbs nor your condescension, your guidance nor your glamour, your tuition nor your tradition. We have our own historical way to follow . . .[30]

The Plebs's historical way took them out of Oxford to Earls Court. By way of comparison, less than 20 years later Arthur Eaglestone left the Yorkshire coalfield for Oxford, where he had won a scholarship. Wholly affiliated to the idea of Oxford as a heartland of the national culture, and travelling alone, Eaglestone's record of his time there is profoundly depressing.[31] His only friends appear to have been Indians and Ruskinites.

A more iconoclastic opposition to state absorption and national identity might have been expected from over the borders. This was not the case. 'Welshness' had first been engulfed by the Tudors, and was recast in our period as a species of Celtic Liberalism which exhausted itself in a rural struggle for Disestablishment and land.[32] 'Scottishness' was politically Whig and culturally Tory. The Highland-Stuart risings of 1715 and 1745 were opposed by the majority of Scots – the lowland bourgeoisie had especially benefited from their later version of 1688. Union of kingdoms under one Parliament in London was sealed in 1707, brutally insisted upon after Culloden, and flourished thereafter, albeit with suitable coatings of Highland patriotism to sugar the national pill.[33]

In 1904 Havelock Ellis produced his *Study of British Genius*. Based upon the recently compiled sixty-six volumes of the Dictionary of National Biography, he counted the share of eminent persons against the size of population. Within the English counties the southern and south midland shires – 'the most anciently civilized' – had produced the greater proportions. Within the United Kingdom, England's ratios were naturally set as standard: Wales had produced less than its share, Scotland more, and Ireland least of all.[34] The respective shares corresponded perfectly to the hegemony of the English 'south country' over the United Kingdom. The Scots (especially their 'geniuses'), who had most welcomed Union, excelled; the Irish, who had least welcomed it, failed. It was hardly surprising. Ellis' findings indicated not British genius but British geniality.

Ireland

Ireland was the weakest point in English power. Liberal history and English freedom were institutions which did not travel well across the Irish Sea. Nor could they be expected to. For the Catholic Irish the seventeenth century represented a grotesque inversion of the Liberal memory. The first Catholic Rising of 1641–42 had been prompted by fears of Parliamentary, not Stuart, tyranny. Cromwell came in 1649, not as protector but as murderer and thief. The Restoration of 1660 restored nothing much. The Glorious Revolution of 1688 was not bloodless. When James II was expelled from England he turned up in Ireland. Parliament's new man, William III, broke the Catholic resistance and brought yet more thefts of land and a cruel penal code – the 'severest laws' against Catholics.[35] What joy could there possibly be for the Catholic Irish in a story of national identity which celebrated Parliament and the first Orangeman?

The Ulster Presbyterians' experience of the English was more complicated but not much less at odds. They were dissenters too. Planted in the north from 1609 these poor lowland Scots were colonists, but they were not the 'Protestant Ascendancy' who lorded it for the English. They were covenanting people. They saw themselves, and in Ireland were encouraged to see themselves, as settlers in an alien territory cleared by their own hard hand. They held out against James' Catholic Lord Lieutenant, Tyrconnell, in 1688–89 until help arrived from the Williamite forces and the tide was turned at the Boyne, but these actions did not especially endear them to London. Their cultural impulse remained independent and although they had some political success, with other fellow countrymen, in the 1770s and 1780s – an Irish Parliament, 1783–1800 – their poverty remained only marginally less than that of the Catholics. London penalized their trade and Dublin Castle played their historic loyalty off against the precarious loyalties of the Catholic majority. The Orangemen were founded by Anglicans in the 1790s to oppose Catholic and Presbyterian radical disloyalties, but they finally found haven in Union after 1801 and grew, laterally, with nineteenth-century Catholic nationalism. By the 1880s the Ulster Orangemen stood by the Union as militant Protestants inside a UK Protestant majority, but their loyalty was not to Parliament, still less to Liberalism. Their loyalty was to themselves. The period 1688–89 had no less a different meaning for them than it had for the Catholics. In a sense they were the only ones who continued to take

Burke at his word. Their William was but a gaudy caricature of Buckle's or
Freeman's or any English William. There was little rhetoric of a developing
freedom in their reading of 1689. 'No surrender' meant no change and no
change meant the continued unfreedom of Catholics. Freedom was for no
one more a petrified *thing* of the late-seventeenth century than it was for the
Orangeman, and his symbols and mottoes were not English, or even British,
but the assertion of one kind of Irishness against another. In its scarlet Popes
and wooden shoes and great gun of Athlone what meaning, other than an
Irish one, could the Loyal Orangeman's toast have for mainland Britain?[36]

In their own way, both Catholic and Orange Irish found their Irishness by
losing their Englishness. Nothing proved this more than home rule. Ireland
was unfree and coerced, but Ireland would not be absorbed. The lengths to
which the Liberal party was prepared to go in order to heal and absorb were
remarkable. Some, like Chamberlain, refused, and split in 1886. Others, like the
ageing John Bright, held on, but against their better judgement: 'I hesitate to
become the assailant of Gladstone though I condemn his policy . . .' But the
'"Party associations" are ready to accept anything apparently'.[37] By 1897
P. J. MacDonell could call for 'due homage' to the Irish Nationalists; he
even thought their 'struggle against English insolence and injustice was a
creditable page in Parliamentary history'.[38] These were generous words, but
on closer inspection they were more generous to the English state than to Irish
Nationalism. MacDonell's confidence in Parliament's powers of absorption
was unbounded, and the Irish home rulers had no choice other than to try
and share that confidence. The problem of Irish refusal to be absorbed lay in
the English state, but the Irish home rulers had to swallow Englishness before
they could be allowed their Irishness. This was not easy. John Redmond, their
leader, was unequivocal about Ireland's 'unconquerable nationality', but he
also saw his country as a 'paralysed and broken' arm *within* the British
Empire.[39] The Irish home rulers had to confide in the Liberal memory for the
success of their scheme:

> England's record of honour, her record of service to freedom is rich and
> ample; but it lies elsewhere.

They could do no other than trust to 'Englishmen . . . as reasonable sons
of Liberty', and to England's 'two great examples of Liberty . . . perfecting
democratic government for herself . . . [and] giving to her dependencies full
freedom of self government'.[40]

Unfortunately for Redmond and his supporters there were other
Englishmen and other Englishnesses who had a Unionist hand in the matter.
The Conservatives made common cause with Unionists and Orangemen.
For Randolph Churchill the way to get at Gladstone, to get 'the old man
hooked', was to play the 'Orange card'.[41] And in each round, with each home
rule bill, in 1886, 1893 and 1912, the stakes grew higher as Orangemen
and Conservatives grew more virulent. By 1912 the argument *against* home

rule was as much based on English imperatives as arguments *for* it – the supremacy of one Parliament and the defence of a British Empire.

> There is not a man in this room who is not a voter, and who therefore is not vitally interested in preserving our Parliamentary institutions and especially the House of Commons . . . that most subtly contrived political machine, the growth of centuries of self government.[42]

But it was not a question of voters at all. In the name of 'loyalty' and Parliament, Orangemen and Conservatives said they were prepared to be disloyal. Historical nations transcended mere majorities. The Ulster Protestants may be an Irish minority but, as Mr Amery said:

> . . . when it comes to questions which go to the very roots of a Constitution, questions of national existence . . . then the counting of heads or votes which suffices for ordinary current legislation ceases to have any meaning.[43]

The Protestant leader, Sir Edward Carson, may have nodded his assent, but if *they* were talking of England, or Britain, or Empire, *he* was thinking of Ulster:

> The first law of nature with nations and governments as with individuals, is self preservation.[44]

The home rule bills broke the Liberal party and polarized the Irish. As D. George Boyce makes clear in his contribution to this volume, no matter how the Liberals tried to present the bills as part of a new 'Britishness' where the different nationalities of the United Kingdom were re-constituted, it was clear Ireland was a special case receiving special measures. As such, the bills represented an ideological defeat for Englishness, an ideological impossibility for Catholics, an ideological treachery for Orangemen. In 1913 – with home rule in the offing but the Ulster Volunteers under arms and the British army said to be an uncertain quantity – by that perversion of Liberal History which Ireland represents, the Conservative leader Bonar Law could compare Asquith to James II. Coming from a Tory, these were hard words for a Liberal to swallow:

> In order to carry out his despotic intention the King had the largest army which had ever been seen in England. What happened? There was no civil war. There was a revolution, and the King disappeared. Why? Because his own army refused to fight for him.[45]

Bagehot, the Liberal interpreter of the English Constitution, had always sensed that home rule was an impossibility as much for the English state as for the Irish people. He thought the Irish home rulers might have been Liberals in detail, but they had not thought the matter through. If they did, with their Liberal allies, they would see that the core of their position was anti-Parliament in a way true Liberals could never countenance:

> The very life of Home Rule, and in a great measure too of Irish Catholicism, springs from want of sympathy with the Imperial Parliament, and though that may show how very desirable it is for English politicians to act cordially with the Home Rulers and the Liberal Catholics on all subjects on which cooperation is really possible, it also indicates how very few these subjects are likely to be.[46]

And yet, Bagehot was hard pushed to suggest a policy. According to him, because the Catholic Irish, – a negated people – had so little 'politics' of their own to offer, and at the same time did not wish to play the English Constitution by English rules, they were a hopeless case. Bagehot's offering of a better-proportioned Union was the political equivalent of the War Office's revised Union Flag of 1900. The new flag restored the cross of St Patrick to equivalent proportions with St George and St Andrew but forgot that the *cross* of St Patrick was an 1800 English invention for a saint who was not a martyr and for a people who had never used it.[47] Because the Irish did not want an English constitution they were said not to want any constitution:

> The truth is that almost all effervescence against civil restraints in matters not obviously moral, is popular in Ireland. . . . Home Rule must be regarded as deriving its popularity hitherto, quite as much from its general irreconcilability with the existing order of things, as from its representing any new order of things with which Ireland would really be content. The Union may be unpopular in itself, but it is also unpopular because it represents the established order.[48]

Empire

Neither Catholic nor Unionist Ireland would be easily absorbed into the English state. But other problems of absorption were gathering. In the generation spanned by the three home rule bills the state had amassed a new Empire in Africa and the Far East of some ninety million people and four and three quarter million square miles. Encompassing the old Empire of India, and the 'white' colonies, the British Empire at the turn of the century numbered around three hundred and forty five million people and eleven and a half million square miles. It was the most extensive territorial claim in the world and it worried many Liberals not only in the scale of its burden (how many Irelands?)[49] but also in its implications for the United Kingdom itself.[50] Liberals like J. A. Hobson had been most worried at how quickly the 'disease' of 'modern Imperialism' had infected the political culture. For Hobson, the South African war had been a national defilement. John Bull was now known for 'The black slime of his malice',[51] and Hobson's question was in whose interest did this Empire exist and for whose interest would the nation declare itself? Would the nation stand by its best Liberal traditions, or would it be led by the nose by the newspaper monopolies, mining companies and finance houses?

> Can a body of interested men upon the spot, business men or politicians, impose their authority upon the Empire so as to utilize the Imperial sources for their particular ends? In the case of South Africa it has been possible. Will it be possible again?[52]

Certainly the prospects did not look bright. The Empire was a large, if shaky, fact and even senior sections of the Liberal party could claim to be in its favour, albeit in a more flaccid way than the Conservatives. But no one, not even Liberal Imperialists, could seriously pretend that the Empire's millions of black and brown peoples were being tutored in the Liberal way. With the questionable exception of Ceylon, self-government, and with whatever constitutional nicety one would care to name it, – representative, home rule, joint controlling, dyarchy, dominion, commonwealth or union – was simply not on the agenda. These peoples could not even be assured of equal treatment under British law even if they were said to enjoy the constitutional perfection of being ruled by a 'King in Parliament'. The first problem of Empire, it may be noted, was not the nationalism of subject peoples but the 'overflow of nationalism' of the metropolis.[53]

Hobson had tried to make a distinction between 'colonialism' and 'Imperialism': colonialism was 'a genuine expansion' of nationality, a settling of old peoples in new lands. Hobson knew it rarely worked; colonial settlement usually ended in tears – rebellion, bondage, 'Imperialism' – but its impulse was different from the rough annexations of soldiers and statesmen.[54] Hobson had to make the distinction because of recent theories of nation and Empire. He was aware of new formulations of Englishness fostered in particular by the Cambridge Regius Professor Sir John Seeley. Seeley and his acolytes had tried to redraw the Liberal map of English History. The origins of the new Englishness were moved back from 1688 to 1588. From the Elizabethan Age the English began their long voyage of world conquest and settlement. Their global success had been unique, they seemed, 'as it were, to have conquered and peopled half the world in a fit of absence of mind'.[55] It had to have been done in this way because these were not the conquests of individuals. Instead, England was now invested with a *geist* which moved and had its being in the historical forces of race, language, and right moral authority. Against this, the Liberal-Whig celebrations of 1688 were considered insular; they represented the contractual satisfactions of lawyers who mistook the building of institutions for the surge of nations.

New historical categories were necessary. For the mustiness of old deals and documents, Seeley offered sea spray and muscle:

> Once we begin to think of England as a living organism, which in the Elizabethan age began a process of expansion, never intermitted since, into Greater Britain, we shall find these divisions altogether useless, and shall feel the want of a completely new set of divisions to mark the successive stages of the expansion.

> To us England will be wherever English people are found, and we shall look for its history in whatever places witness the occurrences most important to Englishmen.[56]

If the new England was where the Englishmen were, who were the English? Here, the new history was aided by the old. The Victorian historians, Stubbs, Freeman and Green had been more attached to constitutional than sea-going matters and they had firmly placed original 'Englishness' in the free moot of the Saxon village. From village moot and forest clearing to national Parliament was essentially a 'Whig' story, but the *origins* of the English species were now in the race, language and custom of a Teutonic people rather than in the metropolitan deeds of elite-Whigs.[57] Stubbs, and Green perhaps unwittingly, shifted the ground of Englishness from being something less about constitutional precedents to being something more about white skins, English tongues, and feelings about being free. This change formed the bridge between the old Liberal rationalism and Imperial *geist*. By it, everyone who could possibly claim to have the right skins, show the right tongues, and be identified with the right feelings, was now invited across to the Whig celebrations – and with some strange results.

Seeley's Empire ignored Africa and Asia. It was, after all, only where the English settled, and for him that meant the paltry ten million in Canada, West Indies, South Africa and Australasia. That many of these were Scots did not matter. In Macaulay and Mill India had had a strong claim on the transmutation of Liberal ideas. For Seeley, India was part of the Empire too, but only as a burden, alien and unsettlable, a duty to be discharged decently. In fact, the United States, 'English in race and character' was closer to us than those under the Union Jack – a view corroborated by influential Americans who, though they 'may not like the English . . . are of the same race'.[58] If Saxon forebears was genealogical news to black and immigrant America, and if the Empire's indigenous peoples were not its true constituents, there were further illogicalities to come. Sir Charles Dilke shared Seeley's vision of a federal Empire was based upon a new Englishness but he was less parsimonious about who should be its citizens. Facing what he saw as a coming world crisis, and overwhelmed by its statistics, Dilke's 'Greater Britain' solution was a concocted idea where the rag-bag of British colonies could, for example, be levelled against the land mass of Russia: 'the British Empire exceeds the Russian Empire slightly in size and vastly in population'.[59] The binding forces of this new state were a language and feeling which could include those lesser races who brushed with that language and feeling:

> But now the English-speaking people have conquered India, almost the whole of North America, the greater part of Polynesia with Australasia, and most of the opened parts of Africa. . . . The increase of the race, and the increase of that larger body who speak its tongue, are both keeping pace with the figures suggested in the dreams and speculations of half a century ago. More than a hundred million people speak English as their chief tongue, and vastly more than that number as one of two languages; while four hundred millions of people are, more or less directly, under English rule.

This view courted the North Americans ('not only in race and language, but in laws and religion and in many matters of feeling – essentially one'),[60] and where language and feeling failed, race might succeed. Dilke toyed with bringing in Germans and Swedes as well.

A vulnerable power: Enemies within and without

The dread of a far-flung Empire impossible to defend – English schoolchildren stared at Mercator's Projection and heard tales of lesser nations rifling John Bull's pockets – was but a symptom of deeper dreads about the insecurity of England itself. Because the essential England lay in the south, even geography conspired to make us vulnerable. Great Britain's mountains were west and north while the lowlands of the south were open and seductive – the historical route of invasion.[61] Images of vulnerability mixed with images of corruption. Hobson's Southern England was a model for decadent world Imperialism – a soft, rentier downland living off the tribute of subjugated peoples. Degeneration lay in the cities. How could the unmanly products of urban life be made into military material? While some fretted over the capacity of an urban working class to defend the Empire, in 1895 Cecil Rhodes feared their capacity to attack it: 'If you want to avoid civil war, you must become imperialists.'[62] Given the complementariness of Rhode's choices, British Imperialism had to be parochial.[63]

There are many examples of this within the politics of the period; for a more forceful example it is perhaps better to go outside political manoeuvrings. The convergence of structures of feeling in Joseph Conrad's *Heart of Darkness* and Jack London's *People of the Abyss* is remarkable. The two writers adhered to very different political-cultural views, but both men had a high regard for the English. Published within a year of each other (1902–03), Conrad's is a classic story of Imperialism and London's is

a classic document of the 'social question'. The natives of Conrad's Congo
and London's Stepney are each ruled by another race, and live in sunless,
torpid lands, uprooted, cast aside, and dying from degeneracy. It is difficult,
at times, to tell Congo and Stepney apart:

> An empty stream, a great silence, an impenetrable forest. The air was
> warm, thick, heavy, sluggish . . .

> Mind and body are sapped by the undermining influences. . . . Moral and
> physical stamina are broken . . . the children grow up . . . without virility
> or stamina, a weak-kneed narrow-chested, listless breed, that crumples
> up and goes down . . .

> They are stupid and heavy, without imagination . . . a stupefying
> atmosphere of torpor, which wraps about them and deadens them . . .

> They were dying slowly . . . nothing but black shadows of disease and
> starvation . . . lost in uncongenial surroundings, fed on unfamiliar food,
> they sickened, became inefficient . . .[64]

In 1898, when the explorer Guy Burrows wanted to tell of Pigmy hooliganism
he lapsed into Cockney slang. Someone appears, 'little arrows' are fired:
'A stranger! "Eave'arf a brick at 'im!"'[65] Both 'Mistah Kurtz' and
Jack London contemplated the liquidation of these unfit peoples. Kurtz's
'"Exterminate all the brutes!"' is more shocking, but London's depiction
of socio-biological scum – 'it is criminal for the people of the Abyss to
marry' – was not less well-intentioned.[66] Stepney or Africa, pigmy Pigmies
or pigmy Cockneys, the state would have to discharge its responsibilities to
both or be dragged down by both. The British state grandiloquently exported
its fear in the form of power and re-imported its power in the form of fear.

Insularity was one response to the paradox of power and fear. The revival
of 'folk' studies, local archaeology, and county history had a profound effect
on regional, sub-national, identities. True to the paradox, folk study went
deep within the English 'way', but the best of it was inspired by colonial
anthropology. In 1910 the Folk Lore Society (f. 1878) called for more
looking-inward, more on the English 'peasant' than the colonial 'savage'.
In 1911 only eleven out of forty English counties had no published field-
work on their customs.[67] The revival represented a flight away from external
threats deep into the nation's racial and rural essence. Aspects of this flight to
the rural are examined in Alun Howkins' chapter in this volume. The revival
fixed the nation on populist lines of race, language, and tradition – as well
as what it took as 'customary' notions of class and gender – not according
to what its people were doing (or might do) but according to what they
had been and were, (and could not be any other).[68] When the Countess of
Warwick introduced that pre-eminent *doer,* Joseph Arch, to the nation in
1898, she described him not as a wage labourer and trade unionist but as a
'Warwickshire peasant' set in a context of old English stock. When the black

American 'cake walk' dance was introduced to the London music halls in the same year, so dreaded was miscegenation with 'old, healthy sensual (but not sensuous) English dances' that cake walking was said to show 'why the negro and the white can never lie down together'.[69] That the South Londoners had mixed cake walking with their own swagger to dance the first Lambeth Walk in 1903 was so much the worse for them. Indeed, it was their genes we had to worry about. The Eugenics movement believed that genetic adaptations to city living had been unfavourable to national molecular grouping. In spite of high level government reports, on 'Physical Training' (1902 Scotland) and 'Physical Deterioration' (1904), which showed the contrary, the movement insisted on the findings of its new 'science'.[70] What can they know of England those who only England know? Quite a lot, it seemed – from *Folk Lore* to *Victoria County Histories* to *Eugenics*.

Indeed, Imperial insularity was introducing a distinct neurosis into the political culture. The growing clamour to censor national uncleanliness (Social Purity Movement in the 1870s, National Vigilance Association in the 1880s) was motivated by sexual and military insecurity. In 1905 Gilbert and Sullivan's *Pinafore* and *Mikado* were banned so as not to upset Japanese allies! Even Kipling was censored for his *Notes of Two Trips with the Channel Squadron* (1898).[71] Promoting healthy literature, on the other hand, was a national duty. The serious study and teaching of history as 'public doctrine', encouraged by German precedents, were advanced by the establishment of the *English Historical Review* in 1886 and the Historical Association in 1906.[72] More seriously, the neurosis came close to producing an early form of English fascism.

Charles Pearson's *National Life and Character* (1893) projected the future without fear or favour. If others could not bring themselves to think objectively – for example, the United States would not save themselves misery by contemplating the shipment of negroes back to Africa – then Pearson could. He would tell Britain where it was going. In fact, nations figured far less in his projections than what he chose to call races. The British were tossed in with an Aryan sludge of White races who could not hold, and would eventually come into conflict with, Black and Yellow sludges from across the oceans. Outbred, outviced, and outsettled by the blacks and yellows, and too genetically delicate for settlement in intemperate climes, the whites would have to be content with what they had. And in order to keep it, the State would need to intervene to the point of what Pearson chose to call 'socialism'. This national socialism would be democratic, but overlaid by a military autocracy with fortress duties. As the state made its citizens healthy and took over responsibility for social planning and religion, its military would defend it. Defend it from what? One may be excused from thinking that the greatest threat lay in Pearson's own neurosis:

We shall wake to find ourselves elbowed and hustled, and perhaps even thrust aside by peoples whom we looked down upon as servile, and thought of as bound always to minister to our needs. The solitary consolation will be, that the changes have been inevitable. . . . Yet in some of us the feeling of caste is so strong that we are not sorry to think we shall have passed away before that day arrives.[73]

State becomes Society

The Greater Britain imaginings of a new Englishness leading to a universally concocted, trans-Atlantically aligned, linguistic-racial federalism was a mess from any point of view – political, cultural, or strategic. However, its importance lay not in any appraisal of geopolitical affairs, still less in any feasible future for the nation, but in the only way Empire ever really mattered to Britain – at home, in the political culture.[74] The new Imperialism relocated the relationships between state and people. Underpinned by ideas coming out of Oxford from the 1860s which stressed the unique responsibilities of the ideal state for enlarging human freedom, Imperialism could come to refer to the state not as an institution on license (no matter how distant) from the people, but as the organic outgrowth of the nation. At Balliol, T. H. Green re-interpreted Greek and German philosophy for a new generation of ruling Englishmen and their state. Green's (Liberal) revision had shown 'scrupulous caution'[75] in the matter of keeping a gap between 'State' and 'Society', but his younger disciples like Bosanquet came to emphasize Hegel to the point of finally closing that narrow gap.

Bosanquet's 'State' was an idealist and heavily theoretical construct of the state as the only true organ of the social will and therefore, the real maker and legitimiser of the social order. Once this was accepted – no matter his dislike of actually existing states – Bosanquet's 'State' became a very lofty affair indeed. For him, rights and principles could best be understood in relation to concrete situations, usually the fluid situations of individual encounters. But the time had come to save the Poor and serve the nation, and only the state, by existing to show that the citizen's duty was 'to a quality, not a crowd' could redefine rights and translate them into reality.[76] Because Bosanquet and the idealists' 'State' was not collectivist – although collectivist measures were another thing – but nevertheless insisted upon the veneration of its power, then its attractiveness to conservative politics was strong. Through their state the English would rediscover their soul:

> Our nation, our country, our State – England, say; what has it always stood for to those who loved it right? For more things than I can tell; but for these at least, honesty, justice, liberty . . .

> Is all this hostile to "the State"? Where did the question come from, "What is man's soul for?" and the answer "To live well"? From the first great

book on the State, did it not? Not the soul of Greek or Jew, but the soul of man. Sovereignty [of the State] will find it hard to accept limitations? Hard, very likely. Sovereignty is there to do hard things. To find your own soul, in helping the soul of man; both of them are hard things; but easier together, surely, than apart. Are they in antagonism? I think not.[77]

T. H. Green had warned that the state should only be challenged 'in fear and trembling' but others like Bosanquet questioned the possibility of challenge altogether. Rather than seeing State and Society as jealous constellations of power, the State was now responsible for Society so as to make and remake the synthetic nation.[78] The new Englishness found a ready role for this philosophy for there was now an awful lot of 'Society' the Imperial 'State' had to be responsible for.

The real fissures in the political culture between 1880 and 1920 lay not in political parties but along a line to do with attitudes to the state. Nearly all the emergent political groupings wanted some form of more state responsibility. The softer view of the state looked to ensuring the freedom, diversity, and continuity of old Liberal Englishness; the harder view would have it defend *and* extend British power. Although the 'soft' position looked more to home, and the 'hard' position abroad, both stances were essentially united on the peculiar, constitutional and/or racial propensities of the English/British to rule others. For those at the bottom of the English/British heap there may have been crumbs of comfort of a racist kind here. For those at the top, the new role of the public schools and ancient universities as tutors in leadership provided a common code and grounding which always threatened to carry them beyond political parties 'in the national interest'. Here, the interpretation of the national interest lay not in the democratic state, but was encoded in a network of personal contacts and informal understandings beyond and behind that state.[79] If feelings about nation drew political positions together, feelings about their major responsibilities – the 'social question' at home, and the Empire abroad – set their focus and direction.

But translating state responsibilities into the party political system was harder than contemplating what they might be. The more one approached the middle-ground – somewhere between Chamberlainite Conservatism and Liberal Imperialism – the more convergent positions became and the more did the electoral system demand a clear break between them. The break eventually came over 'Free Trade' in the 1905 general election, but it did not hide the convergence, and the discourse continued within the political culture throughout the Liberal administrations of 1906–16. Boer War catastrophes had checked Seeleyite optimism, but Joseph Chamberlain had hoped that a mixture of war jingoism and industrial depression would carry his cause for a 'white' Imperial federation bound by economic protection. This was not to be. His protectionism was popular in the Conservative party but not particularly welcomed by the Conservative cabinet or the 'white' colonies.

On the question of federation, those colonies took as much a self-interested view as he did. At the 1902 Colonial Conference they rejected federation and greater defence burdens, and only half accepted trade preference. Lord Salisbury counselled caution, and Chamberlain left the government to stump the country.[80] The 1905 Liberal election victory was a rebuff, but the argument went on into the 1920s in the shape of the Tariff Reform Commission.

In view of inter/intra party views of the state, and idealist-conservative formulations of the state which looked to it for a new national soul, W. A. S. Hewins, the Secretary of the Tariff Reform Commission from 1904, was a pivotal figure. Hewins had been an academic before joining the Commission. He was close to Chamberlain and eventually became a Conservative MP and Under Secretary for the Colonies. The roots of Hewins' Conservatism lay in a rejection of Individualism and a concern for Empire and the 'social question'. Greatly influenced as a student by the organic 'Englishness' of Ruskin, Kingsley, Carlyle and Rossetti, Hewins took to the social sciences as a way of challenging what he saw as the abstract mechanicalism of Liberal Individualism: 'All my friends wanted to break the dominion of the "Manchester School" over the minds of men, and to get a new idealism into public life . . .'[81] When he took his seat on the Commission (alongside Charles Booth) he had no doubt (as they had no doubt) that a visionary state would be the fount of that new idealism. Hewins is worth comparing with someone else who saw the new state differently but wanted it no less. L. T. Hobhouse was an influential 'New Liberal' and his *Liberalism* (1911) was written to translate Liberal ideas for a twentieth-century Englishness. Hobhouse had been a contemporary of Hewins at Oxford, and, like him, he had converted to the social sciences in a university which did not recognize the discipline but had created the intellectual need for it.[82] Also like Hewins, Hobhouse had understood the crudity of old Liberal Individualism for a new age. Although kinder on Liberalism's past (he presented an impeccably 'Whig' history) Hobhouse was no less pessimistic than Hewins about the nation's future unless it reformulated its view of the state. For him, 'liberty without equality is a name of noble sound and squalid result'.[83] The new generation of collectivist Liberals would have to make liberty and equality a positive social and Imperial force. There is no talk of metaphysical states and national souls in Hobhouse. In 1918 he bluntly attacked Bosanquet for his Germanic theories.[84] Hobhouse's was a traditional Liberal discourse of rational contracts, human rights and popular choices; his state dealt with actuality rather than metaphysics. At the centre of his collectivism Hobhouse agonized over how far the state should go; Hobhouse was the scourge of Bosanquet and could never have sat on the same committee as Hewins but it is as well to remember that not all Liberals saw him in this light.

Herbert Spencer and A. V. Dicey spent the period fighting a powerful rearguard action for old Liberal Individualism.[85] Their sense of the historical timing of events differed, but they both saw the new state and its collectivism as a dangerous distortion of Benthamite-Utilitarianism where the 'greatest good' cry had shifted from civil society into the mouth of a vastly equipped state apparatus. Nineteenth-century social problems had forced the state into action; this had initially been a freeing action but as the legislation continued unabated the Leviathan was now threatening to eat civil society and engorge freedom. The wider the franchise and, after Bagehot,[86] the narrower the executive power, the more of what Spencer called the 'divine right of parliaments', and what Dicey called 'democratic despotism', would continue. Their insistence remained on a freedom of discrete units weighed against the power of the state: 'the more there is of the more the less there is of the less'.[87] Spencer had sounded the warning early; he did not mince his words in analyzing where the new shifts in the political culture were leading; state collectivism was a 'New Toryism' for the 'Coming of Slavery'.

If Spencer had lived to see it, he would have regarded the Liberal government from 1906 as his warnings come true. Lloyd George's massive extensions of state collectivism in welfare were tied to Imperial defence: old age pensions went with Dreadnoughts, healthier mothers went with stronger soldiers, 'soft' state merged with 'hard' state. So forceful was Lloyd George's case (involving basic constitutional changes), and so expert was his manipulation of the political culture, the Conservatives were scuttled at three elections and clung to Ireland as their best gambit. State power grew enormously with the Liberals. After all, it was they – the historical admirers of voluntarism in civil society – who deserted the friendly societies in their national insurance scheme, and had tried to incorporate uniformed male youth into a cadet force under the Territorial Army.[88] After all, it was they – the historical admirers of Parliament – who passed an Official Secrets Act which equated the 'interests of the state' with the state apparatus (Whitehall – Ministers – Cabinet) rather than with Parliament. The 1911 Act was intended to go beyond espionage to ensure the ordinary, daily, protection of the State from its own civil servants and whatever perceptions they may have entertained as to their civil duty to Parliament and Crown over State. The government fully intended this blanket covering but did not tell Parliament. In the Official Secrets Act, 'Society' becomes 'State'.[89]

The Liberal government had worried about the socialists. However, mainstream socialism produced collectivist hybrids no more innovative than New Liberal versions except in their willingness to go further and do more, matched by a greater degree of naivety about the State as an agent of new ideals: if you like, more Hobhouse and more Bosanquet. In Blatchford, Hyndman, and the later Sidney Webb, the analysis centred on the failure and injustice of laissez-faire Individualism. The working class would unambiguously benefit from reforms based on, in Blatchford's case, the work of an expert state committee, in Hyndman's case, 'The State, as the organized commonsense of public opinion', and in Webb's case, 'on the concrete administrative necessities of definitely organized commonwealths'.[90] None of them could speak adequately, and not even always politely, about the future agency of the working class itself, and in matters colonial none of them got much beyond a socialist Chamberlainism and the absorbent qualities of the English state. In all of them there was the lingering image of a society of soldier-citizens who are rationally and collectively deployed against the anarchy of the free market. This image serves as solution in William ('General') Booth's *In Darkest England and the Way Out* (1890), where the Poor were to be enlisted, drilled, and kitted-up for their march out into the light.[91]

The collectivism of Sidney and Beatrice Webb can be seen as a tremulation on the political culture of the period. Until after 1914 they stood with no major party in order to move with all major groupings. They called themselves socialists, they were students of Cooperation, local government, and trade unionism, they advocated a kind of New Liberalism in municipal affairs, they tended towards Chamberlainism in colonial affairs, they hoped for an alliance of Liberal Unionists and Liberal Imperialists in national affairs, they steered Conservative education policy in London, they could mix comfortably with protectionists, radicals, Liberals, Conservatives, ultra Imperialists, Germanophobes and race-destiny men in their 'Coefficients' dining club of 1902.[92] As the executor of the will of a Fabian benefactor, Sidney Webb founded the London School of Economics in 1895. Its first Director, and Sidney's personal choice, was the Conservative Imperialist W. A. S. Hewins, later of the Tariff Reform Commission. In 1903 Webb worked closely with the Liberal Imperialist R. B. Haldane to set up Imperial College, just as they had both worked (against the Fabian executive) to set up the L.S.E.[93] Haldane was a friend of A. J. Balfour and nephew of Lord Salisbury. Beatrice's connections had been no less eclectic. Herbert Spencer had been a friend and mentor in her formative years; as a young woman she had been close to Joseph Chamberlain and she had worked for Charles Booth on his London inquiries.

The avowed aim of the Webbs and their Coefficient comrades was national and imperial efficiency. The idea of 'efficiency' had come out of the Booth-Rowntree poverty investigations in the 1890s and had referred to individuals and their health. Now it applied to nation and Empire. In its name the Coefficients could sit down together and do business across the political middle-ground of the state. The war in 1914 tested 'national efficiency' to the limit, narrowed the middle-ground, and hurried on State political processes. The state organized an unprecedented conflict on an unprecedented scale. Huge new ministries were created, basic industries were planned, organized Labour was rushed to a seat at the top, tariffs were set, income tax went up to six shillings in the pound, the size of the civil service doubled, the state had six million British men in uniform, 'The very time on the clocks was changed'.[94] Lloyd George became Prime Minister in 1916 as the man perfectly suited to the acceleration of State processes under maverick political conditions – as did another Liberal Imperialist 24 years later. After the war the state's political middle-ground could open up again, slightly, but now in a much more central position in society. In 1919

Bosanquet considered his theories to have been vindicated: 'There is little, we recognise now as always, with which the State must not in some sense busy itself.'[95] The old Liberals were the inevitable losers, as were the non-statists socialists. Once more, if the interests of the nation demanded it, statesmen could sit down together to do business, as they did in Lloyd George and Balfour's coalition cabinet after 1919, and MacDonald and Baldwin's national cabinet after 1931.

By 1920, in the name of national efficiency the state was entrenched in the midst of a political culture which half-remembered, in order to half-forget, its Liberal descent. This new Englishness was ready to desert the Liberal ethos in the national interest – an interest phrased over the next 20 years in terms of an English political culture but defined in terms of economic efficiency (health) and social order. Some called the new Englishness 'pragmatic', or 'phlegmatic', others used Burke to see it as a continuing 'moderateness', others would come to see it as bumbling through. Northern Ireland was its first political creation.

Notes

I would like to thank Mr Charles Constable, Mr Ron Greenall, and Dr David Reeder, for their comments on versions of this chapter, and Adele Jones for patiently typing it up.

1 R. Hilton, 'Were the English English?' lecture delivered at the History Workshop on English National Identity, Oxford, 10 March 1984.

2 C. Hill, 'Patriotism and the English Revolution', lecture delivered at the History Workshop on English National Identity, Oxford, 10 March 1984.

3 C. Hill, 'The Norman Yoke', in his *Puritanism and Revolution* (London: Panther, 1969).

4 *Special Committee on Unskilled Labour.* Report and Evidence (London: C.O.S., 1908), pp. 102–3.

5 H. T. Buckle, *History of Civilization in England,* vol. I (London: Longman's Green, 1902); John Sparrow, *Mark Pattison and the Idea of a University* (Cambridge: C.U.P., 1967); Henry Thomas Buckle (1821–62); scholar, traveller and linguist, his two volume *History* (1857, 1861) was a great popularizer of Liberal political culture.

6 Buckle, *History of Civilization,* pp. 499, 501.

7 G. B. Adams, *Constitutional History of England* (London: Cape, 1920), p. 358.

8 H. M. Chadwick, *The Nationalities of Europe and the Growth of National Ideologies* (Cambridge: C.U.P., 1945, repr. 1966), p. 110.

9 B. Vincent, *Haydn's Dictionary of Dates and Universal Information*, 23rd edn (London: Ward, Lock, 1904), p. 924. The words are those of Sir Edward Coke.

10 H. Butterfield, *The Englishman and his History* (Cambridge: C.U.P., 1945), pp. 39–79. For a legal account of Coke's struggle for the common

law against the king, see: F. W. Maitland, *The Constitutional History of England* (Cambridge: C.U.P., 1908), pp. 268–75. Frederic William Maitland (1850–1906); educated at Eton and Trinity College, Cambridge where he was President of the Union, Maitland was Downing Professor of the Laws of England, at Cambridge, from 1888 to 1906.

11 T. B. Macaulay, quoted in J. W. Burrow, *A Liberal Descent* (Cambridge: C.U.P., 1981), p. 57; Buckle, *History of Civilization,* pp. 402–3.

12 E. Burke, *Reflections on the Revolution in France,* 12th edn (London: Dodsley, 1793), pp. 27–36; T. Paine, *Rights of Man* (1791–92, Harmondsworth: Pelican, 1977), pp. 63–5.

13 Paine, *Rights of Man,* p. 65.

14 Maitland, *Constitutional History of England,* pp. 275, 282–5, 343, 537; Adams, *Constitutional History,* pp. 359–60.

15 Buckle, *History of Civilization,* pp. 487–503; John and Barbara Hammond's three major histories, *The Village Labourer* (1911), *The Town Labourer* (1917), and *The Skilled Labourer* (1919) were, in their turn, a major influence on E. P. Thompson's *The Making of the English Working Class* (1963; Harmondsworth: Pelican, 1968) – and, in a way, when Thompson defends himself from criticism, he defends them also (p. 934).

16 This self-cleansing of the State is a major element in G. Stedman Jones' revised explanation of the political demise of Chartism as a mass movement: 'The Language of Chartism', in *The Chartist Experience,* eds. J. Epstein and D. Thompson (London: Macmillan, 1982).

17 S. Smiles, *Self Help* (1859; London: Sphere, 1968), pp. 11–12. These sentiments are remarkably similar to ideas in the other great Liberal classic of 1859, J. S. Mill's *On Liberty,* J. M. Robson (ed.), *Essays on Politics and Society by J. S. Mill* (Toronto: U. of Toronto Press, 1977), p. 310.

18 Smiles, *Self Help,* p. 13.

19 Butterfield's argument on English continuities (op. cit.), and his work *The Whig Interpretation of History* (London: Bell, 1931) is important here; Adams, *Constitutional History,* p. 359; S. R. Gardiner, *A Student's History of England,* vol. III (London: Longman's Green, 1892), pp. 813–17, 876–9, 959.

20 A. B. Atkinson, *Unequal Shares. Wealth in Britain* (Harmondsworth: Pelican, 1974), p. 21.

21 Ronald Butt regrets the lack of a moral theory to justify something universal he calls 'capitalism': *The Times,* 21 February 1985. He ought to reconsider the history of nationalism.

22 R. H. C. Davies, 'The Content of History', *History,* 66 (October 1981), 372.

23 *Report on Fabian Policy* (London: Fabian Tract no.70, 1896), p. 4.

24 H. M. Hyndman, *England For All. The Text Book of Democracy* (1881; Brighton: Harvester, 1973), pp. 5–6.

25 Burrow, *Liberal Descent,* p. 22. Burrow's study does full justice to the complexity of the issues.

26 See A. Bullock and M. Shock (eds), *The Liberal Tradition* (London: Adam & Charles Black, 1956).

27   See D. Thompson, *The Chartists* (London: Temple Smith, 1984), ch. 7, and
     B. Taylor, *Eve and the New Jerusalem* (London: Virago, 1984).

28   For the exclusivity of the higher echelons of government see: H. J. Laski, 'The
     Personnel of the English Cabinet 1801–1924', *American Political Science
     Review,* xxii (1928). For early Liberal party overtures to working-class politics
     see: R. Harrison, 'The British Working class and the General Election of 1868',
     International Review of Social History, V (1960).

29   Walter Vrooman, founder of Ruskin, quoted in W. W. Craik, *The Central
     Labour College 1909–29* (London: Lawrence & Wishart, 1964), p. 36.

30   *Plebs* editorial, June 1909, quoted in Craik, *Central Labour College,* p. 81.

31   R. Dataller, *pseud., A Pitman Looks at Oxford* (London: J. M. Dent, 1933).

32   G. A. Williams, *When Was Wales?* (Harmondsworth: Pelican, 1985), p. 228.
     A 1747 statute stated that all Acts of Parliament for England were deemed
     to include Wales: Maitland, *Constitutional History of England,* p. 330. My
     references in this paragraph to Welshness and Scottishness are short. They
     are only intended as comparative preludes to my major argument on political
     Englishness and the Irish.

33   See C. Harvie, *Scotland and Nationalism* (London: Allen & Unwin, 1977),
     pp. 58–9, 40–1; T. Nairn, *The Break Up of Britain* (London: Verso, 1981),
     pp. 110, 148, 151–6, 167; H. Trevor-Roper, 'The Highland Tradition of
     Scotland', in *The Invention of Tradition*, eds. E. J. Hobsbawm and T. Ranger
     (Cambridge: C.U.P., 1984), pp. 15–41.

34   H. Havelock Ellis, *A Study of British Genius* (London: Hurst & Blackett,
     1904), pp. 48–9, 77–8.

35   Liam de Paor, *Divided Ulster* (Harmondsworth: Pelican, 1973), pp. 1–32;
     Maitland, *Constitutional History of England,* p. 334.

36   de Paor, *Divided Ulstexr*, pp. 33–62, 33.

37   Letter, John Bright to Benjamin Armitage, 6 May 1886, Manchester Public Library
     Archives, Misc. 473/1–4. I am grateful to Mr R. L. Greenall for this reference.

38   Six Oxford Men, *Essays in Liberalism* (London: Cassell, 1897), p. 260.
     Sir Philip James MacDonell (1873–1940); president of the Oxford Union
     in 1895, served as war correspondent for *The Times* in South Africa before
     pursuing his career as colonial judge and administrator.

39   J. Redmond, *The Home Rule Bill* (London: Cassell, 1912), p. 99.

40   S. Gwynn, *The Case for Home Rule* (Dublin: Mansel, n. d.), pp. vi–vii, 152.

41   J. Darby, *Conflict in Northern Ireland* (Dublin: Gill & Macmillan, 1976), p. 7.

42   A. J. Balfour, *Aspects of Home Rule* (London: George Routledge, 1912), p. 25.

43   L. S. Amery, *The Case Against Home Rule* (London: West Strand, 1912), p. 62.

44   Sir E. Carson, in S. Rosenbaum (ed.), *Against Home Rule* (London: Frederick
     Warne, 1912), p. 18.

45   Quoted in, de Paor, *Divided Ulster,* p. 72.

46   Walter Bagehot, writing in *The Economist,* 27 November 1895, quoted in,
     N. St John Stevas (ed.), *The Collected Works of Walter Bagehot* (London:
     Economist, 1974), V, 126.

47 E. M. C. Barraclough, *Flags of the World* (London: Frederick Warne, 1971), pp. 22–3.

48 Bagehot writing in *The Economist,* 22 April 1876, quoted in St John Stevas, *Collected Works,* p. 132.

49 Hobhouse worried about the de-liberalizing effect of the Irish problem on the metropolis' own institutions: L. T. Hobhouse, *Liberalism* (1911; Oxford: O.U.P., 1979 repr.), p. 26; Leonard Trelawny Hobhouse (1864–1929); educated at Corpus Christi, Oxford, he was Tutor and Fellow in Philosophy there from 1890 to 1894, *Manchester Guardian* leader writer 1897–1902, and Professor of Sociology at London University from 1902 to his death in 1929.

50 J. A. Hobson, *Imperialism. A Study* (1902; revised 1938, London: George Allen & Unwin, 1961), p. 18; John Atkinson Hobson (1858–1940); educated at Lincoln College, Oxford, Hobson was a prolific and original writer on economics and sociology. A 'New' Liberal who joined other radicals as a regular contributor to *The Nation* between 1906 and 1920, Hobson had been sacked for unorthodox economic opinions from his lectureship with London University extension classes in 1897.

51 Hobson, *Imperialism, Preface*; J. A. Hobson, *The Psychology of Jingoism* (London: Grant Richards, 1901), p. 34. The South African war was seen by many on the 'left', including Hobson, as a war fought on behalf of Jewish financiers.

52 Hobson, *Psychology of Jingoism,* p. 139.

53 C. Townshend, 'Martial Law: Legal and Administrative Problems of Civil Emergency in Britain and the Empire, 1800–1940', *Historical Journal,* 25, i (March 1982), 167–71; Maitland, *Constitutional History of England,* p. 340; Hobson, *Imperialism,* p. 12.

54 Hobson, *Imperialism,* pp. 7–10.

55 J. R. Seeley, *The Expansion of England* (1883; London: Macmillan, 1897), p. 10. J. W. Burrow considers Froude to be a Whig, but I prefer Burrow's references to Froude as a Carlylean Tory. See for instance Froude's comments on the Indian mutiny (Burrow, *Liberal Descent,* p. 238) and Carlyle's on the Governor Eyre case in Jamaica (Townshend, 'Martial Law,' pp. 173–5). Sir John Robert Seeley (1834–95); Professor of Latin at University College, London from 1863, Seeley was Professor of Modern History at Cambridge between 1865 and 1895. A staunch Liberal Unionist, his influential *Expansion of England* was intended to tutor statesmen in the lessons of political history.

56 Seeley, *Expansion of England,* pp. 141–2.

57 Burrow, *Liberal Descent,* pp. 171–85.

58 Seeley, *Expansion of England,* p. 17; Price Collier, *England and the English from An American Point of View* (London: Duckworth, 1912), pp. 355–6.

59 C. W. Dilke, *Problems of Greater Britain* (London: Macmillan, 1890), p. 12. Sir Charles Wentworth Dilke (1843–1911); twice president of the Cambridge Union, Dilke was a rich lawyer and radical Liberal MP who rose to cabinet office under Gladstone (1882) before breaking with the Prime Minister over home rule and losing his seat after a famous divorce case. Dilke's world tours in 1866–67 and 1875 had encouraged his Greater British ideas.

60 Dilke, *Problems of Greater Britain,* pp. 2–3.

61 V. E. Chancellor, *History for their Masters. Opinion in the English History Textbook 1800–1914* (Bath: Adams & Dart, 1970), pp. 129–30; R. Albrecht-Carrié, *A Diplomatic History of Europe Since The Congress of Vienna* (1958; London: Methuen, 1967), p. 254. For the 'staying power' of the 'Southern Metaphor' in the English way of life see, M. J. Wiener, *English Culture and the Decline of the Industrial Spirit 1850–1980* (Cambridge: C.U.P., 1982), ch. 4. It would appear that Southern England has suffered from the problem of standing for the essential England. Lacking the counter assertiveness of provincial England, it has not enjoyed study in its own right. See the Editorial Preface by John Lowerson, *Southern History,* i (1979), 9–10.

62 Hobson, *Imperialism,* pp. 131, 314, 364; Rhodes, quoted in, R. Palme Dutt, *The Crisis of Britain and The British Empire* (London: Lawrence & Wishart, 1953), p. 79.

63 "It is thoroughly parochial. England knows no world but England:" Price Collier, *England and the English,* p. 256.

64 J. Conrad, *Heart of Darkness* (1902; Harmondsworth: Penguin, 1983), p. 66; J. London, *The People of the Abyss* (1903; London: Journeyman Press, 1977), p. 26; London, p. 25; Conrad, p. 44.

65 G. Burrows, *The Land of the Pigmies* (London: C. Arthur Pearson Ltd., 1898), p. 196.

66 Conrad, *Heart of Darkness,* p. 87; London, *People of the Abyss,* p. 24.

67 R. M. Dorson, *The British Folklorists. A History* (London: Routledge & Kegan Paul, 1968), pp. 280–1.

68 There was a huge literature on folklore and county history; for its conservatism of place and gender see, for example, T. F. Thiselton Dyer's *English Folk-Lore* (London: Hardwicke & Bogne, 1878) and *Folk-Lore of Women* (London: Elliot Stock, 1905).

69 J. Arch, *Joseph Arch. The Story of his Life. Told by Himself,* edited with a *Preface* by the Countess of Warwick (London: Hutchinson, 1898), p. vii; W. R. Titterton, *From Theatre to Music Hall,* 1912, quoted in C. Madge and T. Harrison (eds), *Mass Observation: Britain* (Harmondsworth: Penguin, 1939), pp. 148–9. Joseph Arch (1826–1919); a Warwickshire itinerant agricultural labourer from 1835 to 1872, Arch was made secretary of the National Agricultural Labourers' Union in 1872 and led it through the 1870s. He was Liberal MP for N. W. Norfolk in 1885–86 and 1892–1902.

70 R. Soloway, 'Counting the Degenerates: The Statistics of Race Deterioration in Edwardian England', *Journal of Contemporary History,* 17, i (January 1982), 41, 56–7.

71 A. Craig, *The Banned Books of England* (London: George Allen & Unwin, 1937), 22–5 and A. Lyon Haight, *Banned Books* (London: George Allen & Unwin, 1955), pp. 67–8, 78. See also D. Gorham, 'The "Maiden Tribute of Modern Babylon" Re-examined: Child Prostitution and the Idea of Childhood in late-Victorian England', *Victorian Studies,* 21, 3 (Spring 1978).

72 K. Robbins, 'History, The Historical Association, and the "National Past"', *History*, 66, 218 (October 1981), 415–16, 418–19.

73 C. H. Pearson, *National Life and Character. A Forecast* (London: Macmillan, 1893), pp. 84–5. Charles Henry Pearson (1830–94); educated at Oriel and Exeter, Oxford, he was appointed Professor of Modern History at King's College, London from 1855 to 1865, and Lecturer in History at Trinity, Cambridge from 1869 to 1871. In 1871 Pearson emigrated to Australia for health reasons, and became a reforming Minster of Education in Victoria, 1886–90.

74 For the way in which Imperial matters of defence, constitution, and trade, between 1880 and 1932, were phrased in domestic terms with the 'white' Empire, see I. M. Cumpston (ed.), *The Growth of the British Commonwealth* (London: Edward Arnold, 1973).

75 B. Bosanquet, *The Philosophical Theory of the State* (1899, 1919; Preface to 3rd edn. London: Macmillan, 1965 repr.), p. ix. See also D. Reeder (ed.), *Educating Our Masters* (Leicester: Leicester U. P., 1980), pp. 6–29, and E. Barker, *Political Thought in England* (London: Home University Library, 1915), p. 24. Bernard Bosanquet (1848–1923); educated at Harrow, and Balliol (1866–70) where he was greatly influenced by T. H. Green. After eleven years as Fellow at University College, Oxford, Bosanquet moved to London in 1881 to live independently, write philosophy, teach for the London Ethical Society and work for the Charity Organization Society. From 1903 to 1908 he was Professor of Moral Philosophy at St Andrews University.

76 B. Bosanquet, *Social and International Ideals. Being Studies in Patriotism* (London: Macmillan, 1917), p. 291; S. Collini, 'Hobhouse, Bosanquet and the State: Philosophical Idealism and Political Argument in England 1880–1918', *Past and Present,* 72 (1976). See also Barker, *Political Thought,* p. 67.

77 Bosanquet, *Philosophical Theory,* pp. lx–lxi.

78 The traditional Liberal position Bosanquet dismissed as a playing with 'a mere aggregate:' 'The distinction between such a sum of wills, and a will that aims at a truly common interest or good, rests upon the fundamental contrast between a mere aggregate and an organic unity' (*Philosophical Theory,* p. 104).

79 Soviet espionage in the 1920s came to appreciate 'the highly enmeshed web of trusting relationships which were at once the strength and weakness of the class structure in troubled Britain', and tried to penetrate it for its own ends: Andrew Boyle, *The Climate of Treason* (1979; London: Hutchinson, 1982), p. 17.

   For the role of public school sport in teaching boys how to lead, see the quotation from Edward Lyttelton in, P. Bailey, *Leisure and Class in Victorian England* (London: Routledge & Kegan Paul, 1978), p. 127. As Oxford was supposed to train leaders, so it was also blamed for the supposed failure of national leadership, particularly in trade and manufacture: J. Brown, *Business and the Education of a Gentleman in Late Victorian England,* unpublished Stamford University PhD, 1966 (University Microfilms), pp. 9–41.

80 H. E. Egerton, *A Short History of British Colonial Policy* (1897; London: Methuen, 1918). For differences between Metropolitan and settler views on

colonial policy, real and pretended, see R. A. Huttenback, *Racism and Empire* (Ithaca: Cornell U. P., 1976).

81　W. A. S. Hewins, *The Apologia of an Imperialist. Forty Years of Empire Policy* (London: Constable, 1929), I, 3.

82　Oxford University had been relatively quick to create a Chair of Political Economy, filled by Nassau Senior in 1825. For the beginnings of criticism of political economy in favour of 'scientific sociology', at the highest academic level, see Robert Lowe's rejoinder to Mr Ingram of the British Association: 'Recent Attacks on Political Economy', *Nineteenth Century,* iv (1878).

83　Hobhouse, *Liberalism,* p. 48.

84　Hegel is the basis of metaphysical idealism for the State, and Bosanquet was 'his most modern and faithful exponent'. Interestingly, Hobhouse excused T. H. Green, whom he described as a genuine progressive and not a Hegelian: L. T. Hobhouse, *The Metaphysical Theory of the State. A Criticism* (1918; London: George Allen & Unwin, 1960), pp. 18, 118–19.

85　See Spencer's *The Man versus The State* (London: Williams & Norgate, 1885) and Dicey's *Lectures on the Relation between Law and Public Opinion in England* (London: Macmillan, 1914). Herbert Spencer (1820–1903); teacher, engineer, essayist, psychologist, sociologist, and philosopher, Spencer's extreme individualism in social affairs and evolutionism in history had a great influence on the social sciences. Albert Venn Dicey (1835–1922); Fellow of Trinity, Oxford 1860–72, Q.C. in 1890, and Professor of English Law and Fellow of All Souls 1882–1909. Dicey was an ardent Unionist.

86　W. Bagehot, *The English Constitution* (1867; London: Fontana, 1963), pp. 248–9. For qualitative changes in Parliamentary legislation and practice – 'the nineteenth-century Revolution in government' – see H. Parris, *Constitutional Bureaucracy. The Development of British Central Administration since the Eighteenth Century* (London: Allen & Unwin, 1969), especially chs 6, 7 and 9.

87　Spencer, *Man versus The State,* p. 78; Dicey, *Lectures,* pp. 306, 310.

88　The commercial insurance companies were the financial beneficiaries of the scheme: B. B. Gilbert, *The Evolution of National Insurance in Great Britain* (London: Michael Joseph, 1966), ch. 6; J. Springhall, *Youth, Empire, and Society.* British Youth Movements 1883–1940 (London: Croom Helm, 1977), pp. 29–30.

89　Act to re-enact the Official Secrets Act, 1889, with Amendments, ch. 28, Geo. V, 1911; Departmental Committee on Section 2 of the Official Secrets Act 1911 (Franks Report) vol. i, *Cmnd Paper* 5104, *Parliamentary Papers* 1971–72, pp. 25–6.

90　R. Blatchford, *Merrie England* (London: Clarion Press, 1908), p. 133; H. M. Hyndman, *England For All,* p. 6; S. Webb, *Twentieth Century Politics: A Policy of National Efficiency* (London: Fabian Tract, 1908), p. 5.

91　W. Booth, *In Darkest England and the Way Out* (London: International Headquarters of the Salvation Army, 1890), p. 91, *passim.*

92　N. Mackenzie (ed.), *The Letters of Sidney and Beatrice Webb* (Cambridge: C.U.P., 1978) II, 169–70.

93 The Fabian executive, and particularly George Bernard Shaw, was angry with Webb's handling of the bequest. Shaw wanted the L. S. E. to be explicitly collectivist and questioned Webb's explanation that the School was to pursue 'pure' research: 'First, Hewins must be told flatly that he must, in talking to the Guild of St Matthew and the other Oxford Socialists, speak as a Collectivist, and make it clear that the School of Economics will have a Collectivist bias' – Shaw to Webb, 1 July 1895, quoted in E. J. T. Brennan, *Education for National Efficiency* (London: Athlone Press, 1975), pp. 36–7. For his part, Hewins modestly attributed his appointment to personal competence. In spite of Webb's defence of pure and competent research, Hewins worked busily behind Conservative-Unionist scenes throughout his term as Director: Hewins, *Apologia,* pp. 25, 55–8.

94 A. J. P. Taylor, *English History 1914–45* (1965; Harmondsworth: Pelican, 1975), p. 26.

95 Bosanquet, *Philosophical Theory,* p. xii. He was comparing the social attitudes at the time of the new edition (1919) with the criticisms the book received on its publication in 1899.

CHAPTER THREE

The discovery of rural England

Alun Howkins

Since 1861 England has been an urban and industrial nation. The experience of the majority of its population is, and was, that of urban life, the boundaries of their physical world defined by streets and houses rather than fields or lanes. Yet the ideology of England and Englishness is to a remarkable degree rural. Most importantly, a large part of the English *ideal* is rural. A series of 'vox pop' interviews carried out for the television programme *Country Crisis* (Channel 4, 3 January 1984) showed that most people interviewed in London, including two young blacks, identified the country as 'better', and country life as superior to town life.

England is in some respects peculiar in this. In France, for instance, the ideal has, until very recently, been an urban one. Republicanism, arguably the dominant ideology of urban France since at least the 1870s, feared and distrusted the largely Royalist peasantry. Any affection for the countryside and country life in France is a relatively recent phenomenon. It is interesting that Holt's study of sport in modern France did not consider going out into the country as a recreational form until, at the earliest, the Popular Front period from 1934 onwards.[1]

It is important to stress, right from the beginning, that the ideal of England is very specific. Two examples will serve. A recent television advertisement seeks to sell 'Ben Truman' Bitter through identification with a rural England of the apparently recent past. A craftsman leaves his village workshop, walks slowly across a village green, past the church to a half-timbered pub. Another advertisement, this time a hoarding for the Campaign for Nuclear Disarmament, shows a village church, with a spire, peeping through hedges, and over thatched roofs. In the foreground is a missile launcher. The slogan is simply, 'America Rules OK'. What is interesting about these two advertisements is not that they use a rural image to mobilize innocence or purity against an industrial image of corruption or violence, that is obvious enough, but rather the very specifity of the rural image they use.

Essentially both images are those of the south of England – the 'south country'. Thatching for instance, especially straw thatching, is regionally specific, as are village greens and hedgerows.[2] These images, rural and southern, are, by definition, outside the direct daily experience of the vast majority of Britain's population, yet they occur again and again. Of course, there are urban images of an historical kind used in advertising. The Hovis television commercial with the child walking up a steep hill evokes the recent urban past, even if it is shot in Shaftesbury in Dorset, as do the Courage ones set in a London pub c.1925. Both of these link purity of the produce to a particular 'real' environment. But it does not take long to realize that these are exceptional. Purity, decency, goodness, honesty, even 'reality' itself are closely identified with the rural south.

The word *reality* in the last paragraph was chosen deliberately. What our rural image does is present us with a 'real England'. Here men and women still live naturally.[3] The air is clean, personal relationships matter (especially between employer and employee), there is no crime (except 'quaint' crime like poaching) and no violence (which is why the CND hoarding is so powerful). It is an organic society, a 'real' one, as opposed to the unnatural or 'unreal' society of the town.

The purpose of this chapter is to locate the origins of this specific rural vision, and chart, albeit unevenly, its changing form and gradual popularization. It will be argued that a strain emerged within English politics and ideas in the 1880s which linked the rural to a general crisis in urban society and that this in turn produced a cultural response from the 1890s and 1900s which, by 1914, had spread far across English art and letters, music and architecture, producing a ruralist version of a specifically English culture. Finally, beginning before 1914 but reaching its peak in the interwar period, a great movement 'to the outdoors' completed the process by making the countryside an accessible and popular site of leisure.

I

A ruralist strain in English culture is far from new, Raymond Williams dates it back to at least *Piers Plowman* if not earlier.[4] However, the central problem of Williams' kind of writing is that by stressing *genre* and structure it underplays the very real differences of social formation surrounding the production of texts. Let us look briefly at the 'south country'. The actual origin of this notion comes from Hilaire Belloc's poem of that name:

When I am living in the Midlands,
They are sodden and unkind,
I light my lamp in the evening,
My work is left behind;
And the great hills of the South Country
Come back into my mind.[5]

Edward Thomas picked up the notion and used it in 1908 as the title for one of his best prose collections:

Roughly speaking . . . the country south of the Thames and Severn and East of Exmoor, and it includes, therefore the counties of Kent, Sussex, Surrey, Hampshire, Berkshire, Wiltshire, Dorset and part of Somerset.[6]

What is important about Thomas' south country is that it is, in essentials, a unified landscape type. It is rolling and dotted with woodlands. Its hills are smooth and bare, but never rocky or craggy (the male/female word associations are fascinating), in fact, hardly 'great hills' at all. Above all it is cultivated and it is a post-modern countryside. When Clare looked at England there were no hedges; their coming marked the destruction of his landscape.[7] When Wordsworth wrote of nature it was wild, stupendous and uninhabited except for solitary figures introduced simply to be made puny. The landscape of the 'south country' does not conform with earlier ideas of the rural, although it took things from these ideas. Indeed there is no reason why it should since it was the product of an entirely different situation.

However, it is important to remember in what follows that the 'south country' rapidly lost its real existence in the sense that Thomas meant it. What was substituted were a set of yardsticks of 'rurality' by which the observer judged landscape. Thus, Shropshire could be incorporated into the 'south country' but not Cornwall, since parts of Shropshire conformed to the ideal type, whereas practically none of Cornwall did. For instance half-timbering, village greens and hedgerows are all part of the Shropshire landscape. Similarly, much of East Anglia was (and is) excluded from the ideal though there are exceptions like Lavenham and Thaxted. Rural England could find no place for one hundred acre fields and flint cottages even if Clare would have felt at home among them.

This 'south country' was the product of an urban world, and an urban world at a particular point in time – the late 1870s through to the early 1900s. In this thirty-year period a group of factors came together which created a new image both of urban and rural England. From the late 1870s the British manufacturing industry, while remaining relatively powerful, was gradually losing ground in world markets to American and German competition. This was especially so in the metal industries, heavy engineering, and, after the late 1880s, chemical and electrical engineering.[8] Large-scale industrial investment at home had never been the practice of British commercial institutions, especially the City of London, and capital was not available for reinvestment in industry.[9] What this meant was the gradual submerging of the old industrial middle class into the commercial middle class which had always maintained close links with the landed aristocracy. For instance, the number of millionaires *in industry,* as a percentage of the total number declined from 55 per cent in the first half of the nineteenth century to 27 per cent in the first years of the twentieth.[10] From the 1890s a process began which, by the end of the Great War, created a new and cohesive elite 'dominated by the South of England and finance, with its London-based associates of great influence in twentieth-century society, like the Civil Service and the professions'.[11]

The nature of this process was complex and there were difficulties with the dating of it. What interests us here is the perception of that change and its ideological representation. Until the 1860s, if not later, England was seen primarily as an industrial nation whose greatness lay in mythical self-made men, as celebrated by Smiles. To foreign visitors London was a place of idleness and corruption, too much like their homelands, in many cases, to be of interest. The French writer Faucher, visiting England in the 1840s, left an account of London but hurried North to see the real seat of English power. Engels did the same.[12] Even Frederick Olmstead, a Statten Island farmer who visited England in 1850 primarily to see its agriculture, spent some days in Liverpool wondering at the docks and other urban marvels.[13]

As England's economic power failed, albeit gradually, the *perceived* centre of its economy shifted to the south. That this perception preceded the completion of that shift and was concomitant with it is hardly surprising. By 1902, as far as J. A. Hobson was concerned, it was all but complete. When he looked at the south of England in 1902 he saw a country of 'plush parasitism' drawing its tribute from the Empire and Latin America via stocks and bonds held in the City.[14]

The growth in power of the City, as well as the increase in size of its middle class, brought, in the last years of the nineteenth century, a new urban world to the fore, the world of inner London. As Stedman Jones has shown, the 'problem' of London was increasingly the subject of concern and even panic from the late 1870s,[15] while Manchester, England's previous hell, vanishes. But it was more than that. As England's manufacturing aspirations declined, its Imperial designs increased. From the crowning of the Queen Empress in 1876 Imperialism became an increasingly important factor in English life, and London, commercially, politically and culturally, was the heart of that Empire. It was a heart which, from the publication of *The Bitter Cry of Outcast London* in 1884, was believed to be rotten.

Here we must take a brief side-step. When the imperialists of the 1870s and 1880s sought comparisons with Britain's greatness they turned, because of the dominance of classics in the public school and University curricula, to Rome, and Rome taught a terrible lesson. This lesson is in Gibbon's sternly moral view of the Empire's end. In Gibbon, a great Empire, overextended, hugely wealthy and relying increasingly on native and colonial peoples to maintain its wealth, was destroyed because of decay at the centre:

> This long peace, and the uniform government of the Romans, introduced a slow and secret poison into the vitals of the Empire. The minds of men were gradually reduced to the same level, the fire of genius extinguished, and even the military evaporated ... the Roman world was indeed peopled by a race of pygmies when the fierce giants of the North broke in and mended the puny breed.[16]

Gibbon, of course, had no 'scientific' racial theory but the late Victorians did. Thus Gibbon's notion of decay within 'the vitals of the Empire' producing a 'puny breed' found echoes in eugenics and corrupt forms of Darwinism. As Lord Walsingham, a Norfolk landowner and would-be social theorist, wrote to Henry Rider Haggard in 1899:

> Look at the pure bred Cockney – I mean the little fellow whom you see running in and out of offices in the city, and whose forefathers have for the last two generations dwelt within a two-mile radius of Charing Cross. And look at an average young labourer coming home from his days field work, and I think you will admit the city breeds one stamp of human beings and the country breeds another. ... Take the people away from their natural breeding grounds, thereby sapping their health and strength in cities such as nature never intended to be the permanent home of men, and the decay of this country becomes only a matter of time. In this matter, as in many others, ancient Rome has a lesson to teach.[17]

Walsingham made the link between racial degeneration, city life and ancient Rome, but even those who lacked the classical touch nevertheless saw the same process at work. As Stedman Jones writes,

> If the theory of hereditary urban degeneration had been confined to one or two eccentric doctors, there would be little point in examining it. ... But this was not the case. In the 1880s and 1890s the theory received widespread middle-class support and was given authoritative backing by Booth, Marshall, Longstaff and Llewellyn Smith.[18]

What is also important is that although the theory was 'wrong', and indeed Booth's own statistics proved this to be the case, it made little or no difference

to Booth or to his less well-versed contemporaries. The overwhelming opinion
of social observers was that urban degeneration from healthy countryman
to unhealthy Cockney in three generations was inevitable and disastrous. As
Stedman Jones insists,

> the theory of urban degeneration bore little relation to the real situation
> of the London casual poor in the late Victorian period. What it provided,
> was not in fact an adequate explanation of London poverty, but rather
> a mental landscape within which the middle class could recognize and
> articulate their own anxieties about urban existence.[19]

The growing belief in an industrial, urban and racial crisis led to a search
for alternatives to the apparently unbreakable cycle of urban poverty. One
set of these alternatives, the urban ones, are described by Stedman Jones.
But there was another set which dovetailed with these: the set that saw a
solution in terms of rural England.

II

In 1894–96, two decades of agricultural depression temporarily lifted to
reveal that over a hundred years of 'rural over-population' and subsequent
forced migration had worked only too well. There were no men left on the
land. Haggard quotes in *A Farmer's Year,* a letter from an estate agent (estate
steward) in Hertfordshire:

> All the young men have or are quitting the land . . . leaving only the idle
> young men and those of weak intellect (who are of no use anywhere), the
> middle-aged and old men, to work the land, and as these die . . . there is
> no one to take their place.[20]

Reports like this certainly exaggerated the situation but there can be no
doubt that there were serious, if periodic, labour shortages in East Anglia at
least from 1894 onwards.[21]

But it is *perceptions* that matter. Having turned from the problems of
racial degeneration and urban crisis to the purer and more natural rural
areas, contemporary social observers found a crisis there which was as
bad, if not worse, than that of the cities, and from the very early 1900s a
rash of books, pamphlets and articles began to appear on rural conditions.
These writings stressed that the core of the 'national' problem lay with the
countryside and with the problems of agriculture. If London destroyed men
and women in three generations and there were no replacements in the
rural areas, the race was doomed. Nobody seriously questioned agricultural
productivity or even efficiency; the question was, to use contemporary
phraseology, a 'social one'. Country life had to be made attractive and men

and women had to be returned to the land if the nation was to survive. As Lord Milner wrote in 1911:

> We have got to get back to the old conception of the paramount importance of production and productive capacity – no merely material idea ... but the key to the maintenance of a healthy, vigorous and moral race. But of all forms of productive capacity there is none more vital, indispensable, and steadying, than the application of human industry to the cultivation of the soil.[22]

The extent to which nearly all political parties shared these assumptions by the 1900s is remarkable. Between 1910 and 1914 Liberal, Labour and Conservative parties all produced statements and plans for the rural areas. Lord Milner thought that,

> if there is one point at which order seems beginning to emerge from the present confusion of our political and social aims, it is precisely with regard to this fundamental necessity of making a better use of the greatest of all natural resources. "Back to the Land" is a watchword which, in some form or another, is beginning to appeal to serious men of every hue of political thought.[23]

The Liberal Party had the longest record of concern, one which stretched back to the 1880s, and in 1913 they produced a two-volume report on the land which was to form the basis of a land campaign. Its core was the reform of land ownership and country life which would produce a new rural England:

> Under satisfactory conditions, with earnings by the parents sufficient to meet all the children's principal needs ... with arrangements for independent life in country villages which would give all those who can take advantage of it a new outlook and lead some of the best of them to prefer a country life in England to either Urban or Colonial Life, an enormous change might take place.[24]

In 1910 the Conservative Party, whose interest in land reform had by the party's own admission been limited, also produced a land plan, based on small holdings, and written by Sir Gilbert Parker.[25]

Perhaps more surprisingly the socialists also had a position; indeed a rural vision was central to an English socialism which still owed much of its inspiration and theory to William Morris and Edward Carpenter. 'The land calls the people', wrote Bruce Glaisier in 1908, 'and the people unbound hasten to the land'. Socialism would change the physical face of England, it would 'not destroy but recreate and greatly sweeten and ennoble the towns' while, 'village life will be restored, invigorated and enriched'.[26] In 1913 these ideas got a firm shape in the form of a series of proposals which were known as the Independent Labour Party 'Rural Programme', based on land nationalization, small holdings, cooperation, and a minimum wage for agricultural labourers.[27]

In all these 'programmes', as well as in the numerous books and pamphlets not specifically connected to any party, there was a unity. This was that for all groups, in different ways, the land, 'peasant proprietorship', even country life itself, was coming to represent order, stability and naturalness. In contrast to the towns, and London in particular, the country and country people were seen as the essence of England, uncontaminated by racial degeneration and the false values of cosmopolitan urban life. However, the question was not solely or even mainly one of politics or economics but one of the transformation of a whole culture. The cultural history of England had to be rewritten and a new Englishness discovered which accorded with changed perceptions of society. This is *not* to postulate a crude economic determinism; rather it is to suggest that as economic and social change occurred, hand in hand with it, and to some degree influencing it, went a reworking of cultural forms which equally determined the eventuation of change. The rest of this chapter will look at that process of cultural change.

III

To begin with, the recent past was defined as un-English, as dominated by metropolitanism, and as having erected a set of values which were unnatural to this English people. As G. K. Chesterton wrote in his *Short History of England*:

> The ordinary Englishman [was] duped out of his old possessions, such as they were, and always in the name of progress. . . . They took away his maypole, and his original rural life and promised him instead the Golden Age of Peace and Commerce.[28]

The same idea was conveyed yet more clearly in Cecil Sharp's highly influential study of English folk-song:

> Since the death of Purcell [1695] . . . the educated classes have patronised the music of the foreigner, to the exclusion of that of the Englishman. Foreign vocalists, singing in a foreign tongue, have for two centuries monopolised the operatic stage; while English concert platforms have, during the same period, been exclusively occupied by alien singers and instrumentalists, singing and playing compositions of European writers.[29]

This extract from *English Folk Song: Some Conclusions (1907)* indicated two of the main ideas behind the new definitions of Englishness.

First is the notion that recent history had seen the abandonment by the elite of national allegiance. This did not necessarily mean they were unpatriotic, (although it could be argued some were) rather that by stressing international trade and the development of industry and commerce they had 'internationalised' their concerns. Crucially for Sharp, in adopting the music of Mendelssohn or Liszt, or the Gothic of Northern France and Venice, the national elite had created a taste which was that of a European bourgeois rather than specifically English.[30] In this rewriting of the recent past the Smilesian view of progress was turned on its head. The nineteenth century became a period in which the rapacity of international capital had martyred three generations on the wheel of industry. Figures like John Bright and Richard Cobden were seen not as the prophets of a peaceful and prosperous international order, but as weak hypocritical tyrants who in the narrow self-interest of their class had sold the nation's birthright to Jewish bankers and international capitalists.[31] The most famous of these attacks is of course Strachey's *Eminent Victorians* which, although it was not published until after the Great War, was essentially a product of the Cambridge of the 1900s.[32] Similarly, the Hammonds' histories are a record of the effects on England and on English men and women of the creation of an international trading order which sacrificed those 'at home' in the interests of profit.[33]

The second point raised by Sharp, and probably the more important one, concerned 'Tudor England', the source for remedying this evil. Tudor England was not the period in which England was ruled by the Tudor dynasty, 1485–1603, rather it was a construction based on the later years of the reign of Elizabeth, lasting until the 1680s but with gaps, especially the 1650s. The movement away from Victorian 'medievalism' to 'Tudorism' is in itself instructive. It represents a move from the community of the medieval village based on the Church and the Latinate culture, internationalist in some sense and often associated with radicalism, to the more aggressive expansionist, sophisticated and, above all, English world of Elizabeth. This is not to argue that all other elements vanished overnight; Mark Girouard's work on chivalry and Roy Strong's on the 1640s–1660s as subject matter for English painting have shown otherwise. Rather it was a shift in emphasis which grew more popular and eventually replaced the earlier medieval ideal in all but the most radical of writers.[34]

The age of Elizabeth had long held a special place among English historians but it was with Froude that the period began to fill a central role.[35] In the *Nemesis of Faith,* for instance, he wrote, 'the dazzling burst of the Elizabethan era was the vigorous expansion of long-imprisoned energy, springing out in bounding joyous freedom'.[36] Especially in his essays, reprinted as *Short Studies in Great Subjects* in 1898, he presented a view of the late-sixteenth century as dominated by a commonsensical but an expanding and powerful England, firmly believing in her own moral virtue. This view is summed up in his essay 'England's Forgotten Worthies'.

In this essay Drake, Hawkins and the other heroes of Elizabethan navigation leave the

> banks of the Thames and the Avon, the Plym and the Dart . . . out across the unknown seas fighting, discovering, colonizing, and graved out the channels, paving them at last with their bones, through which the commerce and enterprise of England has flowed out over all the world.[37]

Froude's ideas, for long regarded as heretical by a predominantly Whig historical establishment, found increasing acceptance in the 1880s and 1890s, especially when put together with the work of Seeley. As John Burrow says, in his study of the Victorian historians to which I owe much, 'Froude's message found a response in generations which also listened to Dilke and Seeley, recited Kipling and Sir Henry Newbolt, admired Baden Powell and excused Jameson.'[38] The continuing power of the Elizabethan image ensured that increasingly, 'the notion of an Elizabethan golden age passed into popular mythology where it was identified as the authentic site of Merrie England'.[39]

The Tudor construction was an extraordinarily powerful one. Unlike the medievalist construction it encouraged expansion and worldliness. Its heroes were adventurers rather than knights; its physical setting was idyllic without the harshness of monasticism. Above all it was English. Froude's picture of the degenerate French and Spanish[40] fitted well with a society which blamed the corruption of France for Oscar Wilde and the nameless 'greenery-yallery' sins he imported for English youth. Against Wilde the Tudor set Drake, against the inside world of darkened velvet rooms it set the outside horizons of sea and Empire, against the Lily it set the Rose.

The Tudor World was firmly rural. Drake and Hawkins may have created commerce but they did not create, or want, industry. Froude himself made the connection between industry, urbanization and racial degeneration which 'characterised' Rome.[41] In *Oceana*, his last work, he urged the citizens of New Zealand not to 'renew the town life which they leave behind them . . . [and then] they will grow into a nation when they are settled in their own houses and freeholds'. Only the children of the rural colonies can 'seem once more to understand what was meant by merry England'.[42]

IV

This model of history provided precise guidelines as well as generalized ideals. For instance, general to what has been called the 'English musical renaissance' was the rediscovery, setting and performance of pre-eighteenth century music, especially the music of late-sixteenth-century and seventeenth-century England. From the mid-1890s figures like E. H. Fellowes, R. R. Terry and J. A. Fuller Maitland searched for and edited the works of the Tudor and Stuart composers. The *Fitzwilliam Virginal Book* was brought out in 1899; Fellowes' *The English Madrigal School* began its thirty-six volumes series in 1913, and Frederick Keel's *Elizabethan Love Songs* published in 1909 made the songs of Bartlett, Dowland and Campion generally available. At the same time in the heart of the 'south country', at Haselmere, Arnold Dolmetsch began to make and play 'ancient' musical instruments enabling authentic performances of this music to take place.[43]

However, it was not just to a dead past that those who sought to create a new Englishness turned. If the countryside, and the easily accessible 'south country' in particular, was the source of the English race, it was also the source of English culture. Culture was to be found in the arts of the countryside and in its people. To Cecil Sharp, as to most other folk-song collectors, the English 'peasant' was not John Hodge, a backward remnant of a collapsed and inferior pre-industrial world, but the unknowing bearer of the essence of English musical culture.

> In the country, where nowadays the unlettered classes alone survive, the common people still preserve their own music, just as they have kept their own speech. . . . Peasant music is genuine music; peasant speech is genuine speech. . . . For the unconscious output of the human mind, whatever else it may be is always real and sincere.[44]

In musical terms Tudor England and the countryside were to be brought together as a new basis for an English national music. It was not so much that one should write folk songs or madrigals, rather that a concept of nationalism was laid at the centre of the composer's art: 'the art of music, above all the other arts, is the expression of the soul of the nation' as Vaughan Williams wrote.[45] It was the countryside which was to provide the base: 'there, in the fastness of rural England, was the well-spring of English music'.[46]

But a national cultural revival could not only be about music, even to those whose interests were primarily musical. As Mary Neale, folk-dance teacher and one-time associate of Sharp, wrote in 1905:

> The revival of our English folk music is . . . part of a great national revival, a going back from the town to the country, a reaction against all that is demoralising in city life. It is a re-awakening of that part of our national consciousness which makes for wholeness, saneness and healthy merriment.[47]

Another source of inspiration for a national culture were the varieties of vernacular architecture, again especially southern ones, which were so much a part of the ideal rural landscape. By the mid-1870s the Gothic had become contaminated by its association with industrialization, especially its 'vulgar' form. In Bedford Park, the first of the middle-class ruralist suburbs,

Norman Shaw and E. W. Godwin turned to the southern English vernacular tradition.[48]

> The whole place has the snug warm look of having been inhabited for at least a century. This comes partly from the colour and material of the houses, a mellow red brick; partly from their architecture, which may be called "Queen Anne," abounding in gables, and permitting all kinds of inequality in height and irregularities of frontage; and partly from the intermixture of fine old trees looking almost ancient.

In other words, it was a southern, English village. Bedford Park had its green, its 'inn' ('Ye Hostelry' on Shaw's plans) named The Tabard (one assumes after Chaucer's starting-point), and even, on occasions, its May-pole.[49]

More important though than the aesthetes' paradise of Bedford Park was the gradual spreading of the 'English taste' of which it was a forerunner. By the mid-1900s English taste, whether for domestic building or for show, had become all but synonymous with the 'Tudor' – the lowest common denominator of southern English vernacular style. As early as 1900 the British (not English!) Pavilion at the Paris Exhibition designed by Edward Lutyens, probably the most important architect of his generation, was a 'faithful reproduction of Linston House, an elaborate seventeenth-century building at Bradford-on-Avon'.[50] Lutyens again re-created the Tudor in the sixteenth-century street scenes he designed for the 1912 'Shakespeare's England' Exhibition at Earl's Court.[51] By then Lutyens had moved well away from the Tudor but the style itself, linked to what has been called 'counter-urbanisation', came to dominate middle-class private housing.[52] Gradually at first, then more rapidly, half timbering, diamond-paned or bottle-glass windows, gable ends and rustic porches became a national style for domestic building. Through children's books from Beatrix Potter onwards generations learned that home was a cottage and, if not a cottage, then the 'Janet and John' mock-Tudor of the inter-war suburb. This kind of house became infused with a domestic glow suggestive of an earlier and better world of decency and honesty. What King says of the bungalow in his recent study could be applied to all housing of this kind.

> Though introduced as a "country" house (as were many "Tudor" buildings) the bungalow was essentially an urban dwelling. It was *in* the country but not *of* it. It was the product of the despoilation of the city which industrial capitalism had brought about – environmental pollution, overcrowding, and the stresses and strains of urban life.[53]

Even the garden spoke of an imagined rural past. The designs of Gertrude Jekyll, a friend of Lutyens, executed at first for the rich,[54] and the prints from Allingham's *The Cottage Homes of England*,[55] swept away the privet and shrubs, the carefully planted rows of bedding plants, the straight paths and neat borders of the high Victorian garden. In their place, roses, hollyhocks and Sweet Williams pushed themselves to the curving edges of the lawn in an apparently unplanned profusion of colour that came to be known as the 'cottage garden'. Allingham, and her many picturesque imitators, did more to create the ideal than the theories of Jekyll. By portraying homes 'where the banks of hollyhocks and the cottages tumbling under the weight of rambler roses threaten to suffocate the inhabitants',[56] the watercolours, prints and postcards of late Victorian and Edwardian England produced a rural ideal that found reflection in every suburban road.

V

If architects changed the visual environment to accord with 'England', and the composers created a new sound which placed an overwhelming importance on the English and especially the rural, it was the writers of the period who made what was probably the most fundamental contribution to the discovery of Rural England. Further, by interpreting the countryside in particular ways, it was they who created the world of the South Country and fixed it as a part of national ideology. To discuss this contribution in the detail it deserves is well outside the scope of this chapter, but I should like to centre on two or three aspects.

Vitally important was the fact that the character of the countryside created was regionally specific. Probably the most influential of the prose writers was W. H. Hudson.[57] Hudson seldom wrote about England outside the South Country. *A Shepherd's Life, Nature in Downland* and even the apparently more inclusive *A foot in England* seldom go far north of London or west of the Exe. Similarly the majority of the prose writing of Edward Thomas concentrates on the south east, although he did also write on Wales. Others extended the boundaries of the South Country to include areas which were topographically and culturally similar. Thus areas of the south Midlands and even Shropshire were incorporated into the vision, especially after C. R. Ashbee moved to the Cotswolds with the Guild of Handicrafts in 1901.[58] This construction of rural England was one of populated and cultivated landscapes. Even Hudson's beloved Downlands is not wild in the sense of the Pennines or the Yorkshire Moors. It is farmed and peopled and it is often the people who come through most strongly, even in a naturalist like Hudson. Like later ruralists he delighted in village characters he met in pubs. Indeed most of *A Shepherd's Life* grows out of such a man. Even in *Nature in Downland* we find chapters devoted to the human inhabitants as well as the flora and fauna. Again one is reminded of Sharp. To him the countryside was important but it was the human inhabitants who despite themselves contained the essence of the country.

Perhaps not as influential in his time as Hudson, but more enduring, was George Sturt. To Sturt the natural world of the countryside existed only to rear Englishmen. In the following extract from his journals we have a sense of how, to many writers, ruralism was a defence against alienation even in the darkest days of the war. He wrote in 1916:

> For "England" is – what shall I say? the stream, the tradition, the living continuity, of public opinion, public conduct, public intercourse and behaviour of English people towards one another and towards hills and valleys, and waving trees and the fair sunshine of this island.[59]

In books like *Memoirs of a Surrey Labourer, The Bettesworth Book* and *William Smith, Potter and Farmer,* Sturt peopled the South Country with a race which, although it had faults, contained most of what was important in English life:

> Tradition is a form of group life. It tends to composure and conservation in individuals. No industry can long go on without it. Hence it prevails more in the country than in London, where individuality most flourishes. But to name the many ancient industries is to recite the group efforts of the English from time immemorial.[60]

By associating Englishness with a specific social formation, the South Country, the writings of people like Sturt and Hudson gave a political shape to Englishness. This was often unintentional and, like the imitators of Allingham, Lutyens or Vaughan Williams, it was the popularizers who played a greater part than the originators. For instance, Sturt was a radical and had been a supporter of the SDF, Sharp was a socialist, as was Vaughan Williams. Even the high priest of ruralism, the founder and editor of *Georgian Poetry* mixed with Fabians on the Sussex-Hampshire border in the 1880s and 1890s. Yet precisely by constructing an ideal out of a specific rural England they gave credence to its existing political and social structure even if they were critical of it.

Central to this ideal were the ideas of continuity, of community or harmony, and above all a special kind of classlessness. From at least the 1880s the 'agricultural interest' had come to mean less the old aristocracy on the right of the Tory party and more a community of those who shared the plight of agriculture in the Great Depression. The foundation, in the early 1890s, of Lord Winchelsea's National Agricultural Union, which sought to unite farmers, labourers and landowners into a common defence association, is only the organizational manifestation of a view which became stronger and stronger over the next 40 years.[61] Often unknowingly, the ruralists of the 1900s fed into this stream. For example, Edward Thomas, a man who knew the hardships of country life better than most, managed in one of the finest country poems, 'Lob', to combine both a radical and a classless mythology into his symbolic countryman.[62] Lob, like Sharp's singers, carries the traditions of England in his head and in his poem:

> Yet Lob has thirteen hundred names for a fool,
> And though he never could spare time for school
> To unteach what the fox so well expressed,
> On biting the cock's head off, – Quietness is best -
> He can talk as well as anyone
> After his thinking is forgot and done.

He is also a radical, among his names in the past have been Robin Hood and Jack Cade, and it is he who keeps the footpaths open:

> All he said was "Nobody can't stop 'ee. Its
> A footpath right enough . . ."

Like Froude's heroes, Lob had been an Elizabethan.

> . . . This is Tall Tom that bore
> The Logs in, and with Shakespeare in the hall
> Once talked, when icicles hung by the wall.

Like the Morrisite gardener Reginald Blomefield, he knew and preferred the English names for flowers,

> He has been in England as long as dove and daw
> Calling the wild cherry tree the merry tree,
> The rose campion Bridget-in-her-bravery;
> And in a tender mood here, as I guess,
> Christened one flower Love in idleness.

Yet the essence of Lob, and his Englishness, is that he transcends class and incorporates all aspects of country life into his being. He may have 'died at Sedgemoor' with that tragic peasant army, but he also 'Wedded the king's daughter of Canterbury'. In his most recent manifestation, the one who Thomas meets is

> ". . . a squire's son. . . . Who loved wild beast and bird and dog and gun."

It is he who explains to Thomas that Lob is the spirit of Englishness which survives:

> "Do you believe Jack dead before this hour?
> Or that his name is Walker, or Bottlesford,
> Or Button, a mere clown, or squire or Lord?"

No, for Lob lives on, and at the end of the poem he is identified with the 'young Squire',

> . . . one glimpse of his back, as there he stood,
> Choosing his way proved him of old Jack's blood,
> Young Jack perhaps and now a Wiltshireman
> As he has oft been since his days began.

VI

Although the audience for poetry was probably greater in the years just before the Great War than at any time before or since, as testified by the success of the Georgian anthologies, the numbers involved were still very small. What is striking is the way in which this Englishness, which after all could simply have remained another literary or artistic fashion, spread outwards and downwards. This process is complex, and again only pointers can be offered here. By the mid-1920s, for instance, the new mortgage-built estates were dominated by the 'Tudor' vernacular. Ellesmere Road, West Bletchley, the home of Orwell's ruralist hero George Bowling, was such a place with its row upon row of mock Tudor semi-detached houses.[63] The literature of guide books is another area. Hudson, at the beginning of his *A Foot in England,* had a chapter on guide books and remarked on their increasing number,[64] though it is the post-war world which witnessed the height of their popularity, with all the major railway companies, but especially the Southern Railway, selling the countryside through posters, pamphlets and guided rambles.[65] Similarly, post-war Ordnance Survey Maps changed from their 1900s plain, buff covers which made them look like the official, working documents they were, to illustrated covers showing ramblers, cyclists and motorists enjoying rural England with the aid of the map.

In music despite the onslaught of modernism represented by the first London performance of Stravinsky's *Petrouchka* in 1911 and the arrival of the Russian Ballet soon after, the work of Vaughan Williams and others increased in popularity to the extent that folk song as a model became a source of complaint among music critics.[66] Sharp's success was even more remarkable. He sought in *English Folk Song* to reinstate the traditional songs of England in the popular consciousness. He wrote, 'Our system of education is, at present, too cosmopolitan; it is calculated to produce citizens of the world rather than Englishmen.'[67] Music in elementary schools, if it was based on folk song, would 'refine and strengthen the national character'.[68] By 1914, as Vic Gammon points out,[69] Sharp's ideas had become the orthodoxy of musical education. In that year the Board of Education guide to teachers of music said, 'the music learned by children in elementary schools should be drawn from our folk and traditional song'.[70] This was in direct contradiction to an earlier guide, published in 1905, which Sharp attacked in *English Folk Song*.[71] The 1914 circular ended with words that Sharp himself could have written.

> Nor is it always realised how strong and vital a tie between the members of a school, a college or even a nation may be formed by the knowledge of a common body of traditional song.[72]

Again, it was in writing that the popularizing influence was greatest. Robert Blatchford's socialist weekly *The Clarion* with a large circulation among the lower-middle and upper-working classes became increasingly less socialist and more ruralist during the second decade of the twentieth century. By stressing cycling and walking, *The Clarion,* and to a lesser extent other socialist papers, linked enjoyment of the countryside to a socialist future. Further, by creating a national network of clubs, largely devoted to leisure activities, the Clarion organization spread the practical side of ruralism. Despite this shift *The Clarion* remained political at least up to 1915. *Country Life* was never 'political'. Founded in 1897 by Edward Hudson, it was an immediate success not so much among the country gentry as among the largely urban middle class, 'Who . . . were looking into this world from outside.'[73] As Clive Aslet writes,

> before he acquired his fortune or title, Lord Lee of Fareham leafed his way longingly through the pages, dreaming of an ideal country existence which he was not yet able to realise; he later bought Chequers. On the other hand, the nostalgia of the magazine – conveyed in watery photographs of fishermen and other country folk – caused at least one officer in the First World War to have *Country Life* sent out to the trenches as a symbol of what he was fighting for.[74]

Country Life was so successful that it enabled Hudson himself to live out the ruralist dream in a succession of grand country houses including Lutyen's conversion of Lindisfarne Castle.

Along with the success of Hudson and in a different way Blatchford, there came into existence before the Great War a virtual industry of country writing. Edward Thomas was both a worker in this industry and a cynical observer of it. His talent as a prose writer was forced into reviewing, hack writing, and endless commissioned books which gave him little time to develop his own concerns and interests. *A Literary Pilgrim in England,* for instance, he detested. The endless collection of fact and fancy about writers (many of whom he found antipathetic) simply to provide a lightweight literary guide book was against everything he felt to be important. As he wrote to Eleanor Farjeon,

> Homes and Haunts [his sarcastic name for the book] I have got to detest, & I believe I have been doing it intolerably ill through indifference

and haste to be done with it, but in a soberer state of mind I can see that I mustn't throw away £70 or so if I can possibly get it.[75]

However it was, to my mind, the Great War which made the difference not only to Thomas but to Englishness. On 4 August 1914, Englishness went into battle. To Rupert Brooke there was an immediate connection between the war and his beliefs. He had been a ruralist, a reviver of the Tudor in the Marlowe Society at Cambridge, a seeker after country life in a caravan, and a socialist in Blatchford's mould. Yet it was in his Englishness that he found some kind of justification for his life and actions. As Henry James wrote in his preface to Brooke's posthumous *Letter from America*, 'he had found at once to his purpose a wonderous enough old England, an England breaking out into numberless new assertions'.[76] In his most famous poem Brooke makes his position clear,

. . . There shall be
In that rich earth a richer dust concealed;
A dust whom England bore, shaped, made aware,
Gave, once, her flowers to love, her ways to roam,
A body of England's breathing English air,
Washed by the rivers, and blest by the suns of home.

The connections were also clear to Robert Blatchford in his Sussex cottage. He wrote on 5 August 1914:

Then I looked at the opal blue sea and the green curves of the Sussex downs and the gleaming white cliffs of England, and I seemed to hear the dreadful sound of the drums of Armageddon.[77]

To George Sturt in Surrey it was clearer still:

[This] is, indeed of all wars, perhaps the most genuinely religious that ever men fought in: it goes nearer home to our conscience than any struggle ever did. For here, in the sanctity of life . . . here is involved what English folk have been instinctively feeling their way towards since the Reformation; England in her comely village customs, her dear "L'Allegro" attitude: in Wordsworth's outlook, in Gray's, in Tennyson's, and later in Dickens's and William Morris's. It is for music, for skill, for adventure and Romance; for kindliness, for "tea-time" and all the gentleness that involves, for the pleasant cornfields and country lanes.[78]

In Flanders, in the very antithesis of England's South Country, the rural ideal was enshrined by mass slaughter. For the young officers of the New Armies in particular, Englishness meant ruralism and the South Country. These were they who in the years just before the war were the readers of Thomas and

Hudson, the singers and dancers to the tunes Sharp collected, they were the subscribers to *Country Life* or *The Clarion,* and it was they who roamed the Sussex Downs and sat in 'rural inns' reading the verse of de la Mare and Masefield.[79]

But the South Country gave them more than a vision of Englishness; it gave them a model of society – an organic and natural society of ranks, and of inequality in an economic and social sense, but one based on trust, obligation and even love[80] – the relationship between the 'good Squire' and the 'honest peasant'. It was a model which admirably suited the relationship between the young infantry subaltern and the sixty or so men under his command. It would probably be possible to trace through the War the ways in which this exemplary relationship was reinforced by propaganda which increasingly stressed home as rural and southern. An important example is the YMCA anthology, *The Old Country* edited for the Everyman Library by its general editor Ernest Rhys. In the introduction Sir Arthur Yapp of the YMCA wrote of the average soldier, 'In imagination, he can see his village home',[81] clearly an absurd statement since the majority of soldiers came from the cities. However, the contents of this popular anthology stressed the rural to the exclusion of all other images of England. E. V. Lucas' poem 'O England' talks of 'country of my heart's desire, land of the hedgerow and the village spire', and interestingly this poem was also issued as a gramophone record.[82]

A detailed examination of this propaganda process would need to be the subject of another chapter. Here are some points of suggestion for such a chapter. First the external point of reference in most war poems (where there is one) is Southern England or some ideal of the rural. Sassoon, Blunden and Thomas all follow this, especially of course Blunden both in his poems and in *Undertones of War.* The contrasts of 'Home' and Flanders are made constantly in the war diaries of Sassoon. In the entry for 30 March 1917, Sassoon wrote, 'I wish I could write a book of Consolations for Homesick Soldiers in the Field'. He then proceeded to detail his 'dream gallery'. It is a consciously stereotyped vision of the South Country with a 'grey church-tower', 'the village smoke ascending like incense of immemorial tranquility', and fields of flowers like a Gertrude Jekyll garden. At its centre is the 'rose grown porch of some discreet little house' with 'a girl in a print dress . . . waiting, waiting for the returning footsteps along the twilight lane, while the last blackbird warbles from the maytree'.[83] Two months later the diary paints an almost identical scene, only now it is a description of the Kent countryside around Sassoon's home at Weirleigh.[84]

Second, and more importantly, this vision seems to have spread downwards. Many, if not most, soldiers seem to have had good relationships with their immediate superiors. Both Lyn Macdonald's book on Passchendaele and Martin Middlebrook's on the Somme,[85] books which are based primarily on oral testimony, stress the 'love' felt by ordinary soldiers for many of their officers. This created in the trenches, if not when out of the line, a classlessness based upon a shared experience of suffering very like the pre-war metaphors of a united agricultural community working together in the face of adversity. As one soldier wrote:

> The love that grows quickly and perhaps artificially when men are together up against life and death has a peculiar quality. Death that cuts it off does not touch the emotions at all, but works right in the heart of you.[86]

George Coppard, a private in the Machine Gun Corps, noted how an officer's behaviour made all the difference to his platoon,

> If an officer used brutal words, we would loathe him and meditate vengeance. If he spoke kindly to us or did us some service, we would call him a toff or a sport and overflow with sentimental devotion to him.[87]

Third, the ordinary soldiers themselves could not but have had a romanticized vision of home. The antithesis Flanders/England was just as great for them as for the officers, even if they did not articulate it in the same way. The postcards sent from the front show, as well as patriotic motifs, soldiers dreaming of fields and lanes, with wives and children living in rose-covered cottages. More than that, home *had* to be idealized. Even when those in England seemed uncomprehending, heartless or just downright stupid about the War, there simply had to be a world outside Flanders, and this world equally could not be that of 'dark satanic mills', even if that did better represent the reality of home. One only has to look at the enormous increase in plotland and shanty building in the countryside after 1918, much of it done by ex-soldiers, to see the strength of this rural ideal.[88]

This ideal was reinforced by official and semi-official propaganda. As well as the Everyman anthology already mentioned, various anthologies were produced in service editions from late 1916 onwards, which were almost entirely pastoral. Also as many accounts of the war tell us, the boredom of the trenches and life out of the line gave enormous amounts of time for reading. The high level of literacy was important. As Paul Fussell remarks,

> By 1914 it was possible for soldiers to be not merely literate but vigorously literate. . . . On the one hand, the belief in the educative powers of classical and English literature was still extremely strong. On the other the appeal of popular education and "self-improvement" was at its peak and such education was still conceived largely in humanistic terms.[89]

Given this, the Everyman Library, the World's Classics, and the countless cheap editions designed for the pre-War autodidact reached the trenches.[90] Above all, Fussell suggests, was Quiller-Couch's *Oxford Book of English Verse* which 'presides over the Great War in a way that has never been sufficiently appreciated'. This text appears to have been widely available and read, even among ordinary soldiers, and to have conditioned, with its heavily pastoral and ruralist tone, much of the literary response to the War.[91]

VII

By 1918 what had begun as a response among a section of the middle class to the problems of 'outcast London' was well on its way to becoming a permanent part of the national ideology. It was that 'Worcestershire lad', Stanley Baldwin who said in 1924:

> To me, England is the country, and the country is England. And when I ask myself what I mean by England when I am abroad, England comes to me through my various senses – through the ear, through the eye and through certain imperishable scents.[92]

Baldwin went on to associate these responses with 'the very depths of our nature', going back to 'the beginning of time and the human race'. So did the ironmaster's grandson, the archetypal product of the industrial revolution, come to associate his country with the countryside. But it was not just him. Baldwin continued:

> nothing can be more touching than to see how the working man and woman after generations in the town will have their tiny bit of garden if they can, will go to gardens if they can, to look at something they have never seen as children, but which their ancestors knew and loved.[93]

Again the expansion of plotland living after the war supports this. As Hardy and Ward write in their recent study of the plotlands:

> After the First World War, many a survivor suffering from the effects of gas was urged to get out of London, while there were others, terribly disfigured, who wanted to avoid the daily encounters of city living. And there were yet more who, counting themselves fortunate to have survived, resolved not to go back to the life of the urban toiler, but invest the gratuity paid to demobilized soldiers in a new life in the country. . . . Dreams of chicken farming or market gardening may have been easily shattered, but the patch of land and the owner-built house on it remained.[94]

It was not only permanent residence. By the end of the war the notion of the country as a site of holidays and leisure was becoming widespread. Not just the trip to Hampstead Heath or down the Thames to Maidenhead by steamer, but a growing ideal of discovering rural England as it 'really was', unspoilt and natural. As John Prioleau wrote in the dedication of his 1929 guidebook:

> A book for those who prefer country air to town air, road to the street, the face of England to the charm of anywhere else. . . . A book for lovers of the open road, and of England, written by one.[95]

The dedication could be to a book by Hudson or Thomas, but it is not, it is to a book called *Car and Country,* designed to take the owner of the Austin Seven or Morris Minor into real 'rural' England.

Prioleau takes his car owner through 'England', which surprisingly includes the 'Irish Free State' and Wales, but the emphasis is firmly on the South Country. Just over a quarter of the book is given to Kent, Surrey and Sussex. Here real rural England is to be found; Leith Hill is 'one of the most beautiful places in the world', though only thirty miles from Victoria Station; the Sussex Downs are 'pure England'; while the Kent/Sussex border around Rye has become 'the ideal spot for a quiet ramble *by car* [my emphasis]'.[96]

In the ten years between the publication of Prioleau's little guide book and the outbreak of World War II hundreds of publications, like Arthur Mee's *The King's England* (which destroyed Burford for ever) and the *Shell Guides,* sent more and more people, and increasingly working-class people, into the countryside. The south London cyclists sought out the lanes of Kent and Surrey with the aid of their Arthur Mee and an Ordnance Survey Map. The owner of an Austin Seven used his 'Barts Half-Inch' map to get to the villages Kipling wrote about in Puck. The Southern Railways ran excursions and ramblers' specials to the South Downs. In 1939 this generation, who despised Brooke and had grown up under the shadow of Flanders, went to war singing,

> There'll always be an England
> While there's a country lane,
> As long as there's a cottage small
> Beside a field of grain.

Notes

This chapter, which is exploratory rather than definitive, has gone through many forms in the last few years and many people have talked about it with me. I cannot list them all or even remember most of them, but thanks. Helen Walker, whose work on the outdoors in the inter-war period will render much of what I have written obsolete, read the piece with care and made many points which helped enormously. As always though, especially where I ignored advice, the faults are my own.

1   Richard Holt, *Sport and Society in Modern France* (London: Macmillan, 1981), ch. 1.

2   On thatching see John and Jane Penoyre, *Houses in the Landscape: A Regional Study of Vernacular Building Styles in England* (London: Faber and Faber, 1978). For a brilliant discussion of hedgerows and space, as well as ideas about landscape see John Barrell, *The Idea of Landscape and the Sense of Place 1730–1840* (Cambridge: C.U.P., 1972). W. G. Hoskins, *The Making of the English Landscape* (Harmondsworth: Penguin, 1960), deals with this general problem.

3   A marvellous and moving example of this is to be found in Helen Thomas' memoir of Edward Thomas, *As it Was* (London: Faber and Faber, 1926). It also dominates much of Lawrence, especially *Lady Chatterley's Lover.*

4   Raymond Williams, *The Country and the City* (London: Paladin, 1973), especially ch. 1. See also Martin J. Wiener, *English Culture and the Decline of the Industrial Spirit* (Cambridge: C.U.P., 1981).

5   Hilaire Belloc, *Complete Verse* (London: Duckworth, 1970), p. 36. The poem first appeared in *Verses* (1910).

6   Edward Thomas, *The South Country* (1932; new edn, London: Dent, 1984), p. 1. This is an essential source of understanding for many ideas in Thomas and in this section of this chapter.

7   Barrell, op. cit.; §3, *passim.*

8   For some of this, and problems linked to it see fns 9 and 10 and also S. B. Saul, *The Myth of the Great Depression* (London: Macmillan, 1969).

9   See William M. Clarke, *The City in the World Economy* (London: I.E.A., 1965); also P. J. Payne, 'The Emergence of the Large Scale Company in Britain', *Economic History Review*, 2nd. series, XX (1967), 519–42.

10 W. D. Rubenstein, 'Wealth, Elites and the Class Structure of Modern Britain', *Past and Present*, 76 (August 1977), 99–126.

11 Ibid., p. 124.

12 Leon Faucher, *Manchester in 1844* (1844; new edn, London: Frank Cass, 1969). Frederick Engels, *The Condition of the Working Class in England* (Moscow: F.L.P.H., 1962). For example, p. 74, 'In Lancashire, and especially in Manchester, English manufacture finds at once its starting point and its centre.'

13 Frederick Law Olmstead, *Walks and Talks of an American Farmer in England* (1852; new edn, Ann Arbor: U. of Michigan Press, 1967), chs V–VII, *passim.*

14 J. A. Hobson, *Imperialism* (1902; new edn, London: Allen and Unwin, 1938), pp. 150–1.

15 Gareth Stedman Jones, *Outcast London* (Oxford: O.U.P., 1971), especially ch. 16.

16 Edward Gibbon, *The History of the Decline and Fall of the Roman Empire*, ed. J. Bury, 6th edn (London: Methuen, 1911–12), I, 56–8.

17 Quoted in H. Rider Haggard, *A Farmer's Year* (London: Longmans, 1899), p. 466.

18 Stedman Jones, op. cit., p. 128.

19 Ibid.

20 Haggard, op. cit., p. 462.

21 For a more detailed discussion of this see Alun Howkins, *Poor Labouring Men* (London: Routledge and Kegan Paul, 1985), pp. 10–12.

22 Introduction to Christopher Turnor, *Land Problems and National Welfare* (London: The Bodley Head, 1911), pp. vi–viii.

23 Ibid., p. vii.

24 *The Land. The Report of the Land Enquiry Committee, Volume 1. Rural* (London: Hodder and Stoughton, 1913), p. 1vii.

25 Turnor, op. cit., pp. 296ff.

26 *Labour Leader,* 14 August 1908, p. 513.

27 Ibid., 4 September 1913, p. 5; 27 November 1913, p. 3.

28 G. K. Chesterton, *A Short History of England* (London: Chatto, 1917), p. 131.

29 Cecil Sharp, *English Folk Song; Some Conclusions* (London: Mercury Books, 1965), pp. 163–4.

30 This is an enormously complex subject which I can barely touch on. Again I differ from Wiener on dating and interpretation, but it is worth noting that part of the revival of 'Englishness' was a sustained attack on the Gothic.

31 See Wiener, op. cit. especially ch. 3. Also Mark Girouard, *The Return to Camelot* (New Haven and London: Yale U.P., (1981), *passim*. The study of anti-semitism in much of this movement would be interesting. See for example Hobson, and also Rupert Brooke's 'Grantchester'. Again this is outside the scope of this chapter.

32 See Michael Holroyd, *Lytton Strachey: A Biography* (London: Heinemann, 1973). Bloomsbury, too, often seen as European and modernist, largely because of Virginia Woolf's later novels, is profoundly 'English'.

33 Again Wiener, op. cit., pp. 85–7 and fn. 19, p. 189. The Hammonds are more complex than he suggests. I think it is the ideal of how the poor lived before capitalism, especially in *The Village Labourer,* which is so powerful.

34 Girouard, op. cit.; Roy Strong, *And When did You Last See Your Father?* (London: Thames and Hudson, 1978), especially pp. 136ff.

35 For much of what follows see J. W. Burrow, *A Liberal Descent* (Cambridge: C.U.P., 1981), Part IV.

36 Quoted in ibid., p. 275.

37 J. A. Froude (ed.), 'England's Forgotten Worthies', in *Short Studies in Great Subjects*, Vol. 1 (London: Longmans, 1898), pp. 446–7.

38 Burrow, op. cit., p. 282.

39 Ibid., p. 249.

40 Ibid., p. 259.

41 Ibid., pp. 283–4.

42 Quoted in ibid., p. 285.

43 There are two basic accounts of the music of the period, Frank Howes, *The English Musical Renaissance* (London: Seeker, 1966) and Peter J. Pirie with the same title (London: Gollancz, 1971). In my opinion the older book is better. For a further treatment of some of these themes see Alun Howkins, 'Some thoughts on the Genesis of National Music in England', in *Patriotism*, ed. R. Samuel (London: Routledge and Kegan Paul, forthcoming late 1985).

44 Sharp, op. cit., pp. 43–4.

45 Ralph Vaughan Williams, *National Music and Other Essays* (Oxford: O.U.P., 1963), p. 42.

46 Ralph Vaughan Williams, 'Cecil Sharp: An Appreciation' reprinted in Sharp, op. cit., p. vii.

47 Quoted in Vic Gammon, 'Folk Song Collecting in Sussex and Surrey, 1843–1914', *History Workshop Journal*, 10 (Autumn 1980), 81.

48 *The Pioneer,* 22 March 1881, p. 1, quoted in Margaret Jones Bolsteri, *The Early Community at Bedford Park* (London: Routledge and Kegan Paul, 1977), p. 54.

49 Bolsteri, op. cit., *passim.*

50 Clive Aslet, *The Last Country Houses* (New Haven and London: Yale U.P., 1982), p. 157.

51 Ibid., pp. 159–60.

52 See B. J. Berry, *Urbanisation and Counter Urbanisation* (London: Sage, 1976).

53 Anthony D. King, *The Bungalow* (London: Routledge and Kegan Paul, 1984), p. 124.

54 Aslet, op. cit., pp. 289–91.

55 Helen Allingham, *The Cottage Homes of England, Drawn by Helen Allingham and described by S. Dick* (London: Edward Arnold, 1909).

56 Gillian Darley, *Villages of Vision* (London: Paladin, 1975), p. 234.

57 Ruth Tomalin, *W. H. Hudson* (Oxford: O.U.P, 1984) discusses his importance at length.

58 Fiona MacCarthy, *The Simple Life* (London: Lund Humphries, 1981). See also Jan Marsh 'Georgian Poetry and the Land', unpublished PhD thesis, University of Sussex 1976, for the move of some Georgian poets to Herefordshire.

59 George Sturt, *The Journals of George Sturt 1890–1927*, ed. E. D. Mackerness (Cambridge: C.U.P., 1967), II, 767.

60 Ibid., p. 839.

61 For these ideas see Howard Newby, *Green and Pleasant Land?* (Harmondsworth: Penguin, 1980) and Colin Bell, et al., *Property Paternalism and Power* (London: Hutchinson, 1978).

62 For Thomas' feelings about 'Lob' ('very close to his heart') see Eleanor Farjeon, *Edward Thomas: The Last Four Years* (Oxford: O.U.P., 1958), pp. 172–4.

63 George Orwell, *Coming Up for Air* (1939; Harmondsworth: Penguin, 1962), pp. 13–16.

64 W. H. Hudson, *A Foot in England* (Oxford: O.U.P., 1982), ch. 1, *passim.*

65 See John Lowerson, 'Battles for the Countryside', in *Class Culture and Social Change*, ed. Frank Gloversmith (Brighton: Harvester, 1980), pp. 258–80.

66 Vaughan Williams, *National Music*, op. cit., p. 26.

67 Sharp, op. cit., p. 173.

68 Ibid.

69 Vic Gammon, 'Music in the Primary School; Aspects of History and Ideology', Unpublished P.G.C.E. Special Study, University of Sussex 1982.

70 *Board of Education Circular 873* (London: B.O.E., 1914, repr. 1923), ch. 'Teaching of Singing', p. 106.

71 Sharp, op. cit., pp. 171–5.

72 *Board of Education*, op. cit.

73 Aslet, op. cit., p. 42.

74 Ibid.

75 Farjeon, op. cit., p. 48.

76 Rupert Brooke, *Letters from America* (London: Sidgwick, 1916), p. xxx.

77 *The Clarion,* 7 August 1914, p. 6.

78 Sturt, *Journals,* op. cit. II, 702. It is worth comparing this passage with Edward Thomas' 'This is no case of petty right or wrong'.

79 This is a composite but not fanciful picture. For example, see the lives of Rupert Brooke, Lascelles Abercrombie and Edward Thomas among others.

80 For a good discussion of this in a literary sense see Paul Fussell, *The Great War and Modern Memory* (New York: O.U.P., 1975), pp. 164ff.

81 Ernest Rhys (ed.), *The Old Country: A Book of Love and Praise of England* (London: Dent, 1917). Note the title is 'England' not Britain despite the involvement of Irish, Scots and Welsh troops.

82 See Wiener op. cit., pp. 63 and 185.

83 Siegfried Sassoon, *Diaries 1915–18*, ed. Rupert Hart Davies (London: Faber and Faber, 1983), p. 147.

84 Ibid., p. 167.

85 Lyn Macdonald, *They Called it Passchendaele* (London: Macmillan, 1983), Martin Middlebrook, *The First Day on the Somme* (London: Allen Lane, 1971).

86 Quoted in John Ellis, *Eye Deep in Hell* (London: Croom Helm, 1976), p. 200.

87 George Coppard, *With a Machine Gun to Cambrai* (London: H.M.S.O., 1969), p. 85.

88 For an excellent discussion of this phenomenon see Denis Hardy and Colin Ward, *Arcadia for All* (London: Mansell, 1984).

89 Fussell, op. cit., p. 157.

90 See for example, Ivor Gurney, *War Letters*, ed. R. K. R. Thornton (London: The Hogarth Press, 1984), p. 85.

91 Fussell, op. cit., pp. 157–60.

92   Speech at the annual dinner of the Royal Society of St George, 6 May 1924, in Earl Baldwin, *On England* (1926; new edn, Harmondsworth: Penguin, 1937), p. 16.

93   Ibid., p. 17.

94   Hardy and Ward, op. cit., p. 190.

95   John Prioleau, *Car and Country* (London: Dent, 1929), p. v.

96   Ibid., p. 36.

CHAPTER FOUR

The invention of English

Brian Doyle

The crisis of leadership

Between 1880 and 1920 Britain continued to enjoy a large measure of world economic supremacy. While its dominance within international finance was maintained, and even enhanced, the same was not true of industrial production. Though still the world's leading trading nation, controlling 35 per cent of world trade in 1900,[1] it could no longer be assumed that such dominance would continue as a feature of the natural order into a less certain future. The period is marked by a series of initiatives within and on behalf of the ruling class aimed at a revitalization of leadership qualities which were needed to maintain the overseas empire and to govern at home. They involved spasmodic attempts at boosting advanced teaching and research in science and other fields of 'modern' study, especially as applied to industrial organization and technological development. More consistently, though, the machinery of an expanded state engaged with general initiatives in the spheres of 'culture', including non-scientific forms of education. On the whole these efforts carried a national emphasis, as a number of educationalists, politicians, philosophers and political theorists searched for new and more efficient ways of building and disseminating a national sense of ancestry, tradition and universal 'free' citizenship. However, the cultural negotiations involved were problematic since they generated tensions between the ideology of individualism and the investment of cultural authority in the state. Furthermore, while a revitalized ruling and administering class might be seen to require infusions of men of wealth and leadership from slightly lower social layers, this could prove acceptable only under conditions in which new procedures for educational cultivation had been established.[2] While it had become easier for some middle-class men (or their sons) to earn membership of the national ruling culture by Edwardian times, their status as true 'gentlemen' remained equivocal in an atmosphere of continued mistrust of the business community, even if this mistrust was tempered by outbreaks of anxiety over the volatility of the lower orders, which it was felt was the task of their middle-class superiors to defuse.[3]

At the same time as there were initiatives from above – there was a softening of the ambivalent attitude to aristocratic gentility on the part of those business and industrial groups whose culture had been so well sustained by utilitarianism and political economy during the period of Britain's growth to world economic supremacy. These groups were learning to recognize that much was to be gained from the aristocracy's long experience of government and cultural authority. Thus the period between 1880 and 1920 was marked by a sequence of strategies to combine traditions of aristocratic cultural mystique with utilitarian programmes of industrial and social administration. It was strategies of this kind which brought together groups united in a concern for 'national efficiency'. Such groups attempted to establish more effective programmes for educating, governing and mobilizing a majority population to serve the British imperial mission at home and abroad.[4]

This mobilization was built on three main platforms: classification, pacification and cultivation. The working class was seen as the object for 'colonisation' by its cultural superiors in order that 'respectable' members of the class be separated from their 'rough' residue, and the leaders of the class be made fit for a limited role in governing the nation.[5] In this process any shadows of socialist organization were to be dispersed by the radiance of a common culture and heritage. Of course the nation was organized not only in terms of class but also in terms of gender and age-grade. It was conceived as the proper function of the nation's mothers to rear (within families suitably inoculated against any possibility of communism in the home)[6] fine imperial specimens of manhood. Schooling had also a central place in such initiatives. As a crucial feature of their role in cultural reproduction, schools were expected to inculcate in the nation's children a proper sense of patriotic moral responsibility. Insofar as schooling proved too 'mechanical' a procedure for influencing the pupils' subjectivities in the approved manner,[7] efforts were also made to influence home life in a more direct fashion. This was a tendency which coincided with the elimination of mothers and young children from employment in the wake of technological innovations which particularly diminished the kinds of work in which traditionally they had participated.[8]

In sum, the period is characterized by a number of efforts aimed at generating a revitalized leadership which would effectively combine the 'mechanical' qualities of utilitarianism and political economy with those of the more 'organic' traditions of the aristocracy. In many ways the Settlement movement of the 1880s and 1890s provided test sites for this combination. Here young men (some of whom, such as C. E. Vaughan,[9] subsequently were to support the elevation of English within the national system of education) fired by a somewhat secularized 'politics of conscience', engaged in missionary work addressed to the cultural colonization of the great mass of the excluded population.[10] Deep in the heartland of 'unknown England' that was London's East End, they tested their aura of cultural mystique against the potentially demystifying pressures of the East End world.[11] It was upon this forcing-ground that those traditional modes of cultural authority, reinforced by an Oxbridge education, could systematically be reworked in such a way as to govern (or professionally administer) a class-divided industrial society.[12]

The new modes of official and semi-official supervision and government are best viewed in terms of a general 'collectivist' modification of older patterns of 'individualism'. In attempting to develop a new collective sense of Englishness, intellectuals and administrators alike applied themselves to what, at an earlier (and, indeed, later) time, would have been seen as an 'un-English' and idealist version of the national life. This vision was directly concerned with the governing of a (at least potentially) spiritually organic and mechanically efficient nation. In its more philosophical aspects such intellectual work was addressed to providing a theoretical underpinning for a collectivist social outlook which would be immune equally from what it saw as the mechanical vulgarities of statism and the revolutionary demands of socialism.[13] It was only in the context of the theoretical work of T. H. Green and Bernard Bosanquet, and of Fabian 'municipal' revisions of the programme of socialism, that William Harcourt, the prominent Liberal politician, could claim in the 1890s that 'we're all socialists now'. The new philosophy of society moved beyond any simple vision of the state as a set of administrative institutions, towards a vision of it as an almost venerable ideal form: a form which claimed to be able to dissolve political struggle into the larger flow of the national way of life, in the name of common culture and common economic interest.[14]

At a more practical level, but under the shadow of such an ideal, a series of administrative layers were built at the sensitive ideological point between the official state and the mass of the people. It is, indeed, at this very point that the movement to advance the status of 'English' in education must be situated if its particular history as a cultural and administrative form is to be understood. The advance, or invention, of the new English must thus be explained in the context of growth in the number of semi-autonomous professions in fields such as public administration and welfare, journalism, publicity and arts, and the establishment of national cultural institutions geared to providing a schedule for organizing the nation.

From classics to English

The establishment of the new English involved a major reworking of relationships between cultural forms (that is to say, socially produced patterns of meaning, subjectivity and knowledge) and the operation of institutions of social organization and administration (in general, formal relations of political power in society). This can be characterized, as an ideological process in the strict sense that it successfully established an apparently *natural* role for the new English within both formal education and the less formal patterns of public and private life. The object here, then, is to provide a description of this process of cultural and ideological transformation.

In 1880 English did not exist as an autonomous academic discipline. Although since the 1820s a chair of English Language and Literature had been established at University College, London, and a handful of similar chairs (usually under the title of 'English and History') had been added during the intervening decades, such innovations both in their characteristic methods and subject matter reached back to an older tradition of teaching 'Rhetoric' with an added emphasis from the middle of the century on historical and philological studies. The period of real growth and transformation took place after 1880 and coincided with the development of the new 'provincial' college sector outside the ancient universities of Oxford and Cambridge, which set in motion the rise of a number of new departments of 'modern' knowledge. However, by 1920, English in a substantially adapted form when compared with 'English Language and Literature' or 'English and History' had come to be seen by public administrators, politicians, academics and 'men-of-letters' not only as a necessary constituent of a modern national system of education, but even in many cases as its most essential core element.

Such an account is of particular interest today since any adequate understanding of the current operations of English in education must pay attention to historically developing relationships between English and senses of Englishness. While such relationships have now come to be so taken-for-granted as to have been rendered almost invisible (at least until very recently), during the period 1880 to 1920 their articulation around class, gender, age, nationality and ethnicity was much more directly in evidence. It was the ideological work of that moment to institute the relations between English and Englishness as self-evident.

Previously when the term 'English' was used in relation to education it signified one among a number of 'modern' languages whose associated grammar, literature and history occupied only a minor role as an adjunct to classical studies, certainly within the 'higher' sectors. Within 'elementary' education the term covered not only reading and writing but also any other non-classical subjects as were taught. From the 1840s the inferior position of English language and literature began to be questioned, mostly by scholars working outside the ancient universities of England,[15] but it was only during the early decades of the present century that English Studies (or, more simply, 'English') in its recognizably modern disciplinary form began to offer an educationally significant challenge to the intellectual and cultural prestige long invested in classics. As MacPherson has argued, the elevation of the vernacular language and literature within higher education was an attempt to sustain the notion of a 'liberal education' in the face of tendencies towards academic specialization on the one hand, and the dwindling popularity of classics on the other. The introduction of the national language and literature at Oxbridge was seen (at least to begin with) as a broadening and rejuvenation of the 'literary' curriculum which would thereby be sustained as a foundation for more specialized study.[16] Benjamin Jowett (1817–93), Master of Balliol College, Oxford, and one of the modernizing dons who supported endeavours both to extend university education and to attract men from new social classes to Oxford, considered that,

> classical study is getting in some respects worn out, and the plan proposed [the introduction of English Language and Literature at Oxford] would breathe new life into it.[17]

One of the signs of the eclipse of classics by English was the foundation in 1907 of the English Association which was to propound very effectively the view that the new discipline had become 'our finest vehicle for a genuine humanistic education,' and that 'its importance in this respect was growing with the disappearance of Latin and Greek from the curricula of our schools and universities'.[18] However, the eventual transference from the classical curriculum to a modern alternative and the enhancement of English and Englishness which was one of its major products, drew on the raw materials provided by the scholarly work of the middle decades of the nineteenth century. In the process of inventing the new English, these materials were substantially transformed to serve a national and imperial culture. In fact, it was only as a consequence of this earlier work of literary, linguistic and historical categorizing that it became possible for a sense of national and vernacular 'ancestry' to challenge the cultural and educational rule of the classical languages and literatures. Arthur Quiller-Couch, Professor of English Literature at Cambridge in 1916, recalled in one of his lectures the impact of this challenge on his contemporaries several decades earlier:

> Few in this room are old enough to remember the shock of awed surprise which fell upon young minds presented, in the late "seventies and early" eighties of the last century with Freeman's *Norman Conquest* or Green's *Short History of the English People*; in which as through parting clouds of darkness, we beheld our ancestry, literary as well as political, radiantly legitimised.[19]

New cultural strategies

We can now attend to some of the specific ways in which such general initiatives were worked through, from an explicitly cultural standpoint. Histories written from within perspectives formed by the modern discipline of English have tended to depend upon aestheticizing assumptions about the self-evident value of the discipline as such – that is, a value directly derived from the purely aesthetic or 'cultural' qualities seen as inherent within the objects of study (authors, texts and traditions). Alternatively, they have treated the development of the discipline against a background of ideas and a general sense of the spirit of the age.[20] Furthermore, previous histories of the discipline of English have tended to treat the period 1880 to 1920 as a 'pre-historical' one. I am arguing, in contrast, that modern English was a product shaped by initiatives, strategies and procedures which together represented an attempt to build a renewed system of cultural authority in the years between 1880 and 1920.

The notion of 'degeneracy' is important in this context. Around and within this notion a constant play with gender, nationality, self, age and maturity can be traced. The esteemed characteristics were those associated with masculinity, activity and concrete statement, personal poise and self-mastery, together with a concern for racial purity or at least racial vigour. Variants of Social Darwinism were used to authorize British competition with other nations, attempts at racial perfectibility and preferred notions of essential human subjectivity. For example, the idea of advanced education as a process for the 'regeneration of the self' was strongly propounded by modernizing Oxbridge dons such as Mark Pattison, an influential educationalist and Head of Lincoln College Oxford from 1861.[21] For Pattison the essence of the human self (essential subjectivity) was the passive human subject produced by 'nature'. However, a truly 'liberal' or 'higher' education could inculcate a higher subjectivity which transcended nature by offering experiences, feelings and pleasures that were beyond the mindless routines thought to be engaged in by most of mankind.[22] The 'culture' offered by a liberal education could thus control nature by generating a higher form of 'life' – by teaching 'the art to live'.[23] This is one indication of the way in which cultural strategies of the time worked through the whole gamut of cultural processes: from patterns of signification and making sense of self and society, through conceptions of the proper modes of gaining experiences, feelings and pleasures, to more formalized modes of producing knowledge.

This whole cultural ensemble was held together in a manner which bore a striking resemblance to ways of dealing with statism and socialism which have been considered earlier. Collectivist strategies attempted to restrain any tendencies either towards statism or socialism by tempering the full rigours of laissez-faire capitalism through a renewal of state and semi-state institutions. In the case of general cultural strategies, the excesses of full-blown conceptions of Social Darwinism were qualified by re-interpreting self-governing natural processes as capable of cultural modifications (as in Pattison's scheme). This led to a considerable investment of energy in shaping from above the constituents of the national culture and national character; and to the identification and removal of any tendencies towards degeneration within the national 'body'.

Such procedures played a central part in the construction of the new English. They could not, however, have been sustained without the development of parallel general educational initiatives of unprecedented scope. It is important here, though, not to take the notion of 'education' in any narrow sense since the mission of national education as it operated between 1880 and 1920 encompassed institutions, events and locations well beyond the scope of education as it has since come to be formally conceived. Such education took place not only in schools and colleges, but also within the home and at local and national gatherings (as in the case of the National Home Reading Union)[24]; at public galleries and museums; and even within city streets, in the signifying processes encouraged through the erection of monuments of a national flavour in prominent positions within the urban landscape.[25] Nor was the rural landscape omitted from such initiatives: the National Trust was founded in 1895 to secure the permanent preservation of places and buildings of 'beauty' and of 'historic' interest; that is, to sustain the national heritage in its physical and geographical aspects. In 1897 a permanent site for British works of art was established as the National Gallery of Modern Art (the Tate Gallery) at Millbank, London, to display as well as preserve approved works of visual art. Similarly the National Portrait Gallery (1896) and the *Dictionary of National Biography* (1885–1900) stand as counterparts, at the level of individual portrayal and biography, to the work of categorization and charting that went into producing monumental works on the national history, language and literature such as the *Cambridge History of English Literature* (1907–16) and the *New* (later, *Oxford*) *English Dictionary* (1884–1928).

Even within more formal patterns of education, initiatives ranged from those which tended increasingly towards the institutionalization of a national system overseen by the state (Education Acts from 1870 to 1902 and beyond; the formation of School Boards and Education Authorities and a national Board of Education [1899]) to a number of semi-state programmes such as, from the 1870s, the national Extension Movement, the National Council of Adult Schools Association, and, later, the Workers' Education Association. The English Association should also be mentioned here since it showed a considerable overlap of personnel and policies with many of these other initiatives (formal and informal), having particularly close affinities with the National Home Reading Union, the *Dictionary of National Biography* and the National Trust, and occupying an interesting position of relative autonomy from the state Board of Education.

The new English

Specific developments within formal education and their relation to the new English can now be given direct attention. The period saw transformations (mooted from the 1850s) of modes of professional academic organization and administration, teaching, research and publication. In general such transformations involved secularization as much as professionalization and operated not only inwards towards the academy but also outwards towards a new constituency: the nation as a whole. A partial eclipse of religious belief in the face of social relations organized around industry, science and technology, led to greater emphases on a 'lay' ministry and pedagogy, and a search, from the mid-nineteenth century, for new tools of a general higher education.[26] Oxbridge institutions, though, were slow to respond to such trends and it was only towards the end of the century that calls for the ancient universities to accept a 'national' role began to be heeded. By the turn of the century Oxbridge was beginning to service a limited amount of social mobility; but, on the whole, middle-class education continued to be catered for elsewhere, increasingly through the extension movement and the 'provincial' colleges.[27] The challenge by versions of 'science' to the classical curriculum has been mentioned earlier, but one way of dealing with this challenge should be identified here. This was articulated by the scientist, educationalist and parliamentarian Lyon Playfair at a meeting to publicize the establishment of York College in 1875:

> our universities cannot get hold of our great industrial centres in any permanent way unless they raise them in self-respect and dignity by giving them an intellectual understanding of their vocations. . . . [They] have not learned that the stronghold of literature should be in the upper classes of society, while the stronghold of science should be in the nation's middle class.[28]

The 'literature' to which Playfair refers is, of course, classics rather than English literature (which had not yet come to be seen as an adequate instrument of 'culture'). In fact, it was largely through the middle-class and scientific bias of the new provincial colleges that English Language, Literature and History came to serve as a sort of 'poor man's classics,' and it was only at the very end of the century that Oxbridge became sufficiently concerned to begin to succumb to the then 'national demand'[29] for such studies and introduce new 'Schools' and 'Tripos' regulations that would allow the ancient institutions to take a lead in these new areas. Oxbridge, then, was only lifted to the apex of the study of English Language, Literature and History when it was subjected to the demands for national efficiency and leadership.

The foundation of a state Board of Education signalled the acceptance within the official culture of a need for policies that would co-ordinate an efficient and fully national system of education, and also allowed the voices of dons who had been calling for a transformation of the traditional curriculum to carry more weight than ever before. But the 'nationalising' tendency within educational policy-making had to move carefully between claims for education as a universal human right and education as a series of differential provisions along class and gender lines. Even working-class challenges tended to move between these two poles. Some attacked the whole notion of disinterested 'liberal education' as such in the name of class-orientated forms, while others supported the system which propagated the sense of a common cultural heritage with the proviso that wider access be established.[30] In practice, the constituency to which this national education was addressed remained firmly rooted in differential class provision. Indeed, this division was further accentuated when the distinction between the 'elementary' and 'higher' systems was enhanced by the 1902 Education Act.[31]

It was at this moment, and in such a context, that the Board of Education came to see, in the ideas of the modernizing dons and the version of 'culture' proposed by Matthew Arnold, fruitful potentialities for the curriculum of the state-maintained middle-class secondary schools. What were still called the 'English subjects' proved particularly attractive here. The 1904 School Regulations refer to 'the group of subjects commonly classed as 'English' and including the English language and literature, Geography and History'.[32] In contrast, a Circular of the Board published in 1910, 'The Teaching of English in Secondary Schools', deals with 'English' solely under the headings of 'Literature' and 'Composition'. Literature is introduced as follows: 'Real knowledge and appreciation of Literature come only from first-hand study of the works of great writers. The first thing to be done is to draw up a list of such works to be read in school'. And composition is also indebted to literature:

> Composition means arrangement, and English composition is the arrangement, in speaking or writing English, of right words in their right order, so as to convey clearly a consecutive meaning. It thus involves the arrangement, not merely of words, but of the substance of thought which the words are meant to convey. . . . Only through composition can pupils acquire effective mastery of the enlarged vocabulary with which they become acquainted through literature, but which remains inert in their minds without the exercise of applying it to the expression of their own thought.[33]

With the increase of tension between universal education and differential provision, the special qualities of the new English (under the hegemony of English literature), for securing the sense of a common culture while at the same time being suited to differential application across the range of educational sectors, caused the Board to look very kindly on the fledgling discipline and to give a great deal of support to its advancement in schools.[34]

'English', then, by the first decade of the new century, had come to have a multi-faceted character due to its variation of role within the new provincial colleges, Oxbridge, and the national system of schooling. From the 1850s miscellaneous 'general knowledge' about the language, literature and history had been considered appropriate content for examining potential recruits to the Civil Service, and especially the Indian Civil Service. By 1875 seventeen examinations were available to schoolboys covering not only the Civil Services, but also the Armed Forces, the Professions and the Universities, in nearly all of which the English subjects were set.[35] Thus, at least at this level, the English subjects were already well established as minimal testing devices for entry into state, semi-state and autonomous professional organizations. The study of language, literature and history was also substantially influenced by the general process of higher academic specialization which took place during the same period. University College, London and Owen's College, Manchester, were the earliest influences in this respect. Here, apart from reliance on the rigours of a large-scale examination system, new areas of modern knowledge were set up as autonomous academic disciplines with a related German-style system of professoriate, administrative hierarchy, departmental structure, and a commitment to research – none of which was characteristic of the operations of the traditional classical curriculum.[36]

English Language, Literature and History in the colleges was both similar to and different from these other modern disciplines; similar in that, like them, it sought to create for itself a solid and autonomous identity; different (especially from the early decades of this century) in that its predominantly classically trained and often clerical academic proponents increasingly claimed for it a status well beyond that of any mere 'discipline' or 'knowledge subject'. The history of the transition from the 'English Language and Literature', 'English and History' and the 'English subjects' to the simple and all-embracing generic term 'English' is the history of a complex process of cultural extension and elevation. 'English' came to extend its range of operations beyond any disciplinary boundaries to encompass all mental, imaginative and spiritual faculties. In the words of one professor, the object of teaching English literature came to be not the imparting of 'knowledge' but 'the cultivation of the mind, the training of the imagination, and the quickening of the whole spiritual nature'.[37] English was elevated through being imbued with the kind of cultural authority previously invested in classics, but now with the addition of a powerful national dimension that yet somehow transcended nationality. Another professor was reported as stating that,

> literature should be a means of larger experience – a conning tower or
> an upper chamber with a view beyond bounds of class, locality, time or

country. . . . It was clear that literature deepened our sense of the import of nationality by giving the most intense and at the same time most manifold expression of it.[38]

By the early decades of this century English was coming to be called upon to sustain a 'national ideal', which was traced back to Matthew Arnold. Its role was to assist in the educational work of transcending 'individual self-interest' by subordinating the 'individual self' to 'common aims':

> In his educational outlook [Arnold] was a nationalist. . . . Such an ideal, he believed, could be imparted and maintained by a public system of education. . . . Matthew Arnold's great achievement was that he convinced the younger generation among his readers of the necessity for providing throughout England an abundant supply of public secondary schools for boys and girls, schools which would be intellectually competent, attested by public inspection, and aided both by local authorities and the state.[39]

In serving this ideal, one feature which gave the new English its peculiar potency was the cultural mystique bestowed upon it by a vision of the qualities seen as inherent in the national literature. This vision was most dramatically evoked by John Bailey at a Conference of the English Association in 1917. Bailey

> related a story of an officer who read *The Faerie Queene* to his men when they were in a particularly difficult situation. The men did not understand the words, but the poetry had a soothing influence upon them. Nothing better could be said of poetry than that.[40]

In order to understand the genesis of this new cultural form, we must examine some other forces of cultural extension and elevation which provided its preconditions. The history of the 'extension movement' illustrates many of the cultural patterns which influenced the emergence of the new English.

The moves for an extended system of university education reached back to the 1840s when it was aimed at providing more qualified candidates for Anglican ordination, but it was very soon transformed into a more lay-oriented mission. The first practical measures of educational extension were instituted during the 1850s and 1860s when London degrees were opened to all who could pass an 'external' examination, but it was only towards the end of the 1860s that an emphasis on the English language, literature and history became an important feature of the process of extension. In the course of the next two decades Oxford and Cambridge became involved in what one of the Cambridge extension lecturers described as an attempt to provide 'University Education for the Whole Nation by an Itinerant system connected with the Old Universities.'[41] The object of this peripatetic programme from the point of view of Oxbridge was outlined by the Oxford Vice-Chancellor in 1887:

> the lecturers whom we send through the country are a kind of missionary; wherever they go they carry on their foreheads the name of the University they represent. To a great majority of those persons with whom they come in contact it is the only opportunity afforded of learning what Oxford means and what is meant by the powers of an Oxford education.[42]

Of course, what Oxford 'means', and the source of its 'power', a classical curriculum taught within an intimate collegiate system, could hardly be extended. The new 'meaning', therefore, that was preached by the missionaries was embodied in a modern subject: English Language, Literature and History. The ideal of a complete integration of the cultural mission of the universities with English was to be most clearly articulated in the pages of the Newbolt Report of 1921, 'The Teaching of English in England', which was commissioned by the Board of Education:

> The interim, we feel, belongs chiefly to the professors of English literature. The rise of modern universities has accredited an ambassador of poetry to every important capital of industrialism in the country, and upon his shoulders rest a responsibility greater we think than is as yet generally recognised. The Professor of literature in a university should be – and sometimes is, as we gladly recognise – a missionary in a more real and active sense than any of his colleagues. . . . The fulfilment of these obligations means propaganda work, organisation and the building up of a staff of assistant missionaries.[43]

But in earlier days, English was not without rivals. T. H. Green, first chairman of Oxford extension lectures in 1879, favoured a philosophical system which would 'appeal both to the intelligence and to the emotions', and thereby provide 'a rational view of man and society, a theory neither hedonist nor materialist'.[44] Even if philosophy never gained the role Green hoped that it would, Benjamin Jowett was remarkably successful in inculcating his latter-day Platonic guardians at Green's Oxford college, Balliol, with a renewed vision of leadership. Green's own views carried a good deal of influence within another movement of 'extension', the 'settlements' set up from the 1880s in London's East End and other urban areas. The view of citizenship which Green promulgated, and which was supported by Jowett's successor as Master of Balliol college, Caird, was influential in forming the social ideals of a generation of politicians, senior civil servants (including those within the Board of Education), and influential members of the English Association.

The settlement movement has been mentioned earlier. The orientation here was more 'collectivist', and it can be seen as a response to socialist challenges to policies based on political economy and philanthropy. The settlement of Toynbee Hall in the East End of London was founded in 1884 by the Christian socialist Samuel Barnett. The settlement connects with other forms of extension in that it did have an educational aim, but, like Oxford House (another settlement or 'mission' set up in the East End in 1884), it usefully illustrates new initiatives for the renewal of forms of leadership and patterns for social administration upon which the elevation of English largely depended. Barnett saw Toynbee Hall as the potential centre for an East London University; in fact it became, as did the other settlements and extension classes, a centre for members of the middle class.[45] While Toynbee Hall 'expressed the spirit of Balliol', Oxford House came out of the more 'missionary' Keble College, Oxford.[46] Indeed the Federation of Working Men's Clubs set up by Oxford House directly assisted the young Oxford missionary in developing the 'knack of mingling on terms of personal equality with men, while yet by some *je ne sais quoi* in himself', preserving 'their freely accorded social homage'.[47] This was as much the true 'meaning' of Oxford as was any other aspect of the programme of extension. What was at stake was the renovation of modes for achieving freely given cultural consent to a renewed leadership; a leadership capable of entering the world of 'men' on terms of only apparent equality. The first annual report of the Oxford House mission in 1884 set this programme out most clearly: 'Colonisation by the well-to-do seems indeed the true solution to the East End question, for the problem is, how to make the masses realise their spiritual and social solidarity with the rest of the capital and the kingdom'. The report goes on to claim that the people could only be taught 'thrift and prudence' by men who would actually associate with them, thereby ensuring that the influence of 'the imperishable youth of Oxford' would induce them to face 'the elementary laws of economics'.[48]

The same ideological pattern is to be found within the imperial, educational and commercial programme for 'national efficiency' which, from the 1890s, drew in a number of prominent figures from the worlds of politics, business and 'letters'.[49] John Gorst, Conservative M.P., intimate of Barnett and one supporter of this programme, captured the emotions that motivated this ideology when speaking at Glasgow University in 1894. In his view the crowding of 'the destitute classes' into the cities had made 'their existence thereby more conspicuous and dangerous', particularly since they 'already form a substantial part of the population, and possess even now, although they are still ignorant of their full power, great political importance'. The danger was that they might even go beyond 'their lawful power at the polls', especially if stirred up by 'designing persons' and promises of 'social salvation', and attempt to produce change through 'revolutionary action'.[50] Barnett himself saw the problem as one of achieving an amicable peace between rich and poor by finding the cultural means of bringing together the 'two nations'.[51] R. B. Haldane was another important member of the national efficiency group. He was also a keen supporter of extension programmes, and future Lord Chancellor in both Liberal and Labour governments. His views show how the proponents of national efficiency linked a concern for a renewal of leadership qualities with the generation of a cultural mystique through education. In the course of his Rectorial address at Edinburgh in 1907, Haldane asserted that 'when a leader of genius comes forward the people may bow down before him, and surrender their wills, and eagerly obey', since 'to obey the commanding voice was to rise to a further and wider outlook, and to gain a fresh purpose'. To this end, students must live for their work: 'So only can they make themselves accepted leaders; so only can they aspire to form a part of that priesthood of humanity to whose commands the world will yield obedience'.[52]

The English Association was founded in the same year and applied itself to the advancement of the new English within the national culture. One of the principal figures within the Association was to be Henry Newbolt, imperialist poet, celebrant of the mystique of the public school, future chairman of the Board of Education Committee which reported on the state of English in 1921, and – like Haldane – a supporter of the national efficiency group in its aims of planning imperial policy, improving education and recapturing commercial prosperity.[53]

Culture, society and the English Association

Once it is accepted that the cultural politics that shaped English is not synonymous with what has come to be taken as qualities and features intrinsic to the discipline itself, English can then be understood in terms of its especial fittedness to more general cultural and educational strategies. Contrary to many previous historical accounts based upon a problematic generated from *within* the discipline, English is best seen as an invented or constructed cultural form which was a culmination of attempts to produce a truly 'English' theory of society and a prospectus for cultural renewal. In the work of establishing this new form within the national system of education the English Association was a key force.

The Association was set up to promote the maintenance of 'correct use of English, spoken and written', the recognition of English as 'an essential element in the national education', and the discussion of teaching methods and advanced study as well as the correlation of school with university work.[54] From the beginning, personnel attached to the new Board of Education seem to have been sympathetic to the view of English as the most natural candidate to lead a mission of cultural renewal: at any rate, the English Association from its inception set out to ensure that such was the case. George Saintsbury, Professor of Rhetoric and English Literature at Edinburgh, in his presidential address to the A.G.M. of the Scottish branch in 1907, emphasized the importance of bringing the influence of the Association to bear on questions of education when they came before the legislature. In this way the Association 'might really be the means of exercising a not inconsiderable leverage on educational performances and educational arrangements'.[55] Within a few years firm and formal contacts with the Board of Education had been established. Arthur Acland, the Liberal politician and president of the Association, announced in 1910 that the Board of Education 'would welcome help from us in putting forward a scheme for English teaching in Secondary Schools'.[56] This was confirmed by a statement carried in the next bulletin of the Association:

> the Board of Education has now given effect to the intimation conveyed by Mr Acland and vaguely announced by him at the Annual meeting. They have definitely asked for representatives of the Association to confer with their officers in order to discuss a circular which they are preparing on the teaching of English in secondary schools. In this way, for the first time, the Association obtains official recognition.[57]

In 1917 the Association was largely responsible for convincing the Board of the need for a Departmental Committee to investigate the state of the teaching of English in England, and to propose plans for future developments. When the Committee was subsequently formed, eight of its fourteen members were from the Association.[58] It is best to see the new Association not so much as a pressure-group founded to further the professional interests of teachers of English, but rather as a class-based mobilization which drew in not only most professors of English Language and Literature, but also like-minded politicians, administrators and men-of-letters. In the person of the (non-academic) Henry Newbolt, who subsequently was to chair the Departmental Committee, it found a figure who could articulate many of the themes to which both the fledgling discipline and the Association itself adhered. Newbolt was quick to express his hostility to the whole notion of formal 'institutions'. When about to become a member of the Association in 1913, he is reported to have remarked that,

> Nothing in the world caused him such dismay, such instant feelings of antagonism, as catching sight of any institution whatsoever. . . . He was coming inside the English Association with the hope of assuring himself that his own principles were being carried out by it.[59]

As a writer on the early days of the Association subsequently noted, the movement tended to work by modes of informal 'social lubrication.'[60] Throughout the years up to the publication of the 1921 Report, the Association had a policy of alternating the occupants of its presidential chair between men-of-letters (such as Saintsbury, Bradley, Ker, Herford and Gosse) and representatives of the official parliamentary culture (including Acland, Balfour, Morley and Asquith). It also at various times gathered into its ambit important figures within general educational administration (e.g.,

Haddow, Sadler, Barker, Curzon, Mansbridge, and a host of college Heads, Registrars, Provosts and Vice-Chancellors). Perhaps the Association derived its authority from its ability to mobilize such a wide diversity of influential persons on the basis of its anti-institutional stance.

In bringing into relation such personnel, the Association also brought together all of the cultural and institutional themes that have been detailed previously. Members of the Association recognized, for example, potential dangers as arising from the loss of aristocratic leadership, and the rise of a cultural market-place, which urgently necessitated the use of literary culture to bring about an apparently spontaneous consent to a regenerated leadership. As one speaker at the A.G.M. of 1909 put it:

> The old standards have decayed, the aristocracy no longer take the intellectual lead; men of letters and booksellers are left face to face with a multitude of readers whose intellectual appetites and tastes are emancipated from all direct influence and control. If we look at the state of our imaginative literature, we must observe in it a grossness, even an indecency, of conception, and an inflowing tide of slang and vulgarity and other forms of ugliness which tend to corrupt imagination and barbarize language. These are the inevitable results of leaving the merit of a book to be determined exclusively by market value.[61]

But it was also recognized that such circumstances called for different strategies within the respective elementary and higher sectors of education. While for elementary pupils the object was to instil a feeling for the grandeur of the national language and literature, within the higher sector it was felt to be necessary to fire the pupils' and students' imaginations: to provide indirect moral inculcation through pleasurable and even joyous responses to literary values.[62] The Association applied itself to ways of resolving the continuing tension between the utilitarian needs of business and industry and the reinvigoration of a cultural leadership, its avowed objective being to reconcile practical utility, enlightened patriotism and the 'human ideal' in education.[63] It attempted, in fact, the condensation at a practical and institutional level of what theorists had been attempting to think into existence during the latter part of the previous century: that is, the establishment of a depoliticized 'Culture' which would bind the disparate interests within the nation into a single organic unity sharing a common heritage. And, as a number of discussions within the Association show, what gave English its peculiar potency for this cultural project was its apparent potential to reach directly to the roots of subjective human response through modes of 'appreciation' as opposed to mere factual instruction in the manner of the earlier English Subjects and English Language, Literature and History. F. W. Moorman, Professor of English Language at Leeds and an active supporter of the W.E.A., told the annual conference in 1914 that the main purpose of the teaching of English Literature was not to impart knowledge, or to 'equip students for the conquest of the world'; indeed, the object was not to 'teach' at all but to 'delight' and, 'for some, to sweeten leisure'.[64] This should be compared with the substance of the motion moved by P. J. Hartog, Academic Registrar of University College, London, on behalf of the Association at the Federal Conference of Education in 1907:

> That the object of the teaching of English should be to develope [sic] in pupils the power of thought and expression, and the power of appreciating the content of great literary works, rather than to inculcate a knowledge of grammatical, philological and literary detail.[65]

Such an objective involved establishing what, in practice, was to stand as the proper constituents of the new English, and their relation to each other. The record of debates within the Association reveals the gradual emergence of 'literature' (sometimes used as a synonym for 'poetry') at first as an essential feature of English, and then as its primary constituent. The debate which followed Hartog's motion took the form of a 'heated controversy' over the relative merits of grammar, philology and literary detail as opposed to the contents of great works. But these were not the only oppositions registered within the new English during early debates. There were moments at which an older pattern of connotation held the field of debate and supported a direct opposition between the very terms 'English' (in the sense associated with the 'English Subjects') and 'literature', as when a contributor to a debate in 1908 distinguished sharply between the teaching of English and literature on the grounds that the latter involved the 'interpretation of life' and was therefore unsuited for teaching to children as opposed to university students.[66] Discussions directed towards the school sectors commonly worked with a tripartite division of English into language, composition or essay writing, and literature[67]; while, on occasion, 'literature' was conceived as being in polar opposition to language, or composition, or even history.[68] C. H. Herford, Professor of English Literature at Manchester, pointed out in 1918 that 'English' or 'English Language and Literature' was 'a loose name for a group of studies differing in educational aim, and in the faculties they appealed to, and those they demanded for successful prosecution'. Nonetheless, these studies had two chief aspects: the science of language and literature, and the medium of a 'broader culture'.[69] In general, though, there was a clear movement towards substituting for 'English Language and Literature' and the 'English Subjects' the simple all-embracing term 'English', and this was done with the assumption of a new focus. English was essentially seen as concerned with the contents of 'great works' and as the medium for transmitting a 'broader culture', which meant establishing a dominant role for literature. The conception of the centrality of literature could be tacitly and uncontroversially assumed in a 1919 bulletin of the Association where the general goal of promoting 'the exact study of our literature which the English Association has at its heart' is simply stated as self-evident.[70]

Of course, the nature of this 'broader culture' that was to be transmitted by means of English required some consideration, if only by attending to imponderable notions like 'poetry', 'form' and 'style'. In 1910, Herbert Grierson, Professor of English Literature at Aberdeen, was reported as affirming that 'Happily we had come to see that the final justification for English Literature was English Literature', in an address to the Association[71]; while the Principal of the Glasgow Training College went on to confirm (referring to the role of teachers as moral educationalists) that 'their first aim as English teachers was to teach literature as literature'.[72] Nonetheless, while the ultimate value of literature was taken to be guaranteed by the poetic vision or form that inhered in it, the very imponderability of this mode of signification rendered it potentially uncontrollable or even subversive. As Macneile Dixon, Professor of English Language and Literature at Glasgow, reiterated on a number of occasions, poetic inspiration tended at times towards 'madness' and was thus in need of the stable guardianship of 'tradition'.[73] The enthronement of 'literary' or 'poetic' values as the spiritual ruling force within English was completed towards the end of the period, in the wake of two decades of discussion within the Association.[74] And, indeed, those poetic or literary qualities which stood as the validating centre for the new English (what Newbolt called the 'silent tongue' peculiarly available to the ear of the writer)[75] were never those of an out-and-out aestheticism. Many agreed with A. C. Bradley's claim, made in his presidential address of 1912, that while poetry was an end in itself and a source of pleasure, it was also a vehicle for morality.[76] So here was the ultimate source of value in literature as in society: moral authority. The force of this moral authority becomes clearer when discussions within the Association touching specifically upon the pedagogic uses of literature and indeed language are considered. Here the double emphasis upon the need to arrest cultural degeneration and to preserve the national heritage was overridingly in evidence.

For example, the critic and essayist John Bailey was a figure who linked the National Trust with the English Association in his concern equally for the heritage and literary values. Bailey was chairman of the Association from 1912 to 1915 and president in 1925–26. He was also a key figure in the National Trust and chairman of its executive committee between 1923 and 1931. At a meeting of the Association in 1913, Bailey was described by Caroline Spurgeon (the first woman to be appointed to a British university professorship in arts: she was a University of London Professor of English Literature at Bedford College from 1913; and a member of the Newbolt Committee) as 'a treasure keeper' in his role as 'a custodian of some of the greatest and most precious national possessions, England's places of historical interest and beauty'. Had it not been for him and his colleagues at the National Trust many old and historical buildings would have suffered. Now, as chairman of the English Association, 'he was but widening the sphere of his watchfulness'.[77] The care which Bailey lavished on his 'treasures' within the National Trust was at least equalled by his work as activist and propagandist for the 'eternal values' of poetry through the Association[78] and in the pages of the Newbolt Report where his contribution to the section on the universities was particularly notable. Much of what is included in Section VII, 'The Universities' could easily have come from works published under Bailey's name. There is the statement that 'the reading of English poetry' is 'generally recognized as a rational way of spending time . . . a way of educating, of drawing out, the best things in the imagination, the mind and the spirit of anyone, old or young'.[79] Great works of literature 'stand utterly above any history'; literature is 'an art' rather than science or speculation [philosophy], thus – unlike history or philosophy – great literature is 'never superseded'.[80] This should be compared with the claim in Bailey's 1926 English Association pamphlet that

> there is as much stability in aesthetic judgements as in ethical or political or philosophical or scientific; [and] the reputations of poets and artists are not less but more assured than those of biologists or statesmen or metaphysicians.[81]

He then asks how should one recognize authority and answers that 'degrees only prove knowledge; look among those who really love art and literature'. He goes on to conclude that

> the artist, if he really is an artist, possesses absolute value which he cannot lose: the man of science, once refuted or superseded, retains no absolute but only an historical importance.[82]

But the moral authority invested in English literature was not simply 'eternal', it was also resolutely national. Perhaps this was most concisely articulated in the course of the presidential address to the Association by Sidney Lee in 1918. Lee, a key figure not only within the Association since its foundation, but also with the *Dictionary of National Biography* from its earliest days, in referring to the aims of the English Association suggested 'that English be the constant, the unresting ally and companion of whatever other studies the call of national enlightenment and national efficiency may prescribe'.[83] One way in which some members of the Association hoped that English in education would help achieve such ends was by addressing itself to countering linguistic 'perversion'. S. K. Ratcliffe referred in 1909 to the need for the 'preservation, or restoration, of spoken English' under the present conditions of 'rapid degeneration'. He talked of the language going to pieces 'before our eyes', especially under the influence of the 'debased dialect of the Cockney . . . which is spreading from our schools and training-colleges all over the country. In ten years' time the English language will not be worth speaking'.[84] Mr Shawcross, chairman of the examination board of the N.U.T., offered a contribution to this discussion in much the same vein. He spoke of the 'revolutionary change' in the teaching of English in

elementary schools over the previous ten years. He went on (in the words
of the bulletin report) to give 'his experience of Manchester children under
the old system':

> they could parse accurately and analyse poetry, but they spoke the
> perverted Lancashire dialect of the towns, had a narrow vocabulary, and
> could not understand diction. . . . The conditions of the children's home
> life tended to nullify the efforts of the teacher to instil a little culture. . . . It
> was even possible to get children in the slum districts of a great city to
> love such a poem as Wordsworth's "Daffodils". He wished to put in a
> plea for the teaching of pure poetry in the primary school. Get a child to
> love a poem; every word and phrase in it need not be understood at first.
> The understanding would develop as the child grew older, and a clearer
> explanation could be given than was possible in earlier years.[85]

Arthur Acland, then president of the Association, had already stated in his
address to this meeting that in the promotion of 'effective use of the English
language' one of the best means was 'to foster a love of English literature'.[86]
Thus, English literature was seen by members of the Association as the most
effective vehicle for establishing through elementary education acceptable
standards of linguistic usage. The goal was to implant 'standard' English
forms (linguistic and cultural) by inculcating a 'love' of literature (the most
that might be hoped for in the elementary sector).[87] Within the higher
sectors (preparatory, secondary, grammar and public schools; and colleges
of various kinds) the aim was much broader. This involved, at the very least,
the nullification of any middle-class 'hatred' for learning, and its replacement
by a taste for the finer stuff of literature; and, even more ambitiously, a
'quickening' of the whole spiritual nature.[88] This strategy for inculcating a
general love of literature and for more explicit interventions into the flow of
subjective responses, experiences and pleasures, had a great deal in common
with the programme for a renewed Liberalism being developed at this time
by L. T. Hobhouse:

> The heart of Liberalism is the understanding that progress is not a
> matter of mechanical contrivance, but of the liberation of living spiritual
> energy. Good mechanism is that which provides the channels wherein
> such energy can flow unimpeded, unobstructed by its own exuberance of
> output, vivifying the social structure, expanding and ennobling the life of
> the mind.[89]

Returning to Acland's presidential address of 1909, it is notable that he
resumed exactly these themes, but now applied to English literature. In
promoting effective use of the English language, he claimed, one of the best
means was to foster a love of English literature which could be achieved by
removing all 'deadening and mechanical influences' thereby inducing 'a hope

that the movement [centered upon the English Association] would penetrate the homes of the future'. 'Unless the love of literature was developed in the home, little progress would be made', he concluded.[90]

This also introduces another aspect of the Association's cultural programme. It is best described as the attempt to propagate a sense of qualitative, as opposed to functional, literacy; a programme directed through the educational system but aimed, in the final analysis, at home life. As a speaker at the 1913 conference put it, the need was to promote 'that scholarly tone without which even the omnivorous reader might yet remain illiterate'.[91] Since the 'nation' to which the broader cultural mission of the Association was addressed was one of *homes,* the aim was not so much 'to make the nation feel the grandeur of English literature as such', as to make 'English literature a matter for education in English homes and schools'[92] (the words are Montagu Butler's in his presidential address of 1908; he was Master of Trinity College, Cambridge, and a former head of Harrow School).

If the prosecution of a sense of qualitative literacy within the homes of the nation was a fundamental strategy of the Association, in its more ambitious and sophisticated form this strategy aimed at bringing the raw subjectivity of the student or pupil into palpable contact with that very stuff of life considered to inhere within the 'sacred' text. This goal had important consequences for the role given, not only to critical and scholarly commentaries and other incrustations upon the essential text but also, to the teacher: 'In dealing with literature in any full sense, to efface oneself, to stand away, between the child and literature, is the highest and not the easiest of duties which the teacher can undertake'.[93] Walter Raleigh, Merton Professor of English Language and Literature at Oxford, also emphasized this negative role for all intermediaries between text and reader when he warned of the dangers of any 'immodesty' on the part of the teacher. Teachers of literature must avoid any attempt to become 'living representatives of all the mighty dead'. Instead they must facilitate the proper mode of encounter between reader and text, that of 'falling in love'.[94] The pleasures of experiencing that 'joyous thing'[95] that was literature were intended to elevate the student into an affective domain where a higher moral tone might be inculcated. As an ultimate, a more elevated sense of 'good form' or 'style' might be attained.[96] However, some statements by members of the Association reveal that the effacement required by this procedure was no more than a tactical ploy, since one of the dominant assumptions of moral education was 'that morality was to be made a conscious aim of the teacher, but concealed from the pupils, who were to imbibe the influence from literature as habit or experience'.[97]

The programme of the English Association, and of the emergent discipline of modern English, was faced, however, with serious dilemmas. For one thing the attempt to transfer a truly aristocratic sense of *je ne sais quoi,* or 'style', to the vernacular cultural form in the 'mechanical' context of a much-expanded system of formal education, continued to pose problems throughout the period. For another, the willing and living submission of the whole population to the seductions of literary culture was, in practice, subject to much resistance 'from below'. And, indeed, both these dilemmas are clearly registered in the Newbolt Report, and would provide grounds for a substantial assault on the programme from the 1930s.[98]

If the summation of the programme for the new English under the leadership of the English Association is to be found in the pages of the Newbolt Report, its publication stands also at the beginning of a process of transformation and revision within the Association itself. While the Report itself added little that was new to the strategies developed by the Association over the previous couple of decades, it systematized and concretized those strategies into a single developed statement and, in so doing, provided a discursive seal between the Board of Education as a formal state institution and the 'anti-institutional' English Association. Once this had been achieved, little was left for the Association to do. An increasingly professionalized, hierarchized and autonomous set of educational institutions offered little space for the continued influence of a class-based general mobilization like the English Association. In consequence, during the 1920s the Association lost its former unity of purpose and its mobilizing power within the governing and academic cultures. By the following decade it faced a financial crisis and had diverted its energies in two separate directions: it supported scholarship in English (rather than pedagogy), and – in divesting itself of its overt leadership of the mission of education renewal through English – concentrated on 'the popular diffusion of literary culture'.[99]

Conclusions

I have argued that the movement mobilized within and by the English Association drew its energy and force from the apparent capacity of 'English' as a novel cultural form to resolve a number of problems posed for the functioning of national institutions between 1880 and 1920. In one sense, there can be no doubt that total success was achieved, if this is measured in terms of the degree to which the new English came to be established as the core of the modern curriculum at almost all levels of the national education system from the 1920s; indeed, this is the sort of conclusion that most previous histories of English have encouraged. But since the object of the present cultural history is not simply to plot, from within, the development of an academic discipline, it is necessary to assess successes and failures from a different standpoint. The greatest success which flowed from the movement for the advancement of English in this period was in its effects within the professional classes, and the middle classes as a whole, where the new cultural and pedagogic form prepared the ground for, and subsequently helped to sustain, a renewal of modes of public communication (especially within broadcasting, journalism, the cinema and publicity). But as a mobilizing centre addressing the whole nation, the success of English was never other than partial. Nonetheless, in terms of public administration – of the building of administrative layers at sensitive points between the official state and the generalized public – the new English came to occupy a strategically important role. This was notable within the national education system where, from the 1920s, the ensemble of pedagogic practices and knowledges was reordered around a 'modern' curriculum centered upon English. This was in marked contrast to the situation in some other European countries where more formally theoretical disciplines came to be placed at the curricular core of the nation. In Britain, however, English has functioned to provide a substitute for any 'theory' of the national life in the form of an imponderable base from which the quality of the national life can be assessed. While it has never resolved longstanding tensions between discourses on 'culture', 'science', 'philanthropy' (later transmuted to 'welfare'), and 'national efficiency' (later, 'wealth creation'), it has provided a cultural domain apparently immune to the ravages caused by their continuing conflicts. The sense of 'Englishness' that English has come to signify was apparently so free of any narrow patriotism or overtly nationalist or imperialist politics that any debate about the meaning of the term itself seemed unnecessary until quite recently.

Notes

1 Arthur Marwick, *Britain in a Century of Total War* (Harmondsworth: Penguin, 1968), p. 20.

2 Hugh Kearney, 'Universities and Society in Historical Perspective', in *Present and Future in Higher Education*, eds. R. E. Bell and A. J. Youngson (London: Tavistock, 1973).

3 Michael Sanderson (ed.), *The Universities in the Nineteenth Century* (London: R.K.P., 1975), pp. 2 and 188–210; Sheldon Rothblatt, *The Revolution of the Dons* (London: Faber and Faber, 1968), p. 256.

4 Brian Simon, *Education and the Labour Movement, 1870–1920* (London: Lawrence and Wishart, 1965), p. 175.

5 Gareth Stedman Jones, *Outcast London* (Oxford: Clarendon P., 1971), p. 242.

6 Carol Dyhouse, 'Social Darwinism and the Development of Woman's Education in England, 1880–1920', *History of Education*, 5 (1976), 41–58.

7 Joan Burstyn, *Victorian Education and the Ideal of Womanhood* (London: Croom Helm, 1980), p. 95.

8 Miriam E. David, *The State, the Family and Education* (London: R.K.P., 1980), p. 137.

9 Charles Edwin Vaughan (1854–1922) studied at Balliol College, Oxford, 'when T. H. Green was proclaiming the national work of the universities'. (A. N. Shimmin, *The University of Leeds, the First Half Century* [Cambridge: University P., 1954], p. 123). He was, in fact, strongly influenced by Green

(who was his cousin), and by another friend, Arnold Toynbee, with whom he worked in the East End of London. Having been a teacher at Clifton College, Bristol, for 10 years, he moved to Cardiff in 1889 to take the chair of English Language, Literature and History (the title of his chair was changed to 'English Language and Literature' from 1894); then to the chair of English Language and Literature at Newcastle in 1899; and to the chair of English Literature at Leeds in 1904. He was a contributor to the *Cambridge History of English Literature,* and chairman of the Yorkshire Branch of the English Association in 1911. (See *Bulletin*, no.47 [London: English Association, June 1923], hereafter referred to as *Bulletin*.)

10 On the 'settlement movement' see K. S. Inglis, *Churches and the Working Classes in Victorian England* (London: R.K.P., 1963), ch. 4; on the 'secular mission' see Melvin Richter, *The Politics of Conscience: T. H. Green and his Age* (London: Weidenfeld and Nicholson, 1964), *passim*.

11 For an interesting comparative account of the relations between moral prestige, aesthetic emotion and cultural mystique in the respective modes of gentlemanly education of English and Chinese elites, see R. H. Wilkinson, 'The Gentleman Ideal and the Maintenance of a Political Elite', in *Sociology, History and Education*, ed. P. W. Musgrave (London: Methuen, 1970), pp. 126–47.

12 David Kynaston, *King Labour, the British Working Class 1850–1914* (London: Allen and Unwin, 1976), ch. 4.

13 Francis Mulhern, *The Moment of 'Scrutiny'* (London: New Left Books, 1979), pp. 11–14.

14 For an account of the relationship between social administration and the national way of life in the period, see Nicholas Rose, 'The psychological complex: mental measurement and social administration', *Ideology and Consciousness,* 5 (Spring 1979), 5–68. Jacques Donzelot, *The Policing of Families* (London: Hutchinson, 1979) provides a more general and structural model; see especially pp. 16–21 and 55–68.

15 R. W. Chambers, *The Teaching of English in the Universities of England* (London: English Association, July 1922), pamphlet no. 53.

16 Robert G. MacPherson, *The Theory of Education in Nineteenth Century England* (Athens, Georgia: U. of Georgia Press, 1959), p. 116.

17 J. Churton Collins, *The Study of English Literature* (London: Macmillan, 1891), p. 105.

18 *Bulletin,* no. 8, June 1909.

19 Arthur Quiller-Couch, *On the Art of Writing* (Cambridge: C.U.P., 1916), 1928 edn, pp. 139–40.

20 D. J. Palmer, *The Rise of English Studies* (Oxford: O.U.P., 1965); J. H. Newton, 'English in the University', unpublished thesis (University of Cambridge, 1963); Chris Baldick, *The Social Mission of English Criticism* (Oxford: Clarendon P., 1983).

21 Rothblatt, 1968, pp. 246–7 and *passim*.

22 John Sparrow, *Mark Pattison and the Idea of a University* (Cambridge: C.U.P., 1967), p. 131.

23 Sparrow, pp. 129, 146.

24 R. D. Altick, *The English Common Reader* (Chicago: Chicago U.P., 1957), p. 212.

25 For an analysis of the forms of signification mobilized by the Albert Memorial in Kensington, London, see Michael Eaton, 'Lie back and think of England', in *The Left and the Erotic*, ed. Eileen Phillips (London: Lawrence and Wishart, 1983), pp. 159–81.

26 Sheldon Rothblatt, *Tradition and Change in English Liberal Education* (London: Faber, 1976); Ben Knights, *The Idea of the Clerisy in the Nineteenth Century* (Cambridge: C.U.P., 1978); and MacPherson.

27 Sanderson, p. 22.

28 Shimmin, p. 15.

29 According to Henry Nettleship, by the late 1880s Oxford was being subjected to 'a well-founded national demand' for the introduction of English Language and Literature; see C. H. Firth, *The School of English Language and Literature* (Oxford: Blackwell, 1909), p. 29.

30 William W. Craik, *The Central Labour College, 1909–1929* (London: Lawrence and Wishart, 1964), *passim.*

31 Hobsbawm, p. 169; Brian Doyle, 'Some Uses of English', stencilled paper no. SP 64 (Birmingham: Centre for Contemporary Cultural Studies, University of Birmingham, 1981).

32 *Regulations for Secondary Schools, 1904,* extract in J. S. Maclure (ed.), *Educational Documents, England and Wales 1816–1967* (Oxford: O.U.P., 1968), p. 158.

33 *The Teaching of English in Secondary Schools,* Board of Education Circular 753 (London: H.M.S.O., 1910).

34 David Shayer, *The Teaching of English in Schools, 1900–1970* (London: R.K.P., 1970), p. 35.

35 Altick, p. 184.

36 Brian Doyle, 'The Hidden History of English Studies', in *ReReading English*, ed. Peter Widdowson (London: Methuen, 1981).

37 F. W. Moorman (Professor of English Language at Leeds) reported in *Bulletin* no. 22, February 1914.

37 C. H. Herford (Professor of English Literature at Manchester) reported in *Bulletin* no. 35, September 1918.

38 M. E. Sadler (Vice-Chancellor, University of Leeds) reported in *Bulletin* no. 18, November 1912.

40 *Bulletin,* no. 32, September 1917.

41 J. F. C. Harrison, *Learning and Living, 1790–1960* (London: R.K.P., 1961), p. 219.

42 Harrison, p. 226.

43 *The Teaching of English in England,* Board of Education (London: H.M.S.O., 1921), p. 259 (The Newbolt Report).

44 Richter, pp. 135, 360.

45 E. R. Norman, *Church and Society in England 1770–1970* (Oxford: Clarendon P., 1976), pp. 163–5.

46 Inglis, p. 156.

47 Gerrard Fiennes, quoted in Simon, p. 83.

48 Simon, pp. 82–3; Kynaston, pp. 88–9.

49 For a general account of this movement see G. R. Searle, *The Quest for National Efficiency, A Study in British Politics and British Political Thought, 1800–1914* (Oxford: Blackwell, 1971); see also Simon, p. 175.

50 Simon, pp. 79–80.

51 Ibid., p. 79.

52 Ibid., p. 170.

53 Ibid., p. 175.

54 Nowell Smith, *The Origin and History of the Association* (London: English Association, 1942), p. 5.

55 *Bulletin,* no. 3, February 1908.

56 *Bulletin,* no. 10, February 1910.

57 *Bulletin,* no. 11, June 1910.

58 *Bulletin,* no. 37, April 1919; and *Bulletin,* no. 38, September 1919.

59 *Bulletin,* no. 19, February 1913.

60 Smith, pp. 6–7.

61 W. J. Courthope's address to the A.G.M. of the Association, as reported in *Bulletin,* no.7, February 1909. He was author of the influential *History of English Poetry* (see Quiller-Couch). Compare Courthope's remarks with the claim made by Collins in 1891 that 'it is the privilege of Art and Letters to bring us into contact with aristocrats of our race' (Collins, p. 66). Courthope was one of the 'witnesses' called upon by Collins to support his case for the introduction of English Language and Literature at Oxford.

62 See the reports on H. Montagu Butler's speech in *Bulletin,* no. 3, January 1908, and W. Boyd's paper on 'The Mental Differences between the Primary and the Secondary Pupil, and their Bearings on the English Teacher's Work', *Bulletin,* no. 10, February 1910.

63 J. H. Fowler of Clifton College, Bristol, and a member of the original executive committee of the Association, moved the following motion at the Federal Conference of Education in London in 1907:

    'That this Conference urges the importance of the study of the English language and literature as an essential part of School Training on the grounds of practical utility, enlightened patriotism, and the human idea in education' (*Bulletin,* no. 1, July 1907).

64 *Bulletin,* no. 22, February 1914.

65 *Bulletin,* no. 1, July 1907.

66 J. W. Mackail, as reported in *Bulletin,* no. 3, January 1908.

67 F. W. Moorman, as reported in *Bulletin,* no. 22, February 1914.

68 *Bulletin,* no.7, February 1909; *Bulletin,* no. 8, June 1909.

69 *Bulletin,* no. 35, September 1918.

70 *Bulletin,* no. 36, January 1919.

71 *Bulletin,* no. 10, February 1910.

72 Ibid.

73 *Bulletin,* no. 4, May 1908; *Bulletin,* no. 22, February 1914.

74 John Bailey, *A Question of Taste* (London: English Association, 1926), pamphlet no. 65.

75 *Bulletin,* no. 19, February 1913.

76 *Bulletin,* no. 16, February 1912.

77 *Bulletin,* no. 19, February 1913; Bailey's contribution to the Newbolt Report is discussed by R. W. Chambers' pamphlet which also includes a rejoinder by Bailey.

78 *Bulletin,* no. 19, February 1913.

79 *The Teaching of English in England,* p. 198.

80 Ibid., pp. 205–6.

81 Bailey, p. 7.

82 Ibid., p. 19.

83 *Bulletin,* no. 35, September 1918.

84 *Bulletin,* no. 7, February 1909.

85 Ibid.

86 Ibid.

87 Ibid.

88 *Bulletin,* no. 19, February 1913; *Bulletin,* no. 22, February 1914.

89 L. T. Hobhouse, *Liberalism,* quoted by Searle, p. 256.

90 *Bulletin,* no. 7, February 1909.

91 *Bulletin,* no. 19, February 1913.

92 *Bulletin,* no. 3, February 1908.

93 J. W. Mackail, as reported in *Bulletin,* no. 3, February 1908.

94 *Bulletin,* no. 3, February 1908.

95 Ibid.

96 *Bulletin,* no. 6, November 1908; *Bulletin,* no. 8, June 1909.

97 A. M. Williams, Principal of Glasgow Training College, as reported in *Bulletin,* no. 10, February 1910.

98 *The Teaching of English in England,* pp. 252–9; Mulhern, p. 318.

99 Smith, pp. 10–11.

CHAPTER FIVE

A literature for England

Peter Brooker and
Peter Widdowson

If we lie back and think of England and Literature in the period prior to and during World War I, we are likely to name first certain poets as the nation's bedfellows: Kipling or Rupert Brooke, for example. These, after all, are the writers who openly propagandized for Empire, or who glorified war and are remembered still for doing so. Brooke's 'The Soldier' repeats the words 'England' and 'English' six times in its fourteen lines, and contains the phrases 'forever England' and 'an English heaven'. Before we consider what and whose England is being celebrated in such a poem, we might recall that the longer period 1880–1920 produced not only an art for Empire's sake and heroic war sonnets, but also an art for art's sake and a poetry of 'counter-attack', warning of the 'pity of war'; that, additionally, for some five years the anthologies of *Georgian Poetry* (which introduced Brooke and gained a popular audience for a poetry which James Reeves describes as 'markedly English and rural in character')[1] ran in tandem with a more tough-minded Imagist poetics, under the entrepreneurship of Ezra Pound; and that, finally, alongside developments in naturalism and a literature of topical social concern (as in Shaw, Wells, Galsworthy and Bennett) the post-Jamesian novel was turning to the formal experiment and innovation which issued from modernism.

Two general arguments are of assistance to us in examining the diversity of this literature and its expression of ideas of Englishness. First, Hugh Cunningham has suggested that the language and political thrust of a radical patriotism available in the late-eighteenth and early-nineteenth centuries had become etiolated and then, by the turn of the nineteenth century, appropriated by a ruling conservative bloc for its own ends: no longer the source of a critique of corrupt government and capitalist tyranny, patriotism could be appealed to in order to defend British Imperialism against internal divisiveness and foreign foes.[2] Second, Tom Nairn in *The Break-up of Britain* explains the peculiarities of English nationalism and the absence of radical populism in terms of the patrician character of the British state and the continued hegemony of the middle class, newly centered – with the decline of British industry at the turn of the nineteenth century – upon finance capital. Nairn describes nationalism as 'invariably populist':

> People are what it has to go on. . . . For kindred reasons, it had to function through highly rhetorical forms, through a sentimental culture sufficiently accessible to the lower strata now being called into battle. That is why a romantic culture quite remote from Enlightenment rationalism went hand-in-hand with the spread of nationalism. The new middle-class intelligentsia of nationalism had to invite the masses into history; and the invitation had to be written in a language they understood.[3]

The general question this brings us to ask is the extent to which literature was contained by, or resisted the boundaries of, a dominant loyalist patriotism and subservient Romantic culture. What we soon notice, however, is that distinctions have to be made, and were made in the period, between different forms of patriotism. The most salient of these is a distinction between forms of declamatory, cajoling and uplifting patriotism and a non-aggressive, sometimes non-militaristic, patriotism invested in ideas of the national character, its traditions, and a unifying love of country. The latter is adopted by Quiller-Couch in two essays entitled 'Patriotism in Literature'.[4] It is not, says 'Q', the English habit to fling the loud-mouthed patriotism of 'Rule Britannia' back at Germany's 'Deutschland liber Alles'. Contemporary English patriotism resides rather in the 'cheerful irony of the English private soldier' (294) and draws upon the spirit of 'Merry England' sustained in poetry, folk and popular song from Chaucer onwards (304). For the source of this true patriotism an Englishman looks to a 'green nook of his youth in Yorkshire or Derbyshire, Shropshire or Kent or Devon; where the folk are slow, but there is seed-time and harvest' (301). He ends his first essay: 'other nations extend, or would extend, their patriotism over large spaces superficially: ours . . . ever cuts down through the strata for its well-springs, intensifies itself upon that which, untranslatable to the foreigner, is comprised for us in a single easy word – Home' (306). As we shall show, this sentimental love of the mother-country, particularly when traced to recollections of youth and perceptions of rural England, proves central to expressions of Englishness in the literature of the period.

Nairn's remarks present us, however, with an additional question: if Romantic culture in the early-nineteenth century had been quite consistent with a populist patriotism opposed to tyrannous government, why could that culture later take root in right-wing nationalism? In what ways and with what implication had the idioms and inflections of English Romanticism, and not only of patriotism, undergone a mutation in being handed over as a tradition, say, from Wordsworth to William Watson, Walter de la Mare and Wilfred Owen? Two main themes throw some light on the contemporary aspect of this process. The first we associate with the influence of English forms of aestheticism upon the character and tone of the 'Romantic culture' of the period. What this reveals is that literature and literary culture did not simply undergo a change in itself, but, in this phase, facilitated the appropriation of an erstwhile oppositional patriotism. The second theme concerns the literary construction of a myth of England, invested in ideas of the ownership of the land and the heritage of rural England, and is seen most clearly in contemporary nature poetry and 'country-house' fiction. We deal with these themes in four related sections. The first offers a brief account of the making of an emphatically 'English' literary tradition. The second traces the inflections of Romanticism in the poetry of the period, its relations to the forms of patriotism outlined earlier and, in particular, its complicity in the formation of a myth of rural England. We see then in the third section what forms this myth takes in the contemporary concern with the 'condition of England', and in some country-house fiction. Finally we turn to a discussion of the relative strengths of a more critical and dissident literature, emerging from within socialism, feminism and modernism.

Forging the English literary tradition

Of central importance in maintaining, in Tom Nairn's terms, 'the rhetorical forms' and 'sentimental culture' necessary to patriotic nationalism was the shaping of a version of the past by way of a constructed English literary tradition. Probably the most revealing feature of the combined aesthetic, moral and ideological bearings of this tradition in any period is the place and status it accords to Shakespeare. Before and during the Great War, Shakespeare attracted a wealth of impressionistic, biographical, historico-textual criticism, as well as much 'Germanic' scholarship – though this last mode was revealingly ousted both by the war and the establishment of English as an independent university subject. These approaches to Shakespeare, whatever their differences, shared the assumption that his life and work were worthy of all manner of study. Accompanying the typical claim that Shakespeare's impartial genius mirrored as it maximized a distinctly English mentality (his plays, wrote John Masefield in 1911, were 'the greatest thing ever made by the English mind'),[5] was the no less common magnification of his work from the status of national treasure to a set of universal truths, expressing what Masefield called the 'true empire' within man's soul. In addition, this equation of poetry, nation, and spiritual Empire could be seen as rooted in the geographical and linguistic heart of pastoral England. A. J. Furnival and John Munro wrote in *Shakespeare. Life and Work* (1908): 'Near the centre, the heart of England, in one of those Midland shires that gave Britain its standard speech, was the most famous user of that speech, William Shakespeare, the World's greatest poet, born.'[6]

In a more militant vein, Sidney Lee in 1901 had discovered a 'natural instinct of patriotism' in Shakespeare, and Sir M. W. MacCallum in 1910 had recommended the History plays as the 'consummate flower' of 'patriotic enthusiasm'.[7] George Saintsbury saw *Henry V* as cause for rejoicing in 'the triumph of Henry of England'; Stopford Brooke, the same play as an unrestrained paean to 'the honour and greatness of England'; and Sidney Lee, as evincing Shakespeare's choice of 'the fittest representative of the best distinctive type of English character'.[8] In the war years themselves, Shakespeare was more directly recruited to the national cause. J. A. R. Marriott, for example, writing as an Oxford MP and historian in 1916, detected 'a political message' in Shakespeare's chronicle plays, 'the present significance of which cannot, at this moment in our history, be over-emphasised'[9]: the need for 'national unity' which was 'to Shakespeare the one supreme condition of national greatness' (5).

The different emphases emerging in such criticism can be seen in essays by Sir Walter Raleigh (Merton Professor of English at Oxford from 1904) and Sir Arthur Quiller-Couch (King Edward VII Professor of English at Cambridge from 1912). Raleigh's more belligerently chauvinistic reading appeared in two essays in 1916 and 1918. In the first, he claims that half an Englishman's national pride derives 'from his fellowship with Drake, Sidney, Bacon and Raleigh, Spenser and Shakespeare'.[10] Their example had been a source of political unity in the past, and could be now, once again, when England was standing 'against the bloodthirsty vanity of that meaner and poorer tyranny which threatens us today ... the poets are still ahead of us, pointing the way' (44). Shakespeare, who 'speaks for the English race' and 'the creed of England', represents the English practice of tolerance towards Europe and 'the English love of compromise', standing against 'foreign cruelty, pedantry and dogmatic intellectualism' (44–5). In his second essay, Raleigh sets humanity, tolerance and nobility above nation and institution, but in effect offers English (and Shakespearian) virtues as a more direct vindication of English military victory. Thus, 'the wit of our trenches, especially perhaps among the Cockney and South Country regiments, is pure Shakespeare', and in scenes from *The Tempest* we see how the Germans failed to impress the 'incurably humorous' British private.[11] Raleigh, however, appears to move closer in this essay to Quiller-Couch's position, perhaps because at this point an English victory was assured. 'Q' himself, in *Shakespeare's Workmanship,* also published in 1918, openly rejects Imperialism which would 'drag in' God and literature to justify a war against a weaker nation.[12] He admits that the object of *Henry V,* for example, was to present Henry as 'our patriotic darling', but prefers to side with the divinity of poetry under whose ministrations Falstaff, because wronged, became '*ipso facto*, the better man'. In Falstaff he finds the 'jollity of common-folk', something 'as English as Chaucer. . . . In all the great sweep of the plays there is nothing so racy, so English' (158).

Quiller-Couch prefers 'racy' Englishness to Walter Raleigh's pride in the English race. Beyond this, the differences between them were as much between individuals ('Q' the 'fine old English gentleman', Liberal party activist and Liberal Party University appointee; Raleigh the author of the fin-de-siècle *Style* and sometime associate of W. E. Henley), as they were between Cambridge and Oxford English. Ideologically 'Q' is the more subtle, but both men and tendencies were united in their affirmations of Englishness and in 'dragging in' literature by way of its agreed national poet so as to confirm national pride, tradition and character. As members of a liberal-conservative intelligentsia, deliberately employing an informal, conversational discourse, they joined in laying the foundation-stone of an English tradition from which could rise the architecture of a common English syllabus in 'life, literature and thought'.

As a corollary to the construction of a national literature with Shakespeare at its centre, we may note that in the period 1900–14 Thomas Hardy, the 'poet' of Wessex, was emphatically shaped into the English rural annalist *par excellence*. A number of surveyors of his fiction appeared at this time, in most cases constructing a 'Hardy' in terms of the five or so novels (*Tess* and *Jude,* full of 'faults' and 'flaws', remain problematic) confirmed by his own categorization in the Preface to the 'Wessex Edition' of 1912 as 'Novels of Character and Environment'. Other, more recalcitrant, novels are excised from the *oeuvre* in favour of those 'characteristic' works which reveal Hardy's mastery of 'the true romance of country life'.[13] In this reading Hardy is seen as belonging 'by birth and temperament to the soil of England'[14] and his 'peasant characters' as confirming 'that life on the English soil has not changed essentially since Shakespeare'.[15]

The poetry anthologies of the period, too, act as revealing barometers of the contemporary taste and judgement which worked to forge the English literary tradition. After Palgrave's *Golden Treasury,* the most influential anthology was undoubtedly Quiller-Couch's *Oxford Book of English Verse* (which went through 17 reprints from 1900 to 1930). Writing of the 'not merely literate but vigorously literary' culture created by 1914, Paul Fussell suggests in *The Great War and Modern Memory* that 'there were few of any rank who had not been assured that the greatest of modern literatures was the English and who did not feel an appropriate pleasure in that assurance'.[16] The *Oxford Book* as a major supplier of such assurance negotiated seven centuries of English poetry, from which 'Q' chose the 'best', convinced that 'the best is the best', and delivered them up in a size to fit a knapsack and the mental equipment of officers and men alike. The *Oxford Book,* Fussell argues, 'presides over the Great War'[17] as a provider of common literary knowledge, ready allusion in trench verse and letters home, but most importantly as supplying a mode of perception on the conflict. In these different functions the *Oxford Book* was joined by the nine anthologies to which 'Q' himself acknowledged a debt, from *Lyrics from the Elizabethan Song Books* to Churton Collins' *Treasury of Minor British Poetry*. With the advent of war were added such pocket collections of verse and prose homilies as *Keep the Flag Flying* and *Be of Good Cheer, The 'Country Life' Anthology of Verse* (1915) – 'poems of today for the lads who have gone to war' from Henley, Newbolt, Binyon, Bridges and the Georgians – and the selection by Bridges, dedicated to the King, of French and English pastoral: *The Spirit of Man (1916)*. We turn from war, states Bridges in his preface, and 'look instinctively to seers and poets', rejoicing that 'our country is called of God to stand for the truth of man's hope'.

One example of the ideological direction such publications could take was the anthology *Poems of Today* (first issued in August 1915 and reprinted 14 times by the end of 1918). Published by the English Association, so influential in structuring attitudes and practices in English education, this anthology was intended explicitly for use in schools. Among its 147 poems it contained Newbolt's 'Drake's Drum', Bridges' 'I love all beauteous things', Masefield's 'Beauty', Kipling's 'Sussex', Brooke's 'The Old Vicarage, Grantchester' and Yeats's 'The Lake Isle of Innisfree' (there was no Thomas Hardy and no poems by Imagists). The selections were divided into three groups: the first is glossed as being 'of History, of the romantic tale of the world, of our own special tradition here in England, and of the inheritance of obligation which that tradition imposes upon us'; the second as being 'of England again and the longing of the exile for home, of this and that familiar countryside, of woodland and meadow and garden, of the process of the seasons . . .'; third, these themes mingle 'to the music of Pan's flute and of love's viol, and the bugle call of Endeavour and the passing bell of Death' (viii). Here a sentimental literary culture is inextricably bound up with ideas of English virtue and obligation, rural nostalgia, and the nation's heroic past.

The notes of 'Pan's flute', 'love's viol', 'the bugle-call of Endeavour and the passing bell of Death', sound regularly through the other anthologies mentioned, and then resound, all of them, in the representative Georgian, Rupert Brooke. Brooke, says Fussell, was 'full of literature',[18] but we might just as well say that the literature of the war years and after was full of him. As well as appearing in the first two Georgian anthologies (which sold respectively 15,000 and 19,000 copies), Brooke was included in Bridges' *The Spirit of Man, Poems of Today,* and, in due course, in *The Oxford Book of English Verse.* Brooke's first volume, *Poems* (1911), was reprinted in 1913 and then six times in 1915 and four more times by August 1916. By 1932 it had sold 100,000 copies. A second selection, titled *1914 and Other Poems,* went through fourteen impressions between May 1915 and September 1916. A collected edition, with Edward Marsh's memoir, appeared in 1918 and went through sixteen impressions in the next 10 years. There can be little doubt, then, about Brooke's contemporary reputation and popularity, or, as the period had it, his 'legend'. Brooke was an exemplary product of Edwardian culture. As the 'golden-haired', Rugby and Cambridge-educated poet-athlete and poet-soldier, he combined the ruling-class values with which Britain entered the war, giving expression to both the sense of pastoral England as 'Home' and the readiness for self-sacrifice in the service of a nation at war. As Winston Churchill commented immediately after Brooke's death:

> [the war sonnets] are a whole history and revelation of Rupert Brooke himself. Joyous, versatile, deeply instructed, with classic symmetry of mind and body, he was all that one would wish England's noblest sons to be in days when no sacrifice but the most precious is acceptable, and the most precious is that which is most freely proffered.[19]

From a different perspective, S. P. B. Mais in an early essay on Brooke argues that he is John Donne reincarnated, but has matured beyond a 'cruelly cynical stage' into a 'beauty' which 'becomes deeper and more mellow with advancing years'.[20] Of Brooke's 'The Old Vicarage, Grantchester' Mais writes, 'Here is the seeing eye, the inevitable word, the god speaking through the lips of a man; it is magic gossamer-like, almost unbelievably beautiful' (275). Churchill, the liberal politician, prefers Brooke's mobilizing war sonnets; Mais, the liberal reviewer and educationalist, prefers his 'love of country' and 'beauty'. Brooke was the poet for both of them, since in him the two main types of verse, as the two forms of patriotism, co-existed.

The movement from Grantchester to death in 'a foreign field' and the preference in Shakespeare criticism for Falstaff or Henry V suggest the different tones given to celebrations of Englishness, national character and purpose in the vocabulary of liberal, conservative ideology. Those abashed at aggressive Imperialism may have felt more comfortable with a contemplative Englishness and the 'true empire' within; but as forms of nationalistic patriotism these positions and tones were not incompatible, as popular anthologies, poets and poems show. The militaristic beast, in fact, would have had difficulty existing without the aesthetic beauty, just as the kitbag would have sagged without the body of literary tradition to stiffen it.

Romantic culture and patriotism

The last two decades of the nineteenth century saw the appearance of overlapping tendencies in aestheticism, decadence and symbolism, especially in poetry. Roughly characterized, the term *aestheticism* and the related phrase 'art for art's sake' summarized an exclusive devotion to what Oscar Wilde called the 'principle of beauty only'; the term *decadence* referred to a fetishistic cultivation of the erotic and morbid and *symbolism* to a belief in the mystical and sometimes occult power of the symbolic imagination to gain access to an underlying, but superior, reality.

What all three tendencies shared was a provocative rejection of middle-class Victorian values and a belief in artistic autonomy, giving renewed pre-eminence, in a tradition of Romanticism, to the isolated individual poet and to the divinations of a refined poetic sensibility. Arthur Symons had discussed the new poetry in 1893 as a 'poetry of sensation, of evocation', its ideal being 'to fix the last fine shade, the quintessence of things; to fix it fleetingly; to be a disembodied voice, and yet the voice of a human soul'.[21] This soul, long starved, was now to receive sustenance: 'and with it comes the literature . . . in which the visible world is no longer a reality, and the unseen world no longer a dream' (83). In symbolist literature, he writes, there was to be a new spirituality which sets its face 'against exteriority, against rhetoric, against a materialistic tradition'. From this revolt, literature would gain new liberty, but also take upon itself the heavy burden of religion: 'it becomes itself a king of religion, with all the duties and responsibilities of sacred ritual' (84).

The vocabulary of such statements (sensation, shade, soul, dream, ritual, imagination, mood) reveals symbolism's particular antipathy to the many tendencies which made 'the external world . . . the standard of reality'.[22] This critique is at its strongest in Yeats's complaint against 'newspaper government' and the 'scientific movement'; against a loss of 'unity of being and of culture'. In opposition to the degenerate 'formulas and generalisations' and massed vulgarity of the age, Yeats set the coming of the 'new sacred book' of the arts, and the meditative poet's power to be 'continually making and unmaking mankind', thus re-invoking, after the failure of the Victorians, the high authority of the Romantic artist as exiled seer and second-maker under God.[23]

What is of interest is the way in which this combative discourse could be appropriated to reinforce consensual notions of the unity of poetry, the national character and imperial destiny. The explanation for this lies in the curtailed, if oppositional, logic of the aestheticist position; in an inherent limitation, that is to say, which can be traced to its main English source in Walter Pater. Pater and Symons, unlike Yeats, have been thought of as reacting to 'exteriority' with a mildly approving or passive aestheticism.[24] In the end this may be the case, but Pater's austere, amoral aestheticism can be seen, as John Goode has argued,[25] as a decisive quarrel, or 'break', with Romantic theories of organic unity. If Goode's reading of Pater identifies the most progressive potential that could be claimed for it, aestheticism nevertheless yielded, exactly on account of its assertions of artistic autonomy, to the seduction of wholeness, purpose, connection and coherence which ideology offers. The sensations, moods, dreams and myths, the 'fleeting moments' and 'incommunicable ecstasy' of symbolist doctrine, could be enlarged and stabilized in the language of received 'poetical' verse and appreciative criticism it had helped put into circulation.[26] It is true that these artistic movements did not necessarily entail incorporation into 'totalities' of Englishness, as the examples of Yeats and the early T. S. Eliot would show, but clearly neither of these poets developed 'the possibilities of proletarian art' (115) which

Goode sees as potential in Pater's anti-organicist theory. In fact, of course, they reveal the reverse tendency towards aristocratic and conservative ideas of artistic and social order, proving the persistence of ideas of organic form and the persuasiveness of reactionary ideologies. And this is true too of other symbolist inheritors. Symbolism, for all its subversiveness, became, in Goode's phrase, 'a Romantic continuity' (126). For writers such as Henley, Gray, Davidson and Symons, whose best work 'stands opposed, as forms of production, to the hegemony . . . there is an expressive totality – Imperialism, Catholicism, vitalism, mysticism – in which to take refuge' (125).

A revealing example of a writer who took such refuge was W. E. Henley. His imperialist war-cries would seem to be in direct conflict with the tenor of aestheticism, and indeed this was Henley's own understanding in his criticism and later poetry, where in the 'Epilogue' to *For England's Sake* (1900), for example, he sets the regenerative, war-like 'Red Angel, the Awakener' against 'The White Angel' of peace which is responsible for 'a rich deliquium of decay'.[27] The running battle between Henley's Tory *Scots Observer* (subtitled *An Imperial Review*) and Oscar Wilde appears also to be entirely consistent with this. But beneath the bitterness of this exchange – evident particularly in Charles Whibley's vicious review of *The Picture of Dorian Gray* – there was a personal animus, certainly on Henley's part, which suggested something other than an artistic, or even political, antagonism. Wilde was a successful literary rival who provoked Henley's jealousy, but perhaps more than anything he appeared as the decadent doppelgänger to Henley's virile pose as the 'Viking Chief'.[28] Certainly when viewing aestheticism in someone other than Wilde, the *Scots Observer* (renamed the *National Observer* in 1890) could respond more temperately. In the second of two articles on Pater, for example, his doctrine of intense sensation, artistic ecstasy and the pursuit of perfection in life, literature and style was favourably received.[29] Henley's own poetry, moreover, exhibited a pronounced ambiguity. If his work is known now it is likely to be for the masculine resilience of 'Invictus' ('My heart is bloody, but unbowed. . . . I am the master of my fate;/I am the captain of my soul') or for the swashbuckling effusions of *For England's Sake*. But Henley's much earlier *Bric-a-Brac* (1888) had shown him whistling 'the tune of the time' in a set of crafted ballades, rondeaux and villanelles. The concern here with formal contrivance, and in *London Voluntaries* (1893) with musical composition and Turneresque atmosphere, won the admiration of the Rhymers' Club, and from Wilde the remark that the assembled poems of *A Book of Verses* (1888) showed 'a very refreshing bit of affectation'.[30] In this earlier verse Henley had learned from French examples what he termed 'artistic good breeding', 'rhetorical elegance . . . verbal force and glow . . . rhythmic beauty and propriety'.[31] This apprenticeship in style 'grammared' him for the continuing aestheticism of his later verse (*Echoes, Rhymes and Rhythms, Hawthorn and Lavender*), whose cultivation of 'good breeding' was far from incompatible with his political view. 'Toryism', said Henley, as I conceive it, is as much a matter of taste as a body of doctrine, and as much a mental attitude as a set of principles. . . . Toryism, to be plain, is in some sort a matter of aversions – one aversion is for that conspiracy of bad public breeding and individual prurience which "one may call popular culture."[32]

In spite, then, of his apparent enmity towards aestheticism, Henley shared with it a frenetic desire for intensity, an anti-philistinism, and a belief in artistic autonomy ('the interest of art is absolutely incompatible with the sentiment of patriotism'[33] – a statement which *For England's Sake* alone would contradict at every turn). He held consistently to a determined individualism, and to a belief in the 'unconquerable soul' (of the poem 'Invictus'), whether this was the soul of poetic creativity (with which the aesthetes would be unlikely to disagree), or the soul of England. To set the chivalric elegy of the earlier 'Ballade of Dead Actors' beside the imperial rhapsody of 'Pro Rege Nostro' is to see the deeply Romantic inflection informing both an art for art's and art for England's sake:

> Where are the braveries, fresh or frayed?
> The plumes, the armours – friend and foe?
> The cloth of gold, the rare brocade,
> The mantles glittering to and fro?
> The pomp, the pride, the royal show?
> The cries of war and festival?
> The youth, the grace, the charm, the glow?
> Into the night go one and all
> . . . .
> Where shall the watchful Sun,
>   England, my England,
> Match the master-work you've done,
>   England, my own?
> When shall he rejoice agen
> Such a breed of mighty men
> As come forward, one to ten
>   To the Song on your bugles blown
>   England –
>   Down the years on your bugles blown.[34]

Henley's circle of 'Young Men', gathered around the *Scots Observer* and *National Observer*, included Kipling and Yeats (the *National Observer* published both *Barrack Room Ballads* and 'The Lake Isle of Innisfree') and the minor figures Charles Whibley and George Wyndham. Wyndham is of symptomatic interest here. He was an upper-middle-class landowner who emerged from Eton, Sandhurst and the Coldstream Guards to become Under-Secretary of War at the outbreak of the Boer War and Chief Secretary for Ireland in 1900. He contributed to the *National Observer* from 1890, and under Henley's guiding influence edited North's *Plutarch,* Shakespeare's poems and a series of essays on Romantic literature. T. S. Eliot described Wyndham as 'a romantic aristocrat', a man who 'stands for a type, an English type' and more than this, for 'a period and a tradition'.[35] His Romanticism Eliot characterizes as curiosity and enthusiasm, employed 'not to penetrate the real world but to complete the varied features of the world he made for himself' (31–2). The remarkable feature of Wyndham's type was his unity, 'the fact that his literature and his politics and his country life are one and the same thing', and this unity Eliot perceives as a fabricated, fairyland myth generated by and for the individual and type in whom 'Romanticism is incorporate in Imperialism' (32). Wyndham stands then as a typical example of a contrived, ideological coherence thrown over the worlds of politics and letters, which in the forms of Imperialism, *belletrist* appreciation and amateur scholarship is made compatible with an equally fictive England of country houses and riding to hounds. Beyond the double persona of Henley, Wyndham, his pupil, represents an expressive totality of art and ideology – a totality which pure aestheticism eschewed but which, in its continuities with Romanticism and its diluted progeny, it facilitated rather than challenged.

What such examples reveal is not that aestheticism was responsible for imperialist verse, but that its self-conscious removal of art from a common public, its abortive antagonism to 'externalities' and its language of mood, dream and sensation were open to appropriation and completion in the service of received attitudes. Form, we might say, will find a content; and poetry, since it cannot (Verlaine and Pater notwithstanding) assume the non-referential purity of music, will tend towards the 'impurities' of statement, attitude and ideology.

English fields and flowers of verse

At least three overlapping generations of poets can be identified as writing in a distinctly English tradition and as offering an image of Englishness for a wide middle- to lower-class reading public in the years before World War I. The first comprised such poets as Alfred Austin, Henry Newbolt, William Watson and Alfred Noyes, who are commonly thought of, in their own terms, as administering a death-blow to an already defunct 'art for art's sake'; the second included such popular Edwardian luminaries as Robert Bridges, A. E. Housman and Walter de la Mare; and the third, the emerging and nebulously grouped Georgian poets who have been seen in their turn as presenting a liberal revolt to Tory didacticism. It would be foolish to ignore the shifts in literary history which these groups represent, or to ignore differences between individual poets. The argument, however, is at the level of literary ideology and, as such, is a matter of continuities in English Romanticism which seeped (via Tennyson, Swinburne and Meredith particularly) through at least two decades of poetry. As an instance of this,

Ernest de Selincourt, in the firm belief that poetry is 'the highest form of literature', could refer without hesitation, as late as 1915, to the authority of Wordsworth's 1801 Preface for his definition of the poet: 'a man speaking to men: a man, it is true, endowed with more lively sensibility, more enthusiasm and tenderness ... than are supposed to be common among mankind'.[36] Ezra Pound, surveying the results in English poetry of the period, felt that it was far from being *echt* Wordsworth or *echt* anything: 'The common verse in Britain from 1890 was a horrible agglomerate compost, not minted, most of it not even baked, all legato, a doughy mess of third-hand Keats, Wordsworth, heaven knows what, fourth-hand Elizabethan sonority blunted, half-melted, lumpy.'[37] Pound's condemnation was that of a self-publicizing, expatriate imagist, uncomfortable in English literary culture, but his sense of the ill-digested influences and derivative reflexes prompting English poetry is an accurate one. Romanticism in these decades assumed, in Imperialist verse, the forms of a degenerate heroic individualism, a patronizing affectation of the language of men; or, in other directions, a cultivated anti-philistinism, tepid affirmations of aesthetic autonomy or plaintive rural nostalgia, moderation in all things and flowers in all poems. The bardic declamations or pained registering of fugitive impressions, the standard poeticisms and lulling melodious reveries, the use generally in the period of the forms of chant, ballad, shanty, hymn, folk-tale and dream, all these once again contributed to the 'highly rhetorical forms' and 'language they understood' which Nairn sees as aspects of the sentimental culture conducive to nationalism.

This diminished Romanticism, having all the force of an orthodox taste rather than a consciously constructed tradition, was only challenged by the later war-poetry of Owen and Rosenberg and the anti-romantic polemics of T. E. Hulme, Pound and Eliot ('romanticism is a spilt religion', Hulme had said; '"emotion recollected in tranquility" is an inexact formula', Eliot added). But even then its influence was far from overturned. Earlier departures in the direction of what can be called the 'realistic' effects of unadorned observation, free verse, urban subjects, rough ingenuousness and abrasive narrative as in the early poetry of Henley, in John Davidson, W. H. Davies and John Masefield, were incidental and shallow channels off an already narrowed mainstream. Or, more to the point, they were seen as incidental. S. P. B. Mais, for example, wrote how Masefield's 'real genius' lies not in his narrative poems where he was led 'to prostitute his talents', but in the short lyrics of his *Poems and Ballads*.[38] Here Mais finds 'true magic' and 'music of a more poignant and haunting fragrance' (254). An example of this more 'real' poetry is Masefield's 'Beauty' (chosen also by Quiller-Couch for the *Oxford Book of Victorian Verse*) which begins:

I have seen the dawn and sunset on moors and windy hills
    Coming in solemn beauty like slow old times of Spain:
I have seen the lady April bringing the daffodils
    Bringing the springing grass and the soft warm April rain.

Such a poem suits Mais's definition of true poetry: 'the retelling of great events remembered in passivity, heightened by language that could be uttered in no other way, musical, magic from the soul' (256). The source again is Wordsworth, but, revealingly, a Wordsworth filtered through aestheticism. What is of interest, here and generally for the period, is the process of naturalization by which a debased Romanticism was affirmed as received wisdom, with the many assimilations and editings of alternatives this involved. What follows is a sketch of this process.

Writing in defence of himself and other Tory poets who helped establish in the Edwardian period what Ford Madox Ford termed 'the physical force school', Henry Newbolt, with one eye still on the Aesthetes, wrote with staggering assurance of the identity of interests uniting poets and their readers:

> life is their object, and art is not their life. . . . If then they come to the artist it is for something that will help them to the fuller life, and they demand of him not merely that he shall excel in expression but that he shall excellently express feelings such as they can understand and value. They demand that he shall chant to them, for example, their own morality, their own religion, their own patriotism.[39]

Newbolt's final remarks reveal all too clearly what the opening word 'life' means. On the basis of such an unbroken contract poets could indeed be populist and the bards of commonsense. Similarly, the *Quarterly Review* praised Alfred Austin as 'a concrete individual Englishman' whose unoriginal philosophy of life made for a merited 'poetry of commonsense and healthy directness'.[40] Again, Alfred Noyes, calling for a poetry which would co-ordinate 'the whole world of ideas', described the artist as one 'to whom the method of expression has become so natural that he thinks no more about it'.[41]

The poet, the reader, commonsense, philosophy, poetic expression and national interest are perceived and presented as one, in a naturalized harmony which had no difficulty in incorporating an aestheticist blueprint such as Noyes's poem 'Art'. Behind such an apparently seamless whole there stands the very particular and uncommon interests of finance capital and ruling-class power, but between such power and common attitudes there flowed the indispensable pacifying liquid of received assumptions. As regards the judgement of poetry these assumptions were regulated by the leading criterion of 'beauty'.[42] This is an aestheticist premise which threads through the prose of Pater, Wilde, Symons and Yeats. But if for the aesthetes beauty was a matter of both ecstatic sensation and self-conscious formal artifice, and for Yeats the defiant 'end and law of poetry', it becomes in Edwardian and Georgian poetry a naturalized, uninspected and vaguely uplifting convention.

This is exactly demonstrated in a review of Watson, Noyes and Newbolt. They are seen as exemplifying a poetic tradition, now old and undemanding but still to be judged by 'beauty in expression' and the affinity of poetry with music:

> Neither of them insists on any new formula for the definition of poetry. The compass of the old instrument is, in their view, still wide enough to contain modern music. They aim at a quality of beauty in expression which demands no violent re-adjustment of sympathy or taste on the part of the reader.[43]

But the criterion of beauty was by no means only applied to the patriotic Edwardians. It was the high aim also of such poets as Bridges, Sturge Moore, Laurence Binyon and de la Mare.[44] The artist or poet, said Bridges, 'is the man possessed by the idea of beauty', and such an idea, in which beauty was close cousin to the 'the agreeable', corresponded, says David Perkins, 'to the usual idea of poetry among educated people'.[45] Bridges' modest experiments in versification influenced de la Mare, and both in turn influenced the Georgians. But behind them stand the occluded, but more vigorous explorations in 'sprung rhythm', 'inscape' and 'instress' of Gerard Manley Hopkins, and behind Hopkins, the influence, once again, of Pater at Oxford. Bridges withheld and then severely edited Hopkins' poems for publication in 1918, thus accommodating Hopkins' work to a prevailing orthodoxy in the same gesture that he helped orchestrate it. This self-protective editorializing retarded the potential of a dynamic nature poetry, but muffled also a critique of industrialization (Hopkins' 'And all is seared with trade, bleared, smeared with toil'), as well as an intimation of deeper movements in English society. In 1871 Hopkins had written to Bridges:

> I am afraid some great revolution is not far off. Horrible to say, in a manner I am a Communist. . . . But is it not a dreadful thing for the greatest and most necessary part of a very rich nation to live a hard life without dignity, knowledge, comforts, delight or hopes in the midst of plenty – which plenty they make. They profess that they do not care what they wreck and burn, the old civilisation and order must be destroyed. This is a dreadful look out but what has the old civilisation done for them? As it at present stands in England it is itself in great measure founded on wrecking . . . the more I look the more black and deservedly black the future looks.[46]

Hopkins' letters to Bridges, including the explanatory note to the related 'Tom's Garland', were not published until 1935. In the interim, the Edwardian poetry-reading public could be wooed by Bridges' cadenced indeterminacies into accepting an undivided, unchanging England characterized by the critic de Sola Pinto as 'a world of gentle English landscapes, clear streams, downlands, gardens and birdsong haunted by memories of the classics, of music and poetry and decorous Victorian love-making'.[47] From this picturesque indolence it was a step only through de la Mare's Romantic innocence-without-experience to the 'quality of pleasantness' which T. S. Eliot coolly unpicked as the common thread in the Georgian knot.[48]

'Georgianism', said Robert Graves and Laura Riding,

> was an English dead movement . . . politically affiliated with the then dominant Liberal party. . . . Georgian poetry was to be English but not aggressively imperialistic; pantheistic rather than atheistic; and as simple as a child's reading book. These recommendations resulted in a poetry which could be praised rather for what it was not than for what it was. Eventually Georgianism became principally concerned with Nature and love and leisure and old age and childhood and animals and sleep and similar uncontroversial subjects.[49]

Literary history and criticism have since reproduced this uncertain identity, setting Georgianism at some point between 'what it was not' and the stereotypical versifying it was or became.[50] The debate extends to the criteria for membership (were Graves, de la Mare, Lawrence, Owen, Thomas, members?) and to its inheritance (conscious or otherwise) of a specifically English tradition (itself vital or stale, parochial or cosmopolitan) developing from Cowper and Clare to Wordsworth and Hardy. The question, however, is not what Georgianism or the English poetic traditions were or were not, in definitive terms, but their meanings as processes.

Again, to examine the contemporary readings of Hardy is to see something of this, to discover indeed (as in the case of Hopkins) how the tradition is smoothed and rubbed down as it is handed over. Thus Hardy the poet could emerge as a consolation and stay, only if his prosy awkwardness in diction and syntax, his 'unadjusted impressions', 'cunning irregularities' and alertness to the bleak and 'unforeseen' were – ironically – overlooked or chastised.[51] The Georgians, writes David Perkins, relished Hardy's 'contemplativeness, tenderness and piety, his country settings, rustic characters, sense of local tradition, realism, colloquial speech and large authentic personality', turning away therefore from his 'austerity, concentration, roughness of texture, and gargoyle satire'.[52] In place of a difficult relation with Hardy (with the exception perhaps of Edward Thomas, but was he a Georgian?), they preferred what Perkins describes as a 'love affair' with the lads and lasses, the cherry trees, the blue hills, fairs and football of A. E. Housman's Shropshire. Where Hardy was not regarded as simply beyond the pale, as, in Chesterton's phrase, 'the village atheist blaspheming over the village idiot', he was moderated into the contemporary English canon as a shadow to Housman, whose *A Shropshire Lad* boomed from an unnoticed private edition of 500 copies in 1896 to sales of 5,000 in 1918 and 21,000 in 1922. Against this Hardy could show a barely noticed *Selected Poems* in 1916 (containing 120 lyrics compared with the 920 of *Collected Poems,* 1930), and his hard-won inclusion in Palgrave's *Golden Treasury.*

An apparently simple panegyric to the mythic 'land' of England in the form of pure rural patriotism occurs in a letter from Rupert Brooke in May 1914 on his way home from the South Seas: 'Plymouth O blessed name O loveliness!. . . . Drake's Plymouth! English, western Plymouth!. . . O noble train, oh glorious and forthright and English train, I will look round me at the English faces and out at the English fields – and I will pray.'[53] Even more emphatic is an article he wrote after the war had started, 'An Unusual Young Man' (29 August 1914), in which he expresses the meaning 'England' had for him: 'He was immensely surprised to perceive that the actual earth of England held for him a quality which, if he'd ever been sentimental enough to use the word, he'd have called "holiness" . . . He felt the triumphant helplessness of a lover.'[54]

This response to 'English fields' and 'the actual earth of England' was founded on the entrenched association of poetry with Nature. Palgrave's *Golden Treasury* (1908), for example, speaks of the poetic tradition as a 'stream'; of the whole volume as dedicated to 'a harvest of song'; of younger 'singers' as 'blossoms springing up amongst us'; and of lesser talents as 'nightshade and yewberries'.[55] The acceptance of this association is well illustrated in a comment from the rural writer Richard Jefferies. Though otherwise committed to 'describing the realities of rural life behind the scenes', Jefferies could extol English nature poetry for its comprehensiveness, and add that 'our greatest of all, Shakespeare, carries, as it were, armfuls of violets and scatters roses and golden wheat across his pages, which are simply fields written with human life'.[56] Imprisoned in this persistent analogy, poetry of natural description and nostalgic evocation continued to be written, in spite of the heavy urban odds against it. The poems of Bridges, de la Mare and Drinkwater, for example, seek and find the spirit of England in the very act of *not* seeing the signs of rural decline.

It has often been suggested that such conventional assumptions and the accompanying idioms of Edwardian poetry were revealed as outmoded and inadequate with the advent of war,[57] but this is not entirely convincing. Brooke's intended self-irony in 'The Old Vicarage, Grantchester' (a title preferred by the arbiter Edward Marsh to Brooke's 'The Sentimental Exile') is overwhelmed by the poem's air of pampered nostalgia ('And is there honey still for tea?'). While reportedly embarrassed by the poem's 'silly passages', Brooke would not or could not find a more distancing rhetoric. Nor did the 'grim realities of modern war' bring about a sudden and radical adjustment in his own writing or the poetic sensibilities of other writers. The pastoral mode with its guarantees of an English homeland was consistently employed by Edward Blunden as a means of reassurance and ironic counterpart to the immediate shocks of war, just as it was, more intermittently, by Hardy, Aldington, Graves, Binyon and Owen. The ubiquitous flowers of Edwardian and Georgian poetry also continued to punctuate the verse of combatants, though the attention narrowed to English roses and Flanders poppies. Both are referred to in Brooke's pre-war 'Grantchester', with its pointed contrast between regimented German tulips and 'an English unofficial rose', and, as Paul Fussell makes clear, Brooke was drawing here upon a long and continuing tradition of distinctively English poetic imagery and symbolism.[58]

This imagery and connotation were on occasion differently inflected, however, as in Rosenberg's 'Break of Day in the Trenches'; and as the war went on, the myth of heroic England and its accompanying rhetoric were dispelled, at least among the combatant troops and a newer breed of soldier poets. Charles Sorley, in August 1914, had remarked in a letter, 'England – I am sick of the sound of the word'[59]; and his poetry evinces both a sense of waste and futility in war and a sharp mockery of poets, like Housman and Brooke, whose verse assisted in constituting the heroic response.

To look at Edward Thomas is to see less a rejection of this England than a differently inflected patriotism and response to the land, growing intimately out of another tradition – rural prose commentary. Thomas, in fact, shows how it was possible to study under both Jefferies and Pater. Criticism has tended to represent these influences as a contrast between actuality and an obfuscating poetical prose, but for all the perfumed verbosity of his early prose Thomas was both symptom and witness of an increasingly critical dislocation between words and things, language and experience. The heart of the England he recognized thus comprised less a location than a state of mind, a 'symbolic geography',[60] searched for and maintained to meet a psychological and social need. Thomas' own study of Pater properly identifies this dimension, criticizing Pater's lack of engagement not with the 'actual' but with the factors of 'race, age, class and personal experience' by which a writer might 'take hold of another man'.[61] Thomas had recognized, in short, aestheticism's eschewal of ideology. The moment of his own ideological commitment soon followed. In 1914 he began writing poetry, and in July 1915 enlisted. When asked why he was fighting, so the story goes, he picked up a handful of earth and said, 'literally for this'.[62] The meaning behind this symbolic act of patriotism is best expressed in the poem 'Lob', also from 1915. Lob is the ubiquitous, irrepressible spirit of the people and their culture; he is

> Lob-lie- by-the-fire, Jack Cade,
> Jack Smith, Jack Moon, poor Jack of every trade,
> Young Jack, or old Jack, or Jack What-d'ye-call,
> Jack-in-the-hedge, or Robin-run-by-the-wall,
> Robin Hood, Ragged Robin, Lazy Bob.

And the poem ends:

> Young Jack perhaps, and now a Wiltshireman
> As he has oft been since his days began.[63]

Thomas reaches back here through his own Wiltshire associations, and the Wiltshireman Richard Jefferies, to an English Everyman of yeoman stock. As Stan Smith comments: 'Despite its deep conservatism this populist mystique of England here takes on a radical inflection with its implied hostility to a utilitarian, capitalist ethos that would "grind men's bones for bread".'[64] Thomas' 'radical populism' is qualified however by Lob's elusiveness and his unending service as cannon-fodder ('One of the lords of No Man's Land, good Lob, – /Although he was seen dying at Waterloo,/Hastings, Agincourt and Sedgemoor too – /Lives yet').

Lob recalls the tradition of the 'free-born Englishman' but survives only as an anachronistic myth in the face of bourgeois property relations and modern war. As the historian G. M. Trevelyan commented on Sedgemoor,

> One thing is certain, that only in an age when the class of free-hold yeomen formed a large proportion of the population, and employed a part at least of the hired labour, could any district have thus risen in arms against the will of the squires. The land of England was not then owned by the few.[65]

The only land Lob's descendants could lay claim to in the name of the nation in 1915 was No Man's Land. Lob himself – as the embodiment of a 'radical populism' – was trapped in the recesses of the past, unable to step forward as a defiant Tommy Atkins.

The fiction of an essential England

The collusion of aestheticism and literary pastoral with patriotism and the construction of a myth of rural England appeared in much of the fiction and prose of the period, bound up there with a mystical notion of the land and a nostalgia for the traditional rural community centered on the country house or great estate. Constance Holme's *The Lonely Plough* (1914) provides one popular 'regional' example of a resilient adherence to such a social order, and her belief was shared, though with less confidence, by such writers as John Galsworthy and E. M. Forster, as well as the Liberal politician C. F. G. Masterman. The title of Masterman's *The Condition of England* (1909) identifies a major concern for these writers, confronted as they were with signs of class mobility and conflict and a newer English landscape of expanding metropolis, suburbia and industrialism.

These themes informed much of the fiction also of D. H. Lawrence, whose early novels are particularly marked by the influence of aestheticism upon a perception of rural England. In *The White Peacock* (1911), for example, the location Nethermere (the name already suggesting a Romanticized Derbyshire), human relationships and character are consistently viewed through the artistic criteria of the 1890s, and through pictures by Beardsley, Greiffenhagen and the Pre-Raphaelites. In this way the narrator Cyril (and Lawrence himself) can retain an evasive but unifying aesthetic vision, threaded with a mythologized pastoral or rural England. Thus Annable, the gamekeeper, appears like 'some malicious Pan'; Lettie is a 'sable Persephone'; George, the young 'yeoman', is 'picturesque, fit for an idyll'; and the young people's picnic is described as if staged by Theocritus.[66] This organizing aestheticism, moreover, is clearly consistent with an implied organic community (more fully evoked in *The Rainbow*): as Cyril remarks, 'We were the children of the valley of Nethermere, a small nation with language and blood of our own' (273). Later, after Cyril's return from London, Nethermere no longer seemed 'a complete, wonderful little world that held us charmed inhabitants'; the 'old symbols', he feels, 'were trite and foolish' (305). But this and many other signs of change in character, relationships and environment are read only as expressing loss and decline. The young farmer, George, in particular, declines in the narrator's eyes from an animalistic grace through a period of political activism as a socialist into a debilitating alcoholism. Finally he is 'a condemned man . . . like a tree that is falling, going soft and pale and rotten' (367, 368). Earlier Cyril had been depressed at the sight of 'degradation and ruin' presented by the Crystal Palace, and the speech of a 'little socialist' at Marble Arch had threatened him with the vision that 'the World was all East End' and 'all mud' (321). The decadent narrator (and the novel) sees only degeneration and decay. Removed from, and fundamentally unmoved by, the spectacle, Cyril and Lawrence observe from within a self-referential and self-enclosing aesthetic which permits only self-reflection.

Lawrence's later story 'England, My England' (1915) explores rather than submits to these implications. Egbert, the protagonist here, 'talked of literature and music, he had a passion for old folk-music, collecting folk-songs and folk-dances, studying the Morris-dance and the old customs'.[67] The 'born rose' Egbert marries Winifred Marshall who comes of a different, less spontaneous, but still sympathetic, stock: 'she too seemed to come out of the old England, ruddy, strong, with a certain crude, passionate quiescence and a hawthorn robustness' (304). Together they 'were a beautiful couple' whose house at Crockham 'belonged to the England of hamlets and yeomen' (304). They were 'caught there', Lawrence adds, 'caught out of the world' (307). If there is no irony in these descriptions, there is, we begin to feel, a perception of limitations. Egbert, for example, does not work, and neither he nor Winifred sees 'the difference between work and romance' (307). Egbert remains 'amateurish and sketchy', an 'epicurean hermit' who 'would not' (Lawrence adds 'could not') go into the world and work for money, there to oppose his Englishness to the world of business. His power lay in the 'abnegation of power' (a telling description of aestheticism's opposition through abdication) and implies a 'negation of responsibility' (315). His children respond to this spirit of 'liberty' in him, but after an accident where his child falls upon a sickle and is taken to hospital, he is dependent more than ever on his father-in-law for financial aid, just as the child's continued 'liberty of movement' is dependent on the grandparents' effort, money and will. Subsequently, Egbert's own liberty as a man 'born and bred free' is lost as he submits, though opposed to war, to the mechanization and 'mob spirit of a democratic army' (327). Though he had 'no conception of Imperial England, and Rule Britannia was just a joke to him' (326), Egbert pathetically 'stood for nothing' (311). His pure-blooded unaggressive negating Englishness, so steeped in tradition, passes beyond recall in the slow agony and creeping oblivion of his death in Flanders. Egbert's Englishness then (so closely recalling the 'true patriotism' of Quiller-Couch) is shown as impotent. Well-bred though it is, filtered through a dabbling in literature, folk-song and old customs, this idea of personal and national identity has, Lawrence says, no purchase on the world, and gives Egbert no relation to mass feeling other than that of recoil or resignation. Old England and liberty are extinguished finally in the service of a cause Egbert does not espouse.

Geoffrey Marshall, Egbert's father-in-law, represents a more willingly compromised liberal England. With Egbert he shares 'almost the same' instincts, since 'they were two real Englishmen' (327), but Marshall has come to grips with life. With the advent of war he is faced with a choice between 'German military aggression, and the English non-military idea of liberty and the "conquests of peace" – meaning industrialism' (327). He 'asserted his choice of the latter, perforce. He whose soul was quick with the instinct of power' (327). Here a grafted English heritage, Romantically maintained, abandons the 'English non-military idea of liberty' because it must necessarily assent to capitalist gain (and the propaganda of 'the "conquests of peace"') which will accrue from a capitalist war. Lawrence's story confirms how aestheticism, and an aloof Romanticizing, would inevitably be conscripted into general ideology and the national war effort. True-born Englishness, having entered *via* aestheticism a phase of unconnected negation, was in the event impotent to refuse or oppose the war. Having, in Marshall, come to grips with the world of business, an Englishness already relegated to the home and Dickensian stereotype ('there was always a touch of Christmas about him') assented 'perforce' to further incorporation in the world of business' war. The priorities of capital, which the 'true born Englishman' in the spirit of 'liberty' would still in 1914 have instinctively recoiled from, simply cannot be gainsaid.

Neither Masterman, Galsworthy nor Forster writes with the penetration of Lawrence's story, but they recognize nevertheless that what Masterman called 'the essential nation' of 'feudal society, of country house, country village and little country town' has receded. 'No one today', writes Masterman, 'would seek in the ruined villages and dwindling population of the countryside the spirit of an "England" four-fifths of whose people have now crowded into the cities'.[68] In spite of his clear perception of such incontrovertible social change, however, Masterman is typically forced into reaffirmation of a preferred rural ideal:

Nature still flings the splendour of her dawns and sunsets upon a land of radiant beauty. Here are deep rivers flowing beneath old mills and churches; high-roofed red barns and large thatched houses with still unsullied expanses of cornland and wind-swept moor and heather and pinewoods looking down valleys upon green gardens; and long stretches of quiet down standing white and clean from the blue surrounding sea. Never, perhaps, in the memorable and spacious story of this island's history has the land beyond the city offered so fair an inheritance to the children of its people, as today, under the visible shadow of the end. (208)

John Galsworthy's *The Country House* (1907) and Forster's *Howards End* (1910) share Masterman's liberal ambivalence and are shaped, as is Constance Holme's *The Lonely Plough*, by a similarly contradictory affirmation of the reality of the unreal, of the essentiality of the marginal. All are consequently pressed back, whether more or less self-consciously and assertively, upon fictive contrivance so as to enforce a resolution on behalf of a mythical England.

What little plot *The Country House* has concerns the Pendyce family of Worsted Skeynes and the potentially destructive, but in the event inconsequential, affair between their idle son George and the sketchy but piquant *femme fatale*, Helen Bellew. But the real substance of the novel lies in the values and attitudes of a senior set of characters (especially Horace and Mrs Pendyce) and in the evocations and values of the country estate itself. Galsworthy offers here an anatomy of the traditional English gentry and 'old English virtues'.[69] Horace Pendyce, the squire and 'Tory communist' (13), represents in this way a non-aggressive patriotism and source of continuity, full of a sense of responsibility in the face of change; 'country houses are not what they were' he says, 'if *we* go, the whole thing goes' (9). The general tenor of the novel suggests that the way of life and 'inheritance' the squire adheres to is moribund, socially undesirable and doomed; but because of its exclusive concern with a small section of the middle class and its uncertain tone, the satire is continually blurred. Nothing within the novel effectively challenges the centrality of the traditional 'feudal system' (3), and in fact this system is only re-confirmed, particularly through the use of Mrs Pendyce as the agent of narrative resolution.

Mrs Pendyce is a 'lady' and 'a Totteridge' and also a sounding-board for moments of evocative pastoral description. Initially she is seen as a quiet and passive figure in the community, but it becomes apparent as the novel progresses, and the scandalous threat to the inheritance of Worsted Skeynes approaches, that passivity can be the stillness at the centre of a turning world, and quietness the sign of inner resources. Mrs Pendyce has the 'deep' and 'sacred . . . instinct of a lady' (215); in her there was a 'quality', a 'something' which was 'her country's civilisation, its very soul, the meaning of it all – gentleness, balance' (216). The resolution of the novel (Captain Bellew withdrawing his divorce suit) depends upon his respectful recognition of Mrs Pendyce as 'the lady I know' (296); the country house is thus saved not through any modern mechanisms but through the force of blood and true breeding, contrary though this is to Galsworthy's sense of the failings of the traditional social order. Only once is another world noticed outside this one, when Galsworthy refers to the East End as 'that unknown land' (125). As a good liberal reformer and friend of Masterman, writing after Booth, Rowntree and the 'explorers' of that other country, Galsworthy would himself have 'known' it. But as his novel implies, it wasn't 'England'.

Forster's treatment of the 'England' question in *Howards End*[70] is more complex than Galsworthy's, but has many similar features. The house, Howards End, is the symbolic representation of civilized England, and the novel's insistent question is: who are its inheritors? The answer – signalled in the novel's epigraph 'only connect' – resides in the connection of fractions of the middle class in conjunction with the spirit of traditional rural England. The Wilcoxes, Schlegels and Basts are the strands of this selective social fabric; all reference to the aristocracy and the 'unthinkable' very poor is omitted (58). Forster, as an honest and clear-sighted liberal, recognizes that 'culture' depends on 'islands of money' (58), and if it is culture which is of primary importance in the salvation of England, (or even of 'civilised Europe', the Schlegels are of German parentage), then the male Wilcoxes' hard, materialistic world of 'telegrams and anger' must have its place. In the novel's final settlement, the alliance of culture and wealth has been effected through the marriage of Margaret Schlegel, the true 'spiritual heir' (94) of the numinous first Mrs Wilcox, and Henry Wilcox who, while conveniently retaining his wealth, survives as a broken, if not wiser, man. The Schlegel sisters represent different aspects of cultural humanism: Margaret a compromising pragmatism, and Helen a purer and more dangerous idealism. Though Margaret becomes the owner of Howards End, it is Helen who produces an heir to the house, and presumably England, in the child of her 'half-hour' affair with Leonard Bast. Bast belongs with the newly-mobile but precariously-situated lower middle class of the 'clerking' persuasion, also identified by Masterman. Seeking to climb clear of the 'abyss' of poverty and class demotion, Bast aspires to what Forster makes clear is an inappropriate culture, and dies of a heart attack, buried under the toppled volumes of the bookish culture he had desired. Bast has one quality, however, the 'spirit of adventure', which Forster requires for Howards End. Thus it is he who sires an heir who will combine a natural affinity with the land, middle-class wealth and culture, and lower-middle-class ambition.

Howards End itself is explicitly identified by Forster as 'English': 'the wych elm that she saw from the window was an English tree. No report had prepared her for its peculiar glory. It was neither warrior, lover, nor god; in none of these roles do the English excel. It was a comrade' (192). The first Mrs Wilcox is the embodied spirit of the house, who, though not 'high born', possessed (like Mrs Pendyce) 'the instinctive wisdom the past can alone bestow . . . to which we give the clumsy name of aristocracy' (20). The consistent symbolic association of the house with the land and earth, rising at moments to a prose of hushed rhapsody, helps compose a literary myth which can, in the pages of fiction, neutralize and drive back the encroaching reality of 'London' or 'suburbia'. The opening of Chapter 19 is a central passage, from which Forster returns at the chapter's end to the question of who owns England:

> Does she belong to those who have moulded her and made her feared by other lands, or to those who have added nothing to her power, but have somehow seen her, seen the whole island at once, lying as a jewel in a silver sea, sailing as a ship's soul, with all the brave world's fleet accompanying her towards eternity? (165)

His answer is clear if tellingly vague: England belongs to those who 'have *somehow* seen her, seen the whole island at once' through the glow of Shakespearian patriotism which colours his own vision. England, especially Hertfordshire, which 'is England meditative', retains a pastoral aspect, with 'real nymphs' (185) worthy of Drayton, and a social prospect indebted to Matthew Arnold – 'in these English farms, if anywhere, one might see life steadily and see it whole . . . connect – , without bitterness until all men are brothers' (250).

But Forster knows this affirmation is against all the odds, and although he will not deal directly with the dominant realities of English social life before the war, their presence is the informing contradiction of the entire novel. Significantly, the station for Howards End is between two worlds: 'The station, like the scenery, struck an indeterminate note. Into which country will it lead, England or Suburbia?' (16). 'England' – the pastoral 'reality' is set against 'Suburbia' – the real 'illusion'; Forster's exclusive vision has no better statement. But it is London which excites Forster's greatest contempt: it has, he writes, 'no pulsation of humanity. It lies beyond everything: Nature, with all her cruelty, comes nearer to us than do these crowds of men' (102).

The difficulty of Forster's position is revealed, however, in an important passage at the end of the novel, when Helen remarks that 'London's creeping', that its imminent invasion is 'only part of something else', and that 'life's going to be melted down all over the world'. Recognizing the truth of this, Margaret places her hope 'in the weakness of logic': 'Because a thing is going strong now it need not go strong for ever . . . it may be followed by a civilization that won't be a movement, because it will rest on the earth. All the signs are against it now, but I can't help hoping' (316). There can hardly be a better instance of myth being substituted for history; of a preferred pastoral 'civilization' at rest being held against the acknowledged logic of change. London and suburbia have no place in the 'England' of Howards End; and so, at least in fiction, they can be resisted.

Constance Holme's *The Lonely Plough* (1914) is a more vigorously conservative novel, drawing on the traditions of pastoral description and evocation in which houses are integral parts of an estate rather than the farm-house-that-was in *Howards End,* or the suburban edifice built for a nouveau-riche like Soames in *A Man of Property*. Her novel expressly endeavours 'to show the value of the three-cornered relationships between landlord, agent and tenant', and especially 'the difficult position of the steward'. 'Today', the 1931 Preface claims, the continuing problems of property require 'stewards more sound and sensible than ever'; the pull of the land is still 'in our blood' and the need remains 'for honesty and straight-dealing and confidence in our fellows. The land teaches these virtues, for it will be satisfied with nothing less'.[71]

In the novel's central relationship, Lancaster the agent defers with feudal respect and gratitude to the traditional *noblesse oblige* of the aptly-named landowner Bluecaster. Though Lancaster is burdened with managing the whole estate on Bluecaster's behalf, he recognizes the legitimacy a symbolic aristocracy gives to his own stewardship. Upon this reciprocity of trust the survival of the land is seen to depend. In effect, in affirming the bond between 'the spur of race and the steady influence of a good servant' (166), the novel endorses an unequal class alliance in which the middle-class dynamic of the steward (a 'blunt, absorbed businessman of the land', 264) is both indispensable and exploited. Lancaster is sustained in this role by the qualities of the ideal steward ('forethought, vigilance, courtesy, reticence', 164) and above all by his self-effacing devotion to the land; 'the estate's my wife', he says, 'I'll never have any other' (264). As a result, 'class-hatred was almost unknown on this particular property. . . . The balance between landlord and tenant swung sanely and steadily, for both had trust in the hand that held it' (70). This trust is tested and reaffirmed in the building and disastrous failure of 'Lancaster's Lugg', which collapses under the weight of the spring tide. Bound together, even in failure, aristocrat and steward can form a wall protecting rural values against the stress of change and the symbolic threat of the sea which, it is asserted, 'had not won' (384).

As an adjunct to Bluecaster's hereditary and rightful ownership of the land, the novel presents that too of the smaller gentry, significantly in the person of a woman, Harriet Knewstubb, whose 'people belong here – good old yeoman stock, the best in the land. The backbone of England, some of the books call it' (114). Harriet's model farm shows 'no sign of feminine occupation' but has 'the homeliness that clings imperishably to the farmhouse, the fundamental abiding home of all . . . the Holy of Holies of many a past generation' (190). The novel's third constituent of rural England is represented by Hamer Shaw and his daughter. Having made his money outside, Hamer is called back to Westmoreland 'in passionate content' (56), the novel recognizing that his 'sterling worth and fine business capacity' (57) would in time be of service to 'the conservative country'. Unlike *Howards End's* reluctant acceptance of the male Wilcoxes, *The Lonely Plough's* stolidly bourgeois priorities offer no criticism of Shaw, presenting him as the sympathetic inheritor of Watters, an ancient, sentient house, embodying permanent rural values: 'for master and tenant pass away, but the house remaineth' (136).

Finally these connective relationships, and the common acceptance of natural authority and service, have to be sustained on behalf of the entire 'feudal' community in the face of modern influences (urban life, the motor-car, education, government legislation) which evidently have the future on their side. The novel's most telling self-affirmation against this world comes in its closing pages in an attempt to rescue a 'true picture' of its sequestered values from the medievalizing clichés of a newspaper report on the Lugg disaster:

> Into a seething world of clashing interests and warring classes the tale of the Northern property, where the flower of ancestry still sprang purely as well from yeoman and peasant stock as from patrician, where law was less than loyalty, long service a matter of course, friendship and understanding things born of inbred knowledge – dropped like a medieval, blazoned shield into the arena of modern warfare. Men picked it up wonderingly, fitting it clumsily to an unaccustomed arm, only to discard it with a laugh.
>
> "No agreements? *That's* a lie, any how! . . . Landlord's personal charm – tenants' appreciation – sounds like the days of Magna Carta, doesn't it?. . . . I must say these journalists know how to pile on the colour. Amity between agent and farmers – well, I just don't think . . . Scion of Hugh Lupus of the Conquest gives his life for an old trust – feudalism dug up by the spadeful, and plastered on with a trowel! *Lies*!"
> Yet the true picture was there all the time, defying the brush of maudlin sentiment, as a masterpiece glimmers through a daub. (331–2)

The passage reveals, in Forster's phrase, a belief in 'the weakness of logic'. The very terms the novel has employed undermine its defiance of the view the world takes of it, exposing its quarrel with such journalistic embellishment as a matter, not of true against false, but of idiom, perspective and cultural value. As in so much pre-war literature this vulnerable 'true picture' of England can only be defended as a preferred fiction.

Unknown England and nowhere lands

In this section we wish to pursue some of the internal threats to the flexible but resilient hegemony of a mystic 'England', and examine, also, some salient forms of conscious resistance to it. These latter derive from three sources: the shift in British political life which brought versions of socialism on to the national agenda; the agitation for women's suffrage; and the modernist assault upon liberal values and received literary culture.

'Englishness', as we have seen, depends upon assumptions of a unity of identity and purpose. There are moments in the literature of the period, however, when these assumptions appear insecure, and have then to be forcibly reasserted, either in theme, structure or characterization, even to the point of manifest contrivance. The resolution of *Howards End,* where Forster can 'only connect' selective and altered aspects of middle-class England provides one such example in which the novel's plotting is at once both formal and ideological. At another level, as noticed earlier, affinities appear between ostensibly opposed positions and aesthetics; as between imperialist propaganda and aestheticism for example, producing in a figure such as W. E. Henley a fraught literary personality at war with an enemy who threatens as much from within as from without. What we see in such examples are local illustrations of the ways in which hegemony is generally maintained, through aspects of compromise, assimilation, marginalization or repression. An entire range of such negotiations and conflicts comes into view in the period; internally within literary works, more generally, in literary culture and ideology, with sometimes a direct and sometimes an indirect, but no less profound, bearing upon the theme of English identity. Such conflicts reveal both just how far the ideological requirement of a non-contradictory order and coherence was under pressure in the period, and also what kinds of constraining influence ideology could itself exert in return.

The most sensational revelation in fiction of contradiction and doubleness where there was apparent oneness and unity was *The Strange Case of Dr Jekyll and Mr Hyde* (1886) by Henley's one-time close friend, Robert Louis Stevenson. Stevenson here exposes a domain of private misrule, repressed in the interests of public order at the immediate level of character formation, thereby calling into question bourgeois conceptions of individual identity. The respectable public face, his story says, 'hides' a subversive lower form, ugly in appearance and manner but an undeniable kin all the same, who must moreover be released if there is to be a 'scientific' knowledge of the self. Explorations of a divided self multiplied by the turn of the century, appearing across more and less popular fiction from Oscar Wilde's *Picture of Dorian Gray* (1891), Joseph Conrad's *Heart of Darkness* (1902) and Henry James's 'Jolly Corner' (1908) to Bram Stoker's *Dracula* (1897), John Buchan's Richard Hannay stories and Conan Doyle's Sherlock Holmes. Buchan comment that you could no longer 'take the clear psychology of most civilised human beings for granted. Something was welling up from primeval deeps to muddy it'[72] is, in this respect, a representative one. In these examples, threats to the wholeness of the civilized human subject come from below the waist of a prohibitive morality, from a hedonistic primitivism, from unacceptable capitalist rapacity, or from assaults upon rationality, upon a disciplined code of duty, or the methodical regimen of practical work. The unease these fictions register stems from encounters with a dangerously internalized 'other', whether sexual, racial, criminal or supernatural in aspect; provoking thus a fear of reversion to some lower point on the psychic or social or evolutionary scale. Within the vocabulary found for the temptations and terrors of this regression, there is consistent reference to the chamber or pit, to the abyss or mire, into which characters fall or are all but drawn.

In *Dracula,* as one example, the association then follows of darkness with sleep and nightmare, and thence, in the language with which this text veils sexual desire, with madness and evil. In Conrad's *Heart of Darkness*, Kurtz succumbs in the Belgian Congo to the 'spell of the wilderness', drawn 'by the awakening of forgotten and brutal instincts, by the memory of gratified and monstrous passions'.[73] From his 'impenetrable darkness', having 'stepped over the edge', Kurtz pronounces his inscrutable judgement, 'The horror! The horror!' (99, 100). In a surprisingly comparable story, *The Hound of the Baskervilles* (1902), Sherlock Holmes exercises his 'scientific use of the imagination' to dispel the legend of the hound of Hell and so help 'modernise' the failing aristocratic-feudal order at Baskerville Hall. In the process, Holmes is drawn through his implicit affinity with the criminals Selden and Stapleton to inhabit a neolithic cave on Dartmoor (the antithesis to Holmes' metropolitan base) to become, in the eyes of commonsensical Watson, 'the man of darkness' at 'the heart of the mystery'.[74] In the last stage of the chase Holmes is also sucked waist-deep into Grimpen Mire, the common lair of Stapleton (himself the atavistic heir of the dark side of the Baskerville family) and the spectral hound. If in addition we recall Holmes' cocaine addiction, his lethargy when not on a case, his selective and specialist knowledge and his theory that supreme mental concentration implies logically 'getting into a box to think' (358), we see that the enemy he incorporates and represses is not only a criminal *alter ego* but also a close cousin to the stereotype decadent.

Thus order and unity in paradigmatic fictional protagonists, and by extension in civilized society ('All Europe', writes Conrad for example, 'contributed to the making of Kurtz', 71), experience a tremor which shows them to be precarious. The disorienting effects of invasion by the 'other' do not, however, in these texts prompt the generation of a new order so much as a protection of the old, or at most its adjustment, through assimilation, increased self-discipline, or the externalization, detection and elimination of what threatens. Where this does not occur, as in the stories by Oscar Wilde, Stevenson and Henry James, their narratives close with the simultaneous destruction of both self and other, and therefore in a reaffirmation of unity in death. The uncongenial kinships which well up from the 'primeval deeps' of perilous introspection are thus cancelled at the point of an impossible self-knowledge, or held at bay in characters and narrative at the cost of self-deception and fictional manipulation. The formulaic conventions of the detective novel and adventure story, as employed by Conan Doyle and John Buchan particularly, exemplified in this way the structures by which realist fiction can entertain crisis, contradiction and mystery, but move inexorably nevertheless to a point of closure which explains away such potentially undermining features in the person of a knowing and re-unifying individual representative. Stability is therefore regained.

On another level the imagery of threatening darkness and the metaphor of the abyss appeared in the fiction and non-fiction upon 'Unknown England', particularly in association with London's East End.[75] The exploration of 'darkest London' begun in the 1850s and '60s continued in the closing decades of the century in the works of Walter Besant, George Gissing, Arthur Morrison and 'the Cockney School'. Here a schism was opened not only in individual fictional protagonists (though this was also present) but also in the national 'protagonist', the capital city, whose West End opulence and bright lights stood exposed to the gloomy squalor and labyrinthine hell of its East End slums. These works differed in their degree of realism, their use of working-or middle- or upper-class characters, and in their responses to the poverty, passivity and violence they identified. Whereas Walter Besant, for example, (in *All Sorts and Conditions of Men,* 1882 and *Children of Gibeon,* 1886) detected a latent variety and romance beneath the miserable tedium of working-class life in need only of the transfiguring touch of upper-class benevolence and culture, Gissing eschewed philanthropy but could identify no way out of darkest London beyond the exceptional examples of deracinated, predominantly middle-class individuals. The cause of social reform which Gissing had adopted as the author of *Workers in the Dawn* (1880) was lost sight of in his subsequent fiction of the same decade (The *Unclassed,* 1884, *Demos,* 1886, *Thyrza,* 1887, and *The Nether World,* 1889), which came to show a mixed sympathy and contempt for the London poor he described. Neither Gissing nor Arthur Morrison could see any hope for the working class itself beyond a self-defeating daily struggle for decency and respectability in an immured existence where, as Morrison described it, 'every day is hopelessly the same'.[76]

Gissing and Morrison bore powerful first-hand witness to what had been unseen and uncredited, and their accounts of the monotony and economic and cultural poverty of working-class life seriously called into question the bucolic image of England's poor as a humble but contented peasantry. But even as their work pressed fictional realism towards the form of naturalistic observation and sociological report, it confirmed them in a fatalistic view of an unchangeable social order. Unlike Engels, who saw not only 'the passive vegetative existence' of East End workers but, with the events of the Match Girls' Strike of 1888 and the Dockers' strike of the following year, the signs of a change in class consciousness and labour relations in English society,[77] they did not reveal or subscribe to a newer England potentially in the making. As themselves, in Gissing's term, 'unclassed' and disinterested professional writers ('my attitude henceforth', wrote Gissing in 1883, 'is that of the artist pure and simple'; 'there must be no sentimentalism, no glossing over' said Morrison)[78] they were unable to see the working class as capable of organized resistance or as engaged in class struggle.

Jack London was a politically more committed writer than either Gissing or Morrison. In the event, however, his 'socialism' does not extend to a perception of the 'people' of the London abyss as an organized class or as self-determining agents of change who might replace the subject 'peoples' required by nation and Empire. Indeed London does not see them as 'people' at all but as bestial and criminal mutants. They are to him 'a menagerie of garmented bipeds that looked something like humans and more like beasts'; they are 'gutter wolves', 'gorillas', 'apes', 'a new species, a breed of city savages . . . the slum is their jungle, and they live and prey in the jungle'.[79] The question London asks is whether civilization has benefited the average man, his criteria being a matter of profit as against loss, good as against bad management: 'Either the Empire is a profit to England, or it is a loss. If it is a loss, it must be done away with. If it is a profit, it must be managed so that the average man comes in for a share of the profit' (126). London concludes that civilization and Empire are due for the scrap heap; but what is to replace them and how 'the English' are to enjoy 'a broad and smiling future' (9) he does not say or consider.

The emphatically naturalist or documentary modes adopted by Gissing, Morrison and London give to the social reality of working-class and slum life they portrayed the weight of an immovable given, and thus underwrite their limited political perspectives. Under the influence of historical circumstances and forms of English socialist and progressive thought, two potentially alternative fictional modes were, however, pressed into being. A unique example of the first was Margaret Harkness' never-reprinted novel *Out of Work* (1888). In this novel Harkness discovered a typifying mode which could deal, as John Goode has shown, with events and situations rather than with individual lives or scenes and sketches in the manner of classic realism or naturalism.[80] Features of working-class life such as crime, drunkenness and poverty are presented thus as common social situations with related social causes rather than as the stuff of personal failing or tragedy, or of journalistic report. In this way a series of typical circumstances in working-class life are seen as prompting the expression of collective solidarity and mutual aid. The chief event of this kind is the unemployed march upon Trafalgar Square of November 1887: a moment of working-class history which serves to join the novel's often anonymous characters and their fleeting voices. In the words of an unnamed radical dock labourer 'competition has had its day; it *must* give place to co-operation. . . . Everything is possible once you are united' (67). Working people, Margaret Harkness writes, 'exist by the generosity of their fellows, and the only good thing that comes of being unemployed is "I help you, and you help me, because we've no place in society"' (129). This sense of unity in adversity and the acts of unforced generosity it prompts in the novel contrast dramatically with the ostensibly public celebrations of the Queen's Jubilee, the opening of the People's Palace and a hypocritical 'panegyric of the godly nation' delivered by a Wesleyan minister in the novel's early chapters.

A second literary form and political perspective, employing vision rather than directly observed 'truth of detail', was possible within the tradition of utopian writing. The major example before the turn of the century was William Morris' *News from Nowhere* (1890). Here Morris imagines a future, de-industrialized England, reminiscent of the fourteenth century though set in the twenty-first. London's slums have been cleared, its suburbs returned to the country and the gentry's country houses opened for general habitation. 'England', as the sage Hammond remarks, 'is now a garden'.[81] Morris' understanding of Marx, his sense of the emerging labour movement and the experience of class violence exhibited on 'Bloody Sunday', November 1887, lead him to predict a future general strike and civil war before the establishment of a new order of peace and happiness in an England governed by 'pure communism' (288). William Guest, who narrates the story, ends with the hope that his personal dream may become a shared vision, but what is remarkable about *News from Nowhere* is that Morris sees that a return to the present means a return to the conditions of darkness, inequality and alienation which prevail there – even, that it involves a return to the sectarian bickering of the Socialist League which drives the narrator into his frustrated reverie at the story's opening. Morris therefore incorporates the pessimism of a George Gissing, together with a recognition of the contemporary irrelevance of socialist intellectualizing. Without losing sight of either, his story enables him to enlarge upon and transform the personal dimension of the former, and to transcend the latter, in an account of historical change motored by class conflict. Only, his story implies, through such a double recognition of present conditions and of a possible future, resulting from, but utterly transforming, those conditions, can a re-ordered consciousness and a re-organized England be imagined. *News from Nowhere* presents such an England, while at the same time it acknowledges the difficulties of personally maintaining an aspiration towards it, and of holding this in common.

In the new century the tradition of revolutionary socialism produced the singular literary voice of Robert Noonan/Tressell's *The Ragged-Trousered Philanthropists*. The novel's publishing history (a cut and re-arranged edition appeared in 1914 and a second even more abridged version in 1918) is evidence both of the book's underground reputation and of the constraints placed upon oppositional writing by established literary culture. The question, raised earlier, of 'who owns England?' is here set insistently at the point of production and the nexus of class relations. Noonan's vision of an alternative society of dock labourers is indebted implicitly to H. M. Hyndman, Robert Blatchford, Edward Bellamy and William Morris, and appears most fully, after the analysis of capitalism conducted by Frank Owen, the craftsman painter, in the form of a utopian blueprint delivered by the middle-class socialist Barrington. In his 'Great Oration' Barrington describes a co-operative commonwealth to be achieved through the ballot box ('you must fill the House of Commons with Revolutionary Socialists')[82] and a process of out-competing capitalism. Barrington looks forward to 'the Public Ownership of the Machinery and the National Organisation for the profit of a few but for the benefit of all' (512). 'Britain', he concludes, 'should belong to the British people, not to a few selfish individuals' (516).

The echo of Robert Blatchford's *Britain for the British* here, however, creates some confusion. Earlier in the novel young Frankie talks of recommending to the local butcher two texts esteemed by his father and his socialist friends. Their titles, *Happy Britain* and *England for the English,* are clearly Blatchford's extremely popular *Merrie England* and *Britain for the British* by other names (244). The question is whether Noonan is here consciously or unthinkingly endorsing, along with the titles, the chauvinism which led Blatchford as an 'imperial socialist' to defend the Empire in the interests of the British working class.[83] As contrasting evidence there is the ironic chorusing of 'Rule Britannia' between the appearance of slides of sweated labour and slum life in Bert's 'Pandorama' (326), and the defiant singing of 'England Arise' by the Clarion-like socialist vanners (466). In fact the novel is as undecided on the question of nation and Empire as it is unclear in other respects. These uncertainties are the product, in broad terms, of the confused literary and socialist heritage available to Noonan, but the main problem is that while they are present in *The Ragged-Trousered Philanthropists,* they are not recognized there. Unlike Morris, who returns William Guest to a difficult present, Noonan hurries away from the central perception of Owen's difficulties in persuading his work-mates of the simple justice of socialism to the magical solution of Barrington and the dream of a transcendent universal brotherhood which overlooks any question of a united English or British people. It is on this note that the novel ends:

> The gloomy shadows enshrouding the streets, concealing for the time their grey and mournful air of poverty and hidden suffering, and the black masses of cloud gathering so menacingly in the tempestuous sky, seemed typical of the Nemesis which was overtaking the capitalist system. That atrocious system which, having attained to the fullest measure of detestable injustice and cruelty, was now fast crumbling into ruin, inevitably doomed to be overwhelmed because it was all so wicked and abominable . . .
>
> But from these ruins was surely growing the glorious fabric of the Co-operative Commonwealth. Mankind, awaking from the long night of bondage and mourning and arising from the dust wherein they had lain prone so long, were at least looking upward to the light that was riving asunder and dissolving the dark clouds which had so long concealed from them the face of heaven. The light that will shine upon the world wide Fatherland and illumine the gilded domes and glittering pinnacles of the beautiful cities of the future, where men shall dwell together in true brotherhood and goodwill and joy. The Golden Light that will be diffused throughout all the happy world from the rays of the risen sun of socialism. (629–30)

Noonan's language and aspiration here are consistent with the writings of Blake and Shelley, the Chartists and William Morris. As such he represents an example of revolutionary Romanticism opposed to the cultural nostalgia embedded in Romantic Tory or liberal versions of an ideal England that never was. But Noonan's socialist myth shares with these others a lack of anchorage in a lived history; it exhibits what Rupert Brooke came to recognize in a projected long poem as the double 'existence – and non-locality – of England' ('In Avons of the heart her rivers ran. . . . Closed in the little nowhere of the brain.').[84] Again, while Noonan's ending is full of earnest hope, it is heavy too with naturalizing cliché ('the black masses of cloud . . . the long night of bondage . . . the risen sun of Socialism') which assists in an evasion, finally, of the problems of class consciousness and the agencies of radical social change. For these it substitutes a blinding light and a desperate blind faith in historical inevitability (capitalism is 'doomed . . . because it was all so wicked and abominable', etc.). Noonan regenerates a vital oppositional myth against extremely high odds, but his 'dream' (in the terms of *News from Nowhere*) tidies away several difficulties (as Morris does not); not least the problems and possibilities of creating a 'Socialist Nation'. His ending expresses, in short, the glowing but unfocussed potency of a utopian nowhere in the same gesture as it wipes away, too easily, the gloom, poverty and suffering in the darker days of the present with which the passage opens.

In another tradition of English socialism, the Fabian Society could claim the allegiance of two writers, G. B. Shaw, a life-long member who joined the society in 1884, and H. G. Wells, who joined it in 1903 but left in 1908 after a failed attempt to dislodge the Fabian 'old guard' of Sidney and Beatrice Webb, Shaw and Edward Pease. At first sight, Wells, the Romancer, would seem to have lost patience with the Fabian Gradgrinds and to have departed over a difference of style and method. But there was a further aspect to Wells's departure deriving from his and the Fabians' differing appraisals of social class. For his part Wells felt that the 'bourgeoisie' and 'proletariat' of Marxist parlance were 'phantom unrealities'.[85] But although he could appeal, as in 1914, to a 'governing class' of 'prosperous people . . . rulers and owners' to assert a new heroic responsibility in the face of labour unrest,[86] his predictions of the future were based not on an analysis of class relations but upon an evolutionary and technological determinism which enabled him to spot certain behavioural and scientific trends and extrapolate upon them. Beyond the repeated idea of a self-motivating technocratic elite who would guide his more efficient nation and world states once they were in place, Wells was unable to identify any social agency which might bring his future into being. The explanation for this would seem in Wells's own very rapid rise from lower-middle-class beginnings through a butterfly career until he settled in the occupations of successful journalist/novelist. In itself this would suggest that Wells was ideal material for the consciously middle-to lower-middle-class Fabian Society; but his exceptional rise to the ranks of the prosperous intelligentsia impressed upon him a sense of mobility across class lines rather than a class consciousness, and his attachment to science led him to press the claims of specialist knowledge and training rather than the general professional expertise of the lower-middle class increasingly recruited to the Fabian Society. Wells left the society, therefore, because he did not recognize himself, or the group of technologists and engineers with whom he identified, among its ranks.

Wells's campaigning prophecies did not cease in 1908, but his lack of anchorage outside his natural class home is quite clear in the novel *Tono-Bungay,* published in the following year. Here where he turns to change overtaking present English society in a lumpen novel which mixes veiled autobiography, unintegrated adventure story and technical essay, Wells plots the course of the upwardly mobile George Ponderevo from the cancerous decay of a surviving English feudalism through the corruptions and fraud of private enterprise and modern advertising to the discovery of the hygienic truth of science. If George is a pointer to a new world, however, its blessings are mixed, since what he is engaged in building is not a new society but a destroyer. George remarks early in the novel, 'the new England of our children's children is still a riddle to me'[87] and a riddle it remains, since neither George nor Wells has the means to throw off the residual appeal of an older 'social organism of England' embodied in the country house, Bladesover. Bladesover represents an ordered world of purpose and beauty which 'had not altogether missed greatness' (33); it was the 'key for the explanation of England', and declared itself 'to be essentially England' (51). Though it is seen as passing, this traditional England is the only alternative the novel can reluctantly admit to in 'a country hectic with a wasting, aimless fever of trade and money-making and pleasure-seeking' (339), and which above all has 'no plan . . . no intention, no comprehensive desire' (343).

George Bernard Shaw – knowing better than Wells the middle-class 'bias' and methods of Fabianism, and arguably knowing more of the forms of power in English society – settled uneasily for the Fabian pathway of 'the inevitability of gradualness', *faute de mieux.* In common with other leading Fabians, Shaw dismissed the idea of class struggle and proletarian revolution, but in his case this position was arrived at with an important proviso which then shadows his thinking. The early socialist proposal of a 'militant organisation of the working class and general insurrection', he said in 1888, had proved impracticable, and was now abandoned for the Fabian programme of Social Democracy. He adds, however, that socialist revolution had proved 'unfortunately' impossible, that it has not been abandoned 'without some unspoken regrets' and that 'it still remains as the only finally possible alternative to the Social Democratic programme'. As such it commands a respect and admiration far greater than is due to the 'inevitable, but sordid, slow, reluctant, cowardly path to justice'.[88] Such equivocation put Shaw at a distance from orthodox Fabianism of the Webb variety. His plays in no way propagandize for this orthodoxy, nor do they even reluctantly offer to rationalize the case for Fabian realism as against impractical revolutionary idealism. What they do present at their most searching is the power of Capital and Liberal Imperialism and the frustrated impotence of any opposition to it, including his own as dramatist.

One play which illustrates this and bears directly on the question of Englishness is *Heartbreak House* (begun in 1913, but not published until 1919). Here Shaw presents an uncompromising, and in the end frantically anarchistic, analysis of the inner decay of middle-class England. As his Preface makes clear, Heartbreak House is 'cultured, leisured Europe before the war',[89] and Shaw is at pains to warn of the disabling lack of connection between this 'culture' and political power. His evident frustration with a politically irresponsible middle class is for the most part controlled by the play's comedy, but nevertheless breaks through its trivializing farce of mistaken and pretended identities to present the hysterical disorder of the house as a metaphorical ship of state without leadership or direction. This England is 'a madhouse', heading for the rocks. Salvation, Captain Shotover says, lies in learning 'your business as an Englishman'; business is 'Navigation. Learn it and live', he says, 'or leave it and be damned' (156). The assembled representatives of English society are subsequently indeed damned. Shaw prods them towards the precipice of delirious self-destruction, having first exploded the capitalist Mangan and petty-thief Billy Dunn together. Shaw's satire deposits gunpowder everywhere, but he cannot hit the real target – the *absent* numbskull imperialist Lord Utterword, husband to one of Captain Shotover's daughters. It is Hastings Utterword, she says, given 'the necessary powers, and a good supply of bamboo to bring the British native to his senses', who 'will save the country with the greatest of ease' (145). Captain Shotover later concedes, 'The numbskull wins, after all' (153).

As this and plays such as *John Bull's Other Island* (1904) and *Major Barbara* (1905) show, capitalism is, contrary to the Fabian programme, the reverse of permeable. It is capitalism itself in fact which permeates, effectively propagandizes and endlessly incorporates its weaker, if more virtuous, opponents. In *Heartbreak House,* the Imperialist without a heart from the philistine Horseback Hall, who will govern England like the colonies, is untouchable by any in the play, or by Shaw's social comedy, simply because he is out of range. If, beyond this, the ruling order is seen to be so entrenched that it permits in Shaw's terms neither the antics of the 'old barricade revolutionists' nor the 'dream of a peaceful evolution of Capitalism into Socialism', then there is, for Shaw, nothing to be done outside of the political oxymoron of a revolutionary constitutionalism, entrusted to a fighting Fabianism, committed to the use of force. Such is the conclusion Shaw arrived at in a Fabian lecture of 1906, attempting in the terms of the earlier address of 1888 to enlist the militancy of an impossible socialism he admired to the cause of a democratic programme he found wanting.[90]

Shaw's plays themselves, it is true, do not take up this position so much as twist about in the paradoxes which produced it. Above all they show the assimilative and controlling powers of Capital; even more so because its representatives do not have to be clever and cunning in order to succeed.

In this way the absence of any sustained oppositional voice and of any Fabian argument or character sounds as loudly as the influence of the absent Lord Utterword. What the plays reveal beneath their wit and satire is, in the end, a lack of conviction.

An additional source of opposition was derived in the period from the campaign for women's suffrage. In its struggle against sexual stereotyping and the unequal position of women at home and at work, the women's movement offered a challenge which penetrated beyond the constitutional issue of the Vote to strike at the economic order and very texture of English morality and *mores*. The underlying constructions in literary culture of national character can be seen from this perspective to have been marked throughout by a received language and ideology of gender and sexuality. Its influence is apparent, for example, in Henley's masculine bravado; in his, and the quite general, suspicion of the stereotypically effete aesthete; in the male code of camaraderie and honour in battle; and in the doctrine of service and sacrifice for Queen and mother country. The countryside itself and its pastoral depiction were also regularly associated with the feminine attributes of material comfort, growth, bloom and shapely contours, but identified above all with the double female province of 'Home' and 'Beauty'. In Forster and Galsworthy, as we have seen, the quality of traditional England is entrusted to figures such as Mrs Wilcox and Mrs Pendyce who are by birth and instinct 'ladies'. More than this, what Forster seeks to 'connect' in *Howards End* are not only sections of the middle class, but an inner world of feminine moral culture and sensitivity with an outer world of masculine force and business efficiency. In *The Lonely Plough* this combination appears in the mannish Harriet Knewstub whose hearth is a preserve of English virtues.

At another level the land and countryside are employed as metaphors for sublimated sexual feeling, most frequently in the traditional blending of romantic pastoral and the derivative codes of courtly romance. In *The Lonely Plough,* once more, the earth to which Lancaster is 'married' is in moments of solitude a visionary sphere of ethereal mystery, inhabited by an elusive female form, while in its male aspect the land is the simple strength and permanence Lup offers to Francey. In the fiction of Wells and Lawrence sexuality was treated more directly, and seen by both as a key to reconstructed social relationships. Women are in these cases allotted sexual passion, but in the event only re-positioned, their new freedom becoming a freedom to actively accept, rather than passively submit to, lovers, husbands and motherhood, under State or individual male direction.[91] In exploring the theme of sexuality, both writers also separate it, and therefore women, from forms of political action.

Many of these attitudes and the unequal England they helped support were questioned from within the suffrage movement. In fiction, an example of the force of the feminist critique of sexual stereotyping and a patriarchal national identity was Elizabeth Robins' *The Convert*.[92] The heroine, Vida Levering, 'doesn't love England at all' (26). In a world of afternoon-teas and country-house parties, the women's part is to serve, soothe and charm in witty tête-à-têtes with careworn men. One such woman is 'the typical English girl' Hermione Heriot (45, 50). Vida accepts this role with irony until she is prompted to question the ignorant prejudice which sees the suffragettes as 'sexless monstrosities' (60). Her subsequent involvement and work for the Cause serves to overturn the proposed 'aesthetic basis of society' expounded by the idler Paul Filey (63–5). In this extension of diluted aestheticist doctrine, women are, like art, 'perfectly useless' objects of enthroned beauty and purity. In place of this ideal of queenly and powerless womanhood, Vida is converted to, and herself champions, a view of politicized women acting in concert. In the strength of this belief, events in her personal life (desertion by a celebrated Tory politician and the enforced loss of a child) lose significance in one way as they gain it in another:

> One woman's mishap – what is that? A thing as trivial to the great world as it's sordid in most eyes. But the time has come when a woman may look about her and say, what general significance has my secret pain? Does it 'join on' to anything? And I find it *does*. (303)

In the suffragette meetings Vida attends – though hardly any of the class that 'runs England' are present – the speakers demand 'a *stake* in the country' rather than a reward for its defence (101). Speaking in 'vigorous English' in sight of the Reformers' Tree in Hyde Park, one young suffragette consciously reclaims the tradition of what Vida calls 'England's sturdy freeman' (103). She thus re-deploys an English radicalism which provokes as it unsettles the ingrained sexual prejudice of middle- and working-class alike. Stirred by such signs of rebellion 'against other people's control', Vida perceives a future of 'people learning self-control' (145), and comes thus, in a view of women as 'civilisation's only ally' (146), to question the offence of 'an Empire maintained by brute force' (149). At one point she catechizes Wells's 'vision of the New Time'. His *In the Days of the Comet,* she says, betrays 'his old-fashioned prejudice in favour of the "dolly" view of women'. Even his ideal woman is '"only happiness, dear" – a minister of pleasure', but negligible in all other respects. If this is man's highest view of woman, it is reason too 'why all the great visions have never yet been more than dreams'; for the 'City of the Future' cannot be built 'when the best of one of the race are "only happiness, dear"' (208).

It is in these accumulating redefinitions – of English liberty, civilization and Empire, and above all of woman's place, her union with other women, women's stake in the country and the 'New Time' – that the novel's lasting polemical thrust lies. The same might be said generally of the Suffrage movement, particularly as the war and postwar years exposed the eventual shallowness of the constitutional gain of the Vote, and threw into relief the internal divisions between the movement's conservative and socialist-feminist wings. While Emmeline and Christabel Pankhurst committed women to a chauvinistic patriotism, Sylvia Pankhurst consistently opposed patriarchy, the war and capitalism, in principle and practice. Returning from the new Soviet Russia in 1920, she was charged and sentenced to 6 months imprisonment for inciting industrial unrest and sedition in His Majesty's forces. Her response was the poem 'For Half a Year', a sustained indictment of the systematic subjection and injustice in Empire and nation meted out by the ubiquitous male justicer:

> This is the very hub and central spring
> of that I fight, that hoary power of wealth;
> he's its defender, its first magistrate;
> I who attack it, being tried by him,
> to mine antagonist must plead my Cause.

> He hath the power, and he will vengeance take;
> that was decided ere the case was called;
> for me remains one duty one resource;
> to cry a challenge in this Mansion House,
> this pompous citadel of wealthy pride,
> and make its dock a very sounding board
> for the indictment of his festering sins,
> that shall go ringing forth throughout the world,
> and with it carry all my wit can tell
> of that most glorious future, long desired,
> when Communism like the morning dawns.[93]

The poem ends on the note of naturalizing cliché seen in Robert Tressell. Behind it there stands, however, the more concrete inspiration of Bolshevik Russia and Sylvia Pankhurst's own work in the East End Federation for Women's Suffrage, set up in 1913 and, in 1917, renamed the Workers Socialist Federation. Here, with others, she introduced a maternity and infant clinic with free milk and medical provision from a woman doctor, a nursery run on Montessorian lines, a cost-price restaurant and a toy factory (making unwarlike toys), under workers' control and with equal pay.[94] Fraught as it was with difficulties and compromise, this 'offshoot of utopia' established in embryo a system of democratic local welfare provision of which the full vision was a 'cooperative social system' and a 'United States of the World consolidated in a free socialism'.[95] Here, in what was materially more than a dream, was an alternative to the false unities of Empire and the nation at war; a cooperative network built in an effort to redress the real inequalities of class and sex upon which 'essential England' depended. Significantly this initiative came from the united action of women in the 'Unknown England' of London's East End.

The third source of opposition in the period derived from literary modernism. It is commonplace to note that the *dramatis personae* of this movement numbered at a modest estimate two Americans and one Irishman: T. S. Eliot, Ezra Pound and James Joyce. If Henry James, Conrad and W. B. Yeats are included within modernist parameters, then the number of non-English writers involved rises to half a dozen. Only one English-born writer, D. H. Lawrence, might be added to this list, but then it has to be observed that Lawrence's class origins set him outside the mainstream of upper- and lower-middle-class English literary and social life. In spite of their non-English character, the texts of modernism have been commonly valued, however, as the 'great' literature, in English, of the twentieth century. They therefore have a double significance in relation to 'Englishness'. Drawing upon a combination of residual and emergent features in European literature, as well as upon tendencies in European intellectual and political thought, they first exposed the literary parochialism and ideological limits of dominant English liberal culture, but prompted secondly a subsequent mutation in critical ideology, and a quite fundamental alteration in the features of modern English literature.

Modernism did not, however, at all points offer the same challenge, nor did it prove equally assimilable under a newer dispensation. T. S. Eliot and Ezra Pound, the twin demons of poetic modernism, are examples of this difference. Setting themselves quite consciously against the hand-me-down Romanticism of English poetry, they offered *via* a new impersonal poetics to overhaul the poet's relation to his/her work and public and the received tradition. Under their major surgery, the patient emerged with new organs (the Metaphysicals) in place of old (the Victorians, all but Browning); recircuited arteries, looping from the English seventeenth century through nineteenth-century French symbolism; resuscitated members (Pound's Anglo-Saxon recreations); and transplants from Roman, Italian and Chinese literature. The resulting complexion of the poetic tradition was distinctly European, and in some respects international rather than English. In this way Pound and Eliot mounted a radical challenge to the nation's literary self-image, while at the same time, and paradoxically, as American invaders they performed an act of cultural Imperialism on behalf of a nation rapidly losing confidence in its own imperial mission. *The Waste Land* (1922) accomplished both tasks, displaying the 'ruins' of cultural fragmentation, spiritual despair and lack of connection Eliot saw in contemporary society, while it simultaneously 'shored' up these broken remains as earnests of a redeemed cultural totality. His poem appears formless and obscure, but is articulated across submerged links on the assumption that its message of order, though reduced in the present to cryptic shorthand allusion, can be written out in the full syntax of a restored tradition. In effect *The Waste Land* is a modernist *Culture and Anarchy* which conquers anarchy more successfully than Matthew Arnold's text because it releases anarchy within the containing assumptions of a self-repairing 'ideal order'.[96] In this respect the poem was less of an affront to literary orthodoxy than it at first seemed.[97] To use his own term Eliot 'modified' rather than revolutionized the English Literary tradition. In addition, the combination of avant-garde obscurity and cultural conservatism he introduced conducted poetry (and a later accompanying criticism) to the margins of general English culture. In the event it was only in this eccentric position of a conservative minority art (Eliot's later royalism and antediluvian idea of a Christian Britain confirmed the ideological form of this eccentricity) that modernism was to find a secure English home.

Ezra Pound and England proved far less congenial than England and T. S. Eliot. Though he viewed London on his arrival in 1908 as America's cultural capital, and then beavered energetically from that base in the interests of a new literary renaissance, Pound was rankled by pedantic reviewers, timid publishers, and the inveterate complacency of the English literary establishment. By 1913 he described London as 'dead as mutton',[98] and by the end of the decade in *Hugh Selwyn Mauberley* (1920) he had decided that England's literary tradition could no longer be trusted to the English. The war, moreover – fought 'For an old bitch gone in the teeth' – had wasted artistic talent and exposed England as the home of 'lies' and vested interests, beneath which ran the cancer of 'usury age-old and age-thick'.[99] *Hugh Selwyn Mauberley* marked Pound's departure from England and the beginning of his reconstruction in exile of a 'totalitarian' poetic order in *The Cantos*. In the years that Eliot was settling into an English identity, Pound was developing his homeless epic and commitment to Italian fascism. Only at the nadir of this experience, imprisoned on a charge of treason in the military stockade at Pisa, did Pound turn wryly to the memory of a lost Edwardian England ('and God knows what else is left of our London/ my London, your London'), three years after Eliot's affirmation in *Little Gidding* that 'History is now and England'.[100]

Like Pound, both D. H. Lawrence and James Joyce suffered at the hands of a censorious literary establishment (Lawrence's *The Rainbow* was repressed; Joyce's *Dubliners* was banned, and the English serialization of *Ulysses* was suspended before its first publication in France in 1922). All three writers also wrote works of departure – *Sons and Lovers* (1912), *A Portrait of the Artist as a Young Man* (1914) and *Hugh Selwyn Mauberley* – which project their protagonists, and authors, into the realm of art, detached from the social bearings of class, religion and nation. After the self-removal from the working class presented in *Sons and Lovers*, Lawrence's *The Rainbow* (1915) indicts contemporary industrial England for the lack of human community at its centre, embodying this accusation finally in Ursula Brangwen who feels she does 'not belong to Beldover nor to Nottingham nor to England'.[101] Ursula's individual protest can only be broadened (through the novel's leading metaphors of the arch and rainbow) by recourse to the model of harmonious, organic relations at Marsh Farm, richly celebrated in the novel's opening 'poem'. Yet, as the novel's narrative of change over three generations shows, this transcendent myth of rural England is engaged in an uneven contest with the movements of prosaic history which Lawrence might resist but cannot deny.[102] In *Women in Love* (published in 1921, but written in 1916), this myth is forsaken, and Lawrence bids farewell to an England and English nationalism he sees as irrelevant and dying. The only endorsed alternative in the novel appears in the character of Rupert Birkin who feels that the English have 'got to disappear from their own special brand of Englishness'[103] before a new race can come into being. Birkin holds to an embryonic conception of fellowship, to 'creative mystery' beyond 'the old ethic of humanity', beyond the possessions of the home, beyond location and nation. His wish is to find freedom 'with a few other people', to 'just wander about a bit', to 'set off – just towards the distance . . . to get to – nowhere', there to lead a 'sketchy, unfinished existence' (355, 356, 402). Birkin's idea corresponds to Lawrence's own utopian community, Rananim, which was to be a decent, anti-materialist colony, remote from concepts of nationalism and political action, but as deeply imbued with liberal and Romantic ideology as Coleridge and Southey's earlier Pantisocracy.[104] Its real-life equivalent was Lawrence's war-time retreat to Cornwall where, in 1916, he wrote *Women in Love,* at a time when he said, 'the war, the whole world has gone out of my imagination'. At this point Lawrence's resistance to Englishness had become a misanthropic and absolute anti-nationalism and his utopia a community of one, himself, 'without the people'.[105]

James Joyce's hostility towards England was coupled with an unrelenting enmity towards Irish Catholicism.[106] In 'voluntary exile' from Ireland from 1904, he was led, through an acquaintance with examples of European and American anarchist and socialist thought, to see himself as a 'socialistic artist'.[107] The cultural nationalism of the Gaelic League and Irish Literary Theatre was, Joyce believed, parochial and propagandist (it risked, he said, becoming 'all too Irish').[108] In the conviction that Irish literature should on the contrary be Europeanized, Joyce looked, as did Eliot and Pound, to the example of the exiled Dante, and, like Yeats, to the English Romantics, Shelley and Blake.[109] As an 'unacknowledged legislator' he was committed to the artist's 'mental fight' in redeeming Ireland from the spiritual paralysis presented in *Dubliners* (1914). Like Stephen Dedalus in *A Portrait of the Artist,* he was to 'fly by' the nets of 'nationality, language, religion' in defence of artistic liberty. Only thus untrammelled could he 'forge . . . the uncreated conscience of my race'.[110]

Joyce's career and thinking come to present a central problem in the relation of modernist art and politics. In liberating form and language modern avant-garde art was consonant, Joyce believed, with a libertarian social philosophy.[111] The example of Ezra Pound alone, with which Joyce was familiar, ought to have instructed him differently. The naïveté of this belief, however, was revealed in Joyce's own fiction, which displayed nothing so much as the accelerating distance between his artistic self-dedication and the intimate material detail of Irish life and history he worked upon. Significantly, in Joyce's Irish epic *Ulysses,* the meeting towards which everything tends between artistic integrity and progressive collectivist ideas, results in the anti-climactic and desultory encounter between Stephen Dedalus and Leopold Bloom. Joyce proceeded, then, in *Finnegans Wake* (1939), towards a truly anarchistic liberation of polyvalency which opens language in the same gesture that it seals and protects the word and the work from its users. The result is not only a rejection of the double yoke of Church and King, but of the triple tyranny Oscar Wilde had named as Prince, Pope and People in *The Soul of Man Under Socialism* (a text Joyce translated into Italian in 1909). Joyce therefore flew by all nets but one: the self-government of art, pursuing an anarchistic aestheticism to its extreme. His politics of 'style'[112] appears, then, not so much an answer to religious and imperialistic despotism as their consequence.

Unlike Joyce, W. B. Yeats was actively involved in the movements of Irish cultural and political nationalism, though (like Joyce) he resisted the propagandizing tendencies of the first and the tactics of revolutionary insurrection which developed in the second. Yeats's nationalism was, he always claimed, consistent with 'the school of John O'Leary', a Fenian leader whose aim was a democratic Irish Republic.[113] Though Yeats's relation to the Catholic inspiration of Irish nationalism was complicated by his Protestant bourgeois birth and identification with the Irish Ascendancy class, his interest in Irish folk tale, ballad and legend, and his work for the Abbey Theatre (particularly his play *Cathleen Ni Houlihan*) were consistent with Fenian populism. The turbulent years 1914–21, however, which saw in Ireland the Easter Rising, the Anglo-Irish War and then civil war, produced sharp divisions within Irish nationalism and, in Yeats, a growing desire for authoritarian rule. Under the pressure of these events his populism assumed the more aristocratic mode expressed in his admiration of the virtues of 'custom and ceremony' and his idealization of the social order and artistic patronage of the country house, as evinced by Lady Gregory's Coole Park. Yeats's ambivalence towards the changed character of Irish nationalism was revealed in the poems 'Easter 1916' and 'Meditations in Time of Civil War'.[114] In the first the rebels are castigated for their sterile, self-destructive dogma, while Yeats at the same time acknowledges his role as parent to their idealism and gives the executed rebels heroic, mythological stature. In the second 'an affable Irregular' (opposed to the Treaty with England which gave Ireland dominion status) and a soldier from the national army (which supported the Treaty) are both casually greeted at Yeats's door before he turns away from the world of action to 'the cold snows of a dream'. The refrain of 'a terrible beauty' in 'Easter 1916' aestheticizes the politics of the rebellion and the final section of 'Meditations' (as of the related 'Nineteen Hundred and Nineteen') adopts a lofty, visionary perspective upon Ireland's

violent present and future. In his political uncertainty, Yeats turned then
to the convictions of image and symbol. The codification of this belief in
the transforming power of the Romantic poet's symbolical imagination was
A Vision (composed between 1917 and 1925). The dialectic of contraries
upon which this text and much of Yeats's poetry is built, comes from this
point on to affirm Yeats's intimations of apocalypse: a 'second coming', in
the poem of that title, from which will issue an anti-democratic order, at
once 'hierarchical, multiple, masculine, harsh, surgical'.[115] Over the whole
period Yeats's politics consort with both republican and conservative forms
of populist nationalism, alike in their antipathy towards English rule. His
poetry however, though it was inseparable from his politics, expressed a
unique relationship with England, since it was written in English and drew
upon a redefined and reclaimed early English Romanticism, yet was, as
Thomas MacDonagh observed, 'distinctively Irish too'; its differences being
'the difference of race and nationality'.[116]

What distinguished Yeats from other writers discussed in this section
was not his conservative vision or reassertion of Romanticism, but their
combination in a manner antagonistic to English political rule and English
liberalism. The strength of his position derived from the sustaining context of
Ireland's relation to England, which provided him with a cultural, institutional
and political base, sufficient to make him a popular national poet and public
man in a way none of the other oppositional writers were. The careers of
the modernist writers (and of some who were not modernists) were marked
by self-exile and marginalization resulting from their estrangement from
such a secure social base and the frustrations and antipathies thus produced.
Throughout the years we have surveyed, oppositional writers confirm the
truism of an oppositional position; that it is removed from present centres
of power and influence. Literary culture has, at later dates than the period
under review, accommodated the modernist writers (or, more accurately,
it has undergone the modification of accepting parts of their work, often
separated from their social and political views), while socialism and feminism
have honoured the examples of Morris, Tressell, Sylvia Pankhurst, Elizabeth
Robins and Margaret Harkness (to different degrees, and with an interest
often less in their writing than in their political credentials). The more
positive ideas for a newer England derived from these two latter sources
(interestingly the period did not produce a literature of socialist-feminist
modernism). Politically, both socialism and feminism grew in strength from
the 1880s through to 1914 when they were pressed into a more embattled
dissent by the event of the war. In such circumstances it becomes a mark of
the integrity of this opposition that it recognizes its own predicament: that
set in a rhythm of hope and defeat, bedevilled by lack of unity, compromise
and false optimism, it holds to the aspiration of a new society, but sees at the
same time that (to adapt Brecht's maxim) it can start neither from nostalgia
for a good old England, nor simply from the dream of a better future, but
from the present time of a bad new England.[117]

Notes

1   James Reeves (ed.), *Georgian Poetry* (London: Penguin, 1962), p. xv.

2   Hugh Cunningham, 'The Language of Patriotism, 1750–1914', *History Workshop Journal*, 12 (1981), 8–33.

3   Tom Nairn, *The Break-up of Britain* (London: Verso, 1981), p. 340.

4   *Studies in Literature* (London: C.U.P., 1918).

5   John Masefield, *William Shakespeare* (London: Home University Library, 1911), p. v.

6   F. J. Furnivall and John Munro, *Shakespeare Life and Work* (London: Cassell, 1908), p. 9.

7   Sidney Lee (ed.), 'Shakespeare and Patriotism', in *Shakespeare and the Modern Stage* (London: John Murray, 1906), p. 179; Sir M. W. MacCallum, *Shakespeare's Roman Plays* (London: Macmillan, 1910), p. 74.

8   George Saintsbury in *The Cambridge History of English Literature* (London: C.U.P., 1910), V, 195; Stopford Brooke, *Ten More Plays of Shakespeare* (London: Constable, 1913), p. 294; Sidney Lee in *Henry V. A Selection of Critical Essays*, ed. Michael Quinn (London: Macmillan, 1969), p. 56.

9   J. A. R. Marriott, *English History in Shakespeare* (London: Chapman and Hall, 1918), Preface, no page number.

10 Sir Walter Raleigh, 'The Age of Elizabeth', in eds. Walter Raleigh, Sidney Lee, and C. T. Onions, *Shakespeare's England* (Oxford: Clarendon Press, 1916), p. 1.

11 Raleigh, *Shakespeare and England* (London: British Academy Annual Lecture, 1918), pp. 5, 8.

12 Quiller-Couch, *Shakespeare's Workmanship* (London: Fisher Unwin, 1918), p. 157.

13 Edward Wright, 'The Novels of Thomas Hardy', *The Quarterly Review* (April 1904), *Thomas Hardy. The Critical Heritage*, ed. R. G. Cox (London: R.K.P., 1970), p. 347. Cf. The discussion by Peter Widdowson in 'Hardy in History', *Literature and History*, 9 (1983), 3–16.

14 Charles Whibley, 'Thomas Hardy', *Blackwoods Magazine* (June 1913) in Cox, Ibid., p. 411.

15 Harold Williams, 'The Wessex Novels of Thomas Hardy' in Cox, Ibid., p. 428.

16 Paul Fussell, *The Great War and Modern Memory* (London: O.U.P, 1975), p. 157.

17 Ibid., p. 159.

18 Ibid., p. 156.

19 Rupert Brooke, *The Collected Poems with a Memoir by Edward Marsh* (1918, 3rd edition revised November 1942; London: Sidgwick and Jackson), p. clvi.

20 S. P. B. Mais, *From Shakespeare to O. Henry* (London: Richards P., 1977), p. 273.

21 *Arthur Symons. Selected Writings*, ed. Roger Holdsworth (Cheshire: Carcanet P., 1974), p. 21.

22 W. B. Yeats, *Essays and Introductions* (1895; London: Macmillan, 1961), p. 197.

23 'The Symbolism of Poetry', in *Yeats. Selected Criticism*, ed. A. Norman Jeffares (London: Macmillan, 1970), pp. 43, 49, 51.

24 Cf. John Bayley, *The Romantic Survival* (London: Constable, 1957), pp. 45–6; also John Lucas 'From Naturalism to Symbolism', in *Decadence and the 1890s*, ed. Ian Fletcher (London: Edward Arnold, 1970).

25 John Goode, 'The Decadent Writer as Producer' in Fletcher, Ibid., especially pp. 114–15.

26 Cf. the discussion of the predominantly *belletrist* tendencies in contemporary reviewing and criticism in John Gross, *The Rise and Fall of the Man of Letters* (London: Weidenfeld and Nicolson, 1969), especially ch. 5. 'The aesthetes of the late nineteenth century', Gross writes, 'usually turned out to be men of the Far Right. It may be that those whose first aim is to "appreciate" the world are the natural enemies of those whose first aim is to change it' (153).

27 W. E. Henley, *Works* (1908; repr. New York: AMS Press, 1970), II, 158–9.

28 Cf. Andre Guillaume, *William Ernest Henley et son Groupe* (Paris: Librairie Klincksieck, 1973), p. 166.

29 Ibid., p. 168.

30 Quoted in J. H. Buckley *William Ernest Henley* (Princeton, NJ: Princeton U.P., 1945), p. 95; cf. also Guillaume, op. cit., p. 157n.

31 Henley, *Works,* V. 142–3, 146.

32 Quoted in Buckley, op. cit., p. 131.

33 Quoted, Ibid., p. 142.

34 Henley, *Works,* I, 87, and II, 140–1.

35 T. S. Eliot, *The Sacred Wood* (1920; London: Methuen, 1960), pp. 25, 29.

36 Ernest de Selincourt, *English Poets and the National Ideal* (London: O.U.P., 1915), p. 8.

37 Quoted, in *Imagist Poetry,* ed. Peter Jones (London: Penguin, 1972), p. 14.

38 S. P. B. Mais, op. cit., pp. 256–7.

39 Henry Newbolt, 'A New Study of English Poetry', *English Review* (January 1912), 10, p. 292; quoted in C. K. Stead, *The New Poetic* (London: Penguin, 1967), p. 70.

40 Quoted, Stead, Ibid., p. 75.

41 Quoted, Ibid., p. 79.

42 Cf. Stead, Ibid., pp. 59, 63.

43 Quoted, Ibid., p. 56.

44 Cf. David Perkins, *A History of Modern Poetry* (Cambridge, MA: Harvard U.P., 1976), pp. 165–71.

45 Ibid., p. 165.

46 *Gerard Manley Hopkins. Poems and Prose*, ed. W. H. Gardner (London: Penguin, 1953), p. 173.

47 V. de Sola Pinto, *Crisis in English Poetry 1880–1940* (London: Hutchinson, 1967), p. 72.

48 'Asterix' (pseudonym for T. S. Eliot), *The Egoist,* 3 (March 1918), 43; quoted in John Press, *A Map of Modern English Verse* (London: O.U.P., 1971), p. 118.

49 Quoted, Press, Ibid., pp. 118–19.

50 Cf. The discussion in Press, Stead, and in James Reeves' 'Introduction' to *Georgian Poetry* (Harmondsworth: Penguin, 1962).

51 Cf. Lytton Strachey's influential review of 1914, where he pronounced on Hardy's 'flat and undistinguished, clumsy collection of vocables' in which 'cacophony is incarnate,' *New Statesman* (19 December 1914); quoted in *Thomas Hardy. Poems*, eds. J. Gibson and T. Johnson (London: Macmillan, 1979), p. 13.

52 Perkins, op. cit., p. 163.

53 Quoted in Christopher Hassall, *Rupert Brooke: A Biography* (London: Faber, 1964), p. 443.

54 *The Prose of Rupert Brooke*, ed. Christopher Hassall (London: Sidgwick and Jackson, 1956), p. 199.

55 'Preface', no page number (dated February 1897).

56 *Jefferies' England*, ed. S. J. Looker (London: Constable, 1937), p. 256.

57 Cf. *Men Who March A Way*, ed. I. M. Parsons (London: Heinemann, 1965), p. 14.

58 Fussell, op. cit., p. 244.

59 *The Letters of Charles Sorley* (1919), p. 240.

60 W. J. Keith, *The Rural Tradition* (Hassocks: Harvester P., 1975), p. 203.

61 Edward Thomas, *Walter Pater* (London: Martin Secker, 1913), p. 216.

62 Quoted, Eleanor Farjeon, *Edward Thomas. The Last Four Years* (London: O.U.P., 1979), p. 154.

63 *The Collected Poems of Edward Thomas*, ed. R. George Thomas (London: O.U.P., 1981), pp. 56–7.

64 Stan Smith, 'A Language Not to Be Betrayed', *Literature and History*, 4 (1976), 71.

65 G. M. Trevelyan, *England Under the Stuarts* (London: Methuen, 1904); quoted in Smith, ibid., p. 72.

66 D. H. Lawrence, *The White Peacock* (1911; Harmondsworth: Penguin, 1950), pp. 155, 246, 262, 298. Cf. the discussion of Lawrence's aeestheticism in Graham Holderness, *D. H. Lawrence: History, Ideology and Fiction* (Dublin: Gill and Macmillan, 1982), chs 3, 4 and Appendix.

67 'England, My England', in *D. H. Lawrence. The Complete Short Stories* (London: Heinemann, 1955), II, 305.

68 C. F. G. Masterman, *The Condition of England* (London: Methuen, 1909), p. 12.

69 John Galsworthy, *The Country House* (1907; London: Dent, 1953), p. 41.

70 E. M. Forster, *Howards End* (1910; Harmonsdworth: Penguin, 1975).

71 Constance Holme, *The Lonely Plough* (1914; London: World's Classics, 1962), pp. vii–viii.

72 John Buchan, *The Three Hostages* (London: Hodder and Stoughton, 1924), p. 14.

73 Joseph Conrad, *The Heart of Darkness* (1902; Harmondsworth: Penguin, 1973), pp. 94–5.

74 *The Hound of the Baskervilles*, in *The Original Illustrated Sherlock Holmes* (London: Murray, 1979), pp. 405, 407.

75 Cf. *Into Unknown England 1866–1913*, ed. P. J. Keating (London: Fontana, 1976), pp. 11–32; also Keating, *The Working Classes in Victorian Fiction* (London: R.K.P., 1971) and R. Williams, *The Country and the City* (London: Chatto and Windus, 1973), pp. 221–32.

76 Arthur Morrison, *Tales of Mean Streets* (1901; Suffolk: The Boydell P., 1983), p. 23.

77 Engels, 'Letter to E. Bernstein' (22 August 1884), *Marx and Engels on Britain* (Moscow: Progress P., 1962), pp. 566–7.

78 Gissing, quoted in Keating *The Working Classes in Victorian Fiction,* p. 54; Morrison, op. cit., 'Preface' by Michael Krzak, p. 13.

79 Jack London, *The People of the Abyss* (1903; London: The Journeyman P., 1978), p. 114.

80 John Goode, 'Margaret Harkness and the Socialist Novel', in *The Socialist Novel in Britain*, ed. H. Gustav Klaus (Brighton: Harvester P., 1982), pp. 57–62.

81 *News from Nowhere,* in *Three Works by William Morris* (London: Lawrence and Wishart, 1977), p. 254.

82 *The Ragged-Trousered Philanthropists* (New York: Monthly Review P., 1962), p. 538.

83 The description of Blatchford is Bernard Semmel's in *Imperialism and Social Reform. English Social-Imperial Thought 1895–1914* (London: Allen & Unwin, 1960). Semmel describes Blatchford as 'an imperialist, a militarist, a nationalist, a protectionist – everything the pre-war British radical was not. . . . As an imperial socialist he insisted that the need to protect the nation-family was an object far more important than the class struggle of the international socialists' (pp. 231–2).

84 Brooke, *Collected Poems,* op. cit., pp. cxlvi, cxlvii.

85 H. G. Wells, *Journalism and Prophecy 1893–1946: An Anthology*, ed. W. Warren Wagar (London: Bodley Head, 1965), p. 126.

86 Ibid., p. 46.

87 H. G. Wells, *Tono-Bungay* (1909; London: Collins, 1953), p. 25.

88 G. B. Shaw, 'The Transition to Social Democracy', in *Fabian Essays* (1889; London: Fabian Society, 1931), p. 186.

89 *Heartbreak House* (1919; Harmondsworth: Penguin, 1964), 'Preface', p. 7.

90 Quoted, Louis Crompton, 'Shaw's Challenge to Liberalism', in *George Bernard Shaw*, ed. R. J. Kaufmann (New Jersey: Prentice Hall, 1965), p. 98.

91 Cf. Patricia Stubbs, *Women and Fiction: Feminism and the Novel 1880–1920* (Brighton: Harvester P., 1979), chs 11, 13, 14.

92 Elizabeth Robins, *The Convert* (1907; London: The Women's P., 1980), p. 26.

93 'For Half a Year', in *Writ on Cold Slate* (London: Dreadnought P., 1921); reprinted in *Bricklight. Poems from the Labour Movement in East London*, ed. Chris Searle (London: Pluto P., 1980), pp. 189–91.

94 Cf. Sheila Rowbotham, *Hidden from History* (London: Pluto P., 1974), pp. 114–17.

95 Sylvia Pankhurst, *The Home Front* (London: Hutchinson, 1932), pp. 64, 447.

96 In 'Tradition and the Individual Talent' Eliot writes, 'The existing monuments form an ideal order among themselves, which is modified by the introduction of the new (the really new) work of art among them. The existing order is complete before the new work arrives; for order to persist after the supervention of novelty, the *whole* existing order must be, if ever so slightly altered.' (*Selected Essays* [London: Faber, 1932], p. 15).

97 For early responses to the poem cf. *The Wasteland. A Selection of Critical Essays*, eds. C. B. Cox and A. P. Hinchliffe (London: Macmillan, 1968), pp. 29–44.

98 *The Selected Letters of Ezra Pound, 1907–1941*, ed. D. D. Paige (New York: New Directions, 1979), p. 24. cf. also Peter Brooker's *A Student's Guide to the Selected Poems of Ezra Pound* (London: Faber, 1979), for the response of reviewers to Pound's *Lustra*, 'The Seafarer' and '*Homage to Sextus Propertius*'.

99 Ezra Pound, *Selected Poems* (London: Faber, 1975), pp. 100–1.

100 Ezra Pound, Canto LXXX, ibid., p. 178; T. S. Eliot, *The Four Quartets* (London: Faber, 1959), p. 58.

101 D. H. Lawrence, *The Rainbow* (1915; Harmondsworth: Penguin, 1949), p. 493.

102 Cf. Graham Holderness, op. cit., for an extended reading of the novel along these lines (pp. 174–89).

103 D. H. Lawrence, *Women in Love* (1921; Harmondsworth: Penguin, 1960), p. 445.

104 Holderness op. cit., p. 196.

105 Quoted, Ibid., p. 198.

106 Cf. Dominic Manganiello *Joyce's Politics* (London: R.K.P., 1980), esp. pp. 174–89. We are generally indebted in these paragraphs to this study, though we take a different view of Joyce's literary politics.

107 Quoted, Manganiello, ibid., p. 44.

108 Ibid., p. 28.

109 Cf. Ibid., pp. 190–203, 219, 232.

110 *A Portrait of the Artist as a Young Man* (1916; Harmondsworth: Penguin, 1960), pp. 203, 253.

111 'Our Vanguard of politicians', Joyce wrote, 'put up the banners of anarchy and communism; our artists seek the simplest liberation of rhythms', quoted, Ibid., p. 69.

112 To Stanislaus Joyce, Joyce said 'For God's sake don't talk politics. I'm not interested in politics. The only thing that interests me is style', quoted, Ibid., p. 1.

113 Cf. Elizabeth Cullingford, *Yeats, Ireland and Fascism* (London: Macmillan, 1981), p. 4.

114 W. B. Yeats, *Selected Poetry*, ed. A. N. Jeffares (London: Macmillan, 1965), pp. 93–5, 112–19.

115 Yeats, *A Vision* (London: Macmillan, 1962), p. 263.

116 Thomas MacDonagh, *Literature in Ireland* (Dublin: Talbot P., 1916), pp. 23, 241.

117 Brecht's words were, 'Don't start from the good old things, but the bad new ones', quoted in Walter Benjamin, *Understanding Brecht*, trans. Anna Bostock (London: N.L.B., 1973), p. 121.

CHAPTER SIX

The identity of English music: The reception of Elgar 1898–1935

Jeremy Crump

No technical analysis can discover for certain just how he took something from the air of the Malvern Hills, from the banks of the Teme and Severn, from the cloisters of Worcester Cathedral, and turned it into music which speaks immediately and directly of these things to his fellow countrymen. Walk in Worcestershire and the music of Elgar is in the air around you, fantastic as this may seem to the prosaically minded.

MICHAEL KENNEDY *Elgar* (BBC Music Guides 1970)

Elgar's place in English musical history has been unique since the early 1900s. As early as 1898, the *Musical Standard* observed that his cantata *Caractacus* 'definitely determines Mr Elgar's position as the first of modern British composers'.[1] With the success of the *Enigma Variations* the following year, such an opinion became widespread in musical circles. From that time, Elgar's ceremonial music won him a position as musical laureate which has remained without parallel, and which received official recognition in 1924 when he was made Master of the King's Musick.[2] But Elgar has come to be seen by many as a writer of music whose quintessential Englishness transcends its association with great national occasions. At a meeting of the Royal Society of Arts in 1972, a speaker from the floor, a self-confessed patriot, Dr Frank Hansford-Miller, claimed that

> Elgar is loved by the English people as one of the greatest English composers and also for his unique expression of the deep intangible feelings of England.[3]

This is a typical view of the composer, and permeates the writing of several of his biographers. Often, a specific association has been made between the music and the English countryside, an association central to Ken Russell's film *Elgar* (1963), which is itself a potent influence on recent popular responses to the composer.

In reading appreciations, biographies and criticisms of Elgar it is apparent that the view of the music as expressive of a deeper English identity with strong rural associations was generated under specific historical and cultural circumstances, and that the process by which such meanings were generated may be understood through the study of historically constructed critical traditions, the vocabulary used for discussing the music, and the contexts in which it was performed. It is also clear that the Elgar of the current repertoire is the product of selection which cannot be understood solely in terms of an unchanging set of musical criteria. Of particular interest in this context is the critical neglect of Elgar's great popularity during World War I, and of the works he wrote at that time. This chapter sets out to trace how Elgar's music was received as part of English high culture, both before and during World War I, and then to demonstrate how the Englishness of the music was redefined in the 1930s in a form which has remained largely unchanged since. Elgar's career, his remarkable success after 1900, and his war work are most revealing about the role which the musical establishment played in shaping views of national identity. In order to appraise Elgar's music as it was understood when relatively new, it is necessary to be aware of the reinterpretation of his work in the criticism of the 1930s and in Elgarian biographies written since 1950 which have generally reinforced that reinterpretation.[4]

Elgar established: 1890–1914

Musical life in England quickened from the late 1870s. Major institutions were founded or rejuvenated during that time, and musicians strove to increase their social status by promoting a professional code of high standards of education and performance. Among new institutions were the Royal College of Music (1882), the Associated Board of the Royal Schools of Music (1880), the Royal Choral Society (f. 1871 as the Royal Albert Hall Choral Society), the South

Place Chamber Concerts (1887), Henry Wood's Queen's Hall Orchestra (1896; in 1904 it became the London Symphony Orchestra) and Promenade Concerts (1895). In the provinces, new festivals were inaugurated, such as the North Staffordshire Festival (1888), and the competition festival movement spread from small beginnings in Kendal in 1885 to include 72 festivals and 60,000 competitors by 1909. The English Musical Renaissance, as it became known, also witnessed the activity of Parry, Stanford and Mackenzie, among other composers and the growth of music as a university subject. The main thrust was not so much the desire to spread certain forms of music to the working class, something which had been the aim of the mid-nineteenth century tonic solfa and brass band movements, but the establishment of music as a legitimate occupation for the English middle class.[5]

By 1910, William J. Galloway, in his *Musical England*, could write that 'the mass of the public no longer looks on native musicians with suspicion'.[6] Yet in spite of such developments the musical press continued to reflect a widespread view that much remained to be done; English musical life was still dominated by Germans. E. D. Mackerness has identified three areas in which this was particularly so – in composition, performance and the trade in instruments and sheet music. (Musical education in Germany, which Elgar himself had wanted but had been unable to afford, was less eagerly sought after the 1870s.) In the piano trade, German competition had been severe since the same decade, particularly in the high quality domestic and colonial markets. In 1914, one sixth of pianos sold in Britain were German, despite a revival of the native industry. From the 1880s, British piano manufacturers were keen supporters of 'fair trade'.[7]

There was much criticism of English composition, dominated as it was by festival commissions and church music. In his 1905 lecture, *A Future for English Music*, Elgar said that 'we had inherited an art which has had no hold on the affections of our own people, and is held in no respect abroad.' Arnold Bax, recalling his early musical education at the Hampstead Conservatoire in the 1890s, recalled studying works by composers 'who by virtue of their mildness might well have been described as "sheep in sheep's clothing".' Meanwhile, Henry Wood, much to the dismay of the musical press, promoted Russian music at the Queen's Hall. The *Musical Times,* shortly before the first performance of the *Enigma Variations*, was strident in its demands for the promotion of works of native composers.[8]

The demand for English works had a broader base than frustration with the predominance of dull choral music. As Vic Gammon has pointed out, from the 1880s onwards there were signs of an 'aggressive artistic nationalism' coinciding with imperial and industrial rivalry with Germany and the United States. The outbreak of the Boer War in 1899, followed by early British disasters, brought self-doubt in official circles and in the middle-class press. Such fear of external threat was intensified by renewed awareness of the social consequences of life in the poorer districts of cities. As Price observes, the war 'served for a time as the focus for all the fears that many Britons had about their country's future.' The accompanying exaggerated, militaristic patriotism, riotously celebrated at the relief of Mafeking, 'provided the finest excuse for England to throw aside traditional reserve and loudly prove that her people were still the finest race on earth.' In his choice of texts, extensive use of march rhythms and orchestration giving prominence to brass, Elgar, in works such as the *Pomp and Circumstance Marches Nos 1 and 2* (1901) and the *Coronation Ode* (1902), which included the text of *Land of Hope and Glory,* addressed this crisis of national self-assurance. In a wider sense, Elgar's major works of the period 1899–1914 satisfied the musical profession's demand for English music of some standing at home and in Europe. Elgar's music was at the forefront of cultural rivalry. Of particular importance in this context was his acclaim by prominent German musicians including Richter and Strauss.[9]

The reassertion of the independence of English musical life was by no means complete by the outbreak of World War I, nor was it due solely to Elgar. Only the anti-German mood of 1914 purged the profession of German musicians. Nor should the initiatives of Beecham, with his New Symphony Orchestra and championship of Delius, be overlooked. But Elgar acted as a focus for the resurgence of English composition, and a symbol of restored national pride in music. In 1902, the *Daily Telegraph* observed that 'he now occupies the position of a man with whom most people are determined to be pleased', and, three years later, *The Sketch* mentioned that he was recognized by all *competent* critics at home and abroad as 'probably the greatest musician of our time'.[10]

Two events in particular mark the degree of Elgar's acceptance. The three-day Elgar festival at Covent Garden in March 1904, promoted by the Opera Syndicate and attended by the King and Queen, was an unexampled celebration of the work of a living British composer, and was all the more extraordinary in that it preceded the composition of the symphonies and concertos. Four years later, the *First Symphony* was greeted with great enthusiasm. *The Times* recalled at Elgar's death in 1934 that

> Never has a symphony become so instantly "the rage" with the ordinary British public as did this. For some time the regular orchestras of London could not play it often enough, special concerts were arranged for it, enterprising commercialists even engaged orchestras to play it in their lounges and palm courts as an attraction to their winter sales of underwear.

There were eighty-two performances in 1908–09, most of them in Britain.[11]

How then was Elgar's Englishness constructed in this period of his first popularity? His identification with Worcestershire and Malvern was early exploited by those wishing to establish his English credentials, although critics did not at this stage bring pastoral associations to the fore. A seven-page feature on Elgar in the *Musical Times* in 1900 located him in Malvern and described him as 'one who habitually thinks his thoughts and draws his inspiration from those elevated surroundings'. Robert J. Buckley, author of the first monograph on Elgar (for the *Living Masters of Modern Music* series) thought that the composer's house was a 'meet situation for the dreamy tone-poet'. In so far as such invocation of place was more than appropriate scene-setting, it served to distance Elgar from the metropolitan musical establishment, especially from the university and academy men such as Stanford, and their academic music.[12]

Elgar's music could be placed within a specifically English cultural setting not only through such geographical links, but also through his use of the major popular genres of late-nineteenth-century music, other than the music-hall song. Hence he had access, as Stanford did not have, to appreciation by a wide public and could be viewed as a writer of English music in a sense that Delius, for example, was not.

Galloway wrote of the festival choral work as 'a form of entertainment that has taken a peculiarly firm and lasting hold upon the affection of English people'. Much of the compositional effort of the English Musical Renaissance was expended on such works. Some, such as Parry's *Blest Pair of Sirens* (1887) and Coleridge-Taylor's *Hiawatha* (1898–1900) have survived, but most of them were soon put aside. Ernest Newman was frank in his opinion that

> Elgar has done almost all that could be done with this deadly form of British art, the day for which has long gone by.

In later life, Elgar was to tell Delius that he wrote so many oratorios as 'the penalty of my English environment', but there is little reason to suppose that in the 1890s Elgar, for all his complaining to Jaeger (his contact at Novello's) about the poor reward for such work, was antipathetic to the genre as such. He wrote of *The Black Knight* (1892):

> It is too artistic for the ordinary conductor of Choral Societies – I find they are an inordinately ignorant lot of cheesemongering idiots. The chorus and orchestra *go* for my things.[13]

J. P. Nettel, in his account of musical life in the Potteries, describes how successful *King Olaf* was from the time of its first performance in Hanley in 1896, and how Elgar's music continued to be attractive to the North Staffordshire Choral Society. In 1897, Novello's received enquiries concerning the performing rights for the work from over a dozen choral societies.[14] Elgar's later choral works were similarly in demand, and the *Dream of Gerontius* (1900) was to take its place alongside *Messiah* and *Elijah* in the repertoire of all choral societies.

Elgar was no less familiar with the demands of writing for that other ubiquitous form of Victorian entertainment, the military band. His *Imperial*

March, written for the jubilee of 1897, received many performances, and Novello's published an arrangement of it for military band. Elgar wrote to Jaeger in 1898 that he was working on such an arrangement of *King Olaf* and the following year discussed arrangement of material from *Caractacus* for the same medium.[15] Thus even before the success of the first two *Pomp and Circumstance Marches* in 1901, Elgar's music was available for performance by municipal and regimental bands at the seaside and in parks throughout the country. Signs of Elgar's familiarity with band writing pervade his work, not only in the deliberate invocation of both good and bad music in *Cockaigne* (1901), but also in his scoring for wind instruments throughout the orchestral works.

Even more suggestive of Elgar's identification with popular musical genres was the use of a suite from *Caractacus,* arranged by the military bandmaster Lieut. Charles Godfrey, as a test piece at the Belle Vue national brass band competition in 1903. Nineteen bands played the piece, which was considered by the *Cornet,* a brass band journal, to be 'the best selection we have had at Belle Vue for many years'. It provided a good test of performance skills, and made for a much more interesting contest than the usual operatic selections. The selection of extracts seems to have met the aesthetic as well as technical requirements of the bandsmen. The opening march had 'all the vigour and sturdiness which the word "Roman" conveys' while the finale, 'The Clash of Arms is Over', was 'a fine broad chorus, wealthy in grandeur'.[16] There is no evidence in the brass band press to suggest that Elgar's music was quickly taken up into the regular repertoire of bands, nor were there advertisements of arrangements of his works. Elgar himself did not write specifically for brass band until his *Severn Suite* in 1930, but the 1903 piece is suggestive of a sympathetic response to his music from a wide public.

As with any successful composer, Elgar's music was soon arranged for domestic performance. In 1899, the *Musical Times* reviewed arrangements of items from *Lux Christi* (1896) and *Caractacus* for voice and piano, and a piano reduction of the *Enigma Variations.*[17] Elgar had long since displayed his ability to write commercially successful salon music. *Salut d'Amour* (1888) had by 1921 appeared in 25 instrumental arrangements and 12 vocal adaptations, and was a staple of municipal, restaurant and, later, cinema bands.[18] Elgar continued to write similar music concurrently with his major works. *Carissima* and *Rosemary* did not appear until 1914–15.

In part, then, the Englishness of Elgar's music was a product of his use of established forms, many of them the most common in English music making in the 1890s. At the same time, the context of performance of his ceremonial music, including the *Coronation Ode, Coronation March* (1912), and music for the masque *The Crown of India* (1912), together with the unashamed patriotism of many of the texts he chose from *The Banner of St. George* (1897) onwards, established his identity with the official display of the Imperial court. Of course he was not alone in this, but his presentation to Edward VII (1904), knighthood (1905) and OM (1911) set him at the forefront of such composers, as did his dedication of the *Second Symphony* (1911) to the memory of Edward VII.

There were a few doubts as to the musical value of the ceremonial music – and of the literary value of the texts of the pre-1900 choral works. Sir Thomas Beecham, looking back at the period in 1944, thought that in his large-scale orchestral writing:

> he strays with a dangerous ease to the borderline of a military rodomontade that is hardly distinguishable from the commonplace and the vulgar.

Ernest Newman felt that *Caractacus* was made to end 'in a sputter of bathos and rant'. But most contemporary critics did not feel the need to draw a distinction in quality, as opposed to function, between the ceremonial and 'serious' music, nor to apologize for the former. Even Newman found that the *Coronation Ode* had 'a good many analogies with the better patriotic verses of Mr. Kipling', and Buckley was satisfied with Elgar's explanation of the *Pomp and Circumstance* marches as the work of 'a bard for the people', who 'ought to write a popular tune sometimes'. For the music critic of the *Daily Telegraph* in 1903, Elgar was admirable since he neither tried to make 'proselytes to believe in his own powers' nor to cultivate fashionable whim. He was 'sturdily independent, courting nobody'. It is not easy to square these yeoman values, very much a part of Elgar's personal style, with his cultivation of official recognition, honours and the petty ceremonial of robes and court dress. What such commentators were looking for was a native musician whose self-confidence and reserved manner contrasted with the Wagnerian self-possession of foreign composers, notably Richard Strauss. They found Elgar English in bearing as well as in the sentiments expressed in his works.[19]

It requires an effort of some historical imagination to come to terms with the frequent contemporary comments on the startling modernity of Elgar's music. Yet Constance Smedley claimed in the *Daily Chronicle* that of English composers, 'Elgar alone has the reputation of extreme modernity', and Jaeger thought *The Apostles* (1903):

> all so original, so individual and subjective that it will take the British Public ten years to let it soak into its pachydermal mind.

Such comments were especially applied to the major choral works, *Gerontius*, *The Apostles* and *The Kingdom* (1906), which had few rivals among European composers. Ernest Walker went further in his *History of English Music* (1907) when he maintained that 'vividness, courage, modernity inspire every page of the works by which he bids fair to live'. Emphasis placed upon Elgar's modernity served to locate him within the European mainstream, and there was evident pleasure displayed in the press when Strauss dubbed Elgar 'the first English Progressive'. But Elgar's modernity was seen as distinct from that of the Europeans. His works were preferred by many to those of

Strauss and Mahler since they lacked the pretensions of the former and the neuroticism of the latter. Elgar's *Caractacus* was seen as 'a good example of a clever modern work, in which mere cleverness is never allowed to obtrude itself', and the *Musical Times* praised the unconventionality of *Gerontius* as 'the outcome of conviction'.[20]

That Elgar could be celebrated as a modern composer reflects the conservatism and insularity of the concert-going public before 1914. They showed a wilful lack of interest in the Second Viennese School. Henry Wood's first British performance of Schoenberg's *Five Orchestral Pieces* Opus 29 was hissed by promenaders in 1912, and he was unable to find a sponsor for the same composer's *Gurrelieder* the following year. Schoenberg's own performance of the *Five Orchestral Pieces* drew an appreciative audience in January 1914 though, suggesting that greater interest in such music may have developed had war not intervened. As it was, English music remained largely under the domination of Elgar's idiosyncratic use of the vocabulary of late Romanticism until the 1920s.[21]

Elgar was modern in a peculiarly English way; experiment was tempered by genuine if vaguely defined feeling. *Musical Opinion* praised the *Enigma Variations* as 'music that will please and interest the public'. It did not just aim at being admired by 'a few professors here and there who are in a position to grasp its technical exercises'. The subsequent popularity of *The Kingdom* and the *First Symphony* indicates that such modernity held few terrors for audiences.[22]

Elgar and the war effort

English musical life was fundamentally affected by the war. The attempt to exclude all German music from the concert halls did not survive the first week of the war, but music by Germans and Austrians after Wagner was not performed, and the works of composers from allied nations were actively promoted. The total number of concerts declined sharply, German musicians were expelled, and benefit funds for out-of-work musicians were established. Choral societies were affected by recruitment. At the same time, it was hoped that musicians would play a part in the war effort, both in raising morale at the front, which was largely done by concert parties and music-hall entertainers, and by contributing to the propaganda effort at home. Much of the promotion of such events was left to private enterprise and to charitable organizations. Together, these efforts marked the rallying of the musical establishment to the nation's (and the government's) cause.[23]

Elgar's wartime career has received relatively little attention from his biographers. Diana McVeagh's article in the *New Grove* deals with it in two half-paragraphs, while Michael Kennedy includes it in a section of his *Portrait of Elgar* entitled 'Decline, 1914–34'. *The Times's* obituary makes no reference to it. In fact, the years from 1914 until the beginning of 1918, when

Elgar's health was bad and he retired to Sussex, saw him as much involved in performance and composition as at any time, and enjoying an unrivalled position in English musical life. *The Times* commented in May 1916 that 'Since the war began Elgar, more than ever before, has been regarded by the British people as their musical laureate', while the *Sheffield Daily Post* forecast that

> when the history of the great war comes to be written, the name of Edward Elgar will stand out as the one native composer whose music most truly expressed the spirit of our people.[24]

That this period of Elgar's career has received so little attention is in part due to the fact that the works written at that time have not stayed in the repertoire, and because they largely belong to the ceremonial style which later critics have rejected.

Elgar's contribution to the propaganda effort led to an association of the composer with the nation in a new way. Whereas in the years of the first performances of *Enigma, Gerontius* and the *First Symphony* he was upheld for restoring the status of English music in a European context, now he was held to be a focus for that which was unique to the English spirit. His achievement was not to equal that of the Germans, but to prove his own, and by implication his culture's, superiority over them. Elgar himself was dismayed by the treatment of prominent German musicians and patrons of the arts at the outbreak of the war, yet he was able to overcome any scruples and participate vigorously in the war effort.

Elgar's commitment to that effort was enthusiastic. In August 1915, he signed a manifesto of National Service calling for 'an organised effort to carry on the war' in which 'every fit man must be made available . . . for the fighting line, or . . . for National Service at home.' He had already signed up for civil defence duties in Hampstead. Meanwhile his musical abilities were put to patriotic use, and he produced a number of vocal and orchestral pieces with which he toured the country in 1915–17 to great acclaim. At the outbreak of war, Elgar took over engagements of Kreisler, Gerhardt and Nikisch as conductor of the Hallé,[25] and in December 1914 produced *Carillon*, in which his music framed the recitation of a virulently anti-German poem by the Belgian poet Cammaerts. Against a background of German atrocity stories, and the government's use of the Belgian issue to justify British participation in the war, the piece was received with great enthusiasm. Eugene Gossens, then a young conductor in London, recalled that

> the great French actress Réjane came over from Paris to recite the poem, – Queen's Hall never witnessed such a demonstration as ensued after her delivering of the stirring lines. When she intoned "Chantons, Belges, Chantons!!" the scornful fury of the poet's indictment fired the entire audience.

The work received many performances in London and the provinces in 1915–16, when Elgar conducted it on tours by the London Symphony Orchestra organized by the Birmingham promoter Harrison. In August 1915 it was performed twice daily for a week at the Coliseum, and had previously been presented at another West End theatre, Her Majesty's. The piece was praised for its 'sturdy simplicity' and compared to the *Marseillaise* as successful war music. It was regarded as superior to the songs in music hall idiom which otherwise typified music produced during the war. Thomas Dunhill recalled that 'Nobody who heard that piece at that time can possibly forget the thrill which it provoked.' A. J. Sheldon's statement in 1932 that 'I cannot to this day think of Marie Brema screeching out its cry for revenge without shuddering' seems to have had no echo in opinions published at the time.[26]

Elgar wrote two other Cammaert's settings. *Une Voix dans le Desert* was first performed at the Shaftesbury Theatre in June 1916 as an *entr'acte* between *Cavalleria Rusticana* and *I Pagliacci,* with a stage setting depicting the trenches near the River Yser. The tone of the poem is evinced by the Belgian peasant girl's prophecy

> et tonneront nos cloches
> le dur tocsin des Boches.

The piece was performed nightly for a week. At the end of the year, *Le Drapeau Belge* had its première at Oswald Stoll's Coliseum at a benefit for the British Society for the Relief of Wounded Belgian Soldiers, and both pieces were revived in April 1917 for the Belgian King Albert's birthday concert at the Queen's Hall.[27]

One of the peaks of this first, exuberantly patriotic, phase of Elgar's wartime career came in April 1915 when a 'great patriotic concert' was performed at the Albert Hall, an event said to have been unequalled there in terms of splendour since the 1887 Jubilee. Over 400 performers were drawn from army recruiting bands, and the proceeds went to the Professional Classes War Relief Council and the Lord Mayor's Recruiting Bands. The programme included Elgar's 'March of the Moghul Emperor' from *Crown of India, Carillon* and *Land of Hope and Glory* as well as music hall favourites such as *Tipperary* and *Your King and Country Need You*. The concert was an apotheosis of self-confident militarism, preceding as it did the military disaster of the Somme (July 1915) and the increasing pressure for conscription.[28]

During the war, *Land of Hope and Glory* achieved its greatest popularity. The *Manchester Guardian* observed in 1917 that

> Music hall audiences . . . made one of Elgar's compositions their own long ago – the *Land of Hope and Glory* theme; and how fully it conforms to the requirement of permanent communal art may be gathered from the fact that few people are really aware that it is by Elgar.

But while the tune had been popular ever since its 1901 première, *The Times* felt that it was only in the few years before 1918 that the prediction of Arthur Johnstone, music critic of the *Guardian*, that it would become a national song had come true. There are numerous accounts of performances, some impromptu, others in the most formal concert setting. In the patriotic enthusiasm of 1914, a crowd joined in with the words as the band played the march at the changing of the guard outside Buckingham Palace. Shortly afterwards a massive concert by Clara Butt, the best-known concert singer of her day, at the Albert Hall, used the song as the climax of a programme of patriotic songs. The practice of audience participation in the song seems to have been customary at this time, the occasion of a remarkable public display of emotion.[29] There are fewer such reports from the more sombre years later in the war, but at the cessation of hostilities it was as popular as ever. In July 1919, at a Royal Command 'Pageant of Peace' at which representatives from all over the Empire were present, Elgar conducted *Land of Hope and Glory* just before the national anthem at the end of the programme. It was thought by at least one observer to be 'the musical climax of the pageant.'[30]

The song had the function of boosting morale and celebrating victory at public entertainments in England, extending beyond the concert platform into the music hall and presumably to less formal, communal singing. In 1919, suggestions were made that it should become the official national anthem. It also seems to have achieved some currency at the front where, to the dismay of musical commentators, the troops generally preferred music hall songs to patriotic ones.[31] Quite how popular it actually was among soldiers is uncertain. A letter from a private in the Duke of Connaught's Light Infantry describing his reaction to coming under fire, published in the *News Chronicle*, suggests all too comfortable a view of the troops' morale. It shows how Elgar's music had an immediate association with conventional expression of patriotic feelings. The soldier wrote that

> I felt for the first time what is meant by the joy of battle. . . . We almost prayed that they would come, or that we could try and reach their trenches.
>
> I saw across the channel a picture of home, and knew that England depended on us; and the knowledge set me aglow with pride. I wanted to sing *Land of Hope and Glory*.[32]

Of course, such published letters, were written for home consumption, and exceptional individual responses cannot be ruled out, but, on the whole, the evidence suggests that while *Land of Hope and Glory* was well known, it was not a favourite song of the troops. Of the songs which Clara Butt recorded at the time, *Abide with Me*, with its message of consolation, seems to have had the widest currency at the front. The expansionist sentiment of the Elgar song can have had at best an ironic significance for those for

whom 'wider still and wider' meant the struggle over a few hundred yards of
Flanders mud. Sheldon was probably right when he wrote that Englishmen
did not go into battle 'with Elgar's songs on their lips':

> The ditties of the music hall, if they did not inspire, comforted more.
> Elgar sang his songs for those whose lot it was to remain at home.[33]

Nevertheless Elgar's status was greater for the way in which he was
considered to capture the nation's more serious purpose and resolution in
adversity. Newman, whose anti-German statements reached extraordinary
ferocity for a music critic, commented that:

> an older and better civilization looks to its leading artists for something
> different from the German froth and force, bellowing and swagger.

In Newman's view, Elgar achieved this in his Binyon cycle *Spirit of England*
(1916). The serious tone of the settings was reinforced by their frequent
performance on the same programme as *The Dream of Gerontius*. Some of
Elgar's other pre-war works also received prominent performance during the
war. The *Second Symphony* (1912), for instance, was played at the Albert
Hall in June 1915. According to the *Birmingham Daily Post*

> no-one who was present could have failed to be impressed by the manner
> in which it was received by an audience in which an unusual number of
> young officers was conspicuous.

The work was said to have a wider, more profound appeal than *Carillon*.
The Black Dyke Mills Band, meanwhile, fulfilled over 40 engagements with
arrangements for brass band of the symphonies, suggesting that it was not
only the officer class who found them moving.[34]

In November 1915, Percy Scholes, then music critic of the *Evening
Standard*, wrote an 'Appeal to Elgar' in which he regretted the need to rely
on Brahms's *German Requiem* for military funerals and hoped the composer
would write a British requiem in a popular style. It should be:

> a choral piece which shall be wide enough in its verbal utterance to
> express the feelings of us all, whatever our faith, something vocally not
> too difficult for our choral societies. . . . Something we would have that
> can be sung in Westminster Abbey or Westminster Cathedral, in church,
> in chapel and in concert-room, which can be sung here and in Canada
> and Australia and South Africa.

Elgar did not respond to the challenge to compose such a multipurpose
requiem, although his *For the Fallen* (1916) came to fulfil some of these
functions. The sombre mood of London in 1915, as it became clear that

the war was to be a prolonged one, led to an upsurge of interest in the *Dream of Gerontius*, and the Catholicism of its text, by Cardinal Newman, so offensive to critics in 1900, was overlooked. A performance with Clara Butt in the Albert Hall in February 1915 drew a vast Saturday afternoon crowd. It may have been a stimulus to the singer in her promotion of one of the most extraordinary musical events of the war, an Elgar festival in May 1916 in which *Gerontius* was performed on six consecutive evenings at the Queen's Hall, along with two of Elgar's Binyon songs. Elgar conducted. The concerts raised £2,707-11-2 for the Order of St John of Jerusalem and the Red Cross, but Clara Butt's ostensible motive was to provide a focus for the nation's spirituality at a difficult time. She asked:

> Isn't it time . . . that art in England should try to express a new attitude of the English mind towards life after death? . . . We are a nation in mourning. . . . I want people to come to the Queen's Hall . . . and to realise some spiritual truths, and to give them a week of beautiful thoughts.

Elgar's music, she felt, was the most appropriate medium. The festival was preceded by single performances in Leeds and Bradford, and further performances of the *Dream of Gerontius* were given in 1917 and 1918.[35] At times, audiences reacted strongly to the work. At the end of a performance in the Albert Hall in February 1918, the audience went away 'too completely satisfied to want to applaud.'[36]

The Leeds performance of *Gerontius* also witnessed the première of *To Women* and *For the Fallen*, which, together with *The Fourth of August*, made up the cycle *Spirit of England*. These works, despite their current neglect, were seen as among Elgar's finest, and as the best music written in response to the war. Newman, having seen the score of *Gerontius*, wrote before the first performance that 'here in truth is the very voice of England, moved to the centre of her being in this War', and that the work ended appropriately in a spirit 'not of vociferous rapture, but of resignation and chastity.' Newman added later that Elgar had 'voiced the best in us' and, in a chilling review, wrote of the 'cold steel-like anger' and 'national hatred' which many felt at the time against the malevolent spirit embodied in the enemy. Elgar, he said,

> has risen . . . as no mere beating of the patriotic drum could do, to the full height of this sacredness of love and time-transcending righteousness of hatred.[37]

In *Spirit of England* and the *Dream of Gerontius*, Elgar was considered to have explored and consoled the English soul at a time of national grief. His insight was thought to transcend religious barriers and his Catholicism was overlooked. Elgar's music was seen as expressive of national identity in a more profound way than it had been before the war. As Sheldon wrote in 1926,

> The *Spirit of England* trilogy made Elgar our national minstrel in a finer way than the *Land of Hope and Glory* song did.

For the Fallen was performed in the years after the war on Armistice Day, although, despite plans to produce a shortened version at the Cenotaph ceremony in 1920, it was not used at the inauguration of the monument.[38]

Elgar's final substantial piece of war music was his setting of four Kipling poems in the *Fringes of the Fleet* (1917) for four baritones and Orchestra. It was written for performance at some of the Palaces of Variety on Oswald Stoll's circuit, and was performed at Covent Garden, Leicester and Manchester. Examples have already been given of Elgar's association with West End theatres, but in this venture Elgar and the four singers became in effect a variety turn. As the *Leicester Pioneer* noted, 'The appearance of Sir Edward Elgar conducting his own music is a great draw.' The piece was received with great applause, Elgar being called before the curtain after each performance.[39] Elgar had written a four-part unaccompanied song as an encore in anticipation of such a response.

   Why Elgar should have chosen to appear in music halls is unclear. The *Manchester Guardian* saw it as further evidence of a deliberate broadening of the appeal of his music in an effort to 'gain a point of contact with the People'. Others, including Basil Maine, thought that such touring was necessitated by financial difficulties which led in 1920 to the sale of his Hampstead mansion.[40] In either case, Elgar's tour in 1917 was unique among composers of 'serious' music at the time. Like the rest of his activities during the war, it can be seen as Elgar putting into practice a view he expressed at the time of the first performance of *Pomp and Circumstance March No.1*, that a modern composer could still be a bard for the people, accompanying them into battle with his songs. Alongside such romantic fantasy, couched in terms of high-Victorian medievalism, is Elgar's eagerness for self-promotion and commitment to the patriotic cause. At times during the war Elgar was a very prominent public figure and his association with official patriotism was complete. Both the war works and several of the principal works of the previous 20 years, especially *Gerontius* and *Land of Hope and Glory*, were identified with a national spirit which was valued for its freedom from the taint of German culture which had been dominant in pre-war musical life. Elgar did not reject German musical traditions but shared – indeed in *Carillon* and *Le Drapeau Belge* added to – the currency of anti-German feeling.

   The war was of great importance in establishing the independence of English musical life, even if the triumph of English composition was never complete, and German works written before 1880 continued to be played after 1914. There was at least a halt to the influence of new German (and especially Austrian) music. Elgar's wartime career and the uses to which his music was put suggest an attempt to reinforce a self-consciously English identity in music under the peculiar circumstances of wartime.

Neglect? 1920–30

In several accounts of Elgar's life, the 1920s are seen as a period of neglect. This opinion seems to be based on Elgar's own view that his music was no longer wanted, on outraged reports of poorly attended concerts, and statements by younger writers of how old-fashioned Elgar's music had become. Shaw, a champion of Elgar's music and a personal friend of the composer in his later years, claimed in 1929 that although Elgar was one of the world's great composers, 'I do not believe the English are proud of it, and that is the disgusting part of it'.[41]

But it will not do to accept Elgar's self-evaluation uncritically. He had said very similar things before the war and was always insecure about his own achievement. Relative neglect was inevitable given the massive popularity of Elgar during the war. He wrote relatively little following the death of his wife in 1920, so there were few opportunities for the displays of enthusiasm which had greeted earlier premières. Nevertheless, Elgar's official status was secure, and he received further honours – the KCVO in 1928 and a baronetcy in 1931. In 1924 he was made Master of the King's Musick after his own petitioning that the office should not be allowed to lapse. As a result, he was in charge of musical arrangements for the Wembley Empire Festival in 1924. *The Times* thought Elgar particularly appropriate as Master of the King's Musick since he was:

> one who is to the nation at large the personification of British music. . . . To the British public he is known as one who can voice in music the feelings and aspirations of all his fellow citizens.

Yet it was claimed in 1931 by the composer C. W. Orr that Elgar had been given the OM by the King and 'the cold shoulder by the man in the street'. In 1927, *The Times* was baffled by 'the apparent indifference towards works which a few years ago seemed really to have stirred the public imagination'. The same article greatly regretted that such performances as there were tended to be in all-Elgar concerts when in fact Elgar shone best 'in contrast with other minds'.[42]

Such reports come mostly from a fairly brief period in the later 1920s, and neglect the dissemination of Elgar's music through radio and records. As Northrop Moore has shown, Elgar was involved with developments in recording from the time of his first association with the Gramophone Co., in 1914, and worked for them on very favourable terms for the rest of his life. The company paid Elgar a considerable retainer, despite a working loss on his records, and used his name to endorse its products. In 1921 and 1931, Elgar was chosen to open new recording studios.[43]

In 1932, Landon Ronald, then the foremost interpreter of the composer's orchestral works, other than Elgar himself, criticized the BBC for neglecting Elgar.[44] But there is ample evidence to the contrary. In December 1932, the BBC broadcast an Elgar festival consisting of three concerts devoted to his works. The programme produced for the occasion noted that, by then, it had become the tradition that great national occasions, such as Armistice Day and St George's Day, should be marked by performances of Elgar's ceremonial music. Moreover:

> many of the events which mark red-letter days in the ten year history of the BBC have been Elgar concerts – many more than any other composer could claim.[45]

In 1927, for example, *Cockaigne* had opened the first BBC-sponsored season of Queen's Hall Promenade Concerts.[46]

Elgar's standing was under greater critical scrutiny at this time. The performance of works by Stravinsky and Schoenberg made it clear that Elgar, who had not written a substantial work since his *Cello Concerto* (1919), could no longer be championed as one of the vanguard. By this time there was greater knowledge of the music of Delius, and a new generation of English composers, including Bax, Bantock and Vaughan Williams had achieved acceptance. But Elgar's role as a composer of ceremonial music remained unchallenged. *Gerontius* was a standard work for choral societies, and the new media disseminated his work to a far wider public than that found in the concert halls. According to Dunhill, he was more than ever 'a revered figure in English musical life'. When in 1931 Dent, professor of music at Cambridge, gave less space to Elgar than to Parry or Stanford in his article on English music (in Adler's German language history of music), outrage was widely voiced. Shaw, Newman, and many others came to Elgar's defence. This revival of the old rivalry between Elgar and academic musical circles came at a time when the divergence between new European music and the English national school was marked. For the first time, the gap between a conservative public taste and leading composers' innovations seemed unbridgeable. The upsurge of interest in Elgar's music in the 1930s should be seen against this background.[47]

The Englishness of Elgar redefined

From the early 1930s – Elgar was 75 in 1932 – his achievement was evaluated afresh. Elements of his career and his music were used to construct an image of a particular kind of Englishness. This task was achieved through journalism, biography and music criticism, concert programming and the policies of the BBC and record companies. It was a selective reformulation in which critical effort was spent in downgrading once important parts of the canon in order to establish at the centre a number of 'great works'. At this time, certain conceptions of what was English about Elgar became current and these have won a dominant place in the literature.

In 1926, Sheldon wrote of Elgar that 'To-day he is less written about than the callowest of experimenters or imitators.'[48] Within a few years, he was decisively contradicted as there began a regular flow of monographs about Elgar's life and work. Books by Shera (1931), Sheldon (1932), Basil Maine, John F. Porte (1933), Everard Jose (1934), W. H. Reed (1936) and Thomas Dunhill (1938) were accompanied by special editions of periodicals, including the *Musical Times* and *Music and Letters,* to mark both the 75th birthday and his death in 1934. They ranged in content from technical analysis to personal reminiscence and contained numerous contradictions. It is possible to identify a number of recurrent themes relating to the reformulation of Elgar's Englishness. Great public interest was also stimulated at this time by rumours that Elgar was working on a 3rd symphony, something which led the *Daily Mail* to demand that the work be produced, and Shaw to press for a bursary to allow Elgar to devote himself to it. Finally, the BBC commissioned him to write the work at a total cost of £2,000, money which in the end bought only some preliminary sketches.

Much of the commentary written at this time was content to reassert the English character of the music in terms of its ability to 'express the very soul of our race', much as during the war.[49] But it was also at this time that the music was increasingly related to the English countryside, and, despite Elgar's own views, efforts were made to graft him onto the folk-music revival. Of course, there was much to work on – Elgar's Worcestershire origins, his frequently voiced dislike of London's musical life, and the associations of some of his works, notably the *Introduction and Allegro* (1905) and the chamber music, with rural settings. Some of these aspects were referred to in the earliest studies of Elgar in the first decade of the century, but in the 1930s and afterwards such a view received far greater emphasis. Basil Maine's first full-length biography opens with an account of the author's visit with Elgar to the composer's birthplace at Broadheath. In 1934 an Elgar museum was established in the house even though Elgar only lived in it for the first year of his life before his parents moved back to Worcester. Its rural setting and view of the Malvern Hills gave physical embodiment to the notion that Elgar's background was wholly rural rather than county town petit bourgeois.[50]

Elgar frequently rejected the influence of folk music which inspired the next generation of English composers. He stated on one occasion that 'I write the folk-songs of this country'.[51] In 1928 at a dinner in the Hotel Cecil he regretted that:

> instead of inventing our own tunes we were going back to the old folk-songs, which were very fine in themselves. . . . There were people who

pulled down old castles and built houses from them and sometimes pigsties, but there was the satisfaction of knowing that there was an inspector of nuisances. People could take folk-songs and make modern music with them, but there was no inspector of nuisances who looked after that sort of thing.[52]

Elgar used Polish folk material in *Polonia* and a Welsh hymn tune in the *Introduction and Allegro*, but there are no examples of his incorporating English folk songs into his music. In order to associate Elgar with the tradition, Vaughan Williams was forced to argue that although Elgar did not use actual folk melodies, his music was English in that it exploited the musical idiom of the people in a manner analogous to Burns's and Shakespeare's use of the people's speech. In a lecture on 'National Music' in 1932, he claimed that 'Any school of national music must be fashioned on the basis of the raw material of its own natural song' and that this was as true of Elgar and Tchaikovsky as it was of more identifiably 'nationalist' composers. Vaughan Williams found in Elgar:

> that peculiar kind of beauty which gives us, his fellow countrymen, a sense of something familiar – the intimate and personal beauty of our own fields and lanes; not the aloof and unsympathetic beauty of glaciers and coral reefs and tropical forests.

In what Vaughan Williams considered 'the most beautiful and characteristic' music of Elgar, he found the same essence as folk-song had revealed for his generation, not something new, but 'something which had been hidden by foreign matter.' This remains very much an occult quality which cannot be specified in musical terms, much as Elgar's perception of the English soul could not be identified by earlier writers' musical analysis. Porte was equally mystical, describing in 1933 an 'English strain' which could be felt but was not to be identified with folk-song. It was something which he claimed foreign conductors were unable to realize.[53]

Elgar's music became associated with Englishness in a way that went beyond the fact that he was simply a composer in England, wrote for national occasions and used popular musical genres. Eric Fenby noted in 1935 that,

> When I walk about the countryside of England, I seldom, if ever, find myself humming anything of Delius, but always some exquisite passage from Elgar.[54]

Elgar's influence on Bax, Vaughan Williams and others, notably in orchestral technique and writing for strings, had itself contributed to the creation of an English idiom, which in the work of the younger generation was identified with the rural Romanticism of folk music. By a further process of transference, Elgar's music itself acquired pastoral 'meaning' – hence Fenby's comment.

Later generations have had such an interpretation reinforced by the use of Elgar's music and Elgarian pastiche to invoke rural atmosphere in film. In 1955, McVeagh could write of a four-bar phrase of the third movement of the *Second Symphony* as 'one of those fragments that breathe the scent of Severnside to those who know it'.[55]

Not all Elgar's music could be assimilated in this way. From the 1930s, writers began to find in Elgar not only the quiet, enduring spirit of rural England, but also the other land of lost content, the Edwardian era. This was not a view which had been formed immediately after the war. Elgar had provided the basis for such an interpretation in his dedication of the Second Symphony to the memory of Edward VII, and was not averse to writing music with literary titles referring to lost empires and social orders, for example *Froissart* (1890) and *In the South* (1903). For Jose, writing in 1931, the *Coronation Ode*:

> embodied that identical national spirit which carried through the Haldane Army reforms, the ceaseless perfecting of the Navy, and the ultimate great arising at the call of Kitchener.[56]

A similarly literal parallel of music and political events was identified by Maine two years later, for whom:

> the inclusion of that community song tune for the 1st *Pomp and Circumstance* March finds a parallel in King Edward's dignified respect for democracy, the respect which led him, for instance, tactfully to congratulate Mr John Burns on the fit of his Court Uniform.

The Edwardian England which Elgar was said to have invoked was one of opulence, progress and success. As Maine writes:

> Hope and Glory were to be the themes of the coming era . . . and these too are the themes which like jewels in a crown blaze forth from the Edwardian Ode.[57]

The Times, in its obituary, thought that Elgar's music was the product of 'the post-Victorian interlude between the S. African War and the tragedy of 1914' and that as a consequence it exuded an 'air of general well-being, of contentment with leisure in a spacious world', which was not acceptable to the post-war generation. Constant Lambert was unusual in seeing that 'aggressive Edwardian prosperity' created in Elgar's music 'an intolerable air of smugness, self-assurance and autocratic benevolence'.[58] No music writer in the 1930s refers to the widespread social unrest of the period disturbed by Suffragette outrages, constitutional crisis, labour disputes and the Irish question.

For any proponent of Elgar's music at the time, the ceremonial works posed a problem. The association of Elgar with Empire, the War and pageantry since 1918, was a difficulty for those trying to secure the acceptance of the orchestral works in the repertoire as abstract music. It was the more pressing since Cecil Gray's complaint in 1924 in his *Survey of Contemporary Music* that the ceremonial music invaded the symphonies and degraded them.

One response was to deny the integrity of Elgar's output, resorting to what has been called the 'two Elgars' theory.[59] In sympathetic versions, the unfashionable and lesser music was seen as appropriate for its time or its context, but not as inherently bad. Basil Maine, for example, distinguished between the great works and the popular ones, in which Elgar showed himself the greater,

> for his willing submission to popular sentiment and the events of the hour.

All his music was nevertheless equally sincere.[60] Howes, on the other hand, found some of Elgar's music actually bad, meretricious rather than dull. He saw in Elgar what Harold Nicholson had seen in Lord Curzon

> a certain simplicity and understanding of fundamentals persisting behind a façade of splendour and pride in vainglorious inessentials.

Nor did he deny Gray's assertion that the 'Elgar who wrote for brass' at times contaminated the 'Elgar who wrote for strings', 'a vein of tin among a rich vein of gold'. While regrettable, it could at least have the effect of giving Elgar a 'breadth of effective appeal' necessary for a democratic art, something which Gray thought Delius completely lacked.[61] For Sheldon, stripping away the populist Elgar would leave 'a composer of visionary imaginings', the one of real artistic significance.

Others saw no such break. For Porte, the elements in the symphonies which Gray described as vulgar represented 'an aspect of cheery heroism in good English racial fibre' to be set alongside the aloofness which was Elgar's other English trait. Vaughan Williams saw Elgar at one with his countrymen not only in the deliberately popular works (*Land of Hope and Glory, Cockaigne*) but also 'when he seems to have retired into the solitude of his own sanctuary'. He identifies two fundamental tendencies in Elgar, but does not dismiss one as of less worth than the other.[62]

Rare in the literature at this time is any attempt to reintegrate the ceremonial element in an ironic sense, as recessional in the way that Michael Kennedy has sought to do. In this version, Elgar, with considerable prescience, foresaw at the time of the greatest celebration of Imperial splendour before 1914 the decline of English power. The renewed popularity of Elgar in the 1960s and 70s was thus achieved:

> when the Empire disintegrated, and when people heard in the music what had always been there to hear; the funeral march of a civilisation, of a spiritual and artistic life which was decaying.[63]

The music of pomp and circumstance needs neither apology nor dismissal since it is in reality self-critical to an extent which was satisfactory even to the anti-military sentiment of the late 1960s when Kennedy was writing. Elgar had become a prophet of the Winds of Change.

Why was Elgar's music reconstructed in this way in the 1930s? This kind of pastoral was of course by no means specific to the constructed Elgar. Raymond Williams has established links between the literature of rural life, political reaction and 'The self-regarding patriotism of the high English imperialist period.' And Martin J. Wiener has observed that the rural fascination of the elite, already strong before 1914, was intensified by the war and 'spread throughout the middle class after World War I'. The pastoral associations of Elgar shared the vagueness of the Georgian country idiom of Housman. The relationship in Elgar's own life between the Malvern countryside from which he sought inspiration and the metropolitan musical world in which he earned money, recognition and honours fits Williams' model of a rural cultural superstructure based on 'the profits of industrial and imperial development'. But it was only in the 1930s, at the time of the Peace Pledge Union and concern for the League of Nations, when the India Act (1935) marked a commitment to a less expansionist phase of colonial imperialism, that the pastoral became dominant in some interpretations of Elgar. The retreat to rural values was consonant with the view of 'sunset splendour' in the Edwardian Elgar, and coincided with a cultural conservatism, marked in music by the decline in the fashion for superficially experimental works such as Walton's *Façade* (1921). It was in the late 1920s too that full-scale literary revulsion with the War emerged: when works such as Siegfried Sassoon's *Memoirs of a Foxhunting Man* (1928), Richard Aldington's *Death of a Hero* (1929) and Erich Maria Remarque's *All Quiet on the Western Front* (1929) were published.[64]

In such a cultural and political context, a new consolation was sought in Elgar's music; its earlier associations with Empire and the war were dismissed. Although *Carillon* was revived, with new words by Binyon, during World War II, the war works have remained largely ignored, as has most of the music of royal ceremonial. In this guise, Elgar's music could provide a refuge for those whose nostalgia for the Edwardian years was essentially conservative. The break-up of landed estates, loss of Imperial might, and economic crisis all contributed to a yearning for past glories and a mythical, stable social order. Elgar's music, stripped of its more blatant and unfashionable militaristic associations, was redolent of a decent, prosperous and, above all, rural English past. The Elgar canon as established in the 1930s remains largely unchanged, based upon *Enigma*, the symphonies and concertos, the overtures, *Gerontius* and some lesser orchestral works such as the *Introduction and Allegro*. Post-1945 biographers have adopted various strategies to distance Elgar from accusations of jingoism, usually by an unhistorical reading of Elgar's career. Where enthusiasm for Elgar's imperialist vein survives, notably in the singing of *Land of Hope and Glory* at the Proms, the response from musical officialdom has at times been an embarrassed one, culminating in the unsuccessful attempt to remove it in 1969.[65]

Conclusion

Through the process of critical assimilation described earlier, Elgar has become institutionalized; ways of hearing his music have been established. Before one is transported from suburban living room to the Malvern Hills in the golden glow of a late imperial afternoon, it may be of interest for the listener to reflect how a complex series of sound patterns has so specific and literary a significance. Studies of Elgar have usually taken the meaning of his music as an attribute independent of the cultural experience of the listener. The aim in this chapter has been to suggest that during the period 1900–35 that meaning was selectively constructed in a number of ways.

Analysis of classical music places a high value on an awareness of music history; much musical appreciation involves the identification of period styles, and part of the attraction of the music is its ability to 'survive' and supposedly communicate eternal verities. Much popular music is rejected because of its ephemeral nature. The evidence reviewed here suggests that, on the contrary, the survival of music and its establishment in the repertoire, is not simply a function of the inherent qualities of the piece, but an interaction of the music with contingent circumstances which are not all generated within the musical world. There are crucial periods at which music criticism and the music business serve to mediate wider cultural and political forces. In Elgar's case, these included industrial and imperial rivalry, war, post-war disillusionment and imperial self-doubt. Such links between societal forces and changes in musical tastes remain little explored, and have only been approached schematically here, but there is no reason why the insights which have been achieved in the study of music hall, popular music, the record industry and film through the application of the methods of social historians, sociologists and semiologists should not be applied to elite culture too. The values of concert music are themselves a potential subject for historical appraisal.[66]

During the period covered by the present volume, institutions which were responsible for an expansion of musical activity in Britain and the improvement of the status of musicians were established. The same period saw the establishment of English composition as something worthy of respect – at least in England – and Elgar occupied a dominant position at the beginning of the tradition. But it is only by historical research, taking as its sources the work of journalists, academics and writers of musical reminiscence, that it is possible to perceive how the music was received. Our own perceptions of Elgar are the product of our musical experience and of an evolving body of received opinion, the main features of which first came together in the 1930s. Through its association with major events both in British musical life and national ceremonial, Elgar's music became a focus for the development of notions of Englishness in music, but those meanings have not been historically constant. The changing reception of Elgar illustrates a major shift in ideas of Englishness between the wars, from assertive if insecure imperial pride to introspection and retreat.

Notes

I have used Michael Kennedy's *Portrait of Elgar* for basic information concerning Elgar's career. I do not refer to it specifically except when a quotation is taken from it.

Abbreviations: BDP, *Birmingham Daily Post;* DT, *Daily Telegraph;* MO, *Musical Opinion;* MS, *Musical Standard;* MT, *Musical Times;* SDP, *Sheffield Daily Post.*

I wish to thank the curators of the Elgar Birthplace for their helpfulness on my visits to Broadheath, and Dr Robert Meikle, lecturer in Music at the University of Leicester, who read and commented on an early draft of the paper.

1 *MS,* 1 October 1898.

2 On Elgar's role as an official composer, see David Cannadine, 'The context, performance and meaning of ritual: the British monarchy and "the invention of tradition'" c.1820 – 1977' E. J. Hobsbawm and T. Ranger (eds), *The Invention of Tradition* (Cambridge: C.U.P., 1983), pp. 130ff.

3 Quoted in Humphrey Burton, 'Elgar and the BBC', *Journal of the Royal Society of Arts,* (March 1979), 236.

4 For a contradiction of the orthodox view, see Donald Mitchell, review of Jerrold Northrop Moore, *Elgar, a Life, Times Literary Supplement,* 14 September 1984, in which it is claimed that Elgar was impeded, not stimulated by his English background.

   This essay was largely written before the publication of Alan Durant, *Conditions of Music* (London: Macmillan, 1984), which calls for thorough re-examination of the ways in which music criticism and the history of music are written. In particular, Durant argues that it is necessary to look for the meaning of music not in its essence, but in its context since 'Meanings . . . rely upon far broader social relationships and shared conventions to make possible their circulation or exchange' (p. 11). Of special importance in this respect are the institutions in which music is performed and the means by which education about music takes place (p. 12). The present study may be seen as an exploration of ideas similar to Durant's concerning the social production of meanings in music, with reference to an individual composer and the critical discourse associated with his work.

5 Frank Howes, *The English Musical Renaissance* (London: Seeker and Warburg, 1966); J. P. Nettel, *Music in the Five Towns* (London: O.U.P., 1944); E. D. Mackerness, *A Social History of English Music* (London: Methuen, 1964).

6   W. J. Galloway, *Musical England* (London: Christopher's, 1910), p. 7.

7   Cyril Ehrlich, *The Piano: A History* (London: Dent, 1976), pp. 88, 151.

8   Percy M. Young (ed.), *A Future for English Music and other Essays* (London: Dobson, 1968), pp. 33–4; Arnold Bax, *Farewell My Youth* (London: Longman and Co., 1943), p. 28; *MT*, January 1899, *passim*. See also a letter from Alfred Jaeger, who wrote for the *Musical Times,* to Elgar in 1898: 'I suppose there will be a chance for English composers some day at the Queen's Hall.' Percy M. Young (ed.), *Letters to Nimrod* (London: Dennis Dobson, 1965), p. 10.

9   Vic Gammon, 'Folk song collecting in Sussex and Surrey, 1843–1914', *History Workshop Journal*, 10 (Autumn 1980), 76; Richard Price, *An Imperial War and the British Working Class* (London: Methuen, 1980), p. 1.

    There is of course no suggestion that Elgar was chauvinistic in his relationships with foreign musicians. Indeed, he deplored the treatment of German nationals at the outbreak of the war.

10 Sir Thomas Beecham, *A Mingled Chime* (London: Hutchinson and Co., 1944); *DT*, 15 October 1902; *The Sketch,* 22 February 1905.

11 Percy M. Young, *Elgar O. M.,* 2nd edn (London: White Lion Publishers, 1973), p. 127, 137; *The Times*, 15 March 1904, 24 February 1934.

12 *MT*, 1 October 1900; Robert J. Buckley, *Sir Edward Elgar* (London: John Lane, 1905).

13 Galloway, *Musical England,* p. 88; Ernest Newman, *Elgar* (London: Philip Welby, 1906), p. 55; Eric Fenby, *Delius as I knew him* (London: Ican Books, 1966), p. 123; letter from Elgar to Jaeger dated 28 May 1899, in Young, *Letters to Nimrod.*

14 Nettel, *Music in the Five Towns,* pp. 41–2; Young, *Letters to Nimrod,* pp. 4–5.

15 *MT*, 1 August 1900; Young, *Letters to Nimrod,* letters dated 1 November 1898, 28 March 1899.

16 *The Cornet,* 15 August 1903, 15 September 1903; *British Bandsman,* 12 September 1903.

17 *MT*, June 1899, July 1899, September 1899.

18 J. F. Porte, *Sir Edward Elgar* (London: Keegan Paul and Co., 1921), p. 26; Newman, *Elgar,* p. 45.

19 Beecham, *A Mingled Chime*, pp. 110–11. See also Michael Kennedy, *Portrait of Elgar* (London: O.U.P., 1968), p. 191; Newman, *Elgar*, pp. 44, 47; Buckley, *Sir Edward Elgar,* p. 48.

20 *MO*, October 1905; Young, *Letters to Nimrod*, p. 203; Ernest Walker, *A History of Music in England* (London: O.U.P., 2nd edn, 1924), p. 306. Cf. Buckley, *Sir Edward Elgar,* p. 60. Buckley considered *The Dream of Gerontius* 'so revolutionary that all except the most advanced took time to consider'. Also *MT*, June 1902; October 1900; *MS*, 10 October 1898.

21 Henry Wood, *My Life in Music* (London: Victor Gollancz, 1938), pp. 134, 141. I am grateful to Robert Meikle for drawing my attention to the reception given to Schoenberg's works in England.

22 *MO*, April 1905; *MT*, March 1907 states that *The Kingdom* is 'attaining popularity even more rapidly than the composer's previous works'.

23 On music in World War I, see George Bernard Shaw, *Shaw's Music*, vol. III
    (Oxford: Bodley Head, 1980); Wood, *My Life in Music,* ch. XLI; Percy
    Scholes, *The Mirror of Music, 1844–1944* (London: O.U.P., 1947), pp. 887ff.;
    Harriet Winifred Ponder, *Clara Butt; Her Life Story* (London: G. G. Harrap
    and Son, 1928); Eugene Goossens, *Overture and Beginners* (London: Methuen
    and Co., 1951), pp. 113–14.

24 *The Times*, 6 May 1916; *SDP*, 4 May 1916.

25 *MT*, September 1914.

26 Goossens, *Overture and Beginners; BDP*, 10 February 1915; *MT*, February
    1915; *L'Indépendence Belge*, 10 May 1915; unidentified newspaper cutting,
    Elgar's Birthplace collection, 9 February 1915; *The Globe*, 7 September 1919;
    Glasgow Herald, 9 February 1915; A. J. Sheldon, *Edward Elgar* (London:
    Musical Opinion, 1932).

27 *DT*, 25 January 1916, 31 January 1916; *The Referee*, 16 February 1916;
    L'Indépendence Belge, 19 April 1917. A further work, *Polonia* (1915) was less
    successful. Based on Polish musical material, it was thought to be insufficiently
    typical of the composer. In any case, Poland was not such a rallying call for
    anti-German sentiment as was Belgium. See *The Globe*, 7 July 1915.

28 *The Times*, 26 April 1915.

29 *Manchester Guardian*, 15 August 1917; *The Times*, 1 December 1918;
    The Globe, 8 September 1914; *The Referee*, 11 October 1914. Porte,
    Sir Edward Elgar, states that 'So national is this tune in spirit, that it was
    not infrequent . . . for an audience to fervently sing it to the orchestra's
    accompaniment.' For use of the song at a provincial recruitment rally, see
    Leicester Pioneer, 4 December 1914.

30 *Pall Mall Gazette*, 19 July 1919; *The Performer*, 31 July 1919.

31 *BDP*, 10 February 1919; *Pall Mall Gazette*, 18 November 1918; *Observer*,
    29 November 1919; *MO*, April 1917.

32 *News Chronicle*, n.d., 1916, in the Elgar Birthplace collection.

33 Sheldon, *Edward Elgar*, p. 52.

34 *MT*, 1 May 1916; *BDP*, 19 June 1915. On the revival of the First Symphony,
    see *DT*, 25 November 1914. On Black Dyke Mills Band performances, *MT*,
    n.d., Elgar Birthplace collection.

35 *Evening Standard*, 25 November 1915, 1 March 1915; *The Times*, 16 August
    1916; *DT*, 4 March 1916, 25 March 1916; *The Tablet*, 29 April 1916; *MT*,
    June 1916; *Sunday Times*, 14 May 1916. On disillusionment with initial
    enthusiasm for the war in literary circles, see Robert Wohl, *The Generation of
    1914* (London: Weidenfeld and Nicholson, 1980), pp. 94–5.

36 *The Times*, 4 February 1918.

37 *MT*, May 1916; *DT*, 9 May 1916; *Sunday Times*, 19 May 1916; *BDP*, 9 May
    1916; *MT*, July 1917.

38 Sheldon, *Edward Elgar*, p. 52; Percy M. Young (ed.), *The Letters of Edward Elgar*
    (London: Geoffrey Bles, 1956), letters of 16 February 1920, 15 November 1933.

39 *Leicester Pioneer*, 24 August 1917; *The Times*, 12 June 1917; *Manchester City
    News*, 12 August 1917; *Leicester Daily Post*, 21 August 1917.

40   *Manchester Guardian*, 15 June 1917; Basil Maine, *Elgar; His Life and Work* (London: Bell's Musical Publications, 1933), p. 166.

41   Fenby, *Delius as I knew him*; Shaw, *Shaw's Music*, vol. III; *Daily News*, 9 June 1922; *The Times*, 19 February 1927, 19 August 1929; Osbert Sitwell's, *Laughter in the Next Room* (London: Little, Brown & Co., 1944) describes Elgar's music as 'obnoxious, so full of English humour and the spirit of compulsory games'.

42   *The Times*, 5 May 1924, 19 March 1927; *Music and Letters,* January 1931.

43   Jerrold Northrop Moore, *Elgar on Record* (London: O.U.P., 1974).

44   Ibid., p. 172, quoting *The News Chronicle*.

45   Quoted in Burton, 'Elgar and the BBC', pp. 225–6.

46   David Cox, *The History of the Henry Wood Proms* (London: BBC Publications, 1980), p. 151.

47   Thomas F. Dunhill, *Sir Edward Elgar* (London: Blackie and Son, 1938), p. 167; Kennedy, *Portrait of Elgar*, pp. 261ff. See also Constant Lambert, *Music Ho!* (London: Faber and Faber, 1935).

48   Sheldon, *Edward Elgar,* p. 19.

49   Newman in *Sunday Times,* 25 February 1934.

50   Elgar's father owned a music shop in Worcester. Details of the Elgar Birthplace are from *Elgar Foundation Appeal Leaflet* (1973).

51   Quoted in Kennedy, *Portrait of Elgar,* p. 74.

52   *The Times*, 1 February 1928.

53   Ralph Vaughan Williams, *National Music and Other Essays* (London: O.U.P., 1968), p. 41; *Music and Letters,* January 1935; J. F. Porte, *Elgar and his Music* (London: Sir. I. Pitman and Sons, 1933), p. 96.

54   Fenby, *Delius as I knew him,* p. 209.

55   Viz. K. Russell's use of the *Introduction and Allegro* in the Malvern scenes of his film. Diana McVeagh, *Edward Elgar: His Life and Music* (London: J. M. Dent and Son, 1955), p. 166.

56   Everard Jose, *The Significance of Elgar* (London: Heath Cranton, 1934), p. 13.

57   Maine, *Elgar: His Life and Work*, pp. 119–20.

58   *The Times*, 24 February 1934; Lambert, *Music Ho!*, p. 240.

59   E.g. Frank Howes in *Music and Letters,* January 1935.

60   Maine, *Elgar: His Life and Work*, p. 201. Cf. F. H. Shera, *Elgar Instrumental Works*, p. 16.

61   Howes, *English Musical Renaissance;* Sheldon, *Edward Elgar,* p. 16.

62   J. F. Porte, *Elgar and his Music,* p. 68; Vaughan Williams in *Music and Letters,* January 1935.

63   Kennedy, *Portrait of Elgar,* p. 151. This reading is anticipated in Shera, *Elgar: Instrumental Works,* p. 6, and Maine, *Elgar: His Life and Work,* p. 190.

64   Raymond Williams, *The Country and the City* (London: Chatto and Windus, 1973), pp. 258ff., 282; Martin J. Wiener, *English Culture and the Decline of*

the Industrial Spirit, 1850–1980 (Cambridge: C.U.P., 1981), pp. 72–80. On the profusion of war novels and memoirs after 1928, see Robert Wohl, *The Generation of 1914,* pp. 101–11. Wohl, pp. 118–21, distinguishes between this conservative Edwardian mythology and the more radical post-war myth of 'the lost generation', while drawing attention to their common retrospection.

65 Barrie Hall, *The Proms* (London: Allen and Unwin, 1981), p. 168.

66 Durant asserts that, given changes in the conditions of production and consumption of music, there is 'an urgency for broader, if more difficult, arguments than exist at present; reflections on groups of works and conventions of practice, considerations of technology and the interests of capital and leisure in relation to which it is directed and against which other kinds of activity must take place; attention to issues of pleasure in playing and listening to music': *Conditions of Music,* p. 28.

CHAPTER SEVEN

The Englishwoman

Alice Jane Mackay and Pat Thane

A clearly defined, uncontested, image of the Englishwoman is surprisingly elusive in this period of the construction and redefinition of Englishness. The classic English man of the period was held to combine certain qualities, including leadership, courage, justice and honour, which were defined as distinctively 'English'. He has no exact female equivalent.

The qualities of the perfect Englishwoman were publicly discussed, but they were not generally perceived as being specifically English. Rather they were those qualities – essentially domestic and maternal – believed to be universal in Woman. The ideal Englishwoman's special quality was that she practised these virtues in a fashion superior to women of other countries; but Englishwomen, it seemed, had difficulty in living up to that ideal. Not only were they trained and cajoled from their earliest years to recognize the primacy of domesticity, but throughout life faced criticism for the inadequacy of their performance, even in comparison with women of other countries.

With the emergence of feminism and of the 'new woman' in this period, however, the conventional conception of the female role faced a stronger challenge than did prevailing notions of the male role. There was an ever-present danger that women would be tempted away from domesticity, which had to be guarded against; though, as we shall see, the challenge of alternative conceptions of womanhood grew so strong as the period went on that the image of the ideal Englishwoman had to adapt to accommodate them. It should be stressed that women *themselves* created these alternatives. Rather than being simply passive recipients of an externally imposed ideology of 'separate spheres', women achieved modifications of that ideology.

Nevertheless the Englishwoman remains a more shadowy figure than the Englishman, because, as already suggested, women were believed to possess transnational qualities. Nationality, we suggest, played a more significant role in the redefinition of masculinity as it emerged in the later-nineteenth century than in that of femininity; one of the distinctions between male and female was that the concept of nationality was almost always on the male side of the divide. Women, indeed, *had* no fixed nationality. They were made to adopt that of their husband; on marriage to a foreigner they lost their English status and its accompanying rights.[1]

This is not to say that women were not expected to be patriotic, or had no role in the intense contemporary debate about nationhood; rather that they were identified not with nation but with *race*. The role of females, whatever their social background, was to contribute to the preservation, perpetuation and enhancement of the race, both physically and spiritually; the male role was to defend and preserve the nation. (The meaning and uses of the term 'race' were, as we shall see, variable and slippery throughout the period.) The essential distinction was between a female role which was biological and spiritual, dedicated to the production and rearing of healthy children, the support of men and the guardianship of the spiritual and moral values of the English, and a male role which was virile and intellectual, dedicated to the protection and perpetuation of the nation and its institutions through activity at all levels in politics, administration, the armed services, business and finance.

There is a possible relationship between this conception of woman as the embodiment of the spiritual essence of the race and the inclination, noted elsewhere in this volume, to identify the nation and the language as female and maternal.[2] Such usages are to be found in the material we have surveyed. They should, however, be set more systematically than we have been able to do against *male* characterizations of the nation, as John Bull, or the 'British bulldog' (perhaps more common in wartime).

The distinction between male and female roles in relation to nationality was part of a wider but still under-explored reassertion and redefinition of the concept of 'separate spheres' in the later-nineteenth century and early-twentieth century. An enhanced emphasis upon the private, domestic role of the female was evident, for example, in the increased attention given to domestic training in schools, in the spread of institutions for advising mothers on childcare, in the introduction of the 'marriage bar' into certain professional occupations for women, notably teaching and the civil service.[3] It was clearly associated, far more strikingly than were earlier manifestations of 'separate spheres', [4] with arguments about the need to maintain or enhance both the size and the quality of the population in an atmosphere of increased international competitiveness in economic, political and military affairs. The need to maximize the size of the population by reducing the high rate of infant mortality as well as by slowing or reversing the decline in the

birth rate, the need to improve its physical quality through improved feeding
and health care for infants and children, and the greater emphasis upon
physical exercise for all were persistent themes of official and unofficial
publications and statements in the last years of the nineteenth century.
Such statements did not neglect to emphasize that the size of the adult *male*
population was especially affected by the high infant mortality rate, male
infants being more vulnerable than female, just as males had higher death
rates at all ages. The higher rate of emigration among males further increased
the size of the female majority in the population, which was actually rising
throughout this period (from 1055 females per thousand males in 1881, to
1068 per thousand in 1911; 1096 in 1921; 1088 in 1931), a fact arousing in
men and women fears which lurk behind much of the discussion of women
and of the condition of the nation in this period.[5]

In England the pressures to improve the numbers and physical condition of
surviving children reached a peak during and shortly after the Boer War but
were not products of it. Similar concerns were also evident in rival countries
which were not involved in this or equivalent wars. The chief concern in
Britain even before the war was that it should not fall behind Germany,
in particular, in male numbers and physical fitness. Hence the notion of
'separate spheres' was reinterpreted. Earlier in the century motherhood and
domesticity were presented as being desirable in themselves, as providing
stability in the home, which was seen as essential for the maintenance of
harmony within British society as a whole. Secure homes were thought
to produce a contented people no matter what they might suffer outside
the home. But now the notion acquired an additional emphasis. Domestic
harmony, created and sustained by women, was presented as desirable, even
essential, for the defence of Britain against her rivals overseas, indeed for the
defence of the whole British Empire. It was a role demanded of women of all
classes, since healthy soldiers and workers were as vital for national survival
as businessmen and officers, and social stability required contentment at
all social levels. Women of all classes had to be trained in and reminded
of their duty: whereas working-class women might fail due to ignorance,
inexperience or poverty, middle or upper-class women might be lured by
feminism. An ambivalence evident earlier in the century as to whether the
primary role of the working-class woman was indeed in the home or in
the workforce[6] seems in this period to have been resolved in favour of the
former. There appears to have been a more decisive effort than before to
incorporate them into the ideology of separate spheres; and almost certainly
at this time more working-class mothers were withdrawing from the
workforce.[7] Hence rather similar appeals were being made to women of all
classes. The gulf between the nation's expectations of women and men was
greater than the gulf separating expectations of women of different social
classes; in this sphere of experience gender differences were more significant
than class differences. The differential socialization of males and females in

relation to nation and race is especially well illustrated by examining two leading periodicals directed at adolescents in the later-nineteenth century.

The first weekly number of the *Boy's Own Paper* appeared on 18 January 1879.[8] The new magazine, published by the Religious Tract Society, was intended to provide 'healthy boy literature to counteract the vastly increasing circulation of illustrated and other papers and tales of a bad tendency'. The minute books of the Society show how its General Committee discussed its content in great detail; the whole enterprise was based on the belief that what adolescents read had a direct effect on their future character and actions.[9] After the hugely successful first year of the *B.O.P.* a companion paper was produced for girls. Since the first issues of the two magazines would have been vital in setting the intended tone, the differences in the material offered to boys and to girls are significant.

Girl's Own Paper was intended to serve the same function as *B.O.P.* in driving out unwholesome literature. Both were intended initially for a working-class audience but both acquired a predominantly middle-class readership. *B.O.P.* in relation to middle-class boys was only one of a number of similar magazines published from the 1860s, although it was the most dramatically successful of them. The uniqueness of the *Girl's Own Paper* lay in its recognition that middle-class girls could no longer be satisfied by progressing from children's reading to their mothers' magazines of domestic life. Adolescence was now experienced as a period of change and of choice in the lives of girls as well as boys, as they too were being offered the prospect of higher education and professional employment. The very existence of *G.O.P.* testifies to changes in assumptions about women; from the beginning it was forced to grapple with the question of how to reconcile domestic ideology with the new aspirations of women. It was in relation to adolescent girls that these questions were seen as especially critical – they would be the next generation of wives and mothers and were still open to adult influence. *G.O.P.* and subsequent similar publications were at the sharp end of the ideological conflict.[10]

Both publications were produced by an organization devoted to Christian propaganda. Religious bodies had long, of course, paid especial attention to the education and socialization of the young, and the decision of the R.T.S. to produce a periodical initially for adolescent boys was didactic in intent. A debate raged for some months within the Society as to whether the tone of the Paper should be explicitly evangelical or less direct in its religious message. The more subtle approach won, although only after agreement, subsequently broken, that a more explicitly religious tone would be introduced once its popularity was established. It won because the Paper was expected to be bought *by* rather than for adolescents, with their own pennies, and would therefore have to compete in a hard market with commercial publications. An explicitly religious message was unlikely to assist this cause.

It is significant that the R.T.S. was prepared to settle for a periodical whose content was deliberately designed to influence social values and standards of behaviour rather than to explicitly profess Christianity. This suggests a very close identification between what evangelical Christians believed to be the content of Christianity and contemporary norms of respectable behaviour, including attitudes to the nation. This is too large a question to explore here, but it is possible to suggest an almost total congruence, in contemporary eyes, between conceptions of 'Christian behaviour' and 'gentlemanly behaviour' and of both with 'behaviour becoming in an Englishman'. To educate the young to be gentlemen and ladies was assumed to ensure that they would be sound Christians.

Explicitly religious content was more acceptable in popular publications for girls, since the spiritual focus clearly lay within the female sphere, though by 1914 it had much diminished even in such publications. The difference in content between periodicals published by religious or by commercial organizations was less than might be imagined, and both promoted similar ethical and social, including patriotic, values.[11]

The first number of the *B.O.P.* sets the English boy firmly in the context of his nationality. The front page illustration is of a rugby match, and the corresponding story is 'My first football match', in which an 'Old Boy' recalls the first time he played for the school team, and triumphantly justified his selection by scoring the winning try. He describes how he felt before the game began:

> An officer in the Crimean War once described his sensation in some of the battles there as precisely similar to those he had experienced when a boy on the football field at Rugby. I can appreciate the comparison, for one. Certainly never a soldier went into action with a more solemn do-or-die feeling than that with which I took my place on the field that afternoon.[12]

The connection between sport and war is not seen as in any way inappropriate. The public school and the game of rugby football are tokens of Englishness, and, as in so many school stories, from *Tom Brown's Schooldays* onwards, the implication is that the courage required on the field of play is one of the same order as that which may later be required of a boy on the field of battle. A few pages later comes the 'true story' of an Afghan bandit, who, when the English took over his territory, enlisted in a native force, and, on discovering that the English were 'activated by principles of truth and justice', feels impelled to learn more about their religion. He eventually becomes a Christian, active in combatting 'Mohammedanism'.[13] The serial story – an important item in attracting and maintaining a readership – was entitled, 'From Powder-Monkey to Admiral, or, the stirring days of the British Navy.'[14] It was written by the famous writer for boys, W. H. G. Kingston, but was suggested by the acting editor, G. A. Hutchison, who also revised and rewrote it extensively.[15]

The reader of the first *Boy's Own Paper* was thus being shown a connection between his actions as a boy and his future actions in the wider world where conflict would be between nations. The ideal boy or man is the hero who performs deeds of courage, yet always holds to the knightly virtues; the perfect example of such a hero is the man who risks death fighting for his country. The boy's future is presented as one of active struggle and competition, in which he supports and defends the nation. His youthful actions will prove his fitness or unfitness for this role. In fiction and in factual articles, the army and navy appear as the example which will be most attractive and inspiring to the young reader, but the heroic character equally had a role in the economic sphere:

> In the workshop, on the farm,
> At the desk, – where'er you be –
> From your future efforts, boys,
> Comes a nation's destiny.[16]

The heading of the *Boy's Own Paper* shows all the paraphernalia of a boy's outdoor amusements; the heading of the *Girl's Own Paper* is a copy of a statue, 'The Spirit of Truth and Love',[17] with outstretched arms and pupil-less eyes gazing out at the reader. The difference is clear: the essence of girlhood is in spiritual qualities rather than in actions. On every page of the opening number it is emphasized that 'Woman is formed from girlhood's first plan', and that a girl must therefore constantly assess her thoughts and deeds, all of which will affect her character as a woman:

> If Victoria has been a good queen, as well as a good wife, a good mother, and a good woman, this is due, under God, to the training she had in childhood and girlhood.[18]

A feature on cooking echoes this, asserting that girls who succeed in the art of cookery will have 'gone a long way in the road which leads to their being good daughters, good wives, good mothers, and good mistresses'.[19] Goodness is working for other people, first and foremost in the home. A girl's work in her home should satisfy her every ambition:

> Here is our empire, and here will we reign,
> In mansion or cot be our destiny cast.[20]

There is no virtue for a girl in being restless or adventurous. The home was the 'Empire' in microcosm.

This point is frequently reiterated because there were felt to be influences at work on the middle-class girl that might alienate her from her natural duties. In the article, 'Work for little hands', Mrs Floyer, Examiner in Needlework to the London School Board, makes a satirical comment on the blue-stocking, with the implication that needlework is of far greater value to the world than intellectual work. A young girl, asked by her grandmother if she can sew, replies:

> Oh! no. Miss Crammer says she has no time to teach such common things. She has passed first class at Girton, and her time is too valuable for that.[21]

Again, in an anecdote about a family of sisters, the clever and successful ones are outdone by 'the flower of the flock', who is 'bright, sensible, genial, the light of the home, her mother's right hand'.[22] In an article published later in the year, 'What our girls may do', Alice King puts the matter bluntly:

> They may *not* do any of those things which make them imitators of men; they may *not* try to break down the God-appointed fence which divides their department in the world's great workshop from the department of men; by so doing they only lose their own queenliness without gaining a single ray of male royalty in its place. Let our girls aim at being nothing but women.[23]

As a homemaker, a woman is expected to exert moral and spiritual influence over the male members of the family, and so affect their actions in the outside world, but she herself remains removed from all areas of conflict. The mention of 'queenliness' in the above passage is strongly reminiscent of Ruskin's 'Of Queens' Gardens', which contains the classic statement of the nineteenth-century vision of home:

> This is the true nature of home – it is the place of peace; the shelter, not only from all injury, but from all terror, doubt, and division. In so far as it is not this, it is not home; so far as the anxieties of the outer life penetrate into it, and the inconsistently-minded, unknown, unloved, or hostile society of the outer world is allowed by either husband or wife to cross the threshold it ceases to be a home; it is then only a part of the outer world which you have roofed over and lighted a fire in.[24]

Such themes were pervasive in publications for all age and social groups and were often explicitly associated with the imperial role of the Englishwoman. For example, an article 'Englishwomen and Agriculture' in the *Contemporary Review* in 1898 complained of the overemphasis in the education of women of all social levels on intellectual pursuits and their ignorance of practical agricultural skills. Their acquisition of such skills would at once benefit the home economy, further the development of the Empire and help to sustain family life:

> For my part I am convinced that the fault lies not with Englishwomen as a race, but with the only education that has hitherto lain within their reach. Excellent as it may have been within its limits it has been founded

on too narrow a basis. It has given mere booklearning. . . . Until quite recently it has given very little practical preparation for daily life and it has neglected altogether the special needs of our agricultural population. The criticism holds good equally of our high schools and our elementary schools and of all intermediate scholastic establishments. . . . The whole atmosphere of the class-room has tended to foster girlish ambitions in certain well-defined grooves and intellectual quickness has been of infinitely greater moment than general capacity.[25]

Among other things, argued the author, Virginia Crawford, this situation was creating an overstocked and underpaid labour market for women in white-collar occupations, exposing them also to poor urban living conditions, loneliness and, perhaps, to immorality. If 'our surplus female population' was encouraged instead to take up such pursuits as dairy farming they could assist the home economy by reducing dependence upon imports, while achieving perhaps greater financial independence for themselves, in a manner which had the advantage of making both for health and for the sanctity of family life:

> In our zeal for progress we are apt to forget in England that the family is the natural unit round which society revolves, and that family life cannot be preserved without a certain amount of deliberate and appreciative effort. . . . I am old-fashioned enough to believe that the sending away of daughters at an early age from the family hearth to earn a living elsewhere is a . . . regrettable necessity of our social system and that any development which allows girls to follow an active and remunerative occupation whilst living under the paternal roof will make both for individual happiness and social morality.[26]

This was one of many efforts to weld together the national and social imperative of preserving home and family values, the need of 'surplus females' to be self-supporting and their determination to work and to be independent, with the value to the nation of their contribution to the economy. It was indeed the case that excess supply of 'surplus women' was contributing to low pay, poor living conditions and unemployment among the large and growing numbers of women who could not marry. Their condition was made worse because they were restricted by convention to a narrow if slowly growing range of respectable but poorly paid occupations with limited career prospects (in, for example, teaching, nursing, clerical work); and because in general they came from the large social swathe of families above the level of poverty but below the level of prosperity at which unmarried non-earning daughters could be supported. At every census of the period there were significantly more never-married women than never-married men in every age band above 35. In addition widows outnumbered widowers in every age group above 25; by no means all of them inherited adequate incomes. The higher marriage rate among younger females reflects conventional gender differences in marriage ages. In 1911 in the age band 35–44, 169 per thousand men were single compared with 196 per thousand women.[27] It is probable, though difficult to quantify, that the proportion of unmarried women was higher in the middle than in the working class, due to the higher proportion of middle-class men who failed to marry, who married at later ages or who emigrated. A survey made by Clara Collett in 1890 found that in the 35–45 age group there were 36 unmarried women for every 30 who were married in middle-class Kensington, only 9 unmarried to every 76 married in working-class Hackney.[28]

Conditions such as these caused women to demand alternative roles to the domestic one which was unattainable for so many of them. Pressure of such demands brought about changes in the attributes conventionally ascribed to the ideal Englishwoman. The passage just quoted allowed her a positive role as defender and promoter of English economic interests, while insisting that even unmarried women should not forget the centrality of family commitments or demand too much independence. Even when women were conceded a national role they were not to lose contact with their obligation to the race or with spiritual values.

The central female role as guardian of the race was further promoted by influential contemporaries in the social and natural sciences. A number of writers attempted a scientific examination of the nature of sex differences and their role in the development of the human race. General theories of human development, whether in the fields of biology or sociology, tended to take an evolutionary perspective.[29] Most writers assumed that development was synonymous with progressive evolution and that, in relation to the history of humanity, the European 'races' were at the top of the ladder, with those of the remainder of the world on lower rungs of evolution, due either to a slower rate of development or descent from a higher stage.[30] The Woman Question was considered to be highly relevant to the argument since the mother could be assigned a special responsibility for the future and present condition of the race and for the pace at which it rose and fell on the evolutionary scale.

Herbert Spencer suggested in the 1870s that in individual women the evolutionary process ceased earlier in life than in men because energy was diverted from psychic and intellectual development into reproduction. He believed that the women of his day differed from men in the same way that savages did; similar in kind but different in degree, they were fixed in their ideas and quick to draw conclusions.[31] In *Principles of Sociology* (1876), Spencer went on to conclude that the progress of civilization was based on the development of the monogamous nuclear family, in which the husband was the breadwinner and that any large-scale entry of women into employment would have harmful effects. The fullest and best development of society necessitated female devotion to the home. It should be emphasized that Spencer did not suggest that the differential evaluation of women justified their subordination – which he described as a token of a state of barbarism. Though different from men, women were entitled to equal social and civil rights.[32]

In the field of biology, Patrick Geddes published *The Evolution of Sex* in 1889.[33] He identified differences in temperament between men and women which he believed to derive from a basic difference in cell metabolism – the *katabolism* exhibited by the sperm and the *anabolism* exhibited by the ovum produce, respectively, aggression and rationality in the male and in the female passivity and the hoarding of energy suited to the propagation of the race and its spiritual protection. Like Spencer, Geddes did not present women as inferior to men. He believed that they were equal but just as certainly 'different' and that no amount of activity by women's movements would alter that:

> the differences [between male and female] may be exaggerated or lessened, but to obliterate them it would be necessary to have all the evolution over again on a new basis. What was decided among the prehistoric protozoa cannot be annulled by Act of Parliament.[34]

Adolescence, (1904) by the American, G. Stanley Hall, was an especially influential book on both sides of the Atlantic. The full title is *Adolescence: its psychology, and its relations to physiology, anthropology, sociology, sex, crime, religion and education.*[35] Clearly Hall considered his subject to be of general and fundamental importance. He believed that adolescence was the stage of life during which the 'higher' and 'more completely human' traits are developed, and that, with the further development of the stage of adolescence, a yet higher stage of human development might be reached: 'Adolescence is the bud of promise for the race'.[36]

Hall was convinced that the rise of civilization had gone along with the development of greater structural differentiation between the bodies of the two sexes, and that, especially in adolescence, when sexual characteristics were developing, girls and boys should be educated separately, according to their differing needs:

> Our modern knowledge of woman represents her as having characteristic differences from man in every organ and tissue, as conservative in body and mind, fulfilling the function of seeing to it that no acquired good be lost to mankind, as anabolic rather than katabolic. . . . Her whole soul, conscious and unconscious, is best conceived as a magnificent organ of heredity.[37]

Because of her reproductive function, 'woman is a more generic being than man, closer to the race, and less mutilated by specializations or by deformities of body or of soul.'[38] Hall quotes a paper from the journal *Natural Science* which instances 'co-education of the sexes, occupations of a certain kind, and women's suffrage', as all tending to erode the necessary differences between the sexes, and goes on to suggest that this development in highly civilized races 'would not belong to the progressive evolution of mankind.'[39]

This is one of the clearest contemporary statements of the perception of women (of all nations) as conduits of the essence of the race. It should be emphasized, though, that the belief in the differential evolution of males and females, and in their different capabilities, for example in the intellectual sphere, was by no means universally held among natural and social scientists. Where differences in attainment were discernible, there were those who recognized that their origins were as much, or more, social as biological. 'If', as the physiologist Alexander Sutherland pointed out, in an article titled 'Woman's Brain', 'it has always been more or less the practice to discourage the clever woman and encourage the clever boy, there could be no fairness in pointing to the relative frequency of genius in the two sexes as a proof of the disparity of capacity.'[40]

But this remained a minority view in intellectual and popular publications for all age groups. Those writing for adolescent girls in particular were preoccupied with the distinctive meaning of being a woman and with the importance of avoiding behaviour that could in any way be seen as imitating that of males. Appropriate behaviour for Englishwomen was always seen as something requiring to be *taught* to young females, to be struggled for rather than naturally acquired.

Dr Elizabeth Sloan Chesser, in *From Girlhood to Womanhood* (1914), echoing Stanley Hall, declared that 'every girl has a duty to the race':

> For she is the vase of life; she has in her body the power of handing on and on the life-force which has come to her through millions of years. It is a very sacred and serious thought – is it not? – that your life is so vital a matter to others yet unborn, that by your conduct you can help to keep the life-stream pure, help to uplift the race; that, on the other hand, you can hinder the great forces of evolution.[41]

Even *The Girl's Realm*,[42] a magazine for upper-class and middle-class girls, with a progressive stance on higher education and women's entry into the professions (though with a warier attitude towards the suffrage movement), took constant care to give sufficient encouragement to the womanly virtues. Here as elsewhere, the English girl reader was exhorted to take her example from foreigners:

> Russian girls . . . do not often crave for knowledge, and have very few modern ideas about women's rights; the rights they care most for are to be courted and treated with respect and the deference due to them. . . . They are never masculine or mannish, but strive to cultivate all feminine virtues and qualities, for their great idea is to charm and please. . . . The ideal of most of the girls is to be a wife and mother rather than a 'new woman'.[43]

In a later article, the editor, Alice Corkran, comments on the freedom of American girls, who represent the other end of the spectrum. The results of early association with boys can work out well with the 'finest natures', but the results with frivolous girls are 'lamentable': 'A frivolous American is perhaps one of the most frivolous beings in the world.' The compliment she then pays to English girls, that 'England strikes the happy mean between license and law', does not relate to the particular character of English girls, but to the degree of restraint placed on their behaviour according to the conventions of their social environment.[44] The progressive element in *Girl's Realm* is the acceptance that a woman can be a man's intellectual equal without spoiling her feminine nature; but it remains her femininity that justifies her achievements. An article on Elizabeth Barrett Browning includes the comment that,

> now girls are competing with men . . . there is a tendency among some of them to be impatient of domestic tasks, and of adopting a somewhat scornful attitude towards the essentially feminine duties. Mrs. Barrett has taught us that a woman's mind may reach its highest development, and highest energy of production, and still be all womanly.[45]

Girl's Realm represents another sustained attempt to reconcile competing conceptions of the female role, to integrate women's educational and occupational aspirations with a continued emphasis upon the pre-eminence of 'femininity' and 'domesticity'.

The experience of the Boer War intensified the nationalist and imperialist element in discussions of the female role. The fears of national physical 'deterioration' which were deepened by the wartime revelations of the physical inadequacy of volunteers for the armed services, were also reinforced by the Report of the Interdepartmental Committee on Physical Deterioration, 1904. This, by stressing poor health and diet among children and the importance of nurturing future generations of workers and soldiers, dramatically stressed and publicized the national significance of the maternal role. Furthermore, the unprecedented challenge to British hegemony in southern Africa from members of another European 'race' (the Boers), and its near success, intensified discussion of the need to maintain the Empire as the preserve of the English and their values, in which women were expected to play a crucial role.[46]

The nature of this role was notably explicit in the growing volume of propaganda designed to encourage 'surplus women' to settle in the colonies. This had been an active movement throughout the second half of the nineteenth century, but, again, it reached a peak in the feverish reinforcement of British/English rule in Southern Africa following the Boer War. Unmarried middle-class and lower middle-class women had trickled to the colonies throughout the century in search, sometimes successfully, of the independence which society at home denied them – or of husbands among the unaccompanied men of the colonies. From the 1880s, in the peak period of British imperialist sentiment, the numbers of women emigrating from all classes, and the number of organizations devoted to encouraging such emigration, and to training women for colonial life, expanded significantly.[47] They emphasized the practical skills which women as nurses, servants, teachers, or farmers' wives could bring to the colonies.[48] But they stressed still more strongly the 'civilizing mission' of the emigrant Englishwomen, carrying English ideals abroad, protecting male pioneers from the loss of their national heritage in an alien environment. The ideal was the healthy, practical, but cultured, woman with domestic training, 'who will keep up the tone of the men with whom they mix by music and booklore when the day is over'.[49] They could ensure the survival of 'our Anglo-Saxon ideals'[50] in colonies where those ideals were in danger of weakening among people who were two or three generations removed from 'home' and threatened by the influx of Germans, Russians and French. Emigrant women would 'help to keep the British Empire for the British race.'[51] Furthermore emigration would enable 'surplus women' to find husbands and fulfil their desirable destiny.

Emigration propaganda was often explicitly anti-feminist. Early female sponsors of women's emigration had included feminists centrally concerned to provide opportunities for women which were denied them at home. But the emigration societies became dominated by women and men who were convinced that the surplus woman problem in Britain was the cause of feminist unrest (which they abhorred), since it left women idle and unfulfilled or forced them into the public sphere where they acquired unsuitable ideas. Female emigration, they hoped, could destroy feminism by eliminating this problem while enabling women to achieve domestic fulfilment and to foster Britain's imperial mission.[52]

Hence the emphasis upon the female 'civilizing mission' strengthened in the nineteen hundreds:

> Notions of imperial destiny and class and racial superiority were grafted onto the traditional views of refined English motherhood to produce a concept of the Englishwoman as an invincible global civilizing agent.[53]

> It is the Englishwoman who can best teach them the way because they start with all the advantages of that sex privilege which the Briton wraps around the motherhood of his race.[54]

In similar vein, Dora Gore Browne's poem, 'To England's Daughters' (1904), declaimed that Englishwomen, who traditionally 'Bore aloft the torch of freedom', were now entrusted with a higher duty: 'to keep the flaming torch of loyalty on fire,/in the land of your adoption for the honour of your home' as 'future nursing mothers of the English race to be.'[55]

By 1904 it was felt that the flame had to burn especially brightly in South Africa if English values were not to be swamped by those of the

Boers or the blacks. As the war ended, in 1902, one of a series of articles in
The Nineteenth Century on 'The Needs of South Africa' claimed that

> the emigration of women to South Africa has become a question of
> national importance. If that country is in the future to become one of the
> great self-governing colonies of the British Empire, warm in sympathy
> and attachment to the mother country it must be peopled with loyal
> British women as well as British men.[56]

The government had offered settlement to men who had fought in South
Africa, but these men needed also a British home life:

> Without that home life settlers will bring with them none of the peaceful
> influence which will be the surest means to bring about reconciliation
> with their Boer neighbours and fellow subjects.[57]

One means of securing such reconciliation which might have been thought
possible – marriage between Britons and Boers – was ruled out because,
alas,

> as a rule the Boer women of South Africa are devoid of many of the
> qualities which are essential to make a British man's home happy
> and comfortable. Cleanliness is a virtue too often foreign to the Boer
> character and it is not infrequently replaced by an ignorance of the laws
> of hygiene which produces habits of slovenliness both injurious to health
> and distasteful to British ideas.[58]

Such comments give a clue to contemporary perceptions of the qualities of
the good Englishwoman: hygienic, efficient, resourceful, a good homemaker;
also the purveyor of civilization and repose:

> It is women of high moral character possessed of common sense and a
> sound constitution who can help build up our Empire . . . [they can] . . .
> exalt the tone of social life, bring a softening, elevating, intellectual
> influence.[59]

Really dedicated Englishwomen were exhorted to go as governesses into Boer
families where they would have 'a splendid opportunity of serving the Empire
by instilling British principles into the minds of the children . . . helping to
counteract the evil and disloyal influence by which they are surrounded.'[60]
Those braver still might even marry Dutchmen and – naturally – absorb
them into the superior English way of life. The sense of racial superiority,
and of the female role in preserving and nurturing it, was rarely so explicit
as in commentary on South Africa. British women of all classes were thought
capable of demonstrating the desirable qualities; all were needed in the colonies
as wives or servants. In South Africa there was felt to be a particular need for

English servants to prevent children being raised by 'Kaffirs'; for 'daily contact with a lower race must induce a familiarity with lower ideals'.[61]

Most emigration propaganda was consciously aimed at middle-class women among whom, as we have seen, the danger of failure to find a husband was thought to be greatest and whose alternative opportunities were decidedly limited, though increasingly the emigration organizations found themselves assisting even working-class women.[62] The idealized picture of the colonial woman which emerges from their publications took for granted possession of middle-class accomplishments, especially of literary and musical culture. But enthusiasts for female emigration as a means to secure Britain's imperial greatness recognized that working-class women also might possess qualities capable of compensating for their lack of refinement, appropriate for the need of the Empire, and perhaps more obvious to colonials than to the London organizers of emigration societies. Lady Hely-Hutchinson for example, from the vantage point of Government House, Cape Town, felt that South Africa, in 1902, needed the immigration of 'strong, able-bodied, healthy-minded women of the class that general servants are recruited from at home . . . women who do not look on general service as degrading; women with a sense of responsibility who take pleasure and pride in their work and whose traditions and upbringing have taught them at least this wholesome lesson, that work of whatever sort it may be is elevating or degrading according to the spirit of the worker.' She had no doubt that sound working-class women of this type existed and were much preferable to the 'lady help [who] is anxious that it should be understood that she is a lady, that she has been in better circumstances, that she has a small annual income sufficient to do away with the necessity of her finding a situation at once or indeed for her doing any work that is uncongenial to her. She deprecates the very idea of housework or cooking. She is really too delicate to undertake any but the very lightest duties.' She was 'pretentious, delicate, incapable'. She was the very type that the emigration societies sought to encourage.[63]

The Governor's wife recognized that not all distressed 'surplus' gentlewomen were an asset nor all working women a liability to the Empire; she shared the widespread view that women from all backgrounds had an especial contribution to make to the defence of the Empire. In the years immediately before World War I, such arguments received intellectual backing from eugenicists, notably C. W. Saleeby, who urged positive action to preserve both the quality of the race at home and the superiority of the Empire. The two were, he believed, linked by the 'surplus woman' question. The existence of a surplus in Britain speeded up racial degeneration because it forced some women to seek unwomanly activities and assisted the spread of undesirable feminist ideas. In this he agreed with Herbert Spencer, as he did also in asserting that insistence upon the primary mothering role for women was not inconsistent with believing women worthy of the vote or even of becoming Members of Parliament. Women had a particular wisdom to impart to government; but 'being constructed by Nature as individuals for her racial ends, they best realize themselves, are happy and more beautiful, live longer and more useful lives ... as mothers or foster-mothers.'[64] Unmarried women he believed should become 'foster mothers' by working at such characteristically feminine roles as nursing or teaching.

Hence in the 1900s women were assigned a special responsibility for ensuring that England kept first place in the world. There was more overt patriotic sentiment to be found, for example, in the adolescent girls' magazines than before, though little change in the suggestions as to what girls could do for their country. But it was still believed that too few of them attained the ideal, and that they could learn from women of other countries, for example factory girls could learn from the Japanese:

> The factory girl of Japan is of very different type to that of England. In place of the coarseness which seems almost inseparable from the mode of life, one finds refinement; in place of gaudy, tawdry and unkempt raiment, brightness and neatness; and in place of dirt, which seems to be almost hereditary, cleanliness.[65]

The upper classes could learn from the Russians who

> are among the most thoroughly educated, the most intelligent and the most charming that it has ever been my lot to meet. Their knowledge of three, four and five languages and their wide reading in those languages have broadened their sympathies and given them a wider outlook than is often the case with English and German women. They are quite womanly, but added to their womanliness there is a virility that gives a backbone to their character. . . . [They] do not feel that their interests are separate from those of their men nor do they think their sex inferior and imagine that submissive self-effacement is the highest ornament, yet no country in the world has given us more beautiful examples of wifely devotion and self-sacrifice than Russia.[66]

Such judgements are difficult to evaluate, since they were neither systematic nor universally agreed, and indeed have more of the character of random expressions of prejudice (compare for example these comments on Russian women with those quoted earlier).[67] Essentially they are devices for urging Englishwomen to greater effort, though they are interesting in their willingness to concede superiority to other nations. Representative of this and of other conflicting and sometimes confused contemporaneous tendencies was the two-volume Cassell publication *Women of All Nations* (1909), edited by two Fellows of the Royal Anthropological Institute, which analysed the 'Characteristics, Habits, Manners, Customs and Influence' of Women, nation by nation from bottom (Polynesia) to top (The United States and Canada) of the evolutionary scale. The chapter on the British Isles (by

M. H. Morrison – gender unknown) opened with a contribution to the confusion of international comparisons:

> The Englishwoman, it has been said, lags behind her husband, the American woman strides ahead, the French woman walks beside him. Of the American and the French woman the reflection remains true. Of the English woman it is becoming less true and of the Welsh woman apparently hardly true at all.[68]

Thereafter the chapter was torn between welcoming 'the era of enlightenment through which the sex is passing in England' and more traditional responses, a confusion summed up by the comment: 'As to unmarried women of the country apart from the pity of it that there should be so much waste motherhood, it is they who give continuity to every great cause.' The author stressed that, 'the extremely beautiful, rather characterless type of English beauty . . . is giving place to a young womanhood of distinctive personality, liberal education, many interests, wide sympathies.' Still, however, Englishwomen were not yet good enough:

> Our men to-day are not very different from what we would wish them to be. Those of our women who have the interests at heart of nation and of sex try to bring our girls into line. This is conspicuously so among the upper middle classes, whose influence is specially dominant amongst us and is telling in the ranks below and above.[69]

Their achievement in education, sport and politics, even motoring, showed what women could do, yet the volume still insisted that the most important role for an Englishwoman is in 'the English Home.'

> The comfort, the organization and the unbroken peace of a well managed English household are not surpassed, in some details not equalled, anywhere in the world, which is as one would expect in the country of "Home, Sweet Home."[70]

But perfection, it seemed, still eluded English wives and mothers. They were criticized for being, on the one hand, 'a better friend of her husband than of her children . . . children are left too much to the care of nurses and of schools,' while as wives they were too submissive to their husbands: 'She knows nothing of her husband's business: when he fails he simply says "We must go to Australia". "Yes John," she replies submissively, "Just give me time to get my hat".'[71] But they were also criticized for being too sentimental in the upbringing of their children, while taking their husbands, once caught, too much for granted. They could learn most from Dutchwomen:

> In Holland, more than any other country, women have found their earthly paradise . . . unlike the spoilt and selfish yet brilliant American, without

the charm and the attractive dependence of the Spaniard or Italian, not a managing partner in the family household in the same way as the French woman, nor a comrade to her menfolk like the Russian, the Dutchwoman is a citizen with the welfare of her country at heart, her husband's trusted helpmate and her children's best friend.[72]

In the 1900s all Englishwomen were being measured against an even more exacting standard than before. Domestic perfection had to be combined with some, if not too much, of the independence and adventurousness of the new women and even, it was sometimes indirectly suggested, with a certain sexuality:

A man, in other words, ought to be able to say of his wife as of Cleopatra, "Nothing can stale her infinite variety". A wife then should not let her husband tire of her by letting him be too sure he has got her; the guile of the serpent is as useful as the innocency of the dove.[73]

... the future Englishwoman. ... I dream of a possible woman having something of the frank, fearless grace, the self-reliant daring, the open air freedom of the Englishwoman of the past [a mythical pre-industrial creature previously described by the author]. Give her also charm and sympathy and capability of deep passion . . .[74]

The Cassell volumes are also rare and interesting in offering explicit comparisons among women of the different nations within the British Isles, though, once more, they are bewildering to interpret and it is quite unclear how substantial a body of opinion, if any, they represent. The Scotswoman was described as 'proud ... self-respecting ... independent ... hard-working ... thrifty ... she is always well-informed,' but 'above all she is a mother who has given to the Empire many of her ablest sons ... the Scots have many of the fine qualities of the English – only more so. ... The women north of the Tweed are more serious, more tender and more religious than their sisters on this side. ... *British women as a race* are hospitable; but the educated, refined Scotswoman is the most charming hostess in the world' (our italics).[75]

The meaning of the 'British race' in a chapter which stresses the differences between Celts and Anglo-Saxons remains elusive. Pervasively in the 1900s the terms 'race' and 'nation' were used interchangeably, loosely and variously. English writers, then as now, were inclined to use 'British' and 'English' interchangeably (as several of our quotations demonstrate).[76] They assumed Englishness as the norm and, while being very unspecific about the English 'race' in relation to the Scots, Irish and Welsh 'races', they described the Empire as 'British', meaning it to be English even though it was extensively settled by Celts.

While referring to a 'British race' the chapter dwelled upon the cultural differences among the women of Britain, generally to the disadvantage of the English. Even the Irish, described as being at all social levels held back by poverty, are described as more 'sensitive' and possessing greater emotional depth than Englishwomen.[77] And Welshwomen, 'who have not the slightest intention of becoming English,' were, irrespective of class, 'very charming and very clever,' articulate and well-informed; 'unlike Englishwomen who are silent when their husbands talk, the Welsh join in equally.' They are described as 'democratic . . . intensely individualistic . . . not clannish like the Scots nor aggressively nationalistic like the English' (the last is an interesting but undeveloped suggestion).[78]

Yet for all the difference among the Celts of Britain and between them and the English, the existence of a 'British' empire demanded a claim to the existence of 'British race' with some common characteristics which could justify its survival in an age when territoriality was increasingly, no matter how unjustifiably, defended in terms of racial integrity. This raised another unanswered question: what were the limits to the definition of Britishness. In the Cassell volumes 'The girl of the Province of Ontario' was said to 'represent the best features of the British character. She has pluck, endurance and 'grit' and leads a very active outdoor life . . . with all the skill and zest of her male relatives.' Whether from a wealthy urban background or from a poorer farm, 'she can hold her own not only with her sex of other nations but with the hardy men of her race. She is a fine type of Britain's colonial womanhood.'[79] But when did she cease to be British and become Canadian? Is her Britishness a blend of Celtic and Anglo-Saxon characteristics achieved by some unexamined process? How it relates to Englishness is never clear, so conveniently flexible is the rhetoric of nationality.

These anthropological essays indeed demonstrate the pitfalls facing the attempts of the time to define national characteristics precisely. The more conventional emphasis upon the transnational characteristics of womankind presented problems, and it was not peculiar to the imperialists. It was shared, though with different implications, by feminists in the 1900s. For example, Olive Schreiner insisted that women were everywhere inclined to oppose international rivalry and war, not because of some mystical inner quality of womankind or inherent moral superiority, but because, as creators of life and bearers of children, they knew about pain and the cost of loss of life with an immediacy which men did not:

On that day, when the woman takes her place beside the man in the governance and arrangement of external affairs of her race, will also be that day that heralds the death of war as a means of arranging human differences. . . . Men's bodies are our [woman's] works of art. Given to us power of control, we will never carelessly throw them in to fill up gaps in human relationships made by international ambitions and greeds. The thought would never come to us as women 'Cast in men's bodies; settle the thing so.' . . . To the male the giving of life is a laugh; to the female, blood, anguish and sometimes death . . . it is true that the woman will sacrifice as mercilessly, as cruelly, the life of a hated rival or an enemy, as any male; but she will always know what she is doing, and the value of the life she takes. . . . She always knows what life costs and that it is more easy to destroy than to create it.[80]

A novel whose plot links national differences with the woman question is Mary Bradford-Whiting's *Love's Sacrifice,* which was first published in 1904, in the 'Girl's Library' list of the Religious Tract Society. The *Boy's Own Paper* and *Girl's Own Paper* had been radical departures for the Society, but by this date its publications all had an air of the past. The *B.O.P.,* though seen as a national institution, had been outstripped in popularity by more up-to-date rivals, such as *Chums* and the Amalgamated Press magazines, while the *G.O.P.* was beginning to aim at an older audience and to take a more conservative stance. In 1908, the *G.O.P.* was renamed *The Girl's Own Paper and Woman's Magazine,* under its new editor Flora Klickmann, whose own fiction is represented among the 'Girl's Library' titles.[81] *Love's Sacrifice* shows women's lives untouched by the international rivalry which surrounded them in the 1900s.[82]

The English heroine, Rose, visits Germany and falls in love with Moritz Hagen, a German tutor. The subject of the book is Rose's struggle to come to terms with German expectations of the behaviour of a betrothed young woman. The German view is represented by Moritz's two aunts, with whom Rose is living until Moritz's financial circumstances permit him to marry. Mrs Whiting expresses the differences between Rose and the aunts in terms of cultural differences between the two nations, but her real concern is the conflict between modern and traditional beliefs about women's role in the family and in society. Rose is the modern girl, with a distaste for domesticity and reliance on the intellect. The aunts, though they have been compelled to remain single, have found fulfilment in domestic activity, and particularly in looking after their adored nephew. While Rose, for example, speaks of the new opportunities for German women to be trained as teachers and nurses, and to find 'useful work in the world', the aunts disapprove of higher education for women, and see its introduction into Germany as 'the Fatherland yielding to ideas from without.'

In the end, Rose is won over by her recognition of the value of the German women's purely domestic lives, and by Moritz's tolerance and understanding. Mrs Whiting has no qualms about her heroine marrying a German; the important thing is that he has the right attitude towards the relationship between husband and wife, not that he is a foreigner. Rose declines Moritz's offer to let her go back to England before finally deciding to be his wife. By leaving her country for her husband, she has proved her credentials as a woman.

The attempt to work out a new image for women, rather than for Englishwomen, which can incorporate acceptable elements of the modern and traditional, preoccupies upper-class and middle-class girls' and women's magazines throughout the pre-war period. This is in sharp contrast to the attitude of the boys' magazines and the rest of the popular press, in which the likelihood of war, and fiction on military subjects, feature prominently. War stories had always been a staple of boys' magazines, and, by the time war was declared, they became, in many cases, the only item in the diet. Alfred Harmsworth's Amalgamated Press magazines had declared war long before the actual declaration, and in June 1914, a serial story in the *Boy's Friend*[83] had the legions of the Kaiser sweeping down on Ireland.[84] This was more representative of the mood of the times, and of the experience of their readers. In 1910, Claud Cockburn's father told him to stop playing French and English with his tin soldiers, and to play Germans and English instead; 'I thought Uhlans with lances and flat-topped helmets might come charging over the hill any afternoon now.'[85] Robert Graves was being persecuted at Charterhouse for having a German middle name:

> "German" meant "dirty German". It meant: "cheap shoddy goods competing with our sterling industries". It also meant military menace, Prussianism, useless philosophy, tedious scholarship, loving music and sabrerattling.[86]

The *Girl's Own Paper*,[87] on the other hand, could publish, as late as 1913, an article on the Kaiser and his family as an example of happy domestic life.[88] The outbreak of war, in magazines such as this, was treated for the most part in terms of how women should feel and behave, and war as actual armed combat rarely appears in their pages. The *Girl's Realm* for November 1914 contains few items that are not linked in some way with the war, but the emphasis is on survival rather than victory. An article by the editor, on 'The war and women,' exhorts all women to find useful work, for men will die in battle, leaving women without economic support, and the country cannot afford to keep an 'idle womanhood'.[89] Girls are shown how to knit bed socks and kneecaps for Red Cross parcels. Another article is concerned with the effect of the war on fashion: 'It is not a frivolous matter . . . for it affects not only the women of the world who wish to be smartly gowned, but the men of the business world.'[90] The competition pages invite girls to send an answer to the question, 'Should I like my brother to enlist?', a photograph entitled 'News from the front,' a doll dressed as a Red Cross nurse (entries would be sent to Belgian refugee children) or a pair of knitted socks (entries would be sent to soldiers at the front).[91] One item brings the war closer: a schoolgirl's diary tells a 'thrilling narrative of the actual conditions of warfare'.[92]

Girls in reality were by no means cut off from jingoistic attitudes, which they experienced directly and in their brothers' magazines, but magazines which were intended to put forward models for middle-class womanhood delineated a 'girls' realm' in which crude expressions of nationalism had no part. Men go off to war; women preserve the home for them: home 'is the place of Peace'. But the entries to the competition, 'Should I like my brother to enlist?', show the attitudes of some real girls, who do not accept the

division between themselves and their brothers. 'If we have a good sample of
the general opinion', said the report on the competition, 'there is no lack of
enthusiasm for the motherland among the girls of Britain'.[93] Many, in fact,
expressed the wish that they themselves could go out and fight, among them
the winner of the first prize:

> It is a great hardship to many girls, myself included, to know that they
> cannot help their country in the actual fighting line. . . . In our family
> girls predominate, and we all long to be men and fight. We long to "live
> dangerously" for the sake of Great Britain.[94]

In 1915, *Girl's Realm* published a piece written by 8-year-old Mollie Vose
in her school magazine:

> If I caught the Kaiser, I should not shoot him or kill him, anyway. I should
> only take him prisoner and leave him in the barbed wire until he died. I
> should not feed him, either. I'd let him starve.[95]

This active patriotism (or at least, desire for adventure) in English girls became
apparent to Baden-Powell when he founded the Boy Scout movement. The
separate girls' organization, the Girl Guides, was set up to *prevent* girls from
forming their own troops in direct imitation of the Scouts, whose activities
were intended as moral and physical training to build a manly character in the
future defenders of the Empire. For Baden-Powell, as for the other apostles
of 'national efficiency' at the time, improving the younger generation was
the only way to reverse the military decline, and the decline in the health and
morals of the people which the Boer War experience was thought to have
revealed. Scouts were supposed to place class harmony above any notion of
class conflict or criticism of the social order, remembering that they were all
Britons first: 'And a strong united Empire, where all are helpful and patriotic
will bring us power, peace and prosperity such as no Socialistic dream could
do.'[96] In practical terms Scouting offered an opportunity to act out in real life
the adventures of the popular boys' tales – to wear military-style uniform,
to march along the streets, to learn the skills of woodcraft – and to have all
this taken seriously as a contribution to the defence of the nation. The well-
known *Punch* cartoon of 1909 shows a young Scout offering his arm to an
old lady, with the caption:

OUR YOUNGEST LINE OF DEFENCE
Boy Scout to Mrs. Britannia: Fear not, Granma, no danger can befall you
now. Remember, *I am* with you![97]

The image of the England to be defended is that of a helpless female.
    But girls also coveted the active role. 'Girl scouts' often found encouragement.
A comment in the 1909 *Girl's Realm* on 'Girls and Scouts' denies that the

movement has to do with preparation for war; the essential idea is to give girls a training which will help to make them useful women in later life.[98] In January 1910, by which time Baden-Powell had already formulated his plans for the 'Girl Guides,' the editor of the *Girl's Friend,* an Associated Press magazine primarily for working-class girls, replied to a correspondent in a way which almost implied an existing alternative structure:

> The elected secretary should get into communication with the leader of a boys' patrol organised in her district. This leader . . . will be pleased to assist to put the girls' company on the right road to success. He might even suggest that the girls' patrol should work in conjunction with the boys' patrol, which would be a very happy notion indeed. . . . The girl scout is expected to give particular attention to the subject of nursing and other work for which women are particularly adapted.[99]

The suggestion of working in conjunction with the boys would not have seemed 'happy' to Baden-Powell.

The first official code of practice for Girl Guides came in *Girl Guides: a suggestion for character training for girls,* written by Baden-Powell, assisted by his sister Agnes, in 1909.[100] The opening words are uncompromising:

> Decadence is threatening the nation, both moral and physical. . . . Much of this decadence is due to the ignorance or supineness of mothers who have never been taught themselves.[101]

As a result of the failings of modern women, 'Good servants are hard to get; homes are badly kept; children are badly brought up.'[102] Baden-Powell recommended a programme of training in domestic duties, including sewing, cooking, first-aid and nursing, together with moral training to enable girls to become the 'guides' of men. This was aimed, theoretically, at all social classes, in practice it reached the broad middle swathe, from the better-off working-class to the lower reaches of the wealthy. But he also realized that if girls were to turn back to their proper work, it must be made more attractive to them. He was therefore trying to sugar the pill of 'domestic science' with the addition of some of the adventure and excitement that the 'girl scouts' were looking for. This was difficult to achieve.

For the Boy Scouts, the military discipline, the pride in being recognized in public as a smart, well-drilled band of young men, and the vigorous physical exercise, were all integral to the aims of the movement. As in the curriculum of the public school, which Baden-Powell used as his model, moral growth is considered to go along with the training of the body; the Scouts utilized 'natural' male activities. Baden-Powell was also convinced that the boys would eventually be called upon to fight. With girls, the very elements that made Scouting so appealing to them were precisely those which Baden-Powell wanted to minimize in the Guide movement. A girl might be instructed, he went on, 'by means which really appeal to her, and without necessarily making her a rough tomboy,'[103] thus admitting that it was the potentially tomboyish activities that girls were finding attractive. The Guide movement was another attempt to reconcile new female aspirations with a predominantly domestic and spiritual role for women. Baden-Powell attempted to rationalize the combination of domestic and woodcraft training by suggesting that girls would be needed to find and care for the wounded after a foreign invasion. This is given as the first aim of the training, the second being preparation for a possible life in the Colonies. The third aim, though modestly placed, relates more closely to the earlier complaint about the inadequacies of the woman of the day:

> 3. To make themselves generally more useful to others and to themselves by learning useful occupations and handiwork, and yet retaining their womanliness.[104]

The objections to 'girl scouts' were set out in the form of a correspondence, said to be genuine, between a girl at school in England and her mother in India.[105] The girl has taken up 'Scouting' and explains that she believes it to be a good influence on her, as well as being enjoyable. Her mother points out the ways in which her daughter's letter betrays a growth of unwomanly habits, and tells her that she is merely trying to behave like a boy. Violent exercise (encouraged by short skirts) has been known to result in 'harm which was only discovered when the girl had become a *woman* with a woman's duties to perform.'[106] The girl had expressed her enjoyment of being seen as a Scout in public; her mother says she should rather feel uncomfortable: 'that is the warning of instinct and good *breeding* – that means you come of a race of well-born people.'[107] If she whistles she may end up with a man's mouth, 'and perhaps a moustache[!].'[108] Physical exercise, public parades, all the aspects of Scouting that 'really appeal' to girls are therefore, in the end, unsuitable for them. Yet Baden-Powell recognizes that without making use of the girls' desire for the potentially unwomanly side of Scouting, girls would not be attracted to the Girl Guides. In this same pamphlet he plays upon girls' patriotism and longing for action as he explains the aims of the movement:

> Girls! imagine that a battle has taken place in and around your town and village – it is a thing that may very likely happen in the case of invasion by a foreign enemy.
> What are you going to do?
> Are you going to sit down, and wring your hands, and cry? Or are you going to be plucky and go out and do something to help your brothers and fathers who are fighting and falling on your behalf?[109]

The tone of this implies that girls are required to act, and that their action is urgently needed: 'It is too late when the enemy is at your door.'

But the call is to action within very clear limits. A letter in the *Girl Guides' Gazette*[110] of August, 1914 (whose cover proclaims: 'For God, our King, and Empire; the Baden-Powell Girl Guides . . .') exhorts Guides to maintain a background support role in wartime:

> Every Girl Guide must prove her guide-ship now by being a quiet, cheery, useful, self-controlled girl. . . . Remember, women are very useless if they cannot suffer silently and quietly.[111]

Girls and women get similar advice from many other sources. The President of the Girls' Friendly Society advises that English girls – in this primarily working-class organization – should respond to the outbreak of war with

> quiet self-restraint, diligently doing whatever comes to you to be done, and bravely bearing whatever has to be borne. It is for you to uphold the honour and high character of our nation at home.[112]

The *Girl's Own Paper and Women's Magazine,* aiming further up the social scale, concludes, in an article on 'Women and patriotism', that 'a nation is the home'.[113]

At this same time, the *Girl's Reader,* an Associated Press fiction magazine for working girls,[114] had no hesitation in presenting a serial story with a fighting English girl as a heroine. The story, 'Emma Brown of London, or, The girl who defied the Kaiser',[115] was heralded several weeks in advance, and given such prominence that it is clear the editor was expecting it to be popular. Emma is a Cockney servant girl, whose young man, Ernie Dobbs, is at the front. Emma wishes she was a man so that she could also go. She loses her job (with no regrets, because she considers that her employer is 'no true Briton'), and decides to follow Ernie to France. Within a very short time, pausing only to persuade a group of young loafers to join up, she has reached her destination and proceeded to organize a group of 'ineligibles' in a small village, which results in the capture of twenty-five Germans. Her adventures continue in the same vein; when she joins up with the English troops, they are astounded at her exploits. An officer tells his men:

> We've won a brilliant skirmish, but we know who we've got to thank for it – the bravest and most clever little woman who has ever lived since Joan of Arc! Come on, lads! Three cheers for Emma Brown of London![116]

When Emma is taken prisoner and brought before the Kaiser himself, the illustration shows her standing upright, her head thrown back, her arm pointing towards him as he stands cowed before her:

> "Britain's roused now!" – Emma's voice rang out firm and clear – "the British bulldog won't let go until Germany's brought to her knees." . . .

"I – I ain't eddicated. I don't profess to be; but I know what I'm talking about now. I know that we're in the right, and you're wrong. And I know" – she flung up her head – "that Old England is going to win. *Britain always wins!*"[117]

Here is a heroine who is not subject to the restrictions on women's patriotic activity which the middle-class magazines (by which we mean those for which the question of what is proper overrides that of what may be popular) are so careful to maintain. Emma breaks all the rules: she speaks up against her employer, leaves her job without a backward glance, travels alone to a foreign country and leads men in battle. And the soldiers adore her (though she remains true to the good, if ugly, Ernest Dobbs). She must have been designed to represent the fantasies of large numbers of the readers of the magazine, and there is no sign in the way the story is presented that these readers were expected to feel any sense of anxiety about the unwomanliness of such a heroine.

Emma Brown is a fantasy, but during the war many women did take an active part, and male and female attitudes altered. In 1914, Olave Baden-Powell (Robert's wife) had been shocked to see Girl Guides marching alongside Boy Scouts, and reminded the Guides that their 'true womanliness' had no place for militarism or the 'tomboy spirit'.[118] Girl Guides should be seen in public as little as possible. In 1918, now as Chief Guide, she reports in *Girl Guides Gazette* that she has visited the WAAC in France, who, she declares, is taking a real share with the men in the work of winning the war: 'I felt quite as if it was a grown-up Guide army'.[119] In the same issue there is a page listing Brave Deeds, among which is the story of a 19-year-old girl, a brilliant Guide, who caught a chill and died while working as a cook for the WAAC. She was given a military funeral, and carried to her grave by a detachment of the Black Watch, followed by the Dunblane Company of the Girl Guides. But alongside these reports there is still the emphasis on the view of the true woman's role as one of influence rather than direct action. In September 1918, the *Girl Guides Gazette* recounts an anecdote of Baden-Powell's, in which he quotes an officer whom he met at the front:

> The biggest thing you are doing is the Girl Guides, for I am certain that it is the mother's influence that largely shapes a Man's after-character.[120]

This issue also contains a warning by Lady Baden-Powell:

> The women must be strong, strong as the house which was built upon a rock, or the men will ask themselves: "After all, was it worthwhile?"[121]

All of this parallels the wider experience of women in England during the war. At the outset they were not encouraged to take an active or adventurous part, even within their accepted sphere. Women doctors volunteering for the front were told to 'Go home and keep quiet'; commanding officers 'did not want to be troubled with hysterical women.'[122] Ray Strachey, who was prominent among the pro-war section of the suffrage movement, believing that the women's cause had much to gain from their being seen to be as active in their patriotism as in their feminism, wrote:

> The confusion of the first months of war was tremendous. For men the course of action was, on the whole, straightforward, but for women it was perplexing in the extreme. The impulse of vehement patriotism burned in their hearts and the longing to be of service moved them; but there was little they could find to do.[123]

It was symptomatic of the ways in which women's aspirations had changed in the preceding years that after the initial confusion women found a great deal to do, even entering the armed services for the first time, though in 'service' rather than fighting roles, as clerks, administrators, drivers and so on. And, increasingly, the country needed their active participation in the war effort, not only in roles such as these, or in nursing, but also in previously male sectors of the home labour force. But at the same time that Englishwomen were more than ever before being encouraged to be active and adventurous, the maternal role was assuming greater national importance. As ever more young men were lost at the front, and the physical condition of recruits was revealed to be as alarmingly poor as in the previous war, the government demanded more and better motherhood with ever greater urgency. A *Daily Telegraph* leader proclaimed in 1915: 'If we had been more careful for the last fifty years to prevent the unheeded wastage of infant life, we should now have had at least half a million more men available for the defence of the country.' A Voluntary Infant Welfare Propaganda fund was established to encourage and improve maternity and child care. National Baby Week, a week of propaganda on the infant welfare theme, was held in July 1917. The government provided unprecedented subsidies for child welfare clinics, midwife training, and milk for mothers and babies.[124]

Maternal care, if not encouragement to have yet more babies, was another issue upon which feminists and imperialists converged. The Women's Co-operative Guild, the largest organization of working-class women of the period, broadly aligned with the Labour party in its thinking, had long campaigned for safer conditions of childbirth for women. As part of this campaign, in 1915 the Guild published *Maternity,* extracts from one hundred and sixty deeply moving letters from women about their experience of marriage, childbirth and child rearing. It was prefaced by a stirring introduction from the Right Hon Herbert Samuel, President of the Local Government Board and responsible for health matters:

> In the competition and conflict of civilizations it is the mass of the nations that tells. Again and again in history a lofty and brilliant civilization embodied in a small state has been borne under by the weight of a larger

state of a lower type. The ideas for which Britain stands can only prevail as long as they are backed by a sufficient mass of numbers. It is not enough to make our civilization good. It must also be made strong; and for strength numbers are not indeed enough without other elements, but they are none the less essential. Under existing conditions we waste before birth and in infancy a large part of our possible population.[125]

Victory for Britain and her values, it seemed, depended almost as much upon her mothers as her soldiers. During the war England officially endorsed both of the competing conceptions of woman's role, as worker and as mother. The war, however, also gave birth to another role for women, which was less welcome in official eyes, though it was entirely consistent with pre-war notions of women as guardians of moral values and was foreshadowed, in somewhat different vein, in the writings of Olive Schreiner. Pacificism among women grew during the war and became still stronger in the interwar years.

The peace movement stressed women's internationalism. Indeed the first major peace organizations were international. The International Woman Suffrage Alliance formed in 1902 stressed from its foundation the need for enfranchisement of women as a defence against war. On 31 July 1914 leaders of its British branch delivered a manifesto to the Foreign Office and to foreign embassies, 'on behalf of 26 countries and 12 million women . . . when the fate of Europe depends on decisions which women have no power to shape, we, realizing our responsibilities as the mothers of the race cannot stand passively by . . .'[126] In 1915 the international women's peace conference at The Hague had a tiny British attendance due to the withholding of passports and the difficulty of crossing the Channel in wartime, though in autumn 1915 the Women's International League was established in London as the British section of the Association of Women for Permanent Peace, an offshoot of the Hague conference. At its peak it had only 3,687 members in 40 branches in 1918. It was largely middle class in membership, though with strong I.L.P. links. The women's peace movement more generally cut across class and party political lines, from Sylvia Pankhurst's East London Federation to moderate Liberalism, but it never rivalled the Women's Social and Political Union's mobilization of 30,000 women for a pro-war Women's Right to Serve demonstration in July 1915.[127] The larger, more working-class, Women's Peace Crusade was launched on militant Clydeside in 1916 and was led by women who had been active in the rent strikes of the previous year and in local Labour politics. In 1917 they led a demonstration of 17,000 on Glasgow Green. This movement spread through the industrial cities of northern England and Scotland despite bitter opposition. By the end of the war it had 100 branches and perhaps 5,000 members, close links with the I.L.P. and a broader social base than equivalent movements. After the war it went on to speak up for Irish nationalism.[128]

The women's peace movement appeared serious enough to provoke official discouragement of female pacifism from the highest sources. The Home might be promoted as 'the place of peace' but women were not expected to carry their peace-inducing properties outside its walls. The celebrated letter written by 'A Little Mother' to the *Morning Post* in 1916 was shortly afterwards reprinted as a pamphlet, with an endorsement from the Queen, and reached a wide audience. Its arguments are an interesting inversion of Olive Schreiner's (which had been widely echoed by women pacifists). The 'Little Mother' manages to express a militant and uncompromising dedication to the continuation of the war, while maintaining the image of women, especially mothers, as the peace-loving sex. The success of this letter has its basis in the way it utilizes the current mythology of motherhood: a mother's natural feeling for her child is the strongest and purest form of love, and a woman must undergo terrible sufferings when she voluntarily gives up her son to face death in the trenches. The emphasis on the self-sacrifice of the mother masks the fact that the sacrifice is more her son's than her own:

> We women pass on the human ammunition of "only sons" to fill up the gaps, so that when the "common soldier" looks back before going "over the top" he may see the women of the British race at his heels, reliable, dependent, uncomplaining.

The 'Little Mother's desire for victory is a virtue only in so far as it is seen to be against her female nature: 'We gentle-nurtured timid sex did not want the war.' She makes it clear that her aim in pressing for a victorious conclusion to the war is wider than the interests of her own nation:

> It is we who "mother the men" who have to uphold the honour and traditions not only of our Empire but of the whole civilised world.[129]

An English victory is necessary to ensure the continued progress of the human race.

The language of this letter is in a heroic mode, but it is a heroism of sacrifice; 'Little Mothers' gain their effect by influence rather than action. Over the war period, however, there arises a different, though related, image of the patriotic Englishwoman, or, rather, the English girl, which compares her to another image of female patriotism, Joan of Arc. This image is in process of development before the war – one example comes in a book entitled *52 Stories of the Brave and True for Girls*,[130] whose editor comments in the preface:

> There may be no outlet just now for a woman to lead the forces on the field of war, but there is room for any number of girls to show in quiet places the bravery and truth of Joan of Arc.

Joan, on horseback, is illustrated on the book's cover. *Girl's Realm* similarly claimed in 1908 that 'girls possess in the highest degree the capacity for the knightly virtues', which include compassion for the weak, self-sacrifice, patriotism, justice and mercy.[131] During the war the Guides also invoked this image of chivalry and the knightly virtues:

> We try to train girls to be good Guides for the next generation, and to inculcate a high ideal of womanhood by working on that love of romance and admiration for chivalry found in most girls and boys.[132]

The Guide and Scout promises are equated with vows of knighthood. The story of Emma Brown in *Girl's Reader* was advertised as having a heroine who was a latter-day Joan of Arc.

After the war, these heroic elements become integrated into the schoolgirl of the new popular magazines: the typical plot is that of an honourable girl, falsely accused, who will not betray the real culprit, though that person is prepared to see her suffer. The girl as young knight now approximates to the image of the public school boy, and like him, she is distinctively English. In wartime stories of spies in girls' schools (another ubiquitous plot), the disguised Hun gives herself away by small actions that show she is not naturally 'straight'. The English girl is a slim, upright figure, who will stand up against anyone in a just cause, perform acts of bravery (particularly in rescuing people from drowning), but modestly refuse any public acknowledgement of her actions. She will not countenance the slightest deviation from her code of honour. 'The Castlestone House Company', a serial story running from January to October in the 1918 *Girl Guides Gazette,* combines war, school, and Guiding. Here, patriotic schoolgirls express their envy of men, and the passage has an indulgent tone:

> I envy you, awfully. Being a Guide is all very well, and quite nice, but nothing like fighting Germans and being torpedoed, and catching spies, and all that . . .[133]

These are not feelings which would be endorsed in the *Gazette* outside a fictional context, but patriotism makes them acceptable. Indeed, when the girls discuss the founding of a Guide company for their school, it is the idea of wearing a uniform that causes the most excitement:

> "Look at all the pockets", murmured Elsie, admiringly, "it's as good as being a boy."[134]

The two foreigners in the story, Mademoiselle, the French teacher, and the German girl, Estelle, are secretly working against England. Mademoiselle is discovered throwing lumps of mud at the Union Jack; Estelle shows character defects which are seen to be congenital in Germans:

> Estelle does not strike me as up to the mark. She was in some fuss with Dot last term, and she didn't own up, but let Dot take all the punishment;

that wasn't conduct "befitting an officer and a gentleman", was it? Well, she happens to be neither – not even a Guide yet, and, after all, what can you expect from a German?[135]

These same elements – a girl's desire to take a more active part in the war effort, and the inability of a German to sustain the character of an English schoolgirl – are also found in Angela Brazil's school story, *A Patriotic Schoolgirl* (1918). Marjorie, the main character, has a good deal of contact with the war through her family. Her father and three brothers are in the armed forces, and she knows that there are also women at the front:

> She was burning to do something to help – to nurse the wounded, drive a transport wagon, act as secretary to a staff-officer, or even be telephone operator over in France – anything that would be of service to her country and allow her to feel that she had played her part, however small, in the conduct of the Great War.[136]

Her new friend, Chrissie Lang (or Lange, as a slip of the pen later shows it to be), pretends to believe that one of the teachers at their school is a spy, and searches her private correspondence. Marjorie is distressed by her action, but her friend thinks nothing of it:

> "But look here! It doesn't seem quite right – straight, somehow." "Can't be helped in the circumstances," replied Chrissie laconically. Marjorie wondered whether the service of her country really demanded such a sacrifice of honour.[137]

To be dishonourable has now become the ultimate sin. The English schoolgirl is characterized by the virtues of the 'officer and gentleman', and the accent is on this code rather than on the traditional images of femininity.

After the war women were not expected to sustain the active public role enforced by the abnormal demands of war. Indeed, as Vera Brittain discovered on her return to Oxford, though men who had served were regarded as heroes, women who had undergone horrific war experiences – in her case as a nurse – were treated as an embarrassment. They were expected to slip painlessly back into an uncomplaining pre-war female role.[138] But in this respect, as in many others, the clock could not be turned back to 1914. For younger women at least, there had been a permanent change. The unmarried Englishwoman acquired, in visual as well as literary representation, a new image. Not only was she now allowed a muted version of the qualities and capacity for action of the Englishman, but short-haired, flat-chested, short skirted, she was closer in appearance to a young boy than to a pre-war woman. But she was still expected to grow up to be a woman. Following a period of youthful independence she would fall in love, marry, bear children, acquire a womanly appearance and real fulfilment. The two images of women had been reconciled by assigning them to different periods of life.

The idealization of motherhood which had been growing up since the 1880s became even more potent after the war as a focus for anti-feminism and fears for the survival of the Empire. The result of women refusing motherhood would be 'race suicide'.[139] These arguments were related directly to the future of England and the Empire – the 'race' was now more strictly defined – but still the underlying reasoning was in terms of what was 'progressive' for the evolutionary process, and what was 'natural' for woman as a biological creature. Mothers, seen in this light, are still Ruskin's Queens, and the home, though apparently a limited space within which women were confined, was the repository of universal values of religion and morality. Woman as 'the vase of life' must still be set apart from the competitive struggle of the world outside and cannot be defined purely by her nationality, although she is vital to the life of the nation. 'A nation is the home', and men's patriotism exists in the defence of the home, 'and of all that makes life worth living'.

Notes

1 Their civil and social rights were considerably curtailed, including rights to welfare benefits. For example, when the first old-age pensions were paid under the Act of 1908 all aliens and wives of aliens were excluded from the right to claim. Furthermore as Virginia Woolf pointed out:

That they are step-daughters, not full daughters of England is shown by the fact that they change nationality on marriage. A woman, whether or not she helped to beat the Germans, becomes a German if she marries a German. Her political views must then be entirely reversed and her filial piety transferred. Virginia Woolf *Three Guineas* (London: Hogarth P., 1938), ch. 1, fn. 12.

And if he says that he is fighting to protect England from foreign rule, she will reflect that for her there are no "foreigners" since by law she becomes a "foreigner" if she marries a foreigner ... "For" the outsider will say, "in fact as a woman, I have no country. As a woman I want no country. As a woman my country is the whole world."

Three Guineas, ch. 3.

See our later references to women's internationalism and pacifism. We are grateful to Lidwien Heerkens for the above references.

2 See the chapter by Peter Brooker and Peter Widdowson.

3 Lee Holcombe, *Victorian Ladies at Work* (Newton Abbot: David and Charles, 1973), pp. 40, 178–9.

4 Catherine Hall, 'The early formation of Victorian Domestic Ideology', in *Fit Work for Women,* ed. Sandra Burman (London: Croom Helm, 1979).

5 B. R. Mitchell, *Abstract of British Historical Statistics* (Cambridge: C.U.P., 1962), p. 6. Table 2.

6 This is briefly discussed in Pat Thane, 'Women and state welfare in Victorian and Edwardian England', *History Workshop Journal*, 6 (Autumn 1978), 29–51.

7 This is difficult to quantify due to the inadequacy of female employment statistics. There is some suggestive evidence in Elizabeth Roberts, *A Woman's Place: An Oral History of Working Class Women 1890–1940* (Oxford: Basil Blackwell, 1984).

8 *Boy's Own Paper* was issued weekly from January 1879 until August 1914, monthly thereafter. All references to this and to *Girl's Own Paper* and *Girl's Realm* are to annual bound volumes.

9 Minutes of the General Committee of the R.T.S. 1. 1132 (16 July 1878), quoted in Patrick Dunae, '*Boy's Own Paper*: origins and editorial policies', *Private Library*, 2nd series (Winter 1976), 123–58.

10 Dunae, op. cit. Periodicals can be especially valuable indicators of attitudes and of changes in them. Compare Louis James: 'A periodical is a complex organism, constantly responding to the pressure of the times and the audience. . . . For a periodical does not embody only an editorial viewpoint; it communicates . . . through both content and format: it encapsulates a style of living for particular readers at a particular time and place . . . Periodicals are cultural clocks by which we tell the times.' 'The trouble with Betsy: periodicals and the common reader in mid-19th century England', eds. Joanne Shattock and Michael Wolff, *The Victorian Periodical Press: Samplings and Soundings* (Leicester: Leicester U.P., 1982).

11 Dunae, op. cit.

12 *Boy's Own Paper,* 1 (January-September 1879), 1–2.

13 Ibid., p. 5.

14 Ibid., p. 9.

15 Hutchison's part in the story's composition is described in Jack Cox: *Take a Cold Tub, Sir! The Story of the Boy's Own Paper* (Guildford: Lutterworth P., 1982), p. 13.

16 *Boy's Own Paper,* 1 (January-September 1879), 126.

17 *Girl's Own Paper,* 1 (1880), 208. The editor explains the figure in reply to a letter from two girl readers: 'The statue of which our heading is a copy has been greatly admired. It was called by the sculptor, "The Spirit of Truth and Love", and we think this a good motto for our paper.'

18 Ibid., p. 7.

19 Ibid., p. 5.

20 Ibid., p. 12.

21 Ibid., p. 15.

22 Ibid., p. 11.

23 Ibid., p. 462.

24 John Ruskin, 'Of Queens' Gardens', in *Sesame and Lilies, The Two Paths and The King of the Golden River*, ed. John Ruskin (London: Dent, 1907), First pub. 1865.

25 Virginia Crawford, 'Englishwomen and Agriculture', *Contemporary Review*, 74 (September 1898), 427. We have been unable to discover anything about Virginia Crawford.

26 Ibid.

27 B. Mitchell, op. cit., pp. 15–16, table 5.

28 A. J. Hammerton, *Emigrant Gentlewomen* (London: Croom Helm, 1979), pp. 30–1.

29 J. W. Burrow, *Evolution and Society: A Study in Victorian Social Theory* (Cambridge: C.U.P., 1966).

30 Ibid.

31 J. D. Y. Peel, *Herbert Spencer: The Evolution of a Sociologist* (London: Heinemann, 1971), p. 125.

32 Ibid., p. 94.

33 Jill Conway, 'Stereotypes of femininity in a theory of sexual evolution', in *Suffer and Be Still,* ed. M. Vicinus (London: Methuen, 1980), pp. 140–54.

34 Patrick Geddes, *The Evolution of Sex* (rev. edn; London: Williams and Norgate, 1901), p. 286.

35 G. Stanley Hall, *Adolescence*, 2 vols (New York: Appleton, 1904). Quotations are from the 1920 edition.

36 Ibid., vol. 1, p. 50.

37 Ibid., vol. 2, p. 561.

38 Ibid., p. 122.

39 Ibid., p. 568. The article is: A. Hyatt, 'The influence of woman on the evolution of the human race', *Natural Science,* 8 (1897), 89.

40 Alexander Sutherland, 'Woman's Brain', *The Nineteenth Century,* May 1900, p. 808.

41 Elizabeth Sloan Chesser, *From Girlhood to Womanhood* (London: Cassell, 1914), p. 125.

42 *Girl's Realm* (London: Cassell, 1898–1915), Monthly.

43 *Girl's Realm* 1 (1898–99), 804.

44 'On being engaged', by Alice Corkran; Ibid., p. 954.

45 Ibid., p. 1270.

46 *Race* and *nation* could be seen as synonymous terms. Hall, for example (op. cit., vol. 2, 720), in discussing the evolutionary ascent and descent of races, comments: 'Ploetz thinks that the Frenchmen and Yankees are sinking, and most West Aryans, European Jews, English, Dutch and Scandinavians are rising races.' See also, *Report of the Interdepartmental Committee on Physical Deterioration* Parliamentary Papers 1904, vol. 32; Carol Dyhouse, *Girls Growing up in Late Victorian and Edwardian England* (London: Routledge, 1981); 'Social Darwinistic Ideas and the development of women's education in England, 1880–1920', *History of Education,* 5 (1978), 41–58.

47 Hammerton, op. cit., p. 177.

48 Ibid., pp. 148 ff. Arthur Montefiore Brice, 'Emigration for Gentlewomen', *The Nineteenth Century* (April 1901), 601–10.

49 Hammerton, p. 161.

50 Ibid., p. 163.

51 Ibid.

52 Ibid., pp. 168–9.

53 Ibid.

54 Ibid.

55 Ibid., pp. 163–4.

56 The Hon Mrs Evelyn Cecil, 'The Needs of South Africa. II. Female Emigration', *The Nineteenth Century* (April 1902), 683.

57 Ibid.

58 Ibid.

59 Ibid. See also The Hon Lady Hely-Hutchinson, 'Female Emigration to South Africa', *The Nineteenth Century* (January 1902), 71–87, which, written from Government House Cape Town, was mostly about the 'servant problem' in South Africa.

60 Cecil, op. cit., p. 690.

61 Hely-Hutchinson, pp. 71–9. See also Brice, op. cit.; S. Staples, 'The Emigration of Gentlewomen. A Woman's word from Natal', *The Nineteenth Century* (August 1901), 214–21.

62 Hammerton, op. cit., p. 148ff.

63 Hely-Hutchinson, op. cit.

64 Quoted Hammerton, p. 170.

65 T. Athol Joyce and N. W. Thomas (eds), *Women of all Nations. A Record of their Characteristics, Habits, Manners, Customs, and Influence,* 2 vols (London: Cassell, 1909), p. 510.

66 Ibid., p. 689.

67 See p. 16.

68 Joyce and Thomas, op. cit., p. 756.

69 Ibid.

70 Ibid., p. 757.

71 Ibid.

72 Ibid., p. 704.

73 Ibid., p. 757.

74 Lady Mary Ponsonby, 'The role of women in society', *The Nineteenth Century* (January 1901), 76.

75 Joyce and Thomas, op. cit., p. 759.

76 See pp. 17, 17–18, 27, 37.

77 Joyce and Thomas, p. 761.

78 Ibid., p. 762.

79 Ibid., p. 768. Interestingly these are the concluding sentences of the two volumes.

80 Olive Schreiner, *Women and Labour,* 2nd edn (London: Virago, 1978), pp. 170–1.

81 *Girl's Own Paper,* London 1880 to October 1908; continued weekly as *Girl's Own Paper and Woman's Magazine,* November 1908–27, then monthly as *Girl's Own Paper* until 1948.

82 Mary Bradford-Whiting, *Love's Sacrifice* (London: Religious Tract Society, 1904).

83 *Boy's Friend* (London: Amalgamated Press, 1895–1927), weekly.

84 'The Legions of the Kaiser, or, The mailed fist.' First episode in *Boy's Friend,* 13 June, 1914.

85 Claud Cockburn, *I, Claud . . .* (Harmondsworth: Penguin, 1967), p. 10.

86 Robert Graves, *Goodbye to All That* (Harmondsworth: Penguin, 1960), p. 38. First published 1929.

87 Since November 1908, when Flora Klickmann took over as editor, the title of the magazine had been *The Girl's Own Paper and Woman's Magazine.* The entry in the 1914 *Newspaper Press Directory* describes it as 'for women of the better class'.

88 *Girl's Own Paper and Woman's Magazine,* 34 (1912–13), 553.

89 *Girl's Realm,* 17 (1914–15), 45.

90 Ibid., p. 57.

91 Ibid., p. 61.

92 Ibid., pp. 65–8.

93 Ibid., p. 297.

94 Ibid., p. 299.

95 Ibid., p. 609.

96 Robert Baden-Powell, *Scouting for Boys* (London: Pearson, 1908), p. 334.

97 *Punch,* 136 (1909), 147.

98 *Girl's Realm,* 12 (1909–10), 337.

99 *Girl's Friend* (London: Amalgamated P., 1931), weekly, 1 January, 1910, p. 156.

100 Robert Baden-Powell, *Girl Guides: A Suggestion for Character Training for Girls.* Pamphlets A and B (pamphlet B with Agnes Baden-Powell); (London: Bishopsgate P., 1909).

101 Ibid., Pamphlet A, p. 3.

102 Ibid., A, p. 4.

103 Ibid., A, p. 5.

104 Ibid., A, p. 7.

105 Ibid., Pamphlet B, pp. 14–19.

106 Ibid., p. 17.

107 Ibid., pp. 17–18.

108 Ibid., p. 18.

109 Ibid., p. 4.

110 *Girl Guide's Gazette,* London, 1914–27, monthly.

111 *Girl Guide's Gazette,* 1 (August 1914), 8.

112 *Friendly Leaves,* 39 (1913–14), 322.

113 *Girl's Own Paper and Women's Magazine,* 36 (1914–15), 36.

114 *Girl's Reader* (London: Amalgamated P., 1908–15), weekly.

115 First episode in *Girl's Reader,* 24 October, 1914.

116 Ibid., 31 October 1914.

117 Ibid., 14 November 1914.

118 *Girl Guide's Gazette,* 1 (1914), 3.

119 Ibid., 5 (1918–19), 58.

120 Ibid., p. 50.

121 *Girl Guide's Gazette,* 5 (1918–19), 166.

122 Ray Strachey, *The Cause,* 2nd edn (London: Virago, 1978), p. 338.

123 Ibid.

124 J. M. Winter, 'The Impact of the First World War on civilian health in Britain', *Economic History Review,* 30, 3 (August 1977).

125 M. Llewellyn Davies (ed.), *Maternity,* 2nd edn (London: Virago, 1978), 'Preface'.

126 Quoted in Jill Liddington, 'The Women's Peace Crusade', in *Over Our Dead Bodies,* ed. D. Thompson (London: Virago, 1983), p. 182.

127 Much of this is drawn from Margaret O'Brien, 'Women and Peace Movements in Britain 1914–39', M.A. dissertation University of London, 1983. See also G. Bussey and M. Timms, *Women's International League for Peace and Freedom* (London: Allen and Unwin, 1965); Sylvia Pankhurst, *The Home Front* (London: Hutchinson, 1932); Martin Ceadel, *Pacifism in Britain* (Oxford: Clarendon P., 1980).

128 O'Brien, pp. 13–15; Jill Liddington, *The Life and Times of a Respectable Rebel: Selina Cooper 1864–1946* (London: Virago, 1984), pp. 266, 284.

129 Reprinted in Graves, op. cit., pp. 188–90.

130 Alfred H. Miles (ed.), *Fifty-two Stories of the Brave and True for Girls.* This is one of a long series of books published by Hutchinson between 1891 and 1907 with titles beginning 'Fifty-two Stories . . .'. Most of these books were published with parallel titles for girls and for boys; among these pairs were stories of 'courage and endeavour', 'duty and daring', 'grit and character'.

131 *Girl's Realm* 12 (1909–10), 337.

132 *Girl Guide's Gazette,* 5 (1918–19), 62.

133 Ibid., p. 21.

134 Ibid., p. 6.

135 Ibid., p. 84.

136 Angela Brazil, *A Patriotic Schoolgirl* (London: Blackie, 1918), p. 51.

137 Ibid., p. 250.

138 Vera Brittain, *Testament of Youth* (London: Gollancz, 1933), ch. 10, 'Survivors not wanted', p. 467ff.

139 An extreme example of this belief is Arabella Kenealy, *Feminism and Sex Extinction* (London: Unwin, 1920).

CHAPTER EIGHT

'The Marginal Britons': The Irish

D. G. Boyce

Nations, it has been said, may exist for centuries in unreflective silence.[1] Certainly the ease with which the Irish nation was incorporated into the British state to form the United Kingdom of Great Britain and Ireland in 1801 seemed a good augury for the future of the new political entity. A hundred new Irish MPs in the British House of Commons; a handful of peers and bishops; a redesigned Union flag, emblazoned with the cross of St Patrick; a continuing British administrative presence in Dublin Castle – all seemed a small price to pay for the British government's decision to end the existence of the Irish parliament that it was felt could not give political stability to Ireland, and political security to Great Britain, after the rebellion of 1798.

But the United Kingdom did not long enjoy its unreflective silence. The absorption of peoples and traditions proved more troublesome than the rearrangement of political and administrative machinery. The Irish Union, unlike the Anglo-Scottish Union of 1707, was not a bargain struck between negotiating parties. It was achieved by political persuasion exerted by a greater on a lesser partner; and the nature of that process was to influence the perception of the Union in both Great Britain and Ireland. Irish Roman Catholics, who had been led to believe that Union would bring Catholic emancipation, were to see their hopes destroyed. Irish Protestants, who accepted Union as a security for their privileged position, were to see their expectations disappointed by British concessions to the Catholic majority.

The British government had insisted upon Union as a means of securing national unity in the face of internal and external dangers in the wars with France; it was therefore not unnatural for Britain to assume that it would be able to control and regulate the destinies of the lesser partner. These tensions were present in Anglo-Irish relations from the 1820s until the foundation of the Home Government Association in 1870; but they became acute with the rise to power of Charles Stewart Parnell, and his assumption of the leadership of the Irish Parliamentary Party in 1880.[2]

By its skilful use of propaganda and organization that Party succeeded in creating and sustaining a strong sense of group identity in Ireland, an identity that survived even the bitter Parnell/anti-Parnellite split after the public disclosure of the relationship of its leader to Mrs Kitty O'Shea in 1891. And this development reached its peak at a time when the United Kingdom as a political concept had become firmly established. It was instinctive for the English to regard the terms English and British as virtually synonymous; and the author who wrote in the early edition of the Encyclopaedia Britannica 'for Wales: see England'[3] was only expressing an attitude of the English that they applied to the other parts of the Celtic fringe. The whole process of centralization in the British state, the fact that the English parliament had become, gradually and in a haphazard way, the British parliament, the idea of the sovereignty of that institution, the lack of any distinct Celtic representative in the Cabinet, all reinforced the idea that the United Kingdom was, if not the seamless garment that Unionists liked to make it out to be, at any rate a coat that fitted snugly and firmly over all the peoples who dwelt in the British Isles. Thus, before 1886, remedies for Irish problems – and there were many – concentrated on acts of administration and government, social and economic reforms, the application for example of Utilitarian ideas and programmes.[4]

The assumption underlying all *these* assumptions was that the United Kingdom enabled the Scots, the Irish and the Welsh to exchange comfortably enough their nationality for a wider British nationality; and while some English politicians recognized the force and even the danger of Irish nationality, possibly of nationalism, they were not, between O'Connell and Parnell, confronted with a serious challenge to their idea that the United Kingdom was an integrated whole: hence their ability to support Italian or Hungarian nationalist movements without feeling any unease about matters at home. The Irish were not a distinct nation, though they could be on occasion an exceedingly troublesome folk. And anyway, nineteenth-century English politics were also regional politics; Lancashire, the North, Cornwall had their own regional and local political values, elections were fought in an intensely local atmosphere, and not even the fact that MPs all ended up in London could disguise the fact that they got there from what was seen as a highly parochial background. If Ireland was different, so then was Yorkshire; regionalism was not nationalism; and any threat that seemed about to elevate regionalism into something more sinister – any threat like O'Connell's monster meetings of Irish Roman Catholics – was met with firmness and, if need be, force to prevent, as Sir Robert Peel put it in 1843, the dissolution of the empire.[5]

The Parnellite challenge of the 1880s shook these assumptions to their foundations. Here was a movement that denounced the whole principle of the United Kingdom; that was hostile to the British connection, revering those 'gallant sons of Ireland . . . whose blood has sanctified the cause of Irish freedom'; that revealed to Irish Roman Catholics that they need not bear the whips and scorns (real or imagined) of British rule.[6] Or, rather, English rule: for it was the English that were specifically regarded as the controllers of Ireland's destiny. They had first come to Ireland in the twelfth century, establishing a permanent presence there, and bringing eventually the English religion, English laws, English government, the English crown. The fact that the first 'English' to land on the shores of Ireland were Normans, Welsh and Bretons was conveniently ignored as, for that matter, was the Scottish invasion of Ireland two centuries later. Against the notion that the English were the arbitrators of politics, economics, and society, was posed the idea that the Irish, as the majority in Ireland, could make good any political, economic, or social rights they possessed, or deemed themselves to possess. Irish Roman Catholics were fed that most dangerous of all political ideas: that they were members of the rightful majority in their country, and yet were treated as if they were a permanent minority (which they were) in the United Kingdom. To have the aspirations of a majority, and yet to be told to be content with minority status, was to place Irish Catholics in a frustrating and intolerable position. No community could harbour within its bosom at one and the same time minority and majority feelings; at least, not without serious political stress. Such was the fate also of those other 'marginal Britons', the Irish Protestants.

It is impossible to exaggerate the impact of the rise of Irish nationalism on Irish Protestants. Gladstone's conversion to home rule was the final shock to their political belief in the United Kingdom. In 1800 Irish Protestants had accepted the Union only reluctantly, and on the tacit (and more than tacit) promise that it would protect their interests; as one contemporary pamphlet put it, 'The Catholics would lose the advantage of the argument of numbers, which they at present enjoy, and the Constitution of the Empire would agree with the theory.' In short, there would be a Protestant British constitution for a Protestant Irish people.[7] Irish Presbyterians had reacted with complacent satisfaction at the disendowment and disestablishment of the Church of Ireland in 1869. But the prospect of being handed over to a government of a predominantly Roman Catholic character – which was how they saw the first home rule bill of 1886 – united Irish Protestants as never before. Whatever the limitations of the Government of Ireland bill – and these limitations must not disguise the considerable powers that it offered to an Irish parliament – it represented a complete reversal of the Protestant perception of the purpose and place of the Union. Their native land, their Ireland, was now to be placed at the disposal of the Roman Catholic majority. What to England and

Scotland was a 'party question', the reverend Dr Lynd declared at a great Ulster Unionist Convention in June 1892, was 'to us . . . a matter of life and death, a matter of hearth and home.'[8]

But what made the matter worse was that Irish Unionists knew that they were not really a minority at all; they were part of the British and Protestant majority of the whole United Kingdom.[9] And, just as Roman Catholics suffered minority feelings and yet saw the elusive opportunities of majority status, so Protestants suffered minority feelings (but in their case within Ireland) and saw the continuing benefits of majority status (in the United Kingdom as a whole). This might have persuaded the Protestants to present themselves in the role of Britons, West Britons, or whatever; but they were frustrated by the fact that a sizeable proportion of the population in Great Britain sympathized with the Irish Parliamentary Party's demands. Gladstone had committed the Liberal Party to home rule; a British government, in a British parliament, threatened to turn Protestant majority status into Protestant minority disadvantage. Southern Irish Unionists, with their wider perspective and their dual identity – at once Irish and English – might place their faith in their British Unionist allies. Northern Protestants, with their clear territorial area, their greater concentration of population, had a better opportunity to look after themselves. Yet both were placed in the difficult position that, although loyal, they must – or possibly might have to – oppose a decision of the British government and legislature; hence their stress on the British crown as the focus of their loyalty; for Northern Protestants the crown was their equivalent (if the analogy is appropriate) of the French *république une et indivisible*[10]: a symbol of unifying sentiment, common values, and political loyalty:

> No Home Rule shall bind us,
> But traitors ever find us,
> With thousands more behind us,
> For Union and for King![11]

Ulster Protestants in the nineteenth century never ceased to think of themselves as Irish: the Reverend James Cregan of Belfast admitted, at the 1892 Ulster Unionist Convention, that he 'never felt prouder of being an Irishman than I did on Friday June 17th, 1892.'[12] But the Liberal conversion to home rule forced their political ideas and propaganda into a new mould: they had now to emphasize their British heritage; they appealed and entreated Englishmen not to leave them. Their motto was 'quis separabit'. But their popular songs, their political hymns, their rhymes, had a distinctive Irish flavour; even their tunes were indistinguishable from those of their nationalist rivals. This fact is so obvious that it has taken a foreigner to recognize it[13]; but no one who has read and learnt Protestant tunes, for example, can doubt that he is seeing not the opposite but the obverse of Irish nationalism. What then could link Northern Protestants to a British connexion so necessary to their survival, yet so open to the vagaries of political change? Only the crown, a symbol that offered two advantages; it was a rallying cry, visible, yet intangible, real, yet so metaphysical; and it provided a means of remaining loyal yet, if need be, defying the British government and parliament of the day.[14] 'I'm an Irishman – Born in loyal Belfast,' a 'New Loyal Song against Home Rule' began; and it declared that 'Old Ireland's' fate would be ruined by home rule, warning that:

> The men of Ulster won't have it, I say they're quite right,
> If the Home Rule Bill's passed, they're determined to fight.
> We've been true to Old England, the land of the brave,
> But we'll never submit to be treated like slaves.[15]

This special notion of loyalty distinguished Irish from British opponents of home rule. Their respective Unionism, of course, did overlap at many points: the flag, the crown, the firm denial of Irish nationalism as a real or legitimate political force. *Nationalism* was a sham and a fraud; there was no distinct Irish nation, but merely a collection of disreputable, violent and opportunistic politicians, backed by Land Leaguers and Fenian dynamiters. A legislature could not at one and the same time give away power and yet retain it, at least not without continuing friction that would set at nought the Liberal claim that a home rule bill would settle the Irish question for all time, and create a 'Union of Hearts' between England and Ireland.[16] But above all the British Unionist created a special constitutional version of British and English history, in which the making of the United Kingdom was almost an act of providence, for since it coincided with the rise of England to the powerful and respected status that it now enjoyed, it followed that this rise to power and status must be a product of the making of the United Kingdom as a political entity. To break up the United Kingdom would be to unpick the seams of British history and undermine the basis of British power.[17] Thus it was in 1887 that Lord Salisbury told his audience at Derby that the history of Europe was one that had witnessed the making of nations out of separate entities: Germany, France, Italy were unitary nations, yet at one time they had been fragmented regions or small states. The United Kingdom was undergoing the same process, but it was

> necessary that the generations, as they grow up, should believe that the consolidation is inevitable. It is necessary that they should have faith in the fibre and the resolution of the State that desires to weld them into a common whole . . .

And Salisbury had no doubt of the prominence that must be given to England in this welding: 'The issue depends on you – on you, the constituencies of England.'[18] The eminent Unionist intellectual A. V. Dicey wished to combine what he called the 'special gifts' of each part of the United Kingdom 'for the common service of the whole nation'. To him the Unionist party was, in truth, the 'great National party' – 'we only are entitled to the name of Nationalists'.[19] In a world of strong states, the English nation-state could only survive if it successfully made the transition to a British nation-state, with England as the shaper of that unified nation's destiny. Thus the concept of Britishness that was being evolved in the late-nineteenth century was quintessentially English, based on English power, institutions and political necessity.

It is surely one of the ironies of British politics that its Liberal party – a party that might be expected to be internationalist in foreign affairs, and pan-national in matters domestic – should have become between 1886 and 1914 the vanguard of Celtic nationalism: Gladstone, after all, is one of the few British prime ministers to enjoy the privilege of biographical studies written in the Welsh language.[20] Partly this was because of Welsh Nonconformist radicalism that afforded much (if not always welcome) support for the party in political terms. Liberals also had deep roots in Scotland, where Lord Rosebery's aristocratic Scottish Liberalism was strong enough to extract a Secretary of State for Scotland in 1885.[21] But when the Liberal party under Gladstone became specifically identified with the cause of Irish home rule, and committed to a parliamentary alliance with the Irish nationalists under Parnell, it had to present some picture or image of the United Kingdom that could accommodate its new departure. Home rule has been treated by some historians as an episode in 'high politics' with the wily Gladstone searching for issues and votes that would keep himself and his party in power (though it is hard to see why he should have chosen Ireland, a country whose people and politics were not always popular in Victorian Britain). But there was another dimension to home rule; for Liberals had to meet the strenuous Unionist objection that they were conniving at the break-up of the United Kingdom and the destruction of the British empire, and that they were giving power to landlord-killers and Anglophobes. And so Gladstone and his followers offered a new model of Britishness: one that conceived of the United Kingdom as a multi-national state. This state contained within its boundaries certain historic nations with their own political traditions and identities. When Gladstone remarked at Swansea in 1887 that 'I affirm that Welsh nationality is as great a reality as English nationality',[22] his judgement was a major turning point in the description and imagery of the United Kingdom.

Thus, it was alleged, the supporters of home rule placed in the forefront of their argument the assertion that 'we have within the compass of the United Kingdom no less than four real nationalities'.[23] It was not so much that the Liberals were prepared to concede immediate statehood to these nationalities; indeed, Gladstone blew cold over the issue of Welsh home rule in his Swansea speech, and Scotland was obliged to wait in the wings also.[24] Moreover, while Gladstone was prepared to recognize 'nationalities', he was not prepared to refer so readily to 'nationalism', But he had to present convincing arguments for his Irish home rule policy; and what better point could he make than that the Welsh and Scots had reconciled their nationality with a wider British patriotism, their symbols of nationality with the symbols of English nationhood (the crown, the flag) because they had found a comfortable niche within the United Kingdom. 'Scotland, wisely recognised by England, has been allowed and encouraged in this House to make her own laws freely and as effectually as if she had a representation six times as strongly.' The 'mainspring' of law in England, as in Scotland, was identified with the nation; but 'the mainspring of law in Ireland is not felt by the people to be Irish . . . in the same sense as it is English and Scotch.' Using home rule, Gladstone sought to reconcile 'imperial unity with diversity of legislation.' At the same time the 'supreme statutory authority of the imperial parliament remained unimpaired'.[25] A fellow Liberal, James Bryce, took up Gladstone's points in a correspondence in *The Times*. In a question involving national sentiment, 'the opinion of each of the nationalities surviving in our islands is worth regarding'; and the people of Scotland and Wales, still cherishing 'a distinct national feeling, though happily not incompatible with attachment to the greater nationality of the United Kingdom, have shown that they can extend their sympathy to the sentiment of nationality among the Irish and that they do not deem it dangerous to Imperial unity.' An Englishman had 'but one patriotism, because England and the United Kingdom are to him practically the same thing. A Scotchman has two, but he is sensible of no opposition between them.' And Bryce looked to the day when 'the same will be true of an Irishman.'[26]

There was one important difficulty here which an astute critic pointed out; and that was that Charles Stewart Parnell had on at least one occasion contrasted Scottish and Irish nationality, declaring (in response to a toast of 'Ireland a Nation' at a banquet in the Dublin mansion house) that Scotland had 'lost her nationality, and has practically become merged in England; but Ireland has never done this. And she never will.'[27] Bryce denied that this was the case, arguing that Scotland did not 'honour William Wallace and John Knox the less because she can now also claim a share in Simon of Montfort and John Hampden'. Scotland was contented because she had received justice and equality, because she had 'practically been allowed to manage her own affairs. Why should not justice, equality, and the sense of responsibility bear their appropriate fruits in Ireland also?'[28] This argument ignored the essential point of the Irish Parliamentary Party: its satisfaction with home rule was based upon a clear-sighted recognition that, in the circumstances, it was the best Ireland could expect from England. It underestimated also the very different demand of Irish nationalism, in that it sought separate, not equal treatment, and that 'justice to Ireland' might – indeed probably would – mean the end of British rule in that country.

But there was another, important consequence that might arise out of the home rule crisis; and that was the danger to Irish nationalism that the Liberal and Gladstonian tradition might work – that Ireland might indeed become merged in a wider British nationality, that she might forgive and forget, and share in a Union of Hearts between Great Britain and Ireland. This idea – never entirely out of sight after 1886 – was especially taken up by John Redmond, the leader of the Irish Parliamentary Party who united the warring factions in 1900, and led them to the brink of success between 1912 and 1914.[29]

Was home rule then to be a means, not of fulfilling a distinct Irish destiny, but of strengthening a wider sense of Britishness, making Ireland at last a contented province of Britain? The danger was that the Irish home rulers might be undermined by their own successful propaganda; for there seemed no limit to the punishment that the English mind could take, and, in taking, could assimilate and absorb. Even in its nationalism Ireland, like Scotland and Wales, might succumb to the eternal regenerative force of the British/English polity. The home rulers helped foster 'Irishness' – shamrocks, harps and the like – only to see in 1886 the Viceroy of Ireland, that symbol of English rule and domination, and his wife preparing to make the state entry into Dublin with their children dressed in green velvet coats. This was vetoed by officials on the grounds that it was too overtly subversive, and the children wore white Irish poplin instead (with the great coats dispatched to be dyed blue). At her farewell levee a year later, Lady Aberdeen wore a dress of St Patrick's blue poplin (Irish but not subversive) and a bonnet trimmed with rose, thistle, and shamrock. Her children, however, were not yet emancipated from their Irishness, for their portrait was painted showing Dudley and Archie Gordon in 'traditional' Irish peasant outfit of knee breeches, buckle shoes and tail coats, sitting in a wheelbarrow full of potatoes, and set against a wild mountainous landscape.[30]

The danger was, then, not that the Irish might not succeed in their challenge to Englishness, but that they might succeed too well; how could nationalists overthrow an oppressor who fell in love with the oppressed nationality? How could they frustrate the English who not only accepted the 'fact' of Irish nationality, and its symbols, but also its version of history? In the *Nineteenth Century,* July 1889 issue, there appeared an article 'Plain speaking on the Irish Union'. It declared that the Act of Union of 1800 was morally invalid, carried by the jobbery and corruption of the Irish parliament, and made necessary only by the deliberate and fixed policy of the British government in fomenting disloyalty and dissension in Ireland. Fraud and violence characterized the Union; and instruments obtained by fraud were 'voidable at law'. The diatribe concluded with a list of English atrocities committed during the '98 rebellion, in a campaign conducted 'without law, measure, mercy, or restraint', including half-hanging and the pitch cap. The article was not, as might be expected, written by one of Parnell's lieutenants; it was the work of W. E. Gladstone.[31] And its constitutional message was plain. England must acknowledge the invalidity of the Union which could only gain moral force by 'the frank agreement of the eighty-five Nationalist members of parliament, since 1886, to accept the Act of Union on condition of its being modified by the erection of a Statutory parliament for the transaction of her internal affairs.' A new chapter could then be opened in Anglo-Irish relations, and past bloodshed and treachery forgotten. Only then could home rule coexist with a new sense of British nationhood. A constitutional arrangement could be created in which different national traditions were reconciled with the sovereign parliament of the United Kingdom – and the continuing ultimate dominance of English power. Had the Irish Parliamentary Party been politically successful between 1886 and the fall of Parnell in 1891, it would have been obliged to confront the paradoxes of its own position, as an Irish nationalist movement and party in a British political and constitutional context. But the fall of Parnell, and the disreputable scenes of in-fighting between Parnellites and anti-Parnellites, gave a new direction to the search for yet more differences between the English and the Irish.

It is at first sight surprising that Parnell, a profoundly political figure, as profoundly political as he was non-literary, should have inspired what subsequently became known as the Irish literary revival; but Parnell down, and then Parnell dead, established a new tradition of a 'lost leader', a romantic figure, brought to his destruction by petty, self-seeking men. Nothing could have been further from the truth: Parnell's lieutenants only dropped their pilot at the behest of Gladstone, who warned the Irish Parliamentary Party that he could not carry any measure for Irish self-government while a prominent political party was led by a self-confessed adulterer. But the legend of the lost leader, gallantly defying his foes, placed Ireland's greatest constitutional nationalist in the tradition of those other heroes of Irish nationality – Tone, Emmet, the Fenians – who failed because the Irish were hardly worthy of their genius and their courage. Moreover, Parnell's fall had another important implication for the future of Anglo-Irish relations and the Irish sense of national identity. While the home rule movement seemed on the road to success, Ireland's nationalist newspapers and politicians always stressed the importance of the purely political: the time for cultural activities would come when freedom was attained, but until then it was imperative that all patriots put their shoulders to the wheel of self-government. But now that movement had broken down – and the failure of Gladstone's second home rule bill in 1893 seemed to indicate clearly that politics had, for the present, run their course – then the curb that the politicians placed on literary activity was no longer to be respected: Ireland, as W. B. Yeats remarked, would be 'like soft wax for years to come', and those like himself who sought to give Ireland a cultural, and not merely a political, identity, were now offered their opportunity to translate their ideas into practice.[32]

These ideas need not necessarily have threatened the political and cultural unity of the United Kingdom. After all, most of the greatest figures of the literary revival, Yeats, Synge, George Moore, wrote in the English language, and (whether consciously or not) for an English as well as an Irish audience. Their hope was that Ireland would make a significant contribution to European literature with an Irish interpretation of the human experience. How then could a distinctive Irish literary tradition be created? What made an Irish writer an Irish writer? The answer might be that the writer dealt with Irish themes. But what were Irish themes? The answer might be that national themes were Irish, or (more narrowly still) that nationalist themes might be the true distinction between Irish literature in the English language and what was coming to be established in the late-nineteenth century as 'English literature'. The political circumstances of the 1890s reinforced this idea. Parnell had fallen at the command of the English Gladstone and his nonconformist Liberal party; it was not unnatural for Parnellites to claim that the English influence, having destroyed their leader, was equally destructive of all that was worthy in Ireland. And although Parnellites were in a minority among nationally minded people, they exerted an influence far beyond their numbers, especially in those intellectual circles which were creating the new mood in literature. Thus the idea that Irish politics had been contaminated by the English connexion, by the home rulers trooping to Westminster to immerse themselves in an English political atmosphere, played its part in fostering the idea that Irish writers must likewise seek their salvation, not in London, but at home. They must renew their contact with their native environment.

This two-fold desire to create a truly Irish literature, and yet prevent it from becoming too narrowly nationalist, bedevilled the literary movement from the beginning. In 1891 the Irish Literary Society was established in London, reflecting the new sense of Irish identity among the writers there; in 1892 the National Literary Society was founded in Dublin. Both groups involved people of Protestant as well as Roman Catholic background; indeed, it was the middle-class Protestant, like Yeats and Synge, who came to be regarded as the most characteristic figures of the literary revival as a whole.[33] But the movement was parallelled, and could not help being influenced by, another equally significant development which aimed at giving Ireland a distinctive place in the world, marking it out as a separate nation with an indigenous culture. This movement believed quite simply that the true test of a country's national pedigree was its language: that the essence of the Irish identity was a Gaelic and, by implication, a pre-Reformation one. The Gaelic Athletics Association, founded in 1884, sought to revive traditional Gaelic games and took its cue from Archbishop Croke of Cashel who denounced England's 'accents, her vicious literature, her music, her dances, and her manifold mannerisms' which, like her 'fantastic field sports', were 'not racy of the soil, but rather alien, on the contrary to it, as are, for the most part, the men and women who first imported and still continue to patronise them.'[34] It might not at first sight appear that the expulsion of the cricketing fraternity from the shores of Ireland would seriously undermine English influence (some will disagree). But the implications of such a mood, its determination to identify Gaelic and Irish ways of life and thought as synonymous, were important; and they were sharpened by the establishment of the Gaelic League in 1893, with its avowed aim of 'de-Anglicizing' Ireland, making Gaelic the sole national language. 'In Anglicizing ourselves wholesale', Douglas Hyde declared,

> we have thrown away with a light heart the best claim which we have upon the world's recognition of us as a separate nationality. What did

Mazzini say? What do the *Spectator* and the *Saturday Review* harp on? That we ought to be content as an integral part of the United Kingdom because we have lost the notes of nationality, our very language and customs.[35]

The Celtic revival offered a distinctly racial challenge to the idea of a British nation forged by the predominant partner. There had indeed often been racial tones imparted to the controversy, but they had never been made explicit, for to claim that the Anglo-Saxons, say, were a distinct race might lead to the conclusion that the Celts, as another distinct race, could make an irrefutable claim for separation. Unionists could also use the racial argument to prove that the Saxon needed the Celt – the hard-headed realism of the former must be tempered by the romantic temperament of the latter. And the English-speaking Celt was a kind of honorary Saxon, akin in colour and language to the Englishman.[36] Some English might claim that the Irish were comparable to the Indians, needing the smack of firm government[37]; but this was contradicted by the spectacle of Irishmen (Protestant and Catholic) spread throughout the empire busily ruling (and shooting) black and brown races.[38] The colonial analogy never took on serious significance, except in the acknowledgement that an England that could not secure the basis of its own kingdom was hardly likely to govern successfully anywhere else. Canada might be given self-government, but it was a far-away country, not an integral part of the United Kingdom.[39] It is hardly surprising then that the Celtic revival, insofar as it was noticed at all, was given short shrift by English Unionists. 'The men of Tipperary, though characteristically Irish, are believed to be descendants of Cromwellians. There is Huguenot blood', declared Goldwin Smith in a 1905 essay on *Irish History and the Irish Question*. The revival of 'Erse' as a national language was 'surely a patriotic dream'.[40] England must not divest herself of the real, as distinct from the imaginary, Irish characteristics, for

> Ireland is perhaps happy in having been cut off from the prodigious development of luxury and dissipation which . . . has been taking place on the other side of the Channel as well as from the domination of the stock-exchange. She may in this way become a saving element in the social character of the United Kingdom.[41]

The idea of an Ireland, not merely free but Gaelic as well, had nevertheless an exciting purity, and it was to exert a profound influence on the Irish nationalism which, after 1916, challenged the Unionist idea that the United Kingdom was a 'true nation by every test by which you can judge a nation', with Ireland 'an integral part of a greater nation'.[42] But meanwhile the party that represented the idea of cultural and economic self-sufficiency, that emphasized the Mazzinian view of nationality, made little progress. Sinn Fein, founded in 1905,[43] was nothing more than a loose federation of nationalist societies of a separatist tendency, given the 'utmost liberty of action'[44] by Arthur Griffith to work for an independent Ireland by cultural, economic or military means. Its early electoral forays were discouraging; it had no clearly defined aim. But it combined Gaelic symbolism with a skilful journalistic style, and its touchiness and sense of superiority gave it a potentially powerful appeal, especially if the home rulers should stumble at the last hurdle, and England – or at any rate Liberal England – break faith again. It remained a kind of brooding presence in the background, the self-styled keeper of Ireland's conscience. As yet it carried little political weight. Indeed a general reintegration of Celtic with British politics seemed a real possibility. The Welsh nationalist sentiment of the 1890s, which often expressed a similar blend of angry servility and arrogance (Lloyd George was wont, for example, to contrast the noble poetic Celt with the football-loving rowdy Englishman),[45] also declined as the new century wore on. The Edwardian age was one when British Unionists and Liberals alike seemed prepared to abandon their earlier irreconcilable attitudes to Celtic questions in order to seek new, more compromising schemes of administrative devolution and consensus settlements. Unionists were apparently attracted to some form of Irish financial control, and Liberals were prepared to re-examine their Gladstonian tradition of granting parliamentary and executive functions to identifiable 'Celtic' nations. But these developments were inhibited, and then overthrown, by the lack of room for political manoeuvre afforded to British and Irish parties over the fundamental issue of nationalism and the Union. British Unionists must not compromise their stand on the organic unity of the kingdom; Liberals were driven back into the home rule camp if only to save the Irish home rulers from the threat of Sinn Fein. Political absolutism was only briefly out of fashion; the issue was once again, in John Redmond's words, 'between despotism and home rule'.[46]

British Unionists, for their part, now launched their last crusade to keep the Union intact and prevent the decline of Britain as a nation. But they failed to produce a theory of Britishness that could encompass all patriotically minded men and women on both sides of the Irish Sea. The difficulty was that whereas British Unionists could claim that their sovereign parliament was the key to the United Kingdom as a political entity, Ulster Unionists, their British citizenship threatened (as they saw it) by a British parliament, were unable to afford that parliament the same allegiance. Nor could they feel any affection for an institution whose majority was passing a home rule bill designed (as they felt) to thrust them out of the United Kingdom and the empire. British Unionists could go so far with their fellow Unionists in Ulster; but not even A. V. Dicey could regard the Ulster Covenant, pledging Ulster Protestants to resist home rule by all the means that might be found necessary, as possessing the same force in Great Britain as in Ireland. Ultimately the English must bend to the will of their sovereign parliament, and to the wishes of the electorate[47]; and the Unionist demand for another dissolution and another election on the sole issue of home rule was an admission of that principle. Ultimately

Ulster Unionists need not submit to that will. They were not simply a part of the British electoral system, as Dicey admitted, and hoped to remedy, when he advised British Unionists in 1891 to 'take an active part in Irish contests when a Unionist candidate is standing'. He acknowledged that Irish members for their part 'have sometimes done the Unionists a good deal of harm at English elections'; but he always 'rejoiced at their intervention' because 'it was an undeniable admission that they are not aliens but fellow citizens'.[48] But by 1910 the British electorate had to be cajoled into reviving its earlier enthusiasm for Irish affairs: home rule did not hold the same life and death concern for them as it did for Northern Protestants.

Ulster Unionists were often suspicious of their British political allies, and sometimes resented by them. But they could claim that, in the end, they were saving England from itself: if a radical faction had undermined the power of the House of Lords by ending its absolute veto on Commons' legislation, and now threatened to wreck the unity of the Kingdom by granting home rule to Ireland, Ulster Unionists would themselves take on the role of Imperial defenders, standing for One God, One King, One Empire.[49] This sentiment gave them some valuable and influential allies in Great Britain, such as Rudyard Kipling who affirmed that Ulster, in fighting the Empire's battles, would not fall alone.[50] But the sentiment could not survive the test of the ultimately different convictions of British and Ulster Unionists: the British Unionists' recognition that the sovereign British parliament would have its way.

What had Ulster Unionists to offer in place of the Irish nationality that was denied them by their political opponents in Ireland, and the British nationality that Liberals, by destroying the House of Lords veto, revealed was a delusion? The answer was *Ulster political Protestantism,* which, while denying that Irish nationalism had any validity or justification, emphasized certain characteristics that distinguished Ulster Protestants from the Catholic inhabitants of Ireland. This was not a form of Ulster nationalism, for Ulster Protestants still wanted to remain British citizens under the British crown and constitution; nor was it a belief in British nationality, for Ulster Protestants knew that they were fighting for the survival of their community and their own Protestant Province, against the 'transfer of a people's allegiance without their consent.' But the significant words were 'allegiance' and 'consent.' A British government and parliament could hardly transfer an English subject's allegiance and loyalty, with or without consent. The Ulster Unionists could make no such comfortable assumption, and they were aware of the distinction that it implied. In the 1912–14 crisis, Ulster Unionists spoke of the 'British people', the 'gentlemen of England', the 'inhabitants of England', but never of their 'fellow-Englishmen' or 'fellow-Britons'. Yet they frequently referred to Roman Catholics in Ireland as their 'Nationalist fellow-countrymen', whose disagreeable habit of disloyalty was at the root of the problem.[51]

Ulster Unionists had therefore to pick their words carefully when they came to define political Protestantism. They stressed certain traits (real or mythical) of the Ulster people: their loyalty, their honesty, their desire to defend truth and religious liberty. Ulster Protestants lived in a distinct region of the country (but not of course a 'national territory'). And they harboured strong and deeply held convictions about the character that their religion, environment, and way of life imparted to them: they were self-reliant, respectable, tidy, and hard-working.[52] These were of course social as much as political traits: but with the threat of the immediate application of home rule over their heads, they became part of the Ulster Unionists' determined assertion that they were a special breed, Ulster defenders of a British heritage. A characteristic figure of Ulster Unionism was the Protestant Boy: cheery, alert, self-reliant, a loyal friend to England but a formidable foe to anyone who would impose Catholic rule on him against his will: a descendant of the apprentice boys who slammed shut the gates of Derry in the face of King James's Catholic hordes.[53] The Ulster Unionists' allegiance to the British state did not constitute their sense of group identity but merely their necessary legal citizenship – necessary for their survival, and for defending their political rights. But rights that, the Ulster Unionists argued, must be guaranteed, or their political obligation to the British state would be renounced. 'In the eyes of Ulstermen', wrote Ronald MacNeill, 'constitutional orthodoxy is quite a different thing from loyalty, and . . . true allegiance to the Sovereign is by them sharply differentiated from passive obedience to an Act of Parliament'.[54] These attitudes might appear to the observer selfish and contradictory. They are perhaps more easily understood when it is appreciated that Ulster Protestants believed that their fate might be that reserved for all who did not swim with the nationalist tide: assimilation, irredentist effort, emigration, disagreeable minority status.[55]

The United Kingdom seemed released from the inescapable logic of this situation with the outbreak of the European war in August 1914. Irishmen of whatever political persuasion vied with Englishmen, Scotsmen and Welshmen to join the colours and soldier for the king. But the display of national unity, at least as far as Ireland was concerned, was not as simple as it seemed. The desire of the competing groups in Ireland to preserve their political identity was seen in the Ulster Unionists' demand that their contribution to the British army – that of handing over the Ulster Volunteer Force that had been formed in 1912 to resist home rule – must be given separate organizational status as a Division, including its own Ulster flag. The War Office agreed to this, but at the same time refused any such special recognition to the Irish Volunteers, the bulk of whom Redmond, after September 1914, placed at the disposal of the British army.[56] Moreover, while there was undoubtedly a real and genuine enthusiasm for the British cause in 1914, Irish political groups were seeking to place themselves on a better footing with the British government when the war should end and home rule again become practical politics. Patriotism could be a lever to use in any crisis that would come, and the mutual distrust of the British political establishment, the Ulster Unionists, and the Irish nationalists was not to disappear with the temporary mood of British national unity forged in the European crisis. As Sir Edward Carson told the 'British people' in July 1919, 'if there is any attempt made to take away one jot or tittle of your rights as British citizens and the advantages which have been won in this war for freedom, I will call out the Ulster Volunteers.'[57]

In nationalist Ireland the new spirit of British patriotism did not even outlast the war itself. In 1916 a group of separatists – republicans, Gaelic enthusiasts, some socialists and Irish Volunteers – staged their rising in Dublin in an attempt to halt the drift away from what they regarded as the true national spirit, the spirit that had inspired the dead rebel generations. The initial Irish response to the rising, the hostility to the captured rebels, the anger at the stab in the back dealt by the insurgents to the thousands of Irish troops fighting at the front, seemed to indicate that a wider sense of Britishness had been forged by the shared emotions and dangers of the great conflict. This was soon wiped out by the action of General Maxwell who believed that a lesson must be taught in order to deter any future militancy; but the commonplace assertion that Maxwell created sympathy for the rebels is itself an admission that Ireland was still a special case, despite the enthusiasm of the war. British troops were executing Irish patriots; nationalist Ireland had always been taught to hold her patriots in esteem, not necessarily with a view to emulating them, but certainly to admire their love of country, to hold in reverence their spirit of self-sacrifice; and so Irish nationalists quite naturally set the rising and the executions in a context quite alien to British perception.[58] It was part of a tradition of noble and heroic deeds, deeds aimed against the conqueror; and had not the home rulers themselves, while warning against the consequences of political violence, also praised its nobility: a grand thing, but of course not to be done?[59] Now that it was done, and punished by death, the different attitudes to treason in Great Britain and nationalist Ireland became manifest. What to the English was a natural response to rebellion in wartime – and not only natural, but, if anything, mild – was to Irish nationalists at best a blunder, at worst an outrage. It was small wonder that after 1916 Sinn Fein began seriously to challenge the home rulers, and to challenge them on the grounds of how relations between Ireland and England should be conducted.

More significant even than the 1916 rising was the conscription crisis of 1918, which was symptomatic of the failure of the British people and politicians to understand how Irish nationalists thought about political obligation. Irishmen might volunteer for the British army, for that was in the tradition of Irish soldiering; but to be compelled to fight for Britain was a different matter, and was an example of how British expectations of Irishness were one-sided. Home rule and conscription were not regarded as equal trading, for home rule was a long overdue debt owed by England to Ireland. But if it is true that the ultimate test of man's nationality is the uniform he is compelled to wear in wartime, then, by British standards, the Irish in 1918 failed that stringent examination. Large sections of British public opinion were behind the government's determination to equip itself with powers to introduce conscription in Ireland if need be; and it is hard to see how the British people could have thought otherwise in the months of crisis after the great German offensive of March 1918.[60] This outburst of patriotic resentment at Irish 'backsliding' enabled Sinn Fein to supplant the Irish Parliamentary Party in the general election of December 1918.

Sinn Fein claimed that Ireland was an ancient, proud, distinct European nation, seeking to escape from the oppressor; it demanded recompense for the history of Ireland.[61] It adopted the emotions of Easter Week, but at the same time it denied that Sinn Fein stood for the use of violence: it acknowledged the legitimacy of the physical force tradition, but it did not commit itself to emulate that tradition. Sinn Fein was a broad coalition of disillusioned home rulers, more advanced nationalists, and out-and-out republicans, indeed of nationalists of all shades and hues. But one thing was certain, and that was that Sinn Fein rejected the home rule bill and the concept of the pluralist United Kingdom that lay behind it. Their loyalty was not to be bought by a British Act of Parliament; their nationhood was based on Gaelic history and culture, and on interpretation of the Irish past that allowed no accommodation with the British present. Moreover, the British response to Sinn Fein, its deliberate decisions to ignore the Sinn Fein representatives who assembled in Dublin in their own, self-appointed, 'parliament', further weakened the now tenuous bonds that linked nationalist Ireland to the United Kingdom. Sinn Fein did not authorize the gradual development of guerilla warfare by the Irish Volunteers (now generally called the IRA) in late 1919 and early 1920; and the Dail only reluctantly accepted responsibility for IRA operations as late as April 1921. Meanwhile the British government's *ad hoc* response to Republican violence, the recruitment of the Black and Tan and Auxiliary police forces, the apparent acceptance that any means might be employed to put down lawlessness in Ireland (even the breaking of the law by the crown forces in the taking of reprisals against the civilian population), all these responses seemed to indicate that the Irish were not even full-fledged citizens of the British state, let alone members of a British nation.

By 1921 it was clear that the United Kingdom could only maintain its sense of homogeneity by accepting that part of the kingdom was in revolt against British rule and must be allowed to separate from the British state. For the very actions of the crown forces in responding to IRA provocation were at variance with values long held to be inherent in the British way of life: values such as fairness, legality, decency, and above all, right behaviour. The decision to seek a truce and talks with Sinn Fein in June and July 1921 was as much a result of the sense of what British rule stood for, or ought to stand for, as it was the consequence of IRA military action. Once again Ireland had played upon a trait in the English concept of the British national character; there was nothing left but to demonstrate that British values were still held dear, and to come to terms with nationalist Ireland.[62]

But it was not easy for a country that had always denied the fact of Irish nationhood to come to terms with the Sinn Fein demand for recognition;

even the Welsh patriot, Lloyd George, had little sympathy for a movement that proclaimed its distinct nationality and yet could not boast of a living language such as the Welsh possessed: 'they put up names at street corners to the confusion of every honest patriot'.[63] Why should Ireland be allowed to make good a claim that the Welsh denied to themselves? And what was to become of Unionist Ulster? To answer these complex questions, Lloyd George took up a theory that had earlier been propounded in British Unionist circles: the idea that there were in Ireland not one nation but two, as different from each other as any nations in the British Isles[64]; Ulster Protestants were as 'alien' to Ulster Roman Catholics as were the inhabitants of Fife or Aberdeen.[65] They constituted an 'entity'.[66] at least. But it was not an entity that could be maintained as an integral part of the United Kingdom: such a policy would prove highly contentious and divisive for the rest of the British people, since it would imply that they were standing in the way of the now fashionable theories of 'self-determination'. No British Unionist raised his voice against the 1920 Government of Ireland Act which discriminated against Ulster in relation to the rest of the United Kingdom by obliging the loyalists to accept a Stormont parliament which they did not now want, and had never desired.

Thus it was in order to keep the British people united in Irish policy that the British Unionists modified their concept of the organic British nation. But both Unionists and Liberals had to make further adjustments to their models of nationality before they could find a way out of the political impasse that threatened to divide the mainland Britons. And to discover a new nationhood that might accommodate nationalist Ireland, and yet not damage the United Kingdom and the empire irreparably, they turned to a familiar British concept: that of the dominions, Canada, Australia, which were possessed of nationhood, but which were still part of the British tradition, in government, in political symbols. The Irish were not allowed to be a completely separate nation, they could not be Hungarians, but they could be Canadians or Australians or – even – South Africans (whether Boer or British remained unclear). Thus membership of the British family of dominions might succeed where membership of the British family of domestic nations had failed.[67]

It was misleading to dismiss Lloyd George's dominion experiment as doomed to failure, or to declare that Ireland would not necessarily be satisfied with British imperial nationhood, but must seek a political status that was fundamentally different, based on an idea of a glorious but tragic Gaelic past. But certainly the inter-war years saw an intense nationalism in southern Ireland and the weakening of the bonds that united her to the Commonwealth. The Irish Free State had not followed the path of gradual political evolution within the British Empire; she had become an instant dominion with a Gaelic and Catholic national destiny to fulfil, and a government that could give expression to that destiny only by maximizing national freedom at British expense.

As for the Ulster Unionists, their experience of separate statehood – even if that statehood was only of a home rule kind – reinforced notions of a political distinction between themselves and the mainland, a suspicion of British (especially socialist) motives, and a sense that the Northern Ireland parliament was in some way a sovereign body in all the things that mattered for Ulster's survival.[68]

It might be said that all Irish after 1922 were, as before, 'marginal Britons'. But, of course, certain qualifications must be considered. First of all, in many aspects of life, the Irish had much in common with the English, and indeed with all the inhabitants of the British Isles: from food and clothing, to political institutions and language, the Irish were exposed to a deep, and lasting, influence of England. Ireland might be nationalist in politics, but her civil service, her armed forces, her parliament, all bore the ineradicable imprint of the English models that were given to her, or imposed upon her. Even the idea of a central Irish government was an English one, for Gaelic Ireland was particularist and provincial. Before 1914 the southern Irish were as likely to turn out to look at queens, kings and princes as were the northern Irish.[69] When the Irish troops returned from the war in 1919 they were welcomed back through streets festooned with Union flags.[70]

Wherein, then, did the 'marginalization' of these 'Britons' lie? Was it self-imposed, or imposed upon them by English attitudes? How deeply felt was the sense of difference that lies at the root of all nationalism? The answer to these questions is to be found in two separate, but related, circumstances. The first is the Anglo-Irish relationship, and especially the Union between Great Britain and Ireland that promised much, but was felt by Irish Roman Catholics to give little. The Union was not accompanied by Roman Catholic emancipation; it failed to bring British capital to Ireland; it could not provide Ireland with political structures attuned to the deep social and economic problems of the country. A comparison with the Anglo-Scottish Union is instructive. The Union between England and Scotland was at first unpopular, but as time wore on Scotland did benefit from it, and was able to work within it, while at the same time preserving a sense of Scottish nationality.[71] But the earliest manifestations of majority politics in Ireland after the Union, the Emancipation and Repeal movements of Daniel O'Connell, provided Irish Roman Catholics with a sense of solidarity *at the expense of England*: Emancipation was won, and Repeal denied, in circumstances of conflict not negotiation. And while O'Connell might promise that, given good government, the Irish would become West Britons again, his political style and method – his abrasive oratory, his slogan of 'Ireland for the Irish', his portrayal of English government as base, bloody and brutal – worked against any chance of success for such a concept.

There was another sound reason why Irish Roman Catholics should seek to marginalize themselves. They were, after all, a natural and irreversible majority in their own part of the United Kingdom. But they were denied the benefit of this status by the Protestants of Ireland, and also by British

Protestants, for when Irish and British Protestants were added together, the result was a permanent and irreversible Protestant majority in the United Kingdom as a whole. To accept the full implications of British citizenship – let alone British nationality, or West Britonism – was to deprive themselves of what was rightfully the Roman Catholic inheritance: the mastery of Ireland, the right to have things their way, whether this be for the good or ill of the Protestants.

The Anglo-Irish relationship meant also that the Irish, of whatever political persuasion, had to come to terms with the overwhelming influence of a powerful and advanced partner. Much has been made of the tendency of the English to despise and reject the Irish, more particularly the Irish Catholics, and to regard them as inferiors. But this sense of rejection was no more important than that other different, but for Irish nationalism equally dangerous, phenomenon: the English tendency to absorb things Irish, to tame and domesticate them, to integrate Ireland by offering her good government, land reform, an English system of landlord/peasant relations, thus creating what was to English eyes a conservative and well-regulated society on the English model. Such an Ireland might even have home rule; but what if it were a mere carbon copy of England, speaking her language, adopting what Archbishop Croke called her 'masher ways', losing any separate or distinct cultural identity? Hence the search for a distinct Irish cultural tradition that would mark Ireland out as an ancient European nation, in no way sister to, nor even cousin of, the English. But this apparently positive concept of nationhood (as Lloyd George, with his Welsh experience, shrewdly perceived) could not disguise the fact that Irish nationalism in whatever form fundamentally sought to define itself in relation to England and Englishness. It thus ended up by declaring that anything recognizably and identifiably of English origin must automatically be non-Irish – or, to put it another way, that anything Irish must by definition be devoid of the imprint of England. This amounted to a denial of Ireland as she was in return for Ireland as she might have been. But these ideas dominated Sinn Fein, inspired the revolution of 1916–22, and shaped the politics and culture of the newly independent Irish state during the first three decades of its existence.

Irish nationalism convulsed the United Kingdom because it called into existence not one, but two kinds of nationalism, which resembled in many respects what have been described as 'eastern' and 'western' types.[72] The population of Ireland, like that of eastern (or more properly central) Europe, was locked into 'complex multiple loyalties of kinship, territory and religion'.[73] The political and religious divisions within Ireland meant that any attempt to make the state boundaries conform to a particular community would provoke violent reaction from the minority whose political tradition was threatened, and whose very existence seemed at risk. But in the British Isles there also existed the dominant culture of England, pervading almost all aspects of Irish, Welsh and Scottish life. This English-dominated state was protected by the political institution of the sovereign British parliament; but the Irish nationalist challenge shocked the English into the acknowledgement that they had not yet accomplished their Risorgimento, that they had not completed the process of welding the British Isles into a cultural and political unit. This was particularly alarming in the age of Italian and German nationhood; and British Unionists countered Irish nationalists with a version of 'western' nationalism, seeking to ensure that the idea of the British 'United Kingdom' enjoyed the same political protection that was now enjoyed by Italy and Germany. The conflict between Great Britain and Ireland was not one between an 'emergent' colonial people and its masters, but between Irish and English nationalism, with Irish, and especially Ulster Protestants, forced to decide for themselves where their best chances of survival lay.

The Irish challenge to an English-dominated British state had profound effects on the political character of the British Isles. The national sentiments of the Welsh and the Scots were infused with a new vitality and, while they did not have the force and popularity of Irish nationalism, they did make the United Kingdom self-conscious about its composition in an unprecedented way.[74] It was true that the Welsh and the Scots used their national political leverage to seek equality of treatment with the English part of the kingdom; but this was itself significant, for it demonstrated that English politicians must be ready to accommodate, not merely regional or class demands for political benefits, but national demands that might, if badly handled, have embarrassing and expensive consequences. Wales could no longer be placed under England in the encyclopaedias, nor could Scotland be referred to as North Britain. The Celts had made a comeback; but the break-up of Britain in 1922, and more, its traumatic nature, soon pushed them back into their political fringe. The jettisoning of Ireland, and the decline of English nationalism, contributed to the homogeneity of the United Kingdom, whose sense of Britishness was best served when it tried less hard to be British. More than half a century was to elapse before Celtic matters once again came to the fore in British politics; and in 1969 one political scientist was able to remark on the homogeneous character of the British people, and the 'sense of fraternity' between their religious groups.[75]

But however much contemporaries sought to forget the Irish crisis of 1886–1922, and however marginal the Celt once more became, the experience was an important one for the people of these islands. The English and the Irish could not escape the realities of their common connection, the fact that they were individual nations but with a shared political and cultural heritage. England could not, after all, mould Ireland – any part of Ireland – in her own image, nor dissolve her in the melting-pot of Britishness. A Gaelic-speaking, de-Anglicized Ireland was as incapable of realization as was a monoglot British Isles. Nor could Irish nationalists make out of Ulster the fourth green field of *Cathleen ni Houlihan*. Indeed it might be said that the idea of Englishness had much in common with the idea of Irishness: the desire to misrepresent their unique relationship, to flee from the mutual influences they exerted upon each other, and from the reciprocal nature of their history. Thus Irishness and Englishness constituted utopias: forever beckoning, but forever retreating, and, paradoxically, utterly necessary for each other's survival.

Notes

1   Sir Ernest Barker, *National Character,* 4th edn (London: Methuen, 1948), p. 240. First edition, 1927.

2   The name was altered in 1873.

3   K. O. Morgan, 'Welsh Nationalism: the historical background', *Journal of Contemporary History,* 6 (1971), 153.

4   G. O. Tuathaigh, *Ireland before the Famine* (Dublin: Gill and Macmillan, 1972), ch. 3.

5   *Hansard: Commons Debates,* 3rd series, Vol. 69 (9 May 1843), cols. 23–5.

6   T. D. and A. M. Sullivan, *Speeches from the Dock* (1867; rpt. Dublin: T. D. Sullivan, 1887), pp. 7–13, 241. F. S. L. Lyons, *Culture and Anarchy in Ireland, 1890–1939* (Oxford: O.U.P., 1979), p. 7, fn. 12. The use of the expression 'British' is always open to difficulties, and especially so in the Irish context, for Irish nationalists focussed their attention on *English* rather than British influence on Ireland. Similarly, Irish Unionists commonly referred to their loyalty to 'England' rather than 'Great Britain'. I have used the term *English* rather than *British*, except when referring to those institutions (e.g., British parliament or army), political parties (e.g., British Liberals), and people in the formal political sense (British public opinion) to which the adjective British is normally applied.

7   *Arguments for and against an Union between Great Britain and Ireland Considered* (Dublin: J. Milliken, 1799), p. 26.

8   *Ulster Unionist Convention Report* (Belfast: Belfast News Letter, 1892), p. 35. See also *Irish Unionist Alliance Publications* (Dublin, Belfast: Irish Unionist Alliance, 1893), II, 13–14; R. MacNeill, *Ulster's Stand for Union* (London: John Murray, 1921), p. 13.

9   H. S. Morrison, *Modern Ulster: Its Character, Customs, Politics and Industries* (London: H. R. Allenson, 1920), pp. 157–8.

10 N. Johnson, *In Search of the Constitution,* 2nd edn (London: Methuen, 1980), p. 123.

11 P. Buckland, *Irish Unionism, 1885–1923* (Belfast: Public Record Office of Northern Ireland, 1973), p. 169.

12 *Ulster Unionist Convention Report,* p. 111.

13 G. D. Zimmermann, *Irish Political Street Ballads and Rebel Songs* (Geneva: La Sirène, 1966), pp. 304–5.

14 David W. Miller, *Queen's Rebels: Ulster Loyalism in Historical Perspective* (Dublin: Gill and Macmillan, 1978), pp. 108–21; Patrick O'Farrell, *England and Ireland since 1800* (Oxford: O.U.P., 1975), pp. 72–3.

15 Zimmermann, pp. 319–20.

16 Tom Dunne, 'La trahison des clercs: British intellectuals and the first Home Rule crisis', *Irish Historical Studies,* 23 (1982), 166; R. B. MacDowell, *British Conservatism, 1832–1914* (London: Faber and Faber, 1959), pp. 107–12. The phrase 'Union of Hearts' is Gladstone's; see *Irish Unionist Alliance Publications,* III, 334.

17 For a lucid and convenient summary of such views see A. V. Dicey, *England's Case against Home Rule* (London: John Murray, 1886), *passim;* see also, for example, the Duke of Argyll, *The New British Constitution and its Master Builders* (Edinburgh: David Douglas, 1888), and Sir T. Fraser, *The Military Danger of Home Rule for Ireland* (London: Murray, 1912). O'Farrell, *England and Ireland,* pp. 64–5 makes some useful comments.

18 *The Times,* 20 December 1887.

19 *Irish Unionist Alliance Publications,* III, 479–80; see also Dunne, 'La trahison des clercs', pp. 164–5.

20 For example, Griffith Ellis, *W. E. Gladstone: Ei Fywyd a'i Waith* (Wrexham: Hughes, 1898).

21 R. Coupland, *Welsh and Scottish Nationalism* (London: Collins, 1954), pp. 292–6.

22 K. O. Morgan, 'Gladstone and Wales', *Welsh History Review,* 1 (1960–63), 82.

23 *Mr. Gladstone and the Nationalities of the United Kingdom: A Series of Letters to The Times* (London: Bernard Quaritch, 1887), p. 7 (letter of John Lubbock, MP).

24 D. N. MacIver, 'The paradox of Nationalism in Scotland', in *National Separatism,* ed., Colin Williams (Cardiff: U. of Wales Press, 1982), p. 117.

25 Gladstone in the House of Commons, 8 April 1888, quoted in E. Curtis and R. B. MacDowell, *Irish Historical Documents* (1943; rpt. London: Methuen, 1977), pp. 287–92; see also Gladstone's 'Further notes and queries on the Irish demand', *Contemporary Review,* 53 (January-June 1888), 321–39.

26 *Mr. Gladstone and the Nationalities of the United Kingdom,* pp. 14–15.

27 Ibid., p. 22.

28 Ibid., pp. 26–7.

29 D. George Boyce, *Nationalism in Ireland* (London: Croom Helm, 1982), p. 280.

30 Marjorie Pentland, *A Bonnie Fechter: The Life of Ishbel Marjoribanks, Marchioness of Aberdeen and Temair* (London: Batsford, 1952), pp. 56–7. The portrait of 'Two Little Home Rulers' is reproduced in volume one of Lord and Lady Aberdeen, *We Twa* (London: Collins, 1925), facing page 265. See also J. Sheehy, *The Rediscovery of Ireland's Past: The Celtic Revival, 1830–1930* (London: Thames and Hudson, 1980), pp. 103–4.

31 *Nineteenth Century,* 149 (1889), 1–20.

32 J. S. Kelly, 'The fall of Parnell and the rise of Irish literature: an investigation', *Anglo-Irish Studies,* 2 (1976), 1–23.

33 Sheehy, *Rediscovery of Ireland's Past,* p. 95.

34 D. G. Boyce, *Nationalism,* pp. 232, 236.

35 Ibid., p. 238.

36 Sheridan Gilley, 'English attitudes to the Irish in England, 1780–1900', in *Immigrants and Minorities in British Society,* ed., C. Holmes (London: Allen and Unwin, 1978), p. 95.

37 Dunne, op. cit., pp. 172–3.

38 Such as Rudyard Kipling's favourite soldier, Mulvaney, in *Soldiers Three:* Gilley, op. cit, p. 98.

39 E. Wallace, *Goldwin Smith; Victorian Liberal* (Toronto: U. of Toronto Press, 1957), p. 92.

40 Goldwin Smith, *Irish History and the Irish Question* (New York: McClure, Phillips, 1905), pp. 220–1.

41 Ibid., p. 226.

42 L. S. Amery, quoted in R. B. MacDowell, *British Conservatism,* p. 109.

43 The movement that assumed the name 'Sinn Fein' was founded in 1900 under the title 'Cumann na n Gaedhaeol'.

44 Boyce, *Nationalism,* pp. 295–7.

45 H. du Parcq, *Life of David Lloyd George* (London: Caxton, 1912), I, 146–8.

46 'Irish Home Rule and Liberalism', in *The Edwardian Age: Conflict and Stability,* ed. Alan O'Day (London: Macmillan, 1979), pp. 113–32.

47 R. A. Cosgrove, *The Rule of Law; Albert Venn Dicey, Victorian Jurist* (London: Macmillan, 1980), pp. 250–4.

48 Dicey to Lord Selborne, 5 November 1891, MS Selborne 13/59 (Bodleian Library, Oxford).

49 MacNeill, *Ulster's Stand,* pp. 27–8, 46, 50.

50 'Ulster, 1912'.

51 The phrase 'transfer of a people's allegiance without their consent' is to be found in R. MacNeill, op. cit., p. 141; Morrison, *Modern Ulster,* p. 98; MacNeill, op. cit., p. 1; *Ulster Unionist Convention Report,* pp. 7, 35.

52 'An Irishman', in *Is Ulster Right?* (London: John Murray, 1913), p. 240.

53 Taylor Dowling, *The Troubles: The Background to the Question of Northern Ireland,* 2nd edn (London: Thames MacDonald, 1982), p. 68, reproduces a new characteristic Ulster Unionist postcard showing a boy challenging his enemies to 'Come to Belfast and we'll show 'em.'

54 MacNeill, *Ulster's stand,* pp. 3–4.

55 Ernest Gellner, *Nations and Nationalism* (Oxford: Blackwell, 1983), p. 98.

56 Ian Colvin, *The Life of Lord Carson* (London: Gollancz, 1936), III, ch. 3; Stephen Gwynn, *John Redmond's Last Years* (London: Edward Arnold, 1919), ch. 6. Examples of War Office insensitivity (to use the most favourable interpretation) are its failure to respond to a request that the 16th (Irish) Division be presented with its own colours woven by Irishwomen, and that its men be provided with an Irish Volunteer style cap badge (Gwynn, pp. 174–6).

57 Denis Gwynn, *The History of Partition* (Dublin: Browne and Nolan, 1950), p. 184.

58 Boyce, *Nationalism,* pp. 307–10.

59 Ibid., pp. 285–6; see R. G. Collingwood, *Autobiography* (1939; rpt. London: O.U.P., 1959), pp. 140–3.

60 Boyce, *Nationalism,* pp. 286–8; Boyce 'British opinion, Ireland and the War, 1916–1918', *Historical Journal,* 17 (1974), 586–8.

61 See Sinn Fein's 'Manifesto to the Irish People', 1918, printed in A. C. Hepburn, *The Conflict of Nationality in Modern Ireland* (London: Edward Arnold, 1980), pp. 110–12.

62 D. George Boyce, *Englishmen and Irish Troubles: British Public Opinion and the Making of Irish Policy, 1918–1922* (London: Jonathan Cape, 1972), chs 3 and 4.

63 *Hansard, Commons Debates,* 5th series, Vol. 127 (31 March 1920), cols. 1327–8.

64 Miller, *Queen's Rebels,* pp. 111–12.

65 *Hansard, Commons Debates,* 5th series, Vol. 91 (7 March 1917), col. 459.

66 Ibid., Vol. 127 (31 March 1920), col. 1333.

67 Boyce, *Englishmen and Irish Troubles,* ch. 6.

68 J. C. Beckett, 'Northern Ireland', *Journal of Contemporary History,* 6, 1 (1971), 121–34.

69 As, for example, on the occasion of Queen Victoria's visit to Ireland when students in the Catholic University ran to the windows to see what their disgusted lecturer called 'that woman' (D. Ryan, *The Sword of Light* [London: Arthur Barker, 1939], p. 204).

70 Boyce, *Englishmen and Irish Troubles,* pp. 46–7.

71 MacIver, 'The paradox of Nationalism', pp. 112–15.

72 J. Plamenatz, 'Two types of Nationalism', in *Nationalism: The Nature and Evolution of an Idea,* ed. E. Kamenka (Canberra: Australian National University, 1973), pp. 23–36.

73 Gellner, *Nations,* p. 100. This was noticed by a contemporary observer. 'An Irishman' drew his readers' attention to what he called 'South Eastern Europe' with its 'jealousies between Greek and Bulgarian, between Serbian and Austrian' (*Is Ulster Right?,* p. 3).

74 Coupland, *Welsh and Scottish Nationalism,* pp. 222–3; C. Harvie, *Scotland and Nationalism* (London: Allen and Unwin, 1977), pp. 32–42.

75 Richard Rose, *Governing without Consensus: An Irish Perspective* (London: Faber and Faber, 1971), p. 240; the political scientist who remarked that religion had no impact on voting behaviours was Jean Blondel (*Voters, Parties, Leaders* [Harmondsworth: Penguin, 1969], pp. 46, 60–1).

CHAPTER NINE

Englishness and the Liberal inheritance after 1886

Dennis Smith

From Liberalism to Englishness

In 1885, the Oxford historian Edward Freeman wrote:

> I AM A LIBERAL, A CONVERT FROM HEREDITARY TORYISM, MAINLY BECAUSE TORYISM WILL NOT STAND THE TEST OF ENGLISH OR ANY OTHER HISTORY, AND LIBERALISM WILL.... THE MAIN WORK OF LIBERALISM HAS BEEN TO PRESERVE THE EARLIEST PRINCIPLES OF OUR POLITICAL LIFE ... to change boldly where change has been needed, but to change on the old lines. THE OLDEST INSTITUTIONS ARE THE FREEST.... The best school of Liberalism is a careful study of the history of our own country.[1]

One of Freeman's contemporaries at Oxford had been James Bryce, who later held ministerial office as a Liberal.[2] In 1907 Bryce left the sphere of party politics and became British Ambassador to the United States. Later still, on the basis of extensive foreign travel conducted mainly before World War I, Bryce wrote a book called *Modern Democracies*.[3] In this work, he disclaimed 'any intention to serve any cause or party' (I, xii). Adopting the 'mode of investigation ... known as the Comparative Method' (I, 20), Bryce strove for 'accuracy above everything else' (I, 22). One of his conclusions was that,

> abiding foundations of policy glide . . . into principles which have come to so inhere in national consciousness as to seem parts of national character. Such, for the English, are the respect for law as law, the feeling that every citizen is bound to come forward in its support. . . . The traditional love of liberty, the traditional sense of duty to the community, be it great or small, the traditional respect for law and wish to secure reforms by constitutional rather than violent means – these were the habits ingrained in the mind and will of Englishmen. (I, 156–60)

In 1885 Freeman had described his commitment to Liberalism as the outcome of a process of conversion induced by contemplation of English history. Over three decades later, the self-consciously 'factual' and 'accurate' account of English national character presented by Bryce referred to propensities which had been encouraged and valued within the Liberal tradition. However, an important change in perception had occurred between 1885 and 1921. The principles to which Liberals such as Freeman consciously committed themselves had been transformed into 'habits ingrained in the mind and will of Englishmen', which social scientists like Bryce were able to 'observe'. Liberalism had become Englishness. The principles of a party had established themselves as a major element in the self-image of a people.[4]

In fact, all major political parties in the twentieth century have taken for granted the view of Englishness typified by Bryce's description of the national character. Ironically, Liberalism achieved greatly increased influence as a set of assumptions permeating English society and politics in the very decades during which the Liberal party attempted, and ultimately failed, to adapt itself to the new England which was coming into existence. The Party was unable to come to terms with a society which was urban, industrial, imperialistic and increasingly democratic. It ceased to be an effective national force after 1916.[5] Paradoxically, the very success of Liberalism in pervading the atmosphere of English politics meant that it became difficult to resurrect the Liberal party after World War I. To some degree at least, the Conservative and Labour parties have subsequently been in dispute about the strength and direction of the class bias within an essentially Liberal polity.

The decline of the Liberal party was merely one aspect of the continuing and vigorous career of English Liberalism (with an uppercase 'L') or, perhaps, liberal Englishness (with a lower-case 'l'). The complex inheritance of Liberalism imposed a difficult task upon its beneficiaries. This task was to find a way of avoiding both tyranny and anarchy in the political sphere. Various approaches to this task could be adopted within the liberal tradition depending upon your view of human nature and of the grounds upon which political authority should be legitimated. Liberals had to ask themselves: do we have high or low expectations of 'normal' human behaviour within a Liberal society? Do we expect compliance with the rules of such a society to be on the basis of abstract principle or ingrained custom? Such questions, which elicit both moral and practical judgements, are difficult to answer. However, the responses of contemporaries in the late-nineteenth and early-twentieth centuries helped to shape the meaning of freedom in English society.

In spite of its lack of precision, the ideal of freedom was at the heart of Liberalism. This ideal gave equal importance to the imperatives of achieving decency and achieving order: equal weight in the sense that neither decency nor order should be pursued to the extent that the other was placed in danger. A. B. Cooke and John Vincent convey these sentiments nicely in the following comment, taken from *The Governing Passion:* 'Englishmen want their history to be agreeable. By this they mean that problems should have solutions and that Liberals should be in power. If these conditions do not obtain, they wish to know why.'[6] There was also the need to combine or adjudicate the claims of rationality and tradition. The ideal was that liberty should be enjoyed within the law. Liberty and law should be joint expressions of rational authority within the just community. Liberty, law and the community should all be strengthened by the sanction of tradition. It is difficult to imagine that any of the major figures considered in this chapter would have dissented from these statements.

Unfortunately, major difficulties arose from the fact that specific interpretations of 'decency', 'order', 'rationality' and 'tradition' as means and ends of political life tended to contradict each other. For example, was decency placed in greater threat by lapses in bureaucratic rationality or by a disregard for the role of history and tradition in forging the bonds of interest and emotion which provided the cement of communal life? If one decided to stress rationality, might not the elaboration of a bureaucratic political order conflict with the legitimate expectations of rational human beings for a large measure of responsibility and freedom in their lives? In other words, might not decency and order be competing emphases within a commitment to rationality? If the requirements of political order were held to be especially pressing, might not tradition and rationality conflict as potential bases of political authority? What would be the implications of a choice between tradition and rationality for the management of a decent communal life (see the first question)? And so on.

During the late-nineteenth and early-twentieth centuries at least four approaches to the definition of Englishness and the shaping of the new England evolved within the liberal tradition. Within a shared commitment to English 'freedom', each of these approaches expressed a distinctive response to the problems of combining decency with order and adjudicating between rationality and tradition. Each of them has become, so to speak, established as part of the English national repertoire. They are the image of decent traditional English folk conjured up by Stanley Baldwin[7]; the blueprint for a more efficient, centralized and paternalistic state espoused by collectivists;

the civic managerialism whose most committed and effective practitioner in the early-twentieth century was Neville Chamberlain; and the heroic petty-bourgeois vision energetically broadcast by Arthur Mee, a loyal adherent of the Liberal party.

I am going to argue that collectivists such as the New Liberals sought to impose decent conditions upon the population through a strengthened bureaucratic order. They accepted the need to dispense with many aspects of traditional England in order to do this. By contrast, Stanley Baldwin argued that tradition was the very source of decent principles of conduct. Order would flow from trusting the decent inclinations of English people and encouraging them to stick to tried and trusted ways. Neville Chamberlain sought to establish a managerial regime within which exemplary public men and women would deploy the resources of the state in harness with private initiative. Their object would be to encourage moral regularity or internal order in the hearts and minds of their fellow citizens from all walks of life. This would be done by using the energies of the elite, as voluntary workers and managers of public funds, to create social conditions with a moralizing effect upon individuals. High standards of personal morality would make it possible for individuals to recognize, pursue and achieve a decent life for themselves. Public leaders would frequently have to break with traditional ways in order to foster these good ends, the goals of the civic gospel, within the community. As will be seen, an important aspect of Arthur Mee's great popular appeal was that he seemed able to reconcile conflicting tendencies within liberal Englishness. He could praise scientific rationality while expressing devotion to historical tradition. He could act as a passionate advocate of human rights while emphatically pleading the case for control over some areas of morality (especially temperance). For Mee, decency was in some respects (e.g., technological advance) an expression of human liberation. In other respects, decency demanded strict self-control aided, if necessary, by external sanctions.

In recent years, considerable attention had been paid to collectivism and Baldwin.[8] It must not be forgotten that two other versions of liberal Englishness were very prominent. The Chamberlain dynasty loudly insisted that enlightened leading citizens should implement the civic gospel on behalf of the whole urban community.[9] Arthur Mee was the vocal and persistent spokesman of the man and woman in the street. Neville Chamberlain and Arthur Mee were both products of Nonconformity in the Midlands, specifically, Birmingham and Nottingham.[10] In their words and actions they gave shape to aspirations forming at that time among, respectively, the provincial business and professional classes and the lower middle classes. The powerful contribution made by these aspirations to the definition of Englishness through the adaption of the Liberal tradition must be fully taken into account. To omit them from consideration would distort our understanding of a complex process. It would be misleading, for example, to note the emphases placed by Stanley Baldwin and Lord Haldane on the virtues of, respectively, the Countryside and the State, while neglecting the stress placed by Chamberlain and Mee upon the challenges confronted in the City by the Individual. In this chapter the four strands will be distinguished from each other in their approach to the interplay between decency, order, rationality and tradition as means and ends within political life, and in their response to the manufacturing City.

The chapter is organized into five sections. In the section which follows, the ideological tensions which were inherent in Liberalism in the mid-1880s are explored in more detail, with particular reference to the ways in which Englishness and the idea of the nation were perceived by Liberals at that time. Against this background, the second section outlines the fortunes of the Liberal party in the late-nineteenth and early-twentieth centuries. In the third section, I argue that the public arguments presented by the collectivists and by Baldwin were contrasting outcomes of the ideological and political dilemmas of these decades. In the fourth – and longest – part of the paper I carry out a detailed comparative analysis of the ways in which, between the 1880s and the 1920s, Neville Chamberlain and Arthur Mee drew upon the Liberal tradition. In the final section I consider some implications of the overall argument for the period after the mid-1920s.

Before and after 1886

A few months before the Home Rule crisis Arthur Arnold, a Liberal member of parliament, summed up the Liberal approach as follows:

> LIBERALISM IS THE POLITICAL EXPRESSION OF CIVILISATION: THE INCREASE OF CIVIL RIGHTS; THE SHARING WITH OTHERS THE LIBERTIES, THE FRANCHISES, THE PRIVILEGES, WHICH ADMIT OF EQUAL AND PERMANENT DISTRIBUTION.
> It abhors inequality before the law; it seeks to make legislation respected because of its utility and beneficence.
> It never points to the attainment of happiness and comfort as the result of individual effort; and its cardinal doctrine is that those conditions will be most widely enjoyed where the people are instructed, where the avenues to eminence and usefulness are free and open, where the laws are loved because they are self-made, and the well-accepted obligations of a wise and contented nation.[11]

This carefully phrased and occasionally ambiguous statement would probably have commanded assent both from the aristocratic Whig element in the parliamentary party and from its more militant radicals, some with strong manufacturing connections. The moderate centre of the party, staffed by gentlemen and professionals of various kinds, would have found such sentiments congenial. In fact, it was difficult to maintain political harmony except in terms of such a loosely defined 'approach'. Conflict arose when more specific proposals emerged which threatened the vested interests of particular groups not only in Westminster but also in the country. Here, the party relied heavily upon the support of Nonconformists, skilled workers and the provincial press.[12] Gladstone's formidable political skills both in parliament and in the country helped maintain a precarious unity, especially when attention was focused upon some great issue of conscience. However, his great reforming ministry of 1868 was seriously undermined by the profound discontent of Nonconformists (led from Birmingham) with the 1870 Education Act. It also aroused the hostility of trade unionists to the Criminal Law Amendment Act.

Three years before the Liberals returned to office in 1880, Joseph Chamberlain had strengthened his political base in Birmingham through the establishment of the National Liberal Federation. This body was a successor to the National Education League which had helped coordinate opposition to the 1870 Education Act. Chamberlain hoped to win the allegiance of the more radical Liberals in the country. However, Gladstone's Midlothian campaign of 1879–80 re-established his position as the people's champion. These developments caused considerable nervousness among the more conservative, landowning elements within the party, especially in view of Chamberlain's direct attacks upon their class in his speeches of the early 1880s. Management of these tensions was made more difficult by the Reform Acts of 1884–85 which established single-member constituencies. This change put a stop to the convenient practice of running a Whig and a Radical in harness in two-member constituencies.[13]

Some of the conflicts of moral and material interest barely contained within a Liberal 'approach' may be discerned in a publication edited by Andrew Reid, a political writer on the radical side of the party, which appeared in the election year of 1885.[14] Its title is *Why I Am A Liberal: Definitions and Personal Confessions of Faith by the BEST MINDS of the LIBERAL PARTY*. Among the fifty-five contributors are thirteen privy counsellors and eighteen members of the House of Commons. Seven of the privy counsellors are peers. Introductory statements from Robert Browning, Gladstone, Lord Rosebery and Joseph Chamberlain are followed by short essays from a wide range of people beginning (alphabetically) with Joseph Arch and ending with Reverend Edward White.

The tension between tradition and rationality is well expressed in the contributions of Charles Hopwood and Charles Mackay. Hopwood, 'a member of the Liberal Party, first by education, afterwards by conviction,' cherished 'the history of its glorious past' and its continuing concern with 'The happiness of the population, the prosperity of the country and its sons beyond the seas' (60). Mackay, by contrast, refused to rest on the party's laurels. His task was 'to make the world better than he found it', declining all ease while 'Reason retains her seat in my brain, or Conscience continues to regulate my conduct' (74). To some extent the approach adopted by Edward Freeman, quoted at the beginning of this chapter, mediated between the emphases of Hopwood and Mackay. In Freeman's view, free institutions had to be continually restored, rather than created *ab initio* or preserved unchanged: 'In England we have never lost our tie to the past, to the very earliest past, of our nation. We can therefore reform without destroying' (49).

Would order be threatened by acting on the assumption that the people were rational? Were they capable of enjoying freedom responsibly? George Holyoake, a seasoned spokesman for the labouring population, had no doubt: 'AN ENTIRE LIBERAL IS ONE WHO HAS TRUST IN THE WHOLE PEOPLE, AND WHO COUNSELS THE PEOPLE TO HAVE TRUST IN THEMSELVES' (57). By contrast, Lord Mount-Temple assumed a more cautious tone. He compared encroaching democracy to a 'coach' which might be 'going too fast down a hill.' He commented: 'I prefer sitting in front to help the coachman to drive steadily on in the right direction' (78). A typical moderate view, more than once expressed, was summed up by Reverend Henry Ward Beecher: 'REFORMATION IS THE SUREST PREVENTATIVE [sic] OF REVOLUTION' (20).

The dynamic interplay between tradition and rationality was expressed in a social philosophy which combined the language of evolutionism and utilitarianism.[15] Professor J. S. Blackie wrote of 'the grand object and tendency of the divinely moved forces of Nature to produce the greatest amount of richly varied life, and with that the greatest happiness of the greatest number of free individuals' (31). The message of Reverend John Clifford was that 'LIBERAL PRINCIPLES DEVELOP RESPONSIBILITY: responsibility educates and humanises; and the fully-educated man is the most serviceable member of the social organism' (40–1). The metaphor of the evolving 'social organism' combined appeals to tradition and rationality. It also helped to disguise a potential conflict between decency and order. How was it possible to provide the whole people with material means for the proper exercise of freedom without altering the distribution of property in the existing social order? One way of avoiding an unpleasant conflict between the people (desiring decency) and the owners of property (fearing disorder) was to stress the interests shared by both in a more inclusive 'social organism'. This social organism was the nation.

Gladstone had told his audience at West Calder in April 1880 that although Liberals confronted the 'spirit of organised monopoly' in many forms, 'Above all these, and behind all these, there is something greater than these – there is the nation itself.'[16] His criticisms were directed at the landed interest and the clergy, but were in principle equally applicable to organized labour. Five years later, in Reid's volume, Reverend John Page Hopps informed his readers that 'In making a stand for what has come to be called "Liberalism", we are not scrambling for power or fighting for a party; WE ARE ENGAGED IN NATION-MAKING; and we are engaged in Nation-Making because we are endeavouring to elucidate and practically apply the great foundation principles of a civilised nation's life, and notably that of doing equal justice to all, irrespective of class or caste, sex or sect' (59). There were others who put the emphasis elsewhere, such as Reverend Llewelyn Bevan. As far as he was concerned the crucial foci of social life were two: the small local community (or commune) which expressed 'the principle of *voisinage,* or neighbourhood' and, at the other extreme, 'universal humanity . . . without distinctions of race, language or colour' (29–30). However, this was not the dominant note in 1885. More characteristic was the appeal to national pride underlying the comment of Dr Walter Smith: 'What is it that has made the name of an Englishman so distasteful all over Europe but our Tory fraternising with Bourbons and Metternichs and the "unspeakable Turk"?' (90).

The Home Rule crisis in 1886 raised in an acute form the question of nationality. As Paul Adelman succinctly comments: 'Gladstone did eventually attempt, if only with partial success, to see Irish problems through Irish eyes; Chamberlain made no real attempt to view Ireland other than as an Englishman.'[17] Ironically, the party split separated Gladstone not only from those who followed Chamberlain's radical lead but also from Chamberlain's rivals, the Whigs under Hartington. The followers of Chamberlain and Hartington became the major elements in the Liberal Unionist party. They opposed Home Rule in association with the Conservatives and subsequently cooperated with the latter in the general election of 1894.

The Liberal Party failed to win a majority of seats again until 1906. Meanwhile during the decades after the Home Rule crisis the latent division between those Liberals who were most comfortable protesting against the excesses of patriotism and those who emphasized the imperialist mission of the English nation became more clearly defined. Sharp infighting occurred between Little Englanders and Liberal Imperialists, culminating in a bitter dispute over the conduct of the South African War.[18] This conflict should be examined in a broader context.

Peter Clarke has argued that during the 'progressive era' following Gladstone's retirement in 1894, policies of collectivism at home and imperialism abroad evoked a range of overlapping responses from Liberals and Socialists.[19] For example, positive enthusiasm for both types of policy was expressed by Liberal Imperialists such as Sir Edward Grey, H. H. Asquith and Lord Haldane. They were echoed by many Fabians. It is true that Socialists such as Ramsay MacDonald and Liberals such as J. A. Hobson opposed the form of Imperialism represented by the South African War. Nevertheless, Hobson, along with L. T. Hobhouse, was a prominent figure in the 'New Liberalism' of the early-twentieth century. Old age pensions, national insurance and redistributive taxation were among the collectivist policies supported by the 'New Liberals' after 1906. In Clarke's view, such policies were an important aspect of a major adaptation by the Liberals to class politics before World War I.

However, from the onset of war, persisting disagreements within the party disabled it as a candidate for national power. For example, it was seriously split by the formation of a coalition government under the leadership of

Lloyd George in 1916. After the war, according to Clarke, there were similarities between the Liberal and Labour approaches to 'social politics'. Both parties were potential bases for men such as Hobson, Hobhouse and Graham Wallas. In these circumstances it was in the interests of the Labour Party to supplant the rival bearers of a progressive or social democratic tradition: 'Liberals must often have looked ruefully on the way they disseminated their ideas by dissipating their intellectual capital: And gave up for mankind what was meant for party.'[20]

The shift from Liberal to Labour which Clarke charts is one part of a wider pattern. Other channels through which the Liberal tradition entered into the social and political consciousness of English men and women may be discerned. In order to do so, it is worthwhile to divert attention southwards from Clarke's Lancashire, away from the *Manchester Guardian,* C. P. Scott, and the radical articles of Hobhouse and Hobson, and towards the Midlands, the region which produced Stanley Baldwin, Neville Chamberlain and Arthur Mee. In the following sections, I focus directly upon Birmingham, the Chamberlain dynasty and the editor of the *Children's Encyclopaedia*. Before doing that, however, I want briefly to contrast the political approach of the collectivists in the early-twentieth century with the public stance developed by Stanley Baldwin shortly afterwards. This procedure will throw into relief the distinctive features of the Liberalism expressed by Chamberlain and Mee. It will also prepare the ground for noticing some unexpected (but limited) resemblances between Mee and Baldwin on the one hand, and between Chamberlain and the collectivists on the other.

Collectivism and Stanley Baldwin

The 'social politics' of the Liberal Government between 1906 and 1914 expressed a relatively coordinated governmental response to questions such as unemployment, sickness, and poverty among the aged. This represented a new emphasis within Liberalism, one which tended to increase the state's initiative at the expense of the individual. In *Modern Democracy,* published in 1912, the radical social commentator Brougham Villiers remarked that 'Liberalism has been driven by hard necessity further and further away from theoretic individualism. It has been compelled to do so by the force of democracy itself.'[21] The problem was a long-standing one. From at least the 1890s, Liberals had been finding it difficult to reconcile the needs of the nation and the rights of the individuals within it. The Liberal Imperialists had been most preoccupied with the former. Men such as Asquith, Haldane and Rosebery had as their objectives 'national efficiency' and 'sane Imperialism'. They were ready to ditch 'cumbersome programmes' inherited from the Liberal past and 'start with a clean slate'. Haldane's view was that 'Belief in the state as real equally with the individuals in whom it is realised and whom it controls, this is the foundation of orderly government.'[22]

However, the New Liberals retained a strong moral concern for citizenship as well as the state. For example, in 'The ethical basis of collectivism', L. T. Hobhouse wrote: 'The true conception of an organic society is one in which the best life of every man is felt to be bound up with the best life of his fellow citizen.'[23] Collectivist programmes could be justified in terms of a desire to achieve decency – 'the best life in every man' – through imposition of a more effective national order. This entailed the creation of a more centralized and efficient state. In the course of doing this, obeisance to tradition had to yield to the dictates of rationality.

The work of the 1906 Liberal government and its successor during World War I gave the English some direct experience of collectivist measures. Not all of this experience was welcomed throughout the whole population. It is possible that popular recollections of this recent past help to explain the appeal of Stanley Baldwin in the subsequent period. Baldwin was born in 1867 at Bewdley, twenty-one miles south-west of Birmingham. He claimed to have learnt his Conservative politics from the family cook. However, if the Baldwin kitchen was Tory, the drawing room of Baldwin's childhood years was Liberal. His father, Alfred, supported Gladstone in the 1868 election although he later went over to Disraeli. Stanley's uncle, Enoch Baldwin, who looked after the family's ironworks in Stourport, represented Bewdley as a Liberal member of parliament between 1880 and 1885. A powerful strain of Dissent ran through the family tradition. One of Stanley's great grandfathers had been President of the Methodist Conference in 1845. Alfred Baldwin had been schooled at the Wesleyan Collegiate Institution in Taunton. Stanley, himself, like Neville Chamberlain, became a student at Mason College, the nonsectarian science college founded by a Dissenting manufacturer in Birmingham. There is no doubt that Baldwin could claim the liberal inheritance as his own.[24]

In 1923, newly installed as prime minister, Baldwin stood up in front of a Worcester audience and declared:

> I am just one of yourselves, who has been called to special work for the country at this time. I never sought the office. I never planned out or schemed my life. I have but one idea, which was an idea that I inherited, and it was the idea of service – service to the people of this country. My father lived in the belief all his life. . . . It is a tradition; it is in our bones; and we have to do it.[25]

Stanley Baldwin often had occasion to stress 'the continuity of history' in his speeches. Some of these were published in 1926 in a volume entitled *On England*.[26] The theme of the nation's history appears, for example, in his praise of the River Severn whose waters had at one time passed 'through country full of strife and fighting' but now carried 'their healing message into the heart of England' (22). A West Midlands ironmaster by origin, Baldwin made a virtue of his cultivated archaism: 'I have lived for many years in a backwater, and the flood of culture has swept forward far away from me. I speak not as the man in the street even, but as a man in a field-path, a much simpler person steeped in tradition and impervious to new ideas' (108–9). As far as he was concerned, 'England is the country, and the country is England' (16). The English themselves were characterized by 'a diversified individuality' which they would never allow to be 'steam-rollered' (15). In contrast to the collectivist assumption, Baldwin delivered the message that, far from being dispensable, tradition was a supreme value, to be respected even at the expense of some degree of rationality: 'I dislike that word coordination', he once declared (186).

How was the country to be run? Baldwin's answer was that English character could be depended upon: 'Let us be content to trust ourselves and be ourselves' (12). We could 'rely on the innate commonsense, integrity, courage and faith of the common men and women of this country' (72). His recipe in both politics and industry was to cultivate a climate of mutual confidence: 'no mystery, no secretiveness, but a common desire to get at facts, and a common desire to help' (44). In fact, he added, 'The power of managing our own affairs in our own way is the greatest gift of Englishmen' (47). Here is another example of the collectivist message being reversed. Baldwin is not seeking to achieve a common decency through the imposition of order. Instead, he is arguing that a peculiarly English kind of order can be maintained by relying upon the proven decency of ordinary people. The English temperament is attuned not to a rigidly imposed uniformity – 'Uniformity of type is a bad thing' (15) – but to 'the spirit of co-operation, the spirit of fairplay, and "give and take", [and] the habit of working to a common purpose' (48). Drawing upon the same liberal inheritance, but emphasizing different elements within it, Stanley Baldwin conjured up a vision of England and the English which was very different from that of a Haldane or a Hobhouse.

Neville Chamberlain and Arthur Mee

The four offshoots of the liberal inheritance being discussed in this chapter express varying reactions to the city. Acknowledging the city's potential for creating misery and unrest, the collectivists brought in the power of the state to counter-balance it and hold it in check. Baldwin systematically devalued the city and its characteristic virtues in favour of rural ways. By contrast, Neville Chamberlain and Arthur Mee expressed the aspirations of social groups whose greatest achievements and hopes depended upon the vigorous expansion of an urban industrial civilization in England.

Neville Chamberlain, a product of Birmingham Liberalism in the 1870s and 1880s, encompassed the ambitions of many professionals and business managers. Such people were sympathetic to a style of politics in which the strengths of property and technical expertise might be harnessed together, each increasing the capacity of the other. Mee's perspective was not quite the same. It was more meritocratic; less patrician. In 1920, he wrote: 'A race that sticks to the land like a limpet . . . cannot be great, however happy it may be; and the breaking away of the English people from the land was one of their great strides forward; it was as though Labour was then first mobilised.'[27] Mee was the son of an artisan engineer. In his view, technical expertise (or native wit) accompanied by hard work and moral exertion should win their just rewards. The city should be an arena of great opportunity for anyone with intelligence and character. Neville Chamberlain was a scion of the well-heeled business and professional classes, comfortably padded with inherited wealth. Arthur Mee spoke for the rapidly expanding lower middle class which staffed the offices and warehouses of the nation. They, above all, were the beneficiaries of the developing national education system.

Let us consider some other similarities and differences between the two men. Three broad resemblances should be stressed. First, both men looked for the fruits of individual enterprise within communities exhibiting moral consensus. Second, both had a passion for facts and a desire for intellectual and moral order. Third, both combined a deep interest in evolutionary theory with a sense of mission deriving from a Nonconformist background.[28] Both were enthusiastic to impose temperance upon others. When looking after the family's sisal business in the Bahamas as a young man, Chamberlain had 'put down the drink and unlicensed shops with a strong hand'.[29] Mee wielded his influence in a similar way in the corner of Kent where he eventually established himself in some comfort on his earnings from publishing. Annoyed by the fact that he could only transact postal business in the local off-license, he bought a plot of land nearby. Upon this land he built a 'temperance' post office with a tea-room and circulating library attached. Having secured the postal business for his own premises he had a large sign placed above the entrance. It read: 'Do Right and Fear Not'. It is perhaps not surprising that his employer, Lord Northcliffe, used to tease Mee by calling him a 'narrow-minded little Nottingham Nonconformist'.[30]

Mee's career in journalism and publishing was to a great extent built upon the exploitation and public presentation of his own personality. Chamberlain was much more reticent about his own feelings and political approach.[31] One of the latter's few extended discussions of what politics should be about is his adulatory memoir of his young cousin and close friend Norman, who was killed on active service during World War I.[32] I am going to compare Neville's description of his own personal hero, published in 1923 for private circulation, with some of the portraits painted in Arthur Mee's *Hero Book* which appeared in 1921.[33] Following this, I will contrast certain aspects of the two men's careers before the early 1920s.

As far as Neville was concerned, his cousin Norman was a model of enlightened public service. Like Neville, Norman had travelled in the colonies and found there 'a certain tendency to regard the old country as a slow-going and rather decadent nation' (32). He envied Australia and Canada their 'more efficient citizens'. In those countries, he wrote, 'accumulated poverty does not hang like a millstone round the neck of the reformer'. It was possible to engage in 'social experiments' (33). Norman hoped that 'the Englishmen of today [might] profit by the mistakes of the Englishmen, the Spaniards and the Portuguese of history' (33–4). Neville approved of these 'home truths' (34).

Before his death, Norman Chamberlain was consciously trying to get to know and become part of urban society. In 1908 he wrote:

> I've got a most valuable position in Brum – valuable to me, I mean. There I'm in touch with a whole society as well as with a lot of representative institutions and civil reformers, also with a lot of the working classes, and in such a way that I can find out their views and get to learn still better their difficulties and complaints and blessings, etc. I can never get that anywhere else. The relations between a member and his constituency or a professed inquirer and his victims are quite different. Therefore I don't want to leave this *point d'appui* that I have got and that I love so in Birmingham. (45)

In the course of his work in Birmingham, Norman Chamberlain had become especially concerned with the problem of juvenile unemployment. He worked with the Street Children's Union, helped establish labour exchanges and tried to develop an efficient probationary system. However, as he wrote:

> I am doing this personal work (or "philanthropy") *not as an end, but as a means*. I'm not absolutely absorbed by it; it interests me very much because it gives me a knowledge of social and industrial conditions and of the working man's point of view, which are invaluable to anyone wishing to be a public man, indispensable in fact: I do not see a firmer base on which to build up that insight into, sympathy with and above all knowledge of the average mind. It's only by that we can help them *en masse*. (46)

If a man may be known, in part at least, through his descriptions of those he admires, then we may conclude that Neville shared Norman's view that in the new England public men would have to ascertain the feelings of ordinary city dwellers in order to be able to exercise authority over them responsibly and effectively. Compare Arthur Mee's description in his *Hero Book* of his own idol W. T. Stead, the radical Nonconformist editor of *Review of Reviews*:

> He was every inch a noble man; there was no more fearless honesty in the world than his. There was nothing he dared not do that seemed to him right. Life was to him a trust, a force breathed into him by God, to be used for lifting up the world.

> And all his life he was lifting up. None was too low for him to bend and reach. No good cause was too hopeless for him to declare it. . . . He was one of the builders of the kingdom of God. (16–17)

Sir John Hammerton, Mee's friend and biographer, noted resemblances between Mee and Stead. Each sought to be a 'publicist . . . leader of thought [and] . . . crusader for righteousness'. He argued that 'Stead's was a more complex personality, with greater depths, wider experience of life, ampler scholarship, but strikingly similar in his sense of "mission", as also in his undying interest in W. T. Stead.'[34]

Neville Chamberlain admired his cousin for exemplifying 'the fine old maxim *noblesse oblige*' (v). By contrast, Mee's tribute to his fellow newspaperman was included in a chapter of his *Hero Book* entitled 'The Heroism of Everyday'. Most of the accounts in this chapter are about 'ordinary folk' who 'go where England needs them' and who 'dream not that they are great' (209–10): for example, 'The Pony Boy', 'The Foundry Man', 'The Man in the Engine Room', and 'The London Van-Boy'. Another chapter, dedicated to 'The Heroic Spirit of Civilisation: The Men Who Won the War' (273), included the following passage:

> In one of the stories of the war we read that so many little dots were slowly moving into the distance. They disappeared into a trench, and as they went in other moving dots came out from the other end. Each moving dot was a man. Every moving dot had, somewhere in our Island, a home dearer than any other spot of earth, some spot in our Motherland in which all the hopes of the years were centred for them. But they were willing to be spots on a landscape, they were willing to be crests on a wave, they were willing to leap into death and efface themselves if they might carry on the work of England on the earth. The world had given them something, and they would pay it back. (291)

The difference in perspective between Mee and Chamberlain is nicely conveyed by the fact that for several months during 1917 Chamberlain had been Director of National Service and as such directly concerned with the management of men as 'dots' who would make up a 'line', so to speak.[35] Mee stressed the individual men and women within the mass. When young, he had written: 'the world is a vast collection of ones'.[36] By contrast, the Chamberlain approach was preoccupied with the problem of dealing with the population '*en masse*' and acquiring 'knowledge of the average mind.'

Chamberlain had been born in 1869 and spent his childhood in a Birmingham dominated by the municipal elite led by his father. By the time Joseph Chamberlain took up his seat in the House of Commons in 1876 he was able to boast: 'The Town will be parked, paved, assized, marketed, Gas-and-Watered and *Improved* – all as the result of three years' active work.'[37] As is well known, the rhetoric of Birmingham's Liberal masters advertised their sympathy with the views of the working population, contempt for the reactionary attitudes of rural England, and great concern for the interests of the entire local community. The social and political climate of the city was the product of the interplay of a number of factors: there was a very wide range of local occupations employing a highly skilled workforce; trade unions were relatively weak; there were few very large employers; Nonconformity was an important link between many business, professional and (to some extent) artisan families; and the civic leadership around Joseph Chamberlain was ready to use Birmingham as a political base for national campaigns on a series of issues such as education and the franchise.[38]

Neville Chamberlain was a product of the optimistic idealism engendered during this period.[39] As a young man he acquired the rudiments of a scientific education and read widely in the work of Darwin and Huxley. His interest in such issues was still strong when he gave a lecture in Birmingham in 1910 on 'human development under natural selection'. He speculated about the effects of evolutionary processes upon England's 'success-making qualities' as a nation, including her 'courage, earnestness, determination, judgement and sympathy'. Nearly a decade later, his intellectual frame of reference remained broadly the same. Enlightened human intervention was possible to modify the course of evolutionary change: 'Many people have been sceptical about the suggestion that there was to be a new England, and many others have never intended that it should be very different from the old. If they had their way, I think we might have drifted into a revolution.'[40]

Chamberlain did not rush into politics. Until his early forties he worked as a businessman, managing enterprises in the Bahamas and in Birmingham. His diary entry for 24 June 1914 described a day out for his workers at the firm of Hoskins:

> Watched the working man enjoying himself on the scenic railway and then to lunch. Made the people a speech in which I announced a bonus on savings at the end of the year in proportion to profits. [Mrs Chamberlain] and I left immediately after lunch and got home for dinner. Received a note of thanks from the people assembled at tea.[41]

This is Chamberlain the paternalistic, rather distant, employer. By December of that year he was confiding to his diary: 'I can't be satisfied with a purely selfish attention to business for the rest of my life.'[42] He had entered the City Council 3 years earlier. The following year he became Lord Mayor.

Chamberlain was intent on 'following out the tradition in which I have been brought up.' He focused his efforts on the related spheres of housing, town planning and the eradication of disease. As chairman of the town planning committee, he worked for 'comprehensive planning of the whole area of the extended city and the adoption of a consistent policy with regard to the preservation of open spaces, ring roads, radial roads, and the division of districts into residential, business and factory areas.' Soon he had schemes underway in Harborne, East Birmingham, Yardley and South Birmingham. In 1913 Chamberlain became chairman of a committee enquiring into dwellings in the poorer areas. His interim report the following year noted that 'A large proportion of the poor in Birmingham are living under conditions of housing detrimental both to their health and their morals.' He supported rebuilding in the suburbs, preferably on municipally owned housing estates. By 1915, as mayor, Chamberlain was actively exploring the possibility of a municipal milk delivery service and the sale of coal at cost price to the poor.[43]

In 1916 Neville Chamberlain set up a municipal bank which, he hoped, would encourage working people to save. Significantly, several years previously he had objected to the Liberals' Old Age Pension Bill of 1908 as being 'direct discouragement of thrift'. His underlying ambition was to transform the working class by raising it up to decent, orderly habits under the influence of a wholesome environment. In 1916, he addressed the Trades Union Congress in Birmingham. Soon afterwards, he wrote that, in the sphere of labour relations, 'the Midlands are the most likely part of the country for experiments to start in, and the moment may come when there will be work for me to do smoothing the way'. He acquired a reputation for 'persuasiveness and conciliation' among political colleagues and opponents alike. During the war, he encouraged the establishment of the Citizens' Society to coordinate local unemployment relief and a Civic Recreation League to provide leisure facilities for young people.[44]

This vigorous local career was interrupted by an unhappy period as Minister of National Service in 1917. The following year he entered parliament for the Ladywood Division of Birmingham. He had to wait until 1924 before becoming Minister of Health under Stanley Baldwin. In that same year Chamberlain wrote an article entitled 'Personality and the Equipment for Success'. In it, he declared that wealth and honours are valuable only as a measure of effort and of 'conduct . . . regulated by fixed principles'. The nation's industry, he added, could only be restored by men who would 'discipline themselves' and whose characters contained integrity, judgement, courage, sympathy and patience. This characteristic homily provides a link with Arthur Mee, for it appeared as an item in the Harmsworth *Business Encylopaedia*.[45]

Arthur Mee, the son of a militant Baptist from Stapleford, near Nottingham, was born in 1875, 6 years later than Chamberlain. He remained a Liberal throughout his life. The shorthand skills which Mee perfected by taking notes on sermons brought him fame in 1895. During the General Election of that year, he singlehandedly produced a verbatim report of a speech at Derby by Sir William Harcourt, the Liberal leader in the House of Commons, and rushed it to the offices of the *Nottingham Daily Express* for setting up and printing that night.[46] In 1906 he rejoiced that 'the angels of heaven have taken over the House of Commons again'.[47] A few years later he was to be seen in his yellow motor car touring Dartford in support of the local Liberal candidate.[48] In 1923 he was asked by the secretary of the Home Counties Liberal Federation to stand for parliament on his own account. He refused, remarking: 'my business is with the next generation.'[49]

The offer of a constituency is a reflection of the influence Mee had gained by the early 1920s. This influence was a result of his great success in learning to manipulate the new mass media and appeal to an enormous popular market. His career over the past two decades had been a remarkable one. At the age of fourteen he was holding copy for proof readers at the *Nottingham Evening Post*. By the age of twenty he was editing the *Nottingham Evening Post* and had begun to build up the huge collection of carefully filed press cuttings which was to be the basis of his literary fortune. In 1899 he began work in Fleet Street, helping to edit journals such as the *Morning Herald* and *Black and White*. By 1903 he had published three popular political biographies, including one on Joseph Chamberlain.[50] Two years later, Sir Alfred Harmsworth signed him up for the *Daily Mail* and at that point Arthur Mee entered on a period of great success.

He was a key figure in the campaign by Lord Northcliffe (as Harmsworth became in 1905) to capture the loyalty of the rapidly expanding lower middle classes. This was a constituency at least as influential in the expanding electorate as the one represented by the readership of the *Manchester Guardian*. Northcliffe ministered to a clientele which was hungry for knowledge. It was keen to have its world described and explained, and ready to purchase handy guides to self-improvement. Mee set himself the task of supplying these things.

It all began with the inauguration in 1905 of a fortnightly work called the *Harmsworth Self-Educator*. With the help of a large staff and many outside contributors, Mee produced 48 parts each of 136 pages by 1907. Heavily advertised, with Mee's name prominent, the *Self-Educator* repeatedly sold well. There followed the *Harmsworth History of the World* (in 51 parts between 1907 and 1909) which employed highly regarded modern scholars such as Alfred Russell Wallace, Flinders Petrie, Ray Lankester and Frederic Harrison. The first part began with a substantial introduction by James Bryce, at that time British Ambassador to the United States. The history was a comprehensive one, encompassing Africa and the East as well as Europe. Its early chapters were entitled 'The Rise of Man and the Eve of History', 'Birth of Civilisation and the Growth of Races' and 'Making of Nations and the Influence of Nature'. Its last section was entitled 'The Triumph of the Mind of Man'. It contained surveys of topics such as 'The Emancipation of Labour and the State's Duty to the Workmen', 'The Survival of the Fittest', 'Individuality and Progress: Factors in Mankind's Upward March', 'The Future of the Human Race: Scientific Views of the World's Destiny', 'How Will the World End?', 'The Immortality of the Soul', and 'Man's Destiny After Death'.

The advertisements on the covers of this series declared the virtues of products such as 'The New Model Remington Typewriter', 'The Onoto Self-Filling Safety Fountain Pen' (for 'the business man, the office worker, the student, the wife at home handling house accounts and social correspondence') and the 'Elkington English Lever Watch'. By appealing to this market of typewriter-, fountain pen-, and time piece-users, Mee and his collaborators achieved a massive circulation. One delighted publisher associated with the venture presented Mee a new car when his own royalties touched the £10,000 mark. However, Mee had only just got into his stride.[51]

Before the end of 1915, Mee had organized the production of *The Children's Encyclopaedia* (in 50 parts, 1909–10), *The World's Great Books* (in 30 parts, 1909–10), the *Harmsworth Natural History* (in 39 parts, 1910–11), the *Harmsworth Popular Science* (in 43 parts, 1911–13), and the *New Harmsworth Self-Educator* (in 49 parts, 1913–15). In 1919 Mee produced the first issue of the *Children's Newspaper,* a weekly which sold initially at three-halfpence a time. Its circulation eventually went up to a half a million. According to Hammerton, 'With its publication [Mee's] career can . . . be said to have been confirmed as that of the most successful of all literary caterers for the vast audience of young readers throughout the British Empire – and beyond.'[52]

Mee's patriotism was not aggressive but consisted of a deep-embedded conviction of the beauty and moral worth of England. For example, *Little Treasure Island,* which appeared in 1920, was a love letter rather than a chauvinistic manifesto.[53] Using a device also to be found in one of Baldwin's speeches (noticed earlier), Mee turned his favourite river, the Darent, into a symbol of the spirit of England:

> A quiet and gentle stream the Darent is today, gliding slowly through hamlets and meadows and lanes, seeking out the little places, and nowhere touching the busy world until it runs though Dartford to the Thames. Its reverence for the past is seen in its winding ways. Through the silent ruin of the Past it goes, with only the softest murmuring as it creeps by the little church towers it knew in other days. Still it ripples and glides between the banks on which it has seen its proud share of our Island story, but it treasures its secrets in the quiet places. (19)

Mee combined, in a startling way, a profound reverence for tradition and a zest for change. One of his messages was that the modern world offered very many opportunities for creative participation and adventure. He was a second Samuel Smiles for a new England.[54] Mee also exhibited, simultaneously, a deep sense of life's mystery and an insatiable appetite for hard facts. He refused to be overwhelmed by the scale of contemporary scientific discovery and provided hearty reassurance that men and women would advance in their power to do good, under God's benevolent eye.[55]

Earlier in this argument I contrasted the collectivist approach – which favoured rationality at the expense of tradition and sought to produce decency through the imposition of bureaucratic order – with the stance adopted by Stanley Baldwin. The latter, I suggested, emphasized the value of tradition as compared to the deadening effect of an imposed rationality. He also declared his belief that a peculiarly English kind of order was maintained by the widespread decency of common folk. Neville Chamberlain and Arthur Mee represent two other ideological offspring of the liberal inheritance.

Chamberlain certainly believed that a decent society would only be created through an increase in orderliness. However, the agents of this change would be men and women with well-regulated moral characters. In other words, his hope lay in internal order, order within individuals as individuals. Public men would not rely too heavily on externally imposed order as expressed in the collectivist state. Rather, they would give practical encouragement and lead by example.

By the time Chamberlain became mayor, a subtle osmosis had occurred in Birmingham between the civic gospel which his father had espoused and the Anglican paternalism against which he had inveighed. The latter form of traditional authority had given valuable legitimacy to the radical reforms undertaken by Neville Chamberlain in his pursuit of rational improvement. Chamberlain's problem at the national level was to find a way of harnessing his style of political rationality to a comparable source of traditional authority. In this respect, Baldwin was more effective. However, that is to anticipate the argument.

Arthur Mee was free of the constraints imposed upon practising politicians. Secure in his editor's seat, he could weave together the various elements of the liberal inheritance in a manner denied to others. On the one hand, Mee was an enthusiastic devotee of the Biblical tradition of his Nonconformist forebears. For him, Noah was 'a comparatively modern personage.'[56] On the other hand, he combined this providential sense of cosmic history with an evolutionary view of scientific development. Both perspectives reinforced his conviction that progress was unfolding to the benefit of humanity in a gradually revealed pattern. Tradition, rationality, decency and order stood in a balanced relationship in his writing, each contributing to the appeal of his overall vision.

Mee and Chamberlain were united, and set apart from Baldwin and the collectivists, by their positive acceptance of the opportunities offered by the city as an arena of individual development. However, some resemblances must also be mentioned. Mee and Baldwin had a similar tendency to indulge in romanticized patriotic rhetoric. Furthermore, Chamberlain and the collectivists both had confidence in the creative power of public authority in the new England. It is important to identify the extent and limits of these resemblances. Mee's England was sanctified by the people's heroism, past and present. Its beauties were expressions of the ideals for which men and women struggled, often against all odds. By contrast, Baldwin's England was made pleasant by the people's calm wisdom. Its charms reflected a people at peace with itself, not in struggle. Collectivist England was one in which the institutions of public power were to be used to bestow upon the people benefits to which they had a right but which they were incapable of achieving for themselves, perhaps were even incapable of appreciating. By contrast, Chamberlain's England was one in which public men and women justified their property and privileges in two ways. First, they used their talents to help create social conditions under which individuals could develop decent and orderly habits. Second, they showed by example that such habits are beneficial to individuals and to society as a whole. To return to the initial contrast, Chamberlain and Mee both anticipated with optimism the benefits to be gained by persuading the urban population to aspire and act. From another perspective, Baldwin and the collectivists perceived the advantages of a Social Order in which the urban population is relatively passive, largely acquiescent and broadly satisfied.

Aftermath

In conclusion, it is worth briefly considering the question: how did these offspring of Liberalism contribute to the shaping of Englishness after the mid-1920s?

In the Conservative government of 1924 Neville Chamberlain served as Minister of Health. According to A. J. P. Taylor, of Baldwin's ministers 'Only Neville Chamberlain . . . knew his business and supplied . . . the creative element in the government.' In his view, Chamberlain was 'the most effective social reformer of the interwar years'.[57] Many of his reforms were designed to simplify the tangled web of local government. However, he was opposed by a number of Labour councils who regarded him as mean and intrusive. Trade unionists thought of him as the enemy of the poor.[58] This image has stuck. The underlying difficulty was that Chamberlain entered national politics at a time of deep uncertainty and mistrust in class relations, especially in the industrial sphere. In Birmingham Chamberlain's passion for particulars had been one aspect of a widely shared vision of a harmonious community. This community was to be guided by competent public men informed by a self-critical managerial Liberalism. In Whitehall and the nation he was perceived differently. As a biographer wrote in 1940: 'Birmingham business and the counting house: these are, or were, his associations in the public mind. Inevitably it was said that he lacked humanity.' Rather desperately, the biographer stressed Chamberlain's 'country walks . . . and . . . love of flowers and of gardening.' He pointed out the prime minister's devotion to bird watching, and his contributions to *The Countryman*. The longest quotation in the whole political biography is taken from Chamberlain's account in the *Daily Telegraph* of the imitative habits of the blackbird. Furthermore, the Chamberlains were part of 'the backbone of England'. Their 'stock has its roots in the everyday past of England'.[59] Two years earlier, another hagiographical work entitled, significantly, *The Chamberlain Tradition,* had stressed that the family had 'always been English through and through . . . [without] . . . one drop of foreign blood in them'.[60]

The above quotations signify the hold which the evocation of traditional England had obtained over the popular imagination. Baldwin made most effective use of this political imagery in carrying out his self-appointed mission of fostering social peace during and after the labour troubles of the mid-1920s. Chamberlain met with hostility. Baldwin was the great pacifier. This was ironic. The weaving of durable compromises among potentially hostile interests – masters and men, city and countryside, Anglican and Nonconformist, Conservative and Liberal Unionist – had been the peculiar skill of Birmingham's politicians in the late-nineteenth and early-twentieth centuries. Its products had included the widespread use of industrial arbitration, a commitment to civic welfare, a well-integrated local educational system and a keen awareness by the city's leading figures of the need to monitor opinion with great care.[61] Many of these approaches were coming into use at the national level after the mid-1920s. As has been seen, Baldwin, whose background was not very different from Chamberlain's, managed to present himself as a shrewd and seasoned countryman. In this reassuring guise, he played down the radical implications of the trend towards increased institutional cooperation and corporatism which was affecting relations between government, industry, the trade unions and other powerful lobbies.[62] He told an audience in 1930: 'Our political capacity for avoiding upheavals, our gift for "animated moderation" (in Bagehot's phrase), has long been envied by our continental neighbours. They will find once again, I venture to prophesy, that we shall get together and modify presently our institutions to suit the new conditions. We are not good at planning ahead, but we have a gift for improvising and compromising.'[63]

Meanwhile, Arthur Mee continued to write and edit, producing an average of about two books a year between 1925 and 1943, the year of his death. To some extent, his scientific preoccupations yielded ground to religion and patriotism. His last great venture was the historical and topographical survey, *The King's England*. Volumes covering thirty-six counties had been published by 1945. The continuing popularity of Mee, whose high fees were once the subject of gentle public teasing by Stanley Baldwin, should modify our perceptions of the dominance of the rural myth.[64] Mee could eulogize country lanes and rivers as well as the next man but he was equally, if not more, stirred by cities. In his book on London ('heart of the Empire and wonder of the world') in *The King's England* series he described the capital as being 'like the widow's cruse, mysterious and inexhaustible' (19).[65] He went on:

It is older than freedom, but it is ever renewing its youth. When half the world would speak to the other half it speaks through Faraday House. When the troubled world seeks rest it comes to London. The nations go mad, but London keeps its head. The wonder of cities and the centre of the Empire, it stands in cloudy days like an island of calm weather. The storms may beat about it and the winds may blow, but it remains the magnet of the world. (9)

Those words were published in 1937. Two years later, Londoners and others were reading Arthur Mee's *Blackout Book*.[66]

The rhetoric of World War II emphasized the calm resolution of the English population and their determination not to be beaten. It drew upon ideas already deeply familiar to those who had listened to the speeches of Baldwin and read the work of Arthur Mee. Both men were part of a broader movement of sentiment. For example, the latter's view of London was not his own alone. In *England Speaks,* published in 1935, Philip Gibbs had written that in London there was 'enough courage, patience, endeavour, and intelligence to make a good world' (208).[67] Within the city he recognized 'the old traditional character of the English as Shakespeare saw it [which] . . . surges up irresistibly in times of crisis or of pageantry' (208). When Winston Churchill declared that his fellow countrymen were prepared to 'fight on the beaches' he was echoing, albeit not directly or consciously, thoughts expressed in Baldwin's address on 'England' in 1924:

> The Englishman is made for a time of crisis, and for a time of emergency. He is serene in difficulties. . . . He may not look ahead, he may not heed warnings, he may not prepare, but when he once starts he is persistent to the death. It is these gifts which have made the Englishman what he is, and that have enabled the Englishman to make England and the Empire what it is.[68]

Victory in World War II powerfully reinforced the legitimacy of these sentiments. It also established the patriotic credentials of the Labour movement and its friends. J. B. Priestley was as much the voice of England as was Winston Churchill.[69] After the war Labour's leaders wanted welfare and opportunity for their supporters. This meant an increase in bureaucracy and rationalization within the state. However, collectivist innovations were incorporated within a structure whose guiding principles – compromise, adaptation, a stress on continuity – remained substantially unchanged. The relevance of the feelings of national unity engendered by the war should not be underestimated. Since at least the 1880s a shared Englishness had mediated the encounters, gradually widening in scope, between Liberal establishments and the democratic community. The post-war inauguration of the welfare state was, perhaps, the last great act in this process.[70]

Notes

1   Andrew Reid, *Why I Am a Liberal: Being Definitions and Confessions of Faith by the Best Minds of the Liberal Party* (London: Cassell, 1885), pp. 47–9. See J. W Burrow, *A Liberal Descent, Victorian Historians and the English Past* (Cambridge: C.U.P., 1981).

2   Christopher Harvie, *The Lights of Liberalism: University Liberals and the Challenge of Democracy 1860–86* (London: Allen Lane, 1976), p. 156; H. A. L. Fisher, *Life of James Bryce*, 2 vols (London: Macmillan, 1927).

3   This work contained a comparative study of political arrangements in
    England, the United States, Canada, Australia, New Zealand and Switzerland.
    James Bryce, *Modern Democracies,* 2 vols (London: Macmillan, 1921).

4   Another Oxford Liberal of the same vintage as Bryce and Freeman was to
    develop a more pessimistic view of the future of Englishness: 'it is now more
    than probable that our science, our civilisation, our great and real advance in
    the practice of government are only bringing us nearer to the day when the
    lower races will predominate in the world [and] . . . the higher races will lose
    their nobler elements.' Charles H. Pearson, *National Life and Character: A
    Forecast* (London: Macmillan, 1893), p. 344. See also J. Tregenza, *Professor of
    Democracy: The Life of C.H. Pearson 1830–94* (Cambridge: C.U.P., 1968).

5   The fate of the Liberal party during the late-nineteenth century and early-twentieth
    century continues to be a focus of active debate. See, for example, P. Fraser,
    'British war policy and the crisis of Liberalism', *Journal of Modern History,*
    54 (1982), 1–26; K. O. Morgan, 'Lloyd George's premiership: a study in prime
    ministerial government', *Historical Journal,* 13 (1970), 130–57; G. R. Searle, 'The
    Edwardian Liberal Party and Business', *English Historical Review,* 98 (1983),
    28–60; M. Barker, *Gladstone and Radicalism 1886–94* (Brighton: Harvester P.,
    1974); Peter Stansky, *Ambitions and Strategies* (Oxford: O.U.P., 1964); H. V. Emy,
    Liberals, Radicals and Social Politics 1892–1914 (Cambridge: C.U.P., 1973); P. F.
    Clarke, *Lancashire and the New Liberalism* (Cambridge: C.U.P., 1971); P. F. Clarke,
    Liberals and Social Democrats (Cambridge: C.U.P., 1978); Trevor Wilson, *The
    Downfall of the Liberal Party 1914–35* (London: Collins, 1966); Michael Bentley,
    The Liberal Mind 1914–29 (Cambridge: C.U.P., 1977); S. Collini, *Liberalism
    and Sociology: L. T. Hobhouse and Political Argument in England, 1880–1914*
    (Cambridge: C.U.P., 1979) and Michael Freeden, *The New Liberalism: An Ideology
    of Social Reform* (Oxford: O.U.P., 1978). A classic early study is, of course, George
    Dangerfield, *The Strange Death of Liberal England* (London: MacGibbon and Kee,
    1966; originally published in 1935).

6   A. B. Cooke and John Vincent, *The Governing Passion: Cabinet Government
    and Party Politics in Britain 1885–86* (Brighton: Harvester P., 1974), p. 162.

7   On Baldwin, see David Cannadine, 'Politics, propaganda and art: the case of
    two "Worcestershire lads"', *Midland History* (1977), 97–122; Martin J. Wiener,
    English Culture and the Decline of the Industrial Spirit 1850–1980 (Cambridge:
    C.U.P., 1981), pp. 58, 100–1, 120–1. Baldwin's speeches drew on material supplied
    by Arthur Bryant, his biographer, and Rudyard Kipling, his cousin. Wiener, p. 114;
    A. J. P. Taylor, *English History 1914–1945* (Oxford: Clarendon P., 1965), p. 283;
    Arthur Bryant, *Stanley Baldwin* (London: Hamish Hamilton, 1938).

8   See, for example, Wiener, *English Culture;* Emy, *Liberals, Radicals and
    Social Politics 1892–1914;* Freeden, *The New Liberalism.* On the ambiguous
    relationship between Liberalism and tradition, see S. R. Letwin, 'Matthew
    Arnold, enemy of tradition', *Political Theory,* 10 (1982), 333–51.

9   On the civic gospel see, for example, E. P. Hennock, *Fit and Proper Persons:
    Ideal and Reality in Nineteenth-Century Urban Government* (London: Edward
    Arnold, 1973); Asa Briggs, *Victorian Cities* (Harmondsworth: Penguin,
    1968), pp. 184–240; Derek Fraser, *Power and Authority in the Victorian City*
    (Oxford: Basil Blackwell, 1979), pp. 101–10.

10 The social and cultural climate of Nonconformist circles in the Midlands
    during the decades immediately preceding the births of Chamberlain and Mee
    is evoked in J. D. Y. Peel, *Herbert Spencer: The Evolution of a Sociologist*
    (London: Heinemann, 1971).

11 Reid, *Why I Am A Liberal,* p. 17.

12 Basic sources on the social and political composition of the Liberal party
    in this period are: John Vincent, *The Formation of the British Liberal Party
    1857–1868,* 2nd edn (Brighton: Harvester P., 1976); D. A. Hamer, *Liberal
    Politics in the Age of Gladstone and Rosebury* (Oxford: Clarendon P., 1972).

13 For a useful recent discussion, see Paul Adelman, *Victorian Radicalism: The
    Middle-Class Experience 1830–1914* (London: Longman, 1984), pp. 48–123.

14 Reid was a political writer whose other edited books included *Why I Should
    Disestablish* (London: Longman, 1886); *Vox Clamantium: The Gospel of the
    People* (London: Innes, 1894); and *The House of Lords Question* (London:
    Duckworth, 1898). Reid's own view of the 'ideal Liberal' was that such a person
    would 'LOVE THE APPROVAL OF HIS OWN CONSCIENCE MORE THAN
    THE APPROVAL OF THE CONSCIENCE OF THE PEOPLE' – amongst whom
    he would be 'A TEACHER AND A PROPHET'. He would be 'a modern and
    scientific man, in the sense that he will not allow the Past to control him, but he
    will control it'. Reid, *Why I Am A Liberal,* pp. 114, 116, 125.

15 For a discussion of some aspects of the influence of Spencerian thought on
    Birmingham Liberalism, see Dennis Smith, 'Social development, the state and
    education: a structural analysis of Francis Adams's *History of the Elementary
    School Contest in England*', *Prose Studies,* 1 (1977), 19–33.

16 Quoted in John Morley, *Life of Gladstone,* 2 vols (London: Macmillan, 1905),
    II, 218.

17 Paul Adelman, *Gladstone, Disraeli and Later Victorian Politics,* 2nd edn
    (London: Longman, 1983), p. 46.

18 See, for example, H. C. G. Matthew, *The Liberal Imperialists* (Oxford:
    O.U.P., 1973); Richard Price, *An Imperial War and the British Working Class*
    (London: Routledge, 1972).

19 Peter F. Clarke, 'Liberalism', *History Today,* 33 (1983), 42–5.

20 Clarke, 'Liberalism', p. 45.

21 Brougham Villiers was the pen name of F. J. Shaw. He asserted that the
    dominant interest of the working class lay in 'Guarantism', in the development
    of 'an ever-growing, ever more elaborate organisation to guarantee all the
    members of society against the worst evils of poverty'. Brougham Villiers,
    Modern Democracy (London: Fisher Unwin, 1912), pp. 32, 54.

22 Matthew, *Liberal Imperialists,* pp. 138–40.

23 L. T. Hobhouse, 'The ethical basis of collectivism', *International Journal
    of Ethics,* 8 (1898), 145, quoted in Robert Pearson and Geraint Williams,
    *Political Thought and Public Policy in the Nineteenth Century: An
    Introduction* (London: Longman, 1984), p. 150.

24 H. Montgomery Hyde, *Baldwin the Unexpected Prime Minister* (London:
    Hart-Davis, MacGibbon, 1973), pp. 10–11, 19; K. Middlemas and J. Barnes,

Baldwin: A Biography (London: Macmillan, 1969), pp. 4–5; F. W. Burstall and C. G. Burton, *Souvenir History of the Foundation and Development of Mason Science College and University of Birmingham 1880–1930* (University of Birmingham, 1930), p. 57.

25 Stanley Baldwin, *On England* (Harmondsworth: Penguin, 1937; originally published in 1926), p. 28.

26 See previous note.

27 Arthur Mee, *Little Treasure Island* (London: Hodder and Stoughton, 1920), p. 7.

28 Like his father, Neville had taught at the Sunday school of the Church of the Messiah. Although neither father nor son was an active church-goer, in later life Neville had what Feiling described as 'intrinsically a religious mind'. Feiling, *Neville Chamberlain,* pp. 13–14, 125. Arthur Mee inherited the active devoutness of his father, a deacon of his Baptist chapel. A contemporary of Mee senior commented: 'A comfortable sense of approximate infallibility, with assurance of reward, well earned, in the hereafter, conditioned his outlook and fortified him in beliefs and theories which he cherished to the end.' Quoted in John Hammerton, *Child of Wonder: An Intimate Biography of Arthur Mee* (London: Hodder and Stoughton, 1946), p. 23.

29 The quotation is from a letter written by Reverend F. B. Matthews to Archdeacon Wakefield in 1894. Quoted in Feiling, *Neville Chamberlain,* p. 25.

30 Hammerton, *Child of Wonder,* p. 95. During World War I Mee was an ardent temperance campaigner. He crusaded hard in this cause for the Strength of Britain Movement and wrote three books against alcoholic drink. Arthur Mee, *The Fiddlers: Drink in the Witness Box* (London: Morgan and Scott, 1917); *The Parasite* (London: Morgan and Scott, 1918); *Who Giveth Us Victory* (London: Allen and Unwin, 1918).

31 According to Margot Asquith, Chamberlain 'was shy, fundamentally humble, and seldom looked you in the face when he was talking to you'. Margot Asquith [Countess of Oxford and Asquith], *Off the Record* (London: Frederick Muller, 1943), p. 74.

32 See note 30 above.

33 Arthur Mee, *Hero Book* (London: Hodder and Stoughton, 1921). Mee's heroes included Saint Joan, Sir Francis Drake, Walter Greenway, Toussaint L'Ouverture, the passengers of the Mayflower, William Lloyd Garrison, Socrates, Abraham Lincoln, Robert Louis Stevenson, Captain Cook, the men who built the Panama Canal, the scientist Benjamin Harrison, Sir Robert Peel, 'the men who won the war' and a wide variety of 'ordinary folk'.

34 Hammerton, *Child of Wonder,* p. 181. Stead had been one of the main instigators of the popular protests against the 'Bulgarian atrocities'. Later, he stirred the conscience of the American Mid West. Finally, he went down with the *Titanic*. Frederic Whyte, *Life of W. T. Stead,* 2 vols (London: Jonathan Cape, 1925); W. T. Stead, *If Christ Came to Chicago* (London: Review of Reviews, 1894).

35 Feiling, *Neville Chamberlain,* pp. 63–75.

36 This phrase comes from an article Mee wrote in 1895 entitled 'Thoughts at Twenty-One: Impressions of Manhood's First Hour': Hammerton, *Child of Wonder,* p. 67. Fifteen years later, Northcliffe ('your devoted Chief') was writing to Mee that 'the collective strength of the individual is the strength of the nation'. Northcliffe to Mee, 1 November 1910, quoted in Reginald Pound and Geoffrey Harmsworth, *Northcliffe* (London: Cassell, 1959), p. 398.

37 Joseph Chamberlain to Jesse Collings, 26 June 1876, quoted in Judd, *Radical Joe,* p. 67.

38 See Dennis Smith, *Conflict and Compromise: Class Formation in English Society 1830–1914. A Comparative Study of Birmingham and Sheffield* (London: Routledge, 1982). A classic study is, of course, Asa Briggs, *History of Birmingham, Volume 2: Borough and City 1865–1938* (Oxford: O.U.P., 1952). For a discussion of Englishness with particular reference to Birmingham, see Dennis Smith, 'Knowing your place: class, politics and ethnicity in Birmingham and Chicago 1890–1983', in *The Making of Urban Society: Historical Essays on Class Formation and Place,* eds. N. Thrift and P. Williams (London: Routledge, forthcoming). Michael Blanch has examined some of the evidence for 'nationalist ideology and organization' among the working-class youth of Birmingham between 1890 and 1918. He found links to 'the dominant Unionist party'. Michael Blanch, 'Imperialism, nationalism and organized youth', in *Working-Class Culture*, eds. John Clarke, Chas Critcher and Richard Johnson (London: Hutchinson, 1979), pp. 103–20, esp. p. 119.

39 Some of this spirit is captured by Reverend R. W. Dale's address to the city's young Liberals in 1878: 'I ask you to preserve for [Birmingham] the great place which your fathers have won. Remember that your country is greater than your party. Cherish for your country a fervent and passionate loyalty.' He added: 'You and I are the heirs and representatives of those who laboured and suffered in obscurity in order to defend the liberties of the English people.' R. W. Dale, *Liberalism* (Birmingham: Birmingham Junior Liberal Association, 1878), p. 15.

40 Feiling, *Neville Chamberlain,* pp. 12, 41–2, 83 (letter from Chamberlain, 22 March 1919). Several months earlier he had written: 'In the new England to which we look forward when the present period of pain and stress has passed away there will be great changes in social and industrial conditions. The gentler and more human aspects of life will be developed.' Neville Chamberlain, 'Introduction', in William Haywood, *The Development of Birmingham* (Birmingham: Kynoch, 1918), p. 15.

41 *Neville Chamberlain Papers,* NC/2/20. I am grateful to the Librarian at the University of Birmingham for permission to quote from this source.

42 NC/2/20.

43 Feiling, *Neville Chamberlain,* pp. 52–5, 57. The quotations are from pp. 52, 54–5.

44 Ibid., pp. 48, 58–62. The quotations are from pp. 48, 61.

45 Ibid., p. 119.

46 Hammerton, *Child of Wonder,* pp. 43–4, 55–7. For other evidence of Mee's journalistic expertise which was admired by, among others, Keir Hardie, see

the unsigned centenary article in *Nottingham Evening Post,* 21 July 1975. As an employee of the *Nottingham Daily Express* Mee 'interviewed "W.E.G." at a Hawarden picnic, with the innocent candour of a youthful worshipper'. This quotation comes from an unattributed press cutting in the library of the *Nottingham Evening Post.*

47 Letter, 18 January 1906. Quoted in Hammerton, *Child of Wonder,* p. 102.

48 'Arthur Mee's 50 years in journalism. An editor looks back on his aims and achievements,' *Methodist Recorder,* 4 December 1941.

49 Quoted in Hammerton, *Child of Wonder,* p. 176. Details of Mee's career in the next paragraph come from Hammerton.

50 Arthur Mee, *Joseph Chamberlain: A Romance of Modern Politics* (London: S. W. Partridge, 1901); *Lord Salisbury: The Record Premier of Modern Times* (London: Hood, Douglas and Howard, 1901); *King and Emperor: The Life History of Edward VII* (London: S. W. Partridge, 1901). Mee also edited *England's Mission by England's Statesmen* (London: Grant Richards, 1903).

51 The publisher concerned was William Heinemann who owned the rights to the German history upon which the Harmsworth enterprise was based: Hammerton, *Child of Wonder,* pp. 105–6.

52 Enid Huws Jones, 'A million a year', *New Statesman,* 18 July 1975, 89; Hammerton, *Child of Wonder,* p. 171; A. Quinton, 'The happy wonderer', *Times Literary Supplement,* 11 July 1975, 761–2.

53 See note 43.

54 I am grateful to Keith Train for suggesting this parallel to me.

55 For a fascinating example of Mee's lively imagination at work, read his visionary account of radio outside broadcasts: 'Who knows but that in time we may sit in our armchairs listening to the speeches of Her Majesty's Ministers. . . . Then in the cricket season we shall follow our favourite wielders of the willow without risking cold or sunstroke.' A. Mee, 'The pleasure telephone', *Strand Magazine,* 16 (1898), 345.

56 Hammerton, *Child of Wonder,* p. 105.

57 Taylor, *English History,* pp. 221, 237; see also Feiling, *Neville Chamberlain,* pp. 51–62, 126–46; C. L. Mowatt, *Britain Between the Wars 1918–1940* (London: Methuen, 1968), pp. 338–41.

58 There were even riots, F. Miller, 'The British unemployment assistance crisis of 1935', *Journal of Contemporary History,* 14, 2 (1979), 329–52.

59 Derek Walker-Smith, *Neville Chamberlain: Man of Peace* (London: Robert Hale, 1940). The quotations are taken from pp. 12, 18, 42. The passage about the blackbird is on pp. 195–6. When the letter from which this last passage came appeared in 1936, Arthur Bryant wrote: 'In a single short letter [Neville Chamberlain] . . . has done more to capture the hearts of his countrymen than in all the actions and speeches of a long and highly useful political life': *Illustrated London News,* 29 August 1936, 340, quoted in Wiener, *English Culture,* p. 140.

60 Charles Petrie, *The Chamberlain Tradition* (London: Right Book Club, 1938), p. 17.

61 Dennis Smith, *Conflict and Compromise,* esp. ch. 10.

62 See, especially, Keith Middlemas, *Politics in Industrial Society: The Experience of the British System since 1911* (London: Andre Deutsch, 1979).

63 Stanley Baldwin, 'The authentic note of democracy' (lecture at Annual National Conference of the Brotherhood Movement in Coventry, 14 July 1930), in Stanley Baldwin, *The Torch of Freedom* (London: Hodder and Stoughton, 1935), pp. 38–58. The quotation is from p. 49.

64 The incident occurred at a Fleet Street dinner: Hammerton, *Child of Wonder,* p. 179.

65 Arthur Mee, *London* (London: Hodder and Stoughton, 1937).

66 Arthur Mee, *Blackout Book* (London: Hodder and Stoughton, 1939).

67 Philip Gibbs, *England Speaks* (London: Heinemann, 1935).

68 Baldwin, *On England,* p. 13.

69 On Priestley, see Wiener, *English Culture,* pp. 124–5.

70 Earlier drafts of this chapter were seen by Val Riddell. I am very grateful for her comments. I would also like to thank Mary Smith for help in identifying source material relevant to Arthur Mee.

CHAPTER TEN

The Conservative party and patriotism

Hugh Cunningham

I

It is now something of a commonplace to claim that Disraeli's chief contribution to the Conservative party was to identify it with patriotism. The argument has been put most strongly by Paul Smith. After exposing the severe limitations of Disraeli's claims to be a social reformer, Smith argues that with the coming of limited democracy after 1867 the party had both to consolidate its growing appeal to the middle classes and at the same time to win at least a proportion of the new urban working-class voters. Since an appeal to the latter's material interests would alienate the crucial middle-class voters, Conservative party policy and propaganda, so the argument goes, had to be couched in terms which would have national appeal. As Smith puts it, commenting on Disraeli's famous 1872 speech at Crystal Palace:

> The concept of the national party, identifying itself with the country's greatness, appealing to the masses first as Britons, but attending to their vital needs at the same time as it nourished their patriotic pride, was a brilliant comment on the mentality of the British working man, and it was to serve the Conservative party well for more than eighty years.[1]

That was in 1967. In the following year the study of Conservative party propaganda included in Robert McKenzie and Allan Silver's *Angels in*

Marble provided supporting evidence. 'Few democratic political parties', they concluded, 'can have so systematically and ruthlessly called into question the integrity, the devotion to the institutions of the country, and the patriotism of its opponents'. Thus Robert Blake, in his *The Conservative Party from Peel to Churchill* (1970), could endorse Smith's opinion with only slight qualification. 'No one can prove it for certain', he wrote, 'but, apart from straight conservatism – and we should never underestimate its strength in all classes – this [patriotism] was probably the most effective vote-winner for Disraeli and perhaps his most notable long term contribution to the future success of the Conservative party'. 'The "patriotic" card', Blake wrote, 'has usually been a winner when it can be played with any relevance'.[2]

This opinion about the importance of patriotism to the Conservative party has remained not so much unchallenged as unquestioned. In part this is due to the relatively primitive historiography of the Conservative party; the fixation on high politics and rather less on high journalism has made it difficult to do more than speculate about opinion in the constituencies or among the voters. Patriotism, however, cannot simply be invoked as the Conservative party's unproblematic solution to its need to win cross-class support. If the Conservative party was indeed dependent on patriotism we need to know how it was organized, how it was nourished and articulated, and what language and symbols it employed. Was the patriotism to which Conservatives appealed English, or British, or Unionist, or Imperial, or some combination of the four? Could it be evoked most easily by an old-style rhetoric of Protestantism, freedom, roast beef and plum pudding, John Bull and Britannia, or were there new symbols and occasions to which they could appeal? Did patriotism imply particular policies, in domestic as much as in foreign policy? Did the Conservatives find it easy to organize and make electoral capital out of patriotism? It is to these questions that this chapter addresses itself. The answers, tentative though they are, suggest that the patriotic card worked less obviously to the Conservatives' advantage than has often been implied. Patriotism was as likely to divide the party as to unite it.

II

The organization of patriotism was the first issue to come to the fore and in many ways the one which was most easily resolved. Lancashire Conservatism provided both a model and an inspiration, and it was no accident that it was in Lancashire in 1872 that Disraeli had made the first of his famous speeches, proclaiming his trust in 'that unbroken spirit of her people, which I believe was never prouder of the Imperial country to which they belong'.[3] Already by the time Disraeli made that speech the National Union of Conservative and Constitutional Associations was making its first, rather stumbling, efforts to spread the organization of Conservatism among the working class.[4] The Eastern crisis of 1876–78 indicated that support existed but had to be organized, and disciplined; the violent break-up of Liberal and peace meetings had achieved its purpose, but it provided no firm or long-term basis for Conservative organization. Disraeli's return from the Congress of Berlin in July 1878 was the occasion for the reassertion of control. Confronted by a stage-managed presentation of addresses by Conservative Associations, Disraeli picked up the cue and impressed upon his audience 'that organisation is absolutely essential – that organisation is perfectly consistent with the highest sentiments of patriotism, and that although you may be acting under the influence of the most excited feelings at times, that is no reason why you should relax your discipline'.[5]

Ellis Ashmead Bartlett, who had been behind many of the jingo meetings in Hyde Park in the spring of 1878, took up the hint. A former President of the Oxford Union and a recent convert to the Conservative party, he was to be a key figure in the organization and articulation of patriotism over the succeeding 10 years. As we shall see, the initial success and ultimate failure of his career has much to tell us about the position of patriotism within the party. In the autumn of 1878 he drew Disraeli's attention to the role he had played, and suggested that the time might now be ripe for the formation of a Patriotic Association for 'the defence of the honour and interests of England, and the maintenance intact of the British Empire'. The Association would be ostensibly non-party, but would, as Bartlett put it, 'throw all the weight we might have, and all the enthusiasm that may by judicious treatment be evoked in favour of Lord Beaconsfield at the General Election'; it was, Bartlett notes, an 'immense advantage . . . to the Conservative party to have the "Imperial" feeling in the nation on its side'.

Bartlett envisaged a two-pronged role for the Patriotic Association. First it might provide a forum which would ease the transition to the Conservative party of imperially minded Whigs and Liberals. If it was to be effective in this, respectability was of the essence. Bartlett had to shed those 'rather strange co-workers' who, he admitted, had been his accomplices in Hyde Park. Careful inquiry had to be made into the antecedents and background of potential supporters. 'We are extremely anxious,' wrote Bartlett's brother to Monty Corry, Disraeli's secretary, 'not to identify the Association with any doubtful connections'.[6] This drive for social and political respectability had its success; by the time of the 1880 election three dukes, seven earls and a number of high-ranking officers had lent their names to the Association. Liberals, like the Russophobe Duke of Sutherland, were carefully wooed. The tone of resolutions passed at Patriotic Association meetings was measured and above party; thus the retention of Kandahar, occupied by the British under a Conservative Government in 1879 and about to be evacuated by its Liberal successor in 1881, was said to be 'a national and not a party question'. The purpose, however, as Bartlett pointed out privately, was to win over Liberals and keep the Conservatives tied to a Disraelian foreign policy.[7] The transformation of jingoism into a patriotism which was organized and respectable, and at the service of the Conservative party, was rapid and impressive.

The second role envisaged for the Patriotic Association was the mobilization of the masses. Here again Bartlett was not without success. He had a substantial following in the North of England; he was a well-known platform orator, regarded by many as second only to Randolph Churchill; and he was capable of organizing campaigns. In 1881 he was orchestrating demands for the retention of Kandahar and in 1884 for that of Khartoum. Both were occasions for large-scale petitioning in the North of England. As Bartlett noted of the 40,000 signatures on the Kandahar issue:

> The remarkable fact about these petitions is the number of working men that have signed them, showing the increasing interest which that most important section of the community feel in Imperial questions. It is a great mistake, as the Radical party will soon find out to their cost, to suppose that the working men of England are destitute of patriotism, or that they are only influenced by the sordid and miserable considerations for which the wire-pulling snobocracy of the Caucus give them credit. The true English *working* man is proud of his country, is proud of its great past, is proud of its splendid and beneficent empire, and is revolted by the paltry and penny-wise-and-pound-foolish policy of the Birmingham Radicals.[8]

The gathering of these petitions doubtless owed much to the influence of Bartlett's newspaper, *England,* a 1d. weekly aimed at the working and lower middle class, and designed, as Bartlett put it in his first editorial in March 1880, to fill the field of 'patriotism and . . . to aid in maintaining the honour and interests of the British Empire'. With a circulation of some 40,000 *England* was an important medium for the dissemination of patriotism and Conservatism. It was never a financial success, but the party recognized its value; in 1883 Salisbury contributed £1,000 in an attempt to put the paper on a sound financial basis.[9]

All this activity was at its height during Gladstone's government of 1880–85. Subsequently, as we shall see, Bartlett faded from view. His significance lies in his recognition of the importance of new forms of organization and communication in the era of limited democracy inaugurated in 1867. The jingoism on which he had rode to public recognition should now, he hoped, be organized for the service of the Conservative party. To an extent he was right. But there was a cost to be paid. In Bartlett's creations and those which paralleled or succeeded his, such as the Primrose League, organization increasingly subdued spontaneity.[10] The signatures on the petitions mounted up, the literature poured forth from the presses, public meetings dutifully passed patriotic resolutions, but the political impact was much less than it had been when jingoism was young and relatively uncontrolled. Organization was not always as 'perfectly consistent' as Disraeli had hoped 'with the highest sentiments of patriotism'.

There was a further and more substantial problem. Patriotism was not only a matter of 'sentiments'. It quickly became associated with policies, and in particular two policies which were more likely to divide than to unite the Conservative party: fair trade and opposition to 'alien' immigration. The argument that the Conservatives gained from an assertion of patriotism rests heavily on the idea that patriotism as a policy was high on emotional appeal and low on substantial content; its appeal, it is argued, crossed classes because it did not minister directly to anyone's material needs. This was far from the truth. The emergence of the stress on patriotism within the Conservative party was closely linked with particular and diverse policies.

Two of Bartlett's 'rather strange co-workers' in Hyde Park in 1878 were associated with the beginnings of the campaign for fair trade. One of them was C. W. Stokes, who claimed to be Liberal, but may already have been in the pay of the Tories, as he certainly was by May 1878; by then he was treading the by-election circuit – at Hereford in March 1878 he had been introduced with much hyperbole as 'one of the greatest men of the age – a gentleman who was looked upon as one of the greatest orators of the day, and who was well known as a friend of the working man'. A year later Stokes features as the leader of the newly formed and short-lived National Industrial Defence Association whose aim was 'to avert national ruin by taxing foreign agriculturalists and manufacturers to the relief of those British taxes on malt, etc., and income, which enhance the price of British food and manufactures'. Stokes continued to work for the Conservative party, but like so many of his type he felt himself to be ill-rewarded; his career peters out in the familiar series of begging letters.[11]

A more substantial figure in Hyde Park in 1878 was Lt R. H. Armit. Armit was, among other things, an inventor, and the development of his patents had brought him into contact with workmen in 1876, first at the Blackwall Iron Works, and then at other iron works in the East End and elsewhere. These experiences seem to have convinced him of the need for some form of protection for British industry. In four successive issues of the *Monetary Gazette* in February 1878 he contributed long letters attacking what he described as the 'Bright-Gladstone Free Trade Bastard policy'. In March it was Armit as Honorary Secretary who announced a meeting of the National and Patriotic League for the Protection of British Industries to oppose the 'Peace at any Price' meeting in Hyde Park. Thus at the very outset the fair trade movement promoted itself as patriotic and took a leading role in the violent break-up of a peace meeting. In the aftermath Armit developed the National League 'for the preservation of our home industries and the protection of our national labour against unfair competition.' These activities brought him into contact with the Sugar Bounties question and with two men already notorious in trade union circles: Thomas Kelly and Samuel Peters. Fair trade was thus linked not only with patriotism but also with anti-unionism, and in a particularly murky and corrupt form. The National League of 1878 became the working-class wing of the National

Fair Trade League and, in 1881, developed into the General Labour Union, again under Armit's aegis. These men remained in contact with and were perhaps subsidized by the party leadership, but their notoriety can only have harmed the Conservatives. By 1885 R. W. E. Middleton, the party agent, was warning Salisbury that Kelly and Peters were 'utterly untrustworthy'.[12] It did the patriotic cause no good that men of this stamp were so closely involved with it.

There was of course a more respectable side to Fair Trade, but the party leaders wisely kept their distance from it, knowing that the adoption of a Fair Trade policy would split the party much as Ireland had split the Liberals – as indeed in 1903 it did. Ambitious politicians like Churchill might at opportune moments adopt the cause, cautious ones like W. H. Smith might take judicious soundings, but the leaders, Salisbury and later Balfour, though not in principle opposed to fair trade, nevertheless discouraged any open identification of the party with it. The National Union of Conservative and Constitutional Associations openly expressed its support for tariff reform, indicating the popularity of the policy among active Conservative politicians in the constituencies; but for the party as a whole, from the viewpoint of the leaders, fair trade signalled a divided party and a loss of votes. If fair trade was a patriotic policy, then patriotism was a minefield.[13]

Armit's concern for 'the protection of our national labour' suggests the close links between fair trade and anti-alienism. Here was another policy, indubitably patriotic in content, but exceedingly difficult for the party to handle. The issue at stake in the late-nineteenth and early-twentieth centuries was the immigration of Jews from central Europe and its effect on the labour and housing markets. Respectable politicians of all parties had to steer a course between support for those who felt threatened by Jewish immigration and avoidance of anti-semitism; for within the dominant political culture there was a taboo on the expression of openly anti-semitic views. Conservative leaders, therefore, had to tread carefully. It was even doubtful that they would win much support by emphasizing their opposition to alien immigration. In particular constituencies, and especially those in the East End, no candidate of whatever party could ignore the issue, and the evidence that the Conservatives benefited from it is insubstantial. Thus, despite the passing of the Aliens Act of 1905 by a Conservative government, only two out of twelve Conservative East End M.P.s were returned in the 1906 general election. Outside the East End, even in the other major centres of Jewish settlement, Manchester and Leeds, there were no obvious political dividends to be won from anti-alienism. Alan Lee's conclusion on this point was that 'in Britain it seems that antipathy to Jews or even aliens was hardly an available response for the governing class to tap.' On the Conservative side the fear, rather, was that the party might become associated with an unacceptable form of racism. Thus in 1902 anti-alien Conservative M.P.s were encouraged to break their links with the British Brothers League in favour of the more respectable Immigration Reform Association.[14]

For the Conservative party, indeed, it could not be said that there were no enemies on the right. On the contrary, its fundamental strategy under Salisbury and Balfour was to win over moderate Liberals alarmed by the faddishness of Gladstonianism or the radicalism of New Liberalism. To be successful the Conservatives had to present themselves as a party of the centre, moderate and undoctrinaire.[15] The patriotic lobby was all too frequently an embarrassment, violent in method and language, and promoting policies which were divisive, not unifying.

Even on foreign policy issues the leaders doubted that there were electoral benefits to be won by a resolute Disraelian policy. Randolph Churchill and Joseph Chamberlain in the late 1880s were in agreement that the democracy would oppose war. 'Fighting,' as Chamberlain put it, 'can never again be *popular* with the people, with the masses.'[16] Salisbury drew on his long experience to make the same point. In August 1898 at the time of the Far Eastern crisis he tried to restrain the enthusiasm of the Poet Laureate, Alfred Austin, for a forward policy:

> I have known two such critical phases of opinion on foreign policy. The first was the Danish War of 1864. Then, as now, the London papers, clubland, and Society were all in favour of war. But Lord Palmerston, against his own personal wishes, decided the other way. He was rewarded by a majority of 70 the next year. In 1879 the same phenomenon recurred. The London newspapers, clubland and Society were all for a forward policy – a very forward policy. Lord Beaconsfield, in accordance with his own personal views, accepted that policy. He was rewarded by finding himself in a minority of 120 the following year. How will the third investigations of the same problem work out? No one can tell; but I think it will have the effect of splitting the party into two.[17]

Divisiveness within the party was what was feared. Moderation was the way to prevent it. The patriots had to be restrained.

The most effective way to do this was to fob them off with minor office. Ashmead Bartlett's career may stand for the type. In the early 1880s he was seen as one of the rising young men of the Conservative party. Disraeli had secured a pocket borough for him in 1880 but his popularity was such that in 1885 he was able to switch to his northern power-base, becoming M.P. for Sheffield (Ecclesall). Something of the regard in which he was held in the constituencies can be seen in the resolution passed by the Lancashire Union of Conservative Associations in May 1885, tendering their 'warmest thanks' to Bartlett 'for his able, incisive, and patriotic action in the recent damaging criticism of the Government policy.' From 1886 to 1888 he was chairman of the National Union of Conservatives and Constitutional Associations.[18]

Bartlett undoubtedly expected some reward for all this hard work. What he got in 1885 was the offer of the Civil Lordship of the Admiralty. With some hesitation he accepted. With even greater hesitation he accepted the offer of the same office on the formation of the 1886 government. This time he consulted his friends, and reported to Salisbury:

> I am bound to say they are both surprised and concerned, not on my account only, but on public grounds, the importance of which they have ample means of judging. They say that the great difficulty of the Conservative party has been and is to get at and influence the masses, and that it is practically a damper on the enthusiasm of the masses to find that one, who has succeeded in arousing it, receives slight consideration from the leaders whom they have been induced to support.[19]

Bartlett, as the parliamentary correspondent H. W. Lucy noted, was effectively 'gagged.'[20] Salisbury was not unwilling to consider him for further advancement, and in 1891 he was a candidate for the Postmaster-Generalship. 'He has really worked so hard for the party, and that in the most disagreeable way, and I believe has done so much service, that I do not like not rewarding him; but . . . he is entirely without authority in the House of Commons.' This latter point was certainly true, but it merely points to the gap between the parliamentary party and the constituencies.[21] In 1883 Dunraven, prominent on patriotic issues, had argued that 'the active pushing local men must be utilised, must be given an outlet for their energy, and a field for the exercise of their talents.' The field that many of them chose was patriotism, but their efforts were counterproductive so far as the advancement of their own careers was concerned. Ashmead Bartlett never regained the influence he had in the early 1880s, and after the compensation of a knighthood in 1892 he disappeared into an obscurity, darkened by rumours of financial and sexual irregularities.[22] His brother, who as a young man carried off the marriage of the century with the older, wealthy and influential Baroness Burdett-Coutts, had chosen a safer, surer and less arduous road to social and political prominence.

The failure of the patriotic lobby to gain significant advancement within the late Victorian Conservative party foreshadows the better publicized divisions of the Edwardian period. In the early-twentieth century too, the patriots had policies which they pressed upon a reluctant party leadership. The best-known of these, of course, was tariff reform, but it would be a mistake to see the pressure on the leadership stemming solely from erstwhile Birmingham radicalism. Conservatism proper, in the shape of the backwoodsmen, is now being presented with a modernizing, democratic, populist and patriotic face. Lord Willoughby de Broke, whom George Dangerfield memorably dismissed as a man whose face bore a pleasing resemblance to a horse and who was a mere two hundred years behind his time, is now being rescued from the appalling condescension of posterity. According to taste, different writers have discerned in the backwoodsmen a 'radical right', 'radical toryism', 'radical imperialists', 'tory-socialists', 'tory democrats' or 'radical unionists'. These varying diagnoses highlight the divisions in the Edwardian

Conservative party and, perhaps, exaggerate them. For our purposes, however, the important point is that the substantial issues which led to these divisions were similar to those in the late Victorian era and were focused on a cluster of patriotic policies. One difference was that in the nineteenth century the politicians who adopted the divisive policies lacked a leader of the stature of Chamberlain. The similarity is that the divisive policies were seen as interlocking parts of a package of patriotism.[23] From the point of view of the leadership such patriotism should be humoured but in no way encouraged, for to do so would endanger the central strategy of winning over discontented Liberals by the pursuit of moderation.

Moderation, however, was hardly the keynote of the Conservative party under Bonar Law's leadership in the period before World War I. It was, significantly, in these years that patriots could begin to sense that they were at one with the party. Only when the party was uncharacteristically extremist in its policies and its language were the patriots able to overcome their sense of exclusion. Two issues came to the fore at this point. The first was the Conservatives' sense that in the 1909–11 constitutional struggles over the Budget and the House of Lords it was they, not the Liberals, who were the defenders of the constitution and of the people. The populist strain within the party came to the forefront. The second and crucial issue was Ireland. Divisiveness over tariff reform dropped into the background as defence of the rights of Ulster – of the *people* of Ulster – loomed larger. The Conservatives could now fight – and fight is not too strong a word – on the most fundamental of patriotic issues, the territorial integrity of the nation-state. As Unionists they could indeed claim that the United Kingdom was safe only in their hands.

The problem of course was that it was not in their hands and there was no immediate prospect that it would become so. The failure to win power at the two 1910 elections was ominous. In the interests of the nation some were attracted by the idea of national government in the form of the coalition scheme floated by Lloyd George in 1910. Others, the majority, lived in a state of chronic outrage that a government seen as thoroughly corrupt and unconstitutional should set about dismantling the United Kingdom.[24]

War came to their rescue. The benefits which it brought to the Conservatives were not immediate, for they had to see through a period of patriotic opposition up to May 1915, and they only assumed a dominant role in government with Lloyd George's accession to the premiership in December 1916. The partial return to power during wartime, however, reinforced the Conservatives' image of themselves as the patriotic party, and it helped them to remain the dominant party for the next quarter of a century. The identification with patriotism was now unmistakably advantageous. It was, for example, Conservatives who had advocated conscription before the war, and who were much better placed than Liberals to demand it during war.[25]

A proclamation of patriotism, then, was of undeniable advantage to the Conservatives only in the crisis engendered by world war: war was the occasion of their return to power and in its aftermath they were able, in one form or another, to retain it. Initially they did so as the dominant partner in the Lloyd George government, a coalition which they saw, in Law's words, as 'not . . . a bad thing for our Party and a good thing for the Nation'. From 1920 onwards the disadvantages of coalition to the party, and as they saw it to the nation, began to outweigh the advantages. The Conservatives began to fashion a new role for themselves: the Liberals should be abandoned to their fate, and the Conservatives should take a firm stand as the national and moderate party best-placed to oppose the dangers of socialism. Bonar Law in his latter days adopted this stance of moderate and commonsensical patriotism, but it was of course Baldwin who became its incarnation; as Blake puts it, 'Pipe-smoking, phlegmatic, honest, kind, commonsensical, fond of pigs, the classics and the country, he represented to Englishmen an idealised and enlarged version of themselves.' The extreme patriots, and the issues they raised, were once again an embarrassment to the party.[26]

III

It was the essence of Baldwin's patriotism that it should seem to be simultaneously rooted in history and timeless. It had to sound natural. Yet it was in fact the outcome of a period of flux and change in the language and symbols representing nationhood. The basic issue between 1880 and 1920 may be simply stated. The available repertoire for the expression of patriotism in the late 1870s was narrowly English and arguably increasingly obsolescent. The problem was how to replace it by a repertoire which, especially after 1886, could encompass the United Kingdom, and which could extend to incorporate the Empire. The evidence suggests that the Conservatives were less than successful in the period before 1914 in creating a new repertoire which worked to their own advantage, and that the new patriotism which did come into existence, associated with monarchical ceremonial, was available to all parties, or to none.

The old English repertoire of patriotism can be seen in its dying days in the Lancashire Conservatism of the third quarter of the century. The symbols of Englishness, which were in the possession of radicals for much of the late-eighteenth and first half of the nineteenth centuries, passed, after the first phase of Chartism, to the right. Roast beef and plum pudding, the Union Jack, Rule Britannia, John Bull himself were all successfully appealed to by Conservatives up to the 1870s. Whether this happened outside Lancashire we do not know, and within Lancashire less is known about the situation after the 1870s.[27] Much that follows is necessarily tentative.

In essence the Conservatives were an *English* party. To be more precise, the bedrock of their strength lay in southern England. Moreover during this period they became more rather than less dependent on their southern England base. In the years of Conservative hegemony from 1886 to 1902 they made some inroads into Scotland, though Wales and Ireland outside

Ulster were already lost. They also, in this period, had outposts of strength in Western Lancastria and in the rural Ridings of Yorkshire. After the cataclysm of 1906, however, Conservative support shrunk. Thus in the 1910 elections the Unionists won nearly two-thirds of the seats in England below a line drawn from the Humber to the Dee, but less than a quarter of Northern, Scottish and Welsh seats. Put another way, 78 per cent of Unionist seats in January 1910 were south of the Humber-Dee line. That in turn implied that they were a dominantly middle-class and rural or small-town party.[28]

This electoral geography posed a dilemma for the Conservatives. They could either play to their strength, their southern Englishness, or they could try to broaden the basis of their support by stressing that they were the party of the United Kingdom and of Empire. Not surprisingly different voices can be heard at different times adopting both these roles. As a southern English party they were naturally drawn to the language and symbols of Englishness; they could, moreover, depict their opponents as 'un-English'. But equally they had to make it clear that they were not 'Little Englanders.' They somehow had to devise a language which was both English and Imperial. My argument is that they failed to do this, and remained throughout the period in their geographical strength, in their language, and in their outlook, primarily English.

The title of Ashmead Bartlett's paper, *England,* is telling. It was, Bartlett claimed, chosen by Disraeli himself. For a few brief weeks in 1881 there was a new title, *England, Ireland, Scotland.* Perhaps that was too obviously cumbersome. It was in any case inappropriate, for it was to England, to the English race and to the English Empire that Bartlett constantly appealed. Ireland was an Imperial problem, and appropriately treated as such. Scottish and Welsh sensibilities were quite simply ignored. To be able to do this almost certainly strengthened Bartlett's appeal, for in appealing to Englishmen – and it was usually men not women – Bartlett was able to tap part of the inherited repertoire of patriotism: the Protestant Englishman as manly, straightforward, courageous, tenacious and heir to a tradition of freedom which need not be too closely examined. All these ideas were subsumed in the one word 'Englishman,' and were almost certainly conveyed by it. From that base of Englishness Bartlett hoped to widen horizons until they became imperial, a problem to which we shall return in a moment.[29]

In the later-nineteenth century, politicians talked without compunction of England when they meant Great Britain. As Rosebery put it, in an address to Edinburgh students in 1882, England's wealth, power and population

> make her feel herself to be Great Britain, with Ireland and Scotland as lesser gems in her diadem. Therefore, with an Englishman, the love of Great Britain means the love of England – the larger and lesser patriotisms are one. He speaks, for instance, of the English Government and the English army, without condescending to the terms British and Great Britain – not from heedlessness, but from self-concentration.

In the twentieth century there was more pressure on politicians to school themselves to speak of Britain and the British, but the extent of the failure to do so is perhaps indicated by an advertisement in the personal column of *The Times* in November, 1914: 'Englishmen! Please use "Britain", "British", and "Briton", when the United Kingdom or the Empire is in question – at least during the war.'[30] After the war it was a relief to slip back into bad old ways. In Baldwin's famous speech, 'England', delivered to the Royal Society of St George in 1924 – the speech containing the classic lines, 'To me, England is the country, and the country is England' – he stated that, with the particular audience before him, his first thought 'as a public man is a feeling of satisfaction and profound thankfulness that I may use the word "England" without some fellow at the back of the room shouting out "Britain"'. On other occasions Baldwin simply said British when he meant English. In decent obscurity right at the back of the volume which was given the general title, *On England,* are speeches on Scotland, Wales and Ireland. In the speech on Scotland he contrasted the English, 'a prosaic race', with the romance of the Scots. Yet in an Empire Day speech of the same year it was 'We British' who were supposed to be 'a dull, unimaginative race',[31] The adoption of the word British amounted to little more than an anglicizing of the Scots, Welsh, Irish and immigrant communities. In general, however, politicians had not internalized a sense of Britishness, and to their audiences it was a remote and contrived language.

For the Conservatives there was conceivably much to be gained from the retention of the sense of Englishness. As an English party, they were not above appealing to English prejudices. 'Where the distinct English feeling shows itself', noted Rosebery, 'is chiefly in an impatience . . . of Scotsmen and Irishmen', Thus a Conservative party pamphlet of 1892 attacked not only Home Rule for Ireland, but also the setting up of 'a Scotch Grand Committee for Scotch Affairs'. 'They had promised similar committees', the pamphlet continued, 'for Ireland and Wales, but they refused England – by far the largest and most important member of the United Kingdom the same privilege, because in England there is a Unionist majority. So that Englishmen are to have their local affairs controlled by Scotchmen, Irishmen and Welshmen, while these are to be free from the interference of Englishmen'. In 1895 the Liberal government in its last days was described in another Conservative pamphlet as 'the present mongrel political combination of teetotallers, Irish revolutionists, Welsh demagogues, Small Englanders, English separatists, and general uprooters of all that is national and good'. Randolph Churchill appealed to the same sentiments, arguing in March 1886 that the British parliament had been captured by 'Irish repealers and Scotch radicals', and calling on Hartington and others to come over and join a new, 'essentially English' party.[32]

There was a further advantage for the Conservatives in the retention of the idea of Englishness. It allowed them to paint their opponents as 'un-English' or 'anti-English,' whereas it was not easy to think of someone as 'un-British.' It would be interesting to know the origins of un-Englishness. It was certainly alive, and in operation against Cobden and Bright, in the 1850s. Chichester Fortescue noted thus his responses to the speeches of Cobden and others on the China issue in 1857: 'They were so un-English, so ingeniously unfair against ourselves and in defence of the Chinese . . .' Bright, smarting under such accusations, asked in 1858:

> How indeed, can I, any more than any of you be un-English and anti-national? Was I not born upon the same soil? Do I not come of the same English stock? Are not my family committed irrevocably to the fortunes of this country? Is not whatever property I may have depending as much as yours is depending upon the good government of our common fatherland? Then how shall any man dare to say to one of his countrymen, because he happens to hold a different opinion on questions of great public policy, that therefore he is un-English, and is to be condemned as anti-national?[33]

The condemnation, however, continued to be made. Indeed in the 1870s the accusation of being un-English broadened out from reference to Bright, Cobden and pacifists, to include and focus upon Gladstone. Nothing was more common in the Eastern crisis than to dub Gladstone, and by implication the Liberal party, as un-English. Gladstone himself responded to this in the Midlothian campaign, noting how the Conservatives had tried 'to propagate the suspicion that the Liberal party of this country have entirely forsworn and forgotten the land of their birth – that they are a sort of monsters in nature who are willing to lift their hands against the parents from whose womb they sprang'. When the election results of 1880 were known he pointed the moral: 'The party, which termed itself the Constitutional party, the patriotic party, the country party, and the national party, has now seen the NATION rise up and shatter at a stroke the fabric of its power.' For a time indeed, promoting Disraeli as foreign and Jewish, the Liberals accused their opponents of being un-English. Thus in 1883 Sir Edward Hamilton, Gladstone's secretary, described in his diary the habit of wearing a primrose in honour of Disraeli as 'marvellously inappropriate and un-English!' It was not long, however, before the Conservatives could once again throw the taunt of un-Englishness at their opponents: the abandonment of Gordon merited no other description.[34]

A sense of what was properly English and un-English was not confined to foreign affairs. Drawing upon an English ideology of independence, self-reliance and self-help, a stock Conservative response to the issue of social reform was to claim that a socialistic reliance on the state was un-English. In effect Conservatives were trying to utilize the ideology of opposition to the state – to Old Corruption – which had been part of the radical patriotism of the late-eighteenth and first half of the nineteenth centuries; they sought to redirect it towards opposition to collectivism, and to interference by the state in what were seen as the private lives of individuals. 'We English', wrote the Irishman Dunraven, 'seem to be losing all the healthy self-reliance, and preference for self-help instead of State help, that so honourably distinguished our fore-fathers'. The danger to the English, it seemed to many, lay in an increasing reliance on the state, for to do so was to betray the past. 'Their history, their traditions and precedents', wrote the American, Price Collier, in 1909, 'all point away from this modern tendency to lean upon the State. . . . He has studied England in vain if he has not convinced himself that the core of their vigor and enterprise is their independence, their individualism, their willingness and their ability to take care of themselves under all circumstances. This socialistic condition of national life produces men of ignoble economies and timorous patriotism.'[35]

In resisting this encroaching socialism, as they saw it, the patriotism of men like Dunraven was by no means timorous. Possibly it tapped a deep-rooted suspicion of the power of the state. But in its extreme forms it was a type of patriotism of which the Conservative leaders were well advised to be wary. It exposed them, if too vigorously adopted, to the charge that they were opposed to social reform. It suggested indeed that there was an incompatibility between two facets of the creed which Disraeli had proclaimed in 1872: between patriotism and social reform. The Conservative leaders, Salisbury in the van, knew well enough the advantages of playing on the tradition of the Conservatives as the true social reformers. On this issue, indeed, the lines of division within the Conservative party differed from those on other patriotic issues; some patriots, for example Milner, were keen advocates of state-sponsored social reform. In general the patriotism of the self-reliant Englishman was a useful image with which to attack an unknown socialism, but in day-to-day politics it had to be handled with care; there were few working-class votes to be won, and many to be lost, by identification with the Charity Organisation Society.[36] Once again, a patriotic policy was divisive and possibly electorally harmful.

So far we have looked at the language of Englishness and its persistence, and the only limited spread of the concept of Britishness. Connected with this was another conceptual issue which came to the fore after 1886: for what came to be called the Unionist party, the United Kingdom, not England, should have become the focus of loyalty. Initially the label 'Unionist' may simply have facilitated voting for Tories by Liberal Unionists, as a study of Birmingham suggests.[37] Significantly, however, by the early-twentieth century Unionism had come to stand for something wider and more opaque than the maintenance of the United Kingdom. The *Morning Post* in 1908 suggested its possible scope:

> The basis of all Unionist policy is Union. All national questions, whether domestic or Imperial, should be treated in relation to this fundamental principle, implying the union of classes within the State, national union of Great Britain and Ireland, Imperial union of the self-governing nations and dependencies under the Crown.

A Conservative leaflet in 1910 took up the same theme. Unionism meant a United Nation, a United Kingdom, and a United Empire: 'United We Stand'. 'Radical-Socialism' by contrast meant a Divided Nation, a Divided Kingdom, and a Divided Empire. What the voters made of all this we do not know. Possibly the widening of the concept of Unionism was connected with a sense that voters in the early-twentieth century were less alarmed by the idea of home rule than their predecessors had been between 1886 and 1895.[38]

There was, however, a bigger issue than Unionism which the Conservatives, and indeed others, had to face. That was to try to create a patriotism which was imperial rather than national in its scope. The attempt was made in speech after speech, editorial after editorial. It is worth listening to three of the key figures in this campaign of education and instruction. First Bartlett in 1881:

> True liberty, civil and religious, the birthright of Englishmen, has become identified with the supremacy of England in every quarter of the globe. . . . Empire is not less precious than liberty. The possession of Empire is not only of immense advantage to Englishmen, but it serves as a handmaid to liberty. . . . Let the Conservative party then devote itself to these great principles – "Empire and Liberty" – and its future will be assured. To none are they more vitally important than to the toiling masses of these realms. The working men of England are as susceptible of great ideas as any other portion of the community. They are now rallying, as they have not done for generations, to that party which looks to the interest of the nation as a whole, and to the common interests of the beneficent Empire of Britain.[39]

Here is a direct attempt to extend the inherited patriotism of Englishness to Empire, and to appeal on the basis of it particularly to working men.

Turn now to Chamberlain in harder times, trying to promote tariff reform. To a surprising extent his appeal was not to self-interest, but to a wider conception of imperial mission whose leitmotif was sacrifice. 'The British Empire', he declared, 'was acquired by sacrifice from first to last. It was won by sacrifice. It can only be maintained by sacrifice.' The appeal was both to the sanction of the past and to a vision of the future:

> The moral grandeur of a nation depends upon its being sometimes able to forget itself, sometimes able to think of the future of the race for which it stands. England without an Empire! . . . England in that case would not be the England we love.

The evidence is, as Alan Sykes has argued, that in the years 1903–04 Chamberlain failed to mobilize opinion, in particular working-class opinion, which was crucial to his campaign.[40]

Milner, the most thorough-going advocate of an imperial patriotism, was no more successful. He agreed with the saying 'the Empire is my country', hoped that the Empire would become 'a real State', and believed that for a growing number of men 'Loyalty to the Empire is . . . the supreme political duty'; but, 'no word', he noted, 'has yet been coined to describe membership of the body-politic towards which that loyalty is felt. A barbarous term "Britisher" is perhaps an attempt in that direction, but, besides being barbarous, it is not wide enough. . . . Loyalty to the Empire, however inspiring as a motive of action, is not easy to practise at the present time.' Language was again the problem. It was not easy to wean people away from the specifically English patriotism of landscape and cultural tradition in the direction of 'the greater spiritual content of the wider patriotism'. Attempts to liaise with 'patriotic labour' ended in the realization that only isolated and minority sections of the working class would respond to such a creed. It may well be that Milnerism had its attractions for the governing classes who, through the public schools, did come to internalize a sense of imperial patriotism, but outside those sections of the community who had some reason to think of themselves as a great governing race his influence, and the influence of those like him, was minimal.[41]

Or so, at least, largely anecdotal evidence suggests. The working man, claimed H. E. Gorst, son of the party organizer of the 1870s and 1880s, 'never had cared . . . twopence about anything so far removed from cheap beer and improved conditions of labour as imperialism'. H. G. Wells, in *Mr Britling Sees it Through* (1916), thought that 'Nineteen people out of twenty, the middle class and most of the lower class, knew no more of the empire than they did of the Argentine Republic or the Italian Renaissance. It did not concern them.' 'Any allusion to "The Empire"', noted Philip Gibbs in World War I, 'left [the troops] stone-cold unless they confused it with the Empire Music Hall, when their hearts warmed to the name'.[42]

The lack of appeal of Empire is conceded by those who are otherwise keen to argue the link between the Conservative party and patriotism. Thus Blake drew a distinction between patriotism and imperialism: 'the rising tide of imperialist enthusiasm', he wrote, 'did not bring any noticeable electoral dividends to the political party associated with the cause of empire.' It was as a national and patriotic party, not as an imperial party, that the Conservatives stood to gain. Studies of the 1900 election and of the impact of the Boer War have provided evidence for this view, and more recently Patrick Joyce has endorsed Blake's distinction and conclusions: 'The Electorate', he writes, 'did not take the road that led from patriotism to imperialism.'[43]

IV

The failure of the attempt to promote the empire as a focus of loyalty raises key questions about the content and the symbols of patriotism in the age of imperialism. If empire contributed so little towards patriotism, of what then did the latter consist? Did patriots continue to rely on the old symbols, and if so to what effect? What do we make, for example, of the singing of Rule Britannia at strikes and demonstrations?[44]

These are questions which should trouble historians as much as they did contemporaries, for it was not only Conservatives who were concerned about the failure to create a new focus for loyalty in an urban and democratic society. Progressive thinkers pondered the issue with equal anxiety. The dominant social psychology of politics in the early-twentieth century suggested the need for attachments carefully nurtured from infancy upwards. Naturally, it was suggested, a loyalty to family should reach out to the village, and then to the country. But towns were not seen as natural, and in urban civilization patriotism had to be taught in school, and what Reginald Bray called 'a kind of ritualistic patriotism' had to be inculcated. Old games and May Day festivals could play their part.[45] So also, crucially, could song, especially folk song. As Cecil Sharp, the self-proclaimed socialist put it:

> The discovery of English folk-song...places in the hands of the patriot, as well as of the educationalist, an instrument of great value. The introduction of folk-songs into our schools will not only affect the musical life of England; it will also tend to arouse that love of country, and pride of race the absence of which we now deplore.[46]

Graham Wallas was alert to the same needs, and very precisely to those issues of language which I have emphasized:

> We have not even a name, with any emotional associations, for the United Kingdom itself. No Englishman is stirred by the name "British", the name "English" irritates all Scotchmen, and the Irish are irritated by both alike. Our national anthem is a peculiarly flat and uninspiring specimen of eighteenth-century opera libretto and opera music. The little naked St George on the gold coins, or the armorial pattern on the silver coins never inspired any one . . .
>
> The only personification of his nation which the artisan of Oldham or Middlesborough can recognise is the picture of John Bull as a fat, brutal, early nineteenth-century Midland farmer. One of our national symbols alone, the "Union Jack", though it is as destitute of beauty as a patchwork quilt, is fairly satisfactory.

As to the Empire, Wallas argued, the case was even worse.[47]

This concern on the part of progressive opinion to create and promote a cultural patriotism needs to be set alongside the Conservatives' concern with Empire. Neither group felt happy with the outcome of its endeavours. The former never overcame that distrust of the masses which had been deeply implanted during the Boer War, and confirmed by the Chinese slavery issue.[48] The latter were more confident in proclaiming their faith in the masses, but, as the results showed, with little more reason. Both groups were curiously blind to the new focus of loyalty which was at that very time being created: the monarchy. Here, if anywhere, was Bray's 'ritualistic patriotism.' Its creation, as David Cannadine has argued, was largely the work of the three Es: Edward VII, Elgar and Esher.[49] This new emphasis on monarchy was arguably above party – and above class. And it was new. 'Up to the middle of the 'eighties,' Flora Thompson recalled, 'the hamlet had taken little interest in the Royal House. The Queen and the Prince and Princess of Wales were sometimes mentioned, but with little respect and no affection.' The Jubilees changed all that. Throughout the country, and at all social levels, the celebration of royalty took root. Fourteen miles from Manchester at the turn of the century 'in nearly every cottage hung a magnificent almanac portrait of Queen Victoria', and for the coronation of Edward VII Church and Chapel could forget their social differences 'in a wave of heart-felt patriotism'. In the classic slum of Salford a certain prurience lay behind the 'obsessional interest in the life and pedigree of the royal family and aristocracy', but that did not stop coronation days standing supreme among the high days and holidays. In the East End – in Arthur Harding's East End Underworld – 'The people were definitely for the King and Queen. When I saw a royal procession, I used to take my hat off as they went by'.[50]

In 1930 Vita Sackville-West imagined the ideas passing through the heads of the assembled peers waiting in Westminster Abbey for the coronation of George V in 1910:

> It is to be doubted whether one person in that whole assembly had a clear thought in his head. Rather, words and their associations marched in a grand chain, giving hand to hand: England, Shakespeare, Elizabeth, London; Westminster, the docks, India, the Cutty Sark, England; England, Gloucestershire, John of Gaunt; Magna Carta, Cromwell, England.

Outside the Abbey the event doubtless sparked off different associations.[51] But the ritual of monarchy, and the sense of history and of place which it evoked, could overarch a multitude of different and unarticulated thoughts. It was monarchy which provided the new focus for patriotism in the late-nineteenth and early-twentieth centuries. To be successful it had to override, at least at key moments, the loyalties of class, region and party.

V

The Conservative party never ceased to proclaim its patriotism, and the association of the two since Disraeli's time is part of a received wisdom. There were, however, problems in that association. First, while it was relatively easy to organize patriotism, it was more difficult to maintain it at sufficient pitch of enthusiasm; it became a routinized part of machine politics, and consequently lost its force. Second, the adoption of patriotism implied specific and divisive policies. A patriotic lobby within the Conservative party became identified with fair trade, opposition to alien immigration, and an assertive foreign policy. None of these was likely to pay electoral dividends, and the adoption of them exposed the lobby to disreputable elements within the working class. Only in World War I was the identification with patriotism unquestionably advantageous to the Conservatives. Third, the patriotic lobby, whose work on behalf of the party could not be denied, felt a justifiable and expressed grievance at their members' exclusion from the centres of power; they constituted a permanently disgruntled residue within the party. Fourth, the patriotic lobby found it difficult to create a new language and symbolism in an age when patriotism should properly extend to the United Kingdom and to Empire. There were conceivable advantages for a party whose power base was England in an explicitly English patriotism, but such a patriotism was inadequate for those Conservative imperialists who criticized their opponents for their Little Englandism; if Liberal Little Englanders were narrow and inward looking, so also were Conservative English patriots.

None of this implies that parts of the electorate may not, at times, have perceived the Conservatives as the patriotic party, and in accordance with that, voted for them. In truth even the most sophisticated psephological studies leave this question open. What it does mean is that to point to the association between Conservatism and patriotism is to open rather than close the analysis. Patriotism was not unproblematic, and it did not so obviously work to the Conservatives' advantage as it is easy to assume. The Conservative party was not the only focus for patriotic loyalty in an age when few people disclaimed patriotism altogether. Some sought to create a new cultural patriotism out of a newly invented and newly discovered old folklore. But the most potent symbol of the nation, one capable of harmonizing the divergent patriotisms of church, chapel, locality, nation, kingdom and empire was monarchy; and monarchy was above party.

Notes

I am grateful to the owners and keepers of the following manuscript collections for permission to consult and quote from papers in their possession: the Austin Papers at the National Liberal Club; the Chilston Papers in Kent Archives Office, Maidstone; the Hughenden Papers at Hughenden Manor, High Wycombe; the Salisbury Papers at Christ Church, Oxford.

1 Paul Smith, *Disraelian Conservatism and Social Reform* (London: Routledge & Kegan Paul, 1967), pp. 101, 161, 323.

2 Robert McKenzie and Allan Silver, *Angels in Marble: Working Class Conservatives in Urban England* (London: Heinemann, 1968), p. 49; Robert Blake, *The Conservative Party from Peel to Churchill* (London: Eyre & Spottiswoode, 1970), pp. 124, 274; cf. Alan J. Lee, 'Conservatism,

Traditionalism and the British Working Class, 1880–1918,' in *Ideology and the Labour Movement*, eds. David E. Martin and David Rubinstein (London: Croom Helm, 1979), p. 84; 'By the turn of the century the Conservatives were relying increasingly upon a national appeal, shorn of class-specific or other allegiances.'

3 Patrick Joyce, *Work, Society and Politics: The Culture of the Factory in later Victorian England* (Brighton: The Harvester P., 1980), pp. 268–72; R. L. Greenall, 'Popular Conservatism in Salford, 1868–1886', *Northern History,* IX (1974), 123–38; T. E. Kebbel (ed.), *Selected Speeches of the Late Right Honourable The Earl of Beaconsfield,* 2 vols (London: Longmans, Green, 1882), II, 522.

4 See E. J. Feuchtwanger, *Disraeli, Democracy and the Tory Party* (Oxford: Clarendon P., 1968), pp. 122–31.

5 Hugh Cunningham, 'Jingoism in 1877–78', *Victorian Studies,* XIV (1971), 429–54; National Union of Conservative and Constitutional Associations, Publication No. XXXVI.

6 E. Ashmead Bartlett to Corry, 17 November 1878, W. Ashmead Bartlett to Corry, 11 January 1880, Hughenden Papers B/XIV/B/776, 887.

7 E. Ashmead Bartlett to Corry, 9 January 1879 to 2 January 1881, Hughenden Papers, B/XIV/B/790-906; *England,* 27 March 1880; *Times,* 10 March 1881.

8 *England,* 19 March 1881; Reports of the Select Committee on Public Petitions 1881, pp. 93, 116–17, 149–52; for Khartoum petitioning see Reports of the Select Committee on Public Petitions 1884, 21 April–15 July (117 petitions, carrying 33,472 signatures in favour of expedition to save Gordon).

9 *England,* 27 March 1880, 19 and 26 March 1881, 4 February 1882, 8 April 1882, 24 October 1882, 6 November 1886; on the finances of *England,* see Ashmead Bartlett's letters to Salisbury and enclosures, 26 February, 6 March, 10 March, 29 March, 7 July 1883, Salisbury Papers; *Vanity Fair,* 30 April 1887; Richard W. Middleton to Bartlett 21 October 1887, Chilston Papers, 'Political Middleton', Clp. 1, p. 378.

10 On the Primrose League, J. H. Robb, *The Primrose League 1883–1906* (New York: Columbia U.P., 1942) and M. Ostrogorski, *Democracy and the Organization of Political Parties,* 2 vols. (London: Macmillan, 1902), I, 534–52; on later patriotic organizations with Conservative connections see Anne Summers, 'The Character of Edwardian Nationalism: Three Popular Leagues', in *Nationalist and Racialist Movements in Britain and Germany Before 1914*, eds. Paul Kennedy and Anthony Nicholls (London: Macmillan, 1981), pp. 68–87.

11 See my 'Jingoism in 1877–78', pp. 440, 451; *Hereford Times,* 16 March 1878; Benjamin H. Brown, *The Tariff Reform Movement in Great Britain 1881–1895* (New York: Columbia U.P., 1943), p. 16; Stokes' letters to Salisbury, 7 July 1882–85, February 1886, Salisbury Papers; Richard W. Middleton to Sir William Hart Dyke, 15 August 1885 and to Lord George Hamilton, 11 August 1887, Chilston Papers, 'Political Middleton', Clp. 1, pp. 18, 361.

12 See my 'Jingoism in 1877–78', pp. 440–5, 451; Brown, *Tariff Reform,* pp. 31, 37–8, 47–9; John Saville, 'Trade Unions and Free Labour: The Background to the Taff Vale Decision', in *Essays in Labour History*, eds. Asa Briggs and

John Saville (London: Macmillan, 1960), pp. 330–9; Middleton to Salisbury, 16 September 1885, Salisbury Papers.

13　See Brown, *Tariff Reform,* esp. ch. 3; R. F. Foster, *Lord Randolph Churchill: A Political Life* (Oxford: Clarendon P., 1981), pp. 91–2, 108.

14　Colin Holmes, *Anti-Semitism in British Society 1876–1939* (London: Arnold, 1979), pp. 89–93, 104–6; Alan Lee, 'Aspects of the Working-Class Response to the Jews in Britain, 1880–1914', Kenneth Lunn (ed.), *Hosts, Immigrants and Minorities: Historical Responses to Newcomers in British Society 1870–1914* (Folkestone: Dawson, 1980), pp. 107–33; John A. Garrard, *The English and Immigration 1880–1910* (Oxford: O.U.P., 1971), pp. 35–81. For a critique of the view that the Conservatives did not gain from anti-alienism see C. T. Husbands, 'East End racism 1900–1980', *London Journal,* 8 (1982), 3–12.

15　Paul Smith (ed.), *Lord Salisbury on Politics: A Selection from his Articles in the Quarterly Review, 1860–1883* (Cambridge: C.U.P., 1972), pp. 36, 61, 78, 89, 95.

16　Foster, *Churchill,* p. 319.

17　Salisbury to Austin, 17 August 1898, Austin Papers, National Liberal Club.

18　*England,* 30 May 1885; *St. Stephen's Review,* 21 March 1885; obituary in *Sheffield Daily Telegraph,* 20 January 1902.

19　Bartlett to Salisbury, 23 and 25 June 1885, 30 July and 2 August 1886, Salisbury Papers.

20　H. W. Lucy, *The Salisbury Parliament 1886–92* (London: Cassell, 1892), p. 416.

21　Salisbury to Balfour 25 August 1891, quoted in J. P. Cornford, 'The Parliamentary Foundations of the Hotel Cecil', Robert Robson (ed.), *Ideas and Institutions of Victorian Britain* (London: Bell, 1967), p. 295; for Bartlett in Parliament see H. W. Lucy, *The Gladstone Parliament 1880–5* (London: Cassell, 1886), pp. 150–4, 339–40, 451–3; *The Unionist Parliament 1895–1900* (Bristol: Arrowsmith, 1901), pp. 142–6, 246, 384–5; but see also Bartlett to Salisbury, 16 October 1900, Salisbury Papers.

22　The Earl of Dunraven, 'The Future "Constitutional Party"', *The Nineteenth Century,* XIII (April 1883), 684; Bartlett's later career can be followed in his correspondence with Salisbury 1886–1900, Salisbury Papers. The last letter, 2 November 1900, ends pathetically 'I have never had a real chance.' See also Lord Chilston, *Chief Whip: The Life and Times of Aretas Akers-Douglas, First Viscount Chilston* (London: Routledge & Kegan Paul, 1961), pp. 199–200, and *Sheffield Daily Telegraph,* 20 January 1902. For evidence that Bartlett was not alone in feeling excluded from power see Cornford, 'Hotel Cecil', pp. 268–311.

23　G. Dangerfield, *The Strange Death of Liberal England* (London: Constable, 1935), p. 51. The chief contributors to the reassessment of Edwardian Conservatism are G. R. Searle, 'Critics of Edwardian Society: The Case of the Radical Right', Alan O'Day (ed.), *The Edwardian Age: Conflict and Stability 1900–1914* (London: Macmillan, 1979) pp. 79–96, and 'The "Revolt from the Right" in Edwardian Britain', Kennedy and Nicholls, *Nationalist and Racialist Movements,* pp. 21–39; R. J. Scally, *The Origins of the Lloyd George Coalition* (Princeton: Princeton U.P., 1975); Alan Sykes, *Tariff Reform in British Politics*

1903–1913 (Oxford: Clarendon P., 1979), and 'The Radical Right and the Crisis of Conservativism before the First World War', *Historical Journal,* 26 (1983), 661–76; Gregory D. Phillips, *The Diehards: Aristocratic Society and Politics in Edwardian England* (Cambridge, MA and London: Harvard U.P., 1979) and 'Lord Willoughby de Broke and the politics of radical toryism, 1909–1914', *The Journal of British Studies,* XX (1980), 205–24.

24 See John Ramsden, *A History of the Conservative Party: The Age of Balfour and Baldwin 1902–1940* (London: Longman, 1978), pp. 65–86.

25 Blake, *Conservative Party,* pp. 195–6; but see also Ramsden's argument that war was a mixed blessing to the Conservatives (*Age of Balfour and Baldwin,* pp. 110–27).

26 Law quoted in Ramsden, *Age of Baldwin and Balfour,* p. 109; Blake, *Conservative Party,* pp. 216–17. For discontent on the right see Maurice Cowling, *The Impact of Labour* (Cambridge: C.U.P., 1971), pp. 70–90, and W. D. Rubinstein, 'Henry Page Croft and the National Party 1917–22', *Journal of Contemporary History,* 9 (1974), 129–48.

27 Hugh Cunningham, 'The Language of Patriotism, 1750–1914', *History Workshop,* 12 (Autumn 1981), 8–23; Joyce, *Work, Society and Politics,* pp. 292–303; Greenall, 'Popular Conservatism'; Neville Kirk, 'Ethnicity, Class and Popular Toryism, 1850–1870', in Lunn, *Hosts, Immigrants and Minorities,* pp. 64–106; for some non-Lancashire evidence, see John Field, 'When the Riot Act was read: a pub mural of the Battle of Southsea, 1874', *History Workshop,* 10 (Autumn 1980), 152–63.

28 Neal Blewett, *The Peers, The Parties and the People: The General Elections of 1910* (London: Macmillan, 1972), pp. 16–19, 380–9; Blake, *Conservative Party,* pp. 200–01.

29 For Disraeli's choice of the title, *England,* 23 January 1886; for the longer title, *England,* November 1881; for *England's* rhetoric see, for example, 30 September 1882, 3 March 1883, 20 December 1883.

30 Lord Rosebery (ed.), 'The Patriotism of a Scot', in *Miscellanies, Literary and Historical,* 2 vols (London: Hodder & Stoughton, 1921), pp. 111–12; *The Times* cited in H. J. Hanham, *Scottish Nationalism* (London: Faber & Faber, 1969), p. 130.

31 Stanley Baldwin, *On England,* 4th edn (London: Hodder & Stoughton, 1938), pp. 15, 228, 257.

32 Rosebery, 'Patriotism of a Scot', p. 111; McKenzie and Silver, *Angels in Marble,* pp. 54–5; Foster, *Churchill,* p. 259; cf. Searle's comment that the Edwardian Radical Right 'raucously claimed that it stood for an *English* patriotism' (in 'Critics of Edwardian Society', p. 1.86), and Blake's argument that 'Viewed from one aspect the Conservative party should be regarded as the party of English nationalism' (in *The Conservative Party,* p. 273).

33 Fortescue cited by N. McCord, 'Cobden and Bright, 1846–1857', Robson, *Ideas and Institutions,* p. 111; James E. Thorold Rogers (ed.), *Speeches on Questions of Public Policy by John Bright, M.P.,* 2 vols (London: Macmillan, 1869), II, 373–4. For some earlier examples of 'un-English', for which I am indebted to Professor Donald Read, see Norman Gash (ed.), *The Age of Peel*

(London: Edward Arnold, 1968), p. 95, and D. J. V. Jones, 'The New Police, Crime and People in England and Wales, 1829–1888', *Transactions of the Royal Historical Society,* 5th series, 33 (1983), 164.

34 W. E. Gladstone, *Political Speeches in Scotland,* revised edn, 2 vols (Edinburgh: Andrew Elliot, 1880), II, 208, 361; for Liberal attacks on Disraeli, Holmes, *Anti-Semitism,* pp. 10–12; Dudley W. R. Bahlman (ed.), *The Diary of Sir Edward Walter Hamilton 1880–1885,* 2 vols (Oxford: Clarendon P., 1972), II, 425; cf. the Labour candidate's election address in 1906 claiming that the Conservative government 'introduced un-English methods, reversed the most cherished traditions of the British race, left an indelible stain on the honour of old England, and shook the British Constitution to its foundation'. Cited in David E. Martin '"The Instruments of the People?" The Parliamentary Labour Party in 1906,' Martin and Rubinstein, *Ideology and the Labour Movement,* p. 134.

35 Dunraven, 'Future Constitutional Party', p. 697; Price Collier, *England and the English* (New York: Scribner, 1909), p. 423; cf. Ivy Pinchbeck and Margaret Hewitt, *Children in English Society* (London: Routledge & Kegan Paul, 1973), II, 627.

36 Enthusiasts for social reform were always in a minority; see Peter Marsh, *The Discipline of Popular Government: Lord Salisbury's Domestic Statecraft, 1881–1902* (Sussex: The Harvester P., 1978), pp. 161–4, and D. J. Dutton, 'The Unionist Party and Social Policy 1906–1914', *Historical Journal,* 24 (1981), 871–84.

37 C. Green, 'Birmingham's Politics, 1873–1891: The local basis of change', *Midland History,* 2 (1973–74), 84–98; Blewett, *Peers, Parties, People,* p. 15.

38 *Morning Post* cited in Sykes, *Tariff Reform,* p. 195; McKenzie and Silver, pp. 63–4; cf. John Campbell, F.E. Smith, *First Earl of Birkenhead* (London: Jonathan Cape, 1983), pp. 348–9; Blewett, *Peers, Parties, People,* p. 399.

39 *England,* 1 January 1881.

40 Sykes, *Tariff Reform,* pp. 59–61, 77.

41 Lord Milner, *The Nation and the Empire* (London: Constable, 1913), pp. xii, 488–9; J. O. Stubbs, 'Lord Milner and Patriotic Labour, 1914–1918', *English Historical Review,* LXXXVII (1972), 717–54.

42 H. E. Gorst, *The Earl of Beaconsfield* (London: Blackie, 1900), p. 151; H. G. Wells, *Mr. Britling Sees it Through* (London: Cassell, 1916), pp. 207, 425; Gibbs cited in Paul Fussell, *The Great War and Modern Memory* (London: O.U.P., 1975), p. 201.

43 Blake, *Conservative Party,* pp. 163–4; Joyce, *Work, Society and Politics,* p. 301. For the Boer War and the 1900 election, see H. Pelling, *Social Geography of British Elections 1885–1910* (London: Macmillan, 1967) and 'British Labour and British Imperialism', in *Popular Politics and Society in Late Victorian Britain* (London: Macmillan, 1968), and Richard Price, *An Imperial War and the British; Working-Class Attitudes and Reactions to the Boer War, 1899–1902* (London: Routledge & Kegan Paul, 1972). See also the critique of Pelling by K. O. Morgan, 'Wales and the Boer War – a Reply', *Welsh History Review,* IV (1969), 367–80.

44 Raphael Samuel, *East End Underworld: Chapters in the Life of Arthur Harding* (London: Routledge & Kegan Paul, 1981), p. 263; David Cannadine, 'The Transformation of Civic Ritual in Modern Britain: The Colchester Oyster Feast', *Past & Present,* 94 (1982), 115.

45 Reginald A. Bray, 'Patriotism and Education', Lucian Oldershaw (ed.), *England: A Nation – being the Papers of the Patriots' Club* (London and Edinburgh: Brimley Johnson, 1904), pp. 200–33. This book with contributions by G. K. Chesterton, C. F. G. Masterman, R. C. K. Ensor, Hugh Law, Henry Nevinson, J. L. Hammond and Conrad Noel is the best single source for assessing the depth and content of the patriotism of progressive opinion; cf. P. F. Clarke, 'The Progressive Movement in England', *Transactions of the Royal Historical Society,* 5th series, 24 (1974), 159–81.

46 Sharp cited in Dave Harker, 'May Cecil Sharp be Praised?', *History Workshop,* 14 (Autumn 1982), 59.

47 Graham Wallas, *Human Nature in Politics* (London: Constable, 1908), p. 80; cf. Martin J. Wiener, *Between Two Worlds: The Political Thought of Graham Wallas* (Oxford: Clarendon P., 1971).

48 'No student of history or of the psychology of the crowd', wrote G. P. Gooch in 1901, 'can retain illusions as to the wisdom of multitudes'. See *The Heart of the Empire* (London: Fisher Unwin, 1901), pp. 323–4; cf. Wallas, *Human Nature,* pp. 107–8; H. G. Wells, *The New Machiavelli* (London: Fisher Unwin, 1911), p. 278.

49 David Cannadine, 'The Context, Performance and Meaning of Ritual: The British Monarchy and the "Invention of Tradition", c.1820–1977', in *The Invention of Tradition,* eds. Eric Hobsbawm and Terence Ranger (Cambridge: C.U.P., 1983), pp. 120–38.

50 Flora Thompson, *Lark Rise to Candleford* (London: O.U.P., 1971), pp. 261–71; Margaret Penn, *Manchester Fourteen Miles* (Firle: Caliban Books, 1979), pp. 145–9; Robert Roberts, *The Classic Slum* (Manchester: Manchester U.P., 1971) pp. 145–6; Samuel, *East End Underworld,* p. 263.

51 V. Sackville-West, *The Edwardians* (1930; Harmondsworth: Penguin, 1935), pp. 249–50; for other views of the coronation see John Merriman Gaus, *Great Britain: A Study of Civic Loyalty* (Chicago: U. of Chicago Press, 1929), pp. 42–3.

CHAPTER ELEVEN

Socialism, the state, and some oppositional Englishness

Stephen Yeo

Here in England, we have a fair house full of many good things, but cumbered also with pestilential rubbish. What duty can be more pressing than to carry out the rubbish piecemeal and burn it outside, lest some day there be no way of getting rid of it but by burning it all up inside with the goods and house and all?

William Morris, "Art, Wealth and Riches" (1883)

"First point," began Mr. Smollett. "We must go on, because we can't turn back. If I gave the word to go about, they would rise at once . . . Now, sir, it's got to come to blows sooner or later. . . . We can count, I take it, on your own home servants, Mr. Trelawney?"

"As upon myself," declared the squire.

"Three," reckoned the captain, "ourselves make seven, counting Hawkins, here. Now, about the honest hands?"

"Most likely Trelawney's own men," said the doctor; "those he had picked up for himself, before he lit on Silver."

"Nay," replied the squire. "Hands was one of mine."

"I did think I could have trusted Hands," added the Captain.

"And to think they're all Englishmen!" broke out the squire. "Sir, I could find it in my heart to blow the ship up."

Robert Louis Stevenson, *Treasure Island* (1883)

To articulate the past historically, Walter Benjamin said, "means to seize hold of a memory as it flashes up at a moment of danger." For several decades we have been living through a continuous "moment of danger," so that our history and past culture presents itself to a danger-alerted mind, searching for evidence of democratic endurance and resources of cultural strength and growth. And some part of that cultural inheritance cannot but be "national" in character, with its own particular pressures, resilience and idiom; this must constitute not only some part of what we think and feel about but also some part of what we think and feel with. These resources are unusually large and complex in this island; they are, by no means, always resources of strength, but. . . . If a future is to be made, it must be made in some part from these.

E. P. Thompson, "Foreword" (1978) to
The Poverty of Theory and Other Essays

in all probability England will go first – will give the signal, though she is at present so backward.

William Morris, letter to William Allingham, 26 Nov.1884

Keep smiling through

It is tempting to begin this section with a smile. We would situate ourselves, say, in a recent English 'radical populist' moment between 1940 and 1948 when 'Britain in Pictures' books were being produced by Collins (G. M. Young's *The Government of Britain*, Neville Cardus's *English Cricket*, Edith Sitwell's *English Women*, Edmund Blunden's *English Villages* were examples. George Orwell's *The British People* was announced but done as *The English People* [1947]). We would smile, with them, on things English, including Socialism. That was a moment when Englishness seemed to carry with it all kinds of radical possibilities, as in British Way and Purpose booklets issued by The Directorate of Army Education between 1942 and 1944, or as in J. B. Priestley's 1940 'Postscripts' broadcast on the BBC. The smile might be somewhat condescending: it would certainly blur England and Britain. Going about England in a British state which had long been annexing other nations has been a favourite form of mystification here. Behind the myths of 'Englishness' lies the reality of imperialist Britain. One third of the Britain in Pictures books had 'English' in their titles: Priestley came straight out with it, 'and when I say "English" I really mean British'.[1] Nevertheless we would be assenting to a range of things, including a leaning towards the countryside, towards craft, towards 'getting things done' rather than ratiocinating for ever, towards middle-class angst, charm, irony and self-deprecation, towards independence (sturdy), towards the voluntary rather than the compulsory, variety rather than uniformity, towards an openness to the Romantic critique of capitalism and Protestant invention rather than towards scientific authority, towards continuous organizations of working people . . . and so on – all very real, and all capable of articulation in positive ways during positive times. We would be assenting to some of what 'English' culture pitted against Fascism during the 1940s and to some of what George Orwell, for a time, articulated. His subtitle for *The Lion and the Unicorn* (1941) was 'Socialism and the English Genius'.

But in present times (writing late in 1984), and in the present company of this book, such a smile would scarcely be sufficient.

Flesh and Blood, in the cupboard

Would a grimace be any better? Situating ourselves in an earlier moment, the main one of this book (1880–1920), a grimace could also be appropriate. In one of the 1920 Home Office *Reports on Revolutionary Organisations in the United Kingdom,* 'attention is called to the opinions of working men taken at random on the subject of revolutionary agitation'. Under the heading 'What the Working Man thinks':

> A correspondent who has conversed with workers selected at random in various London industries finds that they all have a hearty dislike for the alien and are inclined to resent the dragooning methods of Trade Unions. A linoleum layer remarked that he hated the Unions – they were the bane of the country. England used to be a free country but now, thanks to the Unions, the life of his class was tyranny. He would like to see powder and shot used freely amongst the Labour leaders and the Jews.[2]

Henry Hyndman, leader of the Social Democratic Federation, Britain's pioneer Marxist organization, would then enter, himself grimacing. 'I am', he would say (1883), 'quite content to bear the reproach of Chauvinism in regard to what I say about the English-speaking and Teutonic peoples'. 'We have to base the first real Socialistic combination upon the common interests and affinities of the great Celto-Teutonic peoples in America, in Australia, in these islands and possibly in Germany.'[3] Winds changed over the next thirty years. Hyndman's face got fixed. In 1910 he upheld,

> the right and duty of this nationality to maintain its independence, even under capitalism. . . . There is no mistake about that. If this is to be a jingo, then I am a jingo; if this is to be a bourgeois, then I am a bourgeois.[4]

By April 1916 Hyndman found himself forming a National Socialist Party no less, against those in the British Socialist Party who stood for internationalism.

Then Ben Tillett could enter, speaking at the founding conference of the Independent Labour Party in 1893:

> he would sooner have the solid, progressive, matter of fact, fighting Trades Unionism of England than all the hare-brained chatterers and magpies of Continental revolutionists.[5]

The grimace would turn to sad laughter as we watched the genius of the *Clarion* newspaper, Robert Blatchford, confess in October 1899 that perhaps he too was, after all, a jingo. He had felt obliged to answer Tillett in the *Clarion* in 1893. But in 1899 he gazetted orders to his daughter 'to play Rule Britannia every night while the war lasts'.[6] The blimp had always been one of Blatchford's many faces. John Smith of Oldham, the 'practical working man' to whom the letters expounding socialism in *Merrie England* had been addressed in 1894, had been told that:

> this, then, is the basis of Socialism, that England should be owned by the English, and managed for the benefit of the English, instead of being owned by a few rich idlers, and mismanaged by them for the benefit of themselves.[7]

By the time of *Britain for the British* (1902) nationalism had bitten deeper into the substance of Blatchford's socialism. Our argument would then be, quite correctly, that there was a lot of such 'Englishness' about in labour and socialist circles during the late-nineteenth and early-twentieth centuries.

As examples accumulated we might, however, forget what they are examples of, namely the imbrication of late-nineteenth and early-twentieth century English socialists in a culture which was indeed xenophobic and in which the 'nation' – usable by earlier patriots for radical purposes – had now been partly lost to imperialism.[8] Socialists, unless isolated, do take on the colour of their surroundings. Nationalism *does* penetrate socialism to the extent that the latter is located rather than flown in from the outside. Such facts tell one, maybe, about nationalism and socialism but nothing much, in these bald forms, about Englishness – in its specificity – and socialism.

We might also forget that the intention and sometimes the function of labour and socialist *organization* was, precisely, to produce the possibility of alternative colouration. Thus, one of the reasons for the Socialist League's break with Hyndman in December 1884 was his 'attacks on foreigners as foreigners or at least sneers at them: coquetting also with jingoism in various forms'.[9] Against this William Morris educated, agitated and organized around an exemplary combination of love of place (mainly bits of England) with principled resistance to Nation and to State. Morris loved where he lived. He wished to transform it so that everybody could share his affection, finding in place – as another poet William Carlos Williams did – the 'true core of the universal'. 'I am not ashamed', he wrote in 'Early England' in 1885, 'to say that as for the face of the land we live in, I love it with something of the passion of a lover'. Ben Tillett's outburst in Bradford in 1893 did not go unanswered at the time. Keir Hardie called on Edouard Bernstein, the German fraternal delegate, to reply from the platform.[10] Nor did Blatchford's buffoonery pass unrebuked. Photos of him were defaced in many socialist club rooms after 1899.[11] And Hyndman's 1910 quotation mentioned earlier went on, 'if this is to be an opponent of organised socialist opinion, then I am an opponent of organised socialist opinion'.

Having distanced the modern reader from Second International English Blimpery, which got even uglier between 1914 and 1918, our argument could end by confirming that of course nation-hood, and in particular this England's nation-hood, has nothing to do with the socialist project. We would repeat the litany that socialism is international, nowhere unless everywhere, nothing if not everything, never if not always, etc. This could slide into saying that it was, is, will be, elsewhere but not here. With disdain resembling that of Matthew Arnold writing about the 'Hebraism' of English nineteenth-century nonconformist culture, we would contrast twentieth-century continental 'Hellenisms'/Marxisms with 'the failure of British society to generate any mass socialist movement or significant revolutionary party in the twentieth century – alone among major nations in Europe'. 'In England a supine bourgeoisie produced a subordinate proletariat.'[12]

Before the idea of Englishness, England, and its State

Walking against that particular run means trying to rehearse some of the factual bits about England which have emerged from more ambitious historical work. Such facts cannot but set limits to the theme of this book, and they cannot but affect socialism, particularly in so far as they bear upon the public realm or state, for this realm has been, for the most part, socialism's chosen sphere of operation.

'Facts' make it sound too simple; Engels' 'a contradictory state of affairs' might be a better phrase. Writing in 1892 'On certain peculiarities of the economic and political development of England', he got quite exasperated:

> By its eternal compromises gradual, peaceful political development such as exists in England brings about a contradictory state of affairs. Because of the superior advantages it affords, the state can within certain limits be tolerated in practice, but its logical incongruities are a sore trial to the reasoning mind. Hence the need felt by all "state-sustaining" parties for theoretical camouflage, even justification, which naturally are only feasible by means of sophisms, distortions and, finally underhand tricks.[13]

Such exasperation is all too intelligible now, in England in 1984. Particularly since it followed a time, during the 1840s in Engels' case, when things had seemed so much clearer and more hopeful. Now in the 1980s again 'sore trials to the reasoning mind' are not lacking, after a post-war boom (during the 1950s and 1960s) when to people of my generation (b.1939) things seemed clearer and more hopeful.

Four connected points may serve, not to cut through the exasperation but at least to turn it outwards. The points may best be made in a compressed way first, and then with illustration from a range of recent work. First, in England (along with much else besides), the State is very old. Second, even in its 'modern' or capitalist forms it goes back a long way: not a single event but 'the great arch'. Third, 'it', the State, is not really an 'it' separate from the rest of social relations, but has been integral to the development of those relations even in their 'modern' or capitalist forms. The capitalist 'private' likes to contrast itself with, or even pretend to do without the State 'public' realm; but the two – in their modern forms – are sides of the same coin. Fourth, there have been formidable pressures working against such simple propositions becoming apparent. These include the very age of the State 'thing' itself, making it easy to reify or abstract the State, and the pressures include those versions of capitalist apologetics which suggest that capitalism is a 'private'/'economic' affair, 'free' from the 'public'/'political' realms. These pressures have been breaking up very fast recently. But the consequences for socialism of giving in to them – that is, regarding the State as an 'it' and an ally to boot – have been formidable and are still very much with us. It has come as a considerable shock to contemporary English socialists to realize that the 'public' State is as much of a problem for them (as much a site for reconstruction) as is the 'private' firm.

England had been a State and a Nation for some centuries before the 1880s, the era of the socialism which called itself 'Modern' in order to jettison 'primitive', pre-'scientific', 'utopian' ideas and methods.[14] If all this chapter can do is to put in place, in England, a particular State – at a time when there are formidable pressures to say that it has been weak, disappearing, less than bourgeois (or more), not a problem for socialists, not an instrument for capitalists and the like – that may be a contribution worth making. As a Nation – 'a body of people kept together for purposes of rivalry and war with other similar bodies' – England was building on a domestic empire from at least the thirteenth century. As a State – 'that is, the nation organised for unwasteful production and exchange of wealth'[15] – an English apparatus of modernity (written record, coherent sovereignty, common currency, reliable revenue, lawed property, sanctified contract) was infusing relations of production from about the same period. Things (relations) happened early here. There was a lot for a long time to have ideas of Englishness about.

This is particularly important with reference to the State. The definite article is itself indicative: *the* State – not a State or some States – slips easily onto the page. Socialists as well as everyone else have tended to reach for this definite article, as if to hold the object constant, making it into an 'it'. '"It", in short', wrote Doris Lessing in a terrifying study of disintegration of all relations between citizens and State, 'is the word for helpless ignorance or of helpless awareness. It is a word for man's inadequacy'.[16] By thinking of an 'it' we have helped to deceive ourselves with the notion that 'the State' could be called upon to redress the wrongs of 'private' capital. That capital should get away with calling itself 'private' is part of its achievement in keeping the 'private' capitalist. It has taken the crisis of the 1980s to let us (socialists anyway, others got there before) begin to grasp the distinctively English and then capitalist forms of the public, or State sphere. The public did not, here, completely eclipse the private: indeed in their modern senses they were exceptionally interdependent. Not to grasp this is to allow ourselves to reach for a hand-me-down Thing (not seen as a relation or set of relations) called The State, to miss an epoch of active capitalist formation, and thus to expect The State to be an easy ally in a future non-capitalist project.

One encouragement to such reification or abstraction has simply been the age of the thing (relation) itself, its 'extraordinarily centralised monarchy', 'the oldest centrally organised state in Europe', 'a royal state unrivalled in its authority and efficiency throughout Western Europe'.[17]

> A national economy is a political space transformed by the state as a result of the necessities and innovations of economic life into a coherent, unified space whose combined activities may tend in the same direction. Only England managed this exploit at an early date.[18]

No matter whether it was ever finished, it was in 1279 that Edward I could begin a survey, the stated purpose of which was to settle questions of ownership once and for all:

> Commissioners in each county were instructed to list by name and have written down in books all villages and hamlets and every type of tenement whatsoever, whether of the rich or the poor, and whether royal or otherwise. . . . No enquiry by any medieval government ever exceeded this one in scope or detail.[19]

Philip Corrigan has described successive 'long waves' in the formation of the modern English State from the thirteenth century onwards. In his 1965 essay on 'The Peculiarities of the English' Edward Thompson used the metaphor of a 'great arch' of bourgeois civilization in England, in no way springing from 'industry' alone: he invited us to think of that linguistic mess but coherent force in England, a rural bourgeoisie, in active dalliance with political power not just at 'moments' but over a whole epoch.[20] The distinctively modern idea of the State as 'a form of public power separate from both the ruler and the ruled, and constituting the supreme political authority within a certain defined territory' emerged in England, if traced through language, in 1535.[21] Not surprisingly, longevity has discouraged analysis and imagination from playing upon the object's past.

Since capitalism is all too often associated with industry (rather than with agriculture or with finance), the old clothes the English State possesses and delights in taking out whenever 'state occasion' offers excuse may also serve to conceal its distinctively *capitalist* nature. The usual camouflage is the adjective 'modern'. But 'this is an old European country': 'a substantial body of professionals who were directly employed by the state . . . and whose vocational justification lay entirely in serving the state's needs, as opposed to [sic] private needs' has been noticed before 1730.[22] As phrases about efficient government machines, homogeneous governing classes, improvement, an exceptionally reverenced State and so on are repeated in the literature on the peculiarities of England – and are pushed back to refer to the late seventeenth and eighteenth centuries or before[23] – we have to keep pinching ourselves. This is the site of 'free' capitalism being talked about, this is England, not some Caesarist, State Socialist, Asiatic, Prussian Other Country. How much, and for how long, here, a particular state or form of state (learning to call itself '*the* State') has been imbricated in freeing freedom for those who most call themselves and others (as in 'free labour') free! How much the attachment of Liberty to Property has depended upon a particular construction of 'the State'. And it was so done that it would be *assumed* here: contrary, perhaps, to dominant impressions, Adam Smith's visions were underpinned by such a firm assumption.[24] So was the work of 'more modern capitalists':

> By the end of the Napoleonic Wars, the more modern capitalists in the towns had already achieved considerable strength on the basis of their economic achievements which, as modern historians now stress, had a long history behind them. Under the leadership of the landed classes, much of the road had been smoothed for them. The English capitalists in the nineteenth century did not have to rely on a Prussia and its Junkers to achieve national unity, tear down the internal barriers to trade, establish a uniform legal system, modern currency, and other prerequisites of industrialisation. The political order had been rationalised and a modern state created long before.[25]

'A modern state'. . . . The definite article has gone, but the adjective 'modern' still gets in the way. Because this 'modern state' during the twentieth century *has,* in a certain sense, been inherited or granted (or so it has seemed to many Modern Socialists), there have been formidable pressures not to see it clearly, in fact to take it for granted. Mists have surrounded it, as they do antiquity, suggestive of lies like the one that it was not very important in the making of 'private' capitalism anyway, or like the one that it has been aristocratic and therefore less than fully capitalist, or like the one that it will evolve into something suitable for socialism organically, without human agency or class re-construction.

Recent work in a recent English – and world – crisis (visible from the early 1960s onwards) has been dispelling such mists. Wallerstein has traced 'the emergence of capitalism as a *political* (my emphasis) phenomenon' on a world scale:

> the sixteenth century witnessed the creation of a system of geopolitical states within whose borders production, consumption, and taxation occurred and economic and demographic phenomena played themselves out. . . . In this sense, then, the emergence of the state was as important to the development of capitalism as the loans and advances of the bankers and traders were to the survival of the underfinanced, corruption-ridden states. . . . The formation of nations legitimated, first, the survival and, later, the hegemony of the capitalist system.[26]

It did not need Modern Socialism to assert the primacy of politics. In a brilliant comparative study of 'The State and the Industrial Revolution' in 1973, the current editor of the *Economic History Review,* Professor B. E. Supple, inclined on the whole to stress the role of the market in England. Almost against himself, however, he came to an exceptionally sharp theoretical understanding of the State. He puts most socialists to shame:

> the state becomes an institutional device (perhaps the most important institutional device) by which groups seek to secure ends which, in other circumstances, they might conceivably secure by private means. . . . And the important point to remember is that the state enters the arena of industrial development not as an arbitrary and unpredictable force, but as the agent of "old" or "new" forces or classes within society, acting either in their own self interest or in pursuit of an ostensibly national purpose, within which their role can be rationalised. The state, like the entrepreneur, or the labour movement, is a social phenomenon.

And, in Britain's case, he conceded that 'the very characteristics of the market environment which distinguished Britain's position from that of other European countries' – for instance 'an unmatched degree of political stability and social harmony' – were 'in large part a function of state action'.[27]

Such imbrication of 'the state' in capitalism, it is now widely realized, puts the problem of *a* state squarely back on English socialist and oppositional laps. It requires us to try to break up old and comfortable structures of thought and organization. This can be disturbing whether done from the Left or the Right:

> to regard the state as a potentially (let alone necessarily) democratic form representing in some sense the public as against the private interests is to

succumb to . . . the "fetishism of representation." For if we recognise that capital from its inception always had two spheres of social economy – the market/private property (or commodity) economy on the one hand, and the levy bounty (largely state) economy on the other . . . then it will be clear that the distinction between public and private is a distinction of two forms of capitalist economy . . . the state is no more "democratic" or "representative" of the exploited classes than is I.C.I. – albeit that one represents itself as public and the other as private.[28]

Cut to 1984: The modern Leviathan

How much there is, in England, to go beyond! But what a lot there is (still?) to go beyond with!

As an English representative at an Italian Socialist Party (P.S.I.) historical conference on Trade Unions and the Working Class in the Second International in Turin in 1981, I found myself being interviewed by a correspondent from the Communist daily, *Unita*. The conference had been disappointing, being not only about the Second International period but also enclosed within its categories. It was also lavish, feeling like a demonstration by the P.S.I. that they too could put on prestige cultural events – just like the Italian Communist Party. The journalist pressed me to criticize it. He had a Communist Party axe to grind. Wanting to criticize but not wanting to grind the same axe, I had little time to think. Rather than retreating into the specialist topic of the paper I had brought to the conference I came out spontaneously with something which met with blank incomprehension from him as it would have done from any P.S.I. people. I said that when we found ourselves discussing large forms as pregnant with possibilities of another epoch as things (relations) like Medici banks had been in pre- and early-capitalism, and debating their preliminary performance and future possibilities, we might be getting somewhere towards the goals we said we shared. I said that, maybe, trade unions (the subject of the conference) were such forms, recalling Marx of 1866:

> unconsciously to themselves, the trade unions were forming centres of organisation of the working class, as the medieval municipalities and communes did for the middle class . . . they are . . . important as organised agencies for superseding the very system of wage labour and capital rule.[29]

If so, they were certainly not being discussed in such a way. Where, I asked, were our 'organised agencies' with which, at such a conference, we might be comparing historical notes, as to their roots, opportunities and obstacles? Maybe, I asked him, he thought that actually existing Soviet socialisms were, or contained, such forms? Or the P.C.I. itself, in all its hugeness?

I did not know and nor, it was obvious, did he. All I did know, on reflection, was that I was thinking in these ways not 'spontaneously' (as Sheila Rowbotham wrote recently 'spontaneity requires a lot of organising') but because of a whole spate of recent writing and practising in England which was re-presenting socialist politics. Attempts at theorizing, and practising (in the double sense of that word) 'the transition', were being made in new ways. Their specific gravity, as it were, in the culture, was greater than their actual size. Focussing on the details of the division of labour between mental and manual, conception and execution, men and women; upon class and labour processes and on what a socialist politics of complex cooperation might look like; on the politics of use values from labour's point of view; on the details of the experience of particular associational forms; on the meanings and possibilities of 'private labour' as against capital; on restructuring by and for labour, going through society to the state; all were making it possible to ask questions, to educate, agitate, organize in new places and in new ways. The Robin Murray quotation on the state used above was part of all this, as was a whole cluster of initiatives stemming from a formation known as the 'new left'. This formation now has considerable, if temporary, power in local government, working in *and* against the State.

Certainly, a renewal of thinking on 'a state' or some states in this specific context is central. If it is socialist to think in epochal, revolutionary terms – in terms of a future epoch other than barbarism but as different from capitalism as capitalism's predecessors were – there are, to put it mildly, considerable transformations to make, or to discover. And in England there is a lot of State, as it were, to go beyond. What are or would be socialist forms of commensuration, of private and public relations, of centralism, of locality, law, contract, history, production, making things (relations) – above all, through all, State?

To think like this is to live, in England in 1984, with a profound sense of defeat. I felt it painfully, through a rising sense of personal insignificance, as I wrote out the P.S.I. conference anecdote mentioned earlier.

England is, after all, the place where 1984 could be conceived as such, and not as a commentary only on cold war communisms but also on advanced – even English – metropolitan capitalism. Winston Smith's nightmare has a very English location. And we are now beginning to get a clear, conscious, articulation of the nature of the modern leviathan coming first from the Right and more slowly, from the Left.

The weight of 'Our Island Story' (the H. E. Marshall history book which was my own childhood introduction to the subject) has indeed been considerable, enough to get anyone stuck. If not as jagged as an alp on the brains of the living, it has at least the dull, depressing presence of a line of downs. In its national or Whig version, the story is presented with so much deliberate continuity that results tend to eclipse processes. How dissident it now is (all over again) to see 'our' (*The*) State as an association or union, to be dissolved and returned to its members (us) for reconstruction!

That was Tom Paine's vision. But against him a pasteurized version of Edmund Burke has won the argument down to today, with the counter-revolution of his *Reflections*. Each generation, he proposes, is responsible not to itself but to a future buried in a past, to the dead and the unborn as well as to the living. 'The frame of our commonwealth *such as it stands*' is in trust to us rather than our tool. 'The very idea of the fabrication of a new government is enough to fill us with disgust and horror.' In the name of such fear and novelty, the English State (and then the frozen details of its actual institutions) has been reified as part of 'the great primeval contract of eternal society'.[30] In such a permanent contract all breaches are to be hidden, past as well as future-possible. So, big lies get told, as 'jubilant celebrations of English political continuity' and in very big imposing books. The lies are about the Norman conquest as restoration, about 1688 as an example of continuity rather than change, and much else besides. As late as the 1870s William Stubbs thought that the seventeenth century should not be taught to undergraduates. It was too close to contemporary politics! The lies appeared as myths on town hall walls, in Almanacks and in statues of Victoria and Albert dressed as Anglo-Saxons, as well as in the work of Eminent Historians.[31] The function of such elegant fibs has been to make the nineteenth-century 'transition to democracy' appear to retain – and to an important degree actually retain for 'the Englishman' – some continuity with 'His Past'.[32]

The mystifications have been profound. This Englishman can still remember the satisfaction on his schoolmaster's face and the puzzlement in this 13-year-old brain when the master said in the same (English, as it so happened) lesson two things. He first said that 'we', of course, had no Constitution. Lesser nations had those. But second, the Monarchy was there to take over from the Commons if extremists threatened to win control. The Kilbrandon Report (1973), with the promising title of a Royal Commission on the Constitution, turned out to be about the technical, party consequences of different schemes of 'devolution'. The constitution, in the sense of the sovereign (Parliament), and 'the essential unity of the United Kingdom', remained as given, unquestionable inheritances. The State in the United Kingdom has been allowed to hide behind a sacrosanct Crown-in-Parliament ('Be it enacted by the Queen's most excellent Majesty, by and with the advice and consent of the Lords Spiritual and Temporal, and Commons, in the present Parliament assembled.'), and democracy to hide behind 'Parliamentary democracy as we know it'.[33] As Seeley complained in *The Expansion of England* (1883) 'the temptation of our historians is always to write the history rather of Parliament than of the State and the Nation'.[34] And as Nevil Johnson found when he went *In Search of the Constitution,* almost a century later, 'there is probably no other country in which Parliament occupies such a special place in the political structure and in the language of politics'. 'There are many in Britain who profess to believe that only the British Parliament is a genuine species of the genus

"Parliament" . . . the English often refer to parliament when other people might talk of the law, or the people, or the State'. More recently the government ('of the day'), like the Emperor in the Hans Andersen story, tries to put on the fine robes of the state ('from time immemorial'), and few subjects now dare to laugh in the streets.

The English revolution now gets seen as 'settlement', for Englishmen. Thus *The Times* in 1979 revealed that

> the difference so stubbornly insisted upon in Ulster concerns the most fundamental of all political issues: allegiance, national identity, the legitimacy of the State, matters which Englishmen had settled for themselves by the end of the seventeenth century.[35]

Historians of the extraordinary rupture in human history represented by the 'modern' (capitalist) world also now emphasize that, in the English as in so many revolutions, what came after was cousin to what went before. In his brilliant *Lineages of the Absolutist State* (1974), Perry Anderson knew what 'deep and radical reversal' of the most characteristic traits of prior feudal development 'there was in the transition to the capitalist epoch' in England. But he also showed how 'a centralised monarchy . . . produced a unified assembly'.[36] The degree of centralization which exists in the English, and then British, polity is now widely recognized because it is so firmly insisted upon from that centre, against all comers, and against strongly surviving myths of localism. Even jokes against the French, even with reference to their educational system, look a bit less funny in England in 1984. A unitary state emerged here in the modern era in which the omnicompetence of the sovereign (Parliament) was to become as clear an impediment to constellations of popular power as the divine right of Kings had been:

> The sovereignty of the British state is not in the British people as in most electoral democracies but in this special definition of "Crown in Parliament." British adults are not citizens but, legally, *subjects,* in that old term derived from absolute monarchy.
> . . . in terms of the actual constitution it may not be the House of Lords but the House of Commons that is anomalous.[37]

Parliament is not, of course, omnicompetent. Without referring to it, as William Morris did, as the Westminster dungmarket, some might say that it is not even competent. That is not the point. The point is that its alleged writ runs everywhere; every other Board, sub-Nation, Public Corporation, Authority, local government unit, union, civil servant, branch of the judiciary derives its authority (or is increasingly seen to do so) in the end, and sometimes disturbingly near to the beginning, from it. And not even from it (Parliament). Lines of power called 'responsibility' go direct to Ministers, whose authority is in turn subordinate more and more to the Prime Minister. Nevil Johnson found Ministerial Responsibility to be one of the main sources of uniquely British centralization. Personal rule prevents other clusters of ('constitutional') legitimacy, and Ministers can get very hot under the collar indeed, and about 'the British constitution' too, when they feel it might be being usurped. For a Secretary of State for Defence to appear on television face-to-face with the leader of C.N.D. was seen by Michael Heseltine in 1983 to be unconstitutional. It took a German King, George II, to grasp the realities here. He murmured once to Lord Chancellor Hardwicke, 'Ministers are Kings in this country'. 'That', observed Nevil Johnson (by no means a left-winger), 'is the core of it all'. 'Furthermore', he went on, 'Britain is distinguished from most other comparable societies by having no genuine concept of public law, and thus no proper public law structure which defines powers and by so doing creates barriers.'[38]

'Politics' (and with it 'Democracy'), as part of all this, has been more and more confined to licensed, dominant, official forms thereof: to forms of association which legally cannot, or do not threaten to take 'Politics' capital letter away from it. Thus, forms of delegation which have been elementary components of English, voluntary, working-class, liberal practice for 200 years now get pilloried as 'Eastern European', 'Party rule', 'unconstitutional/ un-English', and they become the cause of seismic splits within the culture, breaking apart the Labour Party. One major cause of the Social Democratic Party rift was precisely these issues, in a tragi-comedy of Shirley Williams saying 'Burke' to imaginary Paines. There was an uncanny anticipation of such splits in February 1906 in the report of a Special Committee of the Fabian Society 'appointed to consider measures for increasing the scope, income and activity of the Society'. At least the Fabians, as they tended to do at that time, made themselves clear:

> Democracy is a word with a double meaning. To the bulk of trade unionists and labourers it means an intense jealousy and mistrust of all authority, and a resolute reduction of both representatives and officials to the position of mere delegates, mouthpieces and agents of the majority. From this point, Democracy would find its consummation in a House of Commons where, without any discussion, divisions were taken by counting postcards received from the entire population on questions submitted to the people by referendum and initiative.
>
> Because the Fabians have given no countenance to this attitude they have been freely denounced as undemocratic and even Tory. Fabian democracy is in fact strongly opposed to it and certain to come into conflict with it at almost every step in the practical development of socialism. We have always accepted government by a representative deliberating body controlling an expert bureaucracy as the appropriate public organisation for Socialism. When asked where government by the people comes in, we reply that Government has to be carried out by division of labour and

specialisation as much as railway management has; and what Democracy really means is government by the consent of the people . . .

Between these two conceptions of the elected person as representative doing the best he can according to his own judgement after full discussion with other representatives of all shades of opinion, and as a mere delegate carrying out previous instructions from the majority of his constituents, there is a gulf which will sooner or later become a party boundary, and this gulf unfortunately cuts the Labour Movement right down the middle.[39]

In a long crisis of democratic theory and practice, 'Representation' in the sense of 'making present in continuing and interactive ways those who are . . . represented' has given way to other, more professional, hierarchical, and symbolic senses of the word.[40] Allegedly Burkean notions of the license due to a representative have been used to conceal a critique of the idea of political representation as such, which was emergent well within nineteenth-century Liberalism. Political re-formation ('the fabrication of a new government') in any extended sense gets classified as dissident, revolutionary, subversive, illegal, the use of industrial/educational/cultural . . . power for political ends. In 'democratic' theory as well as in practice in twentieth-century Britain, the citizens have become the governed, consumers rather than producers of 'policies' displayed intermittently as 'packages' in a political market place (at General Elections) to which only big suppliers have the capital for real access. Democracy has become a set of actually existing institutions to be defended – if necessary at the cost of killing everyone, including the unborn – rather than a process or struggle with a future, as it was within Liberalism. 'Parliamentary' attached to democracy is now, in 1984, 'in effect an excluding adjective to indicate that there is only one real kind of democracy, which operates through the procedures of a parliament'.[41] So, from the Right we get diagnostic phrases like 'elected dictatorship' and from the Left the 'election of a Court'.[42]

If it can now be seen how many spaces have been closed down, the extent to which the Left in general has been an agent in their closure has also become distressingly visible. This will be a major theme in the remainder of this essay. To anticipate, the Labour party in particular may be seen as active in this process of closure. During the twentieth century the party has almost entirely retreated from civil society, and from organizing private labour. Unions are its sources of funds but also, from the leadership's point of view, its main embarrassment. Autonomous action by them (solidarity) is a threat. It has long ignored Co-ops and friendly societies and clubs and other associations-for-Labour. Even its own movement or party or constituency is seen as problem rather than as opportunity. 'Voluntary action' has been seen by the party as a contrast to its politics rather than a component. And in the public, political sphere it chose early on to conform to existing, dominant forms. Keir Hardie was quite open about it, in his advice to the I.L.P. in 1901. Their party, he advised, 'aimed at becoming a great political power in the land'. 'To enable it to do so it must conform as nearly as possible to the political institutions already in existence with which the public mind is familiar.'[43]

To complicate the story once more, it is important not to moralize any of this. Large determinations are involved, going way beyond ideology, intention or simply condemnation. As a result of developments beyond Labour's control, one, and the most available, choice to Labour *has* been to conform. It is through such delicate, agonized, tactical conformity (including electoral pacts, accepting minority power, and then the role of His Majesty's opposition, and attempting to become the natural party of government) that the party has built up its strength. It has indeed become a precondition for one kind of success (electoral, official, legitimate) of Labour politics that it should accept such confinement. And the rewards have been considerable. The party *did* govern, and through the existing State it *did* deliver necessary reforms to working people, securities of a tangible kind, through job protection, welfare, health and safety, pithead baths, spectacles and so on. Sweated trades would never have retreated spontaneously, and to the extent that Labour is weakened such trades will (and are) advancing all over again.

It is just that for some time now it has been a hard argument to mount within the dominant forms of Labour *and* socialist politics that it is the *forms* of State and politics that must be challenged before 'policies' have any hope of being fought for in a sustained way by the people in whose interests the policies have been allegedly formulated. To argue for political *forms* rather than *policies* is to sound obscurantist. But *who does what* will have to have as much to do with working-class socialism as what is to be done. During the second half of the nineteenth century, Liberals went further in challenging emergent forms of capitalist politics than Labour has done since then. They worried about representation, party machines (including the details of canvassing), politics and the manufacturing of opinion much more than twentieth-century Labour has done. Defeat can easily feed despair: a sense of loss of the future, once falsely guaranteed by attaching an evolutionary idea of Progress to socialism, can easily contribute to a sense of loss of *any* future. As sub-nations within the United Kingdom have been outmanoeuvred in the last two decades, and then sub-state associations for labour like trade unions, and then subnational units of ('local') government, it does seem tempting to conclude that we have indeed entered the New Leviathan's cage. Is it all we can do to regret, with Nevil Johnson, 'the absence of any alternative tradition of how to constitute political authority?'[44]

Yeast was in that dough

To recall that futures other than that hugely dominant present have been available within the English past is the historian's special opportunity. 'Nor should you', as Brecht advised, 'let the Now blot out the Previously and afterwards'.

'Such a peculiar mixture of yeast and dough', remarked John Fowles of the English middle class in *The French Lieutenant's Woman,* 'we tend nowadays to forget that it has always been the great revolutionary class; we see much more the doughy aspect'. What was the quality of the yeast, and how available has it been (or is it still) for other baking, other class projects?

How much which is integral to socialist construction was already happening, in England, long before Modern Socialism, within and against capitalism!

a) More generally

To follow such an assertion through is difficult. This is because *contradiction* is involved (back again to Engels' 'contradictory state of affairs') – long moments, in England, of what E. P. Thompson has called 'co-existent opposed possibilities'. And contradiction is always hard to represent at any level of generality.

To realize and to articulate a contradiction is to look for the spaces within which it moves rather than to get impatient and simply negate or 'abolish' it.[45] In so much of the best writing about the transition to modernity/ capitalism in England there is this sense of articulated contradiction, of dialectic, of *not-only-but-also* rather than *either/or.* There is a sense of epoch rather than 'at a stroke' revolution. There is a sense of long *construction* and of one social formation emerging through another. Capitalism is a dynamic system which discloses (and depends for its dynamism upon disclosing) possible successors, especially, perhaps, in its earliest moments: and the more prolonged its 'rise', the longer the disclosure. As capitalism turns the world upside down, for however brief a period before destabilization, its underside is exposed ('prostitute realities laid bare' in Marx's vivid phrase): grooves are cut for it to turn again whoever, by then, may be on top. It is thereafter, as the saying goes, a topsy-turvy world. To the extent that capitalism depends upon breaking relatively simple, customary relations of power, of inherited domination and subordination, it offers the possibility of displacing its first beneficiaries or owners – which is why from very early on, but latterly with more viciousness and hurry, STOP signs, for counter-revolution, have to be put up. From the point of view of the security of the bourgeoisie, it is generally the case that too many people have to be discouraged from taking too many of its (the bourgeoisie's) passages and promises too seriously. It is the bourgeoisie's burden that each of its vehicles clearing its own steep and rugged pathway can (must? anyway in England *did*) carry other, antagonistic social possibilities. Our very idea of 'the transition' to socialism as something (some relations) to have different ideas about – to have debates in the labour movement about – comes, both in idea and in fact, from the transition to capitalism from previous modes. It is this earlier transition which 'must constitute not only some part of what we think and feel about but also some part of what we think and feel with'.

Law, reason, 'freedom', each promises to go beyond exclusivity. The commodity as the 'first citizen of the world' constantly threatens to walk out, beyond nations, states and individual owners – and to become available for socializing in new ways. Alienable 'private' property, 'freely' disposable, is volatile. However often the adjective 'bourgeois' is thrown over the noun 'democracy', it never completely covers it: the noun always seems capable of escaping the adjective, falling into other hands, being transformed, growing bigger, being realized.

The possibility of such goods becoming genuinely public, or universal, is inscribed in their enclosure or privacy. Indeed, in the hands of the bourgeoisie on its long, English march, these goods characteristically promise, at times, in the end – in that favourite capitalist distance, the long run – to include everyone, to become universal. And the *dimensions* (social length, depth and width) of capitalist construction here, in England, made this double-edgedness doubly so. The moments of co-existent opposed possibilities have been many and long. The bourgeoisie, as it were, hung it all out (democracy, law, freedom, etc.) for a long time, long enough for others to get a good look, use, and see beyond. Much which elsewhere in the world in the twentieth century was to be produced hothouse fashion by post-capitalist regimes already had deep outdoor roots in England. This meant that much which, if it was to be produced elsewhere at all, would have to be Socialism's product could, here, have been its tools or even its inheritance.

This includes some of the ingredients of *any* revolutionary State. These were here very early – like class and class struggle for example. According to one authority at least, there was a *class* of capitalist farmers in England by the end of the sixteenth century.[46] To use a colloquialism, a class is a grouping able to get its act together: materially able at least to attempt to construct or to defend ways of making things (relations) which can inform a whole social formation and then make a 'society'. Without this, construction in and against (but also beyond) one society towards another is inconceivable. Class projects are articulated against other social groups or classes, and in England bourgeois class formation/struggle took place in a long social movement *against* an early centre.

In spite of all which has been said so far in this essay, the particular forms of state, here, meant that it could seem – and to an extent actually be – quite local, with representation by place rather than by social layer, local justice being voluntary and so on. Centralization there was indeed, but without some of the things (relations) which went with it elsewhere. A strong standing army was missing, as was a royal absolutism possessing, for any length of time, a taxation base independent of Parliament, as was a ruling bureaucracy 'under which the instruments of public power became exercisable in a uniform way'.[47] It was the concentration of sovereignty *and* its dispersal through real, located, agents – in a material unity of opposites – which made it effective and made it cohere. A degree of self-administration in the counties was a medium for effective royal power even in feudal England, before the much vaunted J.P.s of the early-modern epoch.[48] One of J. H. Plumb's themes in his famous 1966 Ford Lectures was, precisely, the realization (rather than the abolition) of contradictions between accumulations of local power and central authority. Either could have broken apart from the other or never formed part of the same field-of-force. This would have made for a very different subsequent English (and thus British and thus world) modern history.[49]

Clusters of initiative, independence, enterprise ('capital') found room to accumulate but also found, literally, canals to join them. England already formed 'something like a single internal market' by the late-seventeenth century.[50] Like all markets this implied coherence, but also diversity: activity could be diffuse because it was also integrated. Clusters of activity grew in the Country away from but related to the Court, forming 'Civil Society' separable from but defined in relation to a State. 'Civil society as such develops only with the bourgeoisie' (in the German, *bürgerliche Gesellschaft* stands for both the bourgeois and civil society). But precisely because it (civil society) 'transcends the state and nation' and 'embraces the whole material intercourse of individuals within a definite state of the development of productive forces',[51] it is a concourse for change. 'The private spheres' winning 'an independent existence' and out of that 'free' independence constructing novel forms of private-public relations were a very basic passage in human history:

> the political constitution is brought into being only where the private spheres have won an independent existence. Where trade and landed property are not free and have not yet become independent, the political constitution too does not yet exist.[52]

'Independence' may be understood materially, *that is,* as having to do with things like means of association (political constitution), ways of making things (means of production), means of enjoyment, education, exchange, and so on. Understood in this way, its potential for 'private labour' as well as for 'private capital' becomes obvious. As Michael Walzer traced in his *The Revolution of the Saints* (1965), it was indeed a revolutionary step, leading into and beyond capitalism, to construct and associate in the interstices of one social formation in such a way as to necessitate, to enable, (even to plan) another.

The contradictions become exceptionally difficult to elucidate because, as capitalism develops, the lines of future-possible victory for any emergent social formation seem to run closer and closer to the lines of defeat by the dominant host. What is success and what is failure or rather *whose* is the success and whose the failure get harder and harder to distinguish. As systems advance, victory and defeat take place more and more through the same instruments and in the same spaces: for example, through the instruments and spaces of 'the State' 'based on the contradiction between *public* and *private* life, on the contradiction between *general interests* and *private interests*'.[53] The magic formula 'after the revolution' would note that these contradictions will wither away for socialists. State regulation of the hours of labour in nineteenth-century England (Factory Acts, the subject of the longest chapter in Marx's *Capital* volume I), for example, was at once helpful to large-scale industry *and* a germ of future-possible socialization of capital on labour's terms. A reform which was functional for large-scale capitals was also exciting to Marx as the first clear victory of the political economy of labour over that of capital. 'What a great change from that time!' 'The English factory workers were the champions not only of the English working class, but of the modern working class in general, just as their theorists were the first to throw down the gauntlet to the theory of the capitalist.' 'Since the contest takes place in the arena of modern industry, it is fought out first of all in the homeland of that industry – England.'[54]

By the mid-nineteenth century in England, historical materialism could be forged. It could be forged among the mills of industrial capitalism in the 'shock city' of a major moment in capitalist development: Manchester. And it could be forged with and *about* something, some actually existing as well as future possible relations. About what? About how capitalism worked from outside – explanations of its mechanisms with 'here cause, there effect' – but also about how, materially it c(w)ould change, be transformed, from within, through lots of (working) people's own practices and consciousness.

Engels' exasperation at the peculiarities of the English expressed during the 1890s has been quoted already. Fifty years before that, in the period immediately following his first visit late in 1842, those same peculiarities had excited him and educated him (and through him Marx) greatly. He was much clearer about England in the mid-1840s than he became by the 1890s. In a fascinating essay on 'Engels and the Genesis of Marxism' (1977) Stedman Jones has traced Engels' openness to and transmission of crucial raw elements for the theorizing of historical materialism between 1842 and 1845–46. In and from England he learnt of the possible primacy of real social (class) movements rather than abstract 'principles' in the making of a new epoch; he learned of the strength of 'interests' over against 'ideals'/ideologies; and he learnt of just how far actually existing changes in industry, and consequently in the subject matter of large-scale politics, were *already going on* in England:

> the importance of Engels' contribution derived less from his moments of theoretical originality than from his ability to transmit elements of thinking and practice developed within the working class movement itself in a form in which it could be an intrinsic part of the architecture of the new theory.[55]

How much which is integral to socialist construction was already happening, in England, long before Modern Socialism, in and against capitalism!

b) Less abstractly

It might be helpful to be a little less general. As an early British Socialist said, 'the use of abstract, as of general terms, without explanation or limitation, and of similar mystifying, is one of the means employed to delude labourers and hide from them their interest'.[56]

First, we may overhear a mid-eighteenth century dock worker. *Lloyd's Evening Post* for 18–21 July 1760 reported the following 'Dialogue between an Artificer in a dockyard and those who required his vote in the next election for Kent':

> *Officer:* We are come, expecting your vote for Sir William, in the room of Mr. W . . ., made a Lord. . . . The Government espouses Sir William, and you are a Freeholder.
>
> *Artificer:* I am so, but must think myself at liberty to vote as I please.
>
> *Officer:* As you please! Very fancy, truly; don't the Government employ and pay you?
>
> *Artificer:* Yes, and I honour the Government, know my business, and earn my pay with diligence and honesty.
>
> *Officer:* But are you not under their power, and obliged to do as they please?
>
> *Artificer:* Yes, as an Artificer, but not as a Freeholder . . . I am, as an Englishman, at liberty to chuse my representative.
>
> *Officer:* And the Government to turn you out of your bread.
>
> *Artificer:* Not so indeed. I do my duty as they expect, and this is a case where they can have no just reason for resentment . . .
>
> *Officer:* We did not expect this obstinacy; and to prevent its spreading, we will report it, so you have warning.
>
> *Artificer:* I will be as early as I can in reporting it myself, and am glad, Gentlemen, this is all the ill report you can make of me.[57]

Our nameless Artificer worked in the national (royal) dockyards. Before the factory system these were the largest units of industrial organization, indeed 'larger than anything seen in Europe since the fall of Rome'.[58] As often with such exceptionally large capitals they were nationalized. Working in such a place, the Artificer had relative job security. Shipwrights had begun to associate, for themselves. A society or union had started, not as a trade union in the modern sense (though a union of tradesmen) but as a co-operative society.[59] Production on their own account had commenced, with a bakery at Chatham, a butcher's shop in Deptford, and a cornmill in Woolwich. The Red Flag had been hoisted near the mill. Attempts were made by antagonists of the shipwrights to drive such associations out by law. These failed. Then one Sunday night the mill was mysteriously burnt down.

What the Artificer was doing in the reported dialogue was to insist 'as an Englishman' that the historic bourgeois achievement (still of course very much in process in 1760 rather than a finished result) of making the 'economic' relatively autonomous from the 'political' (and thus 'free') could work towards his independence – and that of his fellow 'freeholders' – rather than his subordination. He was taking 'freedom' seriously. It would be a long time – a whole epoch in fact – before, if ever, the economic and the political could be reunited in the interests of everyone equally. Meanwhile, the Artificer implied, 'me too', or rather, 'us too' as far as public-private relations were concerned. To put it another way, he was insisting on some autonomy for himself in a public sphere. Furthermore, 'as an Englishman', because of England and its history, he was confident that his liberty to choose was legitimate: 'I will be as early as I can in reporting it myself.' Being in some waged sense its servant did not, he thought, imply that 'the Government' owned him. He and his co-workers had private spaces to associate on their own account, to make their own societies. And the forms of their association, as the law-suits and arson showed, were to put it weakly, not identical to the capitalist ones around. Extended they might even reconstitute the existing 'public' altogether. But they were, our English Artificer thought, legitimate.

A generation later, in 1796, another artificer – a Shoreditch silversmith called John Baxter – published an 830 page *New and Impartial History of England*. Those were dangerous times for Radicals, members of Corresponding Societies like Baxter: they were days of vigorous, vicious reaction. Baxter himself became a fellow prisoner with Thomas Hardy during the treason trials of the time.[60]

Baxter's book was a kind of *samizdat,* claiming specifically English (back to the Saxons) rights to resistance or subversion. From a shared store of language, myth and precedent he reached backwards in time in order to make going forward legitimate. That there *was* a shared store is the point. 'Baxter's "Saxons" were Jacobins and sans culottes to a man.' '"Pristine purity" and "our ancestors" became, for many Jacobins, almost any constitutional innovation for which a Saxon precedent could be vamped up.' The *New and Impartial History* worked with the idea of an original English constitution subverted by foreign conquest, partly restored at various times including 1688, but with much 'restoration' (which could amount to revolution) still to be done.

Plebeian radicalism, fecund as it was in ideas and associational forms, claimed Englishness, English history, the English constitution, the *nation* and (a key word) 'patriotism' for itself and its class, over and against usurping, parasitic governments. 'The People' (another key phrase) claimed to have English history and the English constitution on their side. One climax in this history was the Chartist Convention of 1839. There was an array of means of political/social production available in England, from the Address, to the

County Meeting, to the Petition, to the Convention, to the emergent Press. New ones such as the Platform were to be added during the nineteenth century. Of them all, Association and Combination are probably the most contested (right through to 1984) and the least understood. The 1839 Convention was assembled to present one of the old constitutional devices, the Petition, – but in a modern, mass, form – to Parliament, on behalf of political reform. If rejected, however, the idea among some activists was to pass on to ulterior measures and to indulge in the fundamental business of a convention-constitution-making. Ulterior measures were proposed. These had mainly to do with withdrawing material support from the existing system, to weaken it and to enable independence.

But an Englishman did not have to be a socialist or even a Chartist to be fanatical about the details of self-government. In the years after 1845 one Joshua Toulmin Smith (1816–69), for instance, took up a sustained and scholarly struggle against utilitarian, Chadwickian 'improvement' and centralization. He took care to distance himself from the Six Points. But he was a dedicated opponent of what he saw as an emergent system of 'Functionarism and Bureaucratic control'. The main enemy, as he saw it, was a collectivism which 'would in fact put the whole earth in commission and deliver over the whole human race saved from the flood to "Inspectors" and "Assistant Commissioners"'. His 'improving' enemies were uncomfortably like some actually existing state systems constructed by Modern Socialists.[61]

And yet to see Toulmin Smith's observations as 'early' is to open a familiar way of marginalizing them. It is to be tempted to say that, for serious opposition, they had to be superceded: a definitive 'break' had to be made with this pre-scientific English stuff, a break often seen as epistemological and as having to do with Mar*xism:* the new science.

Yet Marx himself went on working with the grain of some convergent facts and movements in English capitalism – as well as other capitalisms – through the rest of his working life. Of course, that was part of brushing against the grain of other dominant facts and movements. But there was plenty to work with. 'Only in England', Engels thought during the 1840s,

have individuals as such, without consciously standing for universal principles, furthered national development and brought it near to its conclusion. Only here have the masses acted as masses, for the sake of their interests as individuals; only here have principles been turned into interests before they are able to influence history.

'The democracy towards which England is moving is a *social* democracy,' he thought:

The English, a nation that is a mixture of German and French elements who therefore embody both sides of the antithesis and are for that reason more universal than either of the two factors [German philosophy, French politics] taken separately, were for that reason drawn into a more universal, a social revolution.[62]

In the developing work of Marx and Engels through the next three decades there was a powerful sense of how materially possible it was becoming to alter relations, to endow them with social possibilities (in the sequence from moral to political to social). There was the emergent presence of large-scale industry, in the sequence from simple co-operation, to handicraft, to manufacture to 'machinofacture' which is so basic to the substance of *Capital* volume I (1867). In this adequately-capitalist form of modern production, labour was really subordinate, newly divided from the means of production which now included science of knowledge. In the new relations of production,

> the co-operation of wage-labourers is entirely brought about by the capital that employs them. Their unification into one single productive body, and the establishment of a connection between their individual functions, lies outside their competence. These things are not their own act, but the act of the capital that brings them together and maintains them in that situation. Hence the interconnection between their various labours confronts them, in the realm of ideas, as a plan drawn up by the capitalist, and in practice, as his authority, as the powerful will of a being outside them, who subjects their activity to his purpose.[63]

But in and against such developments there was also the material promise of labour's ultimate 'education', or emancipation, as well.[64] Also in *Capital* I was the articulation of the

> protracted and more or less concealed civil war between the capitalist class and the working class. Since the contest takes place in the arena of modern industry, it is fought out first of all in the homeland of that industry – England. The English factory workers were the champions, not only of the English working class, but of the modern working class in general, just as their theorists were the first to throw down the gauntlet to the theory of the capitalists.[65]

Factory legislation was functional to capital, giving advantage to large capitals in their quest for relative surplus value. It did no harm to productivity, or to the quest for relative surplus value. But it was also, in its later forms, more than a nominal concession won by labour. In 1864, indeed, Marx referred to the Ten Hours Bill as 'the first time that in broad daylight the political economy of the middle class succumbed to the political economy of the working class'. 'An all-powerful social barrier by which they can be prevented from selling themselves and their families into slavery and death by voluntary contract with capital' had been erected. It may have been a 'modest Magna Carta' but 'What a great change from that time!'[66] How excited was Marx with the potential of a class in the act of coming together. As we saw earlier with the unions:

> unconsciously to themselves the trade unions were forming *centres of organisation* [his italics] of the working class, as the medieval municipalities and communes did for the middle class. If the trade unions are required for the guerilla fights between capital and labour, they are still more important as *organised agencies for superseding the very system of wage labour and capital rule.*[67]

Writing in 1864, Marx was also excited by the possibilities of the co-operative movement. The seeds of this had been sown, he thought, in England by Robert Owen. It would get nowhere if 'kept within the narrow circle of the casual efforts of private workmen'. It needed to be national and political in aggregate. This never meant, for Marx, an entire eclipse of the private and economic by the public and political. The revolutionary project is to hold the two together, to reconstruct them both. The third of the Provisional Rules of the International, drafted by Marx, read, 'that the economical emancipation of the working-classes is therefore the great end to which every political movement ought to be subordinate as a means'. The 'value of these great social experiments cannot be overrated.'

> By deed, instead of by argument, they have shown that production on a large scale, and in accord with the behests of modern science, may be carried on without the existence of a class of masters employing a class of hands; that to bear fruit, the means of labour need not be monopolized as a means of dominion over, and of extortion against the labouring man himself; and that, like slave labour, like serf labour, hired labour is but a transitory form, destined to disappear before associated labour plying its toil with a willing hand, a ready mind, and a joyous heart.[68]

In a footnote to *Capital* volume I, Marx played with the 'philistine English periodical, the Spectator' in its reaction to 'the Rochdale co-operative experiments'. '"They showed that associations of workmen could manage shops, mills, and almost all forms of industry with success, and they immediately improved the condition of the men but they did not leave a clear place for masters." Quelle horreur!'[69] In *Capital* volume III it was suggested that 'a new mode of production naturally grows out of an old one'. Socialization of capital on capitalist terms (joint stock, credit, etc.) had made possible transitional forms of socialization on labour's terms, 'transitional forms from the capitalist mode of production to the associated one'.[70]

Marx knew of the formidable class resistances there were and would be to seeing any contradictory forces in capitalism *as* contradictions ('moments of co-existent opposed possibilities'). 'The vulgus is unable to conceive the forms developed in the lap of capitalist production separate and free from their antithetical capitalist character'.[71] Particularly when it was working people acting for themselves, all kinds of denials happened:

> It is a strange fact. In spite of all the tall talk and all the immense literature for the last sixty years, about the emancipation of labour, no sooner do the working men anywhere take the subject into their own hands with a will than up rises at once all the apologetic phraseology of the mouthpieces of present society with its two poles of capital and wage slavery . . . as if capitalist society was still in its purest state of virgin innocence, with its antagonism still undeveloped, with its delusions still unexploded, with its prostitute realities not yet laid bare.[72]

How much yeast there was, for Marx, in that dough!

Working people in England took quite a range of subjects into their own hands during the second half of the nineteenth century, and on a considerable scale. 'Union' had long been a key word, so that even though *trades* union was slow to grow (not reaching majority status till after World War I) other forms became very important. At first under reforming, middle-class, subsidising, 'vice-presidential' patronage, they stood the tensions (e.g., over questions of styles of sociability), and then found ways of casting the patronage off. 'Independence' was another key word. One of the ways to independence was precisely to go *national* through affiliated forms: to find ways of getting small sums from very large numbers of people rather than the other way round: to find ways of spreading the risk, in order to make for *continuous* association, rather than earlier intermittent and local association. They also pressed for political change through Industrial and Provident Society legislation, at the level of the State. Considerable cultural creativity was involved in all this. Indeed it is here rather than in books or other artefacts that we should look for 'Working-class culture' in nineteenth-century England. Going into 'Union' as in the Co-operative Union, or the Working Men's Club and Institute Union, or the Trades Union Congress, or nonconformist 'Unions' (federating earlier sectarian forms) was one such invention, which itself had financial strength. Friendly Societies, Co-operative Societies, Clubs, chapels and educational groupings grew very large, strong and continuous by the early-twentieth century.

Some contemporaries were, almost against themselves, mightily impressed. A visiting Austrian, J. M. Baernreither, studied the culture in some detail. He thought it constituted a 'revolution'. 'It would be an entire error,' he argued, 'to suppose that the English workman does not extend his thought to the distant future, or picture to himself one very different from today; but in his acts and conduct he reckons with present facts, and he employs the freedom of movement which he enjoys without limit in his associations, to obtain one thing after another'. He called it 'the social self-government of the working classes in England'. 'We must not forget that all these associations have become the governing centre for the various branches of social administration which they manage, and that the influence they exercise on the relations of wages, the system of insurance, the food-supply, and the intellectual training and education of the working class collectively, extends far beyond the association itself, and benefits also those who are outside it.'

> England is at present the theatre of a gigantic development of associated life, which gives to her labour, her education, her social intercourse, nay, to the entire development of her culture, a pronounced direction, a decisive stamp. The tendency towards the union of forces and the working of this union are now-a-days more powerful in England than ever, and more powerful than anywhere else. The free union of individuals for the attainment of a common object is the great psychological fact in the life of this people, its great characteristic feature. This union of individual forces has operated even there, where adverse relations have sought to restrain it; but now, freed from all fetters, and yet at the same time under discipline, it has become a mighty moving wheel of social development in general, and especially in the elevation of the working classes. Since the repeal of the laws prohibiting Combinations (1824), which has been the turning-point in the history of the English working class, the working-men's associations have gained immensely in importance; they have become more organized, more enlightened, more firmly established. The power of union, the capacity of submitting to the lead of others, the pertinacity and energy which they display in the pursuit of fixed aims, are amazing. In the course of the last decade these associations have become more and more differentiated, according to their various objects, and are now well-defined, economic, and legal institutions. The combination of the earlier, more scattered and disconnected groups into great centralized associations has extraordinarily increased their power.[73]

Baernreither's ideal English workman went from workshop to Foresters' Hall, from trade union to public meeting, using to the full all the 'private' spaces there were in civil society to move towards a new one, utterly different, he thought, from the exploitative order of the early industrial revolution. His emphasis was on *men* throughout. He held his hand over the unreconstructed family like almost all men of his time, and since. Women were thus kept at home as the doubly exploited gender. J. M. Ludlow, introducing the 1893 edition of Baernreither's book, thought that it was a matter of the public sphere catching up with 'a new class of men':

> The progress made in the methods of production of the present day, which depends on the ever-increasing application of mechanical power,

has brought the working classes everywhere into a wholly new position towards society. . . . Concurrently with this progress should have gone a complete transformation of the relations of this class to society in point of private and public rights; but while the modern modes of production created, so to speak, a new class of men . . . the legislation and the public institutions . . . remained far behind.

Baernreither saw it as a change from working-men's associations being 'narrow-minded representations of self-interest', to them acquiring 'a public character'.[74] Private labour was claiming for itself, collectively, the same rights and the same (but necessarily adapted because multiplied) forms as private capital. The adaptations were necessary and profound. The similarities were not seen as pale imitations but as full-bodied replacements. It was a culture of detail and of connection. Connections were made between spheres of activity kept separate elsewhere, such as education and material consumption and production, or sociality and insurance, or entertainment and collective self-help. The details of how ancillary activities should be run so as not to conflict with central aims were thought out, and accessible forms of democratic control worked for. There was thinking, for instance, on details like *where* voting should take place in quarterly elections, in branch stores or central stores? Would de-centralization mean loss of coherent interest? There was thinking on canvassing, on what forms choirs should take in Co-operative Societies, on attendance at meetings in relation to payment of subscriptions, on whether 'treating' at the bar was a form of patronage, and so on. A special correspondent writing for *The Englishman* in 1910 was impressed by 'The Truth about the Working Men's Clubs.' He claimed that the clubs, more than any other organizations in London, tended to develop 'that class confidence without which the class consciousness of the Socialist is useless. . . . Their success is a signal proof of the capacity to administer and to organise inherent in the working classes'.[75] Some of the sources of 'Englishness' already described were also tapped by these associations, with Co-operative Societies tracing their kinds of direct democracy back to medieval guilds or even to the Saxons, and with Friendly Societies using a lot of medieval, Foresters, 'Robin Hood' type imagery.

Some spokesmen discussed the aims of these associations in relation to Socialism, especially those with Owenite memories. George Jacob Holyoake, for instance, wanted to propose a familiar English lineage:

Persons favourable to the organization of the social state which Robert Owen had incited to action came to be called "Socialists" . . . Continental Socialists meditated rearranging society by force. There never were in England any philanthropists of the musket and the knife. English Socialists expected to improve society by showing the superior reasonableness of the changes they sought.[76]

By the end of the century, J. M. Ludlow was worried. What he understood as Socialism seemed not to be dominant any longer in the culture. 'In these days,' he wrote during the 1890s

> when the term "Socialism" is sought to be narrowed in the using to this or that particular system, and the patent meaning of the word, and its history in this country as well as elsewhere, are so grossly overlooked that "Co-operation" and "Socialism" are actually treated as antagonistic, both by men who call themselves Socialists and by men who call themselves Co-operators, one cannot too strenuously insist upon the cardinal value of Mr. Maurice's declarations. . . . "The watchword of the Socialist is Co-operation; the watchword of the anti-socialist is competition." Anyone who recognised the principle of Co-operation as a stronger and truer principle than that of competition has a right to the honour or the disgrace of being called a Socialist.[77]

But 'socialism' was not a key word in this associational culture. And here we get to the kernel of the rest of this essay. In the above quotation Ludlow was running his finger along a major fracture in English culture, going through 'socialism' and, in effect, breaking it apart. There have been many socialisms here, many competing versions of a related project. For their full, completed realization whole new versions of the public/private, new states, new civil societies, but called something else, new whole societies would have had to be held together in living active tension. These new versions would have had to be as different from their predecessors as capitalist ones had been, still negotiating contradictions, no doubt, but in different spaces, within different fields of force. With all the inheritance of State already described, and with all its connected Civil Society, there *was* a powerful working-class associational culture running through much of nineteenth- and twentieth-century English society, probably at its strongest c. 1870–1930. At various points I have referred to this as 'private labour'.

This constituted a preparation, a major resource, no, a *precondition* for the construction of any society as much of and for working people as capitalism was of and for the bourgeoisie. And it was especially strong in England. But this culture did not, on the whole, call itself 'socialist'. And it tried to pass the State by on the other side. It tended towards anti-Statism. This was partly because those who came to call themselves 'socialist' were either intent on taking over, 'capturing' the State rather than transforming it (Statists). Or they had projects of supervision and transformation, but in the interests of a social group other than the working class. This group, in shorthand, may be referred to as the Professional and Managerial Class, and its project as Collectivism.

To Statism and Collectivism we shall return. In the associational culture, autonomy, collective self-help, independence, an open-ended idea of progress, and connection were key values. The effort was to do without masters as much as possible: if members were to be servants it had to be in a grander cause than existed below stairs. Most people in such movements would probably have voted, if they could vote, Liberal, for most of the time. A quintessential figure like J. T. W. Mitchell (1828–95) – 'the most remarkable personality that the British Co-operative Movement has thrown up' (Beatrice Webb) – would certainly have done so. At the end of his life he stood in local government elections as a Radical Liberal in Rochdale. But to admit him and his project – Chairman of the C.W.S. between 1874 and 1895, and the main actor in its project – into Liberalism is to extend our understanding of the meanings of that term. Holyoake called it 'deliberate Liberalism'. The Co-operative Wholesale Society vision was nothing less than to take over all of production. At the 1887 Co-operative Congress Mitchell saw that

> there was no higher form of co-operative production upon the face of the earth than the Wholesale Society manifested in its co-operative works. . . . He would start productive works, when they would pay, in every centre in the United Kingdom; and would never be satisfied until the Wholesale manufactured everything that its members wore. . . . If co-operation was to be permanently successful we should have to finally settle this question – To whom does profit and the increment of value belong? He held that as it was created by the industrious classes it belonged to them. . . . He advised co-operators never to be satisfied until they got control of the entire producing, banking, shipping and every other interest in the country. The Wholesale had £100,000 in consols, and in course of time co-operators might possess the whole of the National Debt of this country. If co-operators saved their money they might in time possess the railways and canals, besides finding employment for themselves.[78]

Through supplying all the needs of autonomous, but affiliated member stores, the Wholesale would, in the end, get into manufacturing and exchanging and banking everything. The project was to unite capital and labour in the same body. At the Royal Commission on Labour in the early 1890s, one can feel the amazement of a socialist like Tom Mann at Mitchell's cool ambition. And well into the twentieth century the CWS still had a position from which to offer solid critiques of the main directions political labour was taking. Their magazine *The Producer* ('with which is incorporated The Consumer') in 1917 editorialized thus (there had just been a Labour Party Conference in Manchester):

> With all its teaching and agitation, its preaching and writing, its local and Parliamentary representation, the Labour Party does not yet seem to have realised that for the economic betterment of the common people collectively-owned fields, factories and workshops are better than speeches and resolutions; they could, in fact, be made more effective in the economic welfare of the workers than almost any kind of legislation. When we are treading the paths of national legislation we are upon very

uncertain ground, that is apt to give way at any moment. But when we acquire fields and grow wheat, build factories and manufacture goods, erect warehouses and distribute the contents one to another, we know we are getting on solid ground.

The Labour Party does not proceed in this way. It calls for higher wages, and leaves those who supply the commodities of life to exploit the higher earnings by increased cost of living. . . . What is and always had been the failure of the Labour Party from a business point of view? It is that they have asked other people to do things for them rather than do things for themselves. . . . And when all has been said in favour of a high legal rate of pay, what does the term suggest? It suggests that the workers are still dependent upon other people for wages, as they are for the price of the means of life. They are between two oppressive stools – one to keep down wages, one to inflate prices. How can they disentangle themselves from the position? We presume some would say by State action; perhaps by forcing the Government to own and control industry and the distribution of food. But how full of doubt, uncertainty, and perhaps corruption such a course would be. Would it not be better, and as quickly done in the long run for the people to get hold of the machinery of production by co-operative means?

Once that process was anything like complete the workers could then determine by collective action their own rate of pay, their own price of food, clothing and shelter. And co-operators would then be so numerous that they could walk into the Houses of Parliament and take over the reins of government without any further palaver. This is not a dream. It is simply a business problem.[79]

Early in the twentieth century the Co-operative Wholesale Society was 'the most varied if not the largest business enterprise in the world'. It was the most fully developed of the visions by and on behalf of private labour in England (and Scotland) at this time. And it happened away from the State, and away from the social history of dominant meanings of 'socialism'.

Whether they intended to be or not, however, English associations of working men were of considerable interest to 'the State'. That there had to be a Royal Commission on 'Labour' in the early 1890s is indicative in itself. But the interest was much more determining than a single Royal Commission. From the 1850s through to the 1880s there was a great deal of legislative preoccupation (at times obsession) with working-class association.

Such associations have been accused, by those with an obsession with 'positions' in the heady sense rather than positions in the social, relational sense, of being 'corporate' rather than 'hegemonic', that is, of having no ambitions for general, or state, power and living in closed, class-bound worlds. But in fact, whether they intended to or not, the people in this associational culture *did* raise, through their presence and practice, the nature of wider social and productive relations.

The problem for 'the state' was how, or on what terms to admit working-class association or combination. That capitalists could and must combine was axiomatic. But workers? As Hore Belisha M.P. said in 1933 when debating the tax position of co-operative societies, 'there must be some limit to the principle of mutuality'.[80] From the 1850s onwards, Industrial and Provident Society legislation was concerned with the terms upon which large-scale working-class association could be licensed. This had roots back to Combination Acts and to the Friendly Society Acts of the 1790s, and stretches forward to the Labour and Conservative obsession with trade union legislation from the 1960s onwards. How much of what private capital had or did could private labour have or do? At what point would licensing have to give way to suppression? *When* – if at all – could private labour's *powers* (to associate in a whole range of ways) safely be turned into legal *"rights?"* Limited Liability? The right to make exclusive agreements? Assembly? Picketing? Trading? Interference with 'freedom of contract'? What should the tax position of Cooperative Societies or Working Men's Clubs be? After all, as Hore Belisha's speech went on, 'if the whole country were covered by Co-operative Stores the Revenue would receive no income tax at all'. How private should working-class associations be allowed to be? The volume of complaints against them by their private business competitors was great. To what extent should workers' associations be able to tender for, or even administer, universal public services, like National Insurance in 1911: on the same terms as private industrial insurance companies like the Prudential? What about private, working class education: could that be allowed?

The story of the changing answers to these questions from a trade union point of view has become well known as a result of the renewed crisis of trade unionism and the State from the mid-1960s onwards – a crisis which is clearly very much still with us. That there is also a story from the point of view of English associations of working people more generally is less well known. It has as yet scarcely begun to be told. There are fascinating episodes to be unravelled from a class, rather than a Whig/national point of view. A climax from the Working Men's Club point of view were the battles over licensing legislation in the early 1900s. From the Friendly Societies point of view a battle took place between them, private capital and the State, in 1911. The Co-operative Societies were stabbed in the back, as they saw it – and in spite of another mass petition (3 million signatures) – by Ramsay MacDonald and Neville Chamberlain in the Finance Act of 1933. The outline chronology is the same in all spheres. In the 1870s and 1880s working-class association forced the polity – Conservative as well as Liberal – to move over a bit. A settlement was achieved which was enduring enough, for example in the sphere of trade unionism, for Mrs Thatcher and her Ministers still to be trying, in the 1980s to get back behind it in a thorough way. It gave unions too much ground. Then in the 1890s there was a counter-attack, in the courts. It was only partly reversed by Liberals, in the Trade Disputes Act of 1906.

The story of the next, long, period was that of Parliamentary Labour failing to provide an umbrella under which working-class associations could flourish and federate and challenge the State on their own terms. The issue of who ruled Britain was never properly raised through active working-class association. Or rather it was raised, and then quickly and never adequately settled from a working-class point of view by political Labour saying 'We do,' 'We are the State,' 'Leave it to us,' 'We will do it for you.'

Not only did the State have to move over a bit, to accommodate large-scale, ambitious association, but so too did a very big carrier of nineteenth-century political, economic and would-be social discourse: Liberalism. The subjects (or objects) addressed by Marx (which are really much more interesting than Marxism as science) are things (relations) already mentioned more than once in this essay. They are things (relations) like class, and class struggle, working-class movement/combination/association, large-scale industry and its differences from manufactures, exploitation and its varying state and national forms and locations, norms/ideas and power/hegemony. These are the subjects about which Marx and Marxists have had so much to say. What is striking about England, however, is how much of this agenda for thinking and for acting went through Liberalism and not through 'Socialism/ Marxism'. The yeast in the dough, as yeast does, made it expand. What an extraordinary territory late-nineteenth century Liberalism was! It was, for instance, the Hammonds who, of all historians, between their time and ours, came nearest to E. P. Thompson's view of early-nineteenth century history, with their account of that period as civil ('class') war. It was another Liberal, L. T. Hobhouse, who came so near to theorizing what Gramsci came to work on as 'hegemony'; see Hobhouse's work on stratification within the working class, in reaction to the crisis of the Boer War. He was fascinated by the ideas and practices – the whole culture in fact – which kept unorganized labour subordinate at this time. And it was J. A. Hobson who not only took up the chronology of large-scale industry in books like *The Evolution of Modern Capitalism* but who was also so near a cousin to Lenin in his work on *Imperialism*. Liberals too, even Gladstonian ones, were not afraid to face the central difficulty of political 'representation'. They knew the problems of any one person 'representing' another. They were thus nearer to the base camp from which a revolutionary political modernism might have broken through than British Labour or Social Democracy has ever been since. English Associations of Working Men faced this issue too, but in practice. With their careful financial arrangements, careful practice about the relations between centre and localities in their own associations, quarterly units for elections, self-conscious congresses with inventions like the 'block vote', and their tendency to go for mandation and delegation, they contributed enormously to the difficult issues of class and political 'representation'. Political Labour never did. As Keir Hardie said, to succeed, 'We must conform as nearly as possible to the political institutions already in existence with which the public mind is familiar.' Worse than that, Labour has actually worked to repress continued thought and practice on such matters, in its attempt to found a Political, Statist monopoly. But more of that later.

How much yeast was in that dough!

News from somewhere

With all of this behind it and with all of that to go beyond, one might expect some of the socialisms which emerged in England at the end of the nineteenth century to be extraordinary. And so some of them were. Among a few possible examples I shall choose two.

Thomas Kirkup

Thomas Kirkup (1844–1912) was a Northumbrian-born shepherd boy. Through the pupil-teacher system and Edinburgh University, he became an author and publisher's advisor. He is unknown now. In his day, however, he was a much published, re-printed, and well-received student of socialism. And among the three works which Mao Tse Tung said 'especially deeply carved my mind' as he moved into Marxist theory and practice in 1919–20, Kirkup's *History of Socialism* was one.[81]

Re-reading Kirkup today, his late entry into a main artery of twentieth-century 'communalist' socialism is not surprising.[82] He had, to begin with, a strong sense of the epochal (i.e., revolutionary but not necessarily 'sanguinary') nature of the project, combined with a commitment to those in whose interests it was to be undertaken (working people). He hated the divisions of labour (including the mental-manual one) which oppressed them. In the cause of *his* version of the socialist project it was no failure to 'have done efficient work as a navvy or hodman'. He knew about the extent as well as the beneficiaries of the change he was advocating:

> while its basis is economic, socialism implies and carries with it a change in the political, ethical, technical and artistic arrangements and institutions of society, which would constitute a revolution greater than has ever taken place in human history, greater than the transition from the ancient to the medieval world, or from the latter to the existing order of society.

While the 'most thoroughly democratic organisation of society' was the 'political complement' of such transformation, ethics and culture were necessarily involved – culture, for Kirkup, being written into subsistence in a most unusual way. A central aim of socialism was to 'terminate the divorce of the workers from the natural sources of subsistence and culture'. He used the language of association. 'It must be the aim of the socialist movement also to terminate this incessant divorce between labour and intelligence, by providing within the groups of associated workers due scope for the best talent.' There was a personal, class edge to some of his prose. 'In the history and condition of the working people it is a pathetic fact that their sons who have been gifted with exceptional capacity generally go over to the richer classes. Their services are thus lost to the class from which they sprang.'

Fellow travellers needed reminding, he thought, that socialism claims 'to represent the aspirations after a better life of the toiling and suffering millions of the human race'.[83] What he called 'abstract collectivism' might eclipse that. Rural change, for instance, mattered to Kirkup, and abstract collectivism was, he thought, making it 'difficult for [Marx's] followers to draw up a reasonable agrarian policy suitable to the peasantry'. It was also preventing the realization that *struggle* was the instrument, for now, as ever, 'progress must be attained through struggle, and perfection through suffering'.[84] Working people's aspirations were not necessarily neatly programmatic, for 'probably the most striking feature in recent history may be found in the symptoms, that so frequently appear, of a latent and undefined socialism, which only needs a fitting occasion to call it forth, and which forms a serious but incalculable quantity in the social forces of the time'. He was interested in this 'quantity' not only in England but also in Russia, already in 1892. 'We cannot too often emphasise the fact that it is not an abstract system but a thing in movement. It is not wedded to any stereotyped set of formulae whether of Marx or any other, but must be rooted in reality and while moulding facts it must adapt itself to them.' Mao's approval of all this is not hard to imagine. The 'absolute' was to be suspected, for example with reference to the problem of relations between the centre and localities. 'No absolute rules can be laid down for the relations of the two to each other; these must be determined by considerations of time and circumstances.' 'Texts and systems' could not deal with such matters, nor could 'absolute principles': only history and practice. 'It would be a serious mistake to identify socialism with any of its forms, past or present. They are only passing phases in a movement which will endure.'

Two tendencies, thought Kirkup, could be extracted from the living history of this movement. One was broadly *etatist*, the other broadly communal or voluntary.[85] The latter was quite deeply rooted in local possibility – though getting less so he thought, as he watched developments.

It was simply stated. 'The cardinal thing in socialism is the living and active principle of association.' 'Socialism, then simply means that the normal social organisation of the future will and should be an associated or co-operative one':

> Through the fog of controversy we should clearly see that the fundamental principle of socialism is marked by extreme simplicity. The keynote of socialism is the principle of association. Only by associating for the ownership and control of land and capital can the people protect themselves against the evils of competition and monopoly. Only by association can

they control and utilise the large industry for the general good. It means that industry should be carried on by free associated workers utilising a joint capital with a view to an equitable system of distribution. And in the political organisation of society it has for complement a like ideal, namely, that the old methods of force, subjection and exploitation should give place to the principle of free association. Through the application and development of the principle of free association it seeks to transform State, municipality, and industry in all their departments.[86]

'Rationally interpreted', socialism, for Kirkup was 'simply a movement for unifying labour and capital through the principle of association'. Most co-operators, even in the shop-keeping phase of that movement during the second half of the nineteenth century, would have agreed with such a proposition, while not often labelling it as a 'socialist' one. Such a view, of course, had implications for ways of seeing the State which 'by reasonable socialism should be regarded as the association of men on a large scale', the municipality or commune being regarded as the association for local purposes.

When arguing about the State, Kirkup knew he had allies – in England, allies whom he too easily contrasted with Prussians. But he also knew that he had local antagonists. So he went on about it. There were socialists 'too much influenced by the Prussian type of government and theory of the State'. They were keen on hierarchy, management from above, and centralization as an absolute. 'Such a view may suit people that are used to a centralising autocracy and bureaucracy associated with militarism, but is entirely opposed to English ideas . . . an industrial and economic system which would remind us at every step of the Prussian army, the Prussian police and Prussian officialism, is not attractive to those who have breathed a freer air.' One dimension of English capitalist development was being employed here towards Socialism. 'It is . . . most misleading to speak as if socialism must proceed from the State as we know it.'[87] There were those around who did so speak and their voices were getting louder. After all, as one of them said, 'it is easier to get control over existing machinery than to make machinery for yourself'. Quite so! His worry about this got more evident in the last (1909) edition of the *History* to be issued in his own life-time. He had seen England as a resource against abstract collectivism: but he was becoming fearful of the spending of that resource. 'The direct action of the State' and the idea that 'everything will be done by it', grotesque and absurd (his words) though that notion was, had gotten more influential in the minds of critics of socialism but also 'apparently also by some of its adherents'. The Fabians were particularly to blame. 'The State has very great power, but it has no magical power. And it is a grave mistake to regard it too much as the pivot of social evolution. We can trace its rise and progress in history and its record has not been a good one . . . it has too long and too much been an organ for the exploiting of the mass of the people by the ruling minority.' The mistake was being made more and more within 'recent English socialism', wherein the bureaucrat had been identified much too closely with socialism. 'In its propaganda the Fabian Society has too often interpreted socialism in terms of the State and the municipality. . . . In this and in other points the language of the Fabian Basis is too suggestive of the rigid and abstract collectivism set forth in the prevalent socialism.'[88]

We shall see later how one Fabian and a 'quintessential' one at that dealt with such a case!

William Morris

Meanwhile, however, space must be given to one of the most original socialists of the entire Second International period: William Morris. Morris went far enough forward in epochal terms for it *still* to be difficult for anyone (with the exception of Rudolph Bahro) on the left to have caught up with him. And yet he was more evidently rooted in an English radical tradition than a thinker such as Kirkup. 'Our poet starts from a tangible national reality and deduces its future from its past and present. His utopia possesses history and geography.'[89]

Morris oscillated between great hopes and big fears for England so far as any socialism worthy of the name was concerned. His preferred name for the project was Communism. Sometimes he thought that all he longed for could and would happen, uniquely, here. At other times he knew how much, here, there was to stop it, and how much compromise would have to be endured.

In 1887 Morris produced the first of two sustained theorizations or visions of the transition to socialism. In it he contrasted the Policy of Parliamentary Action with what he called the Policy of Abstention.[90] The latter meant the construction of a great 'Labour Combination' powerful enough to replace the capital *P* of Politics. This combination would, Morris thought, require a material life of its own, a productive capacity. 'Its aim would be to act directly, whatever was done in it would be done by the people themselves; there would consequently be no possibility of compromise, of the association becoming anything else than it was intended to be; nothing could take its place: before all its members would be but one alternative to complete success, complete failure.' This combination would constitute a 'Labour Parliament'. As it grew and as the crisis of monopoly deepened, people would ally with its decrees rather than with those of the 'Westminster Committee'. It would have to undertake 'the maintenance of its people' as well as resistance to erstwhile constitutional (because already constituted) authority. 'No mere aggregation of discontent,' it would be 'the representative of the society of production, the direct opposite to the society of exploitation which will be represented by the constitutional government'. The 'vast labour organisation,' the Combined Workers or Federation would set about the active transformation of the 'raw material and instruments of labour' into common property:

> Let them settle e.g. what wages are to be paid by their temporary managers, what number of hours it may be expedient to work; let them arrange for the filling of the military chest, the care of the sick, the unemployed, the dismissed: let them learn also how to administer their own affairs. Time and also power fails me to give any scheme for how all this could be done; but granting the formation of such a body I cannot help thinking that for the last two purposes they might make use of the so-called plan of co-operation.

All this was described in 1887 and extended most fully in an extraordinary chapter, 'How the Change Came' in *News from Nowhere* (1890). In this work it was all *placed* – in the manner of a tapestry – in a very precise English scene. 'Whatever may be said of the possibility of such construction in other countries, in Britain it is possible,' Morris thought, because, even though there were places where the suffrage was more extended, nowhere else had 'the habit of democracy' gained such sway across the whole culture.[91] Occasionally Morris connected such a habit to 'the ancient constitution of the land', to the forgotten tradition of direct assemblies among Germanic peoples, which nourished 'an Englishman's wholesome horror of government interference and centralisation'.[92]

The State was, for Morris, a major problem. All divisions of labour were so; the centralized State tried to 'administer the affairs of the people living a long way off, whose conditions and surroundings they cannot thoroughly understand'. 'It is always and everywhere good that people should do their own business, and in order that they may do it well, every citizen should have some share of it, and take on his shoulders some part of the responsibility.' But as 'society organised for the production and distribution of wealth' (unusually succinct as a formulation on this topic), the State could not, of course, simply disappear:

> The great federal organising power, whatever form it took, would have the function of the administration of production in its wider sense. It would have to see to, for instance, the collection and distribution of all information as to the wants of the population and the possibilities of supplying them, leaving all details to subordinate bodies, local or industrial.[93]

Morris' fear was that theories of reform, which already had a stronghold and which were based upon the enlargement and extension of the existing State, would come to dominate and to define Socialism. He knew how necessary such theories were for capitalism's survival, how inevitable their multiplication was, and what an available mould for counterfeiting socialism they provided. He knew that such theories might easily eclipse all other meanings of socialism and suppress the real, mass, beneficiaries of socialism (communism), in the interests of a newish class, or layer, of persons whom he did not much like. 'I should like our friend to understand', he wrote to a correspondent in *Commonwealth* in July 1885,

> whither the whole system of palliation tends – namely, towards the creation of a new middle class to act as a buffer between the proletariat and their direct and obvious masters; the only hope of the bourgeois for retarding the advance of Socialism lies in this device.

He knew that some socialisms around him did not even intend to transform the relations of production of modern industry from a working-class point of view. They had quite other fish to fry. Of this kind of socialism he wrote:

> It has two faces to it. One of which says to the working man "This is Socialism or the beginning of it" (which it is not) and the other says to the capitalist, "This is sham Socialism; if you can get the workers, or part of them, to accept this, it will create a new lower middle-class, a buffer to push in between Privilege and Socialism".[94]

Some 'revolutionists' around him considered that they could use 'the old bureaucratic states' like the English one 'rather than have any disruption of them prior to the realisation of the new social system'. Such a line, as we have already seen, was very available in England. There was a lot of State to take for granted. But it constituted a terrible separation for Morris of means from ends, or processes from results. But it also had a terrible necessity about it, particularly where he lived. He came to see, here, that there would probably have to be a 'transitional stage of progress'. 'Before the habit of working for the whole was formed some compulsion would have to be exercised. That compulsion would be found in the very remains of competition which would render the state imperfect.'[95] Concessions would be wrung from the masters, but, again, *agency* or *process* or struggle – who did what and how – was fundamental to Morris. Anything given by private capital or by its State and related agencies like Parliament – even though asked for by Labour – should not be internalized by labour and regarded as part of its own working-class project, even though improvements would undoubtedly result. 'We should be clear that they are not our measure.' Legislation might help the conditions of life, and could not be refused. But it should not be mistaken for real socialism. Improvements produced through agencies other than labour's own will and association would be 'damaging to the cause if put forward by socialists as part of socialism'.[96] Property was going to have to pay a ransom. He knew that. So did many other politicians, business men and cultural fit and proper persons around him who scrambled for the socialist label at this time. The trouble was that the ransom was going to be called Socialism by friend and foe alike:

> the great mass of what most non-socialists at least consider at present to be socialism, seems to me nothing more than a *machinery* of socialism, which I think it probable that socialism *must* use in its militant condition; and which I think it *may* use for some time after it is practically established; but it does not seem to me to be of its essence.[97]

A version of the future which Morris contested strongly and which had already invaded and still occupies a lot of socialist space was the hierarchical, technological romanticism which suggested that, as machinery developed, it would entirely supercede handicraft. This flourished in nineteenth-century England. 'While the ordinary daily work of the world would be done entirely by automatic machinery, the energies of the more intelligent part of mankind would be set free to follow the higher forms of the arts, as well as science and the study of history.' 'It was strange,' commented Henry Morsom, citizen of Nowhere, 'was it not, that they should thus ignore that aspiration after complete equality which we now recognise as the bond of all happy human society'. Work was to be a force making for communism and its continuity, not a messy preliminary to it. It was on this point (of production) that hierarchy was based and could so easily be reasserted. It was here also that the most important distinction Morris made – that between Socialism and Communism – was rooted. If Socialism was defined as a 'mere system of property holding', if its task was merely to take over an already existing, well-developed economic, political, administrative cultural machine or state and to develop it in 'rational' straight lines, then it seemed to him hardly an improvement upon capitalism. In some moods barbarism seemed preferable. Working very much within an English context, Morris could see a communism which went way beyond rational statism. But he could also see the developed reality of a depressing, arrested development profoundly confusing to working people. He could see its beneficiaries all around him, wearing socialist livery and being taken too seriously. Apologists for statism and collectivism were all around him, strong enough presences for Morris to theoretically understand them and politically oppose them to a degree rare in the subsequent history of the search for alternatives.

Statism and collectivism would each leave production as a surviving material basis for hierarchy. Under them it would be at best 'from each according to his abilities, to each according to his work', rather than the communist precept of 'from each according to his abilities, to each according to his needs'. Here Morris was drawing on a distinction familiar within the Co-operative tradition, and present for example in the early-nineteenth-century work of William Thompson. How could you relate rewards to work when 'the production of wares and the service of the community must always be a matter of co-operation?' It is not possible,

> really to proportion the reward to labour, and . . . if you were able to do so you would still have to redress by charity the wrongs of the weak against the strong, you would still not be able to avoid a poor-law: the due exercise of one's energies for the common good and capacity for personal use we say form the only claims on the possession of wealth, and this right of property, the only safeguard against the creation of fresh privilege, which would have to be abolished like the old privilege.

'Fresh privilege,' different from but arising out of the transformation of capitalism, was always a distinct possibility for Morris. And privileges could so easily become habits, ways of acting, interests: just like private capital on the one hand or mutual association on the other. Morris was interested in those 'who occupy a middle position between the producers and the non-producers', like 'artists and literary men, doctors, school-masters etc'. 'They are doing useful service, and ought to be doing it for the community at large, but practically they are only working for a class, and in their present position are little better than hangers-on of the non-producing class, from whom they receive a share of their privilege, together with a kind of contemptuous recognition of their position as gentlemen – heaven save the mark.'[98] He feared

> the danger of the community falling into bureaucracy, the multiplication of boards and offices, and all the paraphernalia of official authority, which is, after all, a burden, even when it is exercised by the delegation of the whole people and in accordance with their wishes.[99]

There were whole categories of occupation 'which would have no place in a reasonable condition of society as e.g. lawyers, judges, jailers and soldiers of the highest grades, and most Government officials'.[100] 'Directors of labour,' 'men of genius' and other such people had to be watched. Masterdom based on property in knowledge was as much masterdom as that based in any other kind of property. 'A decent life, a share in the common life of all is the only "reward" that any man can honestly take for his work, whatever it is; if he asks for more, that means that he intends to play the master over somebody.'[101]

There was an available line to which Morris was opposed all through his communist life. This was the line that said that 'revolutionists' could use the old bureaucratic states 'rather than [have] any disruption of them prior to the realisation of the new social system'. To this he proposed that 'while the national systems cannot at present be directly attacked with success as to their more fundamental elements', a process of 'starving out' or 'sapping' should and could go on. More and more responsibility could be taken by local associations, as instruments of transition, and by working-class unions (limbs of a future socialist commonwealth) who, through federation, should already be dealing with 'the details of change'.[102] During the period in which the old political nations were weakening into dissolution,

> the form which the decentralization or Federation will take is bound to be a matter of experiment and growth; what unit of administration is to be, what the groups of Federation are to be, whether or not there will be cross-Federation, as, e.g. Craftsguilds and Co-operative Societies going side by side with the geographical division of wards, communes and the like, all this is a matter for speculation and I don't pretend to prophesy about it.[103]

Aspiration – instinct for socialism – plus active federation from below were, for Morris, the 'only means' for 'bringing about the beginning of the Socialistic system'. These would be the content of the revolution, whatever its day-to-day manifestations might be. 'There must be a great party, a great organisation outside parliament actively engaged in reconstructing society and learning administration' (1887). It was a very delicate, discriminating line to follow. More than most Marxists, Morris knew of the ubiquity of capitalism, evident on the banks of the Thames as well as in factories, in the looks of people's faces as well as in wage payments. But in spite of or even because of this, it could best be replaced while it was still there, not only on the morrow of the revolution. There had to be 'the token', at least, 'of the gradual formation of a new order of things underneath the decaying order'.[104] 'Capacity for administration' would have to grow, even through associations as frail as the Hammersmith Socialist Society, 'so that when the present system is overthrown, they might be able to carry on the business of the community without waste or disaster'.[105] The question of whether any of this could happen through Socialism, as transition to Communism, or whether Socialism might turn off the desire for anything else, was one which haunted Morris. In England it was a very urgent question. Modern Marxist interpreters have probably been too sanguine about Morris' thoughts on this matter, in their eagerness to fit him into a 'two stages' Marxism, which ratifies twentieth century actually existing socialist states. The point here is that Morris did not need 'Marxism', still less specific texts in Engels' top drawer, to make the critical distinctions here. They were already evident way back in the inheritance available to him. Nor did he need Marxism, separate from his own analyses and experience, to see that, with that English inheritance, what he meant by Socialism would happen, but also that what he meant by Communism could happen. Both were inscribed in preceding facts about England, and consequent ideas of Englishness.

> I know there are some to whom this possibility of the getting rid of class degradation may come, not as a hope, but as a fear. These may comfort

themselves by thinking that this Socialist matter is a hollow scare, in England at least; that the proletariat have no hope, and therefore will lie quiet in this country, where the rapid and nearly complete development of commercialism has crushed the power of combination out of the lower classes. . . . It may be that in England the mass of the working classes has no hope; that it will not be hard to keep them down for a while, possibly a long while. The hope that this may be so I will say plainly is a dastard's hope, for it is founded on the chance of their degradation. I say such an expectation is that of slave-holders or the hangers-on of slave-holders. I believe, however, that hope is growing among the working classes even in England; at any rate you may be sure of one thing, that there is at least discontent. Can any of us doubt that, since there is unjust suffering?[106]

So, what went wrong?

An absurd question to put, so late in the argument, without the pages left to do it any kind of justice: 'Unjust suffering,' certainly, continues. 'Hope' is less evident in England now. William Morris was in a hurry, but he knew there would be no rush here. In his own time he thought that 'Making Socialists' was probably all that could be done. By the time 'Guest' arrived in *Nowhere* the society it stands for had been developing for 150 years. The revolutionary crisis described in the text was not seen by Morris, even during the excited late-1880s, as happening until the 1950s. Even so, in 1984, it is hard to see ourselves, with much conviction, as being on the way. Defence against going backwards is now more pressing. It would be hard to say, as Morris did in a piece 'Where are we now?' in *Commonweal* in November 1890, 'the hope of the partial, and so to say, vulgarized realisation of socialism is now pressing on us'. Defeat, or 'the loss of the future' is much more talked about, now, on the left.[107]

So, what went wrong? The main answers to such a question obviously lie way beyond England and way beyond socialism, as well as way beyond the scope of these pages. It would be absurd and unhelpful to moralize the huge violent themes of twentieth-century world history into some 'fault' among socialists in general, let alone among socialisms here in England. In so far as socialists here, however, *have* been party to – or even abetted – what went wrong, it might be helpful to own up. 'No enemies to the left' is not now a helpful slogan for anyone interested in the project described by Marx as 'the associated mode', or lived by Morris 'in essence and in spirit, even now when we cannot be socialists economically'.

In the case of the emergent projects of Kirkup and Morris outlined above, they quite clearly had active and direct antagonists who regarded themselves as being on the left. The fight against Morris has not always been easy to see because so much of it has consisted of attempts at inclusion, trying to incorporate him comfortably into subsequently dominant projects quite other than his own.[108] Communists who want to justify actually existing regimes as staging posts towards real communism; social democrats who want to substitute a bit of brotherhood, plus wholemeal art or even 'English genius' for epochal change, and now even Trotskyites wanting a unique Marxist leverage on 'reformism', have each tried to hitch him to their waggon. Morris was engaged in active critique of many such positions (as well as others) for most of his communist life. He never pulled his punches about Fabianism, or statism (even though he found Anarchism harder to hit). He knew, towards the end, that he was not winning: 'the world is going your way at present Webb' he told Sidney Webb in 1895, 'but it is not the right way in the end'.[109] And punches were not pulled the other way either. He was patronized. But his project was clearly among those 'primitive' ones which Sidney Webb tried so hard to tidy up in a pamphlet on *Socialism in England* in 1893:

> if our aim is the transformation of England into a Social Democracy we must frankly accept the changes brought about by the Industrial Revolution, the factory system, the massing of populations into great cities, the elaborate differentiation and complication of modern civilisation, the subordination of the worker to the citizen, and of the individual to the community. We must rid ourselves resolutely of all those schemes and projects of bygone socialisms which have now passed out of date.

There was a lot of self-consciously 'modern', sweeping-clean, anti-sentimental and often quite viciously anti-working class and antidemocratic, would-be 'scientific' sentiment in and around Fabianism through the late-nineteenth and early-twentieth centuries.[110] I will try, very briefly, to theorize some of it below.

In Kirkup's case, the treatment was nicely direct. The fifth edition of his *History of Socialism,* and the only edition available, for example, to students in the library of the University of Sussex, was brought out in 1913. Its editor was Edward R. Pease, secretary of the Fabian Society for 25 years, author of an early *History* of it (1916). He was dubbed by Margaret Cole as 'the quintessential Fabian'. Pease was convinced in 1913,

> that historians in the future will recognise, as indeed they are beginning to realise already, that the successor to Karl Marx in the leadership of Socialist thought belongs to Sidney Webb. Marx perceived that industry must be the business of the State, but he did not foresee how this could come about. This has been the work of the English School of Socialism, which has for long prevailed here.[111]

This, as we have seen, had been Kirkup's precise worry in his own, 1909, and earlier editions. In the 1913 edition, 'revised and largely rewritten', Pease simply left out Kirkup's worries about Fabianism and the State.[112] In a little-noticed bit of 'permeation', Pease substituted a panegyric of his heroes and their Society. What had been seen by Kirkup as *problem* was frankly written-up as opportunity:

> To the ordinary citizen, and especially to the workman, the Government is a thing apart, a great machine of which he knows little and over which he has no control, except as an elector, and then only, so to speak, by force. The Fabians were many of them in Government service as first division clerks. . . . To Government clerks at Whitehall, even the juniors, Government is a delicate machine whose working they have to control. . . . To men in such service many ways of influencing political action are apparent which the outsider cannot realise. The country is not so much governed by the votes of the electors, as by the ideas put into the heads of official persons whether parliamentary chiefs or permanent civil servants. What is true of government is equally true of outside organisations. The policy of a political association is determined within limits, by the man who drafts its resolutions and reports. Know more than other people, know what you want, and you can make other people carry out your ideas. It is easier to get control over existing machinery than to make machinery for yourself.[113]

It was evidently also easier to get control over existing books than to make them yourself.

There was much more of such repression around in this period than labour historians have yet uncovered, with Fabians fighting (within themselves too) against 'byegone socialisms' – and their carriers – quite ruthlessly. Fabians often called themselves 'collectivists', and minced no words. 'Universal submission' was something (relation) Sidney Webb was capable of advocating.[114] A rank-and-file Fabian, who called his son Bernard Sidney after his two heroes, and who was thought by H. G. Wells to be a good specimen of 'English mentality in the period 1906-14,' found his niche in 1910 as manager of the Leeds Labour Exchange. He had already confided, in an earlier letter,

> I care more for the State than I care for or have ever cared for myself, or for any other human being. . . . I have lost all my dogmas except a passionate faith in the development of a collectivist spirit in relation to property and breeding.

When he got to Leeds he wrote:

> I am enjoying life hugely now. . . . I am getting a passion for studying this place. I have had a unique life in my chances of seeing different classes of society – really getting to know them. I am pushing on this experience in that direction as much as I can. I have even joined the Leeds Club – the exclusive snobbish club of the place – for the purpose of observing the

habits of employers more closely. The only way to be sure of defeating a
man is to be able to beat him at his own game. We have got to be better
capitalists than the capitalists are. When we – that is, the administrative
classes – have more will, more relentlessness, more austerity, more
organizing ability, more class consciousness than they have, we shall
crumple them in our hands. And by God! you and I may live to see the
beginning of the end.
I am more of a puritan than ever. Austerity is what is needed. These
miserable employers are poor creatures in many ways. They eat too
much; they drink too much; they want their women too much. By God!
I will out Bacchus any man when I choose. But it shall be of my free
choice – not of a limp necessity. From day to day my dream shall be of
a new model army, of vigilant administration supplanting property by
organisation, inch by inch, steadily and slowly – with a jovial carouse
to loosen the muscles now and again. And to hell with the snufflers and
the pimps alike. They shall go in pairs, one of each to a hurdle after the
precedent set by Henry VIII.[115]

'Collectivism' can only be characterized very generally here, in a series
of propositions. It was a kind of socialism which regarded itself as quite
'English'. But, by then, Englishness had come to stand for reform against
revolution.[116] It was characteristically located among a 'nouvelle couche
sociale' rather than among workers. As Belfort Bax remarked, 'Fabianism is
the special movement of the Government official just as militarism is of the
soldier and clericalism of the priest.'[117]

This sociology is probably explicable in terms of facts about England
and, consequently, possible ideas of Englishness. There was, as we have
seen, a long inheritance of state service and State Servants 'as opposed
to private interests'. 'The age of improvement' during the first half of the
nineteenth century produced, and was produced by, a remarkable group of
State Servants whose project was cousin to that of Fabian collectivism.[118]
Even a classic text of large-scale industry like Andrew Ure's *The Philosophy
of Manufactures* (1835) made promises not at all unlike a Shavian brave
new world: good wages, clean homes, light work, no responsibility, science
(not your knowledge or experience but *our* expertise), beneficent but stern
supervision, believe us, we are good for you, don't try to understand more
than is necessary, enjoy the division of labour. Within this tradition of a
public, expert state, 'civil' officials made sense: public men (not always, for
women could find professional identity here too) had a place, and a social
and ideological inheritance allowing them to assume an identity between
their own interest and the 'general good'. And there was a prodigious body
of sociology, in blue books and suchlike publications behind them, among
which Fabians were totally at home. Also in England, industrial wealth and
attendant social position was old enough, reaching into its second and third
generations, for its sons and daughters to have the material and the means to

reject it, worry about it and use it for wider, extra-economic, social/political ends. Beatrice Webb's account of her family home and her search for a role outside it in *My Apprenticeship* is classic here.

'Collectivism' at its apogee of self-consciousness, in Edwardian England, was firmly attached to the Nation; 'a body of people kept together for purposes of rivalry with other similar bodies'. In Edwardian England there was a group called the 'Coefficients,' the scandal of whose views from the point of view of *any* connection with a political 'left' has not yet been generally enough exposed. They were elitist, imperialist, racist, eugenicist – just about as far from associationism as they could possibly be – and they included 'Collectivist' socialists.[119] Even after World War I the Webbs were still committed to 'world struggle' and 'scientific truth'.[120] It was against such 'practical men' of the World Market that William Morris spent his spirit.

Collectivists had the confidence of a social group (possibly even a 'new' class) with a definite place in production. They were, as we have mentioned already, writers, first-division clerks, administrators, supervisors, experts – people who could 'put it together', have an over-view, supervise the relations of production characteristic of large-scale industry. So far from being a problem to them, those arrangements were their opportunity. They were nearer to management than to labour, nearer to the cutting edge of large-scale capitalism than to that of associated labour. In the Webb's 'Socialist Commonwealth,' managers must manage, 'it is a matter of a psychology':

> No industrial enterprise . . . has yet made its administration successful on the lines of letting the employees elect or dismiss the executive officers whose directions these particular groups of employees have to obey. . . . It is, in fact, a matter of psychology. The relationship set up between a manager who has to give orders all day to his staff, and the members of his staff who, sitting as a committee of management, criticise his action in the evening, with the power of dismissing him if he fails to conform to their wishes, has been found by experience to be an impossible one.[121]

Who could go against 'psychology'? Who would dare to contest the impossibilities of capitalist 'experience' and 'industrial enterprise'? Whatever their intentions, whatever their professions about the universality of the project, they were not, in the end, on the side of working people.

With the other dominant direction of twentieth-century English socialism it is harder to be precise. What may, for shorthand purposes, be labelled 'Statism' has itself been much less precise in its articulation than Collectivism. 'It is sometimes charged against the I.L.P.,' wrote Keir Hardie in 1908, 'that it has never formulated its theory of socialism. That is true, and therein lies its strength'.[122]

In the case of 'Statism' we are dealing with a set of dominant assumptions and practices, highly characteristic of twentieth-century English Labour Politics, rather than a 'theory' as such. We, the observers, have to do the theoretical work, as it were, as opposed to having it all exposed for us in big books like those of the Webbs. All I can do here is to itemize some of those assumptions and practices, and illustrate them briefly, – to suggest just how antagonistic they have been to the project of associated labour.

What emerged in twentieth-century England, and became dominant against all other 'socialisms', was a strong would-be monopolistic 'Labour' politics, capable from time to time of winning elections, even of aspiring to be the 'natural party of government', and near enough to power for much of the time to think in terms of 'winning' it. Such thoughts naturally, in turn, determined what statists thought power *was* (is) in advanced capitalisms. Many of the impulses of class and association outlined earlier on became annexed to this politics and, I would argue, were thereby attenuated, even deformed.

To answer the question *why* this happened would take far more pages and ability than this writer has at his disposal. The beginnings of an answer, however, may be available in the characteristics of Statism itself. Some of these may be intelligible, if not entirely explicable, in terms of earlier arguments in this essay. It was, for a start, strongly evolutionary. Working with the grain, as they thought, of tendencies already operating in their societies, Statists thought they had time. Indeed it was only a matter of time. Individual humans grew up, from babies to adults: so too societies evolved, through lower to higher stages. And the adult stage of human society (socialism) was to be made available, soon, through the long centuries of English (British) evolution. Others might have to wait longer, but here, and quite soon as well, 'Socialism' of their kind was available. Ramsay MacDonald was the best at articulating this view before 1914.

Second, Statism tended to anthropomorphize the State. There it was, as it were, an available inheritance, to be taken – for granted. We, the workers, no, we (Labour leaders) on behalf of the workers, could simply become it, that State. In 1912 the I.L.P. paper the *Labour Leader* wanted to distance itself from Fred Jowett's pressure for socialist changes in Parliamentary forms:

> We feel, for our part, whilst recognising the disinterested advocacy of Mr. Jowett, that changes in Parliamentary procedure are not the supremely important matter for our movement.... As Mr. Snowden said, *our central grievance is that we ourselves are not the Cabinet.* With the rise of Labour to power many of the Parliamentary difficulties would tend to adjust themselves. [my emphasis][123]

If that was 'the central grievance', by 1946 it had clearly been met. Union leaders were pleased that they would now be negotiating with friends. At the Annual Conference of Trades Councils in that year H. W. Harrison said:

> We are no longer petitioning for a place in the counsels of the State, *we are the State.*)[124] [my emphasis]

This was in the main line of the personalized State which George II talked about with Chancellor Hardwick. If it wasn't a person or persons, the State was sometimes a ship, as in Ramsay MacDonald's *A Policy for the Labour Party* (1920) where he set out some Reform legislation 'to launch the ship of State well manned and well equipped on its future voyages'.

Third, Statism worked wholly within the characteristic confusion already mentioned between Parliament, actually-existing democratic forms and 'the State'. The latter was so much there, that Statists could not see it from a class point of view. They reduced the problem of representation to the fact of elections. They could not see without it, as it were. All they could do was to put on its clothes, and rejoice, as Harold Wilson did when he first got to Downing Street, that it 'worked'. It was all to hand, usable, old, not necessarily or inherently capitalist, quite 'disinterested', effective, and civil.

Accepting an old, available, evolving (they think) State, they, the Statists, also have to go along with the confinement of Politics to narrow, licensed, official forms. With Statism a group (precisely *not* a class in the full Marxist sense) without a direct base in material production seeks to exercise control over circulation rather than production. They accept the great bourgeois achievement of the separation of politics from economics: this separation remains in place. But then they find that reaching out from the top of one to control the other (from its top too) through projects of 'nationalisation' (even Sidney Webb preferred the term *socialization*) does not bring it to heel. On the one hand they have their own movement or party necessary to get them near 'State power' – and important to many of them as a livelihood – and on the other hand there is 'The State.' 'It' may, perhaps, be seen as needing 'strengthening' or its servants replacing by less biased ones, but it is never seen as available for reconstruction through working people's associated (and already emergent 'voluntary') efforts. There are links missing between movement and state, private (civil) action and public (political) action, between economics and politics. Across these gaps ugly, authoritarian styles of politics (Caesarisms) often make great leaps. They can enter from Right or from Left (Margaret Thatcher or David Owen), but Statism's tragedy is that it often seems to have been around beforehand, however unwittingly, preparing the stage.

Statism is, finally, a very public brand of socialism. Working within the inherited English framework of a strong public realm, it dreams that it can itself oppose, even replace, through 'nationalisation', 'legislation' and so on, 'private' capitalism altogether. It neglects contradictions, struggle and growth points within the private sphere. It neglects private labour. I have argued that the spaces for private labour were especially open in England. With the early cutting of 'private' passages by the bourgeoisie, and with the subsequent occupation of large areas of 'civil society' by ambitious working-class associations, I for one, simply do not understand the neglect of all this by Political Labour and Statist Socialism during the twentieth century. Vast areas have been abandoned, the *forms* of production, the *forms* and content of education, sport, 'culture' itself, the means of communication, even the family have been left unproblematized from a class point of view. Brave New Left and feminist movements have had to try to do the work themselves. Statists even suggest, as an article of faith, that 'industrial relations' must be kept free from politics. The result is that Labour has been ambushed by developments in those spheres as they have become more and more characteristically 'capitalist'.

Why is this? Is it because of the seeming imminence, from a late-nineteenth century point of view, through progress and evolution, of socialism in this country? Is it because England has seemed at times so specially available for socialism? Did this lead to a dash for the tape, as it were, by Political Labour – an attempt to go for the line through a Political monopoly? It is hard indeed to explain. It has been worse than neglect: it has been a matter of positive antagonism. It is as though all the yeast has been deliberately thrown away. Autonomous construction and independent struggles by trade unions have been seen as problem not as opportunity by Political Labour: Friendly Societies in effect have been nationalized (in their functions), and left as self-satisfied social circles rather than as cells for future class construction: the same with the Co-operative Movement. It was Ramsay MacDonald who was Prime Minister when a big assault was launched on them, through taxation, in 1933, and it was Social Democrats like Gaitskell and Crosland who were so anxious to define The Co-op as just another business, needing to be more competitive, in the Independent Commission of 1955. Everything which is 'voluntary' has been abandoned to the Right rather than being nurtured by the Left. And even the fractions of the Party itself, its constituency parties and constituents, are still seen as a more pressing problem for Labour than capitalism, let alone the embarrassment of the unions. Strange indeed. Why?

I would particularly like to thank Philip Corrigan. Without his help over recent years I would not have had the courage or the wherewithal to write this chapter.

Notes

1 J. B. Priestley, *Postscripts* (London: Heinemann, 1940), p. 2.

2 Public Record Office, CAB 24/105. Report on Revolutionary Organisations in the U.K., Home Office, 6 May 1920.

3 H. M. Hyndman, *The Historical Basis of Socialism in England* (London: Kegan Paul, 1883), p. 194n, 433.

4 *Justice*, 3 September 1910, quoted in C. Tsuzuki, *H. M. Hyndman and British Socialism* (Oxford: O.U.P., 1961), p. 211.

5 I.L.P. Conference Report (1893), p. 3.

6 *Clarion*, 21 January 1893, *Clarion*, 14 and 28 October 1899. I owe the 1899 references to Logie Barrow.

7 *Merrie England* (London: The Clarion Press, 1894), p. 123.

8 For an outline history here, see Hugh Cunningham 'The Language of Patriotism, 1750-1914', *History Workshop*, 12 (Autumn 1981). It was not, of course, finally lost: Orwell, Priestley and the radical populism of the early 1940s are inexplicable without the felt possibility of its recovery.

9 William Morris to Robert Thompson, 1 January 1885, quoted in Paul Meier, *William Morris, the Marxist Dreamer*, trans. F. Grubb (Sussex: Harvester, 1978), II, 557–8.

10 See I.L.P. Conference Report (1893), p. 5.

11 *Clarion,* 18 November 1899, and Logie Barrow ts. on schemes for Trades Federation in the late 1890s, p. 102.

12 Perry Anderson, *Arguments within English Marxism* (London: Verso, 1980), p. 149, and 'Origins of the Present Crisis', *New Left Review*, 23 (1964), 43. The best way into the Anderson-Nairn versus E. P. Thompson argument of the early 1960s is now the text and footnotes of the latter's 1965 essay 'The Peculiarities of the English', *The Poverty of Theory* (London: Merlin, 1978), pp. 35–91, 399–400. The relevant nos. of *New Left Review* are nos. 23 through 35.

13 In K. Marx and F. Engels, *On Britain* (Moscow: F.L.P.H., 1962). The piece was written on 12 September 1892.

14 'Modern Socialism' was a phrase much used by Lenin and other Second International Socialists. For a local example see R. C. K. Ensor (ed.), *Modern Socialism* (London: Harpers, 1907).

15 The Nation/State distinction in these succinct terms was made by William Morris in his *True and False Society* (1887).

16 Doris Lessing, *The Memoirs of a Survivor* (London: Picador, 1976), pp. 135–6, see also p. 8. The William Morris quotes on State and Nation are from *True and False Society.*

17 M. Clanchy, *From Memory to Written Record, England 1066–1307* (London: Arnold, 1979), p. 6; Nevil Johnson, *In Search of the Constitution* (Oxford: Pergamon, 1977), p. 81; Perry Anderson, *Lineages of the Absolutist State* (London: Verso, 1974), p. 113.

18 F. Braudel, *Afterthoughts on Material Civilization and Capitalism* (Baltimore: Johns Hopkins, 1976), pp. 99–100.

19 Clanchy, *From Memory* ... p. 30.

20 P. Corrigan and D. Sayer, *The Great Arch: English State Formation as Cultural Revolution* (Oxford: Blackwell, 1985); E. P. Thompson, 'The Peculiarities of the English', *Socialist Register* (1965), also in *The Poverty of Theory* (London: Merlin, 1978).

21 Quentin Skinner, *The Foundations of Modern Political Thought* (Cambridge: C.U.P. , 1978), II, 353.

22 'This is an old European country' is underlined as part of the argument of 'The Peculiarities of the English' (1965), p. 349; the quote about professionals comes from Geoffrey Holmes, *Augustan England: Professions, State and Society, 1680–1730* (London: Allen and Unwin, 1982), p. 239. He is analysing what he calls 'new men of English government', p. 250.

23 J. H. Plumb, *The Growth of Political Stability in England 1675–1725* (London: Macmillan, 1967) is a key work here, as is P. Corrigan and Sayer's referred to in n. 20 above.

24 The Morris quote comes from 'Art and Socialism,' *Collected Works XXII*, 208. For Adam Smith see, Donald Winch, *Adam Smith's Politics: An Essay in Historiographical Revision* (Cambridge: C.U.P., 1978).

25 Barrington Moore, *Social Origins of Dictatorship and Democracy* (Boston: Beacon Press, 1966), p. 32.

26 This gloss on Wallerstein comes from D. Levine, *Family Formation in an Age of Nascent Capitalism* (York: Academic Press, 1977), p. 10.

27 The essay is in Carlo Cipolla (ed.), *The Fontana Economic History of Europe* (London: Fontana, 1973), III, 301–57.

28 Robin Murray, in a typescript memo for the Labour Process Group in Brighton. This group was affiliated to the Conference of Socialist Economists and produced much important unpublished work.

29 *Instructions for the Delegates to the Geneva Congress* (1866).

30 Edmund Burke, *Reflections on the Revolution in France* (1790).

31 On the walls of Rochdale Town Hall (1870s) Cromwell appears naturally in the sequence of Monarchs; in Whitakers' Almanack the King was held to be ruling even where he could not reign during the Interregnum, see Christopher Hill, *Some Intellectual Consequences of the English Revolution* (London: Weidenfeld, 1980); for the statue, and much else about English national history, see J. W. Burrow's *Liberal Descent: Victorian Historians and the English Past* (Cambridge: C.U.P., 1981).

32 Herbert Butterfield, *The Englishman and His History* (Cambridge: C.U.P., 1944), pp. 2, 79.

33 For sharp analysis of this see Raymond Williams, *Towards 2000* (London: Chatto, 1983), pp. 102–27.

34 2nd Edition (1899), p. 30, quoted in Burrow, *A Liberal Descent*, p. 295.

35 Editorial for 21 November 1979.

36 *Lineages*, pp. 114–15.

37 Raymond Williams, 'Democracy and Parliament', *Marxism Today* (June 1982), p. 15.

38 W. C. Costin and J. S. Watson, *The Law and Workings of the Constitution: Documents 1660–1914*, I (London: Black, 1952), p. 376; Johnson, *In Search*, pp. 84, 90.

39 This Report was published by the Fabian Society in November 1906. I owe the reference to Ian Bullock's 'Socialists and Democratic Form in Britain, 1880–1914', unpublished D.Phil (University of Sussex, 1981).

40 Raymond Williams, *Keywords* (London: Croom Helm, 1976) on 'Representative', and his 'Democracy and Parliament', p. 16.

41 Raymond Williams, *Towards 2000*, and 'Democracy and Parliament'.

42 The phrases are Lord Hailsham's and Raymond Williams' (*The Long Revolution*) respectively.

43 *Labour Leader*, 23 March 1901.

44 Nevil Johnson, *In Search of the Constitution,* p. 53.

45 For this sense of *realization* of contradictions see Marx, *Capital*, I, Chapter 3, part 2 on 'The Means of Circulation': 'the exchange of commodities implies contradictory and mutually exclusive conditions. The further development of the commodity does not abolish these contradictions, but rather provides the form within which they have room to move. This is, in general, the way in which real contradictions are resolved. For instance, it is a contradiction to depict one body as constantly falling toward another and at the same time constantly flying away from it. The ellipse is a form of motion within which this contradiction is both realized and resolved.'

46 K. Marx, *Capital*, I (Moscow edit.), p. 744.

47 See Nevil Johnson, *In Search of*, and Perry Anderson, *Lineages*. The latter regards Henry VIII's need to pay for his attack on France in 1543 as a turning point here.

48 Perry Anderson, *Lineages*.

49 J. H. Plumb, *The Growth of Political Stability in England 1675–1725* (London: Macmillan, 1967).

50 E. J. Hobsbawm, 'The General Crisis of the Seventeenth Century', T. Aston (ed.), *Crisis in Europe, 1560–1660* (London: Routledge, Kegan Paul, 1965), pp. 47–9.

51 Marx, *German Ideology* in *Collected Works,* V, p. 89: 'Civil society embraces the whole material intercourse of individuals within a definite stage of the development of productive forces. It embraces the whole commercial and industrial life of a given stage and, insofar, transcends the state and nation, though, on the other hand again, it must assert itself in its external relations as nationality and internally must organise itself as state. The term "civil society" emerged in the eighteenth century when property relations had already extricated themselves from the ancient and medieval community. Civil society as such only develops with the bourgeoisie.'

52 K. Marx, 'Critique of Hegel's Philosophy of Right', *Collected Works*, III, 32.

53 Marx, 'Critical Marginal Notes on the Article "The King of Prussia and Social Reform. By a Prussian,"' *Collected Works*, III, 198.

54 The quotations are all from Chapter 10 of *Capital*, I.

55 Gareth Stedman Jones, 'Engels and the Genesis of Marxism', *New Left Review*, 106 (November/December 1977); see also his 'Engels and the History of Marxism', E. J. Hobsbawm (ed.), *The History of Marxism*, I (Sussex: Harvester, 1982).

56 William Thompson, *Labour Rewarded* (1827), p. 23.

57 'Dialogue between an Artificer in a dockyard and those who required his Vote in the next election for Kent,' in *Lloyds Evening Post*, 18–21 July 1760, quoted in C. R. Dobson, *Masters and Journeymen: A Prehistory of Industrial Relations 1717–1800* (London: Croom Helm, 1980), pp. 98–9.

58 Lawrence Stone, 'The new Eighteenth Century', *New York Review of Books*, 29 March 1984.

59 Dobson, *Masters and Journeymen*, p. 98, information from Lloyds 4–6 January, 26–9 May 1758.

60 E. P. Thompson, *The Making of the English Working Class* (London: Gollancz, 1963), p. 86, and chapter IV 'The Free-born Englishman' as a whole.

61 W. H. Greenleaf, 'Toulmin Smith and the British Political Tradition', *Public Administration*, 53 (1975), 25–44, 36–9.

62 The quotations in this paragraph are from Engels' writings of the early 1840s, cited in the Stedman Jones article 1977, see n. 55.

63 *Capital*, I (Penguin edit.), pp. 449–50.

64 'Education' or 'Educated', in the sense of what Marx calls Hegel's 'very heretical views, on the division of labour'. In his *Philosophy of Right* he says: 'By educated men we may *prima facie* understand those who . . . can do what others do', see Marx, *Capital*, I, 485 n. 51. As large-scale industry develops, the proportion of such people, for capital (but potentially also for labour) presumably increases greatly. 'The mass of misery, oppression, slavery, degradation and exploitation grows; but with this there also grows the revolt of the working class, a class constantly increasing in numbers, and trained, limited and organized by the very mechanism of the Capitalist process of production', see *Capital*, I, ch. 24.

65 *Capital*, I, 413.

66 The 1864 reference is to the *Inaugural Address of the International Working Men's Association*: the 'social barrier' quote and the Magna Carta quote come from *Capital*, I, 416.

67 *Instructions for Delegates to the Geneva Congress* (1866).

68 *Inaugural Address* (Penguin edit. 1974 Political writings 3), pp. 79–80.

69 *Capital*, I, 449.

70 *Capital*, III, ch. 27.

71 *Capital*, III, ch. 23.

72 *The Civil War in France* (Penguin edit. Political Writings 3, 1974), p. 212.

73 J. M. Baernreither, *English Associations of Working Men* (London: Sonnenschein, 1889), 1893 edit, pp. 6, 21, 146.

74 Baernreither, pp. xii, 146.

75 *The Englishman,* 7 December 1910, quoted in T. G. Ashplant, 'The C.I.U. and the I.L.P.: Working Class Organisation, Politics and Culture, c. 1880-1914', unpublished D.Phil (University of Sussex, 1983), p. 524.

76 G. J. Holyoake, *Sixty Years of An Agitator's Life* (London: Unwin, 1893), I, 133.

77 A. D. Murray (ed.), *The Autobiography of John Ludlow* (London: Cass, 1981) but written in the 1890s, p. 188.

78 *Report of the Nineteenth Annual Co-operative Congress,* held in Carlisle (1887), pp. 6–7.

79 *The Producer,* 15 February 1917.

80 Quoted in Neil Killingback, 'The Politics of Small Business in Britain during the 1930's' unpublished D.Phil (University of Sussex, 1980), p. 294. The full quotation is in *The Law Times,* 175, 3 (June 1933), p. 428.

81 Edgar Snow, *Red Star Over China* (London: Gollancz, 1937), p. 153, the other two books were the *Communist Manifesto,* and 'the first Marxist book ever published in Chinese, *Class Struggle* by Kautsky'. Kirkup is mis-spelt as Kirkupp in the quote from Mao used by Snow. Incidentally, Kirkup's work was noticed in the *Co-operative News* as well as in the rest of the socialist press. His works were *An Inquiry into Socialism* (London: Longmans, 1887, 1888 and 1907 editions); *The History of Socialism* (London: A&C Black, 1892, 1900, 1906, 1909, 1913 edits.); *Primer of Socialism* (London, A&C Black, 1908 and 1910 edits.); plus an entry on Socialism in the *Encyclopaedia Britannica*. It is the different editions of *The History* which I have used here.

82 The phrase is in Jack Grey's review 'The road that matters' in *New Society,* 25 January 1979. He counterposes communalist socialism with *etatist*: and refers to 'Kirkup's *History of Socialism* in which the description of Robert Owen's socialist community is point by point the precedent of the Chinese commune'.

83 The quotes are from *The History* (1892 edit.), Preface, pp. vi, 5, 7–8, 218, 231–2.

84 *The History* (1913 edit.), pp.405, 412.

85 The quotes are from *The History* (1892 edit.), pp. 216–18, 263, 273.

86 *The History* (1909 edit.), p. 402.

87 *The History* (1892 edit.), pp. 222, 222–3, 4, 272–3.

88 *The History* (1909 edit.), pp. 400–1, 406.

89 Paul Meier, *William Morris: The Marxist Dreamer* (1972), II, 416.

90 'The Policy of Abstention' (1887), May Morris, *William Morris, Artist, Writer, Socialist* (Oxford: Blackwell, 1936), II, 434–53.

91 *Abstention* (1887).

92 Meier, *Morris,* II, 311–16 and all of ch. V 'The Withering Away of the State' collects the main references in Morris to direct democracy. The quotes in the sentence here are from 'What Socialists Want' (1888) and a letter to Dr John Glasse, 23 May 1887.

93 'What Socialists Want' (1888), quoted Meier, pp. 311–13.

94 'Monopoly', in *Collected Works,* XXIII, p. 253.

95 Letter to Rev G. Bainton, 6 May 1888, P. Henderson (ed.), *The Letters of William Morris to his Family and Friends* (London: Longmans, 1950), p. 290.

96 Letter to Joseph Lane, 20 March 1887, in British Library. Add. Ms. 45, 345, quoted in Florence Boos (ed.), 'William Morris's *Socialist Diary*', *History Workshop,* 13 (Spring 1982), 7.

97 'Communism' (1893).

98 'Abstention' (1887).

99 *True and False Society* (1886).

100 'Dawn of a New Epoch' (1885) quoted Meier, II, 308.

101 'Artist and Artisan', *Commonweal,* 10 September 1887. All of Chapter 8 of Meier II: 'To Every One According to his Needs' is excellent on the whole question of work and privilege, and needs versus in-put as criteria for reward.

102 Morris and Bax, *Socialism, Its Growth and Outcome* (London: Sonnenschein, 1896 edit.), p. 282.

103 'How Shall We Live Then', quoted Meier, II, p. 315. In the work of a friend of Morris', John Carruthers, *Communal Commercial Economy* (1883), pp. 323–5 there is a clear attempt at detailing communalism: 'Without pretending to offer a cut-and-dried scheme of communal government, we may here shortly discuss the form that would be most readily evolved from the existing system. . . .'

104 *True and False Society* (1887).

105 'Statement of Principles of the Hammersmith Socialist Society', 10 January 1891, British Museum Add. Mss. 45894, quoted in Meier, II, 301.

106 'Art Under Plutocracy' (1883).

107 See Raymond Williams, 'Afterword' to *Modern Tragedy* (London: Verso, 1979 edit.) and his attempt to write through this loss, towards coming out on another side, ch. V of *Towards 2000* (1983): 'Resources for a Journey of Hope'.

108 These efforts have been well described in E. P. Thompson's *William Morris: Romantic to Revolutionary* (London: Merlin, 1976).

109 Quoted in R. Page Arnot, *William Morris, the Man and the Myth* (London: Lawrence, 1964).

110 It is well-described in Ian Bullock, 'Socialist and Democratic Form in Britain, c. 1880–1914', unpublished D.Phil (University of Sussex, 1981).

111 Kirkup, 1913 edit. Preface, p. ix.

112 Clearly there in, for instance, Kirkup, 1909 edit., pp. 400–02.

113 Kirkup 1913 edit., p. 379, see also pp. 395–6.

114 Admittedly in time of war, but the tone is characteristic: 'If I were in power, and were driven by urgent military needs or political pressure to do something drastic, I should decree Universal Submission to the national need – not young men for the trenches only, but everyone for what he was fitted, and not persons only but property and possessions – everything to be placed at the disposal of the Government,' quoted J. M. Winter, *Socialism and the Challenge of War* (London: Routledge, 1974), p. 210.

115 E. T. (ed.), Keeling, *Letters and Recollections* (1918), pp. 59–60, 62.

116 See Pease's chapter on 'The English School' Kirkup, 1913 edit, pp. 365–402.

117 *Justice*, 9 March 1901; for the couche and the sociology of Fabianism, see the chapter 'The Fabians Reconsidered', E. J. Hobsbawm, *Labouring Men* (London: Weidenfeld, 1964), pp. 250–71.

118 Well studied in Philip Corrigan, 'State Formation and Moral Regulation in 19th Century Britain: Sociological Investigations', unpublished D.Phil (University of Durham, 1977).

119 For this group in its context, see B. Semmel, *Imperialism and Social Reform* (1960), ch. III; H. C. G. Mathews, *The Liberal Imperialists: The Ideas and Politics of a Post-Gladstonian Elite* (Oxford: O.U.P., 1973); G. R. Searle, *The Quest for National Efficiency* (Oxford: Blackwell, 1971). A. M. McBriar, *Fabian Socialism and English Politics 1884–1918* (Cambridge: C.U.P., 1966).

120 *Industrial Democracy* (London: Longmans, 1920 edit.), Preface, p. xxxi.

121 S. and B. Webb, *The Consumers' Co-operative Movement* (London: Longmans, 1921), p. 161. For the changes in the Webbs' views on co-operation and production see D. C. Jones, 'The Economics of British Producer Co-operatives', unpublished D.Phil (Cornell University, 1974).

122 Keir Hardie, *The ILP: All About It* (1908), p. 4.

123 *Labour Leader*, 31 May 1912. I owe this quote to Ian Bullock's thesis.

124 *Annual Conference of Trades Councils, Report* (1946), I owe this reference to Michael Bor's work on Trades Councils.

AFTERWORD

Will Self

Twenty years and a few months ago I wrote an essay for the *Guardian* on English culture – and by extension, Englishness. I entitled it 'The Valley of the Corn Dollies'. Returning to it and the consciousness it exhibits I am struck, of course, not only by the many obvious continuities – the sense I have of Englishness enduring – but also by the transformations that have taken place in England – and by extension within English identity – over the past two decades, and that were quite unforeseen by me. Not that in 1993 I was in the business of writing futurology, still, any attempt to fix a culture in time must pay due heed to the particular nature of its fluxions. This lack of foresight is also matched by the essay's comparable lack of hindsight; by this I do not mean that it displays no concern with where the ideas and practices associated with Englishness may have come from, but that as its author I seem to have had little precise sense of its evolutionary timescale. This is understandable, I suppose; the concerns of a 32-year-old are, one hopes, different from those of a quinquagenarian. I say 'one hopes', although the very adoption of the impersonal first person and the continuous present relocate the aspiration to a nebulous cultural realm, not this England at the beginning of this particular year: the two-thousand-and-fourteenth of the Common Era.

In fact, this very assumption – that generations are capable of individuation and of possessing their own *geist* – is one that the past 20 years have ground away at, and I realize now that implicit in it were notions of the cultural primacy of the young that were altogether demographically contingent. The impact of a rapidly ageing population on English culture – and by extension, Englishness – is something I will return to, but for now it will suffice to remark that while this phenomenon – the banking-up of the Baby Boomer generation into a grey market at the end of the consumerist conveyor belt – may be widespread in the so-called developed world, the impact it is having on England seems especially powerful, given that Englishness itself is almost always conceived of in terms of gradual evolution rather than abrupt change.

In 1993 I was much taken by what I saw as the peculiarly English genius for satire both political and social, and I took this to be evidence of an underlying vigour in its primary institutions – parliament, the law and the media, if not the monarchy and the established church. I located the satiric wellspring as residing still in a class system that had, by and large, resisted essential alteration by skilful cooption – but I suppose I then believed that the dramatic ironies flowing from this were dynamical and might tend towards dissolution. Arguably, an England without the double-speak of snobbery and exclusion might be less funny, but there were surely other things it was possible to laugh about. I now look back on this attitude as being excessively sanguine; a recent review article by the impeccably middle-English novelist Jonathan Coe in the *London Review of Books* nailed shut – for me – the coffin lid on the ghoulishly self-satisfied face of contemporary English satire. To paraphrase Coe's argument: far from standing in a dynamical relation to the exercise of power, the whole tendency in post-war English snook-cocking – from the so-called 'satire boom' of the 1960s, all the way through to the politico-shit-kicking of Armando Ianucci's *The Thick of It* – has been implicitly to legitimate the status quo; for, by attacking the political class en bloc and without distinction, the satirists have both abandoned their own moral compass, and allowed the wielders of power to appropriate the very weapons deployed. The end result is that one of the most high-profile politicians in contemporary England is the seemingly buffoonish Mayor of London, Boris Johnson, whose self-satirising shtick consistently bastes him with buttery public approval.

Another instance of my younger self's myopia was my failure to anticipate the coming era of bidirectional digital media. Perhaps this was forgivable: in 1993 mobile phones were still a rarity, satellite and cable television services remained trapped in the coils of government regulation; and while locally networked personal computers were becoming reasonably prevalent in English offices, the web was too diaphanous to be seen. At least by me – I remember a salesman visiting me at the small business publishing company I ran in the early 1990s, and attempting to explain the benefits of connecting to the internet and thereby gaining access to the emergent web. I sort of grasped what he was talking about, but simply could not see what use my business could make of these innovations: we had all the information we needed at our fingertips already – or so I believed. Again, the shockwave from the subsequent technological revolution is still reverberating around the world, and there seems no reason why English culture should be particularly affected – except that the web and the internet helped to make manifest one of the longer-term, but previously hidden developments in English culture and society. This was the nation's transformation from a manufacturing economy to a mercantile and service-based one; a change that saw the centre of economic power shift decisively to London and the southeast from the northern industrial cities, and was accompanied by the rise of a commercial bourgeoisie that viewed its own prosperity as intrinsically related to transnational capital flows, even as its loyalty became more fervidly attached to symbols of nationhood such as the monarchy and the armed forces, that within the context of a declining Empire – and still more so after the Treaty of Rome – should have increasingly appeared as rhetorical tropes.

But of course, nationalism is itself *always* a rhetorical trope, and while England may have a curiously contrary way of articulating its self-belief – proceeding, one might say by an apophatic process, whereby Englishness is given greater focus and intensity by mounting up affirmations of all that it is not – nonetheless there is a core English identity to be discovered, one that – as the essays in this volume amply demonstrate – solidified in the late-nineteenth and early-twentieth century; one that has proved remarkably resilient throughout the past turbulent 100 years; and one that shows every sign of remaining intact even as the original factors that brought it into being are changed out of all recognition. It is instructive to map my own rather naïve speculations of 1993 on to the current dispensation, but it is more productive by far to examine the period 1980–2020 in terms of the equivalent span a century before; such an overlay may also mean that I do not look back in 2034, appalled by what I missed.

This late-nineteenth-century shift in the locus of power – from north to south, and from land and manufactures to retail and finance services – was accompanied initially by the ascendancy of the collectivist and Utilitarian tendency in English liberalism. World War I enacted the suppressed ideological premise of this faction, hammering home with the monstrous cacophony of the guns the idea that to be a free Englishman (and despite the Suffragists the accent was still on men at this stage), was to have ones liberties underwritten by the positive interventions of the state. John Bull's green and pleasant island, where vinous-faced squires rode to hounds and do what thou will was nine-tenths of the law remained as a sort of organic reverie, inhering in an invented English countryside of rolling hills and productive mixed-arable and dairy farming. This Englishness – which was subscribed to as wholeheartedly by utopian socialists, as it was by belligerent Tories – was a gestalt unconsciously devised to counter the standardized torments of mass villadom; and it finds its fullest spatial articulation in the Arts and Crafts semi standing in a suburban cul-de-sac, replete with unique features. That simulacra of these houses are being built to this day – and indeed, that the current rowdy debate on the paucity of housing still concentrates on this stock-brick-castellated ideal – tells you almost everything you need to know about Englishness – the principal reason for its endurance lies in the very fictitiousness of its premises.

The twentieth century looks momentously transformative for England on paper: the near-decimation of a generation between 1914 and 1918; the loss of imperial grip in the interwar years and its complete abandonment after 1945 (to be replaced by another fictive gestalt: 'the Commonwealth'); the final attainment of universal adult enfranchisement in 1927; the second great spasm of collectivisation in 1939–45, and its sequels in the form of free-collective bargaining, the National Health Service, universal state education and a burgeoning public housing sector – and so on. But with the benefit of our centennial overlays on the overhead projector we can see that these are as nought when compared with the way ideal Englishness continues to inform and legitimate the real exercise of power. Writing at a time when Burkean Tories and Benthamite Liberals share the Cabinet table, and the Prime Minister declares that the British army's mission in Afghanistan has been successfully completed, it is difficult not to feel trapped within the farcical phase of history's repetition.

Englishness, taken to be the lowest common denominator of what any given individual identifies about his or herself as an English person, remains overwhelmingly located in these rhetorical tropes: the supervening political wisdom of the Head of State (who is at once magnificently disengaged and fully apprised); the immemorial beauty of the countryside (which is paradoxically tied to its anthropic character: we have English Heritage, the United States has wilderness); the bivalent concept of 'fair play', which unites the negative libertarianism of John Bull with the positive state engagement of Messrs Clegg and Milliband; and – most important this – a complex and often contradictory understanding of inclusiveness, which is seen as served just as well by cooption to elites (black and brown coronet-sporters in the Hose of Lords), and impersonation (Hackett-clad hacks out hacking, Burberry-clad members of the chavistocracy fine dining). For the English, the ability of any given individual to assimilate has been taken as a confirmation of the nation's essential inclusiveness; and the way to 'get on' is to accede to a tokenism that will, given time, fade to grey. The unparalleled success of English Jews in achieving this ideal was as marked in the 1900s as it is in the 2000s. The Marconi scandal of 1913, which had a solid undertow of anti-Semitism, was complemented by the insider trading scandal of the Guinness Four in the 1980s, by which time to mention that all the defendants were Jews was as infra dig as alluding to the Semitic origins of half of Thatcher's inner-cabinet.

In the period 1880–1920 concerns with 'the other' were focussed in part on the Ashkenazi Jews, refugees from Russian pogroms who at that time were settling in the East End of London. But far more significant was the apophatic uses to which the Celtic fringe could be put – in particular John Bull's other island. Whether as the unwelcome *Gastarbeiter* of their day, or as fractious malcontents rocking the Imperial vessel, the Irish – fey and improvident at the very best – shored up the immemorial citadel of Englishness. In my 1993 *Guardian* piece, with the Easter Accords still in the future, I quoted an Irish friend – the writer Robert McLiam Wilson in fact – saying what a reliable appetite the English had 'for hearing what shite they are'. I took this – like the satirical sostenuto – to be a good quality, and evidence of a productive dialectic in English culture and character; it does not look that way to me anymore. In fact, like any individual who tolerates such abuse, the English, taken collectively, hide their bullying and their arrogance behind a willingness to hear what shite they are; low self-worth is not a recipe for a happy nationalism – ask the Italians . . . or the Egyptians for that matter. The absolute intractability of the Irish question for successive waves of the English Liberal consensus remains with us, at least in the diminuendo of Ulster, to this day; but revolving round this primum mobile of colonialism (and recall: Ireland was put to the sword by Parliament, not monarch) are all the other crystal spheres of the expansive English cosmos; the fundamental problem for the English – how do they reconcile a recent history typified by violence, exploitation and rapacious greed with their overwhelming sense of fair play – must be staged again and again, because the tension of these opposites can only possibly find resolution – like any other shtick – through its re-enactment. Twenty years ago, with devolved government for Scotland and Wales still in the future, and Irish people of all stripes reminding us of what shite we were, I paid the traditional obeisance: acknowledging the separateness of these cultures, and applauding their ability to still shine in the dark shadow thrown by their behemoth of a neighbour. But I also had to be clear: London was a whirlpool worthy of an Edgar Allen Poe story, sucking in all the raw talent that ventured anywhere near it; culturally speaking, the Celts could only hold their mournful tune if they kept well away from the cacophony.

In 2014 all possible forms of alterity are faced down by the English with the same Biblical stare: either go with the goatish adherents of political Islam, or be herded with the rest of the sheep into the pastures beloved of J.M.W. Turner, where ye shall lie in peace down beside the British lion. The rise and – for the most part – the acceptance of identity politics in England plays to the advantage of traditionally constituted Englishness, an ideology that thrives on physiological metaphors, and which allows for different groups – 'communities' in the modern idiom – inasmuch as they are prepared to become 'sustainable' organs generating 'growth' within the body politic. The Edwardians who hushed up the Cleveland Street scandal, while sending Wilde to jail, would have appreciated an England within which being flamboyantly gay could be squared with being outrageously conformist; no doubt, in time, they could have got used black men with dreadlocks sitting in the House of Lords, or women who profess feminism taking their strident turn at the despatch box. What they understood is that there can always be an England so long as these 'communities' can be persuaded not to see themselves as part of a larger one: the community of the dispossessed. The question of whether or not the English Muslims will hurry up with their assimilation, or persist with their tiresome religio-cultural revanchism, is of course intimately bound up with Englishness itself; an Englishness that – as that other economic sponger-cum-migrant Karl Marx understood only too well – cloaks its cold mercantile heart in swathes of chiffon sentiment. Knowing the price of everything is . . . exhausting, and it is a tedium vitae that persuades the English to indulge in successive cultural – and even spiritual – devaluations; anything but allow Englishness to find its true level in the world.

Earlier I said that bidirectional digital media had made manifest the century-old north-south power shift; now I should explain. In 1993 I was much exercised by 'retail services' the huge English export of which I chose to see, through Panglossian spectacles, as to some extent synonymous with the undoubted English brilliance at purveying popular culture – street fashions, dance music, etc. The truth is that it's *financial* services that were the real export earner then, and despite – or arguably *because* of the 2007–08 ruction – they remain so now; and moreover, courtesy of the tax payer, are fully engrafted in the state apparatus as the largest and most symbiotic instance of a public-private finance initiative. Popular culture is merely the shop window-dressing: like the film director Danny Boyle's lavishly-staged charade in the fiscal melting pot of the Olympic stadium. It follows that England – and by extension the true Englishness – exists if at all in an accommodation with this dispensation, which is really only the *kulturkampf* of that self-same commercial class that first pioneered capital flight a century ago.

To be English is to subscribe at some level to this debt-financing model of national character; the mortgaged heart of oak labours sclerotically on, while a billion Twitters and Facebook status updates are its exaggerated cardiogram, evanescently recording the peaks and troughs of its Kate Middletonesque narcissism. And of course, given that Englishness is the genius loci of an imaginary place – the green and pleasant land through which runways are forever bulldozed, and in which high-speed rail lines are entrenched – it follows that it is a bespoke national character for the ageing: in this relaxed-fit, red-white-and-blue garment they call 'British' the English can punch at, above, or well below their weight on the international stage. Again, as I write, in the immediate aftermath of the conviction of Lee Rigby's crazed killers, and with the Parliamentary committee with responsibility for their oversight making the usual doomy pronouncements on the parlous state of the armed forces, it is worth noting that those selfsame servicemen and women have never been so popular. Only with a national character as capable of being altered on the hoof could a decade's worth of defeats and withdrawals be a cause for such rejoicing; yet even with a possible Scottish secession (taking with them if not the actual formations and materiel, at least the long and honourable tradition of providing the immiserated recruiting office for Imperial hard men), I feel confident that the English will carry on being British when it suits them. It may be that historians developed the army-nation concept to explain successive crises in the legitimacy of twentieth-century French regimes, but the relationship of the British army to Englishness is just as significant, for, like the English constitution, its permanent condition of crisis may in fact be its abiding strength.

It would be comfortingly simple to substitute the role the European Union plays in the English collective psyche in 2013 for that of the British Empire in 1913; but given that the English prize both comfort and simplicity let's do just that. Both are hinterlands to which loyalty is accorded on the basis of trade and profit alone, both are great seething sumps of potential emigrants, both evince a troubling inclination to believe themselves to be dog-wagging tails, and both stir up the ancient fudge of the English settlement. One of the most popular sub-genres of Edwardian English literature was the invasion fantasy – the most famous examples of which are Childers's 'The Riddle of the Sands', and Wells's 'War of the Worlds'. The zeitgeist – whether paranoiac or real – plays little part in the contemporary literary consciousness, which prefers to flee to the Tudor period (or a version of it, at least); and instead we have real-life invasion fantasies courtesy of the John Bull *de nos jours*, Nigel Farage, and his Greek-debt-crisis chorus: The English Defence League. The irony of this embattled Englishness would not have escaped the Edwardians, who, following in the wide wake left by their portly sovereign, were only too happy to attend Shavian debunkings, or consume a Wildean diet of hearing what shite they were, but who nonetheless still had a sense of themselves as being at the very centre of the world.

In 1917, when the doughboys entered the Flanders trenches, that centre decisively shifted to the West; it was an invasion of England via Belgium that none of the science fiction writers foresaw, mostly because the neoliberal faith that in time became incorporated in invaders' ecclesiastical institutions – Breton Woods, the IMF, the Federal Reserve – was already shared, in embryo, by the conquered. No one needs to be a seer to foresee that by 2020 the world cynosure will have just as decisively shifted to the southeast – but not England's. The emergent Chi- or BRICK world will impact just as powerfully on Englishness in the twenty-first century as the hegemonic United States did in the twentieth; yet having already masterfully performed the trick of retaining a sense of metropolitan pre-eminence while becoming parochial, there seems no reason to think that Englishness would not keep calm and carry on. This year's centenary of the outbreak of World War I will give the ageing English – wearing their habitual British costume – the opportunity to stage their favourite sort of mummery: the glorification of machine-made death and destruction on a colossal scale. Already minister after minister is rising to the despatch box to declare that while World War I should not be prettified, and the commemorations should be an opportunity to educate the young; notwithstanding, those selfsame young should be made to comprehend the terrible existential threat faced by their beloved homeland in 1914.

And finally: a word about food – and newsprint. In my 1993 essay I drew the central motif of Englishness from an instance of marketing: in Richard Eyre's 1983 film *The Ploughman's Lunch* (scripted by Ian McEwan), the MacGuffin is thematic rather than narrative. During a conversation between the protagonist – a cod-idealistic television journalist – and the much older advertisement director whose lefty wife he has just cuckolded, the ad man tells him that the ploughman's lunch, far from having been some timeless titbit of the English peasant, was in fact invented in the 1960s to vitalise pub-snacking. I could say a lot more about The Ploughman's Lunch – which in turn attempts to say a great deal about the fellow-travelling English character during the Thatcher revolution – but let's just focus on the food. In 1993 – let alone 1983 – food was still largely conceived of as a form of sustenance. In 2014 it has become the primary way that the English take their culture: to be English is to eat; to eat out, to eat many different cuisines (the English having none of their own worth the ascription), to watch cookery programmes, and to have an opinion on the alleged drug-taking habits of celebrity chefs. It follows that Englishness itself is a gastronomic affair – and I think what I have written above bears this out: Englishness is at once a praxis: a way of going about things; and a way of transforming what is not English – *shish kebabs*, onion *bhajis*, ackee and salt fish – into what is. The problem for Englishness is that it tends to eat too much, and too indiscriminately – and that's not healthy for the ageing national character. Of course fish and chips (an inspired example of English praxis: Belgian fried potato mixed with Ashkenazi fried fish) was traditionally served in newspaper; but it isn't my partisan status as a journalist that leads me to believe that the English would have done well to hang on to the wrapping and discard the food. At least, I would've wished them to have done this, if their great and passionate belief in the freedom and independence of their press wasn't – like so much that is English to the core – something of a myth.

INDEX

Lightning Source UK Ltd.
Milton Keynes UK
UKHW022135290422
402243UK00004B/65